CURRENT
PLUS
DICTIONARY OF
IDIOMS

CURRICULUM PLUS

DICTIONARY OF IDIOMS

**Curriculum *Plus*
Publishing Company**

PUBLISHED BY THE PRESS SYNDICATE OF THE UNIVERSITY OF CAMBRIDGE
The Pitt Building, Trumpington Street, Cambridge, United Kingdom

CAMBRIDGE UNIVERSITY PRESS
The Edinburgh Building, Cambridge CB2 2RU, UK
40 West 20th Street, New York, NY 10011–4211, USA
10 Stamford Road, Oakleigh, VIC 3166, Australia
Ruiz de Alarcón 13, 28014 Madrid, Spain
Dock House, The Waterfront, Cape Town 8001, South Africa

© Cambridge University Press 2003

This book is in copyright. Subject to statutory exception
and to the provisions of relevant collective licensing agreements,
no reproduction of any part may take place without
the written permission of Cambridge University Press.

Printed in Hong Kong, China

Typefaces: Nimrod, Frutiger

Page Design and Composition: dataformat.com, LLC

First published 2003

Library of Congress Cataloging-in-Publication data

Cambridge dictionary of American idioms / Paul Heacock, editor in chief.
    p. cm.
  Includes bibliographical references (p.) and index.
  ISBN 0-521-53271-X
  1. English language—United States—Idioms—Dictionaries. I. Heacock, Paul.

PE2839.C36 2003
423'.1—dc21

2003053233

ISBN 0-521-54283-9
Curriculum Plus Dictionary of Idioms

Cambridge Dictionary of American Idioms

Editor in Chief
Paul Heacock

Executive Editor
Cynthia A. Barnhart

Senior Editors
Carol-June Cassidy
Sidney I. Landau

Lexicographers
Carol G. Braham
Orin Hargraves

Illustrator
Andrew Lange

Study Section
Sidney I. Landau

Subject Index Compiler
Carol-June Cassidy

Database Development and Administration
Stephen Perkins, dataformat.com, LLC
Paul Hayslett, dataformat.com, LLC

Systems Development
Andrew Harley
Dominic Glennon

Cambridge International Corpus
Ann Fiddes, corpus controller
Robert Fairchild, software development
Dominic Glennon, software development

Editorial Consultant
Bernard D. Seal

Text Review
Margot F. Gramer

Proofreader
Anne Garrett

Editorial Assistant, Defining Vocabulary
Sarah Chasse

Editorial Reviewers
Michael McCarthy, Professor, Dept. of Applied Linguistics, University of Nottingham, UK
Don R. McCreary, Professor, Dept. of English, University of Georgia, USA
Carol Cornett, ESL Instructor, Wright State University, USA
Deborah Crusan, Assistant Professor, Wright State University, USA
Suzanne House, Director, English Language Instititue, Lakeland College, USA
Bennett Paris, Adjunct ESL Instructor, Hudson County Community College, USA
Ching-Ping Wang, Lecturer, Dept. of Foreign Languages and Literature, Tunghai University, Taiwan
Yu-Ling You, Assistant Professor, Dept. of Applied Foreign Languages, National Yunlin University of Science and Technology, Taiwan

Project Development Reviewers
John D. Battenburg, Professor, English Dept., California Polytechnic State University, USA
Li-Hung Michael Chang, Wen Tzao Ursuline University of Modern Languages, Taiwan
Grover K. H. Yu, Professor, National Kaoshiung Normal University, Taiwan

Focus Group Participants
Judy Gex, LaGuardia Community College, USA
Sheila Hakner, St. John's University, USA
Dolly Litvak, Nassau Community College, USA
Joan Palmieri, Jewish Vocational Service
Linda Pelc, LaGuardia Community College, USA
Diane Pinkley, Columbia University, USA
Frank Tang, New York University, USA

Contents

What is an idiom?	ix
What is a corpus-based idioms dictionary?	ix
How to find an idiom in this dictionary	x
The parts of an entry	xii
Labels, abbreviations, and words in parentheses	xiv
A–Z	1
Study Section	237
Subject Index	483

What is an idiom?

An idiom is a phrase whose meaning is different from the meanings of each word considered separately. These phrases have a fixed form – they usually cannot be changed – and they are often informal, but they can also be slang, rude slang, or even slightly formal. Many idioms are used in spoken English, but they also appear in newspapers and magazines, in books, and even in academic writing.

Not all fixed phrases are idioms. For example, *close your eyes* is a common fixed phrase, but it is not an idiom because each word in it is used in its standard meaning. The phrase *keep your shirt on* is an idiom, however, because the phrase does not mean "do not take off your shirt" – it means "stay calm."

What is a corpus-based dictionary?

A corpus is a collection of texts stored on a computer. This dictionary was created by a group of editors using sophisticated software tools to search the Canadian and American English parts of the Cambridge International Corpus for words and phrases, and to analyze the results.

Cambridge University Press has assembled a corpus that includes 600 million words of written and spoken English texts. The texts in the CIC come from newspapers, novels, non-fiction books on a wide range of topics, websites, magazines, junk mail, TV and radio programs, recordings of people's everyday conversations, and many other sources. The Canadian and American English parts of the CIC include 175 million words of written texts, 22 million words of spoken English, 7 million words of adademic texts, and 25 million words taken from business texts.

Although idioms in general are used frequently in both speech and writing, each individual idiom is not used frequently. For example, the idiom *give up the ghost* occurs approximately once in every seven million words of corpus texts. (By comparison, the word *give* occurs approximately 3,300 times in every seven million words.) Because there are many more idioms in English than we could include in this book, we decided to include only idioms that occurred at least once in every 10 million words of corpus texts.

The idioms included in the *Curriculum Plus Dictionary of Idioms* have been carefully checked in the Canadian and American English parts of the CIC. Our editors have checked to make sure that each idiom is really used in current Canadian and American English, that it is used often enough to include in this book, and that the information we give about each idiom describes what people mean when they say or write it.

How to find an idiom in this dictionary

Idioms are placed under an alphabetical list of headwords

> **inquire**
> **ins**
> **inside**
> **inside track**
> **insult**
> **intent**
> **intents**
> **interference**

The decision about which headword an idiom is placed under was made using the following rules:

If the idiom includes a noun, it is placed under the first noun.

> **irons**
> several irons in the fire

If the idiom includes a compound noun, it is placed under that compound noun.

> **kitchen sink**
> everything but the kitchen sink

If the idiom includes a possessive noun followed by another noun, it is placed under the noun following the possessive.

> **notice**
> at a moment's notice

If the idiom includes no nouns but does include a verb, it is placed under the first verb (other than auxiliary verbs such as *can*, *have*, *must*, or *would*).

> **keep**
> keep abreast of *sth*

If the idiom includes no nouns or verbs but does include an adjective, it is placed under the first adjective.

> **good**
> as good as

If the idiom does not include a noun, verb, or adjective, it is placed under the first word other than *a*, *the*, or a subject (*you*) or object (*sth*).

almost
  almost never

been
  been around (the block) slang

might
  you might as well (do sth)

not
  not for nothing

this
  this and that

to
  to and fro

Idioms are not placed under any words that are given in parentheses.

The parts of an entry

Idioms are placed under *headwords*. (See p. x for more information.)	**nail** **hit the nail on the head** to be right about something ♦ *Mike hit the nail on the head when he said most people can use a computer without knowing how it works.*
Other forms of the same idiom follow the main form.	**nails** **(as) tough as nails**, *also* **(as) hard as nails** strong and determined ♦ *She is a warm and friendly person, but she is also as tough as nails.*
A *label* gives information about when an idiom is used. When a label applies to only one meaning of an idiom, it is given after the definition number and before the definition.	**needs** **who needs *sth*** *esp. spoken* what was mentioned is not important or helpful ♦ *I wouldn't do it for the money – who needs money?*
One or more *definitions* explain the basic meaning of every idiom. One or more *example sentences* show how the idiom is typically used.	**nothing** **nothing but *sth*** **1** only something ♦ *During spring vacation, he ate nothing but canned beans.* ♦ *The police were praised for showing nothing but the highest degree of professionalism.* **2** completely something ♦ *The story was nothing but lies.* ♦ *My car is nothing but trouble.*
Other idioms that have the same meaning are given immediately after the definition.	**relate** **relate to *sb*** to understand and feel sympathy for someone; = **identify with *sb*** ♦ *The kids need a teacher who can relate to them.*
Usage notes give additional information about how people usually use the idiom. When a usage note, origin note, or cross reference applies to only one meaning of an idiom, it is given before the next definition number.	**serve** **serve *you* right** you deserve the punishment that you received ♦ *After the way she treated him, it would serve her right if he left her.* USAGE: often said with an attitude of pleasure because someone you do not like is suffering

The parts of an entry

share
have *your* share of *sth*
to have enough of something ♦ *My husband and I have had our share of job changes and periods of unemployment in recent years.* USAGE: sometimes, for emphasis, used in the form **have more than your share** (= have too much): *This community has more than its share of kids in trouble.*

Usage notes also give slightly different forms of an idiom.

roll
on a roll
1 experiencing a period of success or good luck ♦ *They were on a roll, winning nine games in a row.* ♦ *With a growing economy and a dropping crime rate, the city has been on a roll.* ♦ Related vocabulary **have a good thing going** at THING

Other idioms that have a related meaning are given, followed by the headword they are placed under.

running
in the running
having a chance to win ♦ *This movie must be in the running for best documentary.* USAGE: said about a competition or election ♦ Opposite **out of the running**

Other idioms that have the opposite meaning are given. If no headword is shown, it means the opposite idiom is placed under the same headword.

shoot
shoot daggers at *sb* See at DAGGERS
shoot from the hip See at HIP
shoot hoops See at HOOPS

gantlet
run the gantlet See at GAUNTLET

*Idioms that are entered under another headword in the dictionary are listed. Some headwords, like **go**, do not have any "see at" references because there are too many idioms in the dictionary that include the word *go*.*

caboodle
the whole caboodle See **the whole kit and caboodle** at KIT

References to idioms that are placed under a more common spelling or form are listed.

saddle
in the saddle
in control ♦ *It looks like those who oppose environmental controls are going to be in the saddle.* ♦ Related vocabulary **in the driver's seat** at SEAT

ORIGIN: based on the idea that someone who is in the **saddle** (= seat fastened on the back of a horse) controls the horse's movements

Origin notes explain how an idiom developed, whether from a literal meaning or a literary source or from use in relation to an activity or situation.

Labels, abbreviations, and words in parentheses

Labels
Idioms are usually used in informal writing and speech, and can be used in most situations. When an idiom should not be used in most situations, a label is given to show how its use is limited. Although most idioms in this book do not have labels, there are four labels used in this dictionary.

slightly formal – idioms that are used in polite conversation, formal speeches, and writing for school or work

esp. spoken – idioms that are mostly used in conversation, although they are sometimes also used in writing

slang – idioms that are acceptable in conversation with friends or people of the same age or social position, but which should not be used when talking with people you do not know well. Idioms labeled *slang* are not usually used in writing, except in very informal writing, such as an e-mail to a friend.

rude slang – idioms that are often offensive to other people

Abbreviations
Only one abbreviation is used in the definitions in this dictionary:

esp. = especially

A few abbreviations are used in idioms. When the idiom is used, a particular person or thing is often named instead of using the word *someone* or *something*.

sb = someone
sth = something
sb's = someone's
sth's = something's

The following abbreviations also appear in the text:

B.C.E. = before the Christian era
C.E. = the Christian era

Other words in italics are also used in idioms: *you, your, its, itself, somewhere*. These words are sometimes replaced by someone or something particular when the idiom is used.

Words in parentheses
Some idioms in this book include words that can be included or omitted when using the idiom without having any effect on the meaning.

check in (with *sb***)**
have *sth* **coming out (of)** *your* **ears**

A, a

A

from A to Z
including all the things involved ◆ *I know that my parents will take care of everything from A to Z if I ask them for help.*

(as) easy as A, B, C See **(as) easy as pie** at PIE

ABCs

the ABCs of *sth*,
the basic information about a subject ◆ *These young students are learning the ABCs of cooking.*

abide

abide by *sth*
to accept or obey an arrangement, decision, or rule ◆ *It is a good thing that most drivers abide by the rules of the road.* ◆ Related vocabulary **adhere to** *sth* at ADHERE, **go by** *sth* at GO

about

about to
1 almost ready to ◆ *One of my friends at work is about to have her second baby.*
2 planning to ◆ *I was about to tell you a joke, but I won't because it's not really very funny.*

not about to
not willing to ◆ *Alice was not about to stand around and watch while Jim and Nan argued.*

above

above all (else)
most importantly ◆ *He loved hunting, skiing, and above all, he loved his family.*

all of the above
everything mentioned ◆ *Struggles for control of a company may involve financial drama, personal loyalties, physical confrontation – or all of the above.* USAGE: often used in tests in which different possible answers are given, one of which is **all of the above** (= all of the answers provided are correct): *The city's major commuter routes are backed up because of (a) construction, (b) fog, (c) heavy traffic, (d) breakdowns, or (e) all of the above.*

above and beyond *sth*
more than or in addition to something ◆ *She has things she wants to accomplish above and beyond another championship.* ◆ *Our products are manufactured under the strictest guidelines, above and beyond what government regulations require.* ◆ Related vocabulary **(above and) beyond the call of duty** at CALL

none of the above
not one of the possibilities mentioned ◆ *Given the choices in the election, I've been thinking about voting for none of the above.* USAGE: often used in tests in which different possible answers are given, one of which is **none of the above** (= not one of the answers provided is correct): *Are you part of Generation X, Generation Y, Generation 1.5, or none of the above?*

above the law See at LAW

above suspicion See at SUSPICION

accord

of *sb's/sth's* **own accord**
without being asked or forced to ◆ *My mother thought something was wrong when I cleaned up my room of my own accord.* ◆ *My legs seemed to move of their own accord.*

account

account for *sth*
1 to explain the reason for something ◆ *More police on the streets accounted for less street crime.*
2 to form the total of an amount of something ◆ *In Florida, people over*

ache

60 account for more than 25 percent of the population.

call to account slightly formal
to be forced to accept responsibility for something ◆ *Davis published top-secret government information, but he was never called to account for this.*

on account of *sth*
because of something ◆ *Mrs. Popper's vacation in Frankfurt had to be cancelled on account of her husband's illness.*

take *sth* **into account**, *also* **take account of** *sth*
to include something when making a decision or judgment ◆ *Salespeople have to take into account the differences between their customers.* ◆ Related vocabulary **allow for** *sth* at ALLOW, **make allowances for** *sb/sth* at ALLOWANCES ◆ Opposite **take no account of** *sth*

take no account of *sth*
to not consider something ◆ *Some teachers seem to take no account of their students' interests or experience.* ◆ Opposite **take** *sth* **into account**

ache

ache for *sb/sth*
to feel desire or regret about someone or something ◆ *I ache for home, the smell of bread baking, rain hitting the porch roof – even the smell of the hen house.* ◆ *We ache for the victims of war who have lost family, friends, and their homes.*

act

act out
to behave badly because you are unhappy or upset ◆ *These kids are very angry and act out because their lives are a mess.*

> ORIGIN: based on the idea of **acting out** a story (= telling a story through physical actions)

act up
1 to behave badly ◆ *Sometimes kids act up because they just want attention.* USAGE: usually used to refer to children
2 to operate badly ◆ *My computer began acting up and I lost a whole day's work.*
3 to become active ◆ *Her allergies acted up when she went hiking in the woods.* USAGE: usually used to refer to a medical condition

a tough act to follow
so good that whatever happens next is not likely to seem as good ◆ *The last mayor was one of the most beloved in the city's history, which means Mike Ransom has a tough act to follow.*

catch *sb* **in the act**
to see someone doing something illegal or wrong ◆ *If you are speeding and one of our officers catches you in the act, you will get a ticket.*

clean up *your* **act**
to improve your behavior ◆ *He used to drink a lot, but he seems to have cleaned up his act.*

get into the act, *also* **get in on the act**
to become involved in something that is happening ◆ *Most of these products are made in the US, but other countries are also getting into the act.*

get *your* **act together**
to become better organized ◆ *If I'm going on a trip, I usually get my act together the night before so I'm packed and ready to go in the morning.* ◆ *The very fact they keep talking about how they have to get their act together is a bad sign.*

action

in action
active or working ◆ *It was interesting to see the UN in action.* ◆ *They could make better ESL books if they observed students in action.*

out of action
not able to work or be active ◆ *That accident forced my boss out of action for almost a month.* USAGE: also said

of machines or systems: *The explosion put the ship out of action.*

take action
1 to do something ♦ *Travelers want the airlines to take action to make flying safer and more comfortable.*
2 to begin legal activity against someone ♦ *Today, the environmental group took action in federal court against the mining companies.*

a piece of the action See at PIECE

actions

actions speak louder than words
what someone does is more important than what someone says ♦ *You have to prepare for what your opponents could do, not what they say they'll do, because actions speak louder than words.*

add

add up esp. spoken
1 to be reasonable ♦ *His story of what happened to him just doesn't add up.* USAGE: usually used with **not**, as in the example
2 to increase in expense ♦ *With five kids in the family, our medical bills really add up.*

add up to *sth*
to result in something ♦ *The details don't add up to a complete picture of what caused the explosion.* ♦ Related vocabulary **amount to *sth*** at AMOUNT

adhere

adhere to *sth* slightly formal
to behave in a way demanded by an idea or rule ♦ *Housing groups that do not adhere to the new fire regulations may lose government money.* ♦ *He followed no specific religion, but adhered to the basic beliefs of Christianity.* ♦ Related vocabulary **abide by *sth*** at ABIDE, **go by *sth*** at GO

ado

much ado about nothing
a lot of trouble or excitement about something that is not important ♦ *His opponents have questioned his role in obtaining the contract, but he claims he did nothing wrong, and that it's much ado about nothing.*

ORIGIN: from the title of a play by William Shakespeare

without further ado slightly formal, *also* **without more ado**
without any more talk or activity ♦ *Without further ado, here is my list of the ten best restaurants in St. Louis.*

advance

in advance (of *sth*)
before something happens ♦ *Tickets cost $6 in advance and $8 on the day of the show.* ♦ *Police checked over the building in advance of the president's visit.*

advantage

take advantage (of *sth*), *also* **take full advantage (of *sth*)**
to use an opportunity to get or achieve something ♦ *He took advantage of the prison's education program to earn a college degree.* ♦ *There are peaches and strawberries grown on the farm, and I sure take full advantage of them.* USAGE: often said of someone who has opportunities that others do not have: *The rich can take advantage of clever accounting tricks to avoid taxes.*

take advantage (of *sb*)
to use someone's weakness to improve your own situation ♦ *Mr. Smith often takes advantage of my friendship and leaves the unpleasant tasks for me to do.*

to advantage
in a way that helps you ♦ *We had to learn to use the landscape to advantage in combat.* ♦ *She chose a dress that would show her fine figure to advantage.*

again

again and again
many times; = **over and over (again)** ◆ *I've told you again and again that I don't know anything about what started the fight.* ◆ Related vocabulary **time after time** at TIME

age

come of age
1 to become an adult ◆ *Your son's children have now come of age.* ◆ *Of all the kids who come of age this year, how many will actually vote?* ◆ Related vocabulary **grow up** at GROW

2 to develop completely ◆ *The idea of equality in the workplace has come of age.*

agree

agree to disagree
to decide not to argue about something any more ◆ *The two countries can agree to disagree on this issue and still have a cooperative relationship.*

I couldn't agree more
I support that very strongly ◆ *I couldn't agree more with the opinions stated in your recent editorial.* USAGE: sometimes used in the form **somebody couldn't agree more**: *Lots of people think the use of hand-held phones while driving should be outlawed, and state lawmakers couldn't agree more.*

ahold

get ahold of *sb* esp. spoken
to communicate with someone; = **get hold of *sb*** ◆ *I'm trying to get ahold of everyone to tell them the party is at 9 tomorrow.*

get ahold of *sth* esp. spoken
to obtain something; = **get hold of *sth*** ◆ *I finally got ahold of that novel you said I should read.*

air

clear the air
1 to explain something that someone disagreed with or did not understand ◆ *To help clear the air, Mills will meet with all employees to discuss the new contract.*

clear the air

Myra realized that Bob misunderstood her, and she wanted to clear the air.

2 to remove any doubt about something that happened ◆ *An investigation may be needed to uncover the facts and clear the air.*

disappear into thin air, *also* **vanish into thin air**
to suddenly become impossible to see or find ◆ *Police say the suspect seems to have disappeared into thin air.* ◆ *When Jim opened his eyes, the bear had vanished into thin air.*

in the air
able to be felt or noticed ◆ *Spring is in the air, and many people's thoughts are turning to travel.*

off the air
1 not broadcasting ◆ *The radio station went off the air at midnight.*
2 not being broadcast ◆ *Many people were angry when they heard the program was off the air.*

on the air
1 broadcasting ◆ *Channel 4 stayed on the air all night to cover the breaking news.*
2 being broadcast ◆ *At least for this season the program will still be on the air.*

out of thin air, *also* **from thin air**
from nowhere or nothing ◆ *How can magicians produce coins out of thin air?* ◆ *Pascal's discoveries did not come from thin air – they're based on the work of earlier mathematicians.* ◆ Related vocabulary **out of the blue** at BLUE

up in the air
not decided or completely developed ◆ *We have no idea which school she'll be attending in September – everything is still up in the air.* ◆ *Will a strike take place? That's up in the air.* ◆ Related vocabulary **leave sth hanging** at LEAVE

walk on air
to be very happy ◆ *Editors of the school's newspaper were walking on air when they heard that the "Tigers News" was judged the best in the country.*

aisles

rolling in the aisles
laughing loudly ◆ *The group, considered by many to be one of the funniest in Canada, had its audiences rolling in the aisles at last night's concert.*

> ORIGIN: based on the idea of uncontrollable laughter causing the people watching a show to fall on the floor in the **aisles** (= the long narrow spaces between rows of seats in a theater)

alive

alive and well, *also* **alive and kicking**
1 involved or active ◆ *As long as our star players are alive and well, this championship isn't over yet.*
2 having influence or importance ◆ *Traditional jazz is still alive and well in New Orleans.*

all

after all
1 despite what happened or was the situation before ◆ *Now that I know what upset you, maybe we can figure out how to work together after all.* USAGE: used to emphasize a change
2 because of the reason given ◆ *We were very afraid—after all, he was armed.* USAGE: used to emphasize a fact with the hope that others will accept it

all along
the whole time ◆ *Do you think he's been cheating us all along?*

all at once
1 happening or done quickly and without any warning; = **all of a sudden** ◆ *All at once I felt dizzy and had to lie down.*
2 at the same time ◆ *I've had to deal with too many problems all at once.*

all but sth
1 everyone or everything except those mentioned ◆ *All but the weakest plants survived the hot weather.*
2 almost ◆ *In some places, bus service has all but disappeared.*

all for *sth* esp. spoken
strongly approving of something ◆ *Americans are usually all for freedom of speech.* USAGE: often used in the form **I'm all for it**: *If the new law will keep guns out of the hands of kids, I'm all for it.* ◆ Related vocabulary **in favor of** *sth* at FAVOR

all in all slightly formal
considering everything ◆ *All in all, it was an especially bad year for farmers, who were hit by low prices and bad weather.*

all of *sth*
only ◆ *His book has sold all of 200 copies.* USAGE: used to suggest that it would be foolish to expect more

all over
in many places ◆ *My family is spread out all over.* ◆ Related vocabulary **all over town** at TOWN

you are** sb/sth **all over
similar to someone or something in every way ◆ *When it comes to worrying, you are your dad all over.*

all over (again)
another time, starting from the beginning ◆ *I cleaned the kitchen, the dogs tracked in mud, and I had to do it all over.*

all that
very or really ◆ *I'm not all that used to eating in fancy restaurants.*

all too
extremely, very ◆ *My bus is delayed all too often.*

all very well
good but not good enough ◆ *It's all very well to fully discuss a problem, but finally you have to stop talking and do something about it.*

and all esp. spoken
and other similar things ◆ *I was expecting snow and all when I went to Boston last winter.* USAGE: also used in the form **and all (of) that**: *We spent a few hundred dollars last weekend, including motel and meals and all that.*

at all
1 to any degree ◆ *Some plants do not grow at all in that climate.* ◆ *Did she ever hear from Linda at all?* USAGE: also used in the forms **any at all** (= any amount whatever) and the negative **(not) much at all** (= not to any great degree): *The problem wasn't getting good health care but getting any at all.* ◆ *I never knew much at all about fine art.*
2 under any conditions ◆ *She would not have been happy there at all.*

for all *sth*
despite ◆ *For all their problems, great improvements were made in the country's literacy rates and medical system.* ◆ *For all the difficulties they had getting it produced, the play is a huge success.* USAGE: used to introduce a fact that is completely different than the information that follows it

for all that
despite everything; = **even so** ◆ *Her writing is odd, even eccentric, but for all that it's not particularly interesting or intelligent.* ◆ Related vocabulary **be that as it may** at BE

not all there
not mentally clear ◆ *He has periods when he's just not all there, which is a common symptom of his condition.*

alley

(right) up *your* **alley** esp. spoken, *also* **(right) down** *your* **alley**
suited to your abilities or interests ◆ *Harry knows a lot about computers and software, so this job is right up his alley.*

allow

allow for *sth*
to consider particular facts that relate to something ◆ *If you own stock, you must allow for the possibility that it will lose value.* ◆ Related vocabulary **make allowances for** *sb/sth* at ALLOWANCES, **take** *sth* **into account** at ACCOUNT

allowances

make allowances for *sb/sth*
to consider particular facts relating

to someone or something ◆ *We try to make allowances for our students' different language backgrounds.* ◆ *When planning a trip, you have to make allowances for things that you can't know ahead of time, such as crowds or bad weather.* ◆ Related vocabulary **allow for** *sth* at ALLOW, **take** *sth* **into account** at ACCOUNT

allude
allude to *sb/sth* slightly formal
to refer to someone or something briefly or indirectly ◆ *In his letter, Dick alluded to problems the company was facing, but he never suggested they were going out of business.*

almost
almost never
very rarely ◆ *Documentary films almost never win prizes.*

along
along with *sth*
and also something; = **together with** *sth* ◆ *She keeps her pills in her bag, along with her money and her comb and lipstick and the usual junk.*

***sb* will be along**
someone is coming ◆ *The author will be along soon to autograph copies of her book.*

altar
sacrifice *sth* **on the altar of** *sth*
to destroy something in order to obtain something else ◆ *He sacrificed his family life on the altar of his ambition and greed.*

amends
make amends
to do something because you did not do it when you should have ◆ *Wendi hopes that by winning today's match she will make amends to her fans for losing such an easy match yesterday.*
USAGE: often followed by a phrase that begins with **to**, **by**, or **with**, as in the example, or used at the end of a sentence: *She embarrassed her family and wants to make amends.*

amount
amount to *sth*
to be the same as something else ◆ *A decrease in student aid amounts to an increase in tuition fees.* ◆ *She thought he was wrong to take what amounts to a stand against greater freedom.* ◆ Related vocabulary **add up to** *sth* at ADD

amount to the same thing See at THING.

analysis
in the final analysis, *also* **in the last analysis**
when all the facts are considered ◆ *In the final analysis, the failure of the rescue mission was the result of bad timing and bad weather* ◆ Related vocabulary **at the end of the day** at END, **in the end** at END, **when all is said and done** at SAID

angle
angle for *sth*
to try to get or achieve something in an indirect way ◆ *He's working as a consultant with several companies that are angling for business in Hong Kong.*

answer
answer for *sth*
to admit responsibility for causing a problem or situation ◆ *He may not go to jail, but someday he is going to have to answer for what he did before God.* ◆ *If you mix art and politics critics get upset and you have to answer for it.* ◆ Related vocabulary **have a lot to answer for** at LOT

answer to *sb*
to be responsible to someone else ◆ *If you own your own company, you do not have to answer to stockholders.*

***sb*'s answer to** *sb/sth*
something intended to be as good as another similar person or thing ◆ *The European Film Awards are*

answers

Europe's answer to the Academy Awards.

not take no for an answer
to be unwilling to accept a refusal ♦ *She sent faxes, made phone calls, sent e-mail – she just wouldn't take no for an answer.*

the answer to *your* prayers
exactly what is needed or wanted ♦ *These new artificial hearts are amazing, but are they the answer to our prayers?* USAGE: sometimes used in the form **the answer to something's prayers**: *Each new technology has been introduced as the answer to education's prayers.*

answers

have all the answers, *also* **know all the answers**
to be ready with all the available information about something ♦ *There's one kid in my class who always has her hand up and always has all the answers.* ♦ *I don't know what can be done – I don't have all the answers, but I do have a lot of questions.* USAGE: often used to describe someone who wants other people to recognize their intelligence: *I used to date someone who had all the answers, and he was such a bore.*

ante

up the ante, *also* **raise the ante**
1 to raise the cost or risk of an activity ♦ *By adding new inspectors, the customs service is upping the ante for smugglers.*
2 to increase the quality of something ♦ *Foxx says he intends to up the ante in nightclub entertainment by introducing new, extremely talented performers.* ♦ Related vocabulary **raise the stakes** at STAKES

ORIGIN: based on the literal meaning of **up the ante** (= to increase the amount of money each person must risk in a card game or other activity involving the risk of losing money)

ante up *sth*
to give money or something of value ♦ *She refused to ante up the personal and financial information that she was asked to provide.* ♦ *Every member of the team anted up $50 to pay for equipment.*

ants

have ants in *your* pants
to be very excited or worried about something ♦ *I've got ants in my pants – I can't wait to get started on my experiment.*

anything

anything but
not ♦ *The minister and the church leaders are all deaf, yet the service is anything but silent.* USAGE: used to emphasize that something is the opposite of what you might expect

for anything (in the world)
not under any conditions ♦ *I know some guys who are police officers, and I wouldn't take that job for anything.* ♦ *Bill said he wouldn't trade the experience of living in Guatemala for anything in the world.*

apart

apart from *sth*
except for something; = **aside from *sth*** ♦ *Apart from its wonderful kitchen, that house needs a lot of work done on it.*

ape

go ape slang
to become very excited or angry ♦ *Did you go ape over Tim's latest film, or did you just get disgusted, like me?* USAGE: also used in the form **go apeshit**, which has the same meaning but is considered rude slang

apologies

make no apologies
to believe that what you have done is acceptable ♦ *Browner makes no apologies for his performance as manager so far, but also says there is always room for improvement.*

appetite
whet *sb's* appetite
to cause you to want more of something ◆ *Her work on this show has whetted her appetite to do theatrical sets for other shows.* ◆ *Predictions of defeat only seemed to whet his appetite for battle.*

apple
the apple of *your* eye
the person someone likes most or is most proud of ◆ *Harry was his first child and the apple of his eye.*

apple pie
as American as apple pie
having qualities that are thought to be typical of the US or of the people of the US ◆ *Blue jeans are as American as apple pie.*

apples
compare apples and oranges
to examine the similarities of things that are completely different ◆ *Comparing the average wages of workers and managers is like trying to compare apples and oranges.* USAGE: usually used to explain that two things cannot be compared

arm
an arm and a leg
a lot of money ◆ *Everything the restaurant offers tastes good, and it doesn't cost an arm and a leg.* USAGE: usually used with the verbs **cost**, **pay**, and **charge**

the long arm of the law
the ability of the police and courts to force people to obey the rules ◆ *Many people believe that any kind of marriage law extends the long arm of the law too far into private matters.*

twist *sb's* arm
to strongly encourage someone to do something they do not want to do ◆ *If he doesn't want to go, you've just got to twist his arm to get him to do it.*

a shot in the arm See at SHOT

keep *sth* at arm's length See at LENGTH

arms
bear arms
to carry weapons ◆ *The court stated that the right of an individual to keep and bear arms is not guaranteed by the Second Amendment.* USAGE: usually used in the phrases **right to bear arms** and **keep and bear arms**

get *your* arms around *sth*
to feel confident that you have a good understanding of something that is complicated ◆ *There are so many different aspects of the energy situation that it's hard to get your arms around it.* ◆ Related vocabulary **get *your* mind around *sth*** at MIND

take up arms slightly formal
to fight with weapons against an enemy ◆ *They took up arms only after other means of resolving their differences failed.*

up in arms
very angry ◆ *Local businessmen are up in arms over the new parking regulations which will make shopping very inconvenient for customers.* USAGE: often followed by a phrase beginning with **over**, as in the example, or **about**: *Why aren't we up in arms about children who are not being educated?*

with open arms
with happiness or enthusiasm ◆ *After suing the organization, I know I'm not going to be greeted with open arms.* USAGE: often used with the verb **welcome**: *A lot of our customers wouldn't be welcomed with open arms in other stores.*

around
around and around
in a circle; = **round and round** ◆ *The skater twirled around and around, faster and faster.* ◆ Related vocabulary **go around and**

arrest

around at GO, **go (around) in circles** at CIRCLES

arrest
under arrest
held by police in connection with a crime ◆ *Police claim they have one of the gunmen under arrest.*

arrival
dead on arrival
without any chance for success; = **dead in the water** ◆ *Five years ago the industry appeared dead on arrival.* ◆ *The idea of legalizing some drugs is a concept that's dead on arrival in many law enforcement circles.* USAGE: often used in referring to something that must be voted on: *Healthcare reform was dead on arrival.*

> ORIGIN: based on the literal meaning of **dead on arrival** (= not alive when brought to a hospital)

arrive
arrive at *sth*
to come to a decision or agreement about something after serious thought or discussion ◆ *The town council needs to explain how they arrived at their plan for future development of the town.*

> ORIGIN: based on the literal meaning of **arrive at** (= to come to a place)

article
an article of faith
something that is accepted as being true ◆ *The importance of a balanced budget had become an article of faith among conservatives.*

as
as for
1 considering or speaking about ◆ *I am still working, and as for my health, it is very good.*
2 slightly formal ◆ and in the same way for ◆ *For Hawthorne, as for Borges, his writing was a reaction to his cultural situation.*

USAGE: often used to start a sentence that changes or adds to the subject of the last sentence: *My wife and I are well. As for our work, it is not going well.*

as if, *also* **as though**
like something was actually so ◆ *The pain was so bad, he felt as if a knife were sticking between his shoulders.* ◆ *When my mother came to visit, I tried to make everything as though she were on vacation.*

as is
without any changes ◆ *I think that sentence is ok – just leave it as is.* USAGE: Sometimes used to say that something being sold may not be perfect or may not work: *We do not guarantee that the camera can be repaired – it is sold as is.*

as of slightly formal
at the time mentioned ◆ *The price was not finalized as of this morning.* ◆ *Alex told his boss that as of the end of this month, he wouldn't be working here.*

as to
about ◆ *Of those who have read it, perhaps none will ever agree as to what it means.* USAGE: often followed by **how**, **what**, **whether**, or **why**

as well
also ◆ *They advertised the new movie on television and in newspapers as well.*

as well as
and also ◆ *We sell books to individuals as well as to schools.*

aside
aside from *sth*
except for something; = **apart from** *sth* ◆ *I watch some public television shows, but aside from that, I pretty much turn the TV off.*

ask
ask for *sth*, *also* **ask for it**
to behave in a way that is likely to cause something bad to happen ◆

You know you're asking for a punch in the nose, don't you?

you couldn't have asked for (anything) more, also **you couldn't have asked for anything better** this is the best thing of its type you can imagine ♦ *My career has been terrific. I couldn't have asked for more.* ♦ *Our daughter's babysitter turned out to be wonderful – we couldn't have asked for anything better.*

don't ask you do not want to know, esp. because the information is embarrassing or upsetting ♦ *The movie has lots of scary parts, and a particularly nasty suicide – don't ask.* USAGE: used to say that you do not want to give any more information about a subject

don't ask me I do not know ♦ *"Who's in charge around here?" "Don't ask me. How would I know?"* ♦ *He stole his neighbor's underwear once. Don't ask me why.* ♦ *Related* vocabulary **go figure** at GO

ask for trouble See at TROUBLE

asking

for the asking easily available ♦ *There are a lot of organizations that have scholarship money for the asking.*

asleep

sound asleep in a deep sleep ♦ *He knew she would be sound asleep after an exhausting day of work.*

asleep at the switch See at SWITCH
asleep at the wheel See at WHEEL

aspersions

cast aspersions on *sb*/*sth* to say that someone's character or work is bad ♦ *When the exhibit of his paintings opened, some critics cast aspersions on both his art and character.*

ass

***your* ass off** rude slang with great effort ♦ *I'm working my ass off right now on my chemistry homework.* USAGE: often follows -**ing** forms of verbs, like **working**, **laughing**, or **talking** ♦ *Related* vocabulary ***your* brains out** at BRAINS

cover *your* ass rude slang to make sure that you cannot be blamed or criticized later for something ♦ *The police were more interested in covering their asses than in finding the killer.*

get *your* ass *somewhere* rude slang to move yourself from one place to another, esp. as an order ♦ *Tell Schall to get his ass out here.* USAGE: sometimes used with a modifier: *I'll give you five seconds to get your lazy ass out of here.*

kick ass esp. spoken to be very exciting or effective; = **kick butt** ♦ *The DVD of that war movie truly kicks ass.*

kick (*sb's*) ass rude slang
1 to fight someone and hurt them; = **kick (*sb's*) butt** ♦ *"You do that again and I'm gonna kick your ass,"* he yelled at the terrified boy.
2 to defeat someone completely; = **kick (*sb's*) butt** ♦ *I want to kick their ass, just like any other team we face on the field.*

kick (some) ass (and take names) to threaten someone with physical violence; = **kick (some) butt (and take names)** ♦ *Detectives had to kick some ass and take some names in order to get information from their sources on the street.* ♦ *Saying that our country is going to go in and kick ass and take names is the easy part – doing it could turn out to be a nightmare.*

kiss (*sb's*) ass rude slang to praise someone more than is reasonable ♦ *I usually have to kiss ass just to get these musicians to show up.* USAGE: usually said about praise

at

intended to make someone like you or do something you want

make an ass of *yourself* slang
to behave in a way that makes you or an organization look foolish ♦ *I have made an ass of myself more times than I can count.* USAGE: also **make an ass of itself**: *Our own party made an ass of itself during the last campaign.*

not give a rat's ass rude slang
to not care at all ♦ *Frankly, I don't give a rat's ass about her.*

you bet your (sweet) ass slang
yes ♦ *Do I have any complaints? You bet your ass I do.* USAGE: used to emphasize your agreement with something ♦ Related vocabulary **for certain** at CERTAIN, **for sure** at SURE, **you bet** at BET

a pain in the ass See at PAIN

at

at it
doing something ♦ *Our school's staff includes new teachers and teachers who have been at it for a long time.* USAGE: often used with the verbs **be** and **go**, and sometimes used to mean that people are arguing, fighting, or having sex: *When I turned around, the boys went at it again.* ♦ *It sounded like the couple next door were going at it all night.*

at that
because of what was said or done ♦ *She called him a fool, and at that he stormed out of the room.*

while *you* **are at it**
at the same time you are doing something else ♦ *Come visit us next month, and while you're at it you can help us move to our new apartment.*

attack

on the attack
forcefully criticizing or energetically competing against someone ♦ *Flynn went on the attack against his rivals, finally bringing some life into a very dull campaign.*

ORIGIN: based on the literal meaning of **on the attack** (= using force against an enemy)

under attack
being acted against physically or with words ♦ *She said cuts in spending put education in America under attack.* ♦ Related vocabulary **under fire** at FIRE

ORIGIN: based on the literal meaning of **under attack** (= having physical force used against you)

attend

attend to *sb*
to give care to someone who is ill ♦ *Malone flew home to attend to his wife, who was in the hospital.*

attend to *sth*
to deal with something ♦ *Firefighters attended to a smoking car outside the building.*

attribute

attribute *sth* **to** *sb* slightly formal
to say that someone else was responsible for creating something ♦ *Any quotation included in your writing has to be attributed to the person who originally wrote it.* USAGE: usually said about a piece of writing or an idea

attribute *sth* **to** *sth* slightly formal
to say that one thing is the result of something else ♦ *The company attributed its decline to some bad investments.*

authority

have it on good authority
to believe that certain information is true because it came from a person or document you can trust ♦ *I have it on good authority that their business is not doing well.*

automatic pilot

on automatic pilot, also **on automatic**
doing something without thinking about how or why you do it ♦ *All the actors in this play seemed to be oper-*

ating on automatic pilot, and none of them was very good. USAGE: also used in the form **on autopilot** with the same meaning: *I was so tired, I was simply running on autopilot.* ♦ Related vocabulary **running on empty** at EMPTY

> ORIGIN: based on the literal meaning of **automatic pilot** (= a system that flies a plane without human effort)

avail

avail *yourself* **of** *sth*
to use something for your own benefit ♦ *Many students avail themselves of government loan programs to help pay for college.*

to no avail
without any benefit or result ♦ *The boy pushed against the door to no avail – something heavy was holding it shut.* USAGE: sometimes used in the phrase **to little avail** (= having almost no benefit or result): *Security forces tried to disperse the crowd, but to little avail.*

average

on the average, *also* **on average**
usually ♦ *Health conditions were on the average pretty good.* ♦ *Women on average tend to be more interested in shopping than men are.*

> ORIGIN: based on the literal meaning of **on average** (= when two or more amounts are added together and divided by the number of amounts)

average out to *sth*
to equal an amount over a period of time ♦ *I think our hotel costs would average out to thirty-five or forty dollars a night per person.*

awake

wide awake
1 completely awake and thinking clearly ♦ *My mother came into my bedroom at 7 a.m. and found me wide awake.*
2 completely aware ♦ *You need to be wide awake to the danger of leaving your belongings unattended.*

awe

in awe (of *sb/sth***)**
admiring someone or something very much ♦ *I was a kid during World War II, and I was in awe of the guys who flew these planes.*

ax

have an ax to grind, *also* **have an axe to grind**
1 to have a selfish reason for saying or doing something ♦ *The best reporting is done by people who don't have an ax to grind.* ♦ *After you get the same complaints from a number of people, you begin to think it may not be just people who have personal axes to grind.*
2 to have a strong opinion about something that influences your actions ♦ *I don't have an ax to grind about the fact that Christmas has become commercialized.*

get the ax
to be forced to give up your job ♦ *Which employees are most likely to get the ax when the company downsizes?* ♦ Related vocabulary **get the boot** at BOOT

B, b

babe

a babe in the woods
someone who has not had much experience in life ◆ *A few of the players were just babes in the woods, fresh out of high school.*

baby

throw out the baby with the bath water
to lose the good parts when you get rid of the bad parts of something ◆ *You can't close the airport because one airline has problems – that's just throwing out the baby with the bath water.*

back

back away (from *sth*)
to stop supporting something ◆ *Congress backed away from the plan to cut taxes.*

back down
to decide not to do something because others say you should not do it ◆ *Most of the speakers opposed the budget cuts, but the mayor said she would not back down.* ◆ *We demanded an end to the weapons tests, and we thought they had agreed to back down.*

back off
to not do something you intended to do ◆ *They had been unwise when they backed off from making changes to the law.* ◆ *Another boss might have told the editor to back off and not pursue the story.*

ORIGIN: based on the literal meaning of **back off** (= to move away)

back out (of *sth*)
to refuse to do something agreed to earlier ◆ *I said I'd help, and I can't back out now.*

back to back
each immediately following the other ◆ *They were the first team to win three championships back to back.*

ORIGIN: based on the literal meaning of **back to back** (= with your back pressed against another person's back)

back up *sb*, also **back *sb* up**
to support someone ◆ *The special operations forces would be backed up by infantry and air power.* ◆ *I keep telling her it's true, but she doesn't believe me – will you back me up here?*

back up (*sth*), also **back (*sth*) up**
1 to state the truth of something ◆ *The last speaker backed up what most of the other people said.*
2 to make an electronic copy of information in a computer so that it can be stored separately ◆ *We back up our files on a disk every day.*

behind *your* back
when you are not present ◆ *I often wonder what they say about me behind my back.*

break the back of *sth*
to destroy something ◆ *Police are hoping they can break the back of these gangs.* ◆ *Experts say we will have to live in a state of high alert until we break the back of terrorism.*

ORIGIN: based on the idea that breaking the back of an animal or person usually kills it

get *sb* off *your* back slang
to rid yourself of someone who is annoying you ◆ *I was willing to do almost anything to get her off my back.* ◆ Related vocabulary **(get) off *sb*'s case** at CASE ◆ Opposite **on *your* back**

in the back of *your* mind, also **at the back of *your* mind**
understood or known but not actively considered ◆ *I'd like to believe we can still be friends, but in the*

back of my mind, I know that's not true.

know sth like the back of your hand
to be very familiar with something ◆ *He knows the nighttime sky like the back of his hand.* ◆ Related vocabulary **know sth backwards and forwards** at KNOW

> ORIGIN: based on the idea that you know what your own hand is like very well

on your back
regularly criticizing you or trying to force you to do something ◆ *My mom is always on my back about leaving my clothes lying around the house.* ◆ Related vocabulary **on sb's case** at CASE, **get after sb** at GET ◆ Opposite **get sb off your back**

stab sb in the back
to do something secretly to harm someone ◆ *A lot of women in this business think they have to stab each other in the back to get ahead.* ◆ *By supporting civil rights, some senators believed Truman had stabbed the southerners in the back.*

turn your back on sb/sth
to refuse to help or be involved ◆ *How can we turn our backs on people who have no homes, no jobs, no hope?*

watch your back
to be careful of what is happening around you ◆ *You have to watch your back all the time in this neighborhood.* ◆ Related vocabulary **watch your step** at STEP

when sb's back is turned, also **while sb's back is turned**
when someone is not watching what is happening ◆ *When my mother's back was turned, my grandmother would give the dog candy.*

with your/its back against the wall, also **with your/its back to the wall**
in a serious situation with few ways to react to it ◆ *Many of these schools find themselves with their backs against the wall, and unless they get more funding, they'll have to fire some teachers.* USAGE: sometimes used in the form **have your/its back against the wall**: *The Mexican team has its back against the wall and must win tonight's game.*

backseat
take a backseat (to sb)
to let someone else deal with something ◆ *I was happy to take a backseat and let my brother deal with the family crisis.*

> ORIGIN: based on the idea of sitting in the backseat of a car and letting someone else drive

take a backseat (to sth)
to be considered to be less important than something else ◆ *For many kids, homework takes a backseat to sports.*

bacon
bring home the bacon
1 to earn money to live on ◆ *If Jo's going to stay at home with the kids, someone else will have to bring home the bacon.*
2 to do something successfully ◆ *Holtzman pitched poorly, and he was followed by McNamara, who didn't bring home the bacon either.* USAGE: usually said about playing sports

save your bacon
to prevent something very bad from happening to you ◆ *It's a short book but it could save your bacon when you're traveling overseas.*

bad
not bad
reasonably good ◆ *Thirteen bucks – that's not bad for lunch.* USAGE: often used in conversation: "*How are you?*" "*Not bad.*" ◆ also used in the forms **not too bad**, **not that bad**, and **not so bad**: *It takes me about an hour to get to work, which*

is not that bad. ♦ Related vocabulary **not half bad** at HALF

(it's) too bad, *also* **(that's) too bad**
1 I am sorry ♦ *It's too bad parents don't have the chance to read these reports.*
2 I do not care ♦ *I try to help these kids learn the basics, and if they don't have the patience to learn, too bad.*

bag

in the bag
safe or certain ♦ *When the score reached 12 to 2 we knew the game was in the bag.* USAGE: usually said about the result of a competition or election

leave *sb* holding the bag
to make someone else take all of the responsibility ♦ *If we loan the company money we want to be sure it won't fail and leave us holding the bag.*

***sth* is *your* bag** slang
you like or care about something ♦ *There are some good jobs available if marketing is your bag.* USAGE: often used with **not**: *Camping is not my bag.*

let the cat out of the bag See at CAT

bags

have bags under *your* eyes
to have dark circles under the eyes ♦ *I can always spot the new parents – they're the ones who have bags under their eyes.*

pack *your* bags
to leave a place or a job and not return ♦ *Several members of the city council feel the chief of police should pack his bags.*

bail

bail out (of *sth*)
to stop doing something or being involved in something ♦ *Bad working conditions have caused many nurses to bail out of the profession.* ♦ *The TV show triggered a number of protests, and some of the sponsors bailed out.*

> ORIGIN: based on the literal meaning of **bail out** (= to jump out of an aircraft with a parachute)

bail *sb* out, *also* **bail out *sb***
to help someone out of a difficult situation by providing money ♦ *When the airlines began to fail, they asked the government to bail them out.*

> ORIGIN: based on the literal meaning of **bail out** (= to use a container to remove water from a boat)

jump bail, *also* **skip bail**
to fail to appear in court after giving money to obtain your release before trial ♦ *McPhee jumped bail and was never heard from again.*

bait

> ORIGIN
> These idioms are based on the literal meaning of **bait** (= food used to attract and catch animals or fish).

fish or cut bait
to act or decide you are not going to do anything ♦ *The time has come when you have to fish or cut bait – either you help us plan what to do or we will decide and go ahead without you.*

rise to the bait
to react to something that was said just to make you react ♦ *Tony keeps saying that women are bad drivers, but I refuse to rise to the bait and don't answer him.*

take the bait, *also* **swallow the bait**
to accept something that was offered to get you to do something ♦ *I flirted with Kate, teased her some, but she never took the bait.* ♦ *Others tried to focus on our disagreements, but we didn't take the bait and instead talked about what we can do together.*

balance

hang in the balance
to depend on something for success or continued existence ♦ *With thousands of jobs hanging in the balance, there's a lot of competition to attract new factories.* USAGE: sometimes used without **hang**: *They don't think we should get involved, even if lives are in the balance.*

off balance
surprised or confused ♦ *Policy makers were caught off balance by the speed and success of Canada's efforts to ban the weapons.* USAGE: often used with **keep** or **throw**: *The stories were part of an effort to keep the antiwar movement off balance.*

> ORIGIN: based on the literal meaning of **off balance** (= likely to fall)

on balance
after considering everything ♦ *They felt sure that, on balance, they had made the right choice.*

tip the balance
to cause a change, esp. in making something more likely to happen; = **tip the scales** ♦ *One or two senators can tip the balance of power on almost any issue.*

ball

carry the ball
to do the work necessary to achieve something ♦ *The people who carried the ball for her campaign were mainly volunteers.*

a different ball of wax
something not at all similar ♦ *Sports are very popular but the Olympics are a different ball of wax.* ♦ Related vocabulary **a (whole) new ballgame** at BALLGAME

drop the ball
to fail to keep working to reach a goal ♦ *Public schools have pretty much dropped the ball on arts education.*

> ORIGIN: based on games like football in which all play stops if the ball is dropped

get the ball rolling, *also* **start the ball rolling**
to begin something ♦ *We've been*

tip the balance

She said that no one thing tipped the balance when she was deciding which job to take.

ballgame

trying to get the ball rolling on construction of a new playground. ◆ She was hoping that a meeting with senior managers would get the ball rolling.

have a ball
to enjoy yourself very much ◆ She's running the company now and having a ball.

on the ball
active and aware of things ◆ Their staff seems to be really on the ball, able to get projects done on time. ◆ Related vocabulary **keep *your* eye on the ball** at EYE

play ball (with *sb*)
to agree to do something the way someone else wants you to ◆ Critics say the agency has been pressured to play ball with drug companies. ◆ Related vocabulary **go along (with *sb/sth*)** at GO, **play along (with *sb/sth*)** at PLAY

> ORIGIN: **play ball** is said to start a baseball game by the official who controls the game

the ball is in *your* court
you need to react or answer ◆ We made a reasonable offer for the house, and now the ball is in their court.

> ORIGIN: based on the sports meaning of **court** (= the playing area in games like tennis)

the whole ball of wax
everything ◆ She started working on the project in 1999, and within six months she was responsible for the whole ball of wax. ◆ Related vocabulary **the whole bit** at BIT

ballgame

a (whole) new ballgame
a completely different situation ◆ The teenage world is a whole new ballgame for most parents. ◆ Related vocabulary **a different ball of wax** at BALL

ballistic

go ballistic
to become extremely upset and excited ◆ It took almost an hour to get our food, and Mike almost went ballistic when they brought him the wrong thing. ◆ Related vocabulary **blow *your* top** at TOP

ballpark

in the ballpark
within an acceptable or similar range ◆ We weren't even in the ballpark – we offered $170 million, but the offer they accepted was for $350 million.

in the same ballpark
of a similar nature ◆ When it comes to budget cuts, tourism just isn't in the same ballpark as education and public safety.

bananas

go bananas
to become very emotional ◆ I just went bananas when she told me she wanted to move out.

bandwagon

jump on the bandwagon, *also* get on the bandwagon
to support something that is popular ◆ Publishers jumped on the CD-ROM bandwagon even though they didn't know if they could sell CD-ROMs.

bandy

bandy *sth* about, *also* bandy about *sth*
to talk about something without being careful about facts ◆ The number $31 million was bandied about at the time, although actual losses might have been much lower.

bang

bang away
1 to use the keys of a computer or piano ◆ We found this old piano and started banging away.
2 to emphasize something ◆ This

book bangs away at the seriousness of the situation.

> ORIGIN: based on the literal meaning of **bang away** (= to make a loud noise by repeatedly hitting something)

bang for the buck, *also* **bang for your buck**
value in exchange for money or effort ♦ *This is a great little red wine that gives you plenty of bang for the buck.* USAGE: often used with **more**, **bigger**, and other adjectives: *For most users, these new computers provide more bang for the buck.*

> ORIGIN: based on the slang meaning of **bang** (= excitement) and **buck** (= money)

bank
bank on *sth*
to depend on something ♦ *All I can bank on is that when I tell Dad what happened, he'll know what to do.*
break the bank
to cost too much ♦ *Having a winter vacation in the sun without breaking the bank is a dream come true.*

banner
under the banner of *sth*
using the support or protection of a belief or idea ♦ *They're part of a group that goes under the banner Youth Against Crime.*

bar
bar none
without omitting anyone or anything ♦ *Terrell is the best player in the division, bar none.* USAGE: used when comparing someone or something to all others of the same type

bargain
drive a hard bargain
to make someone agree to an arrangement that benefits you ♦ *The bank was able to drive a hard bargain because the company badly needed cash.*
in the bargain, *also* **into the bargain**
in addition ♦ *It was a very powerful horse and stubborn in the bargain.*
more than *sb/sth* **bargained for**
something in addition to what was expected ♦ *The pain caused by the operation was much more than I bargained for.* USAGE: often used with **get**: *Sarah was looking for a challenge, but she may have gotten more than she bargained for in this job.*

barge
barge in
to enter a room suddenly and unexpectedly ♦ *How can you barge in here like this and start shouting insults at me!*

bark
sb/sth **has more bark than bite**, *also* *sb's/sth's* **bark is worse than their/its bite**
something is not as unpleasant as you expected ♦ *The storm turned out to have far more bark than bite.* ♦ *My boss sounds tough, but her bark is much worse than her bite, and she's actually pretty easy to work for once you get to know her.*

barking
barking up the wrong tree
believing the wrong explanation for something ♦ *He had nothing to do with the robbery – the cops are really barking up the wrong tree this time.*

barrel
over a barrel
in a situation in which someone has no choice about what to do ♦ *The software company has you over a barrel – if you don't accept the li-*

barrels

over a barrel

"Now get us the money, Mr. Peters."

The bank really has me over a barrel – I can't repay the loan if they won't let me get to my money.

cense, you can't use the software.
USAGE: usually used with **have**, as in the example

> ORIGIN: based on the idea of making someone lie on a barrel (= a large, curved container) so they will be unable to move freely

the bottom of the barrel See at BOTTOM

barrels

with both barrels

with as much energy as possible ◆ *I always get in trouble for not letting you talk, and now I'm getting it with both barrels because I did let you talk.*

> ORIGIN: based on the idea of shooting with a gun that has two barrels (= tubes from which bullets are shot)

bars

behind bars

in prison ◆ *It's impossible to imagine what it would be like to spend your whole life behind bars.*

> ORIGIN: based on the literal bars used to build a prison

base

off base

wrong ◆ *You're way off base if you think that teaching the basic skills is a waste of time.*

touch base (with *sb*)

to talk briefly to someone ◆ *I'll touch base with him later today to tell him about the meeting.*

get to first base See at FIRST BASE

bases

cover all the bases

to deal with every possibility ◆ *Those movie awards cover all the bases – best villain, best fight, best kiss, best everything.*

basics

back to basics

returned to the main principles of something ◆ *She got back to basics on her last album, using just a guitar and piano to produce some won-*

bay

derful music. USAGE: often used with **go** or **get**, as in the example

ORIGIN: based on the idea of learning **the basics** in school (= reading, writing, addition, subtraction)

bat

bat around *sth*, *also* **bat** *sth* **around**
to discuss an idea or opinion ◆ *A bunch of us batted around ideas at the annual meeting.*

go to bat for *sb/sth*
to give help or support to someone or something ◆ *She's one of my closest friends in the world – I'd go to bat for her any day.*

ORIGIN: based on the literal meaning of **go to bat** (= to position yourself to hit the ball in a baseball game)

like a bat out of hell
very fast ◆ *Ben yelled at the guy and he took off like a bat out of hell.*

(right) off the bat
immediately ◆ *Let me say right off the bat that I don't blame you for this problem.* ◆ *I know who you mean, but I can't think of his name right off the bat.*

not bat an eye See at EYE

bath

take a (financial) bath
to lose money on an investment ◆ *Investors took a bath when they had to resell the bonds at lower prices than they had paid.*

bathroom

go to the bathroom
to urinate or excrete the contents of the bowels ◆ *Mommy, I don't need to go to the bathroom.* ◆ *I took the dog out to go to the bathroom.*

batteries

recharge *your* **batteries**
to rest and get back your energy and interest in things ◆ *They took a short vacation to recharge their bat-*

teries before starting work on their next project.

ORIGIN: based on the literal meaning of **recharging a battery** (= adding more power to a device that stores electricity)

battle

do battle (with *sth***)**
to compete or argue with someone ◆ *We plan to teach groups that normally do battle with each other to cooperate.* ◆ *Jessie liked to do battle with her brother.*

ORIGIN: based on the literal meaning of **do battle** (= to fight against a military force)

fight a losing battle
to try hard but fail ◆ *For years it seems we have been fighting a losing battle against poverty and hunger.* ◆ *In an old house, you're always fighting a losing battle with dust and dirt.* USAGE: sometimes used without **fight**: *Many teachers feel they are in a losing battle for learning and order.*

a running battle (with *sb/sth***)**
an argument or fight that continues for a long time ◆ *Flynn has fought a running battle with the tobacco company over its advertisements.*

draw (the) battle lines
to clearly show the differences between two ideas or opinions ◆ *Churches generally draw battle lines over moral issues.* USAGE: often used in the form **the battle lines are drawn**: *The battle lines are being drawn between many patients and their health-care providers.*

ORIGIN: based on the literal meaning of **battle lines** (= the positions of two armies prepared to fight)

half the battle See at HALF

bay

keep *sb* **at bay**, *also* **hold** *sb* **at bay**
to prevent someone from moving

closer ◆ *He held the police at bay with a gun for several hours.*

keep *sth* **at bay**, *also* **hold** *sth* **at bay**
to control something and prevent it from causing you problems ◆ *She fought to keep her unhappiness at bay.* ◆ *In the garden, there's no security system to keep the rabbits at bay.* ◆ *Experts hope the economy will slow enough to keep inflation at bay.*

be

(so) as to be slightly formal
that it is or that they are ◆ *These crimes happened so long ago as to be of little importance now.* ◆ *They will carry as little as possible so as to be able to move quickly.*

be that as it may slightly formal
although it may be true ◆ *We are close to achieving our goals, but be that as it may, we still have problems that must be solved.* ◆ Related vocabulary **for all that** at ALL, **even so** at EVEN

be *yourself*
to act in a manner that suits your personality ◆ *The goal is to get our employees to stop trying to impress their bosses and just be themselves.* ◆ *Now she can be herself again, wear purple eyeshadow, and dress however she wants.*

so be it
nothing can be done about this ◆ *Start with the most important thing you need to do, and if nothing else gets done, so be it.*

be-all

the be-all and end-all
the best or most important thing ◆ *Professional tennis was never the be-all and end-all for me.*

beam

beam *sb/sth* **down**, *also* **beam down** *sb/sth*
to send someone or something to earth as waves of energy ◆ *A few people liked my idea, but most just looked at me as though I'd beamed down from outer space.*

beam *sb/sth* **up**, *also* **beam up** *sb/sth*
to send someone or something into space as waves of energy ◆ *Mission Control beamed up pictures of the spaceship taken from the space station.* ◆ *The ads show aliens beaming up a cow.*

> ORIGIN: based on the literal meaning of **beam** (= a line of light) and made popular by the TV show "Star Trek," in which people would ask to be transported by saying **beam me up**

beans

spill the beans
to let secret information become known ◆ *My husband was afraid to spill the beans about the cost of his purchases.*

not know beans about *sth*
to know nothing about something; = **not know the first thing about** *sth* ◆ *I don't know beans about computers – I've never even used one.*

bear

bear down (on *sb/sth***)**
1 to use all your effort to do something ◆ *Our students will have to bear down if they want to pass their exams.*
2 to push or press on something ◆ *When washing your car, try not to bear down too hard or you'll take off the paint.*
3 to move toward someone or something in a threatening way ◆ *Another storm is bearing down on northern California.* ◆ *The car gathered speed and bore down on him, so he jumped into the ditch.*

bear fruit
to produce a result that is wanted or desired ◆ *Some of the changes in the election laws are already bearing fruit.*

ORIGIN: based on the idea that getting results is like getting fruit from a plant

bear out *sth*, *also* **bear** *sth* **out**
to support the truth of something ◆ *Every opinion poll taken bears out our belief that a different jury would have reached a different verdict.* USAGE: often used in the form **borne out by**: *Her theories were not borne out by the research I did.*

bear up
to be brave ◆ *I wonder where she finds the strength to bear up under so much unfair criticism.*

bear with *sb/sth*
to be patient with someone or something ◆ *Just bear with me while I finish downloading this file.*

bearings

get *your* **bearings**
to feel sure of your abilities ◆ *Lonely and upset, she moved in with her parents to try to get her bearings.* USAGE: the opposite meaning is expressed by **lose your bearings**: *For a short time after my mother died, my father seemed to lose his bearings.*

ORIGIN: based on the literal meaning of **bearings** (= your position in relation to other things)

beat

beat back *sth*, *also* **beat** *sth* **back**
to reduce the power or importance of something ◆ *People who experience a disaster have to beat back the fear and sadness all over again when another disaster strikes.* ◆ *Once again, health-care reform has been beaten back in Congress.*

beat *sb* **down**
to make someone tired or unable to continue doing something ◆ *I like the work, but the schedule just beats me down and wears on me.* USAGE: often used in the form **be beaten down**: *Paul was so beaten down by his debts that he couldn't even think.*

beat down on *sb/sth*
to come from the sky with great force ◆ *We lay in bed listening to the rain beat down on the metal roof.* ◆ *Even early in the day a blazing sun beat down on them without mercy.* USAGE: said about rain and sun

beat it slang
to go away immediately ◆ *I told the kid to beat it, and that's the last I saw of him.* ◆ *She said she was going to pack her bag and beat it back to Tennessee.* USAGE: often used as an order: *Go on, beat it!*

ORIGIN: based on the phrase **beat a retreat** (= leave a battle quickly)

beat *you* **to it**
to do something before someone else can ◆ *You had better tell her what happened before someone else beats you to it.*

beat *sb* **up**, *also* **beat up** *sb*
1 to strongly criticize someone ◆ *The candidates spent the time beating each other up instead of talking about how to improve the economy.* USAGE: sometimes used in the form **beat up on someone**: *Sanchez beat up on Brown for problems with street repairs.*
2 to easily defeat someone ◆ *The Rangers beat up Kansas city, 7–3.*

ORIGIN: based on the literal meaning of **beat someone up** (= to hurt someone badly)

not miss a beat, *also* **not skip a beat**
to not pause ◆ *George didn't miss a beat when we asked him what kind of car we should buy for our daughter.* ◆ *Even when she's asked embarrassing questions, she doesn't skip a beat.* USAGE: sometimes used in the form **without missing a beat**: *Ella forgot the words she had memorized but, without missing a beat, she made up new ones.*

ORIGIN: based on the idea of the regular beat of music or the heart

beating

take a beating
1 to be severely defeated in a game or competition ♦ *The Knights really took a beating in last night's game.*
2 to lose a lot of money ♦ *The company took a beating last year, losing about $50 million.*
3 to be severely criticized ♦ *The president took a beating from environmental groups yesterday.*
4 to be damaged by something ♦ *The southeast took another beating from the weather yesterday.* ♦ Related vocabulary **take a licking** at LICKING

> ORIGIN: based on the literal meaning of **take a beating** (= to be hit and badly hurt)

beats

(it) beats me *esp. spoken, also* what beats me
I do not know or understand ♦ *It beats me how he managed to survive for three weeks alone in the mountains.* USAGE: often said in answer to a question: *"How should we explain this?" "Beats me."* ♦ sometimes used in the form **beats the hell out of me**: *So why am I waiting in line to get into this movie? Beats the hell out of me.*

beauty

the beauty of *sth*
a quality that makes something good, easy, or of value ♦ *The beauty of the Internet is its openness.* ♦ *One of the beauties of soccer is that you don't have to be big to play the game.*

because

because of *sth*
as a result of something; = **due to** *sth* ♦ *The flight was delayed because of bad weather.*

beck

at *sb's* beck and call
ready to do whatever someone asks ♦ *Imagine what it's like to have a cook and a maid at your beck and call.*

become

what will become of *sb/sth*
what will happen to someone or something ♦ *Investigators are trying to figure out what became of a collection of rare books worth several million dollars.* ♦ *What would become of those kittens if we didn't find homes for them?* USAGE: also used in the form **what had become of someone/something**: *I always wondered what had become of Jean.*

bed

go to bed with *sb*
to have sex with someone; = **sleep with** *sb* ♦ *She invited him over for dinner and was hoping to go to bed with him.*

in bed with *sb*
1 secretly helping someone and receiving help from them in return ♦ *The senator isn't the only person in Washington who's in bed with military equipment manufacturers.* USAGE: usually used negatively about a political relationship, as in the example
2 having sex with someone ♦ *She found her husband in bed with another woman.*

sth is not a bed of roses
something is not easy and without troubles ♦ *He soon discovered that living in a foreign country is not always a bed of roses.*

make (up) the bed
to smooth and arrange the covers on a bed so it is ready for someone to sleep in ♦ *It took me the whole morning to make the beds and do the wash.*

put *sth* to bed
1 to finish dealing with something ♦ *This is an opportunity for us to put some of these problems to bed.*
2 to get a newspaper, magazine, or book ready to be printed ♦ *You put the paper to bed and you're proud of it, but the next morning you find the world has changed while it's been printed.*

3 to clean a garden after the plants have died ♦ *It takes about two weeks to put the garden to bed.*

> ORIGIN: based on the literal meaning of **put someone to bed** (= to help someone get ready to lie down in bed and sleep)

bee

have a bee in *your* bonnet
to talk a lot about something you think is important ♦ *Martin has a bee in his bonnet about recycling.*

beef

beef up *sth*, also **beef *sth* up**
to make something stronger or more effective ♦ *The city is beefing up police patrols, putting more cops on the street where they can be seen.*

have a beef with *sb/sth*
to think someone or something should be changed ♦ *I've got nothing against advertising, but I do have a beef with how many bad ads there are on TV.*

beeline

make a beeline for *sb/sth*
to move quickly and directly toward someone or something ♦ *When the train finally arrived, cold and weary travelers made a beeline for it.*

> ORIGIN: based on the idea that a bee travels in a direct path to its hive (= place where it lives)

been

been around (the block) slang
had experience ♦ *I know because I've worked in lots of programs and I've been around.* ♦ *He's a former cop who's been around the block and knows what it's all about.*

been had
to have been deceived ♦ *If you paid much for this radio, you've been had, pal!*

been there, done that
I have experienced that before ♦ *If your attitude toward Las Vegas is been there, done that, perhaps it's time to try a different vacation spot.*
USAGE: sometimes used in the form **been there, done that, got the T-shirt**: *Our manager promises things will change, but a lot of us have been there, done that, got the T-shirt, so we don't plan to stick around.*

beg

beg off
to excuse yourself from something ♦ *I had the chance to spend the day at the beach, but I begged off, saying I had too much work on my desk.*

beg to differ (with *sb*) slightly formal, also **beg to disagree (with *sb*)**
to have a different opinion ♦ *Some people think losing that game brought the team together, but I beg to differ – the team has always been together.* ♦ *Many believe our planet is in danger, but I beg to disagree – it's not our planet but human existence that's in danger.*

beg the question See at QUESTION

(I) beg your pardon See at PARDON

begging

go begging
to be available ♦ *Good jobs still go begging in the health care and teaching fields.*

begin

to begin with
first or most importantly ♦ *To begin with, I don't have enough money to take a trip to Europe this summer.* ♦ Related vocabulary **for openers** at OPENERS, **for starters** at STARTERS

beginning

the beginning of the end
the first part of a process that will finish something ♦ *Several brilliant plays marked the beginning of the end for the challengers.*

behalf

on behalf of *sb*, *also* **in behalf of *sb***
for the benefit or support of someone ◆ *A team of lawyers sued the company on behalf of the workers who lost their jobs.*

behavior

on *your* best behavior
not causing any difficulties ◆ *The two candidates were on their best behavior, giving serious answers to questions from a group of citizens.* USAGE: usually used to refer to children, but also often used to describe the actions of adults in uncomfortable situations

behind

behind in *sth*
not finished at the expected time ◆ *Jed was behind in school and didn't graduate with the other kids his age.*

believe

believe it or not esp. spoken
this is surprising but true ◆ *She's back in college and, believe it or not, she's planning to get a degree in philosophy!*

believe me esp. spoken
this is really true ◆ *And believe me, I was scared!* USAGE: used to emphasize a statement

you better believe it esp. spoken, *also* **you'd better believe it**
yes, without any doubt ◆ *When I asked Springer if those folks still needed help, he said, "You better believe it. They need all the help they can get."*

make believe See at MAKE

not believe *your* ears See at EARS

not believe your (own) eyes See at EYES

bell

ring a bell
to seem familiar ◆ *"We live in Walnut Creek." "I don't know why that rings a bell."* ◆ Related vocabulary **have a familiar ring (to it)** at RING

ring a bell

"I'm looking for someone named Jeanne O'Conner – does that name ring a bell?"

bells
set off alarm bells, *also* **ring alarm bells**
to warn of trouble and the need for action ◆ *The report about worldwide climate change should sound alarm bells in every community.*

with bells on
with a lot of enthusiasm ◆ *"Are you going to the party tonight, Michael?" "I'll be there with bells on."*

belly
go belly up
to fail ◆ *My company announced layoffs, so I found another job, and then my new company went belly up.* USAGE: usually said about business and other organizations

> ORIGIN: based on the idea of a dead animal found lying on its back, with its belly (= stomach) facing up

belt
below the belt
not fair ◆ *That new advertisement really hits below the belt.* USAGE: often used with **hit**, as in the example

> ORIGIN: based on the idea of hitting someone below the belt in boxing, which is against the rules

belt out *sth*, *also* **belt** *sth* **out**
to sing loudly and with enthusiasm ◆ *After five decades, Brother Ray can still belt out a soulful song.* USAGE: sometimes used to describe enthusiastic talk: *Keyes has belted out speeches warning about the need to rebuild the nation's moral fiber.*

under *your* **belt**
already achieved or experienced ◆ *She had fourteen years as a manager under her belt and knew the job as well as anyone.* ◆ *He has several literary awards under his belt.*

tighten *your* **belt**
to spend less money ◆ *I've had to tighten my belt since I stopped working full time.*

bench
on the bench
1 waiting to play in a game ◆ *He went from spending all his time on the bench to being a starter.*
2 serving as a judge ◆ *Garman was the first woman in her law school and the first on the bench in Illinois.*

bend
bend over backwards
to try very hard; = **lean over backwards** ◆ *We want your business and will bend over backwards to keep it.* USAGE: usually used to describe efforts to help or please someone ◆ Related vocabulary **fall all over yourself (to do sth)** at FALL

bend *sb's* **ear** See at EAR

bend the rules See at RULES

benefit
give *sb/sth* **the benefit of the doubt**
to decide you will believe someone or something ◆ *People tell me I shouldn't trust him, but I'm willing to give Simon the benefit of the doubt and wait and see what he actually offers.* ◆ *The American people are usually willing to give the government the benefit of the doubt.*

bent
bent on *sth*
determined to do something ◆ *He was bent on quitting that job even though he was making a lot of money.*

bent out of shape See at SHAPE

berth
give *sb/sth* **a wide berth**
to keep far away from someone or something ◆ *He believes that his neighbors give him a wide berth because he is black.* USAGE: sometimes used in the form **give a wide berth to something**: *Consumers continued to give wide berth to shopping malls last month*

beside

beside *yourself*
extremely upset or excited ◆ *My mother was beside herself with curiosity.*

beside the point See at POINT

best

as best (as) *you* can
as well or as good as is possible in a particular situation ◆ *You have to live your life as best you can and not worry about what people are going to say.*

at best
in the most satisfactory conditions ◆ *This truce could last only a short time at best and, at worst, would fall apart in a week.* ◆ Opposite **at worst** at WORST

at *your* best
showing your most positive characteristics ◆ *It was kind of a bad day for me and I wasn't at my best.*

do *your* (level) best
to try very hard ◆ *Tickets are hard to get, but I'll do my best to find you one.* ◆ *Work is easy – you show up in the morning, do your level best for eight hours, then you go home.*

for the best
well ◆ *I was rejected by one college, but I really like where I am now, so I guess things worked out for the best.* ◆ *Everyone was asleep by 9, and that turned out for the best because the sun woke us at 6 the next morning.* USAGE: often **hope for the best** (= wish something ends well): *We try to make sure we've planned for the worst, but we're hoping for the best.*

get the best of *you*
to control your behavior; = **get the better of *you*** ◆ *Dad had a bad temper and he often let it get the best of him.*

make the best of a bad situation
to do as well as possible under conditions that are not satisfactory ◆ *The only way to survive being jailed is to make the best of a bad situation.*

the best of both worlds
the most enjoyable or attractive features of two different things ◆ *I have the best of both worlds because I live in the country but have a very large metropolitan area only an hour away from me.* ◆ Opposite **the worst of both worlds** at WORST

the best of the best
the most excellent example of something ◆ *When the award was made for his book, the presenter said that without a doubt, it was the best of the best.* ◆ Related vocabulary **cream of the crop** at CREAM

the best of the lot
the most excellent of all people or things considered as a group ◆ *The world is bursting with good young violinists, and one of the best of the lot is Vengerov.*

give *sth your* best shot See at SHOT

know best See at KNOW

on *your* best behavior See at BEHAVIOR

put *your* best foot forward See at FOOT

with the best of them See at THEM

bet

don't bet on it
you should not believe this is likely ◆ *He says he'll play again next season, but don't bet on it.* ◆ Opposite **(you can) bet on it**

(you can) bet on it
it is very likely this will happen or be true ◆ *Sales will go up – you can pretty much bet on it – because if there's one thing Americans know how to do, it's shop.* ◆ Opposite **don't bet on it**

you bet
I agree ◆ *"I think people in that neighborhood are snobs." "Oh, you bet."* ◆ Related vocabulary **for certain** at CERTAIN, **for sure** at SURE, **you bet your (sweet) ass** at ASS

bet the farm See at FARM
bet the ranch See at RANCH
you (can) bet your bottom dollar See at DOLLAR
bet your life See at LIFE
(do you) want to bet See at WANT

bets
hedge *your* bets
to protect yourself against making the wrong choice ◆ *Forecasters were hedging their bets about the storm, saying that it could bring lots of snow, or it could head away from us.*

better
even better, *also* **better still**
more satisfactorily ◆ *Put a goal in front of me – or even better, tell me I can't get something done – and I'll work twice as hard to do it.* ◆ *If you can't get rid of the spots, try using a razor blade or better still a liquid that dissolves gum and paint.*

better late than never
it is good this happened now although it should have happened sooner ◆ *I guess it's better late than never, but getting the award after he died strikes me as less than satisfactory.*

better off
in a more satisfactory condition or situation ◆ *I think you'd be better off if you bought a new car and didn't try to repair your old one.*

better safe than sorry esp. spoken
being careful is probably more desirable than risking a bad result ◆ *Concerned about the attacks, he sent his son out of the village, figuring, better safe than sorry.*

for better or (for) worse
this could be good or bad ◆ *We now have a new government, for better or for worse.* USAGE: said about things you think are not likely to be very good

for the better
into an improved condition ◆ *Jackson believes we can change America for the better.*

get the better of *you*
to control your behavior; = **get the best of *you*** ◆ *I didn't like what I had heard about this man, but my curiosity got the better of me and I had to meet him.*

had better
should or must ◆ *I thought I had better destroy the list so that no one else would see it.* ◆ *You'd better get moving if you want to catch your train.* USAGE: **had** is sometimes not said: *If we have a problem you better hope somebody is there to help you.*

so much the better
it will be more satisfactory ◆ *People like a good story, and if it's a strange and scary story, so much the better.*

against *your* better judgment See at JUDGMENT

do one better (than *sb/sth*) See at DO

go one better (than *sb/sth*) See at GO

have seen better days See at DAYS

know better (than to *do sth*) See at KNOW

the better part of *sth* See at PART

think better of it See at THINK

you better believe it See at BELIEVE

between
(just) between you and me
without telling anyone else ◆ *Between you and me, I think she made up the whole story about being robbed.*

beyond
***sth* is beyond me**, *also* **it's beyond me**
this is impossible to understand ◆ *How they thought they could come in and out without anyone noticing is beyond me.*

bidding
do *your* bidding, *also* **do the bidding of *sb***
to do what someone tells you to do ◆ *In some societies, men still*

big

believe their wives are there to do their bidding. USAGE: based on the literal meaning of **bid** (= to ask)

big

big in *sth*
very successful or famous in a particular activity or place ♦ *Iced tea is big in the summertime.* ♦ *The band is still unknown in the US but they're very big in Japan.*

big on *sth*
believing that something is good or important ♦ *He's very big on jazz.* ♦ *She's not big on sales and marketing and all that.*

big deal See at DEAL
big time See at TIME
bite the big one See at BITE
have bigger fish to fry See at FISH
make it big See at MAKE
the big picture See at PICTURE
think big See at THINK

bill

a clean bill of health
1 news that you are healthy or well ♦ *Johnson was given a clean bill of health by his doctors earlier this month.*
2 news that an organization is operating correctly ♦ *The airline received a clean bill of health from federal investigators.*

> ORIGIN: based on the literal meaning of a **clean bill of health** (= a statement from a health official that all the people working on a ship are in good health)

fit the bill, *also* **fill the bill**
to have the qualities or experience that are needed ♦ *If you want quieter entertainment, there are many excellent museums in town that will fit the bill.*

foot the bill
to pay money owed ♦ *Who's going to foot the bill for all the repairs?*

sell *sb* **a bill of goods**
to lie about something ♦ *He sold the FBI a bill of goods to stay out of jail himself.*

pick up the bill (for *sth***)** See **pick up the tab (for** *sth***)** at TAB

bind

in a bind
forced to deal with a difficult situation ♦ *Ashworth felt he was in a bind, with two completely different sets of directions he was supposed to follow.* ♦ Related vocabulary **in a tight spot** at SPOT, **put** *sb/sth* **in a hole** at HOLE

bird

a bird in the hand
what you have or know is better than something you do not have or know ♦ *Investors are focused on the bird in the hand, and not looking for new opportunities very much these days.* USAGE: based on the full form, **a bird in the hand is worth two in the bush**, which is rarely used

> ORIGIN: based on the idea that a person should catch one bird that is easy to catch rather than hoping to find more somewhere else

a bird's eye view See at EYE

birds

for the birds
without value ♦ *"What do you think of the new system?" "I think it's for the birds – it won't work."*

> ORIGIN: based on the idea that birds eat seed, which is not worth much

kill two birds with one stone
to do two things at the same time using the effort needed to do only one ♦ *I killed two birds with one stone and saw some old friends while I was in Louisiana visiting my parents.*

birth

give birth to *sth*
to cause or be the origin of something ♦ *The popularity of the car*

eventually gave birth to the interstate highways. ◆ Related vocabulary **give rise to** *sth* at RISE

> ORIGIN: based on the literal meaning of **give birth** (= to have a baby)

bit

a bit (too) much
unreasonable or unfair ◆ *I think it's a bit much to expect anyone to play three tennis matches in one day.* ◆ *Bill went at four in the morning and had to wait four hours to get in, but that was just a bit too much for me.*

bit by bit
in small amounts; = **little by little** ◆ *I still don't know just how all this new software works, but I suppose I'll find out bit by bit.*

champ at the bit, *also* **chomp at the bit**
to be very eager ◆ *The phone companies are champing at the bit to expand into these new lines of business.*

> ORIGIN: based on the idea of a horse chewing on the **bit** (= piece of metal in its mouth that allows a rider to control its movements) when excited or nervous

do *your* **bit**
to do your share of an activity; = **do** *your* **part** ◆ *I just want to come to work and do my bit and not talk to anybody about my personal life.* ◆ Related vocabulary **do** *your* **share** at SHARE

every bit as
exactly as ◆ *The Euro may become every bit as attractive and secure an investment as the US dollar.* USAGE: always followed by an adjective, as in the example

not a bit, *also* **not one bit**
not in any way ◆ *I'm not a bit happy with this bag – it was very expensive and already needs repair.* ◆ *That movie is not one bit scary, but then I haven't seen a movie yet this year that really is.*

quite a bit
a large number or amount ◆ *She had quite a bit to say to him when he finally showed up.*

the whole bit
all of something, including everything connected with it ◆ *When I have a meeting I wear a suit and tie and the whole bit, but otherwise, it's old jeans and a T-shirt.* ◆ Related vocabulary **the whole ball of wax** at BALL

bitch

bitch and moan rude slang
to complain ◆ *Don't start bitching and moaning again about what I pay you.*

bite

a bite to eat
a small meal ◆ *You'll feel better once you've had a bite to eat.* USAGE: often used with **quick**: *I usually sleep late and just have a quick bite to eat when I get to work.*

bite off more than *you* **can chew**
to try to do something that is too big or difficult to do ◆ *The key to success lies in not biting off more than you can chew.*

bite the big one slang
to be very bad ◆ *That movie really bites the big one.*

take a bite out of *sth*
to reduce something ◆ *Work is taking a bite out of his free time.* USAGE: often used about money: *Rising energy costs would take a bite out of people's wallets.*

bite the bullet See at BULLET
bite the dust See at DUST
bite the hand that feeds *you* See at HAND
bite *your* **tongue** See at TONGUE
sb/sth **has more bark than bite** See at BARK

bits

blow *sb/sth* **to bits**
to completely destroy someone or something in an explosion ◆ *Do you*

black

know what's left over after a large star has blown itself to bits?

black

black and white
a very clear choice that causes no confusion ♦ *When you're flying a plane, it's black and white – you can't be wrong, you've got to be right.*

> ORIGIN: based on the clear difference between the colors

in black and white
1 in written or printed form ♦ *Your offer sounds good, but I want you to put it in black and white.*
2 as involving clear choices ♦ *She tends to view the political world in black and white, with good guys and bad guys.*

> ORIGIN: based on the idea of black printing or writing on white paper

black out
to stop being conscious ♦ *I blacked out right after the accident.* ♦ Related vocabulary **go blank** 2 at BLANK

black out sth, also **black sth out**
1 to stop delivering or receiving electricity ♦ *The power failure blacked out all of northern Illinois.*
2 to keep from being broadcast or printed ♦ *Tonight's game has been blacked out on local television so you have to buy tickets to see it.* ♦ *The local papers blacked out news of the disaster.*

> ORIGIN: based on the literal meaning of **black something out** (= to keep something from being seen by covering it with black)

in the black
in a situation in which you are earning more money than you are spending ♦ *Some states have legalized gambling as a way to put their finances in the black.* ♦ Opposite **in the red** at RED

blah

blah, blah, blah esp. spoken, slang
the usual or expected remarks ♦ *You know how it goes, everyone says, "Oh Elise is so sweet and I just love her and she's such a good student and blah, blah, blah."*

blame

lay the blame on sb/sth, also **lay the blame at sb's door**
to say that someone or something is responsible ♦ *The president seemed to lay the blame for the shootings on video games and TV shows.* ♦ Related vocabulary **lay sth at sb's door** at DOOR

blank

draw a blank
1 to forget something ♦ *When Phil asked Lee which airline they were flying on, Lee drew a blank.*
2 to be unable to get information ♦ *Hoover asked the investigators to find out about Byrne, but they drew a blank.*

go blank, also **blank out**
1 to forget ♦ *He let his mind go blank and kept on walking, thinking about nothing at all.*
2 to become unconscious ♦ *He remembers trying to get up, and then he went blank until he woke up the next morning with a roaring headache.* USAGE: sometimes used in the form **everything went blank** (= someone became unconscious): *I heard a noise behind me, and then everything went blank.* ♦ Related vocabulary **black out** at BLACK
3 to stop receiving a television picture ♦ *There was a popping sound, and then the TV screen went blank.*

blast

> ORIGIN
> These idioms are based on the sound and strength of a literal **blast** (= explosion).

a blast from the past
something that makes you suddenly remember an earlier time in your life ◆ *Here's a blast from the past – the 1960s group the Mamas and the Papas were inducted into the Rock and Roll Hall of Fame this week.*

blast away
1 to be very loud ◆ *The radio blasted away with sad country and western songs.*
2 to strongly criticize or attack with words ◆ *People with no sense at all blast away on talk radio all day.* ◆ *The prosecutor blasted away at him without letup.*

full blast
1 with enthusiasm and energy ◆ *When he's here and going full blast, we're all worn out by his energy.* ◆ Related vocabulary **go all out** at GO
2 with as much power as possible ◆ *She's been running her air-conditioners full blast for months.*
3 as loud as possible ◆ *Somebody put on "The Star Spangled Banner" and turned the volume up full blast.*

have a blast
to enjoy doing something very much ◆ *Sky watchers are having a blast keeping track of the comet.* ◆ *They had a blast poking around the farmers' market looking at all the food.*

bleed

bleed *sb/sth* **dry**
to use up everything someone or something has available ◆ *The city is losing money at a rate that eventually will bleed it dry.* ◆ *I'm worried that the medical bills will bleed my parents dry.*

> ORIGIN: based on the idea of a person losing so much blood that they die

bleed for *sb/sth*
to suffer for someone or something ◆ *My father said that when he was in college he was a hopeless liberal who bled for causes.*

> ORIGIN: based on the literal meaning of **bleed for someone/something** (= to be injured or killed while supporting an idea or protecting your country)

bless

(God) bless you
may you have good health ◆ *"The road just stops and – ah-choo!" "Bless you." "Thank you."* USAGE: said to someone who has just sneezed

blessed

blessed with *sth*
lucky to have a special quality or character ◆ *She's been blessed with the sort of slim figure and very good looks everyone else wishes they had.*

> ORIGIN: based on the literal meaning of **blessed with something** (= to be given something with God's help)

bless *your* **heart** See at HEART

blessing

a blessing in disguise
something that at first appears to be bad or unlucky but is actually good ◆ *Losing my job was a blessing in disguise – I never would have found this one if it hadn't happened.*

blessings

count *your* **blessings**
to realize your good luck ◆ *Seven climbers are counting their blessings after surviving a sudden snowstorm yesterday on Mt. Rainier.*

blinders

have blinders on
to not be able to recognize or accept what is happening around you ◆ *I don't know why I thought he was innocent – I guess I had blinders on.* USAGE: sometimes used in the form **put blinders on** (= to refuse to accept something): *They put blinders on because they found it easier to*

blink

have blinders on

You'd have to have blinders on to think there are no problems in that neighborhood.

ignore her behavior than to do something about it.

> ORIGIN: based on the literal meaning of **blinders** (= pieces of material attached next to a horse's eyes to keep it from seeing anything on either side)

blink

in the blink of an eye
extremely quickly ♦ *There was a huge "boom" and in the blink of an eye the buildings were gone.*

on the blink
not operating well ♦ *The computers in the accounting department are always on the blink and the bills don't get paid on time.*

block

block out *sth*, also block *sth* out
1 to ignore something ♦ *After a while you become good at forcing yourself to block out the pain.* ♦ Related vocabulary **blot out** *sth* at BLOT

2 to make time available ♦ *When was the last time you blocked out two hours to do whatever you felt like doing?*

on the block
for sale ♦ *The radio station has been on the block for a year, but no one seems to want to buy it.*

> ORIGIN: based on the **auction block** (= the surface from which a public sale of goods or property to the person willing to pay the most happens)

a chip off the old block See at CHIP

the new kid on the block See at KID

blocks

out of the (starting) blocks
at or from the very beginning; = **out of the (starting) gate** ♦ *The company wanted to be first out of the blocks with the newest video game format.*

ORIGIN: based on the literal meaning of **starting blocks** (= blocks a runner's shoes are placed against at the beginning of a race)

blood

blood is thicker than *sth*
family relationships are stronger and more important than something else ♦ *We were old friends, but I couldn't side with her against my parents – blood was thicker than friendship to me.*

ORIGIN: based on the saying **blood is thicker than water** (= family relationships are strongest of all)

(make) *your* blood run cold
to be very frightened ♦ *The thought of the damage such a bomb could do made my blood run cold.*

draw blood
to make someone very angry or upset ♦ *He always draws blood with his film reviews.*

get blood from a stone, *also* **get blood out of a stone**
to do something very difficult ♦ *Jesse tried to get a loan from her parents, but that's just trying to get blood from a stone.*

have blood on *your* hands
to be responsible for violent injuries or deaths ♦ *If you are honest about this situation, both sides have blood on their hands.* ♦ Related vocabulary **have sb/sth on *your* hands** at HANDS

in *your* blood
as a basic part of your qualities or characteristics ♦ *She always seemed to be acting, but she had the theatre in her blood, and performing was as natural for her as breathing.* ♦ Related vocabulary **born to *do sth*** at BORN

in cold blood
intentionally and without emotion ♦ *The jury must now decide if the two men are guilty of killing their parents in cold blood.* USAGE: most often used with the verbs **kill**, **murder**, and **shoot**

ORIGIN: based the figurative meanings of **cold** (= lacking in feeling) and **blood** (= emotion)

sweat blood
to work very hard ♦ *Some students sweat blood over their dissertation, and others write it in a couple of months.*

taste blood
to achieve a small victory, which makes you want or expect an even greater one ♦ *I could taste blood after the first day of the trial and I knew we would win in the end.*

blot

blot out *sth*, *also* **blot *sth* out**
to make something stop upsetting you ♦ *I twist the pillow over my head to blot out the horrible sounds.* ♦ *She closed her eyes, trying to blot out the memory of the day's events.* ♦ Related vocabulary **block out *sth*** 1 at BLOCK

ORIGIN: based on the literal meaning of **blot** (= to cover something with drops of ink)

blow

blow sb away, *also* **blow away sb**
1 to cause someone great pleasure or surprise; = **knock sb off *their* feet** ♦ *Everyone I tell that story to, I mean everyone, is just blown away.* ♦ *That new exhibit of ancient gold objects at the museum is so amazing, it will blow you away!* ♦ Related vocabulary **blow *your* mind** at MIND
2 to defeat someone completely ♦ *The Warriors ended an 11-game losing streak by blowing away the Boston Beans 101–87.*
3 slang ♦ to kill someone ♦ *It's basically a dull movie except for the scene where Francie gets to blow away some bad guys.* ♦ *You know, it probably won't be an accident that blows me away but some health*

blows   36

problem. ♦ Related vocabulary **blow *sb*'s brains out** at BRAINS

blow hot and cold
to be enthusiastic one moment and not interested the next ♦ *It's impossible to have a healthy relationship with someone who blows hot and cold all the time.*

blow it slang
to lose an opportunity ♦ *Most people think Congress blew it on the environment by not acting quickly on the president's proposals.* ♦ Related vocabulary **throw away *sth*** at THROW

blow *sb* off, *also* **blow off *sb***
to not meet someone you planned to meet ♦ *Bates blew me off this morning but then asked me to meet him tonight.*

blow off *sth*, *also* **blow *sth* off**
1 to get rid of something ♦ *The old millionaire blew off one marriage to wed his new partner.* ♦ *Your average worker can't just blow off his credit-card debt.*
2 to consider something to be unimportant ♦ *Some students will simply blow off exams they don't think will be part of their records.*

blow out *sb*, *also* **blow *sb* out**
to defeat someone completely ♦ *Sometimes you play really badly and get blown out.*

blow out *sth*, *also* **blow *sth* out**
to make something stop working ♦ *I turned on my new television and blew out the picture tube.*

blow over
to be forgotten because something else happens ♦ *This scandal will never blow over unless something even worse happens.*

> ORIGIN: based on the literal meaning of **blow over** (= to be pushed down by wind)

blow up
to become suddenly very angry ♦ *He may blow up when he finds out how much money I spent.*

blow up *sth*, *also* **blow *sth* up**
to make something larger ♦ *Could you blow this picture up to 8 by 10?*

soften the blow, *also* **cushion the blow**
to make a difficult experience less unpleasant ♦ *Special relief funds have been set aside to soften the blow to families that lost someone in the disaster.*

strike a blow against *sb*/*sth*
to help defeat or destroy someone or something ♦ *Supporters of the law said that it would strike a blow against gun violence.*

strike a blow for *sb*/*sth*
to help or support someone or something ♦ *The court's decision strikes a blow for every little guy that's ever been kicked around by a big company.* ♦ *Don't you wish you could think of a good way to strike a blow for change?*

blows

come to blows
to have a fight or a serious argument ♦ *Protesters nearly came to blows with the police.*

blue

out of the blue, *also* **out of a clear blue sky**
happening suddenly and unexpectedly ♦ *Then one day, completely out of the blue, I had a letter from her.* ♦ *The attack came out of a clear blue sky.* ♦ Related vocabulary **out of thin air** at AIR

between the devil and the deep blue sea See at DEVIL

like a bolt from the blue See at BOLT

once in a blue moon See at MOON

(until *you* are) blue in the face See at FACE

blues

sing the blues
to complain ♦ *Computer programmers are singing the blues because business is bad and no one is hiring.*

ORIGIN: based on the type of music called **the blues** (= a musical form in which songs often are about difficulties or bad luck)

bluff
call *your* bluff
to make someone do what they said they will do ♦ *He said he would help, and now his opponents have called his bluff and asked him to provide the funds.*

ORIGIN: based on the literal meaning of **calling a bluff** in a card game (= forcing someone to show the cards they hold)

bluff *your* way See at WAY

blush
at first blush
when first learning or thinking about something ♦ *At first blush, the house seemed perfect until we discovered we had no heat or hot water.* ♦ Related vocabulary **at first glance** at GLANCE, **at first sight** at SIGHT

board
across the board
including all parts of something ♦ *The new law reduces taxes on products across the board, from wheat to cars to cell phones.*

go by the board
to stop existing ♦ *Alsop complained that the world he knew as a young man had gone by the board.* USAGE: also used in the form **go by the boards**

on board
1 supporting something ♦ *While most of us might be OK about interracial dating, some people aren't on board with the notion.*
2 working with someone ♦ *It's a well-financed organization, and it has some well-known people on board.*

ORIGIN: based on the literal meaning of **on board** (= on an aircraft, train, or ship)

boat
don't rock the boat
do not upset people by trying to change a situation ♦ *You shouldn't sit there and say everything's fine, don't rock the boat.* USAGE: sometimes used without **don't**: *Of course you'll want to rock the boat.* ♦ Related vocabulary **keep *your* nose clean** at NOSE, **make waves** at WAVES

miss the boat
1 to lose an opportunity that could lead to success ♦ *He thinks we're missing the boat on improving relations with Russia.*
2 to not understand the importance of something ♦ *I believe that people who think this issue is simply going to disappear have missed the boat.*

in the same boat
experiencing the same situation or condition ♦ *Suddenly Paul was in the same boat as any other worker who had lost a job.*

whatever floats *your* boat
do what makes you happy ♦ *If you want to have five children you should have five – whatever floats your boat.* USAGE: also used in the form **what floats your boat**: *By the time you've finished high school, you've probably figured out what floats your boat.*

body
over my dead body esp. spoken
I will never let this happen ♦ *"Wouldn't it be cool if Dad's band played at your party?" "Over my dead body!"* USAGE: said in reaction to what someone else has said

bog
bog down *sb/sth*, also **bog *sb/sth* down**
to cause someone or something to

boil

stop developing or moving forward ◆ *The film bogs down after a really great beginning.*

> ORIGIN: based on the idea of being trapped in a **bog** (= area of soft, wet earth)

boil

boil down *sth*, *also* boil *sth* down to *sth*
to reduce something to its most basic or important parts ◆ *I am supposed to boil down this ten-page report to half a page.* ◆ *The whole question boils down to how will we pay for this?*

boil over
to become uncontrollable ◆ *Anger boiled over when the police ordered the protesters to leave.*

> ORIGIN: based on the idea of liquid in a pan being heated until it boils over the side of the pot

bolt

like a bolt from the blue, *also* **like a bolt out of the blue**
suddenly and unexpectedly ◆ *Quinn's announcement that he is quitting came like a bolt from the blue.*

> ORIGIN: based on the idea of a **bolt** (= flash) of lightning that comes suddenly from the sky

bolt upright
vertical and straight ◆ *She suddenly awoke from her nightmare and sat bolt upright in bed.* USAGE: usually used with **sit** and usually used after the verb, as in the example

bombard

bombard *sb* with *sth*
to continually send someone something, esp. to inform or influence them ◆ *Every day it seems as if we are bombarded with e-mail messages warning of computer viruses.* ◆ *Stuart bombarded her with flowers, phone calls, and faxes just to get her to say she would go out for dinner with him.*

> ORIGIN: based on the literal meaning of **bombard** (= to attack a place with continuous shooting)

bone

a bone of contention
a matter of disagreement ◆ *Legal costs have continued to be a bone of contention between the two groups.*

a bone to pick with *sb*
a small disagreement with someone ◆ *My sister and I had a bone to pick with our parents over where we'd go on vacation.*

bone up (on *sth*)
to study or improve your understanding of something, esp. for a test ◆ *The test includes history, math, and languages, so I'll have to bone up on a lot of subjects.* ◆ *With new developments in medicine happening all the time, doctors continually need to bone up.*

close to the bone
very personal or offensively honest ◆ *He said he was only joking, but his comments were so close to the bone they weren't funny at all.*

not have a *type of* bone in *your* body
to have none of the characteristic described ◆ *He was friendly and kind and didn't have a mean bone in his body.*

to the bone
as completely as possible ◆ *Over the past 10 years, music programs in the public schools have been cut to the bone.* ◆ *When the wind whips around the house, even with the heat turned up I get chilled to the bone.*

> ORIGIN: based on the idea of cutting all the meat from a bone, which leaves nothing that can be eaten

bones

feel *sth* in *your* bones
to know something is true, al-

though it cannot be proved ♦ *I knew something terrible was going to happen – I could feel it in my bones.*

make no bones about *sth*
to say clearly what you think or feel about something ♦ *He made no bones about how bad he thought the food was.*

book

by the book
as the rules demand ♦ *Judge Neil runs his courtroom efficiently and by the book.*

not judge a book by its cover
to not be able to really know about someone or something by simply looking at them ♦ *She doesn't look very bright, but you can't judge a book by its cover.*

an open book
available for anyone to see or know about ♦ *Your health secrets will be an open book to anyone who can do an online search.*

throw the book at *sb*
to punish or criticize someone severely ♦ *After several arrests for drunk driving, the judge finally threw the book at him.*

hit the books

books

cook the books
to keep false financial records for an organization ♦ *We're not going to cook the books or lie about the health of our business.*

hit the books
to study ♦ *To learn English, she not only hit the books but also practiced conversing with others every day.*

off the books
without being included on official financial records ♦ *Waiters, cashiers, and busboys often work off the books, getting paid in cash.* USAGE: sometimes used with **keep** or **take**: *Officials have kept their expenses off the books.*

one for the books
something unusual or unexpected ♦ *My sister stayed in on a Saturday night! There's one for the books.*

> ORIGIN: based on the idea of a record book that contains information about the most unusual, largest, strangest events or things that happen during a particular period of time

I went to class in the morning and worked all afternoon, so I was in no mood to hit the books when I got home.

boot

on the books
part of the law ♦ *These changes would add little to the civil rights laws now on the books.*

boot
boot up
to start a computer ♦ *I have eight computers in my office and each one of them boots up differently.*

get the boot
to be forced to leave a job ♦ *Which congressmen will get the boot from the voters in the next election?* ♦ Related vocabulary **get the ax** at AX

to boot
also ♦ *She said she liked living at home, and she was saving money to boot.*

border
border on *sth*
to be similar in quality or character ♦ *I thought the author's criticism bordered on rudeness.* USAGE: usually used about negative qualities

born
born to *do sth*
to have the natural ability to do something ♦ *This sweet-voiced artist was born to sing.* ♦ Related vocabulary **in your blood** at BLOOD

born to be *sth*
to strongly show a quality in your behavior ♦ *Ellen was born to be organized.*

bosom
in the bosom of *sb/sth* slightly formal
in a safe or comfortable place, esp. with family ♦ *How often had I dreamed about being back in the bosom of my family?*

> ORIGIN: based on the idea of a mother holding her baby against her **bosom** (= breast)

boss
show *sb* **who's boss**
to make clear who has more power ♦ *When you're trying to get kids to be-* have, *you have to show them who's boss.*

boss *sb* **around**
to tell someone what to do ♦ *States and communities have complained that they're being bossed around by Washington.*

bothered
sb **can't be bothered to** *do sth*
someone has decided it is not important to do something ♦ *If I'm just going to the gym in the morning, I can't be bothered to put on makeup.* USAGE: sometimes used in the form **someone could not be bothered with something**

bottle
bottle up *sth*, also **bottle** *sth* **up**
1 to not express something ♦ *She bottled up her emotions throughout the tournament.* ♦ *The more you bottle that anger up, the more likely it is that it will explode.*
2 to keep something from making progress ♦ *The French navy had bottled up the British navy.* ♦ *Lawmakers in key positions can bottle things up for months.*

hit the bottle
to drink too much alcohol ♦ *I was disgusted with myself for having hit the bottle again.*

bottom
bottom out
1 to reach a level that is as low as it will be ♦ *Temperatures will bottom out in the teens tonight and reach the mid-20s by noon tomorrow.*
2 also **hit bottom** to become as bad as it will be ♦ *Has the economy bottomed out, and how fast will it recover?*

from the bottom of *your* **heart** esp. spoken
with sincere feeling ♦ *And I say from the bottom of my heart, I am so happy to be back in South Africa.*

get to the bottom of *sth*
to discover the truth about something ♦ *The electric company has not*

yet gotten to the bottom of why we had such a huge blackout.

the bottom fell out (of *sth***)**
something suddenly lost value ◆ *When the bottom fell out of the real estate market, a lot of people lost a lot of money.* USAGE: usually used in the past tense

the bottom of the barrel
the worst or least able members of a particular group ◆ *He described them as the bottom of the barrel of American society.* ◆ *There were only 40 students in the new class, and I think the admissions office was getting to the bottom of the barrel.* USAGE: sometimes also in the form **scrape the bottom of the barrel**: *I think the awards committee is really scraping the bottom of the barrel if they're giving this award to me.* ◆ Opposite **the cream of the crop** at CREAM

the bottom of the heap, *also* **the bottom of the pile**
the lowest rank within a group ◆ *Being near the bottom of the heap, the company has nowhere to go but up.* ◆ *Those at the bottom of the heap feel that no one cares about them.* ◆ Opposite **the top of the heap** at TOP

the bottom of the hour
30 minutes past the hour on a clock ◆ *We'll have more on these stories at the bottom of the hour.* ◆ Related vocabulary **the top of the hour** at TOP

the bottom of the ladder
the lowest rank ◆ *Because she was just out of college, her job was at the bottom of the ladder.* ◆ Opposite **top of the ladder** at TOP

from top to bottom See at TOP

bounce

bounce back (from *sth***)**
1 to become healthy again ◆ *I bounced back in just a few days after the operation.*
2 to return to a good condition ◆ *The economy seems to have bounced back from the recession very quickly.*

> ORIGIN: based on the idea of a ball or sounds bouncing back (= returning to a particular place)

bound

bound and determined
completely serious ◆ *The women of the town were bound and determined to have a school built.*

bound up in *sth*
to be completely involved in or connected with something ◆ *These guys' lives are completely bound up in baseball.*

bound up with *sth*
to be connected to something else ◆ *The secretary pointed out that US security is absolutely bound up with the security of Europe.*

duty bound to *do sth* See at DUTY

bounds

> ORIGIN
> These idioms are based on the literal meaning of **bounds** (= a limit or line on a field on which games are played).

out of bounds
not allowed or approved ◆ *The judge ruled that the lawyer's questions were out of bounds.* ◆ *Most military bases are totally out of bounds for reporters.*

know no bounds slightly formal
to have no limit ◆ *Tom's determination to succeed knows no bounds.*

overstep *your/its* **bounds,** *also* **overstep the bounds**
to do more than you are allowed to do or should do ◆ *Many believe that Congress overstepped its bounds in passing this new gun control law.* ◆ *Some of his colleagues may have overstepped the bounds of good taste.*

bow

bow down (to *sb/sth***)**
to obey someone or something ◆

bowl

The old man expects me to bow down to him, but I won't do it.

> ORIGIN: based on the literal meaning of **bow down** (= to show obedience or respect by bending the head down or the body forward)

bow out (of *sth*)
to not to do something you said you would do ◆ *An accident forced Billy to bow out of the show just before the first performance.*

bow to *sth*
to accept something without really wanting to ◆ *The government says it will not bow to pressure to allow untested drugs to be used.*

bowl

bowl *sb* over, *also* bowl over *sb*
1 to cause someone to fall by hitting them with your body ◆ *Reagan burst through the door, practically bowling over Jeanne.*
2 to completely surprise someone ◆ *I was totally bowled over by the beautiful gift from the office staff.* ◆ *The party completely bowled him over.*

> ORIGIN: based on the game of **bowling**, in which a ball is rolled toward a group of wooden objects with the intention of making them fall

box

think outside the box, *also* think out of the box
to develop ideas that are different and unusual ◆ *We need to think outside the box if we are going to come up with something really new.* ◆ *These guys are incredibly creative – they really know how to think out of the box.* USAGE: sometimes used with verbs other than **think**: *You need to look outside the box and see what you can come up with.*

> ORIGIN: based on the idea that limiting your thoughts is like thinking inside a box which can contain only a certain number of ideas

boy

boy oh boy *esp. spoken, also* oh boy
I am excited or surprised to say ◆ *Everyone said it would be fun, so I went to the party, and, boy oh boy,*

think outside the box

Her boss likes her because she's always thinking outside the box.

was it great! USAGE: usually said to emphasize something good, but also sometimes used to emphasize something negative: *I had a cold and, oh boy, I felt terrible.*

boys
boys will be boys
it is expected that men will behave badly ♦ *It's not enough to say boys will be boys, and then let them behave in whatever way they like.*

one of the boys
someone who is accepted as part of a social group ♦ *He tried to be one of the boys, but he just wasn't interested in sports.* USAGE: usually used to refer to a group of men who are friends or who work together

brains
beat sb's brains out
1 to seriously hurt someone ♦ *I was afraid he was going to come back and beat my brains out.*
2 to severely criticize someone ♦ *How could I win the election with that guy on the radio beating my brains out every day?*

blow sb's brains out
to shoot someone in the head ♦ *He pulled out his revolver and blew her brains out.* ♦ Related vocabulary **blow sb away** 3 at BLOW

your brains out
as much as possible ♦ *The people in this town want to go to the game and scream their brains out all afternoon.* ♦ Related vocabulary **your ass off** at ASS

pick sb's brains, also **pick sb's brain**
to get information and advice from someone ♦ *The new kids can pick the brains of guys who have played against these teams before.*

rack your brains, also **rack your brain**
to try very hard to remember or think of something ♦ *She racked her brains for a subject they could discuss without an argument.*

the brains behind sth
the person who provides ideas and plans for an activity ♦ *Someone very clever must be the brains behind such an organized group of thieves.*

brakes
hit the brakes
to suddenly slow down or stop a vehicle ♦ *Maggie hit the brakes, making her car go out of control.*

put the brakes on sb/sth
to slow or stop the progress of someone or something ♦ *People who live here want to put the brakes on plans to build so many new houses.* ♦ *More than a foot of snow on the ground put the brakes on travel in the region.*

branch
branch out, also **branch off**
to become involved in a wider range of activities ♦ *Women are branching out into leadership roles at many levels in the army.*

> ORIGIN: based on the literal meaning of **branch** (= the part of a tree that grows out from the main part)

brass tacks
get down to brass tacks
to start talking about the basic facts of a situation ♦ *Let's get down to brass tacks – who's going to pay for all of this?*

breach
step into the breach
to do work that someone else is not able or not willing to do ♦ *Other institutions are stepping into the breach to make loans where banks will not.* USAGE: also used in the form **throw someone into the breach**: *Friedman was thrown into the breach when our head coach suddenly quit.*

bread
your bread and butter
something that provides you with regular income ♦ *Our customers are*

our bread and butter, so treat them with respect.

break bread (with sb) slightly formal
to eat ◆ *There were several chances for politicians and celebrities to meet and break bread with each other.*

the greatest thing since sliced bread, *also* **the best thing since sliced bread**
wonderful ◆ *My kids think their new puppy is the greatest thing since sliced bread.*

break

break away (from sb/sth)
1 to escape ◆ *George's excited horse broke away and ran off into the field.*
2 to separate from the control of someone or something ◆ *Scotland isn't going to suddenly break away from the rest of Great Britain.* ◆ *We're trying to break away from the idea that men should not be affectionate with their children.*

break down
1 to stop working ◆ *Sometimes the heating system simply breaks down.* ◆ *Talks between the two countries broke down.*
2 to become very emotional ◆ *I didn't know anyone who was killed, but I still broke down and cried when I heard about the bombings.*
3 to lose strength or determination ◆ *He didn't want to go, but in April he broke down and accompanied his wife and two children to Disneyland.*

break down sb, *also* **break sb down**
1 to weaken someone ◆ *I felt so good, I felt like nothing could break me down or make me sick.*
2 to cause someone to become emotional ◆ *Andy broke down and cried several times during his retirement speech.*

break down sth, *also* **break sth down**
1 to divide something into smaller parts ◆ *The quickest way to get this job done is to break it down into a number of specific steps.*
2 to explain something ◆ *Let me break it down for you – when a dog shows its teeth, it's about to attack you.*
3 to cause something to weaken or decay ◆ *Temperatures were high enough to break down the chemicals.* ◆ *One sniff of that chocolate was enough to break down my determination not to eat sweets.*

break even
to earn as much money as you spent ◆ *Some of the books we publish do not sell enough copies to break even.*

break in
1 to interrupt ◆ *During the day they break in about every half hour to give the latest news.*
2 to enter illegally ◆ *While she was out somebody broke in and stole everything she had.*

break in sth, *also* **break sth in**
to make something comfortable by using it ◆ *They're great shoes because I've already broken them in.*

break into sth
1 to begin suddenly to do something ◆ *Then he broke into a run and we just couldn't catch him.* ◆ *Onishi broke into sobs and covered his eyes with a handkerchief.* ◆ Related vocabulary **burst into sth** at BURST
2 to enter a place by using force ◆ *His apartment has been broken into twice, even though he had good locks on the door.*
3 to interrupt something ◆ *Fanny's low voice broke into Nancy's pleasant thoughts.*
4 to illegally get access to a computer system ◆ *Spies have been trying to break into the army's computers for years, but no one has stolen any important data yet.*
5 to divide something into smaller pieces ◆ *For the next basketball season there will be 24 teams broken into four divisions.*

break loose
to escape ♦ *People are worried that they would be unsafe if that tiger ever broke loose.* ♦ Related vocabulary **(all) hell breaks loose** at HELL

break off (*sth*)
to end something suddenly ♦ *Our third meeting broke off after an hour, but our fourth lasted three days.* ♦ *I just broke off with a guy I've been going out with for eight months.*

break open *sth*, *also* **break** *sth* **open**
to suddenly and clearly begin to win a competition ♦ *Several quick goals helped Hewlett break open a close game and beat the Tigers by 10 points.*

break out
1 to begin suddenly and with force ♦ *A fight broke out in the dance club.* USAGE: usually used to describe a fight, argument, or war
2 to escape from a place or a situation ♦ *Two inmates broke out of prison and are still at large.* USAGE: often used with **of**, as in the example
3 to suddenly have spots on the skin ♦ *Detergents make the skin on my hands break out.*

break out *sth*, *also* **break** *sth* **out**
to make food or drink available ♦ *Break out the champagne and drink to the couple's health!*

break *sb* **up**, *also* **break up** *sb*
to make someone laugh or cry ♦ *He was the kind of comedian who broke up an audience with perfect accents and extremely funny impressions.* ♦ *Both of their parents died in that car crash, and it breaks me up just to think about it.*

break up with *sb*
to end a romantic relationship with someone ♦ *Many times I was ready to break up with Bill, and then he'd be nice and I'd decide I shouldn't.*

break with *sb/sth*
to end a friendly relationship with a person or organization ♦ *In Nadia's version of events, she was the one to break with Howard.* ♦ *Barnhart broke with other tobacco companies when he announced that he was settling several major lawsuits.*

give me a break *esp. spoken*
it is difficult to believe this is true or real ♦ *This guy is going around saying he's from another planet and getting paid for it – I mean, give me a break!* ♦ *You're going to run in tomorrow's marathon? Give me a break!*

breakfast

eat *sb/sth* **for breakfast**
to deal with someone or something easily and completely ♦ *People say she eats her competitors for breakfast.* ♦ *He is a level-headed guy who eats pressure for breakfast.*

breath

(like) a breath of fresh air
pleasantly different ♦ *Selena was a talented and beautiful entertainer, a breath of fresh air in an industry full of people all trying to copy each other.*

catch *your* **breath**
to stop for a short time to rest or think about something ♦ *We needed to catch our breath after she told us the news.* ♦ *She sat down on a rock to catch her breath after climbing to the top of the hill.*

hold *your* **breath**
to wait for something ♦ *I've been just holding my breath and hoping they'll call me back for an interview.*

> ORIGIN: based on the literal meaning of **hold your breath** (= to stop breathing)

in the same breath
at the same time ♦ *How can you say that you are against the death penalty but in the same breath say we may need to use it now?* USAGE: said when comparing two state-

breathe

ments that seem to have opposite meanings

not hold *your* breath
to not expect something to happen quickly ♦ *She wants the company to apologize for damaging her reputation, but she isn't holding her breath.* USAGE: often used in the form **don't hold your breath**: *If you're waiting for the next big cut in computer prices to buy that powerful new machine, don't hold your breath.*

> ORIGIN: based on the idea that it will take longer for the thing you are waiting for to happen than the amount of time you can **hold you breath** (= stop breathing)

out of breath
breathing with difficulty ♦ *Bill was completely out of breath after moving the desk upstairs.*

save *your* breath
to not say anything ♦ *She figured that they might as well save their breath – her mind was made up.*

take a deep breath
to pause ♦ *Companies want you to buy these high-tech security devices, but you should take a deep breath before you spend your money on them.*

take *your* breath away
to be extremely surprised ♦ *We have landscapes so grand they will simply take your breath away.* ♦ *She was strolling along the street, and just seeing her took his breath away.* USAGE: said especially about people or things that are surprisingly beautiful

under *your* breath
to say something quietly so that others cannot hear your exact words ♦ *The passenger next to me was angry over the delay and kept grumbling about the airline under his breath.*

waste *your* breath
to say something that is likely to be ignored ♦ *You'd be wasting your breath reporting it to the police because they don't look for stolen bikes,*

even expensive ones. USAGE: often used in the form **don't waste your breath**: *Don't waste your breath – I've already asked her to help and she said no.*

with bated breath
while nervously waiting ♦ *We watched with bated breath to see if the mother bear would bring her baby back to safety.*

breathe

breathe easy
to relax ♦ *Baseball fans can breathe easy now that the players' strike is over.*

breathe *your* last slightly formal
to die ♦ *Jay made the trip north to be with his mother when she breathed her last.* USAGE: also used to describe the end of a organization, belief, or relationship: *Amtrak may shortly breathe its last – without more funding, it may have to shut down next month.*

breathe (new) life into *sth* See at LIFE

breeze

breeze through *sth*
to do something easily or quickly ♦ *Lisa breezed through her homework, then started practicing for the play.*

breeze through *somewhere*
to move through a place quickly ♦ *Folks living close to the border could breeze through customs in those days.*

shoot the breeze
to have a relaxed conversation ♦ *Hank and his pals spend a lot of time drinking beer, shooting the breeze, and thinking about girls.*

bridge

cross that bridge when *you* come to it
to not worry about a possible problem until it becomes an actual problem ♦ *I might need a lawyer, but I'll cross that bridge when I come to it.* USAGE: also used in the form **cross the bridge** or **cross a bridge** (= to

begin to deal with a problem): *We crossed the bridge when we decided we needed to discuss these issues.*

bridges
build bridges
to increase understanding between different people or groups ◆ *They wanted to build bridges and believed that an international conference would be the best way to start that process.*

burn *your* bridges
to permanently and unpleasantly end your relationship with a person or organization ◆ *Welles had burned his bridges so badly with the movie studios that they laughed when you mentioned his name.*

> ORIGIN: based on the military action of burning a bridge you have just crossed to prevent the enemy from crossing it after you

brief
in brief
described in a clear and short way ◆ *This, in brief, was the historical background out of which Zen Buddhism emerged.* ◆ Related vocabulary **in short** at SHORT, **in a word** at WORD

bright
bright and early
very early in the morning ◆ *You'll have to be at the airport bright and early to make that flight.*

bring
bring back *sth*, *also* **bring** *sth* **back**

1 to cause something to become popular again ◆ *He's trying to bring back disco music.*

2 to cause someone to remember something ◆ *That music always brings back happy memories.* ◆ Related vocabulary **bring to mind** *sb/sth* at MIND

bring down *sb/sth*, *also* **bring** *sb/sth* **down**
to remove a person or a government from power ◆ *The demonstrations reminded me of the troubles that brought down the president.* ◆ *The students were not just asking for reforms, they wanted to bring down the government.*

burn your bridges

Harry really burned his bridges when he left his last job.

bring sth down, *also* **bring down sth**
1 to reduce something ◆ *Drugs can bring your blood pressure down.*
2 to cause something to fail ◆ *Dozens of Web sites were brought down by these software programs.*

bring sth down (on sb), *also* **bring down sth (on sb)**
to cause something to have influence or power over someone ◆ *Why would you bring down that kind of attention if you were trying not to be noticed?* ◆ *We don't bring violence down on people. People bring it down on themselves.*

bring forth sth, *also* **bring sth forth**
to make something available ◆ *Maddie brought forth a new line of clothes.*

bring sth forward slightly formal, *also* **bring forward sth**
to make something known ◆ *During the trial, evidence was brought forward that proved the wrong person had been arrested.* USAGE: often used in the form **something was brought forward**, as in the example

bring sth home (to sb)
to make something more clearly understood ◆ *Her visit to the war memorial brought home to her the suffering the war had caused.* USAGE: usually said about something that is difficult or unpleasant ◆ Related vocabulary **hammer home sth** at HAMMER

bring in sth, *also* **bring sth in**
to earn money ◆ *She brings in about $600 a week.*

bring it on
to begin a fight or competition ◆ *If this is the worst you can do to us, I say bring it on – we can defend ourselves.*

bring off sth, *also* **bring sth off**
to succeed in doing something ◆ *Only a megacorporation has the resources to bring off this kind of deal.*

bring on sth, *also* **bring sth on**
to cause something to happen ◆ *People who are sick often wonder what they did to bring this on.* ◆ *The attacks brought on fears that the political process might be overtaken by violence.*

bring out sth, *also* **bring sth out**
to make something obvious ◆ *Sometimes a crisis brings the best out in people.* ◆ *Oil polish brings out the grain of this beautiful old wood.*

bring sth to bear
to use something to achieve a result ◆ *She said that they were attempting to bring additional pressure to bear on the government.* USAGE: sometimes used in the form **something was brought to bear**: *It will be a major issue for the community because such strong arguments can be brought to bear on both sides of it.*

bring sb up short
to cause someone to suddenly stop what they are doing ◆ *A sharp stab of pain in my right knee brought me up short.*

brink

on the brink of sth
almost ready to do or experience something ◆ *Because of competition from television news, a number of newspapers are on the brink of collapse.*

broke

go for broke
to risk everything and try as hard as possible to achieve something ◆ *You can't possibly go for broke if you're afraid of what might happen if you don't succeed.* ◆ Related vocabulary **go all out** at GO

if it ain't broke, don't fix it esp. spoken, *also* **if it's not broke, don't fix it**
it is a mistake to try to improve something that works ◆ *He hasn't made a lot of changes to the team since taking over as head coach, figuring if it ain't broke, don't fix it.*

brunt

bear the brunt of *sth*
to get the greater amount or larger part of something bad ♦ *Ordinary citizens will bear the brunt of higher taxes.* ♦ *The oldest parts of the town bore the brunt of the missile attacks.*

brush

brush aside *sb/sth*, *also* **brush** *sb/sth* **aside**
to not give someone or something serious consideration ♦ *I saw this happen, and you can't just call me crazy and brush me aside.* ♦ *Her friends worried that she might be arrested, but Nancy confidently brushed aside their concerns.*

brush off *sb/sth*, *also* **brush** *sb/sth* **off**
to not accept someone or something as being important ♦ *When she told me my project would be a better television film than a feature film, I thought she was brushing me off.* ♦ *But the prime minister brushed off that criticism, saying it was just talk.*

> ORIGIN: based on the literal meaning of **brush something off** (= to remove something from a surface by moving your hand quickly over it)

brush up (on *sth***)**
to study again something you learned before ♦ *Brushing up on computer skills can be important for any worker thinking about getting a new job.*

paint *sb/sth* **with the same brush**, *also* **tar** *sb/sth* **with the same brush**
to say that someone or something has the same bad qualities as someone or something else ♦ *When one swimmer uses banned substances, you feel sorry for the others because they are all tarred with the same brush.*

bubble

bubble up
to appear suddenly ♦ *When she laughs, a happy child's laugh bubbles up out of her.* ♦ *The most interesting ideas in education have bubbled up in places as different as New York and Arizona.*

> ORIGIN: based on the literal meaning of **bubble up** (= to rise to the surface of a liquid)

burst *sb's* **bubble**, *also* **burst the bubble of** *sb*
to tell someone unexpected bad news ♦ *I don't want to burst her bubble by telling her we won't have a vacation this summer.* ♦ *He tries to burst the bubble of anyone who believes population growth is not a problem.*

on the bubble
equally likely to experience either of two results ♦ *The Cougars, who looked like they'd definitely be in the tournament a week ago, are suddenly a team on the bubble.* ♦ *Some states will vote for the Democrats, and some are likely to vote for the Republicans, but Arizona is on the bubble.* ♦ Related vocabulary **(live) on the edge** 1 at EDGE

> ORIGIN: based on the idea that something on the surface of a bubble is as likely to roll in one direction as in another

buck

buck up (*sb***)**, *also* **buck (***sb***) up**
to encourage someone to be energetic and positive ♦ *I told the kids when they had colds to buck up and tough it out.*

pass the buck
to make someone else responsible for something ♦ *Bus companies say their drivers are causing delays, but they are just passing the buck again.*

the buck stops with *sb*, *also* **the buck stops here**
someone takes responsibility for a

situation or problem ◆ *I approved the plan, I'm responsible for it, and the buck stops with me.* ◆ *I didn't feel the article misrepresented me. I mean, the buck stops here – I did write about those things.*

bang for the buck See at BANG

buck the system See at SYSTEM

bucket

kick the bucket
to die ◆ *Didn't you hear? He kicked the bucket – had a heart attack, I think.*

buckle

buckle down
to do the work you need to do ◆ *Schools, parents, and students need to buckle down and find ways to reach the new standards.*

buckle up
to fasten a strap that holds you in your seat in a vehicle or aircraft ◆ *Four out of five children are not correctly buckled up.* ◆ *The pilot asked the passengers to buckle up because we were flying through a storm system.*

bud

nip *sth* in the bud
to stop something soon after it has begun ◆ *If this problem isn't nipped in the bud, it will soon get totally out of hand.*

> ORIGIN: based on the literal meaning of **nip** (= to cut) and **bud** (= the part of a plant that develops into a flower)

buff

in the buff
without clothes on ◆ *Sasha appeared in the buff in some magazine ads.*

bug

bug out slang
1 to become upset and excited ◆ *I said I would do it, and then I started thinking and I was kind of bugging out about the whole thing.*
2 to leave suddenly ◆ *When it was time for him to show up for his army service, he bugged out for one of the islands.*

build

build in *sth*, also **build *sth* in**
to include a feature when something is being put together ◆ *You should build in some way to cancel the contract if things don't work out.* ◆ *Software developers built in a word processor.*

build *sth* into *sth*
to make a feature part of the design of something ◆ *We have built new data security into the software design.* ◆ *The schedule has a lot of free time built into it.*

build on *sth*, also **build upon *sth***
to add another thing to something that already exists ◆ *In his new book he builds on his own discoveries, and he builds on current theory.* ◆ *The president is building upon the extraordinary commitment to volunteerism Americans have.*

bulk

bulk up *sb/sth*, also **bulk *sb/sth* up**
to make someone or something stronger or more powerful ◆ *National Guard soldiers were bulking up airport security in the state.* ◆ *We have to be careful with his weight training not to bulk him up too much.*

bull

take the bull by the horns
to forcefully attack a difficult situation ◆ *I took the bull by the horns and confronted him about his drinking.*

> ORIGIN: based on the idea that holding a **bull** (= male cow) by its horns is a brave and direct action

(as) strong as a bull See **(as) strong as an ox** at OX

bullet
bite the bullet
to do or accept something difficult or unpleasant ♦ *We've all experienced unpleasant moments when we had to bite the bullet and apologize for something we did.*

> ORIGIN: based on the literal action of biting on bullets that was done by soldiers in the past who were operated on without drugs

bump
bump into *sb/sth*
to unexpectedly meet someone or find something ♦ *Last week, Jill bumped into an old college friend she hadn't seen in years.* ♦ *The story is about an amateur detective who lives in Maine and has an amazing ability to bump into real-life murder stories.*

bump off *sb*, also **bump *sb* off**
to kill someone ♦ *Unbelievable as it is, this woman decided that she was going to bump off her husband's girlfriend.*

bumper
bumper to bumper
having almost no space between cars and moving very slowly ♦ *Traffic is bumper to bumper from the Midtown Tunnel all the way out to exit 17 on the Turnpike.*

bundle
bundle up (*sb*), also **bundle *sb* up**
to put coats and other warm clothes on someone ♦ *In the winter you have to bundle up, because it gets really cold.* ♦ *Her mom bundled her up in a down parka, with a knit cap under the hood.*

burgers
flip burgers
to do work that does not pay well, esp. at a cheap restaurant ♦ *Instead of playing baseball, the boys might be flipping burgers and earning a little cash.*

burn
burn out (*sth*), also **burn *sth* out**
to stop working because of damage ♦ *The new motor burned out because they used the wrong type of oil.*
USAGE: usually said about a motor or engine

> ORIGIN: based on the literal meaning of **burn out** (= to stop producing a flame)

burn out (*sb*), also **burn *sb* out**
to stop being effective because of too much work or stress ♦ *Most of these people will burn out within 10 years and be replaced by younger employees who don't mind working nights, weekends, and holidays.* ♦ *This work burns me out so much that by the end of the day I can't even decide what I want to eat for dinner.*

burn *sb* up, also **burn up *sb***
to anger someone a lot ♦ *I was really burned up by her comment.*

burn up *sth*, also **burn *sth* up**
1 to use all of something ♦ *Commuting to and from my job burns up all my free time.*
2 to use a lot of a system ♦ *The singer's fans have burned up the Internet with speculation about her cancelled tour.*

burn *your* bridges See at BRIDGES
burn *your* fingers See at FINGERS
burning the midnight oil See at MIDNIGHT
burn the candle at both ends See at CANDLE
burn *sth* to a crisp See at CRISP
crash and burn See at CRASH
have money to burn See at MONEY

burner

> ORIGIN
> These idioms are based on the idea that on an old-fashioned stove, the temperature at the back is lower and food cooks more slowly or is kept warm there.

burst

on the front burner, *also* on *sb's* front burner
getting or needing immediate attention ♦ *We want to make sure that aid for Africa is on the front burner.* ♦ *Retirement planning hasn't exactly been on Kessler's front burner.* USAGE: sometimes used with **put**: *The president has finally put this issue on the front burner.* ♦ Opposite **on the back burner**

on the back burner
not getting or needing immediate attention ♦ *After months on the back burner, the debate about e-mail privacy is about to be renewed.* USAGE: often used with **put**: *She decided to attend Harvard, where she would study political theory and put her acting career on the backburner.* ♦ Opposite **on the front burner**

burst

> ORIGIN
> These idioms are based on the literal meaning of **burst** (= to suddenly break apart).

burst in (on *sb/sth*)
to enter or appear suddenly or unexpectedly ♦ *She was in the middle of teaching her writing class when the head of the English department burst in.* ♦ *"Sorry to burst in on you like this,"* Nick apologized to the room full of surprised people.

burst into *sth*
to begin to produce a lot of something ♦ *The children burst into tears when they saw their ruined toys.* ♦ *The car burst into flames.* ♦ *The whole situation was so ridiculous, I simply burst into laughter.* ♦ Related vocabulary **break into** *sth* 1 at BREAK

burst out *doing sth*
to suddenly begin making sounds ♦ *Everyone burst out laughing.* ♦ *I collapsed in a heap and burst out crying.*

burst out of *somewhere*
to suddenly appear from somewhere ♦ *Suddenly I burst out of the tangled brush onto the pavement.* ♦ *The silvery jet burst out of the dark clouds above.*

bursting

bursting at the seams
extremely full or crowded ♦ *The courts are bursting at the seams and might not be able to handle more arrests.* ♦ *The city is absolutely bursting at the seams, and one of the biggest complaints people have is the number of cars.*

bush

beat around the bush
to avoid talking about what is important ♦ *Quit beating around the bush and tell me what you really think about my idea.*

bushes

beat the bushes
to search everywhere for someone or something ♦ *We don't have to beat the bushes to get good photographs – they mostly come to us from photographers we know.*

> ORIGIN: based on the practice in hunting of having someone hit bushes with a stick in order to force birds hiding in them to fly up into the air to be shot

business

business as usual
doing everything in the ordinary way ♦ *Serious problems such as depression can make business as usual impossible for most people.* ♦ *She says we have to deal with the AIDS epidemic because business as usual is killing too many people.*

get down to business
to begin seriously doing what you need to do ♦ *They both knew they did not have much time, so they got down to business and began to discuss the issues that needed to be settled.* USAGE: sometimes used without **get**: *Our professor is very down to business and very well prepared.* ♦

Related vocabulary **get down to it** at GET

go about *your* business
to do what you usually do ♦ *How could she make such a big mistake and then go about her business as if it never happened?* ♦ Related vocabulary **go about *sth/doing sth*** at GO

sb is in business
someone is able to begin doing something ♦ *Making one of these instruments looks like a simple process – find the right kind of plant, cut off the stalk, and you're in business.* USAGE: sometimes used in the form **back in business** (= able to start doing something again): *To clean the air filter, just take it out and rinse it, and you're back in business.*

in the business of *doing sth*
to have something as your main purpose ♦ *Film makers are in the business of creating illusion.* USAGE: sometimes used in the form **not in the business of doing something**: *Our organization is not in the business of helping people break the law.*

like nobody's business
very quickly, very easily, or very well ♦ *Kids can work the Internet like nobody's business.*

make it *your* business to *do sth*
to decide you will take responsibility to do something ♦ *He made it his business to find out what happened to the money.*

mean business
to be serious ♦ *After she scored that point, I realized that she meant business.* ♦ *We hope that the government means business and will really do something about the lack of affordable housing.*

mind your own business
do not be so interested in what other people are doing ♦ *If she asks where we're going, tell her to mind her own business.*

mix business with pleasure
to combine work and social activities ♦ *Weekend getaways that allow you to mix business with pleasure have become fashionable.*

none of *your* business, *also* **nobody's business**
do not interest yourself in matters that do not involve you ♦ *"Those children should never be left alone." "Don't tell me what to do – it's none of your business."*

the business end of *sth*
the part of a weapon or tool that does something ♦ *She screamed when she found herself facing the business end of his gun.*

butt

butt in
to interrupt ♦ *Sorry to butt in on you like this, but there's an important call.*

butt out
to not get involved in something ♦ *Teens usually think their parents should just butt out of their lives.* USAGE: often used as an order: *This is none of your business, so just butt out!*

kick butt esp. spoken
to be very exciting or effective; = **kick ass** ♦ *The new system really kicked butt, catching several cheaters the first day it was used.*

kick (*sb's*) butt, *also* **kick some butt**
1 to fight someone and hurt them; = **kick (*sb's*) ass** ♦ *Lyle claimed she could kick my butt, and then decided she had better start training in case anybody asked her to prove it.* ♦ *The cops in this city don't just want to kick down doors and kick some butt.*
2 to defeat someone completely; = **kick (*sb's*) ass** ♦ *Even when Barry was hurting, he was not only on the field but also kicking butt.* ♦ *We hope they come back because we want to kick their butt again.*

kick (some) butt (and take names) See **kick (some) ass (and take names)** at ASS

butter

butter sb up, *also* **butter up sb**
to praise someone in order to get them to like you or do what you want ♦ *The magazine tried to get her to write an article by buttering her up.*

butterflies

have butterflies in *your* stomach
to feel very nervous ♦ *Her mouth was dry, there were butterflies in her stomach, and her knees were shaking so much it was hard to walk on stage.*

buttons

push sb's buttons
to do exactly the right thing to get people to act the way you want ♦ *He was an extremely good speaker and knew just how to push an audience's buttons to keep them interested.* USAGE: also used in the form **know what buttons to push**: *People in your own family know exactly what buttons to push to upset you.* ♦ Related vocabulary **yank sb's chain** at CHAIN

buzz

buzz off esp. spoken
go away ♦ *I can't believe he would tell a senator to buzz off.* USAGE: often used as an order: *Buzz off and leave me alone!*

give sb a buzz esp. spoken
to telephone someone; = **give sb a ring** ♦ *I was just wondering if you were up for dinner tonight so give me a buzz if you're around.*

by

by and by slightly formal
soon ♦ *I know you want to hear what happened last night, and I'm coming to that by and by.*

bygones

let bygones be bygones
forget about unpleasant things that have happened in the past ♦ *There is a feeling here that we should let bygones be bygones and move on to more important things.* USAGE: sometimes used in the form **bygones are bygones**: *What is past history is history, what is done is finished, and bygones are bygones.*

C, c

caboodle
the whole caboodle See **the whole kit and caboodle** at KIT

cage
rattle *sb*'s cage
to make someone angry on purpose ◆ *I rattled his cage by telling him I hated his art.*

> ORIGIN: based on the idea of **rattling** (= making a noise by repeatedly hitting) the cage to annoy the animal inside it

cahoots
in cahoots (with *sb*)
working secretly with someone ◆ *She was in cahoots with this guy who was smuggling drugs across the border.* USAGE: usually said about doing something dishonest

cake
have *your* cake and eat it too
to do or get two good things at the same time ◆ *I worked at home so I could raise my family and still earn money. It let me have my cake and eat it too.*

***sth* takes the cake**
something is the most extreme example ◆ *I've known some jerks but you take the cake.* USAGE: usually said about something bad

the icing on the cake See at ICING

call
(above and) beyond the call of duty esp. spoken
much more than should be expected ◆ *If your waiter goes beyond the call of duty, leave a bigger tip.* ◆ Related vocabulary **above and beyond *sth*** at ABOVE

> ORIGIN: first used about police officers, fire fighters, or soldiers who were injured or killed while doing their jobs

call for *sth*
1 to demand something ◆ *Officials called for an investigation.*
2 to require something ◆ *The recipe calls for 12 pounds of tomatoes, onions, sausage, and some herbs.* ◆ *I didn't know if that kind of comment was what was called for.*
3 to calculate in advance ◆ *The weather forecast for Friday calls for wind and rain.* ◆ *Economic forecasts called for a 4.4% increase in the growth rate.*

call in *sb*, also **call *sb* in**
to demand that someone come to do something specific ◆ *The mayor called in the police to provide extra security for the conference.* ◆ *I can't afford to call the plumber in every day!*

call in sick
to telephone work or school to say you are ill and will not be there ◆ *I woke up with a terrible cold and had to call in sick last week.*

call it quits
to stop doing something ◆ *A number of county fairs have called it quits because of a lack of interest.* USAGE: often said about an effort to accomplish something: *Brant called it quits this morning after traveling nearly 12,000 kilometers in the balloon.*

call off *sth*, also **call *sth* off**
to decide not to do something that was planned ◆ *Why should I call off the trip when I've already paid for it?*

call on *sb*
1 to ask someone to do something ◆ *The governor called on the public to use less water during this dry weather.* ◆ *The teacher called on me with a tough question, and I didn't know the answer.*
2 to visit someone ◆ *Part of my job was to go out and call on farmers, to see how they were doing.*

call up sb, *also* call sb up
1 to order soldiers to begin active service ◆ *The secretary of defense called up more reserves, which brings the total number of troops on active duty to 29,000.*
2 to choose someone to play at a higher rank of a sport ◆ *Herman was called up to the major leagues a month later.*

call up sth, *also* call sth up
1 to find and bring information to a computer screen ◆ *Your computer may freeze when you try to call up the file.*
2 to cause something to be remembered ◆ *The attacks called up thoughts of how Americans reacted after the bombing of Pearl Harbor.*

close call
1 a very difficult decision ◆ *Apparently it was a close call, but after a long debate the jury convicted her.*
2 something bad that almost happened; = **close shave** ◆ *Sam had several close calls while he was learning to drive with his dad.*

no call for sth *esp. spoken, also* no call to do sth
it is not reasonable ◆ *Some movies throw in some violence, even though there's no call for it in the story.* ◆ *You have no call to be jealous.*

on call *esp. spoken*
available and ready to work or do something at any time ◆ *Working for Mitnick was a lot like being a doctor – I was constantly on call.*

pay a call on sb/sth
to go somewhere to see someone or something ◆ *The president paid a call on US troops stationed in the region on Sunday.* ◆ Related vocabulary **pay (sb/sth) a visit** at VISIT

sth to call *your* own
something that you own or control ◆ *I've been renting this house for several years and now I want a place to call my own.* USAGE: sometimes used with periods of time to say that someone is too busy: *With a full-time job and a family to take care of, I don't have a minute to call my own.* ◆ also used with **can** or **could**: *Children need a little money they can call their own in order to learn its value.*

too close to call
impossible to guess the result in advance ◆ *Tonight's semifinals match is too close to call.* USAGE: usually said about a competition or an election

calm

the calm before the storm
a quiet period immediately before a period of great activity or trouble; = **the lull before the storm** ◆ *For most teachers, the days just before the school year begins are the calm before the storm.*

camp

break camp
to fold up and pack a tent and other equipment used to camp ◆ *We broke camp yesterday and hiked to town, where we caught a bus back to the city.*

camp out
1 to live in the open air for a time, often in a tent ◆ *When I was in high school, during the summer we would camp out at the lake.*
2 to live in a place temporarily without many possessions ◆ *The floods forced people from the city to camp out with relatives or even in public parks.*

can

in the can
1 completed and ready to be shown ◆ *Sarandon has another movie in the can.* USAGE: usually said about a film or television show
2 *slang* in prison ◆ *The last time he was in the can, he attacked another prisoner.*

open (up) a can of worms
to create a situation that will cause trouble or be unpleasant ◆ *The in-*

vestigation into how these expensive trips were paid for certainly opened a can of worms. USAGE: sometimes used without **open up**: *I don't think her plan will work – it seems like kind of a can of worms to me.*

candle

burn the candle at both ends
to regularly stay awake late and get up early because you are too busy ◆ *I'm busy trying to get ready for the holidays and burning the candle at both ends.*

sb/sth can't hold a candle to sb/sth else, *also* **sb/sth doesn't hold a candle to sb/sth else**
someone or something is not as good as someone or something else ◆ *For Walter, basketball and football can't hold a candle to baseball.* USAGE: sometimes used in the form **something can hold a candle to something else**: *Not one of her drawings can hold a candle to yours.*

candy

like taking candy from a baby
extremely easy ◆ *Selling my mother something I made is like taking candy from a baby – she can't say no.*

cap

cap sth off, *also* **cap off sth**
to complete an experience in a particularly good or bad way ◆ *We went to the beach, strolled around town, and capped off our visit with a fireworks display that evening.* USAGE: sometimes used in the form **cap it all off**: *There's been bad economic news all year, and to cap it all off, now oil prices are increasing.* ◆ Related vocabulary **to top it all (off)** at TOP

capital

with a capital *letter*
to an extreme degree ◆ *That makes me feel OK with a capital O.* ◆ *If you want culture with a capital C, you can go to an art museum or a concert.* USAGE: used to emphasize the meaning of a particular word

cards

hold all the cards, *also* **have all the cards**
to have what is needed to control a situation ◆ *He holds all the cards in our office – he even decides where the water coolers are located and what kinds of pencils we have.*

> ORIGIN: based on the idea of **holding** (= controlling) the most valuable cards in a card game

in the cards, *also* **on the cards**
very likely to happen ◆ *I think winning the World Series this year is definitely in the cards for Boston.* ◆ *Some reports suggest that a tax cut is still on the cards.*

> ORIGIN: based on the use of **tarot cards** (= a set of cards with pictures representing different parts of life) that are believed to be able to show what will happen in the future

play *your* cards right
to do the correct things to achieve a desired result ◆ *If I play my cards right, I could be hired as a consultant on that project.*

> ORIGIN: based on the idea of **playing** (= choosing and putting on the table) the right card at the right time in a card game

put (all) *your* cards on the table, *also* **lay *your* cards on the table**
to truthfully explain what you know or think ◆ *I could only put my cards on the table and say I don't know what happened to this child.*

> ORIGIN: based on the idea of showing other players your cards in a card game

care

sb couldn't care less, *also* **sb could care less**
someone does not care at all ◆ *Most fans couldn't care less about it.*

take care (of yourself) esp. spoken goodbye; = **take it easy** ◆ *"It was* nice talking with you." "It was nice talking to you, too." "Okay, take care." ◆ "Good-bye," she said to him, "take care of yourself." USAGE: usually said as part of ending a conversation

take care of sb/sth
1 to be responsible for someone or something ◆ *Our parents spent a lot of time taking care of us when we were young.* ◆ *My mother-in-law fell and could not take care of herself anymore.* ◆ *My wife takes care of paying the bills.*
2 to deal with a difficult situation or person ◆ *I was forced to take care of all the financial reports, lawyers, and contracts.* ◆ *The principal usually takes care of students who won't follow the rules.* ◆ Related vocabulary **look after sb/sth** at LOOK

cares
who cares? esp. spoken
I am not interested in or upset by something because it is not important ◆ *I overslept and missed the class, but who cares?*

sweep something under the carpet

carpet
sweep sth under the carpet
to hide something embarrassing; = **sweep sth under the rug** ◆ *The problem is usually ignored or swept under the carpet.*

carried
carried away
made very emotional or enthusiastic; = **swept away** ◆ *I got carried away and bought four new shirts.* ◆ *Not everyone was carried away by the news that the team had won.*

carrot
a carrot and stick (approach)
rewards and punishments that influence someone's behavior ◆ *Our company uses a carrot and stick – more money is the carrot, loss of your job is the stick.* USAGE: used in different forms to describe different combinations of rewards and punishments: *Management's proposed deal is all stick and no carrot.* ◆ *The latest round of peace talks offers both sides the carrot as well as the stick.*

She felt that some aspects of our history should be swept under the carpet.

> ORIGIN: based on the reward of a **carrot** (= a long orange vegetable) and the punishment of using a **stick** to encourage a horse to move

carry

carry off *sth*, *also* **carry** *sth* **off**
to succeed in doing something ◆ *A shaggy dog named Bugsy carries off some of the most amusing moments in the play.* ◆ *She said she never lies because she doesn't have a good enough memory to carry it off.*

carry on
1 to continue to do or be involved in something ◆ *Dianne is carrying on the family tradition by becoming a lawyer.* ◆ *It's hard to carry on a business and take care of a small child at the same time.*
2 to continue behaving in a particular way ◆ *You've got to carry on as though nothing happened.*
3 to behave in a manner that is not controlled ◆ *The kids have been carrying on all day.*
4 to continuously complain about something ◆ *My grandmother carried on about the bad language she hears on TV.*

carry out *sth*, *also* **carry** *sth* **out**
to do a job or complete an activity ◆ *Astronauts planned a spacewalk to carry out major repairs on the space station.* ◆ *The agency doesn't have the funds or the know-how to carry out its duties.*

carry over *sth*, *also* **carry** *sth* **over**
to allow something you deal with to continue existing ◆ *I try not to let my problems at work carry over into my private life.* ◆ *She couldn't pay the full amount she owed, so she carried over part of it to the next month.*

carry *sb* **through** (*sth*)
to help someone continue to exist in a difficult situation ◆ *People stocked up on food, fuel, and candles to carry them through the storm.* ◆ *She puts her trust in God and believes He will carry her through.*

carry through *sth*, *also* **carry** *sth* **through**
to complete something successfully ◆ *We'll need a qualified and experienced planner to carry through the study.* USAGE: often used in the form **carry through with something** or **carry through on something**: *I think they lack the will to carry through with their attack.* ◆ *She felt no need to carry through on what she signed up for.*

carry a tune See at TUNE
carry the ball See at BALL
carry the day See at DAY
carry weight See at WEIGHT

cart

cart *sb/sth* **away**, *also* **cart away** *sb/sth*
to take someone or something somewhere ◆ *We cleaned out the garage and carted tons of stuff away.* ◆ *Investigators were carting away boxes of material from her office.*

cart *sb* **off**, *also* **cart off** *sb*
to take someone or something somewhere ◆ *Rioters smashed windows and carted off televisions, shoes, car tires, and anything else they could carry.* ◆ *He was carted off to jail.*

(put) the cart before the horse
to do something that should happen later before other things ◆ *Barnhart is putting the cart before the horse by building a stadium before a team has agreed to play there.*

carve

> ORIGIN
> These idioms are based on the literal meaning of **carve** (= to cut something into slices or pieces).

carve out *sth*, *also* **carve** *sth* **out**
1 to create a reputation, rank, or job through skillful activities ◆ *She carved out a reputation for herself as a high-powered lawyer.*
2 to get a part of something ◆ *Those*

case

companies carved out a sizable share of the imported pasta market.

carve up *sth*, also **carve** *sth* **up**
to divide something into parts ♦ *The new owner carved up the company and sold off several divisions.* ♦ *Local leaders have carved up the forest and turned the land over to a company that built homes on it.*

case

(a) case in point slightly formal
one example of this ♦ *Elliott is one of the best rappers around, and her new album is a case in point.* ♦ *Boston is such an unpredictable team – their victory over Indiana yesterday is a case in point.*

get off *sb's* **case**
to stop criticizing and annoying someone ♦ *They think he was trying to cheat them, so they're not going to get off his case.* ♦ Related vocabulary **get** *sb* **off** *your* **back** at BACK

in any case
whatever happens; = **in any event** ♦ *You should be able to catch a bus, but in any case you can always take a taxi home.* ♦ *In any case, you should test drive the car before buying it.* USAGE: the same meaning can be also expressed by **come what may**, **come hell or high water**, **at (the very) least**, and **either way** ♦ Related vocabulary **one way or the other** 2 at WAY

in case
if ♦ *I don't expect much traffic, but in case there is some, I think we should leave early.*

in case of *sth*
if something unusual or unexpected should happen ♦ *In case of fire, go immediately to the nearest emergency exit.* ♦ Related vocabulary **in the event of** *sth* at EVENT

I rest my case esp. spoken
you have proved that what I just said is true ♦ *Ned's mother said he needs to leave home or he'll never be independent. His sister said, "But he can't even do his wash!" and his mother replied, "I rest my case."*

just in case
only if something happens ♦ *We keep a lot of food on hand, just in case there's a storm.* USAGE: often used without any following clause: *Make sure you have extra batteries available, just in case.*

make a case for *sth*
to explain why something should be done ♦ *Everything seems to be going pretty well, and she has yet to make a case for change.* USAGE: also used in the form **make a case that** (= to explain that something is true): *It is easy to make a case that he's one of the best baseball players around.*

> ORIGIN: based on the legal meaning of **make a case** (= to show that what you say is true)

on *sb's* **case**
telling someone what to do or criticizing what they do ♦ *You're always on my case about my smoking.* USAGE: often used with **get**: *Perry had been drinking a lot lately, and Beth started to get on his case.* ♦ Related vocabulary **get after** *sb* at GET, **on** *your* **back** at BACK

on the case
doing what needs to be done ♦ *There is definitely a problem, and we are on the case – that's all I can say for now.*

cash

cash in (on *sth***)**
to make money doing something ♦ *Companies developing this technology are not necessarily cashing in.* ♦ *Criminals cannot cash in on their crimes by selling their stories to the newspapers.*

cash out (*sth***)**
to sell something you bought as an investment ♦ *Most of the early investors cashed out as the business became increasingly complicated.* ♦ *You should avoid cashing out your retirement plan.*

cast

cast about (for *sth*)
to try to find something ♦ *She spent years casting about for a career before she opened her own restaurant.*

> ORIGIN: based on the idea of someone who fishes by **casting** (= throwing) a line or net in first one pool of water and then another

cast doubt on *sth*
to cause uncertainty about something ♦ *New DNA evidence has cast doubt on the guilty verdict.*

cast off *sth*
to get rid of something ♦ *Shirts and ties were being cast off in favor of informal clothes for business.*

> ORIGIN: based on the literal meaning of **cast off** (= to unfasten the ropes holding a ship)

cat

cat got *your* tongue
why are you not speaking ♦ *After she finished the story, I kept silent. "What's the matter, cat got your tongue?" she asked.*

let the cat out of the bag
to tell something that is a secret, often without intending to ♦ *Amazingly, not one of the people who knew about the surprise let the cat out of the bag.*

play (a game of) cat and mouse
1 to repeatedly try to make someone react in a way that will cause them problems ♦ *Enemy warplanes have been playing a deadly game of cat and mouse, trying to bring American fighter planes into range of their missiles.*
2 to try to find someone who is hiding from you ♦ *Border agents played cat and mouse with people trying to enter the country illegally.*

> ORIGIN: based on the way a cat plays with a mouse before killing it

catch

catch as catch can
achieved any way that is possible and not in a planned way ♦ *Without a school to go to, her education was catch as catch can.*

catch *sb* off guard
to surprise someone ♦ *He's used to being interviewed and it seems that no question catches him off guard.*

catch up on *sth*
1 to do whatever you have not had time to do ♦ *I have to catch up on my reading.*
2 to find out about something ♦ *Most folks stop here for a cup of coffee while they catch up on the day's news.*

catch you later esp. spoken
goodbye ♦ *I just called to say hi and hopefully we'll talk tomorrow – catch you later.* USAGE: used at the end of a conversation or message

cats

raining cats and dogs
to be raining in great amounts ♦ *It was raining cats and dogs by the time I got home.*

caught

***sb* would not be caught dead**
someone would never do or wear something ♦ *I wouldn't be caught dead doing ads for that company.* ♦ *My father wouldn't have been caught dead in a white suit.*

> ORIGIN: based on the idea that something very bad would make even a dead person uncomfortable

caught short
not prepared for something ♦ *Airlines were caught short of fuel because of the oil workers' strike.* USAGE: often used when someone does not have enough money: *The cash machines aren't working and I'm really caught short.*

(get) caught up in *sth*
to become completely involved in something ♦ *You get caught up in*

cause

the excitement of the moment and don't think a lot about what happens next.

cause

make common cause slightly formal
to work together to achieve something ◆ *A number of groups have made common cause with local people to stop the highway from being built.* ◆ *The two countries have begun to make common cause against shared enemies.* ◆ Related vocabulary **have sth in common (with sb/sth)** at COMMON

caution

throw caution to the wind, *also* **throw caution to the winds**
to take a risk ◆ *As a young man he was always ready to throw caution to the wind.*

cave

cave in (to sb/sth)
to agree to something after originally opposing it; = **give in (to sb/sth)** ◆ *If the pressure from your parents becomes too strong, you might cave in and go to graduate school.*

> ORIGIN: based on the literal meaning of **cave in** (= to suddenly fall inward)

ceiling

hit the ceiling See **hit the roof** at ROOF

center

center on sb/sth, *also* **center around sb/sth**
to be the person or thing that is most noticed ◆ *The movie centers on one man's struggle to deal with his father.* ◆ *Much of this region's economy centers around a large oil field.*

the center of attention
someone or something everyone notices ◆ *Frost was the center of attention in the week before the game.*

cents

put *your* two cents in, *also* **put in *your* two cents**
to give your opinion ◆ *She believes it's her duty to vote and put her two cents in.*

for two cents
without needing much encouragement ◆ *You're so spoiled and nasty that for two cents I'd throw you out in the street.*

certain

of a certain age
who are not young ◆ *Adults of a certain age might want to spend a couple of hundred dollars more for a larger monitor that will be much easier on their eyes.* USAGE: used to avoid saying **middle aged** or **old**

for certain
without any doubt; = **for sure** ◆ *The only thing Jack could say for certain about Jill was that she was a complete mystery to him.* ◆ Related vocabulary **you bet** at BET, **you bet your (sweet) ass** at ASS

chain

yank sb's chain, *also* **pull sb's chain**
to upset someone ◆ *She knows that playing that music really yanks my chain.* ◆ Related vocabulary **push sb's buttons** at BUTTONS

chair

pull up a chair
to move a chair so you can sit with others in a group ◆ *We're just talking about the picnic on Saturday – why don't you pull up a chair?* USAGE: often used as an invitation, as in the example

chairs

play musical chairs
to move people from one organization or job to another ◆ *The teams play musical chairs at that position – all of the top punters have played for at least two teams.* USAGE: also used in the form **a game of musi-**

cal chairs: *Buckley was reassigned in a game of corporate musical chairs Thursday.*

> ORIGIN: based on the children's game in which there is one more player than there are chairs and the players walk in a circle around the chairs until music stops playing, at which time they hurry to the nearest empty chair

chalk

chalk up sth, *also* **chalk sth up**
to record something special ♦ *Many banks chalked up large profits from their loans to internet companies.*

> ORIGIN: based on the idea of keeping a record on a chalk board

chalk sth up to sth else, *also* **chalk sth up to sth else**
to say that something is caused by something else ♦ *She doesn't even bother to say thank you, but I just chalk it up to bad manners and try not to let it bother me.*

chance

fat chance
there is very little or no possibility of that happening ♦ *Will Hal make you laugh? Fat chance.* USAGE: usually used as a separate sentence to remark on what was just said, as in the example

given half a chance
allowed any opportunity ♦ *Given half a chance, most writers would rather talk about a project than work on it.* USAGE: also used in the form **give someone/something half a chance**: *If we give Geoff half a chance, he could paint that kind of portrait.*

have a fighting chance
to have a reasonable likelihood ♦ *The Socialist Party has a fighting chance to win control of the French government.* USAGE: often used in the form **not have a fighting chance**: *If they don't like the way you perform in practice, you don't have a fighting chance of getting into a game.* ♦ Related vocabulary **level the playing field** at PLAYING

not a chance *esp. spoken, also* **no chance**
it will not happen ♦ *Will classroom volunteers solve America's reading problems? Not a chance.* ♦ *"I'd like to see us win easily for a change." "No chance, not against this team."* USAGE: usually used as a separate sentence to comment on what was just said, as in the example

not have a (snowball's) chance in hell *esp. spoken*
not have any possibility ♦ *It quickly became clear that I didn't have a snowball's chance in hell of finding my lost wallet.* USAGE: sometimes used in the form **have no chance in hell**

> ORIGIN: based on the idea that a **snowball** (= snow pressed into a round shape) would melt in hell

on the off chance
because it is possible but unlikely ♦ *I bought a first edition of the book on the off chance that it might be valuable someday.*

stand a chance
to have the possibility of being successful ♦ *If you're thinking about suing someone, talk to a lawyer to see if you stand a chance.* USAGE: often used in the form **not stand a chance**: *Shy students don't stand a chance in such a large class.*

stand a chance of doing sth
to have the possibility of doing something ♦ *Do you think he stands a chance of beating Mark?*

chances

take your chances
to depend on luck ♦ *I would rather take my chances than try some drug no one knows much about.*

change

a change of heart
a decision that what you thought

earlier is not true or right now ◆ *He'd been active in the organization for years, but after a change of heart, Yang left the group.* ◆ *He never wanted a movie made about him, but three months before he died, Chavez suddenly had a change of heart.*

a change of pace
a different activity than what came before ◆ *People need to get up and move around at lunchtime – they need a change of pace, and a chance to socialize.* ◆ *He decided to take the role because it was a nice change of pace from his last few movies.*

for a change
as something different ◆ *Rhodes felt calm and almost happy, for a change.* ◆ *Why don't we eat dinner on the porch for a change?*

quite a change
something very different ◆ *Claudia's new school is quite a change from her old one.*

chapter

chapter and verse
all the facts ◆ *I know all about it, chapter and verse.* USAGE: often used with the verbs **give**, **quote**, or **recite**: *She can recite chapter and verse about her problems with insurance companies.*

> ORIGIN: based on the idea that proof of an idea can be found in the Bible, which is divided into chapters and verses (= parts)

charge

in charge (of *sth*)
responsible for something ◆ *Who's in charge here?* ◆ *Now that Mr. Bully has been fired, I wonder who will be in charge of the office.*

charged up
excited and full of energy ◆ *Tim was so charged up about tomorrow's game, he couldn't sleep.*

get a charge out of *sth* esp. spoken
to enjoy something very much; = **get a kick out of *sth*** ◆ *He still gets a charge out of being able to please his audience.*

charm

work like a charm
to operate perfectly ◆ *The modem is easy to install and works like a charm in my computer.* ◆ Related vocabulary **like a dream** at DREAM

charts

off the charts
1 much more than is usual ◆ *Basketball's TV income is already off the charts.*
2 much better than usual ◆ *Groncki's newest restaurant is totally off the charts.*

> ORIGIN: based on the literal meaning of **chart** (= a way of presenting numbers or information in vertical rows)

chase

cut to the chase
to say what is important without delay ◆ *The engine is the only thing wrong with the car – to cut to the chase, it is loud, really loud.*

> ORIGIN: based on the idea that, when describing a movie, the writer can **cut** (= interrupt) the story and explain the exciting parts, which usually involve a chase

cheap

on the cheap
for not much money ◆ *In Paris you can eat on the cheap in some good Left Bank restaurants.*

cheat

cheat on *sb*
to have a sexual relationship with a person while you are married to someone else or are having a relationship with someone else ◆ *It's hard to believe that he cheated on you.*

check

in check
within reasonable limits ♦ *I've been spending all my salary and have got to find a way to keep my expenses in check.* USAGE: often used in the form **hold something in check**: *Sometimes it's hard to hold your emotions in check.*

check in
to give your name when you arrive at a place ♦ *With all these security measures, you have to check in at least two hours hour before your flight.* USAGE: usually said about giving your name at a place you will be staying, such as a hotel, or before traveling on an aircraft

check in (with *sb*)
to communicate with someone, esp. regularly ♦ *When traveling, I am supposed to check in with my boss at least once a day.*

check *yourself* into *somewhere*
to enter a hospital for medical care ♦ *He had chest pains and checked himself into the hospital.*

check off *sth*, also check *sth* off
to look at a list of names or items and mark them if correct ♦ *He checked off their names as the passengers got on the bus.*

check out
1 to pay what you owe for having stayed at a hotel ♦ *The Gardners checked out early this morning and left for Europe.*
2 to seem to be true or in agreement with other facts ♦ *Her statement checks out with most of the reports from other people who saw the accident.*

check out (*sth*), also check *sth* out
to pay for something you are buying or to let someone record what you are borrowing ♦ *To complete your online purchase, check out by clicking on the icon below.* ♦ *Ty checked another three books out of the library this afternoon.*

check out *sb/sth*, also check *sb/sth* out
to discover the facts about someone or something ♦ *Not one of the places I checked out seemed right for the wedding.* ♦ *We checked out his story, and his boss says he really was at work that day.* USAGE: often used in the phrase **check it out**: *She said it was a good movie so we thought we'd check it out ourselves.*

check up on *sb*
to try to discover what someone is doing, esp. secretly ♦ *I think he stops by my office to check up on me, to make sure I'm actually working.*

cheek

cheek by jowl
very close together ♦ *Business and residential buildings have been developed cheek by jowl in this city.*

> ORIGIN: based on the idea that the **cheek** and **jowl** (= parts of the face) are very close to each other

turn the other cheek
to decide not to do anything to hurt someone who has hurt you ♦ *When someone attacks you personally, the best approach may be to turn the other cheek.*

> ORIGIN: based on the Biblical instruction to **turn the other cheek** (= if someone hits you, a better response than hitting them is to turn your face so that they can hit you on the other side)

cheer

cheer up (*sb*), also cheer *sb* up
to feel happier, or to cause someone to feel happier ♦ *We've cheered up a lot since we found a great place to swim.* ♦ *Jack stopped at her apartment every day to bring her food and cheer her up.*

chest

get *sth* off *your* chest
to tell someone about something that has been worrying you ♦ *I sometimes discuss my problems*

with someone else just to get them off my chest.

child
with child
pregnant ◆ *She went back to her parents' home when she discovered she was with child.* USAGE: used by people who think it is not polite to say pregnant, or for humorous effect

chill
chill out slang
to relax ◆ *I like to come home from work, have dinner, chill out for a little bit, and then go to bed.* USAGE: often said to someone who is too excited or upset: *I was worried about the kids, and he told me I should just chill out.*

chime
chime in
to enter a conversation, esp. by interrupting ◆ *Everyone at the table began to chime in with their own ideas.*

chip
chip in (*sth*)
to pay for part of something with other people ◆ *They each chipped in $50 to take their parents out to dinner at a fine restaurant.*

a chip off the old block
someone who is similar in character to their father or mother ◆ *She enjoys bossing people around just like her mother used to do – she's a real chip off the old block!*

a chip on *your* shoulder
a tendency to be easily angered or upset ◆ *He always acted as if he was better than us and went around with a chip on his shoulder.*

chips
let the chips fall (where they may)
to not worry about the effects of your actions ◆ *We just try to enforce the law fairly and let the chips fall where they may.*

when the chips are down
when you are in a difficult or dangerous situation ◆ *When the chips are down, you need people around you that you can depend on.* ◆ *He's like that special best friend from high school you go to when the chips are down.*

choir
preach to the choir
to talk about something with a group of people who already agree with you; = **preach to the converted** ◆ *I realized that all I was doing was preaching to the choir – the men who really need to hear about this don't come to these groups.*

choke
choke off *sth*, also **choke *sth* off**
to suddenly stop the movement or progress of something ◆ *He told his staff to stop talking to the press, hoping to choke off the bad publicity.*

choke (*you*) up
to have difficulty speaking because you feel great emotion ◆ *During his farewell talk the coach got all choked up and started to cry.*

chops
lick *your* chops
to be eager to do something that you think will be satisfying or pleasant ◆ *Their team was so much better than ours that when they played us, they were just licking their chops.*

> ORIGIN: based on the literal meaning of **lick your chops** (= to lick your lips when thinking of something good to eat)

chord
strike a chord
to cause you to realize that something is connected to you in some way ◆ *The characters in the play strike a chord because their speech and their reactions are like ours.*

chorus
in chorus slightly formal
together at one time ◆ *Many people who stutter are able to speak normally when reading in chorus with others.*

Christ
for Christ's sake rude slang, *also* **for Christ sakes**
I am surprised or annoyed by this; = **for God's sake** ◆ *For Christ's sake, Julie, what are you doing here?* ◆ *This dress makes me look like a little old lady, for Christ's sake.* ◆ *It's two in the morning, for Christ sakes! Why are you calling me now?* USAGE: used for emphasis ◆ Related vocabulary **for crying out loud** at CRYING, **for goodness' sake** at GOODNESS, **for Pete's sake** at PETE

ORIGIN: based on the literal meaning of **for Christ's sake** (= in the name of or for Christ)

chunk
a chunk of change
a large amount of money ◆ *He's probably got enough money to buy a little ranch somewhere and still have a chunk of change left over.* USAGE: often used with **big**, **huge**, or other modifiers: *You'd have to agree that $80 million is a big chunk of change by anyone's standards.*

churn
churn *sth* **out**, *also* **churn** *sth* **out**
to produce something in large amounts and without much thought ◆ *Rosco churned out a book a year for 13 years and earned a lot of money doing it.*

cigar
close, but no cigar
almost but not exactly what you had hoped for or wanted ◆ *Vince never got that big win he wanted – it was always close but no cigar.*

ORIGIN: from games of skill or chance in which the person who won would get a cigar as a prize

circle
come full circle
to return to the same situation or attitude you originally had ◆ *I left publishing, tried teaching, and now I've come full circle back to publishing.* USAGE: also used in the form **bring something full circle**: *The film starts in the present, then moves to the past before bringing the story full circle back to the present.*

square the circle
to solve an unusually difficult problem ◆ *To get both sides to agree to anything at all meant we had to square the circle.* ◆ Related vocabulary **have it both ways** at WAYS

ORIGIN: from the problem in geometry (= a branch of mathematics) of constructing a square that is equal in area to a circle

circles
go (around) in circles
to be very active but not achieve anything ◆ *His mind went in circles around the problem, but he couldn't seem to find a solution for it.* USAGE: sometimes used in the form **talk in circles** (= speak a lot but without saying anything important): *Every time the mayor speaks he seems to talk in circles.* ◆ Related vocabulary **around and around** at AROUND, **go around and around** at GO, **round and round** at ROUND

circumstances
under certain circumstances
because of particular conditions ◆ *Your insurance will pay for that surgery, but only under certain circumstances, for example if it's an emergency.*

under no circumstances
not for any reason ◆ *Abby's mother said that under no circumstances could Abby go out with her pals.*

under the circumstances, *also* **under these circumstances**
because of the particular situation

claim

♦ Going to see the scene of the explosion was, under the circumstances, a really stupid thing to do. ♦ The storm was very dangerous, so under the circumstances I think we were lucky to have had only one tree blown down. USAGE: also used in the form **under those circumstances**: *There is an ongoing investigation, and under those circumstances, it wouldn't be right for me to comment.*

claim
sb's claim to fame
the reason why someone is famous ♦ *Chan's claim to fame is that he does his own stunts in his movies.* USAGE: sometimes used of places: *The restaurant is Philadelphia's latest claim to fame.*

stake a claim (to *sth*), *also* **stake *your* claim (to *sth*)**
to show that you believe something is yours ♦ *In recent years, several big stores have staked a claim to the wealthy shoppers in this area.* ♦ *Stevens has staked a claim to a new brand of techno music with a series of exciting concerts.*

> ORIGIN: from the idea of marking land that is not owned by someone with **stakes** (= pointed sticks) to show it is yours

clam
clam up
to refuse to talk or answer ♦ *Every time I think he's going to tell me what's bothering him, he just clams up.*

> ORIGIN: based on the behavior of a **clam** (= a sea creature), which quickly closes its shell when something touches it

(as) happy as a clam
very happy ♦ *I am happy as a clam living all by myself in this little house by the sea.*

> ORIGIN: based on the full form of the phrase, **happy as a clam in mud at high tide** (= a clam that cannot be dug up and eaten, which therefore could be considered happy)

clamp
clamp down on *sth*
to act to stop or limit something ♦ *Police here have finally clamped down on speeding.*

class
in a class by *itself*
the best or only one of its kind ♦ *The High Desert Museum was in a class by itself.* USAGE: also used in the form **in a class by yourself**: *Among jazz singers, she was in a class by herself.*

clean
clean *sb* out
to take everything from someone ♦ *Thieves took my bank card and absolutely cleaned me out.* ♦ *I'd offer you something to eat, but Sean was here last night and he cleaned us out.*

clean up
to win or earn a lot of money ♦ *We cleaned up playing the slots at the casino last night.* ♦ *The computer giant cleaned up with its new, easy-to-use operating system.*

clean up *somewhere*
to remove illegal or dishonest activity from a place ♦ *Having more police on the street has helped clean up the city.*

a clean bill of health See at BILL
clean up *your* act See at ACT
come clean See at COME
keep *your* hands clean See at HANDS
keep *your* nose clean See at NOSE
wipe the slate clean See at SLATE

cleaner
take *sb* to the cleaners
to cheat someone of money ♦ *Some*

people say the company took them to the cleaners by charging double for some services.

clear

in the clear

1 not guilty of a crime ◆ *The government investigated charges against the company and decided it was in the clear.*

2 not experiencing something bad ◆ *Just when I thought I was in the clear, I came down with the flu.*

clear out

to leave a place, esp. quickly ◆ *We have to clear out of here soon to get to the airport on time, but you can stay around.*

climbing

climbing the walls

to be extremely nervous or upset ◆ *If your kids are climbing the walls, they need to get out and work off some of that excess energy.*

clock

around the clock

all day and all night without stopping ◆ *One lane on the bridge is closed around the clock for the next three months.*

punch a clock

1 to record on a special clock when you arrive and leave work ◆ *In some offices, if you don't punch a clock, you don't get paid.*

2 to go to work every day ◆ *Someone who is retired doesn't have to punch a clock or commute.*

turn back the clock, *also* **roll back the clock**

to make things the same as they were at an earlier time ◆ *I cannot vote for someone who promises to turn back the clock to better days because that's impossible.* USAGE: sometimes used in the form **turn the clock back**

a race against the clock See **a race against time** at RACE

clockwork

like clockwork

1 at regular times ◆ *I change my car's oil like clockwork every 3,000 miles.*

2 without problems ◆ *Most of the performance went like clockwork, but there were a few little things that weren't perfect.*

close

close to home

having a direct personal effect on you ◆ *Her novel about a teenager's drug addiction hit a little too close to home for my taste.* USAGE: usually said about something that upsets or embarrasses you, and often used with the verb **hit** as in the example ◆ Related vocabulary **too close for comfort** at COMFORT

closet

come out of the closet

1 to be willing to talk in public about something that was kept secret ◆ *The biggest surprise was that so many viewers came out of the closet and publicly supported the show.*

2 to announce that you are attracted to people of the same sex; = **come out** ◆ *Not all gays come out of the closet, either because they don't want to or don't need to.*

USAGE: sometimes used without **come** in both meanings: *We're bringing adoption out of the closet and trying to make people more comfortable with it.* ◆ *He's out of the closet with his friends, but not at work.*

cloth

cut from the same cloth

to be very similar ◆ *These new songs are clearly cut from the same cloth as the band's earlier tunes.*

(made up) out of whole cloth

to be completely invented ◆ *The whole article was a fairy tale, made up out of whole cloth.*

cloud

cloud
a cloud on the horizon, *also* **(dark) clouds on the horizon**
a problem or difficulty that is likely to happen in the future ♦ *For farmers, another cloud on the horizon is higher prices for fertilizer and fuel.* ♦ *Even when everything is going perfectly, Bruce can see dark clouds on the horizon.* ♦ Related vocabulary **on the horizon** at HORIZON

on cloud nine
very happy ♦ *She just bought her first new car and she's on cloud nine.*

under a cloud
thought possibly to be involved in something illegal or criminal ♦ *Several people at my company have suddenly left under a cloud and are being investigated by the police.*

clue
clue *sb* in, *also* **clue in *sb***
to give someone information they need or want ♦ *I asked David to clue us in on what needed to be done first.* ♦ *He hung the painting to clue in visitors that this was a different kind of place.*

not have a clue, *also* **without a clue**
to have no knowledge or information about something ♦ *The guy doesn't have a clue what forestry is all about.* USAGE: sometimes used in the form **have a clue**: *Before most doctors have a clue about what a new drug can do, it's being sold to the public.*

coast
the coast is clear
1 there is no danger of being seen ♦ *We had to wait until the coast was clear to slip out of the building, which was being watched.*
2 there is no danger of anything more happening, esp. trouble ♦ *Now that the killer has been arrested, the coast is clear and people can go out without fear.*

from coast to coast
everywhere or all across a country ♦ *Winter storms are making life difficult from coast to coast.*

> ORIGIN: based on the literal meaning of **coast to coast** (= east to west or north to south, one border to another)

coattails
ride *sb's* coattails, *also* **ride the coattails of *sb***
to use your connection with someone successful to achieve success yourself ♦ *I don't think she would get promoted without riding her boss's coattails.* ♦ *My opponent is riding the coattails of the popular governor of Massachusetts.*

coffee
wake up and smell the coffee
to pay attention and do something about a situation ♦ *Some parents just deny their kids are having problems, and they'd better wake up and smell the coffee.*

cold
come in from the cold, *also* **bring *sb* in from the cold**
to become accepted by society ♦ *I think that country is coming in from the cold – they deal with the outside world a lot more these days.* ♦ *The government wants to see some proof that the rebels want peace before bringing them in from the cold.* USAGE: usually said about political groups or spies (= people who secretly gather information about other countries)

leave *you* cold
to fail to interest you ♦ *Most of the programs on TV leave me cold.*

leave *sb* (out) in the cold
to ignore or not include someone ♦ *If you can't be pleasant to other people, then you will most certainly be left out in the cold.*

blow hot and cold See at BLOW

give *sb/sth* the cold shoulder See at COLD SHOULDER

go cold turkey See at COLD TURKEY

in a cold sweat See at COLD SWEAT

in cold blood See at BLOOD

throw cold water on *sth* See at WATER

cold shoulder
give *sb/sth* the cold shoulder
to show no interest in someone or something ♦ *Our town council has given the cold shoulder to a proposal to build a public swimming pool.* ♦ *I'd love to know why Bill gave the cold shoulder to Janice.*

cold sweat
in a cold sweat
very frightened or worried ♦ *I dreamed I'd lost our plane tickets and woke up in a cold sweat.*

cold turkey
go cold turkey
to suddenly and completely stop doing something, esp. a bad habit ♦ *Finally she went cold turkey on a 23-year smoking habit and hasn't smoked since.* USAGE: also used in the form **quit cold turkey** with the same meaning: *The big organizations suddenly quit cold turkey, leaving the work to volunteers.*

collar
hot under the collar
angry ♦ *The criticisms seemed unfair to me and I got pretty hot under the collar when I thought about them later.*

colors
with flying colors
with great success ♦ *She took a driving test and passed with flying colors.* ♦ *My brother always managed to get through his courses, although not always with flying colors.*

ORIGIN: based on the small and colorful flags flown (= hung in the wind) on boats and ships in a race or when coming into port

show *sb's/sth's* true colors, also **reveal *sb's/sth's* true colors**
to let others see what someone or something is really like ♦ *Hal's wife showed her true colors by getting a second job when he lost his.* ♦ *Workers felt the company revealed its true colors during the crisis.*

come
as *sth* as they come
as much of a particular characteristic as is possible ♦ *Eric is as competitive as they come and always trying to win.*

come across (*sb/sth*)
to happen to find someone or something ♦ *I was looking through a magazine and came across an interesting article on American artists.*

come across (as)
to appear to have a particular attitude or character ♦ *Sometimes he seemed like a good old pal, but other times he came across as an angry and unpleasant man.*

come again esp. spoken
what did you say ♦ *Come again? I didn't hear that.*

come along
1 to develop or improve ♦ *Thomas is more relaxed and his skills are coming along.*
2 to appear or be available ♦ *Sometimes an album comes along that just sounds better than anything else you've heard in a long time.*

come apart
to stop working effectively ♦ *Parents are saying that the school has come apart since the principal left.* ♦ *If the agreement comes apart, we'll just have to put a better one together.* ♦ Related vocabulary **come apart at the seams** at SEAMS

come around
to visit ♦ *Some people are going to come around and see what we do in our department.*

come around (to *sth*)
to change your opinion of some-

come

thing ♦ *I want to go, and I think she'll come around and we'll actually take a vacation.*

come between *sb*
to cause a relationship to become less close ♦ *It wasn't religion that came between them but their very different personalities.*

come by (*sth*)
1 to obtain money, wealth, or goods ♦ *Mitchell had acquired some wealth, although whether he came by it honestly or dishonestly is not clear.* USAGE: often used in the form **hard to come by**: *Fresh meat and fish were hard to come by.*
2 to learn a skill ♦ *I had to work hard to learn to skate. I didn't come by it easily.*

come clean
to tell the truth about something you have tried to hide ♦ *I should probably come clean now and admit that I don't really know how to cook at all.*

come down on *sb/sth*
1 to criticize someone or something ♦ *It seems that if you give an opinion about something, people come down on you.*
2 to have an opinion about someone or something ♦ *It was hard to know where he would come down on the issue.* ♦ Related vocabulary **come down on the side of** *sb/sth* at SIDE

come down to (*sth*)
to be recognized as the most important thing ♦ *It comes down to simply teaching the basics to these kids—they don't know anything.*

come down with *sth*
to become ill with a disease ♦ *Twenty-two pupils came down with flu.*

come forward
to offer help or information ♦ *The police hope that some witness to the shooting will come forward with information.*

come home (to *sb***)**
to become completely clear to someone ♦ *The reality of his loss finally came home to him.* USAGE: usually said about something that is difficult or unpleasant ♦ Related vocabulary **hit home** at HIT, **strike home** at STRIKE

come home to roost
to cause problems for you ♦ *He said some stupid things and now those remarks were coming home to roost.* USAGE: said of problems that result from your own mistakes, and sometimes used with **chickens**: *Nobody felt sorry for him because it was a case of the chickens coming home to roost.*

> ORIGIN: based on the habit of chickens and other birds that return to their nesting places

come in for *sth*
to receive criticism ♦ *The report came in for some sharp remarks from several experts.*

come in handy
to be useful ♦ *My son's wagon comes in handy when I have to move anything heavy.*

come into *sth*
to receive money or property from someone who has died ♦ *She came into a fortune when her father died.*

come into *your/its* **own**
to achieve success and respect ♦ *By the time he was 25, Fox had come into his own as an international soloist.*

come off
to happen and be successful ♦ *No one is sure if the jazz festival planned for this summer will come off.*

come off (as)
to appear to have a particular attitude, intention, or character ♦ *I didn't want to come off as weak.*

come off it esp. spoken
stop saying or doing that ♦ *Come off it, Pete, there's no reason to be scared of asking her for a date.*

come on *esp. spoken*
tell the truth ♦ *Oh, come on – you have no idea who stole your credit cards.*

come on strong
1 to act in a forceful way ♦ *I didn't want to come on too strong, so I tried not to seem angry.* ♦ *The opposition came on strong with rallies and protests and an e-mail campaign.*
2 to be popular ♦ *Animal movies have come on strong again.*

come on to *sb*
to try to attract someone romantically or sexually ♦ *She felt bold and confident enough to come on to him at the party.* ♦ Related vocabulary **hit on** *sb* at HIT

come out
1 to be made public ♦ *There have been so many different medical reports coming out.*
2 to announce that you are attracted to people of the same sex; = **come out of the closet** ♦ *A lot of people were surprised when the senator came out.*
3 to become available ♦ *In my business you have to be aware of what new music has come out.* USAGE: said especially about a movie, book, or recorded music

come out swinging, *also* **come out fighting**
to strongly defend yourself or something you believe in ♦ *Both candidates came out swinging in the televised debate Sunday night.*

come over *sb*
to change or influence someone's behavior ♦ *No one knows what came over Bill, but he stopped smoking.*

come true
to happen as hoped for ♦ *The good things we've been hoping for are actually coming true.* ♦ Related vocabulary **a dream come true** at DREAM

come unglued
1 to become very upset and lose your confidence ♦ *He never showed any signs of coming unglued, even when it looked like they would lose.* ♦ *After Dan's death, she came unglued and was never herself again.*
2 to fail ♦ *A year later, the local chemical industry began to come unglued.*

come unstuck
to start to fail after some progress had been achieved ♦ *His plans for the company came unstuck when there wasn't enough money to buy new machinery.* ♦ *Their deal seems to have come unstuck.*

come up
1 to be mentioned or talked about ♦ *The issue will come up in the meeting on Monday.*
2 to happen unexpectedly ♦ *I don't care how well you planned, something always comes up that you didn't think of.* ♦ Related vocabulary **crop up** at CROP, **show up** 2 at SHOW

come up with *sth*
to think of, develop, or find something ♦ *They've tried to come up with a solution.* ♦ *Over the summer they're hoping to come up with 100,000 volunteers.* ♦ Related vocabulary **pony up (*sth*)** at PONY

come upon *sb/sth*
to find or meet someone or something, esp. unexpectedly ♦ *We came upon a farmer setting a fire to clear off dead grass from the pasture.*

come what may
whatever happens; = **come hell or high water** ♦ *The peace-keeping force will be sent home in six months, come what may.* USAGE: the same meaning can be also expressed by **at (the very) least**, **either way**, **in any case**, and **in any event**

comfort

too close for comfort
worrying because of a possible direct effect on you ♦ *When people start saying our local elections are corrupt, that's a little too close for*

coming

comfort. ◆ Related vocabulary **close to home** at CLOSE

coming

where *sb* is coming from
what causes someone to have a particular opinion ◆ *I can understand where he's coming from, but I don't completely agree with him.*

have another think (coming) See at THINK

have *sth* coming out (of) *your* ears See at EARS

have it coming See at HAVE

not know if *you* are coming or going See at KNOW

see it coming See at SEE

up and coming See at UP

what's the world coming to See at WORLD

commission

out of commission
1 broken or not working ◆ *The explosion put the engine out of commission.*
2 not able to do the usual things ◆ *After her knee surgery, she was out of commission for about eight weeks.* USAGE: used to refer to a person who is ill or injured

common

have *sth* in common (with *sb/sth*)
to share interests or characteristics ◆ *What these very old objects have in common is that they were all stolen and smuggled out of the country.* ◆ *What does the new model have in common with earlier versions?* USAGE: also used in the forms **have nothing in common** and **have a lot in common**: *The two women had absolutely nothing in common.* ◆ *The two men had a lot in common and got along well.*

make common cause See at CAUSE

company

in good company
similar to someone who is better known than you are for their achievements or experience ◆ *Einstein didn't do so well in school, so you're in good company.* USAGE: often refers to a negative situation or problem, as in the example

keep *sb* company
to stay with someone so they are not alone ◆ *I kept him company while he was waiting for the bus.*

keep company (with *sb*) slightly formal
1 to be connected with someone ◆ *There are rumors that the singer keeps company with some very dangerous criminals.*
2 to spend time together in a romantic relationship ◆ *They've been keeping company for a year and plan to marry in the spring.* USAGE: often used in this sense for a humorous effect as an old-fashioned expression for beginning a relationship with the intention of marriage

part company (with *sb*)
1 to end a relationship ◆ *Rick and I parted company a long time ago, and I'm seeing someone else now.* ◆ Related vocabulary **parting of the ways** at PARTING
2 to disagree ◆ *That is an issue on which many people part company with the president.*

comparison

pale in comparison (with *sth*), *also* **pale by comparison (with *sth*)**
to seem lacking in importance or quality than something else ◆ *I thought I had a frightening accident, but mine pales in comparison with yours.*

complain

can't complain esp. spoken
to admit that things are mostly all right ◆ *My job gives me a month's vacation, so I really can't complain.*

compliment

return the compliment
1 to do something for someone because they have done something

for you ♦ *Our neighbors looked after the house while we were away, and we'll return the compliment when they go on vacation.*
2 to do or say something unfriendly to someone because they have made you angry ♦ *The batter was thrown out of the game, so he returned the compliment by calling the umpire a fool.* ♦ Related vocabulary **return the favor** at FAVOR

concerned
as far as *you* are concerned, *also* **so far as *you* are concerned**
in your opinion ♦ *The prime minister said that as far as he's concerned, the next elections would be held as scheduled.*

so far as *sth* is concerned, *also* **as far as *sth* is concerned**
in considering something ♦ *So far as benefits are concerned, the most important to me today would be health care.* ♦ Related vocabulary **for that matter** at MATTER

concert
in concert (with *sb/sth*) slightly formal
together or in agreement with someone or something ♦ *Several companies are working in concert to improve delivery of electricity.* ♦ *Our government should not act alone, but in concert with its allies.*

conclusion
in conclusion slightly formal
finally ♦ *He said in conclusion that cooperation between investigators had helped catch the suspects.*
USAGE: used by a speaker or writer to begin a final statement

conclusions
jump to conclusions
to judge a situation without enough information about it ♦ *The investigation isn't finished, so let's not jump to conclusions about what caused the plane to crash.*

concrete
set in concrete
firmly established and very difficult to change; = **set in stone** ♦ *The basics of the financial plan are set in concrete.* USAGE: sometimes used in the form **written in concrete**: *Nothing is written in concrete – we can still make changes.*

confidence
in (the strictest) confidence
trusting that something said will not be told to anyone else ♦ *She told me her plans in confidence, and I really can't talk to anyone about them.*

conk
conk out
1 to stop working or fail suddenly ♦ *My radio conked out again, so I couldn't hear the weather reports.* USAGE: usually said about a machine or engine
2 to go to sleep very quickly ♦ *I was so tired, I conked out on the couch and never even made it into bed.*

connection
in connection with *sth*
having to do with a particular thing ♦ *The police have questioned many people in connection with the fire in the shopping mall.* ♦ Related vocabulary **in relation to *sth*** at RELATION

conscience
in good conscience slightly formal
without feeling guilty ♦ *I could not in good conscience recommend a family member for the job.*

consequences
face the consequences
to deal with the results of something you have said or done ♦ *The law should force this man to face the consequences of running out on his family.*

suffer the consequences
to experience the effects of something you have said or done ♦ *The*

contrary

witness decided to tell the truth and suffer the consequences. USAGE: sometimes used in the form **take the consequences**: *Sometimes we have to take the consequences for our beliefs.*

contrary

on the contrary
just the opposite, esp. of something said or believed ◆ *The evidence of history, on the contrary, shows that these ancient people had a very advanced culture.* USAGE: often used to disagree with someone or something and to present new information

to the contrary
suggesting or showing that the opposite is true ◆ *Unless you have specific information to the contrary, it is obvious that she is lying.*

control

out of control
unable to be managed or limited ◆ *The weeds in the garden are out of control.*

convenience

at *your* convenience
when you want to or are not busy; = **at your leisure** ◆ *She left these samples for us to try out at our convenience.*

at *your* earliest convenience
as soon as you can ◆ *Call me back at your earliest convenience.*

converted

preach to the converted
to talk about something with a group of people who already agree with you; = **preach to the choir** ◆ *Many websites seem to only preach to the converted, but others attract all sorts of people.*

cook

cook up *sth*, also cook *sth* up
to invent something to produce a result you want ◆ *Freddy cooked up a great story so that Jane wouldn't know she was on her way to a sur-*prise party for her birthday. USAGE: often **cook up** means to invent something that is dishonest or illegal: *I'd like to find out who cooked this scheme up.*

ORIGIN: based on the idea of cooking food to make a meal

cooking

what's cooking esp. spoken
what is happening? ◆ *Hey, you guys, what's cooking? Is the party still on for tonight?*

cool

cool down, *also* **cool off**
to stop feeling angry ◆ *After the girls were kept apart for a while, tempers cooled down and the shouting stopped.* ◆ *I was really angry, so I left the house and took a walk to cool off.*

cool it
to relax or calm down ◆ *The best thing both sides can do is to cool it and then get back to talking about the problem.* ◆ *Hugh stepped between the two boys and told them to cool it.* USAGE: often used as an order: *Nikki, leave your brother alone, and, Josh, cool it!*

keep *your* cool
to be calm despite danger or difficulty; = **keep *your* head** ◆ *Somehow I kept my cool even though Seldon's remarks were unfair and made me angry.* ◆ Related vocabulary **keep your shirt on** at SHIRT ◆ Opposite **lose *your* cool**

lose *your* cool
to suddenly become very angry and start shouting ◆ *I try to be patient with her but she made so many irritating comments, I absolutely lost my cool.* ◆ Opposite **keep *your* cool**

play it cool See at PLAY

cord

cut the (umbilical) cord
to end support of someone or something, esp. financial support ◆ *He needs to cut the umbilical cord, get away and find his own place in the*

world. ✦ *By criticizing his party so strongly, he cut the cord and now has to raise campaign money on his own.*

ORIGIN: based on the literal meaning of **cut the umbilical cord** (= to separate a baby that has just been born from the tube that connects it to its mother)

core

to the core
completely or totally ✦ *A showman to the core, Chuck arrived at my party wearing a white headdress and a long purple cape.* USAGE: often used in the form **rotten to the core** (= totally bad or evil): *That kid is rotten to the core.*

corner

around the corner
close ✦ *Lighter and smaller laptops are just around the corner.* ✦ *Spring is here and baseball season is just around the corner.*

back *sb* into a corner
to force someone into a bad situation ✦ *The company backed its workers into a corner by hiring replacements during the strike.* USAGE: sometimes used in the form **get backed into a corner**: *When that team gets backed into a corner, they aren't afraid to fight their way out.*

from the corner of *your* eye, *also* **out the corner of *your* eye**
not seen completely, only briefly noticed ✦ *From the corner of his eye he thought he saw a large dog, but it was actually a coyote.*

in *your* corner
supporting you ✦ *It makes a big difference to have a crackerjack, experienced lawyer in your corner.*

paint *sb/yourself* into a corner
to do something that takes away all of your choices ✦ *They've painted themselves into a corner by promising to announce the results of their investigation.* ✦ *The army painted the rebels into a corner, and the only choice they had was to fight.*

turn the corner
to improve after going through something difficult ✦ *I wonder if the country has really turned the corner in this crisis.*

corner the market See at MARKET

corners

cut corners
to do something in the fastest or cheapest way ✦ *We couldn't get the money we needed, so we had to cut corners to make the film – and it shows.*

the four corners of the earth, *also* **the four corners of the world**
every part of the world ✦ *The giant company plans to bring coffee and soft drinks to the four corners of the earth.* ✦ Related vocabulary **to the four winds** at WINDS

cost

at any cost
no matter how difficult; = **at any price** ✦ *Even if I'm sure I am right, I will avoid an argument with most people at any cost.* ✦ Related vocabulary **at all costs** at COSTS

costs

at all costs
no matter what dangers or difficulties are involved ✦ *The country must defend its borders at all costs.* ✦ Related vocabulary **at any cost** at COST, **at any price** at PRICE

cotton

cotton to *sb/sth*
to like someone or something ✦ *The public did not cotton to her new CD.*

cough

cough up *sth*, *also* **cough *sth* up**
1 to pay money unwillingly ✦ *I had to cough up $35 for administration fees.* ✦ *Martinez's lawyers knew the banks had the money, and pushed them to cough it up.* ✦ Related vocabulary **fork over *sth*** 1 at FORK
2 to allow an opponent to take the lead in a competition ✦ *Sele got a*

could

3–0 lead in the second inning but then coughed it up in the third.

could

could do with *sth*
to want or need something ◆ *You look as if you could do with a haircut.*

counsel

keep *your* own counsel slightly formal
to not tell other people your thoughts ◆ *He was a quiet man who kept his own counsel no matter what was going on around him.*

count

count down (to *sth*)
to count backwards to the time when something is expected to happen ◆ *They had a clock that counted down the days, hours, and minutes to the new year.* ◆ *If you're counting down, spring is just ten days away.*

count me in esp. spoken
include me in your activity or plan ◆ *You can count me in – I haven't been to a ballgame in years!* USAGE: also used in the form **count someone in** (= include someone): ◆ *Dennis said the coach could count him in for Saturday's game.* ◆ Opposite **count *me* out**

count on sb
to expect someone to help you when you need them ◆ *I'm counting on you to tell me everything they say.* USAGE: sometimes used to show that you expect a problem: *You can always count on Michael to screw things up.*

count on *sth*
to expect something to happen ◆ *You may be disappointed if you count on getting that loan.*

count me out esp. spoken
do not include me in your activity or plan ◆ *Count me out – I'm not going swimming when it's this cold!* USAGE: also used in the form **count someone out** (= do not include someone): *She shouldn't count her* brother out yet – he might still decide to come. ◆ Opposite **count *me* in**

courage

have the courage of *your/its* convictions
to do or say what you think is right no matter who disagrees with you ◆ *He has the courage of his convictions to do what is right even when other disagree.* ◆ *"What is needed is a political party with the courage of its convictions," Chad said.* ◆ Related vocabulary **stand up and be counted** at STAND

screw up (*your*) courage, also **pluck up (*your*) courage**
to force yourself to be brave ◆ *Jimmy screwed up his courage and gave Lisa a heart-shaped box of chocolates on Valentine's Day.*

course

in due course slightly formal
after a certain period; = **in due time** ◆ *They're working on the plan and will announce it in due course.*

of course
1 esp. spoken obviously yes ◆ *"May I use your telephone?" "Of course, go right ahead."* USAGE: often used in the phrase **of course not** (= obviously no): *"Is she really going to leave without paying?" "Of course not."*
2 it is obvious ◆ *Of course you should call the doctor if she starts feeling worse.*

off course
not moving forward as wanted or expected ◆ *The opinion polls show that voters think the government has gone off course.* ◆ Opposite **on course**

ORIGIN: based on the literal meaning of a ship or spacecraft going in the wrong direction

on course
moving forward as desired or expected ◆ *Are we on course to finish this book on time?* ◆ Opposite **off course**

ORIGIN: based on the literal meaning of a ship or spacecraft going in the right direction

run its course
to continue until finished ◆ *Unfortunately, a cold has to run its course.* ◆ *It was a wonderful show, but I think this play has run its course.*

stay the course
to continue doing something, even when it is difficult ◆ *I will stay the course and finish the job I was hired to do.*

ORIGIN: based on the literal meaning of a ship continuing in the same direction, even in bad conditions

par for the course See at PAR

court

hold court
to attract people who want your attention ◆ *The actress held court with the reporters and photographers who followed her everywhere.*

ORIGIN: based on the idea of a king who **holds court** (= surrounds himself with people of high social rank and people who give advice)

cover

blow *sb*'s cover
to make secret information about someone known ◆ *Herman had been a spy for 20 years before someone blew his cover.*

cover up *sth*, also cover *sth* up
to keep something secret or hidden ◆ *Others accused her of covering up her financial dealings.* ◆ *I was amazed that the building contractors we hired tried to cover up the problems they had.*

ORIGIN: based on the literal meaning of **cover up** (= to put a cloth or other object over someone or something)

read *sth* (from) cover to cover
to read something from the beginning to the end. ◆ *The newspaper comes before breakfast and my husband reads it cover to cover while he's eating.*

cover all the bases See at BASES
cover a multitude of sins See at MULTITUDE
cover *your* ass See at ASS
cover ground See at GROUND
cover the waterfront See at WATERFRONT
cover *your* tracks See at TRACKS
not judge a book by its cover See at BOOK

cow

have a cow
to be very worried, upset, or angry about something ◆ *The record companies were having a cow over downloadable music files.* USAGE: the opposite meaning is expressed by **don't have a cow**: *Don't have a cow, Mom, I'll clean up my room.*

holy cow
1 what a surprise ◆ *"I was paying 23 percent interest on that credit card." "Holy cow!"*
2 how wonderful ◆ *"A friend of mine is in Hollywood filming a movie this month." "Holy cow, that must be so cool."*

cows

until the cows come home esp. spoken, *also* **till the cows come home**
for a very long time ◆ *You can diet until the cows come home, and you still won't be a size 4.*

crack

at the crack of dawn
very early in the morning ◆ *We had an eight o'clock flight so we were up at the crack of dawn.*

crack down (on *sb/sth*)
to take strong action to stop something bad from continuing ◆ *The university is taking steps to crack*

down on underage drinking on campus. ♦ *Countries that used to ignore terrorist groups in their midst are starting to crack down.*

crack up

1 to laugh ♦ *She was very funny and we cracked up every time she said anything.*

2 to become mentally ill ♦ *I lost my appetite, became unable to sleep, and worried that I was cracking up.*

have (the) first crack at *sth*, *also* **get (the) first crack at** *sth*

to have the first chance to try to do something ♦ *If you want to sell your share of the business, our company would have first crack at buying it.* USAGE: sometimes used in the forms **get a crack at something** or **have a crack at something** (= have a chance to do something): *He was lucky to get a crack at managing the firm.*

take a crack at *sth/doing sth*

to try to do something; = **have a go at** *doing sth* ♦ *Ford said he had always wanted to take a crack at writing a novel.* USAGE: sometimes used in the forms **take another crack at something** or **have another crack at something**: *He couldn't go this year but plans to have another crack at it next year.*

crack the whip See at WHIP

cracked

not all it is cracked up to be, *also* **not what it is cracked up to be**

not as good or special as people said or believed ♦ *The general opinion is that love affairs aren't all they're cracked up to be.*

cracking

get cracking

to begin working without delay ♦ *If you plan on growing these flowers from seed, you better get cracking now.*

cracks

fall through the cracks, *also* **slip through the cracks**

to be not noticed or dealt with ♦ *Obviously too many young people fall through the cracks in the healthcare system.*

cradle

from the cradle to the grave, *also* **from cradle to grave**

during the whole period of your life ♦ *Free medical care might not be with us from the cradle to the grave, as we once hoped.*

> ORIGIN: based on the idea that the **cradle** (= small bed for a baby) represents the beginning of a life, the **grave** (= burying place) represents the end of a life

crank

crank out *sth*, *also* **crank** *sth* **out**

to produce something continually, like a machine ♦ *He regularly cranks out one movie a year and hasn't shown any signs of slowing down.*

crank up *sth*, *also* **crank** *sth* **up**

to increase something ♦ *To meet the demand for their baked goods, the plant has cranked up the speed of the production lines.* ♦ *The volume was cranked up so high that he had to scream in order to talk to the woman next to him.*

crap

crap out

to stop performing well ♦ *Our new lawn mower just crapped out.*

cut the crap

stop saying things that are not true or not important ♦ *We need to tell them, "Hey, guys, cut the crap – you need to work toward a solution."* USAGE: often used as an order, as in the example

full of crap rude slang

completely wrong, false, or worthless; = **full of shit** ♦ *He promises me things all the time but he's full of* *crap.* ♦ Related vocabulary **full of it** at FULL

crash
crash and burn
to fail suddenly and completely ♦ *Gil lost his job and his pension when the company crashed and burned.* ♦ *She watched her parents' marriage crash and burn.*

> ORIGIN: based on the image of a crash followed by a fire that completely destroys a vehicle or aircraft

craw
stick in *your* craw
to be unacceptable and therefore annoying to you ♦ *She went to prison even though she was innocent – that case has stuck in my craw ever since.*

> ORIGIN: like something you cannot swallow, based on the literal meaning of **craw** (= the throat of a bird)

crawling
crawling with *sth*
full of something ♦ *Because the Internet is crawling with sports fans, the league thinks it can build an international audience online.*

> ORIGIN: based on the literal meaning of **crawl with something** (= to be covered by insects or other small creatures)

crazy
crazy about *sb/sth*
to like or love someone or something very much; = **mad about *sb/sth*** ♦ *He was my first love, and I was crazy about him.* USAGE: often used in the negative form **not crazy about** to express a lack of enthusiasm about someone or something: *I'm really not crazy about TV, but I occasionally watch a ballgame.*

like crazy
1 a lot; = **like mad** ♦ *She itched like crazy.*

2 very quickly; = **like mad** ♦ *The cucumbers here grow like crazy.*

cream
the cream of the crop
the best of a particular group ♦ *This editorial staff isn't the cream of the crop, but it's not as bad as you say.* ♦ Opposite **bottom of the barrel** at BOTTOM

> ORIGIN: based on the idea that cream is the best part of milk

credit
credit *sb* with *sth*
to believe that someone has a particular quality or ability ♦ *I credited her with more sense than she showed.*

do credit to *sb*, *also* **do *sb* credit**
to bring praise and respect to someone for something they have done ♦ *Her achievements do great credit to her parents.* ♦ *His patience and hard work do him credit.*

to *sb*'s credit
deserving praise and respect ♦ *Jackson, to his credit, talks about real problems facing real people.*

creek
up the creek (without a paddle), *also* **up a creek**
in an extremely difficult situation ♦ *All those people who have money invested in it are going to be up the creek.*

> ORIGIN: based on the idea of being in a small boat in a stream and not having a **paddle** (= short pole with a wide, flat part) with which to move it

creeps
give *you* the creeps
1 to make you feel frightened or nervous; = **give *you* the willies** ♦ *This old house gives me the creeps.*
2 to cause someone to feel dislike or disgust ♦ *My neighbor gives me the creeps.*
USAGE: also used in the form **get the**

creeps: *The moment she met Billy, she got the creeps.*

crisp

burn *sth* to a crisp
to burn something very badly ◆ *He burned the sausages to a crisp.* ◆ *I played a little golf yesterday and my neck got burned to a crisp.*

crock

a crock (of shit) rude slang
useless or false information ◆ *My sister told me if I wore dresses I'd have more friends, but I think that's a crock of shit.* ◆ *She called the charges against her "the biggest crock I've ever heard."*

> ORIGIN: based on the literal meaning of **crock** (= a container)

crop

crop up
to appear by chance ◆ *Officials fear that the virus could crop up in the United States.* ◆ *Interest in international issues has cropped up on many university campuses.* ◆ Related vocabulary **come up** 2 at COME, **show up** 2 at SHOW

cropper

come a cropper
to fail or be less successful than before ◆ *I don't feel sorry for them – took a risk and it came a cropper for them.*

crossfire

caught in the crossfire
to be hurt by opposing groups in a disagreement; = **caught in the middle** ◆ *As politicians and educators debate school funding, it's students who are caught in the crossfire.* ◆ Related vocabulary **in the cross hairs** at CROSS HAIRS

> ORIGIN: based on the literal meaning of **caught in the crossfire** (= trapped between two groups that are shooting at each other)

cross hairs

in the cross hairs
in a position to be criticized or attacked ◆ *Her independence put her in the cross hairs of some local politicians.* USAGE: usually the situation results from holding opinions that are not popular or are too independent ◆ Related vocabulary **caught in the crossfire** at CROSSFIRE, **caught in the middle** at MIDDLE

> ORIGIN: based on the literal meaning of **cross hairs** (= crossed lines used to aim a gun)

cross purposes

at cross purposes
with different intentions ◆ *The two groups of advisors seemed to be working at cross purposes during this crisis.*

crossroads

at a crossroads
at the point where a decision must be made ◆ *We are at a crossroads where we must choose between more talk and plain old hard work.* USAGE: usually used with the verb **be**, as in the example

> ORIGIN: based on the literal meaning of **crossroads** (= the place where two roads come together and lead off in different directions)

crow

as the crow flies
measured in a straight line ◆ *It's only about 100 miles as the crow flies to great ski country.*

eat crow
to publicly admit you were wrong about something ◆ *Charles had to eat crow and tell them they were right all along.*

crowd

stand out from the crowd
to be very obvious or unusual ◆ *We try to stand out from the crowd by*

stand out from the crowd

Wearing an outfit like that, he knew he'd stand out from the crowd.

producing movies and TV programs that no one else would produce.

crunch

when it comes to the crunch, *also* **when the crunch comes**
when a situation becomes serious or an important decision has to be made ♦ *You know that when it comes to the crunch, she will do what needs to be done.* USAGE: also used in the form **at crunch time** with the same meaning: *She's the kind of player who's going to score at crunch time.*

cry

cry out for *sth*
to need something badly ♦ *The conflict cries out for international action to resolve it.*

a far cry from *sth*
very different from something ♦ *Playing in a comedy is a far cry from playing a criminal in a mystery.*

crying

for crying out loud esp. spoken
I am annoyed or surprised by this ♦ *No, I haven't bought her a present yet. Her birthday is a month away,* for crying out loud. USAGE: used for emphasis ♦ Related vocabulary **for Christ's sake** at CHRIST, **for God's sake** at GOD, **for goodness' sake** at GOODNESS, **for Pete's sake** at PETE

it's a crying shame See at SHAME

cucumber

(as) cool as a cucumber
very calm and in control of your emotions ♦ *When everything seems to be going wrong, she stays as cool as a cucumber.*

cue

> ORIGIN
> These idioms are based on the literal meaning of a **cue** (= a signal for an actor to say or do something in a play or movie).

(right) on cue
as if planned to happen exactly at that moment ♦ *We were traveling up a narrow river in East Africa when, right on cue, a hippopotamus thrust its head out of the water.*

take *your* **cue from** *sb/sth,* also **take a cue from** *sb/sth*
to be strongly influenced by some-

cuff 84

one or something else ◆ *The national assembly takes its cue from the president and seldom challenges her policies.* ◆ *His new tunes take their cues from the music of Africa and Cuba.*

cuff

off the cuff
without any planning ◆ *I could give an opinion off the cuff, but I'd rather think about it.* USAGE: usually said about spoken statements

cup

not *sb*'s cup of tea
not what someone likes or is interested in ◆ *I realize a fantasy computer game is not everyone's cup of tea, but this one is amazing.* USAGE: also used without **not**: *I like suspense in movies. It's my cup of tea.*

curtain

the curtain falls (on *sth*), also ***sb/sth* rings down the curtain on *sth***
the end comes to something, esp. a job or activity ◆ *Brown managed to get a lot done before the curtain fell on his political career.* ◆ *This year rings down the curtain on more than 50 years of broadcasts.* USAGE: also used in the phrase **the final curtain falls**: *His admirers want to honor the singer before the final curtain falls on his career.*

> ORIGIN: from the large curtains above the stage in a theater that are brought down at the end of a performance

curve

throw *sb* a curve, also **throw a curve at *sb***
to surprise someone with a problem or something unexpected ◆ *Bill threw me a curve by asking me to go to the theater with him instead of a hockey game.* USAGE: also used in the form **throw someone a curveball**

> ORIGIN: from the curve in baseball (= a type of throw to the person at bat that does not travel in a direct route)

cushion

cushion the blow
to do something that reduces harm ◆ *The way to cushion the blow is to raise prices slowly, not all at once.*

> ORIGIN: from the idea of making the force of one thing hitting another less damaging by surrounding it with something soft

cut

a cut above *sb/sth*
better than other people or things ◆ *The songs on his new album are definitely a cut above the ones on his last CD.*

cut across *sth*
to include many different groups ◆ *The appeal of these coffee places cuts across all social levels.*

cut and run
to avoid a difficult situation by leaving suddenly ◆ *He had learned as a boy that there is a time to stay and fight and a time to cut and run.*

cut in
to interrupt ◆ *"Let me tell you why I didn't call," Randy began. "No need," Geri angrily cut in.*

cut it out, also **cut that out**
stop talking or doing something ◆ *His friends kept fooling around, and he kept hoping they'd cut it out.* USAGE: often used as an order: *Nora, stop it. Cut it out.*

cut loose
to behave or express yourself in a free or forceful way ◆ *As we crossed the lobby, Charlie cut loose with a yell that made everyone stop and stare at us.*

cut *sb/sth* loose
to get rid of or release someone or something ◆ *He made it in baseball to the major leagues, but the Sox cut him loose because he could not hit.* ◆

Many workers will be cut loose in the upcoming staff reductions.

cut out *sth*, *also* **cut** *sth* **out**
to end or stop something ◆ *You should cut out eating ice cream and get more exercise.* ◆ *We cut out cable TV and have saved a lot of money.* ◆ *She wants to cut meat out of her diet altogether.*

cut out for *sth*
to be the right type of person to do something ◆ *Ron tried college a couple times, but he finally decided he wasn't cut out for higher education.*

cut through *sth*
to make clear something that has been made difficult to understand ◆ *She cut through all the political talk and outlined what was wrong and what could be done to fix it.*

not cut it
not able to deal with problems or difficulties satisfactorily. ◆ *We were playing against some young people who were strong and fast, and we couldn't quite cut it.* ◆ Related vocabulary **not cut the mustard** at MUSTARD

the cut and thrust of *sth*
the different opinions expressed with enthusiasm ◆ *I don't mind the cut and thrust of argument, but I prefer friendlier and more relaxed conversation.*

cutting room

on the cutting room floor
not included ◆ *Some real ballplayers were used in the movie's baseball scenes, but they ended up on the cutting room floor.* ◆ *In the rush to finish this session, legislators left some very important bills on the cutting room floor.*

cylinders

firing on all cylinders
operating as powerfully and effectively as possible ◆ *Doctors say Mary will be firing on all cylinders after two months of physical therapy.* USAGE: based on the literal meaning of a car engine using all of its **cylinders** (= the parts that produce power)

D, d

daddy

who's your daddy slang
am I not more powerful than you ◆ We were arguing, and then he picked me up and put me over his shoulder and said, "OK, who's your daddy?" USAGE: said to express pride in your power or authority

daggers

shoot daggers at *sb*, *also* **look daggers at** *sb*
to look very angrily at someone ◆ I put a cigarette in my mouth and saw her shooting daggers at me from all the way across the room.

damn

damn it slang, *also* **God damn it**
this is very annoying ◆ No, damn it, you wait a minute. ◆ I was thinking, God damn it, the man said he'd write, so why doesn't he send me a letter? USAGE: sometimes spelled **dammit**: But, dammit, what did she expect me to do?

give a damn (about *sb/sth***)** slang
to be interested or involved ◆ He sent his son to parochial school because he believes that those schools give a damn. USAGE: also used with verbs like **could** and **might** to mean someone is not concerned about something: A significant portion of kids in class could give a damn.

not give a damn (about *sb/sth***)** slang, *also* **not give a tinker's damn (about** *sb/sth***)**
to not be interested in someone or something; = **not give a shit (about** *sb/sth***)** ◆ The beginning was so boring, I really didn't give a damn what happened in the rest of the movie. ◆ We didn't give a tinker's damn about justice. USAGE: although always suggesting a negative meaning, sometimes used without **not**: Who really gives a damn about the details?

worth a damn slang, *also* **worth a tinker's damn**
to have value ◆ Kids in this city aren't getting an education that's worth a damn. ◆ I haven't asked enough people for my research to be worth a tinker's damn, but everyone I've talked to thinks it's a good idea.

damned

sth **be damned**
this thing is not important ◆ They tend to select the best software packages available, and costs be damned. ◆ If you repeat a lie often enough, people will think it must be true, facts be damned. USAGE: usually used with plural nouns, as in the examples

damned if *you* **do and damned if** *you* **don't** slang
criticized whatever you decide ◆ It doesn't matter if the president's wife uses the power of her position or not – she's damned if she does and damned if she doesn't.

I'll be damned slang
I am surprised ◆ "Well, I'll be damned," he said when he saw that a thousand people had come to hear him speak.

I'll be damned if I *do sth* slang
I will not let something happen ◆ I'll be damned if I let her tell me that I don't belong here.

damnedest

do *your* **damnedest** slang, *also* **try** *your* **damnedest**
to try very hard ◆ This was the first time I volunteered for anything so I was going to do my damnedest to help.

damper

put a damper on *sth*
to make something less enjoyable ◆ The terrible weather put a damper on this year's New Year celebrations.

> ORIGIN: a **damper** is a device that reduces the loudness of sound, esp. on a piano, or controls the temperature of a fire

dare
don't you dare esp. spoken
I will be very angry at you if you do ◆ *"I'm going to tell Billy what you said about him." "Don't you dare! "*
how dare you *do sth* esp. spoken
I am very surprised and shocked by what you are doing ◆ *How dare you show up at my wedding?* USAGE: usually shows that you think someone's behavior is very wrong: *How dare he accuse us of lying!*
I dare say slightly formal
I am quite certain ◆ *Oh, I dare say Caroline and I will find some way to fill the time while you go off shopping.*

dark
keep *sb* **in the dark**, *also* **leave** *sb* **in the dark**
to not tell someone about something ◆ *Congress complained about being kept in the dark about the peace talks.*

date
bring *sb* **up to date**
to provide someone with the most recent information or developments ◆ *Aides brought the governor up to date on the negotiations.*
bring *sth* **up to date**
to change something to include the latest information or developments ◆ *He brought the book up to date by adding a new section on environmental policies.*
drop-dead date
a time by which something must be done ◆ *Glickman said the drop-dead date is December 31 – after that, no funds will be available.*
keep *sb/sth* **up to date**
to provide the latest information to someone or for something ◆ *Every week I have to keep the lists up to date by adding or deleting names.* ◆ *The company has a computer wizard on the staff who keeps us up to date on the latest in electronics.*
to date
to this time ◆ *I wrote to you two months ago, but to date I have not received a reply.*

dawn
dawn on *you*
to suddenly understand something ◆ *It finally dawned on him that she'd been joking and he was worried for no reason.*

day
a day late and a dollar short
not enough to be useful ◆ *The government's attempts at reform were a day late and a dollar short.*
(as) plain as day
easy to see or understand ◆ *The secret to our success is as plain as day – make a good plan and stick to it.* ◆ *I looked at the list and there, plain as day, was my name on the list of winners.* ◆ Opposite **(as) clear as mud** at MUD
call it a day
to stop some activity ◆ *All professional athletes know they will reach a point when they have to call it a day.*
carry the day
to win or succeed ◆ *Senators in favor of cutting taxes carried the day.*
day after day
repeatedly for many days ◆ *No one seems able to explain why the same problems keep coming up day after day.* ◆ Related vocabulary **week after week** at WEEK, **month after month** at MONTH, **year after year** at YEAR
day and night
all the time; = **night and day** ◆ *It takes a while to get used to hearing traffic noise day and night.*
day by day
every day ◆ *Day by day things seem to get more expensive.* ◆ Related

day   88

vocabulary **week by week** at WEEK, **month by month** at MONTH, **year by year** at YEAR

day in, day out, *also* **day in and day out**
one day after another ✦ *I am so bored! I do the same thing day in, day out.*

day of reckoning
a time when something must be dealt with ✦ *Taking out another loan to cover your debts will only postpone the day of reckoning.*

> ORIGIN: based on the Biblical **day of reckoning** (= the day when God will judge everyone)

from day one
from the very beginning ✦ *We were told from day one that the army will not tolerate racism.*

have *your* day in court
to have the opportunity to make a complaint publicly and to have it judged fairly ✦ *The attorneys said they were pleased that their clients got their day in court.*

in this day and age, *also* **(in) this day and time**
now ✦ *In this day and age you must have computer skills if you want to get a job.* ✦ *The girl was held under conditions that are hard to imagine in this day and time.* USAGE: used to emphasize a difference between this time and time past

just another day (at the office), *also* **just another day's work**
an ordinary or typical event ✦ *It was just another day of arguing with my teenage son.* ✦ *When we won in Seattle, everyone was thrilled, but in Buffalo, every win was just another day at the office.* USAGE: often used to emphasize the idea that **just another day** for one person is not, for most people, an ordinary series of events at all

late in the day
delayed almost too long ✦ *Isn't it rather late in the day to say you're sorry?*

make my day esp. spoken
make me happy by trying to do that ✦ *You want to fight? Go ahead, make my day.* USAGE: used as a humorous way to show that the person you are speaking to knows it would be a big mistake to **make your day**

> ORIGIN: made popular in the movie "Sudden Impact" with Clint Eastwood

make *your* day esp. spoken
to make someone happy ✦ *Go on, tell him you like his jacket. It'll make his day!* ✦ *Peter's letter really made my day.*

not *your* day
a bad day; = **one of those days** ✦ *I missed my train and forgot my glasses – I guess it's just not my day.*

one day, *also* **some day**
in the future ✦ *I'd like to go to Mexico one day.*

save (*sth*) for a rainy day
to keep something, esp. money, for a time in the future when it might be needed ✦ *It looks like people may be saving a little more for a rainy day.* USAGE: sometimes used with verbs other than **save**: *They made little effort to put anything aside for a rainy day.* ✦ *You're going to need that money for a rainy day.*

save the day
to do something that solves a serious problem ✦ *Naturally, the hero saves the day by shooting the kidnappers and rescuing the hostages just in the nick of time.*

that'll be the day esp. spoken
it will never happen ✦ *A raise in pay? That'll be the day!* USAGE: said esp. to emphasize something you wish would happen

the other day
recently ✦ *She phoned me just the other day.* USAGE: also used in the forms **the other night** and **the**

other week: *I saw him the other night.*

win the day
to achieve complete success ◆ *New products grab headlines, but useful products that give good value often win the day.*

all in a day's work See at WORK
at the end of the day See at END
have a field day See at FIELD DAY
not give *sb* the time of day See at TIME
see the light of day See at LIGHT
the order of the day See at ORDER

daylight

in broad daylight
when anyone can see what is happening ◆ *These robberies took place in broad daylight and not one person has been arrested for them!* USAGE: often used to show great surprise that something evil could be done without any effort to hide it

days

***sb's/sth's* days are numbered**
someone or something will not exist for much longer ◆ *I know my car's days are numbered, but I hope it will last just a little while longer.* ◆ *My days are numbered, but I hope I can live long enough to see my grandchild.*

have seen better days
something is in bad condition because of heavy use ◆ *The airport building had seen better days and needed a lot of repairs.*

one of those days
a bad day; = **not *your* day** ◆ *I missed breakfast, got to work late, and got caught in the rain at lunchtime – it was just one of those days!* USAGE: often used in the phrase **it was just one of those days** with the same meaning

those were the days
life was better in the past ◆ *The band's new songs are nowhere near as good as their '80s tunes. Man, those were the days.* USAGE: used for

emphasis when talking about something particular in the past

dead

dead set against *sth*
completely opposed to something ◆ *She wanted to move to Los Angeles but her parents were dead set against it.*

in the dead of night
during the middle of the night ◆ *The fire broke out in the dead of night.*

dead of winter
in the middle of winter, when it is very cold and dark ◆ *Behind the house was a garden with curving flowerbeds that were beautiful, even in the dead of winter.*

deal

a done deal
a final decision or agreement ◆ *We've already hired someone for the position, so this is a done deal.* USAGE: often used in the forms **it's a done deal** or **it's not a done deal**: *We told them we needed more time to think about it, so it's not a done deal.*

ORIGIN: based on the literal meaning of **done** (= finished)

a great deal (of *sth*), *also* **a good deal (of *sth*)**
a large amount of something ◆ *He offered me a great deal of money.* ◆ *Keeping the house really meant a good deal to me.*

big deal
something important or special ◆ *They made a big deal about inviting the president to the reception.* USAGE: often used to say that something represented as important is in fact only ordinary: *"I ran five miles this morning." "Big deal! I ran ten."* ◆ *They called him a hero, but he said it was no big deal.*

cut a deal
to make an agreement or an arrangement ◆ *There was pressure on both of them to cut a deal on the*

death

budget. USAGE: usually said about business or political agreements

death

bore *sb* to death
to make someone lose interest completely ♦ *Herman was bored to death by the stories Arlie told.*

love *sb* to death esp. spoken
to feel extremely strong affection for someone ♦ *She is easy to work with, and everyone in the office loves her to death.* ♦ Related vocabulary **dote on *sb*/*sth*** at DOTE

put *sb* to death
to kill a person ♦ *The bomber will not be put to death, but he will spend the rest of his life in prison.* USAGE: most often used to refer to legal punishment for murder

scare *you* to death esp. spoken
to make you feel extremely frightened; = **scare the hell out of *you*** ♦ *David suddenly appeared like a ghost in the doorway and scared me to death.* ♦ Related vocabulary **scare the pants off *you*** at PANTS

scared to death esp. spoken
extremely frightened ♦ *My dog is scared to death of thunder and firecrackers.*

sick to death of *sth* esp. spoken
extremely bored with something ♦ *We are sick to death of the constant talk of a baseball strike.* ♦ Related vocabulary **sick (and tired) of *sb*/*sth*** at SICK

tickled to death esp. spoken
very pleased ♦ *We were tickled to death that she finally got the Tony award for best actress.*

at death's door See at DOOR

deal *sth* a death blow See at DEATH BLOW

sound the death knell for *sth* See at DEATH KNELL

death blow

deal *sth* a death blow
to take an action that causes something to end or fail ♦ *New attacks dealt a death blow to the peace talks.*

death knell

sound the death knell for *sth*
to cause something to end ♦ *Everyone likes e-mail, but it hasn't sounded the death knell for snail mail quite yet.*

> ORIGIN: based on the literal meaning of **sound the death knell** (= to ring a church bell slowly to announce a person's death)

deck

on deck
ready or available ♦ *The TV audience expects something good on deck after the news.*

> ORIGIN: based on the idea of being on the **deck** (= flat surface) of a ship, ready for whatever must be done

deck out *sb*/*sth*, also **deck *sb*/*sth* out**
to decorate someone or something in something special ♦ *The stewards were decked out in beautiful new uniforms.* ♦ *Some salesman had decked the car out, giving it racing wheels and stripes on the sides.*

hit the deck
to fall to the ground suddenly to avoid danger; = **hit the dirt** ♦ *At the sound of gunfire, we all hit the deck.*

stack the deck, also **the deck is stacked against *you***
to arrange something so that it is unfair to someone ♦ *We wanted to make sure no one was stacking the deck in their favor.* ♦ *The deck truly is stacked against the poor.*

> ORIGIN: based on a way of cheating in a card game by secretly arranging the cards so that you will win

decks

clear the decks
to finish what you are doing in order to do something more important ♦ *His company is clearing the decks to begin work on a major new product.*

> ORIGIN: based on the literal meaning of **clear the decks** (= prepare a ship to fight by putting away everything that is not necessary)

deep
deep down
strongly felt ◆ *Deep down, she knew that she had cheated her friend and it was wrong.*

defer
defer to *sb*
to accept the opinion or judgment of someone else ◆ *In the end, you must defer to your boss, because the boss is always right.*

definition
by definition
because of the nature of someone or something ◆ *Circus performers are, by definition, delightful show-offs and risk takers.*

degree
to the nth degree
as much or as far as possible ◆ *It was a perfect evening – the parking, the dining, the service, everything worked to the nth degree.* ◆ *She pushed dance traditions to the nth degree.*

degrees
by degrees
in small stages ◆ *By degrees the country began to question the decisions their leaders were making.*

demand
in demand
needed or wanted ◆ *When the storm hit our area, snow shovels were so much in demand that the stores ran out of them.* ◆ *Engineering and science graduates are in great demand this year.*

on demand
at any time that you want or need something ◆ *With cable, you can order movies on demand, but naturally you have to pay for them.*

dent
make a dent in *sth*, *also* **put a dent in** *sth*
to have an effect on something ◆ *All the talk about kids eating too much sugar hasn't seemed to make a dent in the candy business.* USAGE: sometimes used without **in**: *Technology cannot fix education – no amount of technology will make a dent.*

depth
in depth
in a complete way that includes everything; = **in detail** ◆ *There wasn't time to go into each problem in depth, but we did get a short description of every case.*

out of *your* **depth**
knowing very little about a subject ◆ *I know I'm out of my depth with teenagers.*

depths
plumb the depths (of *sth***)**
to carefully examine something in order to understand or explain it ◆ *Who would want to plumb the depths of the criminal mind?*

> ORIGIN: based on **plumb line** (= a cord with a heavy piece of metal attached to it, used to measure the depth of water under a ship)

detail
go into detail
to explain or discuss each feature or every part of something ◆ *Begin the research paper with a general introduction and then go into detail.* USAGE: often used in the form **not go into detail**: *The band needed a rest from performing but wouldn't go into detail about why.*

in detail
in a complete way that includes everything; = **in depth** ◆ *I can't talk about public education in detail, but in my opinion it is generally very good.*

devices

leave *you* to *your* own devices
to allow you to decide for yourself what you do ◆ *Most of the time, the prisoners were left to their own devices by the guards.* ◆ *When the two sides were left to their own devices, they managed to agree on terms for a new contract.*

devil

between the devil and the deep blue sea
having only two very unpleasant choices; = **between a rock and a hard place** ◆ *Our country is caught between the devil and the deep blue sea – our leaders cause great suffering, but an invasion aimed at overthrowing them would bring many other problems.*

go to the devil
stop annoying me, I do not want to deal with you any more; = **go to hell** ◆ *The girl's father said if she didn't stop seeing "that boy," she could go to the devil for all he cared.*

speak of the devil esp. spoken
the person we are talking about has just arrived ◆ *Well, speak of the devil, here's Patrick now.*

diamond

a diamond in the rough
someone or something whose good qualities are hidden ◆ *This film is one of those diamonds in the rough, a wonderful gem that almost no one has noticed.*

> ORIGIN: based on the idea that you cannot see the beauty of a **diamond** (= jewel) when it is rough (= not yet cut and filled with brightness)

dibs

(first) dibs on *sth* esp. spoken
to have the right to do or get hold of something ◆ *I had first dibs on dessert and took the pie.* USAGE: usually used with the verb **get** or as an interjection: *Dibs on the ice cream!*

dice

no dice
this result did not or will not happen; = **no go** ◆ *The Giants could have made it an exciting ballgame, but no dice, they didn't even score.*

die

die down
to become quieter or less easily noticed ◆ *By morning the storm died down.* ◆ *Anger over the attacks on the refugee camps has not died down.*

die hard
to end with difficulty ◆ *Old friendships die hard.* USAGE: often used in the phrase **old habits die hard**: *He no longer needs to work, but old habits die hard, so he's at the office every day.*

die off
to die one after another until no members of a particular group are left ◆ *She was ninety-two and said all her friends had died off.*

die out
to stop existing ◆ *Bird-lovers thought a number of songbirds had died out, but they are back and noisier than ever.*

the die is cast
a decision is made that cannot be changed ◆ *When the first shot was fired, the die was cast and a revolution began.*

> ORIGIN: based on the idea that after you **cast** (= throw) a **die** (= small square block with a number on each side) you cannot control its movement

to die for slang
extremely good ◆ *We had apple pie and it was to die for.* ◆ *He had a smile to die for.*

never say die See at SAY

difference

difference of opinion
a disagreement ◆ *My father and I*

had our differences of opinion about the war.

make a difference
to have an effect ♦ *It is exciting to do something that really makes a difference in your community.* ♦ *People don't realize that their vote can make a difference.* USAGE: often used in the form **make no difference**: *It makes no difference to me if the game is televised or not.*

make all the difference (in the world)
to have an important effect; = **make a world of difference** ♦ *Our team has a fine coach, and that makes all the difference.*

same difference esp. spoken
the same thing ♦ *Either he's a genius or he's crazy – same difference, really.*

split the difference
1 to accept only part of what was originally wanted ♦ *When they don't agree, she's always trying to get them to split the difference so everyone will be happy.* ♦ Related vocabulary **meet sb halfway** at HALFWAY
2 to each pay half of an amount ♦ *I told the owners that we could split the difference between their price and my offer.*

make a world of difference See at WORLD

dig

dig in
to start eating, esp. with enthusiasm ♦ *Jack tossed some salt and pepper on the omelet and dug in.*

dig out sth
to search for something ♦ *I dug out a faded picture of my parents playing on the old tennis court.*

dig up sth
to find something, esp. from storage ♦ *We dug up the old dairy records that showed how much milk each cow produced every day.*

ORIGIN: based on the literal meaning of **dig something up** (= to remove something from the ground, esp. with a tool)

dig up (some) dirt (on sb) See at DIRT

dime

a dime a dozen
commonly available ♦ *Remember, editors are a dime a dozen, so if she causes trouble, fire her.*

stop on a dime
to end movement very quickly ♦ *The car stopped on a dime to avoid slamming into a truck.*

turn on a dime
to change direction very quickly ♦ *The economy is not likely to turn on a dime between now and the end of the year.* ♦ *We never knew what our father would decide because his opinions could turn on a dime.*

dint

by dint of sth
as a result of or because of something ♦ *By dint of hard work, I had risen to the position of district principal.*

dip

dip into sth
to use a small amount of something ♦ *The local government voted to dip into the emergency fund to pay for repairing the old town hall.*

dirt

dig up (some) dirt (on sb)
to look for and find unpleasant or embarrassing information about someone ♦ *They tried to dig up some dirt on their political enemies.*

ORIGIN: based on the slang meaning of **dirt** (= negative information about a person)

dish the dirt (on sb/sth)
to talk about other people without worrying about being truthful ♦ *E-mail us and dish the dirt on anyone*

disadvantage

– *husbands, kids, whoever.* ♦ *Did you know that now astronauts can dish the dirt from space?* ♦ Related vocabulary **dish out** *sth* at DISH

> ORIGIN: based on the phrase **dish out** food (= to serve food) and **dirt** (= negative information about a person)

hit the dirt
to fall to the ground suddenly to avoid danger; = **hit the deck** ♦ *The kid next door threw a rock at him, but Ted hit the dirt and the rock didn't hit him.*

treat *sb* **like dirt**
to deal with someone in a manner that shows no respect for them ♦ *If you treat your customers like dirt, they won't come back to your shop.*

disadvantage

at a disadvantage
in a position that gives one person an advantage over another ♦ *Having too little money to spend has put me at a disadvantage with my friends.*

dish

dish out *sth*
to give something too freely and in large amounts ♦ *The mayor was famous for dishing out political favors to his pals.* USAGE: often it is criticism or unfriendly remarks that are **dished out**: *She dished out insults as easily as some of us dish out praise.* ♦ sometimes appears as the full expression **you can dish it out but you can't take it** (= you can give criticism freely but you cannot deal with it yourself): *I try not to argue with him because I know he can dish it out but he can't take it.* ♦ Related vocabulary **dish the dirt (on** *sb/sth***)** at DIRT

> ORIGIN: based on the literal meaning of **dish out** food (= to serve food)

dispense

dispense with *sth*
1 to free of something unwanted ♦ *People who believe we can dispense with government services don't realize how much they need them.*
2 to not use something ♦ *We dispensed with our second car and have saved a lot of money.*

disposal

sb **is at** *your* **disposal**
someone is available to help you ♦ *I know there is plenty of work to do, so my daughter is at your disposal.*

sth **is at** *your* **disposal**
something is available to be used by you ♦ *The committee has limited resources at its disposal.* ♦ *We have $100,000 at our disposal to provide food for homeless people.* USAGE: sometimes used in the form **at the disposal of someone**: *More powerful guns are at the disposal of criminals than ever before.*

dispose

dispose of *sth*
to end a problem ♦ *We need to dispose of the threat from diseases that can be easily controlled by vaccination.*

dispute

in dispute, *also* **under dispute**
doubted or causing argument ♦ *Her ability to do the job is not in dispute.* USAGE: sometimes used in the form **open to dispute** (= still in doubt): *Her story of what happened is still open to dispute.*

dissolve

dissolve into *sth*
1 to end in an unpleasant or disorderly way ♦ *The discussion quickly dissolved into nasty accusations about her business dealings.* USAGE: often said about something that has begun pleasantly or without disagreement
2 to lose control and express strong emotions ♦ *She dissolved into tears when she saw the damage to her*

home. ♦ *Everyone dissolved into gales of laughter at my sister's remark.*

ORIGIN: based on the literal meaning of **dissolve** (= to be absorbed by a liquid)

distance
go the distance
to continue doing something until it is successfully completed ♦ *The pitcher went the distance and has now won eight games in a row.* ♦ *The project would be difficult, but I agreed I would go the distance.*

keep *your* distance (from *sb/sth*)
to avoid becoming too friendly or emotionally involved with someone ♦ *I've seen her around the office, but she keeps her distance from most of us.* ♦ *The boy carefully kept his distance from the growling dog.* ♦ Related vocabulary **keep *sb/sth* at arm's length** at LENGTH

within striking distance (of *sth*), *also* **in striking distance (of *sth*)**
1 very close to something ♦ *The great thing about the house is that the ocean is within striking distance.*
2 very close to achieving something ♦ *The Republicans are within striking distance of winning the election.*
USAGE: sometimes used in the less polite but stronger form **within spitting distance of something** (= very near): *They live within spitting distance of my house, but luckily I don't see them much.*

distraction
drive *you* to distraction
to cause you to be unable to think or work ♦ *That constant buzzing noise is driving me to distraction.* USAGE: sometimes used in the form **do something to distraction** (= to be unable to think of anything else): *It is obvious that he loves her to distraction.* ♦ Related vocabulary **drive *you* up the wall** at WALL

dive
dive into *sth*, *also* **dive in**
to start something enthusiastically without first thinking about it ♦ *Our mistake was to dive into the work without much preparation.*

ORIGIN: based on the literal meaning of **dive in** (= to go head first into water)

dividends
pay dividends
to produce good results or advantages ♦ *My Spanish lessons have finally begun to pay dividends, and I can carry on a simple conversation!*
USAGE: often used to refer to something you do now that will benefit you in the future: *All your work will pay dividends – you'll see.*

ORIGIN: based on the literal meaning of **pay a dividend** (= to pay someone who owns shares in a company a part of a company's profit)

do
do away with *sb*
to remove someone from a position or job ♦ *Blake was disliked by everyone in the office, and Morse did away with him by firing him.*

do away with *sth*
1 to remove or destroy something ♦ *New treatments for your teeth should do away with the dentist's drill – no more cavities, no more pain!*
2 to kill an animal ♦ *The hunter did away with the injured rabbit.*

do *sb* in
1 to make someone very tired ♦ *The five-mile hike really did us in.*
2 to kill someone ♦ *That snake's bite is so poisonous, it can do you in within a few minutes.* ♦ *If I really wanted to do him in, I wouldn't need to have a gun.*

do one better (than *sb/sth*)
to do more or be better than someone or something else; = **go one better (than *sb/sth*)** ♦ *Several com-*

doctor

panies developed similar software, but ours did one better than the rest by making it user-friendly. USAGE: sometimes used in the form **do someone one better** or **do something one better**: *Jones did him one better and beat the record for the 100-meter dash.*

do *sb* out of *sth*
to cheat someone of something of value ◆ *The CEO's theft of company funds did many workers out of thousands of dollars in retirement benefits.*

do over *sth*, also do *sth* over
to decorate a place in a new way ◆ *We plan to do the kitchen over next year.*

do without (*sb/sth*)
to manage to work or act without someone or something ◆ *I guess I'll just have to learn how to do without your help.* ◆ *They have relied on Henry for so long, I wonder how they will do without him.* USAGE: often used in the form **not do without someone or something**: *My driver really annoys me, but I know I can't do without him.* ◆ Related vocabulary **go without (*sth*)** at GO

it's do or die
to try to achieve a goal or fail making the effort ◆ *It's do or die – if the computer system isn't working by Monday, we'll lose the contract.*

nothing to do with
not connected in any way ◆ *This is a problem for our neighbors but has nothing to do with me.* ◆ Opposite **something to do with**

something to do with
connected in some way ◆ *How a ball travels after it is hit has something to do with the laws of physics.* ◆ *I wonder if cell phones have something to do with people bumping into things when they walk.* ◆ Opposite **nothing to do with**

doctor

just what the doctor ordered
exactly what is wanted or needed ◆ *An evening without the kids was just what the doctor ordered.* ◆ Related vocabulary **just the ticket** at TICKET

does

easy does it
do this slowly and carefully ◆ *Easy does it going down the stairs, Mom.*

dog

as sick as a dog
very ill ◆ *She was as sick as a dog after eating the stew.*

the hair of the dog (that bit you)
See at HAIR

doghouse

in the doghouse
in a situation in which someone is annoyed with you because of something you did ◆ *The president's aide is in the doghouse over remarks she made to the press.* USAGE: the opposite is **out of the doghouse**: *She won't be out of the doghouse until she apologizes.*

> ORIGIN: based on the idea of being punished like a dog who is forced to stay in a **doghouse** (= a shelter used by a dog), away from people

dogs

call off the dogs, also **call off *your* dogs**
to cause people to stop attacking or criticizing someone ◆ *It's time to call off the dogs and let her get back to doing her job.*

go to the dogs
to become worse in quality or character; = **go to hell (in a handbasket)** ◆ *He was a marvelous actor, but his drinking problems caused his career to go to the dogs.* ◆ *It is sad to report that this once first-class hotel has gone to the dogs.* ◆ Related vocabulary **go to pot** at POT

doing

nothing doing
I will not do that or agree to that ◆ *She wanted to come to the dance*

tonight but her father said nothing doing.

doldrums

in the doldrums

1 lacking activity or progress ◆ *When the economy is in the doldrums, every business feels the effects.*
2 feeling sad and lacking the energy to do anything ◆ *He's been in the doldrums since his girlfriend left for college.*

USAGE: the opposite is **out of the doldrums**: *Maybe inviting him to dinner will get him out of the doldrums.*

> ORIGIN: based on the literal meaning of **the doldrums** (= the part of the world's seas near the equator where there is little wind, making it difficult to sail)

dollar

you (can) bet your bottom dollar

you can be very sure ◆ *If there's anything he can sue you for, you can bet your bottom dollar you'll be in court.*

in the doghouse

> ORIGIN: based on the literal meaning of **bottom dollar** (= your last bit of money, which you would not risk losing)

dollars

like a million dollars

extremely good ◆ *All I need is a shower and a good night's sleep and I'll feel like a million dollars.* ◆ *She turned around, still smiling, and looking like a million dollars.*

done

done for

about to fail, suffer, or die ◆ *If we have to rely on Warren for a solution, we are done for.* ◆ *With rockets flying overhead and machine guns shooting at us, I thought we were done for.*

USAGE: usually used after the verb **be**, as in the example

done in

too tired to do any more ◆ *He looked completely done in when he arrived at work.*

not done

not socially acceptable ◆ *Where he comes from, saying no to someone*

When he forgot their anniversary, Andy was really in the doghouse.

door

who wants to help is not done. USAGE: often used after **just** or **simply**: *In 1932, living with someone you weren't married to was simply not done.*

well done *esp. spoken*
I am very pleased ♦ *OK, you've learned to use the computer. Well done!*

a done deal See at DEAL

been there, done that See at BEEN

easier said than done See at SAID

over (and done) with See at OVER

door

at death's door
dying or very ill ♦ *He literally was at death's door when a liver became available for transplant.*

close the door on *sth*
1 to prevent something from happening ♦ *We shouldn't be too quick to close the door on change.* ♦ *I'm trying to decide what to do next, and I'm not going to close the door on anything.*
2 to end a situation or event ♦ *The court's decision closes the door on a shameful episode in the country's history.*

door to door
1 from one place to another ♦ *The trip takes an hour door to door.*
2 at or to every house ♦ *Harris ran a classic political campaign, visiting with folks door to door.*

lay *sth* **at** *sb's* **door**
to blame someone for something; = **lay** *sth* **on** *sb* ♦ *The error in the notice about the date of our next meeting must be laid at my door.* ♦ Related vocabulary **lay the blame on** *sb/sth* at BLAME

open the door to *sth*
to allow something to happen ♦ *The meeting opened the door to real peace talks between the two sides.* ♦ Related vocabulary **open doors (to** *sb/sth***)** at DOORS

show *sb* **the door**
to make someone leave ♦ *Jones made the mistake of complaining about the boss and was shown the door.* ♦ *Dick was rude to my family and I simply showed him the door.*

through the back door, *also* **by the back door**
illegally or dishonestly ♦ *Bennett had many friends in city government and was known for getting jobs for his friends through the back door.*

doornail

(as) dead as a doornail
1 obviously dead ♦ *The fox in the road was dead as a doornail.*
2 not active at all ♦ *Nothing ever happens in our town – it's as dead as a doornail.*

> ORIGIN: based on the literal meaning of **doornail** (= a nail with a large head)

doors

behind closed doors
privately or secretly ♦ *The serious meetings took place behind closed doors and not during social events.* ♦ *Politicians still decide on candidates behind closed doors.*

open doors (to *sb/sth***)**, *also* **open doors (for** *sb/sth***)**
to provide new opportunities or possibilities ♦ *These days, it's cable TV that is opening doors to talented young people and giving them a chance to succeed.* ♦ *When I was a student, a college diploma was guaranteed to open doors.* ♦ Related vocabulary **open the door to** *sth* at DOOR

doorstep

on *your* **doorstep**, *also* **at** *your* **doorstep**
very near to you ♦ *Most people do not want war on their doorstep and will do everything they can to prevent it.* ♦ *People who live with poverty at their doorstep think about today, and not what the future will be like.*

dot
on the dot *esp. spoken*
exactly ♦ *You've got to be here at 9 on the dot or we won't make the train.* USAGE: used mainly of time and in the form of the example

dote
dote on *sb/sth*
to love someone or something a lot, sometimes foolishly or too much ♦ *The world is full of people who dote on their pets.* ♦ Related vocabulary **love** *sb* **to death** at DEATH

dots
connect the dots
to understand the relationship between different ideas or experiences ♦ *It took years of hard work to connect the dots between the murder and the suspect.*

> ORIGIN: from a children's activity in which a picture can be seen when you draw lines to connect numbered **dots** (= small, round marks)

double
double over, *also* **double up**
to suddenly bend forward and down, usually because of pain or laughter ♦ *A sudden, sharp pain made him double over.*

double up (with *sb*)
to share a room or living situation with others ♦ *The two boys will have to double up in the front bedroom.*

on the double
very quickly ♦ *Two doctors arrived on the double to treat the victims of the accident.*

doubt
no doubt
1 certainly ♦ *No doubt you have already heard about the terrible storm we just had, but did you know it blew down the steeple of the old church?* USAGE: sometimes used in the form **without (a) doubt**, with the same meaning: *Without doubt, he is the funniest man I know.*
2 probably ♦ *The schools should no doubt spend twice as much on teachers as they do now.*

no doubt about it *esp. spoken*
it is certainly true ♦ *The Wizard 5100 is an amazing machine, no doubt about it.* USAGE: usually used at the beginning or the end of a sentence, for emphasis

down
down on *sb/sth*
feeling angry or disappointed with someone or something ♦ *Dad's been down on me since I scraped the car backing out of the garage.*

dozen
by the dozen
in large numbers ♦ *He would sit all day in the dark watching videos by the dozen.*

> ORIGIN: based on the literal meaning of **by the dozen** (= in groups of twelve)

half a dozen
a few of something ♦ *I've got half a dozen fishing poles that I never use.* USAGE: used when the exact number is not important

drain
down the drain
wasted or lost; = **down the toilet** ♦ *I'm scared I'm going to be out of a job, and my 12 years of experience will be down the drain.* USAGE: often used with **go**: *We cannot afford to let our train system go down the drain.*

draw
draw on *sth*
to get ideas or facts from something ♦ *The second half of the book draws on new discoveries in the field of microbiology.*

draw *sb/sth* **out**, *also* **draw out** *sb/sth*
to persuade someone to express their thoughts and feelings ♦ *She was good at drawing out young*

people and getting them to talk about their dreams. ◆ She worked hard to draw out all the different opinions people had.

draw *sth* out, *also* **draw out *sth***
1 to make something last longer than is usual or necessary ◆ *I can't see any reason to draw the investigation out any longer.* ◆ *She paused to draw out the suspense.*
2 to completely explain something ◆ *Historians have to draw out, analyze, and judge the importance of the actions of others.*

draw *yourself* up
to make yourself stand straight ◆ *He drew himself up and stood by the window, thinking over what I had just said.* USAGE: sometimes **draw yourself up to your full height**: *She drew herself up to her full height and told me why I was wrong.*

draw up *sth*, *also* **draw *sth* up**
to prepare an agreement or other document in writing ◆ *The lawyers drew up a contract over the weekend.* ◆ *After they draw everything up we'll have a chance to read and correct it.*

quick on the draw
able to react quickly to a situation ◆ *He was quick on the draw answering the reporter's questions.* USAGE: sometimes said about a person who reacts too quickly to a situation and makes serious mistakes

> ORIGIN: based on the literal meaning of **quick on the draw** (= able to take out and shoot a gun quickly)

draw a blank See at BLANK
draw a line in the sand See at LINE
draw blood See at BLOOD
draw fire See at FIRE
draw (the) battle lines See at BATTLE
draw the line See at LINE
draw a veil over *sth* See at VEIL
the luck of the draw See at LUCK

drawing board

go back to the drawing board
to start something again because the previous attempt failed ◆ *Researchers went back to the drawing board to find where they went wrong.* USAGE: sometimes used without **go**: *When we thought we were finished, he sent us back to the drawing board and asked us to completely redo it.* ◆ Related vocabulary **back to square one** at SQUARE ONE

dream

a dream come true
something that has been desired for a long time that has happened as hoped for ◆ *Our vacation by the ocean was a dream come true.* ◆ Related vocabulary **come true** at COME

dream on *esp. spoken*
what you want will not happen ◆ *"I've got a feeling I'll win the lottery this week." "Dream on!"* USAGE: usually said to answer someone else, as in the example.

dream up *sth*, *also* **dream *sth* up**
to invent or imagine something ◆ *She's dreamed up a great new way to waste time.* ◆ *The Gerbils is an odd name for a baseball team – who dreamed it up?* ◆ Related vocabulary **think up *sth*** at THINK

like a dream
so well or so good that it cannot quite be believed ◆ *The suit only cost $100 and it fits like a dream.* ◆ *Our first date was like a dream.* ◆ Related vocabulary **work like a charm** at CHARM

not dream of *doing sth*
to know something is wrong and therefore have no intention of doing it ◆ *When I was a girl, my parents wouldn't dream of letting me stay home alone.*

dreams

wildest dreams
the things that you have imagined,

expected, or hoped for ◆ *His company has succeeded beyond his wildest dreams.* ◆ *Never in my wildest dreams did I think she'd actually carry out her threat.*

dredge

dredge up *sth*, *also* **dredge** *sth* **up**
1 to remember something from the past ◆ *He hates it when people dredge up the crimes that happened here 20 years ago.* ◆ *You're not dredging that old idea up again, are you?* USAGE: often said about something unpleasant
2 to find something after a lot of looking ◆ *We've finally dredged up enough money to have a proper lab with proper equipment.*

dress

dress down
to wear informal clothes ◆ *I dress down if I know I'm just going to be moving boxes of documents at work.* USAGE: often said about wearing informal clothes at work

dress *sb* **down**, *also* **dress down** *sb*
to tell someone angrily what they have done wrong ◆ *She dressed him down in front of a large group of his co-workers.* ◆ *He dresses down players on their performance in the games.*

dress *sth* **up**, *also* **dress up** *sth*
to make something look better or different than it really is ◆ *No matter how you dress it up, the fact is that we lost.* ◆ *His business record is a string of failures dressed up as successes.* USAGE: often followed by **as**, as in the second example

ORIGIN: based on the literal meaning of **dress up** (= to wear more formal clothes)

dressed

dressed to kill
wearing clothes that are intended to make people notice you ◆ *The crowd was young, hip, and dressed to kill.*

dressed to the nines
wearing very fashionable or expensive clothes ◆ *The door opened to reveal a small woman, dressed to the nines for an evening of partying.*

dribs

in dribs and drabs
in small amounts ◆ *She says she keeps getting information in dribs and drabs.*

drift

get the drift, *also* **catch the drift**
to understand in a general way what someone is telling you ◆ *I usually read the first page of a report just to get the drift.* USAGE: sometimes used in the form **get someone's drift**: *She said something about going home, but Len didn't get her drift at the time.*

drill

drill *sth* **into** *sb*
to have something repeated very frequently ◆ *You learn vocabulary by having it drilled into you.* ◆ Related vocabulary **hammer home** *sth* at HAMMER

know the drill
to know what needs to be done or what usually happens in a situation ◆ *You know the drill – cut the grass, bag the clippings, and leave them at the curb.*

drink

drink to *sb* esp. spoken
to wish good health or good luck to someone ◆ *Let's drink to Jessica's new job.* USAGE: usually said as a **toast** (= a short statement celebrating something and followed by everyone present drinking some wine or other liquid)

drive *sb* **to drink**
to make someone regularly drink a lot of alcohol ◆ *The death of a spouse can be enough to drive some people to drink.*

drive

drive *you* crazy, *also* **drive *you* nuts**
to make you upset ◆ *Until you get used to a new computer, the software will drive you crazy.* ◆ *Because I am not a patient person, I am quite sure that editing a dictionary would just drive me nuts!* USAGE: also used in the form **drive you mad**

drive a hard bargain See at BARGAIN

drive a wedge between *sb/sth* See at WEDGE

drive *sb* to distraction See at DISTRACTION

drive *sb* to drink See at DRINK

drive *you* up the wall See at WALL

driving

what *sb* is driving at
the meaning of what someone is saying ◆ *I didn't answer her because I wasn't sure what she was driving at.*

drop

a drop in the bucket
a very small or unimportant amount ◆ *What we were paid for our work was a drop in the bucket compared to what the company earned.*

at the drop of a hat
suddenly, without any planning and for no obvious reason ◆ *He'd buy her expensive clothing at the drop of a hat and worry about how he would pay for it later.* ◆ *I hate to speak in public, but she'll get up on stage at the drop of a hat.* ◆ Related vocabulary **at a moment's notice** at NOTICE, **on the spur of the moment** at SPUR

drop dead slang
go away ◆ *What do you want me to do, tell Don to drop dead?* USAGE: usually used to show you do not like someone

> ORIGIN: based on the more literal meaning of **drop dead** (= to die suddenly)

drop everything
to suddenly stop what you were doing ◆ *You can't just barge into my office when I'm busy and expect me to drop everything.*

drop in, *also* **drop by**
to visit briefly ◆ *About 100 guests dropped in to celebrate the publication of his book.*

drop off
to go to sleep ◆ *I must have dropped off during the show, because I don't remember how it ended.*

drop off *sb/sth*, *also* **drop *sb/sth* off**
to leave someone or something at a particular place ◆ *"Discovery" dropped off supplies and picked up an American astronaut who had spent four months on the space station.* ◆ *Parents drop their kids off at daycare early in the morning.*

drop out (of *sth*)
to stop doing something ◆ *He dropped out of school when he was 16.* ◆ *She dropped out the night before the race, saying she had an injury.*

***you* could hear a pin drop** See at PIN

drop a hint See at HINT

drop *sb* a line See at LINE

drop-dead date See at DATE

drop-dead gorgeous See at GORGEOUS

drop *your* guard See at GUARD

drop the ball See at BALL

***your* jaw drops** See at JAW

drown

drown out *sth*, *also* **drown *sth* out**
to make it impossible to hear something ◆ *The plane was flying so low, the roar of its engines drowned out our conversation.*

drum

beat the drum
to attract attention ◆ *The president said he will beat the drum to build public support for his education program.* USAGE: sometimes fol-

lowed by **for**: *Who is beating the drum for the parents' rights act?*

drum *sth* into *sb*
to teach something to someone by frequent repetition ◆ *Firefighters rely on training that's drummed into them through repeated exercises.*

drum *sb* out of *sth*
to force someone to leave a job or organization ◆ *A lot of writers and directors were drummed out of the film business in the 1950s because they were suspected of being communists.*

drum up *sth*
to create interest in something ◆ *The best way to drum up excitement for a book is to get people to talk about it.*

drummer

march to a different drummer
to be different from other people ◆ *As long as the schools that are marching to a different drummer just serve poor kids, no one really cares how they try to teach their students.*

march to a different drummer

dry

dry up
to disappear ◆ *Many of those jobs dried up in the 1990s.* ◆ *Funding has all but dried up for new research in the field.*

bleed *sb/sth* dry See at BLEED

hang *sb* out to dry See at HANG

leave *you* high and dry See at LEAVE

not a dry eye (in the house) See at EYE

run dry See at RUN

duck

duck out (of *somewhere*)
to leave a place quickly and without being noticed ◆ *The press was waiting for us in front of the hospital, so we ducked out a side door into the car.* USAGE: often said about leaving before an event is finished: *She ducked out of the dinner to watch the last quarter of the game.* ◆ Related vocabulary **slip away** 1 at SLIP

Anna has always marched to a different drummer – it's something everyone likes about her.

ducks

have *your* ducks in a row, *also* **get *your* ducks in a row**
to organize things well ◆ *I thought Mike was extremely smart and always had his ducks in a row.* ◆ Related vocabulary **put *your* (own) house in order** at HOUSE

due

due to *sth*
as a result of something; = **because of** *sth* ◆ *Due to computer problems, the checks cannot be mailed this week.* ◆ *Our flight was late due to the bad weather.*

give *sb* their due
to recognize something good about someone ◆ *This wonderful musician was finally given his due when he was honored at this year's jazz festival.* USAGE: sometimes used in the form **give something its due**: *It took more than 200 years to give the book its due, but it's now regarded as a classic.*

in due course See at COURSE

in due time See at TIME

with all due respect See at RESPECT

dues

pay *your* dues
to earn respect because you worked hard to develop a skill ◆ *She paid her dues playing in small clubs in New York before an album made her famous.*

> ORIGIN: based on the literal meaning of **dues** (= money paid to belong to an organization)

duke

duke it out
to compete against someone or something ◆ *The airlines are duking it out, offering better service and cheaper fares as a way of attracting passengers.* USAGE: often used in newspaper writing to describe competition between political candidates: *Candidates are still duking it out in state primaries, with no one the clear winner yet.* ◆ Related vocabulary **fight it out** 2 at FIGHT, **slug it out** at SLUG

> ORIGIN: based on the slang meaning of **duke** (= to hit or fight someone with your hands)

dumps

down in the dumps
unhappy ◆ *She's down in the dumps because all her friends are out of town.*

in the dumps
not successful ◆ *The movie business remains in the dumps, perhaps because of the huge increase in ticket prices.* USAGE: often said about a lack of financial success

dust

bite the dust
to stop existing ◆ *Back in the '50s we had many competitors, but most have bitten the dust.* ◆ *Another fashion fad has bitten the dust.*

dust *sth* off, *also* **dust off *sth***
to make something usable after it has not been used for a long time ◆ *It's a good time to dust off your resume and see if you can get some work.* ◆ *Byrne dusted off some of the band's classics in Tuesday's concert.*

dust *yourself* off
to prepare yourself to continue doing something you unexpectedly stopped doing ◆ *Everyone wonders if the nation can dust itself off after the disaster.*

> ORIGIN: based on the literal meaning of **dusting yourself off** (= cleaning dirt off yourself) after you fall

gather dust
to be forgotten or not used ◆ *Hugh's tennis racket has just been gathering dust since he hurt his back.*

leave *sb/sth* in the dust
1 to move quickly away from someone or something ◆ *If a big truck*

bears down on you from behind, this powerful car can leave it in the dust. **2** to replace someone or something with something new ◆ *This new computer virus left last year's killer virus in the dust.*

when the dust settles
after an activity stops ◆ *We always believed that when the dust settled, the court would rule in our favor.* USAGE: sometimes used in the form **until the dust settles**: *You meet lots of people when you travel on business, and until the dust settles, you don't know what you've actually accomplished.*

duty

do double duty
1 to do two jobs at one time ◆ *Kudrow does double duty in the show, playing her regular role and the character's twin sister.* **2** to be used for two different activities ◆ *Three conference rooms do double duty as dining rooms when the main dining room is full.*

duty bound to *do sth*
required to do something ◆ *Investigators are duty bound to find out what happened and make a report.*

off duty
not working ◆ *She goes off duty at midnight.* ◆ *The police officer was charged with robbing Castillo while he was off duty.* USAGE: usually said about soldiers, police, medical workers, and people who work a scheduled period of time

on duty
working ◆ *A physical therapist is on duty in the fitness center from 7 a.m. until 9 p.m.* ◆ *He didn't have time to talk about it right then because he was on duty for another three hours.* USAGE: usually said about soldiers, police, medical workers, and people who work a scheduled period of time

dwell

not dwell on *sth*
to not spend a lot of time thinking or talking about something ◆ *I knew how important this test was but I didn't want to dwell on it.* ◆ *My mother's advice always was, "Don't dwell on it, do something about it!"* USAGE: also used without **not**: *She dwells on the past a little too much.*

E, e

each

to each *their* own
it is obviously right for someone else, although you cannot understand why ♦ *Some people who work at home continue to dress in office clothes – well, to each his own, but I'd never do that.*

ear

bend *sb's* ear
to talk to someone for a long time ♦ *She spent the day at a conference bending the ears of some high school teachers.*

grin from ear to ear, *also* **smile from ear to ear**
to give a very big smile ♦ *He was grinning from ear to ear, as if he had just won the lottery.*

have an ear for *sth*
to be especially good at hearing and repeating sounds ♦ *The author has a good ear for ordinary speech and writes realistic dialog.* USAGE: said especially of speech or music ♦ Related vocabulary **have an eye for *sth*** at EYE

have the ear of *sb*
to be able to share your opinions with someone important or powerful ♦ *With a Latino as secretary of commerce, the Hispanic community finally had the ear of the president.*

have *your* ear to the ground, *also* **keep *your* ear to the ground**
to watch and listen carefully to what is happening around you ♦ *We've had our ear to the ground, but we haven't learned anything about the company's plans.*

in one ear and out the other
heard but not remembered ♦ *I'd remind him about something and he'd let it go in one ear and out the other.*

keep an ear out for *sb/sth*
to be prepared to hear someone or something ♦ *We are working on some new songs, so keep an ear out for those.* ♦ Related vocabulary **keep an eye out (for *sb/sth*)** at EYE

lend an ear to *sb/sth*
to listen carefully and with understanding to someone or something ♦ *Bush lent an ear to a group of oil executives who came to the White House.* ♦ *Aunt Rosalie lent a sympathetic ear to my troubles.*

play *sth* by ear, *also* **play (it) by ear**
1 to play a piece of music after hearing it and without written music ♦ *My brother can play anything on the piano by ear.*
2 to deal with a situation as it develops and without a plan ♦ *I'm not sure if I can go bowling or not, I'll just have to play it by ear.* USAGE: sometimes used with other verbs: *I write by ear, and rarely with any exact notion of how I want it to come out.*

turn a deaf ear to *sth*
to ignore what someone is saying ♦ *The Supreme Court said there was a need for action, but Congress has turned a deaf ear to the Court.* ♦ *Meiling's father turned a deaf ear to any criticism of how he had taught his daughter.*

turn *sth* on its ear, *also* **set *sth* on its ear**
to change a type of activity in a surprising and exciting way ♦ *He's turned the diving world on its ear – natural talent like his comes along only once in a lifetime.*

earful

get an earful
to have a lot to listen to ♦ *His fans got quite an earful – several well-known pieces spiced up with new arrangements.* USAGE: often said about criticism or unwanted suggestions: *I got a very unpleasant*

earful from a truck driver who thought I was in his way.

early
early on
shortly after the beginning ♦ *He decided early on that this was the perfect school for him.*

it's early days (yet)
it is too soon to make a judgment about something ♦ *It looks like we will earn a profit, but it's early days yet and we can't be sure.*

earnest
in earnest
with full effort and attention ♦ *Peace talks began in earnest after four days of bloody fighting in September.* USAGE: usually used to emphasize a change from a period of less effort or attention: *The presidential campaign began in earnest on Labor Day.*

ears
all ears *esp. spoken*
very eager to listen to what someone is going to say ♦ *I'm all ears, waiting to hear your latest excuse for not getting this job done!*

not believe *your* ears
to be very surprised by something that someone tells you ♦ *We couldn't believe our ears when we heard that our tickets weren't waiting for us at the airport ticket counter.*

have *sth* coming out (of) *your* ears *esp. spoken*
to have a lot of something ♦ *Ask him for a loan, he's got money coming out his ears.*

***sth* falls on deaf ears**
a statement, opinion, or suggestion is ignored ♦ *Jennifer suggested that Harold should get a job, but of course her advice fell on deaf ears.*

prick *your* ears up, *also* **prick up *your* ears**
to listen carefully ♦ *If you hear my name mentioned, prick up your ears – I want to know what you find out.*

wet behind the ears
young and not experienced ♦ *The job put a lot of responsibility on someone who was still wet behind the ears, but he learned fast.*

music to *sb's* ears See at MUSIC

earth
back to earth
returning to a more usual condition ♦ *I was excited to get the job, but I came back to earth pretty quickly when I realized that I would have to move.* USAGE: used with verbs like **bring**, **come**, and **drop**

on earth
in any conditions; = **in the world** ♦ *What on earth makes you say that?* ♦ *Why on earth would she ask you to join them?* ♦ *How on earth did you survive the heat?* ♦ *Who on earth would want to collect rocks?* ♦ *Where on earth could Casey have learned such behavior?* USAGE: used to express great surprise that something could happen or exist

off the face of the earth See at FACE

go to the ends of the earth See at ENDS

heaven on earth See at HEAVEN

hell on earth See at HELL

move heaven and earth (to do *sth*) See at HEAVEN

the four corners of the earth See at CORNERS

the salt of the earth See at SALT

ease
at ease
relaxed and comfortable ♦ *The girl behind the bar was completely at ease, chatting with her customers as she mixed their drinks.* USAGE: often used in the form **put someone at ease** (= make someone comfortable): *We were greeted by a young woman who immediately put us at ease.* ♦ Opposite **ill at ease**

ill at ease
worried and uncomfortable ♦ *The old gentleman obviously felt ill at*

eat

ease while he waited to have his hair cut. ◆ Opposite **at ease**

eat

eat *you* alive
1 to cause you to suffer ◆ *Without my own lawyer, the defendants' lawyers would have eaten me alive in court.* ◆ *The state income tax is just eating me alive, so I think I may move.*
2 to bite you repeatedly ◆ *The only bad thing about camping by the river was the mosquitoes that ate us alive.* USAGE: used only of insects, as in the example

eat away at *sth*
to reduce something by a little at a time ◆ *These bank fees eat away at my savings every month.*

eat *you* up esp. spoken
to spoil your life ◆ *The danger of a busy professional life is that it will eat you up.*

ORIGIN: based on the literal meaning of **eat something up** (= to use something so there is little or nothing left)

eat it up, *also* **eat *sth* up**
to enjoy something completely ◆ *She has the kind of cheery voice that adults might dislike but little kids just eat it up.* ◆ Related vocabulary **lap up *sth* 1** at LAP

ORIGIN: based on the literal meaning of **eat something up** (= to finish the food you have)

a bite to eat See at BITE
eat *sb/sth* for breakfast See at BREAKFAST
eat crow See at CROW
eat *your* heart out See at HEART
eat like a horse See at HORSE
eat *sb* out of house and home See at HOUSE
eat *your* words See at WORDS
have *your* cake and eat it too See at CAKE
the proof of the pudding (is in the eating) See at PROOF

eating

what's eating *you* esp. spoken
what is making you angry ◆ *What's eating him today – pressure from work or problems at home?*

ebb

the ebb and flow of *sth*
the continually changing character of something ◆ *There is a normal ebb and flow in nature, for example, when there is just the right amount of rain and when there is not enough.* USAGE: often said about something that regularly gets larger and smaller: *There's a constant ebb and flow of traffic on the highway.* ◆ Related vocabulary **ups and downs** at UPS

at (a) low ebb slightly formal, *also* **at its lowest ebb**
below the usual condition or standard ◆ *The divorce comes at a time when Jackson's career is at a low ebb.* ◆ *Support for the arts has reached its lowest ebb and we hope it won't go any lower.* ◆ Related vocabulary **up to par** at PAR

eclipse

in eclipse slightly formal
thought of as less important or as having less value ◆ *By the time he died, the novelist and his work were in eclipse.*

edge

keep *you* on the edge of *your* seat, *also* **keep *you* on the edge of *your* chair**
to make you very excited or nervous because of uncertainty ◆ *It was one of those movies that was so suspenseful, it kept you on the edge of your seat right through to the end.*

(live) on the edge
1 to be in an uncertain situation or one that could cause harm ◆ *I do not believe a person has to live on the edge in order to be a creative artist.* ◆ Related vocabulary **live dangerously** at LIVE, **on the bubble** at BUBBLE

2 to be very poor ✦ *Too many children live on the edge, without proper food or medical care.*

lose *your* edge
to no longer have the determination or skills that made you successful in the past ✦ *Long ago, Foster figured out you could act like a gentleman and still not lose your edge.*

on edge
nervous or worried ✦ *You're always on edge waiting for an important call, because you don't really know when that phone will ring.* USAGE: often used in the forms **set you on edge** or **put you on edge**: *The accident set us on edge for several days.* ✦ Related vocabulary **set *your* teeth on edge** at TEETH

on the cutting edge (of *sth*), *also* **at the cutting edge (of *sth*)**
in front of others with what is new ✦ *Some people on the cutting edge of fashion have one strip of hair dyed one color and the rest another color.* ✦ *University Hospital is at the cutting edge of medical technology.* USAGE: also used in the form **on the edge**: *This band used to be on the edge, but it's much less exciting these days.*

over the edge
into a condition of extreme emotional or mental suffering ✦ *I worry that someone as upset as she is could easily be pushed over the edge and cause herself great harm.*

take the edge off *sth*
to reduce the effect of something, esp. something unpleasant ✦ *Ceiling fans can take the edge off summer heat.* ✦ *The memorial service didn't bring my husband back to life, but it took the edge off my sorrow.*

effort

spare no effort to *do sth*
to work as hard as possible to achieve something ✦ *Emergency services have spared no effort to help people whose homes were destroyed by the tornadoes.* ✦ Related vocabulary **spare no expense** at EXPENSE

egg

have egg on *your* face
to be embarrassed ✦ *If the computer problems continue, then the software giant will have egg on its face.* USAGE: also used in the form **with egg on your face**: *People who supported him came away with egg on their faces.* ✦ Related vocabulary **blow up in *your* face** at FACE

eggs

put all *your* eggs in one basket
to risk your money or your reputation in support of one idea or plan ✦ *I didn't want to put all my eggs in one basket, so I played five different lottery games, but lost all of them.*

> ORIGIN: based on the idea that if all the eggs you got from your chickens are in one **basket** (= container) and you drop it, you will lose all your eggs

eggshells

walk on eggshells
to try very hard not to upset someone or something ✦ *Everyone at the company was walking on eggshells until we heard that no one would be fired.*

> ORIGIN: based on the idea that **eggshells** are easily broken

eight ball

behind the eight ball
in a difficult situation ✦ *Simpson's thoughtless remarks put him behind the eight ball, and many people thought he should resign.*

> ORIGIN: from the game of pool (= a game played on a special table with sticks and numbered balls), in which you do not want to have any ball positioned behind the black ball marked with a number 8

elbow

at *sb's* elbow
very near and convenient ✦ *My kitchen is small and efficient with*

everything right at my elbow. ♦ *Does the president have enough advisors at his elbow?*

elbows

rub elbows with *sb*
to meet or be with someone socially; = **rub shoulders with *sb*** ♦ *As Ms Quasebarth's personal assistant, Celia has rubbed elbows with singers and DJ's and even presidents.*

element

in *your* element
doing something you like very much and are comfortable with ♦ *Paul is in his element when he's working in the office, but when he's making sales calls, he's miserable.*
USAGE: the opposite meaning is expressed by **out of your element** (= doing something that makes you very uncomfortable or unhappy): *Grant was a great general, but as president, he was out of his element.*

else

if all else fails
if nothing succeeds ♦ *Miki spoke a little English, I used a lot of hand signals, and if all else failed, we would look in a phrase book.*

or else
or ♦ *We need to be there by eight or else we'll find it hard to park the car.*
USAGE: when spoken after a demand, **or else** can be a mild threat: *Turn down that radio or else I'll take it away from you!* ♦ *You better remember to bring the wine, or else!*

embarrassment

an embarrassment of riches slightly formal
more of something good or pleasant than you need ♦ *The Internet presents us with an embarrassment of riches when you want information, but how much of it is accurate?*

empty

running on empty
lacking energy or enthusiasm ♦ *He's been running on empty for months now – a vacation will do him good.* ♦ *The program to build low-cost housing has not attracted much support and is running on empty.* ♦ Related vocabulary **on automatic pilot** at AUTOMATIC PILOT

> ORIGIN: based on the literal meaning of **running on empty** (= operating a car with almost no fuel)

end

an end in itself slightly formal
satisfying no other purpose than the enjoyment of doing it ♦ *Memorizing facts can become an end in itself and not a way of understanding something.*

at the end of the day, *also* **by the end of the day**
finally; = **in the end** ♦ *We interviewed many people for the job, but at the end of the day, we didn't think any of them could handle it.* ♦ Related vocabulary **in the final analysis** at ANALYSIS, **when all is said and done** at SAID

at *your* wit's end
so upset that you do not know what to do ♦ *I have a problem that has me at wit's end, and I'm hoping you can help.*

end it all
to kill yourself ♦ *Overcome with grief, he ended it all.*

end of story esp. spoken
all that can be said or reported about something ♦ *That's right, your contract will not be renewed, end of story.*

end up
to reach a final place or position; = **wind up** ♦ *I began work as an accountant and ended up writing advertising.* ♦ *We ended up the evening drinking and dancing at a club downtown.*

get the short end (of the stick)
to feel that you are being treated particularly badly in comparison with other people ♦ *When the mayor*

cut our budget almost in half, I felt like we were getting the short end of the stick. ✦ I always feel like I'm getting the short end, that I'm being cheated out of something.

go off the deep end
to become so angry or upset that you cannot control your emotions ✦ Tom will go off the deep end if Jerry can't pay him the money he owes.

in the end
finally; = **at the end of the day** ✦ Despite all the problems of putting on the play, it was a grand success, and that was all that mattered in the end. ✦ Related vocabulary **in the final analysis** at ANALYSIS, **when all is said and done** at SAID

never hear the end of it
to have to listen for a long time to talk about something embarrassing or annoying ✦ If you don't send your aunt a thank-you letter, you'll never hear the end of it from your mother!

no end esp. spoken
very much ✦ I just didn't like the color of the carpet at all, and it just upset me no end. ✦ That kid loves soccer no end!

no end in sight (to sth)
lacking the possibility of any change ✦ There seems to be no end in sight to quicker and better computers.

no end of sth
a lot of something ✦ The twins were no end of trouble.

not the end of the world
not the worst thing that could happen ✦ If I don't get the job, it won't be the end of the world.

on end
continuously; = **at a stretch** ✦ She practices the violin for hours on end. USAGE: **on end** is used with **hours**, **days**, **weeks**, and other units of time: He's often away for weeks on end.

on the receiving end, also **at the receiving end**
feeling the unpleasant effects of something ✦ She'd been on the receiving end of his temper a few times and knew how nasty it could be.

put an end to sth
to stop something; = **put a stop to sth** ✦ The lights went out, and that put an end to our game of cards.

the end of the line, also **the end of the road**
the last part of something ✦ He knew he had reached the end of the line when performing started to be more tiring than satisfying. ✦ Our friendship reached the end of the road with a nasty fight.

to the bitter end See **stick it out** at STICK

endow

endowed with sth
born with a particular quality ✦ He was endowed with an exceedingly quick mind.

ends

at loose ends
not knowing what to do esp. because of some upsetting change ✦ He was at loose ends when their long-term relationship broke up.

> ORIGIN: based on the idea of a string or rope with ends that are not neatly tied together

follow you to the ends of the earth
as far as possible ✦ You cannot leave me because I will follow you to the ends of the earth.

go to the ends of the earth
to do as much as possible ✦ Most people would go to the ends of the earth to make sure their child had the best possible doctor.

make ends meet
to have enough money to pay for your basic expenses ✦ To make ends meet, she runs a day-care center out of her home.

enemy

your own worst enemy
doing things yourself that prevent

enough

you from being liked or successful ◆ *As a young player, Michael was his own worst enemy, arguing with the coach and other players and generally being unpleasant.* USAGE: sometimes used in the form **its own worst enemy**, referring to something: *The company has made a number of bad decisions that have made it its own worst enemy.*

enough

(say) enough is enough
this must stop ◆ *The movie was so boring that I decided enough is enough and got up and left.* ◆ *I am tired of being treated badly, and I say enough is enough.* USAGE: usually said of something that is not interesting or pleasant

envelope

push (the edge of) the envelope
to move beyond the limit of what has usually been done or was the accepted standard ◆ *TV shows are really pushing the envelope by showing so much sex and violence.*

envy

green with envy
wishing very much that you had what someone else has ◆ *Sharon's going off to the south of France for three weeks and we're all green with envy.*

equals

first among equals slightly formal
the best or most important of a similar group ◆ *The solo violin was first among equals in the midst of all the stringed instruments.* ◆ *Because she is the chairman of the committee, she is, of course, first among equals.*

errand

run an errand, also **run errands**
to make a short trip for a particular purpose ◆ *I've got to run a few errands and then stop by my mother's house.* USAGE: usually to buy or deliver something

error

see the error of *your/its* ways slightly formal
to accept that you have been wrong about something ◆ *What can we do to make Tim see the error of his ways?* ◆ *The industry needs to see the error of its ways and adopt these new safety standards.*

green with envy

Josie's victory made me green with envy.

escape

it escapes *me*
1 I do not notice something ♦ *If there was something important in that package, it certainly escaped me.*
2 I do not remember something ♦ *I knew his name a minute ago, but now it escapes me.*

essence

of the essence
most important ♦ *When someone has a heart attack, time is of the essence – you need to begin treatment immediately.*

even

even if only
just ♦ *I still like to keep in touch with friends, even if only occasionally.* ♦ *If you are angry and disappointed, you might as well admit it, even if only to yourself.*

even so
despite everything; = **for all that** ♦ *This place fills up with tourists in the summer, but even so, there are plenty of places for them to stay.* ♦ Related vocabulary **be that as it may** at BE

event

in any event, *also* slightly formal **at all events**
whatever happens; = **in any case** ♦ *I hope to meet her this afternoon, but in any event I have to return home tomorrow.* USAGE: the same meaning can also be expressed by **at (the very) least, come hell or high water, come what may**, and **either way** ♦ Related vocabulary **one way or the other** 2 at WAY

in the event of *sth*, *also* **in the event that *sth* happens**
if something should happen ♦ *In the event of war, we have to be prepared to send in troops.* ♦ *Travel insurance protects you in the event that you have to cancel your trip.* USAGE: sometimes used in the form **in the unlikely event** (= if something should happen that you do not expect to happen): *In the unlikely event of a fire, alarms will sound and you should exit immediately.* ♦ Related vocabulary **in case of *sth*** at CASE

every

every last
each ♦ *Every last bit of the meal was delicious.* USAGE: used for emphasis: *The lawyer explained every last detail of the contract.*

every other *sth*
omitting the next but including the one after that, as a series or repetition of something ♦ *Our discussion group meets every other Friday at eight o'clock.* ♦ *It seems like every other shop in the village is a cafe.*

every so often
sometimes; = **(every) once in a while** ♦ *We still get together for lunch every so often.* ♦ Related vocabulary **(every) now and then** at NOW

evidence

in evidence
obvious ♦ *Police and ambulance crews were in evidence all over town after the storm.* USAGE: sometimes used with **much** or **very much** for emphasis: *Good sportsmanship is always very much in evidence in these competitions.*

example

make an example of *sb*
to punish someone for doing something so that other people will not do the same thing ♦ *They want to make an example of him by keeping him in prison under very difficult conditions.*

excuse

excuse me esp. spoken
1 I am sorry to interrupt you ♦ *Oh, excuse me, I didn't know you were busy.*
2 that was not what I intended to say or do ♦ *As a kid growing up, my*

family grew strawberries, excuse me, grew tomatoes.
3 I did not hear you ◆ *Which office do you work in? Excuse me?* ◆ Related vocabulary **pardon me** at PARDON

expense

at the expense of *sth*
with the loss of something ◆ *Time is spent preparing students for state tests at the expense of other, important instruction.*

at *your* expense
1 causing embarrassment ◆ *They had a joke at her expense.*
2 with you paying for something ◆ *I can have the ROM on my computer expanded at my expense.*

spare no expense
to not consider the cost of something ◆ *The team spared no expense in hiring players last year.* ◆ Related vocabulary **spare no effort to** *do sth* at EFFORT

explain

explain away *sth*, *also* **explain** *sth* **away**
to invent reasons why something is unimportant ◆ *You will find it hard to explain away all these mistakes.* ◆ *Rather than face the truth, we try to explain it away.*

eye

a bird's eye view
the appearance of something seen from above ◆ *The large painting offers a bird's eye view that shows the layout of the ancient city.* USAGE: sometimes used to show how an animal's view is different: *A basement window gives you a dog's eye view of the world – all you see is the bottom of the fire hydrant and passing feet on the sidewalk.*

catch *sb's* **eye**, *also* **catch the eye of** *sb*
to attract someone's attention ◆ *Out of all the beautiful things in the garden, the fountain was what really caught my eye.* ◆ *It's a good car, but it doesn't catch the customers' eye.*

have an eye for *sth*
to be able to understand and appreciate something ◆ *She certainly had an eye for art, which explains, of course, why she was a successful art dealer.* USAGE: also used in the form **with an eye for something**: *I think I was born with an eye for beauty.* ◆ Related vocabulary **have an ear for** *sth* at EAR

have *your* **eye on** *sb*
to watch someone carefully ◆ *I've had my eye on her for some time, and I believe she is the best person for the job.*

have *your* **eye on** *sth*
to admire and want to have something ◆ *The museum had its eye on the painting for many years, hoping its owner would sell it some day.*

in the public eye
known and talked about by many people ◆ *The former senator remained in the public eye even after retirement.* ◆ *We need to keep education in the public eye if we want support for improvements in our schools.* USAGE: the opposite meaning is expressed by **out of the public eye**: *Illness kept the actor out of the public eye for eighteen months.*

keep an eye on *sb/sth*, *also* **keep** *your* **eye on** *sb/sth*
to watch or give your attention to someone or something ◆ *The mother sat on the edge of the sandbox, keeping an eye on her sons as they played.* USAGE: sometimes used with an adjective: *The woman kept a close eye on her purse.*

keep an eye out (for *sb/sth***)**, *also* **keep** *your* **eye out (for** *sb/sth***)**
to watch carefully for someone or something; = **keep** *your* **eyes peeled (for** *sth***)** ◆ *Three aircraft kept an eye out for the submarine while waiting for help to arrive.* ◆ *I always kept my eye out for strangers.*

♦ Related vocabulary **keep an ear out for** *sb/sth* at EAR, **keep (a) close watch on** *sb/sth* at WATCH

keep *your* eye on the ball esp. spoken
to give your compete attention to what you are doing or want to achieve ♦ *We need to keep our eye on the ball and continue to encourage our students.* ♦ Related vocabulary **on the ball** at BALL

keep one eye on *sb/sth*, *also* **have one eye on** *sb/sth*
to give part of your attention to one person or thing ♦ *Jim continued to talk to me, but he kept one eye on the clock to be sure he wouldn't be late.* USAGE: sometimes used in the form **with one eye on someone or something**: *She read her newspaper with one eye on arrivals board to see is his train had come in.*

more (to *sb/sth***) than meets the eye**
more interesting or complicated than someone or something appears at first ♦ *There is more to her death than meets the eye – she was probably murdered.* ♦ *There must be more to him than meets the eye, or else why would she be interested in him?* USAGE: also used in the form **less than meets the eye** (= not as interesting or complicated as it appears): *Unfortunately, with her boyfriend, there is less than meets the eye.*

not a dry eye (in the house)
everyone is crying or feels strong emotion ♦ *When he sang the beautiful old Austrian folksong, there wasn't a dry eye in the house.*

> ORIGIN: based on a special meaning of **the house** (= the people attending a performance in a theater)

not bat an eye, *also* **not bat an eyelid**
to not show any reaction ♦ *Mom didn't bat an eye when I told her I was getting married.* USAGE: also used in the form **without batting an eye** with the same meaning: *She can give a formal dinner for thirty without batting an eye.*

see eye to eye
to agree with someone ♦ *My father and I see eye to eye on most things.* USAGE: often used in the form **not see eye to eye**: *We don't see eye to eye on a lot of things.*

the eye of the storm
the center of a disagreement ♦ *The man in the eye of the storm is accused of selling secrets to the enemy.*

> ORIGIN: based on the literal meaning of **the eye of the storm** (= the middle of a mass of severe weather)

turn a blind eye (to *sth***)**
to ignore something; = **close *your/its* eyes to** *sth* ♦ *Sometimes a store might sell stolen goods because the owner has turned a blind eye to where they come from.*

with an eye to *sth*
for the purpose of something ♦ *All college applications that we receive are read with an eye to finding the most promising students.* ♦ *This new factory was designed with an eye to providing a better work environment.*

from the corner of *your* eye See at CORNER

eyebrows

raise (some) eyebrows, *also* **raise a few eyebrows**
to cause disapproval or worry ♦ *The styles now favored by many teenagers have raised a few eyebrows among parents.*

eyeful

get an eyeful
to see as much as or more than you want to see ♦ *Visitors to Halifax are getting an eyeful of whales this summer.* ♦ *When he pulled his pants down, we got quite an eyeful.*

eyelid

not bat an eyelid See **not bat an eye** at EYE

eyes

all eyes
with a lot of interest in something or someone you see ◆ *The kids were all eyes, taking in every detail of the new house.*

all eyes are on *sb*/*sth*
everyone is watching someone or something ◆ *All eyes are on the top three tennis players.*

close *your*/*its* eyes to *sth*, also **shut *your*/*its* eyes to *sth***
to ignore something; = **turn a blind eye (to *sth*)** ◆ *As a cop, I can't close my eyes to illegal drugs, even when I'm not working.* ◆ *The church cannot close its eyes to suffering.*

cry *your* eyes out
to be extremely unhappy and cry a lot ◆ *A friend told me my house was destroyed in the fire, and I cried my eyes out.* USAGE: sometimes used in the form **cry your heart out**

***your* eyes pop out of *your* head**
esp. spoken
to show surprise ◆ *My sister showed me the ring Jim gave her, and my eyes popped out of my head, it was so beautiful.*

feast *your* eyes on *sb*/*sth*
to look at someone or something with pleasure ◆ *We spent one whole day feasting our eyes on paintings I never thought I'd have the chance to see.* USAGE: sometimes used in the form **a feast for the eyes** (= someone or something that is pleasing to look at): *Potter's film is a feast for the eyes.*

hit *you* (right) between the eyes
to be very easy to notice ◆ *The song's catchy lyrics and bright melody hit him right between the eyes.* ◆ *I think the quality of our product is going to hit people right between the eyes.*

in the eyes of *sb*, also **in *your* eyes**
in another person's opinion ◆ *Young kids admire this ballplayer, want to be like him, and in the eyes of most of them, he can't do anything wrong.* ◆ *My mother was always a true hero in my eyes.*

in the eyes of the law
legally ◆ *Our legal system is based on the idea that all people are equal in the eyes of the law.* ◆ *In the eyes of the law, you are responsible for what happened.*

keep *your* eyes peeled (for *sth*)
to watch carefully for someone or something; = **keep an eye out (for *sb*/*sth*)** ◆ *Keep your eyes peeled for a taxi.*

lay eyes on *sb*/*sth*, also **set eyes on *sb*/*sth***
to see someone or something ◆ *She did not want to lay eyes on this man ever again.* ◆ *My mother had fallen in love with my father when she first set eyes on him.*

not believe *your* (own) eyes
to think that something you see is not likely to be real ◆ *She looked so different in a uniform, I couldn't believe my eyes.* USAGE: sometimes **scarcely** or **hardly** are used instead of **not**: *When he found the ring in the grass, he could scarcely believe his eyes.*

only have eyes for *sb*/*sth*, also **have eyes only for *sb*/*sth***
to be interested in just one person or thing ◆ *They only had eyes for each other.* ◆ *A hunter has eyes only for the animal being hunted.*

open *your* eyes (to *sth*)
to cause you to understand or be interested in something ◆ *Working with disabled children opened my eyes to how hard they work to do things most of us do so easily.*

do *sth* with *your* eyes closed, also **do *sth* with *your* eyes shut**
to do something very easily; = **do *sth* with one hand tied behind *your* back** ◆ *I've filled in this form*

so many times, I can do it with my eyes closed.
with *your* eyes (wide) open understanding the true character of someone or something ♦ *I knew Bill for a long time, and I went into this relationship with my eyes wide open.*

eyeteeth
give *your* eyeteeth for *sth* esp. spoken
to want to have or do something very much ♦ *Right now I'd give my eyeteeth for a chocolate ice cream soda!*

F, f

face

blow up in *your* face, *also* **explode in *your* face**
to unexpectedly fail ♦ *The military does not rush into a situation that could blow up in their faces.* ♦ *Carey's efforts to explain the need for staff reductions exploded in his face.* ♦ Related vocabulary **have egg on *your* face** at EGG

face to face with *sb/sth*
with someone or something in front of you ♦ *As I was going into the restaurant, I came face to face with my teacher, who was just leaving.* ♦ *Suddenly, I was face to face with a panther.*

face to face with *sth*
having to deal with something unpleasant ♦ *Carol came face to face with the problem of getting proper care for her mother.*

fly in the face of *sth*
to be the opposite of what is usual or accepted ♦ *His decision to start his own business certainly flies in the face of good judgment.*

get out of my face esp. spoken
go away ♦ *Just get out of my face and stop criticizing everything I do!*

in the face of *sth*
1 despite something ♦ *She left home in the face of strong opposition from her parents.*
2 when threatened by something ♦ *In the face of clear evidence that the printing company did what it was supposed to do, the publisher lost the lawsuit.*

in *your* face esp. spoken
rudely annoying you ♦ *The reporter was in her face day after day, asking personal questions.*

(let's) face it
we must accept the truth of this; = **face facts** ♦ *Let's face it, he was a big hunk of a man and a good-looking guy.* ♦ *Lots of people do not read for pleasure and, face it, not all the books you have to read are ones you would choose.* ♦ Related vocabulary **get real** at GET

lose face
to not maintain your reputation and the respect of others ♦ *The sales manager lost face with his customers when he continually promised items he couldn't deliver.* ♦ Opposite **save face**

make a face (at *sb/sth*), *also* **make faces (at *sb/sth*)**
to change the expression on your face to show dislike or get attention ♦ *She made a face like she'd eaten a lemon.* ♦ *The child was making faces, and I wanted to laugh.*

off the face of the earth, *also* **from the face of the earth**
completely gone ♦ *I enjoy boxing but wouldn't miss it if it dropped off the face of the earth tomorrow.* USAGE: most often used with the verbs **drop**, **disappear**, and **wipe**

on the face of it
when first considered ♦ *On the face of it, the new system just moves our company into the computer age, but it may be more complicated than that.*

on the face of the earth
existing ♦ *He is probably the nicest man on the face of the earth.*

put on a brave face
to act confident in a difficult situation; = **put up a brave front** ♦ *The engineers have put on a brave face, saying the telescope can easily be repaired.* USAGE: sometimes used in the form **put a brave face on something**: *She puts a brave face on everything, but you know that she is worried.*

save face
to keep your reputation and the respect of other people ♦ *The school board needs to reach an agreement*

that allows both sides to save face. ♦ Opposite **lose face**

screw up *your* **face**
to make an unpleasant expression with your face ♦ *"This milk is sour," she said, screwing up her face.*

set *your* **face against** *sth* slightly formal
to oppose something ♦ *Mother had set her face against my having music lessons with this teacher in the city.*

show *your* **face**
to choose to be seen by other people ♦ *You need to go out, show your face, chat to people.* ♦ *After the awful way you behaved, I wonder how you can show your face here.*

stare *you* **in the face**
to be obvious ♦ *The answer to this problem was staring him in the face, although at first he couldn't see it.*

stare *sth* **in the face**
to deal with something directly ♦ *We have stared hatred and prejudice in the face and seen what they can do.*

stuff *your* **face** slang
to eat continuously ♦ *They're home watching the ballgame on TV and stuffing their faces with potato chips.*

to *your* **face**
directly to you ♦ *I already knew the answer, but I wanted him to say it to my face, even if it embarrassed him.*

(until *you* **are) blue in the face**
for a long time ♦ *The attorneys can talk until they're blue in the face, but I don't think they'll convince the jury that this guy is innocent.* ♦ *You can argue yourself blue in the face but it isn't going to change my opinion.*
USAGE: used to suggest that someone will not listen to what is being said

what's his face esp. spoken, *also* **what's her face**
a person whose name is forgotten or not known ♦ *They were thinking about hiring what's his face, the guy with the yellow shirt.*

(written) all over *your* **face** esp. spoken
showing what you think of something by your expression ♦ *You see anxiety written all over his face at the thought of doing something completely new and different.* ♦ *Absolute happiness was all over her face.*

keep a straight face See at STRAIGHT FACE

take *sth* **at face value** See at FACE VALUE

face value

take *sth* **at face value**
to accept that something is exactly what it appears to be ♦ *This is good research that can be taken at face value by readers.* ♦ *You have to understand that you cannot take gossip at its face value.*

> ORIGIN: based on the idea that the **value** (= worth) of a piece of money is exactly the amount shown by a number on its **face** (= front)

fact

in (point of) fact
actually; = **as a matter of fact** ♦ *Steve decided not to come with us, and in fact he has already left for New York.* ♦ *In fact, we visited the school last week.* ♦ Related vocabulary **in reality** at REALITY, **in truth** at TRUTH

is that a fact
really ♦ *"The more I read about elephants, the more I realized they are very complicated animals." "Is that a fact?"*

facts

face facts, *also* **let's face (the) facts**
we must accept the truth of this; = **(let's) face it** ♦ *You have to face facts – when your boss tells you she doesn't like your report, you'd*

fail

face facts

"Let's face the facts – we don't have any money to spend on vacation this year."

better rewrite it. ◆ Related vocabulary **get real** at GET

fail

without fail
certain to happen ◆ *Sarah sends me a card on my birthday without fail.*

fails

if all else fails
if nothing succeeds ◆ *If all else fails, we can always spend the weekend at home.* ◆ *You should try to discuss this with your employer, but if all else fails, you need to speak to a lawyer.*

fair

fair and square
honestly ◆ *We played very well and won, fair and square.*

fair enough
all right ◆ *The town is full of tourists, which is fair enough because they spend a lot of money here.*

faith

keep faith with *sb/sth* slightly formal
to be loyal to someone or something ◆ *It is unusual for any official to keep faith with promises made when trying to win an election.*

take *sb/sth* **on faith**
to believe someone or something without proof ◆ *You will have to take it on faith that the information I am asking for is really important.*

fall

break *your* **fall**, *also* **break the fall**
to stop you from going down ◆ *He reached out, trying to break his fall, and ended up breaking his arm.*

fall apart
1 to stop working or fail completely ◆ *Her marriage fell apart after about ten years.* ◆ *The deal to sell the company fell apart last summer.* ◆ Related vocabulary **go to pieces** at PIECES
2 to break into pieces ◆ *Cook the tomatoes until they begin to fall apart.* ◆ *When the roof wasn't repaired, the building really began to fall apart.*

fall all over *yourself* **(to** *do sth***)**, *also* **fall over** *yourself* **to** *do sth*
to put too much energy into some-

thing in order to get attention or approval ◆ *Janice fell all over herself trying to impress my parents.* USAGE: usually used in a negative way, as in the example ◆ Related vocabulary **bend over backwards** at BEND

fall back on (*sth*)
to depend on something after a loss or failure ◆ *The family has no savings to fall back on.* ◆ *I fell back on skills I had learned years ago when I had to earn a living for myself.*

fall flat (on *your* face)
to fail completely ◆ *Most of her jokes fell flat and her act was a disaster.* ◆ *It used to be an amazing magazine, but it's fallen flat on its face.*

fall for *sb*
to find someone attractive and begin to love them ◆ *They met at a friend's house and fell for each other immediately.*

fall for *sth*
to believe something that is not true ◆ *I stupidly fell for his story until someone told me he was already married.* ◆ Related vocabulary **hook, line, and sinker** at HOOK

fall off
to become less ◆ *Sales of handguns fell off sharply after the gun control law went into effect.*

fall out with *sb*
to argue ◆ *The head of the research lab fell out with his boss over pay for the people who worked there.* ◆ *I don't want to fall out with you over something so silly.*

fall short (of *sth*)
to not reach an amount or standard ◆ *Earnings from the farmer's market fell short of what we had expected.* ◆ *Your behavior the other night fell short.*

fall through
to not happen ◆ *Our plans for the weekend fell through.*

take the fall (for *sb/sth*)
to accept responsibility for something ◆ *The team's general manager takes the fall when the team loses but gets a lot of credit when they do well.*

fall afoul of *sb/sth* See **run afoul of *sb/sth*** at RUN

family

in the family way, *also* **in a family way**
pregnant ◆ *Have you heard that Jean's in the family way?* USAGE: used by people who think it is not polite to say pregnant, or for humorous effect, and sometimes used in the form **put someone in the family way** (= to make someone pregnant): *They plan to get married now that he's put her in the family way.*

run in the family, *also* **run in *sb's* family**
to be a common quality among members of a particular family ◆ *His father and uncle were basketball stars in college, so athletic ability runs in the family.*

fan

fan out
to spread over a wide area ◆ *The police fanned out across the park.*

> ORIGIN: based on the literal meaning of **fan** (= a device you open and wave in front of you to cool yourself)

***sth* hits the fan** slang
bad things develop or suddenly become known ◆ *After I learned I had cancer, I realized you need laughter more than ever when things hit the fan.* ◆ Related vocabulary **the shit hits the fan** at SHIT

fancy

strike *sb's* fancy, *also* **catch *sb's* fancy**
to seem interesting or pleasing to someone ◆ *She has enough money to buy whatever strikes her fancy.* USAGE: sometimes used in the form **tickle someone's fancy**: *Look through the gift catalog and see if anything tickles your fancy.*

take a fancy to *sb/sth*
to start liking someone or wanting something very much ◆ *I think my sister has taken a fancy to you.*

far

as far as, *also* slightly formal **(in) so far as**
to the degree that ◆ *As far as I know, he isn't coming to the party.* ◆ *The city once went so far as to threaten to shut off the building's water supply.* ◆ Related vocabulary **as far as** *sth* **goes** at GOES, **as far as possible** at POSSIBLE

> ORIGIN: based on the literal meaning of **as far as** (= the same distance as)

by far, *also* **far and away**
to a great degree ◆ *She is by far the shortest student in the class.* ◆ *She is greater by far than anyone playing today.* ◆ *He is far and away the greatest tennis player I've ever seen.*

far and wide
1 many places ◆ *People came from far and wide to see the parade.*
2 across a large area ◆ *They searched far and wide for the missing dog.*

far be it from me to *do sth*
it is not my responsibility do or say a particular thing ◆ *Far be it from me to tell you when you should leave, but it's getting very late.* USAGE: usually said before making an argument or telling someone to do something

far from *sth*, *also* **far from** *doing sth*
not at all ◆ *We were far from disappointed when they canceled the invitation.* ◆ *Far from declaring victory, he was thinking of what to do if he lost.* USAGE: usually used to show that a result of action was not expected or wanted ◆ Related vocabulary **a far cry from** *sth* at CRY

far from it
almost the opposite is true ◆ *You think he's selfish? Far from it!* USAGE: used as an answer when you think someone has said something that is not true

go so far as to *do sth*, *also* **go as far as to** *do sth*
to be extreme in talking about or doing something ◆ *They went so far as to threaten violence if we did not pay them.*

so far
at this time ◆ *Only one drug has been approved so far to treat the disease.* ◆ *So far, I am the only editor in the department, although we need several more.*

so far, so good esp. spoken
at this stage of the process it is satisfactory ◆ *So far, so good, he thought, trying to make himself feel more cheerful.* ◆ *"How's your new job?" "So far, so good."* USAGE: said of things that are not finished

thus far slightly formal
until now ◆ *We haven't had any problems thus far.*

a far cry from *sth* See at CRY
as far as *you* **are concerned** See at CONCERNED
as far as *sth* **goes** See at GOES
as far as I can see See at SEE
as far as possible See at POSSIBLE
few and far between See at FEW
so far as *sth* **is concerned** See at CONCERNED

farm

bet the farm
to risk everything you have because you are certain of something; = **bet the ranch** ◆ *No matter how confident you are in the future, you should never bet the farm on one idea.*

farm out *sth* **(to** *sb***)**, *also* **farm** *sth* **out (to** *sb***)**
to give work or responsibilities to other people ◆ *Magazines often farm out articles to freelance writers.* ◆ *If you can't finish the reports by next week, you should farm them out.*

farm out *sb* **(to** *sb***)**, *also* **farm** *sb* **out (to** *sb***)**
to give someone to someone else who will take care of them ◆ *She farmed out her children to her brother for two weeks.*

fashion
after a fashion
1 to some degree but not very well ◆ *I can paint after a fashion, but I'm certainly not as good as you.*
2 almost but not completely ◆ *What he said is true after a fashion, though a few of his facts were wrong.*

fast
fast and furious
quickly and with excitement and energy ◆ *Changes came fast and furious in the early days of the program.*

play fast and loose with *sth* See at PLAY

pull a fast one (on *sb***)** See at PULL

fast lane
in the fast lane
doing things that will lead to success ◆ *Their purchase of the company put them in the fast lane of the personal computer industry.* USAGE: often used with **put**, as in the example ◆ Related vocabulary **on the fast track** at FAST TRACK

> ORIGIN: based on the literal meaning of **fast lane** (= a marked path for vehicles traveling faster)

fast track
on the fast track, *also* **on a fast track**
advancing quickly and certainly ◆ *The principal made sure these kids got on a fast track toward graduation and college.* ◆ Related vocabulary **in the fast lane** at FAST LANE, **life in the fast lane** at LIFE

> ORIGIN: based on a **fast track** in horse racing (= a dry, smooth surface that is easy to run on)

fate
a fate worse than death
a very bad or unpleasant experience ◆ *She felt that having to move to a small town was a fate worse than death.* USAGE: often used in a humorous way to describe something that is not too serious: *Spending a day with my aunt would be a fate worse than death.*

seal *sb's/sth's* **fate**, *also* **seal the fate of** *sb/sth*
to decide the future of someone or something ◆ *His father's illness sealed his fate, making it impossible for him to go to college.* ◆ *The election of Abraham Lincoln sealed the fate of slavery.* USAGE: usually refers to an unsuccessful or unpleasant future

tempt fate
to take a foolish risk because you are depending too much on luck ◆ *She didn't want to tempt fate by turning down the job and hoping something better would be offered.*

fault
to a fault
more than is necessary ◆ *She was generous to a fault, taking me out to dinner and buying me expensive gifts.* USAGE: used after an adjective that describes one of someone's good characteristics

favor
curry favor (with *sb***)**
to try to make someone like you or support you by doing or saying things to please them ◆ *The candidate has promised lower taxes in an attempt to curry favor with the voters.*

do *yourself* **a favor**
to do something that will have a good effect on you or give you an advantage ◆ *Why don't you do yourself a favor and take a vacation this summer?*

in favor of *sth*
because you prefer something ◆ *Her*

favors

offer was rejected by the company in favor of a much better deal. ♦ Related vocabulary **all for sth** at ALL

return the favor
to do something similar to someone who has behaved badly to you ♦ *The other team's fans are nasty to us, and our fans can't wait to return the favor.* ♦ Related vocabulary **return the compliment** at COMPLIMENT

> ORIGIN: based on the literal meaning of **return the favor** (= to do something similar for someone who has done something good for you)

favors

not do sb/yourself any favors
to do something that will have a bad effect on you or someone else ♦ *We are not doing our children any favors by giving them unrealistic ideas of how the world works.* USAGE: often said about something that is intended to be helpful or kind but that has the opposite effect

fear

put the fear of God into sb
to frighten someone very much ♦ *There's no question that this wrestler puts the fear of God into his opponents.*

fear the worst See at WORST

feast

(either) feast or famine
either too much or too little of something ♦ *It's feast or famine – last week I had no work, and now I am too busy!* USAGE: often used in the form **it's (either) feast or famine**, as in the example

feast your eyes on sb/sth See at EYES

feather

a feather in your cap
an achievement that you can be proud of ♦ *An order for 28 new aircraft is quite a feather in Boeing's cap.*

feather your (own) nest See at NEST

feathers

ruffle (sb's) feathers
to make someone annoyed or upset ♦ *Her spokeswoman wouldn't say whether the lawsuit has ruffled the singer's feathers.* ♦ *He tries not to ruffle feathers, and people seem to like to work with him.* USAGE: sometimes used in the form **smooth ruffled feathers** (= to make someone feel less annoyed or upset): *The candidate went out of her way to smooth ruffled feathers.*

> ORIGIN: based on the idea of a bird whose feathers are not smooth because of fear or excitement

fed

fed up (with sb/sth)
annoyed by someone or something; = **sick (and tired) of sb/sth** ♦ *Some people are fed up with so much violence on television.* ♦ *I'm fed up with her – she always keeps me waiting.* USAGE: usually said about something that you have accepted for too long

feel

a feel for sth
an understanding or ability in a particular subject or activity ♦ *I studied piano for a year, but I never really got a feel for it.* ♦ *She has a real feel for language, so her books are a pleasure to read.* USAGE: usually said about a natural skill that you cannot learn and often used with **get** or **have**, as in the examples

cop a feel rude slang
to touch someone's body without their permission ♦ *He tried to cop a feel and she threw him out the door.*

> ORIGIN: based on the slang meaning of **cop** (= to steal or take something)

feel for *sb*
to experience sympathy for someone ◆ *I know she's unhappy, and I feel for her.*

feel free (to *do sth***)** esp. spoken
to know that you have permission to do something ◆ *Please feel free to pour yourself some more coffee.*

feel like *sth* esp. spoken
1 to seem likely to do something ◆ *It feels like rain.*
2 to have a desire to do or to have something ◆ *I feel like Chinese food.* ◆ *Carol doesn't feel like a movie tonight.*

feel (more) like *yourself*
to feel as healthy or happy as you usually are ◆ *After the accident, it took a year for me to feel like myself again.* USAGE: often **not feel like yourself** (= to feel ill or upset): *When she woke up in the morning, she didn't feel like herself.*

feel *sb* **out,** *also* **feel out** *sb*
to try to find out someone's opinions or thoughts without being obvious ◆ *Why don't you feel them out to see if they'll invite me too?* ◆ *I need to feel out the boss before asking for more money.*

feel *sb* **up** rude slang, *also* **feel up** *sb*
to touch someone in a sexual way, usually with their clothing on ◆ *You didn't try to feel her up, did you?* USAGE: usually said of a man touching a woman

get the feel of *sth*
to become familiar with something ◆ *This software is a little complicated to use, but you'll soon get the feel of it.*

feel *sth* **in** *your* **bones** See at BONES
feel *your* **way** See at WAY

feelers

put out feelers
to try to discover what people think about something that you might do ◆ *She was thinking of running for mayor, so she started putting out feelers.*

ORIGIN: based on the literal meaning of **feelers** (= the two thin parts attached to an insect's head, used to touch things)

feelings

no hard feelings
I am not angry ◆ *It just didn't work out. No hard feelings.* ◆ *Brad said after the game that he had no hard feelings toward Sean.* USAGE: sometimes used in the form **any hard feelings** (= an unfriendly attitude): *Does Katherine have any hard feelings toward you because of the accident?*

feet

drag *your***/***its* **feet**
to do something slowly because you do not want to do it; = **drag** *your/its* **heels** ◆ *He knows he should make a decision, but he's dragging his feet.*

your **feet on the ground**
a realistic understanding of your own ideas, actions, and decisions ◆ *It is hard to keep your feet on the ground when you suddenly become famous.* USAGE: sometimes used in the form **both feet on the ground**: *She's a woman with both feet on the ground, who knows what's what.*

find *your* **feet**
to become familiar with a new place or situation ◆ *New students need a little time to find their feet.*

get *your* **feet wet**
to experience something for the first time ◆ *If you've never invested money in the stock market, now is the time to get your feet wet.* USAGE: said especially about something that involves taking a risk

hold *sb's* **feet to the fire,** *also* **put** *sb's* **feet to the fire**
to cause someone to feel pressure or stress ◆ *I think reporters really should hold the president's feet to the fire about this issue.*

in *your* **stocking feet**
wearing socks but not shoes ◆ *They*

hurried down the hall to the doctor's room in their stocking feet.

jump in with both feet, *also* **jump with both feet into** *sth*
to become involved in something quickly and completely ♦ *When she decides to get involved, she jumps in with both feet.* ♦ Related vocabulary **jump in** at JUMP

knock *sb* **off** *their* **feet**
to cause someone great pleasure or surprise; = **blow** *sb* **away** ♦ *Here's a film that knocks you off your feet with its first images.* ♦ *He was knocked off his feet when he heard those rumors.* ♦ Related vocabulary **blow** *your* **mind** at MIND

land on *your* **feet**
to be in good or improved condition after a difficult experience ♦ *It may take a few months to get a job, but I'm sure you'll land on your feet.*

on *your/its* **feet**
feeling better or being in better condition ♦ *He's the one who put the company on its feet again.* USAGE: often used in the form **back on your feet**: *After his mother died, it took him a few months to get back on his feet.*

put *your* **feet up**
to relax and do very little ♦ *After working all week, you deserve to put your feet up on the weekend.*

> ORIGIN: based on the literal meaning of **put your feet up** (= to sit with your feet supported above the ground)

six feet under
dead and buried ♦ *You're just waiting until he's six feet under so you can get his money.*

> ORIGIN: based on the idea that dead people are traditionally buried six feet under the ground

stand on *your* **own (two) feet**
to provide yourself with all the things that you need without asking for help ♦ *It's time that kid learned to stand on his own two feet.*

sweep *sb* **off** *their* **feet**
to cause someone to fall suddenly and completely in love with you ♦ *You kind of expect to get swept off your feet on Valentine's Day.*

think on *your* **feet**
to think and react quickly ♦ *An ability to think on your feet is important for a comedian.*

fence

on the fence
not able to decide something ♦ *Many consumers are still on the fence, waiting to see if a better, less expensive computer will come along.* USAGE: often used with **sit**: *Most people sit on the fence and would rather say "maybe" than "yes" or "no."*

fences

mend (*your***) fences**
to repair a relationship with someone ♦ *The mayor is trying to mend fences with members of the city council so they will approve his plan.*

fend

fend for *yourself*
to take care of yourself ♦ *The girl took everything she could carry and left the boy all alone to fend for himself.*

fend off *sb*, *also* **fend** *sb* **off**
1 to stop someone from coming too near to you ♦ *She was never very good at fending off the boys.*
2 to stop someone from hurting you ♦ *The young woman was able to fend off the robber.* ♦ Related vocabulary **ward off** *sb/sth* at WARD

fend off *sth*, *also* **fend** *sth* **off**
to prevent something from happening ♦ *A politician has to learn how to fend off unfriendly questions, especially from the press.* ♦ Related vocabulary **stave off** *sth* at STAVE

ferret

ferret out *sth*, *also* **ferret** *sth* **out**
to discover something after careful

searching ♦ *Officials say they will ferret out abuses in the welfare program.* ♦ *If you're looking for owners of abandoned property, it can take years to ferret them out.*

fever

run a fever
to have a high body temperature caused by an illness ♦ *He developed a very bad ear infection and ran a fever for a couple of days.*

few

a few fries short of a Happy Meal
not very intelligent ♦ *I could tell he was a few fries short of a Happy Meal, but unfortunately you can't arrest someone for being stupid.*
USAGE: this idiom appears in many different forms, including **a few cards short of a full deck**, **a few bricks short of a full load**, **a few clowns short of a circus**, and **a few Cokes short of a six-pack**, all with the same meaning

few and far between
not very many or not appearing very frequently ♦ *He grew up at a time when jobs were few and far between.*

quite a few
a large number ♦ *We watched quite a few of the World Cup matches on TV.*

fiddle

fiddle away *sth*, also **fiddle** *sth* **away**
to waste time doing nothing in particular ♦ *Billy fiddles away hours on end arranging his model cars.*

fiddle with *sth*
1 to be busy with something without a special purpose; = **fool with** *sth* ♦ *Don't fiddle with the remote control – you'll break it!*
2 to try to fix or use something complicated; = **fool with** *sth* ♦ *The report says that computer users spend about one-third of their time fiddling with the operating system and organizing files.* ♦ Related vocabulary **fuss with** *sth* at FUSS, **mess with** *sth* at MESS

field

play the field
to have many romantic or sexual relationships ♦ *After leaving that guy she lived with for five years she's now ready to play the field.*

level the playing field See at PLAYING FIELD

(way) out in left field See at LEFT FIELD

out of left field See at LEFT FIELD

field day

have a field day
to be able to do something you enjoy a great deal, esp. criticizing someone ♦ *The newspapers would have a field day if his drinking was ever widely known.*

fifth

take the fifth (amendment), also **plead the fifth (amendment)**
to avoid answering a question, esp. that could cause embarrassment ♦ *I plead the fifth – I don't know where your girlfriend went!*

> ORIGIN: based on the **Fifth Amendment** of the US Bill of Rights which says you do not have to answer questions about yourself in a court if your answers could show you are involved in a criminal activity

fight

fight it out
1 to argue fiercely until agreement is reached ♦ *For at least two years these two companies have been fighting it out over who holds the trademark.*
2 to compete against a team or organization until one side wins ♦ *Seattle and Phoenix fought it out up to the last day of the regular basketball season.* ♦ Related vocabulary

figment 128

duke it out at DUKE, **slug it out** at SLUG

> ORIGIN: based on the literal meaning of **fight it out** (= to fight to end a disagreement)

fight off *sth*, *also* **fight** *sth* **off**
1 to get rid of something, esp. an illness ◆ *Her body couldn't fight the infection off.*
2 to keep yourself from doing something you should not do ◆ *I was trying to fight off the urge to sneak into the kitchen for something to eat.*

> ORIGIN: based on the literal meaning of **fight off** (= to use physical force against someone)

pick a fight (with *sb***)**, *also* **pick fights (with** *sb***)**
to intentionally start a fight or argument with someone ◆ *When she was first in Congress, she foolishly picked a fight with a very powerful politician.*

spoiling for a fight
to be very eager to fight or argue ◆ *He says what he thinks, and so people think he always seems to be spoiling for a fight.*

fight a losing battle See at BATTLE

fight fire with fire See at FIRE

fight (*sb/sth***) tooth and nail** See at TOOTH

have a fighting chance See at CHANCE

figment

a figment of *your* **imagination**, *also* **a figment of the imagination**
something created by your mind ◆ *I thought I saw someone standing in the shadows, but it was just a figment of my imagination.*

figure

cut a figure
to create an image ◆ *Wielding a knife and covered in blood, the actress cut a figure that was terrifying.*
USAGE: usually used with an adjective before **figure**: *He was tall and slim and cut a handsome figure.*

figure on *sth*
1 to expect something ◆ *I'd better not figure on staying with them if they already have weekend guests.*
2 to plan something ◆ *I had figured on serving ten people dinner and had just the right amount of food.*

figure *sb* **out**, *also* **figure out** *sb*
to understand why someone behaves the way they do ◆ *I've never been able to figure her out.* ◆ *Could anyone ever figure out my parents?*

figure out *sth*, *also* **figure** *sth* **out**
to understand something by thinking about it ◆ *After I figured out that I would earn only eighty cents an hour, I said forget it.* ◆ *She spent an hour trying to install the software, but John finally figured it out.* ◆ Related vocabulary **puzzle out** *sth* at PUZZLE

file

on file
stored in a particular place and arranged so it can be found easily ◆ *The fingerprints on file with the police matched those taken from the body.*

fill

fill in (for *sb***)**
to do someone else's job temporarily ◆ *He discovered his love of acting when he filled in for a sick friend in a college play.*

fill *sb* **in**, *also* **fill in** *sb*
to give someone information that they want or need ◆ *We filled her in on all the latest family news.* ◆ *I've asked Andy to fill in the marketing team about plans for the fall.*

fill in *sth*, *also* **fill** *sth* **in**
1 to give written answers to questions on a computer or on paper ◆ *Fill in the entire form and then click "submit."* ◆ *If you have left out a date, first name, or other information, fill it in.*
2 to complete a plan or idea ◆ *That's*

the basic idea, but we still have a lot of details to fill in.

fill out *sth*, also **fill** *sth* **out**
to provide information on paper or on a computer ♦ *Please fill out the form before you call for an appointment.* ♦ *Print the document, fill it out, and bring it with you.*

get *your* **fill (of** *sth***)**
to have or experience as much as you want of something ♦ *I never got my fill of her cream puffs.* USAGE: sometimes used to say that you do not want any more of something, esp. in the form **have had your fill of** something: *I have had my fill of violent movies.*

fill *sb's* **shoes** See at SHOES

fill the void See at VOID

find

find *yourself*
to discover your particular abilities and interests ♦ *Only after she became an actress did she find herself.*

find *your* **feet** See at FEET

find the time to *do sth* See at TIME

fine

fine by *sb*
acceptable or satisfactory to someone ♦ *Judy got the bill and said she'd charge it to the company, which was fine by me.* ♦ *I rarely called her by her first name, and that was fine by her.*

not to put too fine a point on it
See at POINT

fine art

to a fine art
in a way that is based on highly developed skill ♦ *This restaurant elevates the sandwich to a fine art.*

fine print

read the fine print
to know all the information contained in a document; = **read the small print** ♦ *This new law will disappoint a lot of voters once they have had a chance to read the fine print.* ♦ *You should always read the fine print before signing a contract.*

> ORIGIN: based on the idea that often what is printed in very small type in a document is the most important information

fine-tooth comb

go over *sth* **with a fine-tooth comb**, also **go through** *sth* **with a fine-tooth comb**
to examine every part of something very carefully ♦ *My accountant is going over my tax return with a fine-tooth comb.* USAGE: also used in the form **fine-toothed comb**

finger

a finger in every pie
involved in or influencing many different activities ♦ *You could say that this town wouldn't function without him, because he has a finger in every pie.* USAGE: often used to show disapproval of someone whose influence or power is too great

your **finger on the pulse (of** *sth***)**
knowledge of what is happening now in a particular area ♦ *They've got their finger on the pulse of popular culture in Latvia.*

give *sb* **the finger**
to make an offensive sign at someone by raising your middle finger toward them ♦ *When the kids were told to leave the store, they gave the manager the finger and ran off.*

lay a finger on *sb*
to touch someone as a threat of hurting them ♦ *If you so much as lay a finger on my sister, I'll break your arm!*

not lift a finger
to refuse to make even a small effort ♦ *He spends all day stretched out on the couch and doesn't lift a finger to help.*

point the finger at *sb*
to blame someone ♦ *Critics were quick to point the finger at the directors when the theater started losing money.*

put *your* finger on *sth*
to know the reason for something, esp. something that is a problem ♦ *There's something wrong with his story, but I can't put my finger on what it is.*

fingers

burn *your* fingers, *also* **get (*your* fingers) burned**
to have a bad result from something, esp. to lose money ♦ *Many investors burned their fingers on those stocks.* ♦ *The museum has gotten burned on several paintings purchased recently that have turned out to be fakes.*

cross *your* fingers, *also* **keep *your* fingers crossed**
to hope for good luck ♦ *At this point, they can only stand back, cross their fingers and wait to see if the fireworks go off perfectly.*

> ORIGIN: based on the practice, esp. of children, to put one finger over the next one either as a sign of hope for good luck or to avoid punishment

let *sb* slip through *your* fingers
to allow someone to escape from you ♦ *The police let the main suspect slip through their fingers.*

let *sth* slip through *your* fingers
1 to waste an opportunity to achieve something ♦ *This is my big chance to make a career in journalism and I can't let it slip through my fingers.* USAGE: sometimes used without **let**: *He has seen the world championship slip through his fingers twice.*
2 to fail to get or keep something ♦ *The team lost one of their star players to Seattle last year, and didn't want to let another slip through their fingers.*

fingertips

at *your* fingertips
convenient or easy to find ♦ *Every fact and figure he needed was at his fingertips.*

finish

finish *sb/sth* off, *also* **finish off *sb/sth***
to destroy or completely defeat

let something slip through your fingers

Shirley tried not to let her savings slip through her fingers.

someone or something ♦ *Lack of water finished off the agricultural communities in the valley.* ♦ *He insisted that the disease was not going to finish him off.*

fire

draw fire
to attract criticism ♦ *The advertisements have drawn fire from parents' groups.*

fight fire with fire
to deal with someone in the same way that they are dealing with you ♦ *In the face of stiff competition we had to fight fire with fire and cut our prices.*

fire off *sth*, *also* **fire** *sth* **off**
to write and send something quickly ♦ *He fired off an e-mail to his publisher.*

light a fire under *sb*
to make someone work better or harder ♦ *It's time you lit a fire under those guys or they'll never finish painting the house.*

open fire (on *sb/sth***)**
to begin shooting at someone or something ♦ *Do not open fire until you hear the command.*

play with fire
to do something that could cause you great trouble later ♦ *Don't you know you're playing with fire when you get involved with someone who's already married?*

under fire
being criticized ♦ *The court is under fire for being too political.*
USAGE: often used with **come**: *Mr. Johnson has come under fire for gossiping about his clients.* ♦ Related vocabulary **under attack** at ATTACK

add fuel to the fire See at FUEL

hold *sb's* **feet to the fire** See at FEET

in the line of fire See at LINE

out of the frying pan (into the fire) See at FRYING PAN

set the world on fire See at WORLD

several irons in the fire See at IRONS

where there's smoke, there's fire See at SMOKE

firing line

on the firing line, *also* **in the firing line**
in a situation that attracts criticism ♦ *The judge found himself on the firing line from women for remarks he made about discrimination in the workplace.* ♦ Related vocabulary **in the line of fire** at LINE

first base

get to first base
to begin to have success, esp. in the early stages of something ♦ *They won't even get to first base with the directors if they propose something like that.*

> ORIGIN: based on the literal meaning of **first base** (= the first place a player must run to after hitting the ball in a game of baseball)

fish

a fish out of water
someone who is uncomfortable in a particular situation ♦ *After living in Hong Kong for most of his life, Lee was a fish out of water in Los Angeles.*

have bigger fish to fry, *also* **have other fish to fry**
to have something more important or more interesting to do ♦ *I couldn't spend a lot of time on the problem – I had other fish to fry.*

fish or cut bait See at BAIT

fit

have a fit, *also* **throw a fit**
to become very upset or angry ♦ *My mother had a fit when she saw the mess we'd made.*

fit in
to belong ♦ *Once you find where you fit in best, school goes much better.*

fit in *sb/sth*, *also* **fit** *sb/sth* **in**
to include an activity or person ♦

fits

Where do you find the time in your day to fit in your children?

fit (*sb/sth*) in with *sb/sth*
to belong with something ◆ We must fit new buildings in with the styles and scale of buildings that have been here for two hundred years. ◆ She will fit in well with those high-powered environmental lawyers.

fit (*you*) like a glove See at GLOVE

fit the bill See at BILL

see fit See at SEE

fits

in fits and starts, *also* **by fits and starts**
without regular activity or progress ◆ Though it moves along in fits and starts, this story is so imaginative it is a lot of fun to read.

fix

fix *sb* up (with *sb/sth*), *also* **fix up *sb* (with *sb/sth*)**
to arrange something for someone ◆ If they want to work, I can fix them up. ◆ I thought you didn't like her and had fixed her up with your friend Paul.

get a fix on *sth*
to understand something ◆ It's not easy to get a fix on this new era we've entered. USAGE: sometimes also used in the form **have a fix on something**: After reading that biography, I felt I really had a fix on Jefferson.

fizzle

fizzle out
to end in a disappointing way ◆ I dated him a for a while, but our so-called romance fizzled out rather quickly.

flag

flag down *sb/sth*, *also* **flag *sb/sth* down**
to signal someone or something to stop by waving ◆ A police officer flagged us down to check our vehicle registration and date of inspection.

wave the flag, *also* **show the flag**
to defend and support someone or something ◆ Marsalis waves the flag better than anyone and attracts new fans to jazz all the time. ◆ Brown's job is to show the flag for the president and remind voters that he is working for them. USAGE: also used in the form **fly the flag**: When she was in jail, several newspapers flew the flag for her.

wrap *yourself* in the flag
to say that your beliefs or actions are only to benefit your country ◆ Politicians are usually happy to wrap themselves in the flag and avoid the issues.

flames

fan the flames (of *sth*)
to cause an increase in negative feelings ◆ These images of war could be used to fan the flames of hatred against our country.

> ORIGIN: based on the literal meaning of **fan the flames** (= to cause air to flow toward a fire)

go down in flames, *also* **go up in flames**
to fail or end suddenly and completely ◆ We've seen two big mass-transit plans go down in flames in the last two years. ◆ The idea of self-respect went up in flames a long time ago. ◆ Related vocabulary **go up in smoke** at SMOKE

> ORIGIN: based on the literal meaning of a plane that **goes down in flames** (= falls to the ground and burns)

flare

flare up
to happen suddenly ◆ Severe thunderstorms flare up there at almost any time during the summer. ◆ You may not feel like chopping vegetables when the pain in your hands flares up.

> ORIGIN: based on the literal meaning of **flare up** (= to suddenly burn brightly)

flash

> ORIGIN
> Both of these idioms are based on the literal meaning of **flash** (= sudden bright light).

a flash in the pan
briefly successful or popular ◆ *At first, some of the major record labels thought rock 'n' roll was just a flash in the pan.* USAGE: sometimes used in the form **no flash in the pan** (= successful or popular for more than a brief period): *This trend is no flash in the pan.*

in a flash
suddenly ◆ *She remembered the answer in a flash.* ◆ *I heard her scream and in a flash was back in the house.*

flat

flat out
1 clearly and without confusion ◆ *The coach told me flat out, "You're too small."* ◆ *I don't want to flat out say I never did it when maybe I just don't remember having done it.*
2 as fast as possible ◆ *The painters have been working flat out to get the job finished.* ◆ *She drives as though her car has only two speeds – flat out and stopped.*

fall flat (on *your* face) See at FALL

flavor

flavor of the month
suddenly but temporarily popular ◆ *This rap artist is pop music's current flavor of the month.*

> ORIGIN: based on the custom of selling a different special flavor of **ice cream** (= frozen sweet food) every month

flesh

flesh out sth, also **flesh sth out**
to explain something more completely ◆ *She sketches a character's outline in just a few words and then vividly fleshes out her portrait as the book goes along.*

> ORIGIN: based on the idea of adding flesh to a picture that shows only the bones of a creature

in the flesh
physically in front of you ◆ *I have seen her in films and on TV but never in the flesh.*

press the flesh
to meet and talk with people ◆ *He believes he should get out and press the flesh if his campaign is going to succeed.*

> ORIGIN: based on the use of **press the flesh** to mean **shake hands** (= to take someone's hand in yours as a greeting)

flex

flex *your/its* muscles
to act in a way that shows power or strength ◆ *This very poor nation is beginning to flex its muscles as an important producer of coffee.* ◆ *Conservatives are flexing their muscles in local elections this fall.*

flip

flip out
to suddenly become excited, frightened, or crazy ◆ *He didn't just flip out and start shooting, he planned to kill them.* ◆ *The first time I saw that film, I absolutely flipped out.* USAGE: also used in the form **flip someone out**: *I am not easily scared, but this totally flipped me out.*

flip burgers See at BURGERS

flirt

flirt with sth
to consider something briefly and not seriously ◆ *At one time he flirted with the idea of running for the presidency, though nothing came of it.*

> ORIGIN: based on the literal meaning of **flirt** (= to behave in a way that makes another person think you are attracted to them)

floodgates

open the floodgates
to make it possible for something

to happen ✦ *The court's decision could open the floodgates for large numbers of other cases involving war crimes.* USAGE: usually used to describe activities that had been difficult or illegal but which are now easier or allowed and expected to be done by many

> ORIGIN: based on the literal meaning of **open the floodgates** (= to allow water that had been held back to flow freely)

floor
floor it
to drive as fast as you can ✦ *Some drivers seem to believe a yellow traffic light means floor it and rush through an intersection as fast as possible.* ✦ Related vocabulary **(put) the pedal to the metal** at PEDAL

> ORIGIN: based on the idea that you push the **pedal** (= part worked with the foot) down to the floor of a car to go as fast as you can

(get) in on the ground floor See at GROUND FLOOR

on the cutting room floor See at CUTTING ROOM

flow
go with the flow
to do what other people are doing or agree with their opinions ✦ *In large organizations, there's always a tendency to go with the flow.* ✦ *I never know what to expect when I'm with them, so I've learned that the best thing to do is just go with the flow.* USAGE: the opposite meaning is expressed by **go against the flow**: *Not basing my life on making money has meant having to go against the flow of our culture.*

flunk
flunk out (of school)
to be forced to leave school because of failing work ✦ *He had been a computer-science student before he flunked out of a California university.*

flush

> ORIGIN: Both idioms are based on the literal meaning of **flush out** (= to force water through something to clean it).

flush out *sb/sth*, also **flush** *sb/sth* **out**
to force a person or animal to stop hiding ✦ *The military stormed the building and set it on fire to flush out the militants hidden inside.* ✦ *A hunting dog's job is to flush out whatever it is you're hunting.*

flush out *sth*, also **flush** *sth* **out**
to cause something to become obvious ✦ *We ran the new computer system for a week to flush out any problems with the software.*

fly
a fly in the ointment esp. spoken
someone or something that spoils a good situation ✦ *What remains a fly in the ointment is the fact that the UN has not approved the peace plan.*

> ORIGIN: from a Bible story which explains that dead flies spoil ointment (= medicine spread on the skin)

a fly on the wall esp. spoken
someone who can secretly see and hear what happens ✦ *I would love to be a fly on the wall at that meeting.*

not hurt a fly
not injure or upset anyone or anything ✦ *She said the arrest was a mistake, that her husband wouldn't hurt a fly.* USAGE: also used in the forms **can't hurt a fly**, **couldn't hurt a fly**, and **would never hurt a fly**: *He was so gentle he would never hurt a fly.*

on the fly
in a hurry ✦ *You can't make this dinner on the fly, you need a whole day.* ✦ Related vocabulary **wing it** at WING

sth will never fly
something will not succeed ✦ *People told him it was a great story, but it would never fly as a movie.*

fly by the seat of *your* pants See at SEAT
fly in the face of *sth* See at FACE
fly off the handle See at HANDLE
let fly (with) *sth* See at LET
sparks fly See at SPARKS

flying
flying high
1 doing very well ◆ *All those companies were flying high at first, and next thing you knew they had all crashed to the ground.*
2 to be very excited or happy ◆ *He just heard that he got the scholarship and is really flying high.*
off to a flying start See at START
send *sb/sth* flying See at SEND
with flying colors See at COLORS

fob
fob *sth* off on *sb*, also **fob off *sth* on *sb***
to trick or persuade someone to take something ◆ *Do you think we can fob the children off on Grandma this weekend?* ◆ *This guy fobbed off a fake diamond on me.* ◆ Related vocabulary **palm off *sth*** at PALM

fog
in a fog
confused or not aware ◆ *I was in a fog for several days after my son's accident.*

foist
foist *sth* on *sb*, also **foist *sth* upon *sb***
to force someone to accept or experience something ◆ *We even foist junk food on children in school cafeterias.* USAGE: sometimes in the form **foist something off on someone**: *You cannot foist this ridiculous plan off on the public.*

follow
follow through (on *sth*), also **follow through with *sth***
to continue something until it is completed ◆ *It was an unpopular idea, but he followed through on it anyway.* ◆ *I am sorry now that I didn't follow through with music lessons when I was younger.*

> ORIGIN: based on the sports meaning of **follow through** (= to continue the movement of a swing, even after hitting a ball)

follow up (on *sth*)
1 to act on something ◆ *Some students said they were going to collect clothing, but they didn't follow up.* ◆ *You have to follow up on your application.*
2 to discover more about something ◆ *I'd like to follow up on Rita's question because I'm not sure I understood your answer to her.*
follow up with *sb*
to continue talking to or working with someone ◆ *I left Cynthia a message and asked her to follow up with Mr. Harley about his computer problem.* USAGE: usually used when you talk to someone to be sure a problem is solved or a suggestion is acted on
follow up with *sth*
to do something after having done something else ◆ *The gymnasts perform compulsory routines today and follow up with individual events tomorrow.*
a tough act to follow See at ACT
follow in *sb's/sth's* footsteps See at FOOTSTEPS
follow *your* nose See at NOSE
follow suit See at SUIT
follow *you* to the ends of the earth See at ENDS

follows
as follows slightly formal
in this way or arrangement ◆ *Treatment of your injury is as follows – wash the cut and change the bandage daily.*

food
food for thought
something worth thinking about seriously ◆ *Thanks for your suggestion – it gave us lots of food for thought.*

fool

fool around
to waste time doing something without a particular purpose; = **mess around** ◆ *It was a serious academic school, not a place to fool around.* USAGE: often used in the negative to mean to not waste time but to act with a serious purpose: *The coach was in no mood to fool around, and the team knew it.* ◆ Related vocabulary **fuck around** at FUCK

fool around with *sb*
to have sex with someone other than your husband, wife, or usual sexual partner; = **mess around with *sb*** ◆ *It's hard to believe that any man can get caught fooling around with another woman and still manage to keep his wife on his side.*

fool around with *sth*
to amuse yourself by doing or saying something that is likely to cause trouble; = **mess around with *sth*** ◆ *You don't want kids fooling around with matches.*

fool with *sb*
to deceive or annoy someone for your own amusement ◆ *He often made promises, but usually he was only fooling with us.* ◆ Related vocabulary **fuck with *sb*** at FUCK, **mess with *sb*** at MESS

fool with *sth*
1 to try to fix or use something complicated; = **fiddle with *sth*** ◆ *I'm not an expert, but I've spent 14 years fooling with computers and thought I could handle this problem.* ◆ *Don't fool with those papers! I've got them in a particular order.* USAGE: usually if you **fool with something**, you will spoil or break it

2 to be busy with something without a special purpose; = **fiddle with *sth*** ◆ *Sammy was always fooling with his model trains.* ◆ Related vocabulary **fuss with *sth*** at FUSS, **mess with *sth*** at MESS

make a fool of *yourself*, also **make a fool of *sb***
to do something which makes you appear ridiculous ◆ *If you're afraid to make a fool of yourself, you will never be a successful performer.* ◆ *My former husband thought it was fun to make a fool of me.* ◆ Related vocabulary **make a spectacle of *yourself*** at SPECTACLE

play the fool
to behave in a silly way, often to make people laugh ◆ *Teenagers will often play the fool in class when they don't know the answers.*

fools

not suffer fools (gladly)
to be unwilling to deal with stupid people ◆ *Phyllis is intelligent and impatient, and she does not suffer fools gladly.*

foot

foot the bill
to pay all the costs for something ◆ *We ended up having to foot the bill for a new roof because our insurance didn't cover storm damage.*

get *your* foot in the door, also **have *your* foot in the door**
to have an opportunity ◆ *This part-time work has allowed Frank to get his foot in the door and he hopes it will lead to a full-time job.*

get off on the right foot
to begin doing something in a way that is likely to succeed ◆ *We like to start our meetings on time, and we got off on the right foot this morning.* ◆ Opposite **get off on the wrong foot**

get off on the wrong foot, also **start off on the wrong foot**
to begin doing something in a way that is likely to fail ◆ *Holly's new secretary really got off on the wrong foot by being rude to visitors.* ◆ Opposite **get off on the right foot**

have one foot in the grave
to be likely to die soon ◆ *He had one foot in the grave when he volunteered*

to receive the world's first artificial heart.

my foot *esp. spoken*
not possibly; = **no way** ♦ *They call it the Thrifty Supermarket. Thrifty my foot – every time I go in there, it costs me a fortune.* USAGE: used after a word or phrase to show you disagree with its meaning

not put a foot wrong
to not make any mistakes ♦ *The author never puts a foot wrong as she tells this tangled story filled with complex characters.*

put *your* best foot forward
to act in a way that causes other people to have a good opinion of you ♦ *All I could do was put my best foot forward and hope I made a good impression.*

put *your* foot down
to decide something and express your decision ♦ *Mom put her foot down and said I couldn't use the car until my grades improved.*

set foot in *somewhere*, *also* **set foot on *somewhere***
to visit or go to a place ♦ *Most people who live in New York have never set foot in the Statue of Liberty, which is, of course, right in the middle of New York harbor.*

shoot *yourself* in the foot
to do or say something that causes problems for you ♦ *My brother has shot himself in the foot twice by turning down buyers for his house.*

foot the bill See at BILL

not touch *sth* with a ten-foot pole See at POLE

the shoe is on the other foot See at SHOE

wait on *sb* hand and foot See at HAND

footsteps

follow in *sb's/sth's* footsteps, *also* **follow in the footsteps of *sb/sth***
to do something that was done

follow in someone's footsteps

Kim decided to follow in her father's footsteps and attend the Air Force Academy.

before ♦ *My mother told us never to follow in her footsteps, that we should always try to do better.* ♦ *The company is following in the footsteps of other great research organizations.*

for

for nothing
for no reason ♦ *They didn't call him a big gorilla for nothing.* ♦ Opposite **not for nothing** at NOT

in for *sth*
going to experience something ♦ *Hockey fans are in for a real treat.* ♦ *Fasten your seat belts – we're in for a bumpy flight.* USAGE: used in connection with a problem: *When I saw his report, I knew we were in for trouble.*

force

in force
in effect and in use ♦ *The law has been in force for two years.* USAGE: used when referring to laws, rules, agreements, and systems

in full force
with all members of a particular group present ♦ *The firefighters turned up for the funeral in full force to pay tribute to their chief.*

a force to be reckoned with, *also* a force to reckon with
a powerful and influential person or thing ♦ *In my new job, I felt like a force to be reckoned with.*

force *sb's* hand See at HAND

fore

to the fore
to a position that cannot be ignored ♦ *Whenever he is challenged, his stubbornness comes to the fore.* ♦ *The doom and gloom guys are sure trade wars will rise to the fore again soon.* USAGE: often used in the form **bring to the fore**: *Dry conditions have brought water use to the fore.*

forest

not see the forest for the trees
to pay too much attention to details and not understand the general situation; = **not see the wood for the trees** ♦ *Company officials were so involved in the talks, they couldn't see the forest for the trees and didn't realize their employees were willing to strike.*

forewarned

forewarned is forearmed
paying attention to a warning allows you to prepare for trouble ♦ *Viruses can ruin any computer and antiviral programs give protection – forewarned is forearmed!*

forget

forget about *sth*
do not expect something ♦ *The hotel has room service, but forget about anyone wheeling an elegant meal into your room.*

forget (about) it esp. spoken
1 do not even ask about it ♦ *People point at our car when we drive down the road, and when we stop somewhere, forget about it.* ♦ *I enjoyed dinner, but as for the party, well, forget it!* USAGE: used to say that something was so extreme it would be impossible to describe it, and sometimes humorously spelled **fuggedaboutit** to show how it is said
2 do not think or worry about it ♦ *Want to have it all? Forget it! It can't be done.* ♦ *One editor's attitude was, if you understood all of it, fine, and if not, forget about it.*

forgive

forgive and forget
to accept and not think about what someone has done to you ♦ *If they can admit they were wrong, then they can surely forgive and forget.*

fork

fork over *sth*, *also* fork *sth* over
1 to pay money ♦ *We headed into the theme park after forking over $45 each.* ♦ Related vocabulary **cough up** *sth* **1** at COUGH
2 to give something to someone un-

willingly ◆ *The cops knew he had a knife, and they made him fork it over.*

form

true to form
as can be expected ◆ *True to form, he tried to get out of helping wash the dishes.*

in any way, shape, or form See at WAY

foul

foul up
to make a mistake ◆ *I'm sorry, I fouled up – I meant to send the last message just to Frank, not the whole group.*

foul up *sth,* also **foul** *sth* **up**
1 to spoil something by making a mistake or doing something stupid ◆ *It takes the same amount of time to do things right as to foul them up.*
2 to damage a machine or system ◆ *Too much aspirin can really foul up your stomach.*

foundations

shake the foundations of *sth*
to cause a person or organization to question the truth of something it strongly believed ◆ *For a time his grief over his son's death shook the foundations of his religious faith.*

fours

on all fours
with both hands and both knees on the ground ◆ *I got down on all fours to look for her contact lens.*

fray

above the fray
not involved in a particular argument ◆ *The president will try to stay above the political fray.* USAGE: often used with **stay**, **keep**, or **remain**: *He's remarkably good at remaining above the fray at the office.*

enter the fray, also **join the fray**
to become involved in a very competitive situation ◆ *Cable TV companies have entered the fray, using their high-speed lines to provide Internet access.*

freak

freak (*sb***) out** slang, also **freak out (***sb***)**
to become very excited or emotional ◆ *There was a bomb scare at the school, and parents were freaking out about their kids' safety.* ◆ *Her latest album just freaked me out.*

free

free and clear
without debt or legal claims ◆ *He owns a home in Mexico free and clear.* USAGE: usually said about houses and property

feel free (to *do sth***)** See at FEEL

get off (scot-free) See at GET

give *sb/sth* **(a) free reign** See at REIGN

home free See at HOME

freeze

freeze out *sb/sth,* also **freeze** *sb/sth* **out**
to prevent someone or something from being involved in an activity ◆ *The company tried to freeze out its competition by buying up all the gas stations in the area.* USAGE: usually said about an unfair way of preventing involvement

fresh

fresh from *somewhere*
having just arrived from somewhere ◆ *As a 16-year-old fresh from Argentina, she won two important music competitions in three weeks.*

> ORIGIN: based on the literal meaning of **fresh** (= newly produced or made)

fresh from *sth*
having just finished something ◆ *The South African president is set to begin a trip to the United States fresh from a key election victory.* USAGE: from the literal meaning of **fresh** (= newly produced or made)

fresh out of *sth*
1 having just completed something ◆ *We hired her fresh out of law*

freshen

school. USAGE: often said about someone who has just completed an educational program
2 having just finished or sold all of something ◆ *Sorry, we're fresh out of grapefruit juice. Would you like orange juice instead?*

freshen

freshen (*yourself*) up
to wash your hands or face or use the toilet ◆ *Velma said she needed to freshen up before supper.*

freshen up *sth*, *also* **freshen *sth* up**
to add to something to make it better or more interesting ◆ *She decided to wear her large silver pin to help freshen up the black dress.* ◆ *I'm getting another drink – can I freshen yours up?*

friends

friends in high places
important people whom you can ask for support and help in getting what you want ◆ *If you want to get to see the mayor, it helps to have friends in high places.*

fritter

fritter away *sth*, *also* **fritter *sth* away**
to waste money, time, or an opportunity ◆ *He was known to fritter away huge sums betting on the horses.* ◆ *I didn't do anything over vacation – I just frittered it away.* USAGE: usually used to show disapproval

fritz

on the fritz
not working in the usual way, or not working at all ◆ *The washing machine is on the fritz.* USAGE: usually said of machines

front

in front of *sb*
while other people are present ◆ *Why did you have to embarrass me in front of all those people?*

on the front burner See at BURNER
on the front line of *sth* See at FRONT LINE
put up a brave front See **put on a brave face** at FACE

front line

on the front line of *sth*, *also* **on the front lines of *sth***
leading others in an effort to change something ◆ *For years the group has been on the front line of efforts to educate people about global warming.* ◆ *Doctor Tay is on the front lines of improving treatment for people with head and spinal injuries.*

ORIGIN: based on the military use of soldiers **on the front line** or **front lines** (= closest to the enemy and very important but also those most likely to be hurt or killed)

frown

frown on *sth*
to disapprove of something ◆ *You can wear jeans, but I think the restaurant frowns on shorts and sneakers.*

fruit

bear fruit
to produce successful results ◆ *Opening a new store in San Francisco has already borne fruit for the company.*

fruitcake

(as) nutty as a fruitcake
crazy ◆ *She's as nutty as a fruitcake.*

frying pan

out of the frying pan (into the fire)
from a bad situation to an even worse one ◆ *Many kids who run away from unhappy homes discover they've jumped out of the frying pan into the fire when they try to live on their own.* USAGE: often used with **jump**, as in the example

fuck

> **USAGE**
> People will often use **mess around/mess up/mess with** or **screw around/screw up/screw with** for any of the meanings given for the idioms below to avoid the use of rude slang:
>
> *These guys don't mess around – they take their security very seriously.*
>
> *She's been fired twice, taken back twice and told she'd better not screw up again.*
>
> *No one should mess with a member of our family.*

fuck around rude slang
to waste time or behave in a way that is not serious ♦ *We're not here to fuck around – we have work to do.* ♦ *You're just fucking around with small improvements when we need to make major changes.* USAGE: the opposite meaning is expressed by **not fuck around**: *Pat pulled out a gun and said, "I'm not fucking around, man."* ♦ Related vocabulary **fool around** at FOOL

fuck up *sb* rude slang, *also* **fuck** *sb* **up**
1 to harm someone ♦ *Then he got into drugs and fucked himself up.*
2 to upset someone very much ♦ *She's been really fucked up since her parents' divorce.*

fuck (*sth*) up rude slang, *also* **fuck up (*sth*)**
1 to do something very badly ♦ *I asked you to buy some milk and bread – how could you fuck that up?*
2 to damage something ♦ *He made a number of bad decisions and really fucked up the company.*

fuck with *sb* rude slang
to annoy, anger, or hurt someone intentionally ♦ *If you look a little crazy, the guys will be less likely to fuck with you.* ♦ Related vocabulary **fool with** *sb* at FOOL

fuel

add fuel to the fire
to make a situation worse than it already is ♦ *Should the government warn the public of terrorist threats, or is this merely adding fuel to the fire?*

full

full of *yourself*
thinking that you are very important in a way that annoys other people ♦ *Brooks could be pretty full of himself but, because he's such a star, people were still thrilled to see him.*

full of it esp. spoken
completely wrong, false, or worthless ♦ *Sometimes he's right, but on this topic, he really is just full of it.* ♦ Related vocabulary **full of crap** at CRAP, **full of shit** at SHIT

fullness

in the fullness of time slightly formal
after enough time passes ♦ *She feels the shortage of women judges is a temporary problem that will change in the fullness of time.* ♦ *Carol is sure everything will be ready in the fullness of time.*

fumes

running on fumes
continuing to do something when you have almost no energy left ♦ *After two straight games against top teams, the Tigers were running on fumes and lost on Saturday night.*

fun

in fun
not meant to be taken seriously ♦ *For us, volleyball is competitive, but it's all in fun.*

make fun of *sb/sth*, *also* **poke fun at** *sb/sth*
to make someone or something seem ridiculous by making jokes about them ♦ *When she first moved north, some people made fun of her*

fuss

southern accent. ◆ Related vocabulary **goof on** *sb* at GOOF

getting there is half the fun See at HALF

fuss

fuss with *sth*
1 to be busy with something without having a particular purpose ◆ *Jack had spent hours fussing with the old car.*
2 to try to fix something complicated ◆ *It's a mistake to fuss with your computer.* ◆ Related vocabulary **fiddle with** *sth* at FIDDLE, **fool with** *sth* at FOOL, **mess with** *sth* at MESS

G, g

gales
gales of laughter
sudden, loud happy sounds made by people when they are very amused ◆ *I heard gales of laughter coming from the conference room.*

game
ahead of the game esp. spoken
in a good situation to achieve progress ◆ *With everyone looking for new business, how does your company stay ahead of the game?* USAGE: usually used with the verbs **keep**, **be**, and **stay**

at *your* own game
using the same methods as someone else ◆ *Hire a good advertising company and you can beat the competition at their own game.*

back in the game
active again ◆ *All of a sudden Jack was back in the game and running the department.*

***sb* has got game**
someone is able to do something very well ◆ *These guys aren't all-stars, but they've still got game.* USAGE: usually said about someone's ability in sports

play the game
to act in the correct or expected way ◆ *Some people do well just because they know how to play the game.*

the only game in town
the one there is of its type ◆ *Before cable, broadcast TV was the only game in town.*

a (whole) new ballgame See at BALLGAME

games
play games
to lie or behave in a way that is not completely honest ◆ *We're not playing games when we say we need more help to finish this project.*

gamut
run the gamut
to include everything within a group or type ◆ *Our discussions ran the gamut from wealth to war and education to the environment.* USAGE: often used with **from**, as in the example

gang
gang up on *sb*
to unite as a group against someone ◆ *It seemed like my creditors were ganging up on me.*

gantlet
run the gantlet See at GAUNTLET

gap
bridge the gap
to make a connection where there is a great difference ◆ *He promises to change the tax laws to bridge the gap between the rich and poor.* USAGE: often used with **between**, as in the example

garden path
lead *sb* down the garden path, also **lead *sb* up the garden path**
to deceive someone ◆ *Our country has been led down the garden path by the politicians in office.*

> ORIGIN: based on the idea that a path in a garden is very pleasant, so someone who is brought along it can be deceived without noticing it

gas
gas up (*sth*), also **gas *sth* up**
to put fuel in a vehicle ◆ *We stopped at a service station to gas up the car and clean the windshield.* ◆ *Gas it up and check the oil.*

run out of gas
to lose the energy or interest to continue; = **run out of steam** ◆ *I think our team ran out of gas*

gate

toward the end of the game's first quarter.

> ORIGIN: based on the idea that when a vehicle has no more fuel it will stop moving

step on the gas
to hurry in order to get something done quickly; = **step on it** ◆ *If we're going to get this done today, it's time to step on the gas.*

> ORIGIN: based on the literal meaning of **step on the gas** (= to make a car go faster by giving the engine more gas)

gate

out of the (starting) gate
at or from the very beginning; = **out of the (starting) blocks** ◆ *The Jayhawks scored the first twelve points out of the gate.*

> ORIGIN: based on the literal meaning of **starting gate** (= a set of doors that open at the same time to allow horses to begin a race)

gauntlet

run the gauntlet
1 to experience severe criticism or great difficulties ◆ *Every idea that is presented must run the gauntlet of the Review Committee, and such reviews are never pleasant.*
2 to have to move by a line or group people trying to get your attention ◆ *Before you get to the beach, you have run the gauntlet of shouting souvenir sellers and dirty snack bars.* USAGE: sometimes spelled **gantlet**

> ORIGIN: based on the old-fashioned military meaning of **run the gauntlet** (= to punish a soldier by forcing him to run between two lines of men who hit him as he goes by them)

gear

in gear
working well ◆ *I'd just awakened and I didn't have my brain in gear yet.* USAGE: often used in the form **get something (back) in gear**: *Leaders from both sides will meet in Washington in an effort to get peace talks back in gear.*

> ORIGIN: based on the idea of an engine with **gears** (= machine parts that help an engine move or operate a machine or vehicle)

in high gear, *also* **in full gear**
at the highest level of operation ◆ *Preparations for the convention started weeks ago and are now in high gear.*

gears

shift gears, *also* **switch gears**
to suddenly change what you are doing ◆ *I'd like to shift gears now and talk about a personal concern.*

> ORIGIN: based on the idea that a vehicle will change speed when you change **gears** (= machine parts)

general

in general
1 in most cases ◆ *In general, women live longer than men.* ◆ Related vocabulary **at large** 1 at LARGE
2 as a whole ◆ *He wrote about drama, art, literature, and the cultural scene in general.*

genie

the genie is out of the bottle
something has become known ◆ *Efforts to ban cloning cannot succeed – the genie is out of the bottle.* USAGE: often used in the form **put the genie back in the bottle**: *Once people got used to e-mail, it was impossible to put this genie back in the bottle.*

> ORIGIN: based on the story of a **genie** (= magic being) who was released from a bottle and then helps the person who let it out

get

don't get me wrong esp. spoken
you should clearly understand what I mean ◆ *Don't get me wrong – we're*

glad to have a couple of star players – but it's the team that wins games.

get across *sth*, *also* **get** *sth* **across**
to successfully communicate something ◆ *As a coach, I have to get across to the players what I want from them.*

get after *sb*
to criticize what someone does ◆ *I get after my mother about what she eats because I really love her.* ◆ Related vocabulary **on** *sb's* **case** at CASE, **on** *your* **back** at BACK

get ahead
to achieve success ◆ *Everyone who works here should be able to get ahead.*

get along (with *sb***)** esp. spoken
to have a good relationship ◆ *My kids and their cousins really get along with each other.*

get around *sth*
to find a way to avoid a problem ◆ *He was trying to get around paying tax on that income.*

get around to *doing sth* esp. spoken
to find time to do something ◆ *I wanted to see that movie but never got around to it.*

get at *sth* esp. spoken
1 to say or suggest something in an indirect way ◆ *What is he trying to get at? Is he saying I don't work hard?*
2 to find or understand something ◆ *They are trying to get at the truth by interviewing anyone who saw her before she disappeared.*

get away from it all
to go somewhere completely different from what is usual ◆ *Sometimes I want to get away from it all, and other times I want to know what's going on.*

get away with *sth*
to avoid blame, punishment, or criticism for doing something bad ◆ *She cheated on the test and thought she could get away with it.*

USAGE: often in the form **get away with it**, as in the example

get back at *sb*, *also* **get even (with** *sb***)**
to punish someone who did something to you ◆ *I think he's trying to get back at her for what she said in the meeting.* ◆ Related vocabulary **stick it to** *sb* at STICK

get behind *sb/sth*
to encourage or help someone or something ◆ *I can get behind a creative idea and fight for it.*

ORIGIN: based on the idea of helping something move forward by pushing it from behind

get by
to exist and have just enough of what you need ◆ *I think a lot of families can't get by with just one salary.* ◆ *He gets by on snacks.* USAGE: often followed by **with** or **on**, as in the examples

get down to it
to consider the most important features or facts ◆ *You'd think it would be easier to live in this city, but when you get down to it, the people here are not friendly or helpful.* ◆ Related vocabulary **get down to business** at BUSINESS

get even (with *sb***)**, *also* **get back at** *sb*
to punish someone who did something to you ◆ *She wants to get even with the guy who hit her with the ball.* ◆ Related vocabulary **settle a score** at SCORE, **stick it to** *sb* at STICK

get (*you***) going**, *also* **get (***you***) started**
to cause you to become excited or interested ◆ *My Dad was the one who really got me going on baseball.*

get in
to arrive at a place ◆ *What time did you say his plane gets in?*

get in *sth*, *also* **get** *sth* **in**
to find time to do something ◆ *I'd*

like to get in some skiing while we're in Colorado.

get it esp. spoken
1 to be punished ◆ *When Mom finds out you skipped school yesterday, you're going to get it.*
2 to understand ◆ *She explained it to me several times but I still don't get it.*

get it together
to become organized ◆ *We would have liked to go to Dallas, but we couldn't get it together to drive there.*

get it up rude slang
to become sexually excited so that you have a hard penis ◆ *Walt can still probably get it up occasionally.*

get lost slang
go away ◆ *Those kids told the new girl to get lost.* USAGE: sometimes used as an order: *Get lost, Gary. We don't want you coming with us.*

get *sb* off
to help someone avoid punishment ◆ *Milligan was charged with fraud, but his lawyer got him off.*

get off easy esp. spoken, *also* **get off lightly**
1 to have less difficulty than is usual ◆ *The Midwest got off easy with little snow this winter.*
2 to receive less punishment than expected ◆ *It's not right that someone can commit a major crime and get off lightly.*

get off on *sth*
to become excited by something ◆ *He seems to get off on deliberately shocking his friends.*

get off (scot-free)
to avoid punishment or an unpleasant responsibility ◆ *She got off with just a small fine.* ◆ *If you don't go to the police about it, he'll get off scot-free!* ◆ *She was left to care for her parents while her brother got off scot-free.* ◆ Related vocabulary **beat the rap** at RAP

get on with *sth*
to begin or continue something ◆ *This will be a long meeting, and I think we ought to get on with it.* ◆ *Smaller classes would help failing students improve so they could get on with their education.*

get out of *sth/doing sth*
to find a way to avoid something that you should do ◆ *If I can get out of going to the meeting tonight, I will.* ◆ *She has play practice this evening, and there's no way she can get out of it.*

get *sth* out of *sb*
to cause someone to provide information ◆ *If you don't tell me what happened I'll just get it out of your sister.* ◆ *It was not easy to get the truth out of her.*

get *sth* out of *sth/doing sth*
to experience something as a result of an activity ◆ *What did you get out of reading this book?* ◆ *We get a lot of pleasure out of travel.*

get over *sth* esp. spoken
1 to feel better after an illness or bad experience ◆ *She's just getting over the flu.*
2 to accept a fact or situation ◆ *I can't get over how short he is.* ◆ *They're upset that you didn't call, but they'll get over it.*

get *sth* over with esp. spoken
to finish something ◆ *I'll be glad to take the exam and get it over with.*

get real
to accept the truth and not deceive yourself ◆ *Voters want Congress to get real and pass a bill to revive the economy.* USAGE: also used as an order: *You expect me to ignore data like that? Get real!* ◆ Related vocabulary **face facts** at FACTS, **(let's) face it** at FACE

get somewhere
to make progress ◆ *After months of tests, the doctors think they're finally getting somewhere.*

get through (to *sb*)
1 to communicate with someone by telephone ◆ *If you're having trouble getting through, you should try e-mailing him.*

2 to make someone understand or believe what you mean ♦ *Pictures can sometimes help you get through to people more effectively than writing can.*

get to *sb*
to have an effect on someone ♦ *The heat was beginning to get to me, so I sat in the shade for a while.*

get up *sth*, *also* **get** *sth* **up**
to emotionally prepare yourself to do something ♦ *I finally got up the courage to let her read some of my poetry.*

get-go

from the get-go
since the beginning; = **from the word go** ♦ *It was a popular movie from the get-go.* USAGE: sometimes written as **from the git-go**

get-out

as all get-out
to an extreme degree ♦ *I know this sounds as strange as all get-out, but I feel like I met you before.* USAGE: used after an adjective

getting

getting on (in years)
becoming old ♦ *She's getting on in years, but she's healthy.*

getting on toward, *also* **getting on for**
almost at a particular time ♦ *School had started and it was getting on toward Thanksgiving.* USAGE: sometimes used without **toward** or **for**: *It was getting on 8:00 a.m.*

ghost

a ghost of a chance
a very small possibility ♦ *There's not a ghost of a chance that he'll be promoted.*

give up the ghost
1 to die ♦ *My great-grandfather gave up the ghost a week after moving into a nursing home.*
2 to stop operating ♦ *He had not been to town since spring because his car had given up the ghost.*

3 to stop trying ♦ *She'd been trying to break into acting for ten years without success and was just about to give up the ghost.*

give

give and take
the exchange of some of what you want for some of what someone else wants ♦ *We reached an agreement after many hours of bargaining and give and take.*

give as good as *you* **get**
to treat people the same way they treat you ♦ *When you are working with a lot of strong-willed people, you have to be able to give as good as you get.* USAGE: often used to describe an argument or a fight: *Pat had a black eye and a couple of bruises, but he gave as good as he got, or better.*

give *sb/sth* **away**, *also* **give away** *sb/sth*
to tell or show something that is private or secret ♦ *She didn't want us to know she was upset, but the look on her face gave her away.* ♦ *I haven't seen the movie yet, so don't give away the ending.* USAGE: said about something you do whether or not you intend to do it

give in (to *sb/sth*)
to agree to something after originally opposing it; = **cave in (to** *sb/sth*) ♦ *Brown shrugged his shoulders and gave in, surrendering to the police without a word.* ♦ *For a second she was tempted to give in to their whining, then thought they should learn how to wait – quietly.* ♦ Related vocabulary **knuckle under (to** *sb/sth*) at KNUCKLE

give it to *sb* **straight**
to tell someone something unpleasant directly and honestly ♦ *Just give it to me straight – how badly is he hurt?*

give or take (*sth***)**
approximately the amount mentioned ♦ *The length of my house from front to back is 100 feet, give or*

given 148

take. ◆ *The army spent two billion dollars, give or take a few million, to develop the new fighter plane.*

give out
1 to be completely used or finished ◆ *I'd lend you my calculator, but the battery gave out.*
2 to stop working ◆ *Is it worth it to keep running until your knees give out?* ◆ *Something in the motor gave out.*

give up
1 to admit defeat or failure ◆ *Humans always mess things up, but we can't give up – we have to keep trying.* ◆ Related vocabulary **hang it up** at HANG
2 to stop trying to guess the correct answer ◆ *"Guess what I'm doing." "Reading?" "Nope." "I give up."*

give up *sth*, also **give** *sth* **up**
to stop doing or having something ◆ *She says she would give up eating before she gave up her cigarettes.* ◆ *You never give up looking for survivors of a disaster.* ◆ *He wasn't good at tennis, but he didn't want to give it up.*

give up on *sb/sth*
to stop expecting anything from someone or something ◆ *Some officials seem to have given up on our public schools.* ◆ *Lee was about to give up on ever getting to that party.* ◆ *Cook's supporters gave up on him a week before the election.*

given

given to *doing sth*
to be likely to do something ◆ *Members of the academic community are given to attending meetings and conferences.* USAGE: usually used after **be**, as in the example

given half a chance See at CHANCE

glance

at a glance
almost immediately ◆ *The guide shows at a glance the amount of each type of food that most people need.* USAGE: often used in newspapers and magazines as the title of a list of important facts: *State budget at a glance*

at first glance
when first looked at ◆ *At first glance the deal looked great, but after reading the contract I wasn't so sure.* ◆ *The twins seem, at first glance, very similar, but they're actually very different.* ◆ Related vocabulary **at first sight** at SIGHT, **at first blush** at BLUSH

glass

> USAGE
> These idioms are really two parts of a phrase that describes two different ways of understanding the meaning of a situation. The two parts can also be used together: *I think the glass is half full, not half empty.*

see the glass (as) half empty
to believe that a situation is more bad than good ◆ *Some economists looking ahead to the second half of the year see the glass as half empty.* USAGE: also used in the form **the glass is half empty** (= the situation is seen as bad or not hopeful): *A lot of people are unhappy with the way the organization is run – they say the glass is half empty.*

see the glass (as) half full
to believe that a situation is more good than bad ◆ *I'm an optimist – I see the glass as half full and think we'll come through this difficult time OK.* USAGE: also used in the form **the glass is half full** (= the situation is seen as good or hopeful): *To some people, the glass is always half full.* ◆ Related vocabulary **half a loaf** at HALF

glasses

through rose-colored glasses
with an attitude that things are better than they really are ◆ *Looked at through rose-colored glasses, the story of women's role in the state's politics could be considered a suc-*

the glass is half empty/full

Nick sees the glass as half full, but to Nora the glass is half empty.

cess. USAGE: usually used with **see something** or **look at something**: *The magazine had a habit of looking at social issues through rose-colored glasses.*

gleam

a gleam in *your* eye, *also* **a gleam in *your* eyes**
something that is thought about or planned but not yet started ♦ *I remember when that invention was just a gleam in his eyes.*

> ORIGIN: based on the literal meaning of **a gleam in your eye** (= a sudden expression of an emotion in your eye)

gloom

gloom and doom, *also* **doom and gloom**
the feeling that a situation is bad and is not likely to improve ♦ *There's been so much gloom and doom here, I think we should try to provide a smile.*

glory

glory in *sth*
to be very pleased or proud about something ♦ *Her parents gloried in her success as an artist.*

in (all) *sb's/sth's* glory
in a very happy, successful, or beautiful state ♦ *When he dropped out of the race, his opponents were in their glory.* ♦ *The garden in all its glory is now open to the public.*

the glory days (of *sth*)
a time in the past when something was very successful ♦ *The pace of American dance music has slowed considerably since the glory days of disco.* USAGE: sometimes also used in the form **someone's glory days**: *The song is a joyous nod to the group's glory days.*

gloss

gloss over *sth*
to fail to deal with the importance of something ♦ *The report praised the managers but glossed over the high cost of the project.* USAGE: usually said about a problem or fault: *The State Department's reports for the period glossed over the worst human-rights problems in the region.*

glove

fit (*you*) like a glove
to be perfectly suited to you ♦ *My wife bought me a custom-made fishing rod, and it fits like a glove.*

> ORIGIN: based on the literal meaning of **fit like a glove** (= to fit your body perfectly)

work hand in glove with *sb/sth* See at HAND

treat *sb* with kid gloves See at KID GLOVES

gloves

take the gloves off
to argue or compete without controlling your actions or feelings ♦ *If they're willing to take their gloves off, US peanut producers could compete with anyone in the world.* USAGE: also used in the form **with the gloves off**: *In this fearless essay, she goes at some respected poets with the gloves off.*

glued

glued to *sth*
giving something your full attention ♦ *During football season, he's glued to the TV.* ♦ *She has her ears glued to her CD player all the time.*

glutton

a glutton for punishment
someone who does a lot of something that most people find unpleasant ♦ *I told my brother he could ask his best friend to come along to the movies with us – I really must be a glutton for punishment.*

> ORIGIN: based on the literal meaning of **glutton** (= a person who eats or drinks too much)

go

go about *sth/doing sth*
to do something ♦ *We'd like to help but we're not sure how to go about it.* ♦ *How do you go about getting a visa?* ♦ Related vocabulary **go about *your* business** at BUSINESS

go after *sb/sth*
1 to try to get or obtain someone or something ♦ *There are a lot of people going after a piece of the budget, and some of them won't get any funding.* ♦ *I know I'll never fall into the trap of going after the big bucks.*
2 to attack or try to hurt someone or something ♦ *The candidate went after his opponent in a very personal way.*

go ahead (with *sth*), also **go ahead and *do sth***
to begin or continue an activity without waiting ♦ *We knew what the dangers were but decided to go ahead anyway.* ♦ *Mary said we should go ahead with the meeting on Monday.* ♦ *Why not just go ahead and release the documents?* USAGE: usually said about an activity that has been delayed

go all out
to put all your energy or enthusiasm into what you are doing ♦ *Supporters are going all out for him in this campaign.* ♦ *Huff was one of the toughest guys I've ever seen play the game – he just went all out on every single play.* ♦ Related vocabulary **full blast** 1 at BLAST, **go for broke** at BROKE

go along (with *sb/sth*)
to accept something someone else wants ♦ *The agreement will make them the highest-paid pilots in the industry, if union members go along.* ♦ *The president has announced a plan to cut taxes, and Congress is likely to go along with it.* ♦ Related vocabulary **play along (with *sb/sth*)** at PLAY, **play ball (with *sb*)** at BALL

go around
to be enough for everyone ♦ *For women over 40 there simply aren't enough men their own age to go around, she says.* ♦ *She believes there's plenty of hope to go around.*

go around and around
1 to move in a circle ♦ *The space sta-*

tion doesn't go anywhere, it just goes around and around in orbit.
2 to talk about something without making a decision ◆ *We were talking about what songs we would play, and we went around and around for 20 minutes.* ◆ Related vocabulary **around and around** at AROUND, **go (around) in circles** at CIRCLES, **round and round** at ROUND

go astray
1 to fail to arrive where it should ◆ *I don't understand how my e-mail went astray.*
2 to stop doing something in the way that you should ◆ *Sometimes even the most well-thought-out plans go astray.* ◆ Related vocabulary **lead sb astray** at LEAD

go at sb, also **go at it**
to attack or fight with someone ◆ *All of a sudden the boys went at each other with sticks.* ◆ *The neighbors went at it until someone called the police.*

go at sth, also **go at it**
to do or work on something energetically ◆ *Stewart went at the math problems and solved them very quickly.* ◆ *She liked the work and went at it with a lot of enthusiasm.*

go at it
to have sex ◆ *One couple was going at it in the back seat of their car.* ◆ Related vocabulary **at it** at AT

go back on sth
to fail to do what you promised you would do ◆ *The mayor has gone back on several promises.* ◆ *Once I said I'd come I couldn't go back on it.* USAGE: usually used in the form **go back on your word**: *The president pledged to protect Social Security and does not want to be seen as going back on his word.* ◆ Related vocabulary **break your word** at WORD

go by sth
1 to act according to particular rules, directions, or information ◆ *Men are still going by what's expected of them.* ◆ *That's what Cheryl told me. I'm just going by that.* ◆ Related vocabulary **abide by sth** at ABIDE, **adhere to sth** at ADHERE
2 to be known as something ◆ *He's a gang leader who goes by the street name of Candyman.*

go down as sth
to be remembered in a particular way ◆ *I think he will go down as one of the most important thinkers in this century.* ◆ Related vocabulary **go down in history** at HISTORY, **make history** at HISTORY

go easy on sb
to treat someone in a gentle way ◆ *The movie goes easy on her, but in real life she behaved like a tyrant.* USAGE: often said about someone who does not punish others severely if they have done something wrong: *He complains about judges who go easy on criminal defendants.*

go easy on sth
to not take or use too much of something ◆ *Go easy on coffee and alcohol when you fly.*

go figure
I do not understand this ◆ *The paint was really good, so they stopped making it – go figure, right? ◆ A bus station is where a bus stops. On my desk I have a work station. Go figure.* USAGE: used after making a statement to show that you think the situation you described is silly ◆ Related vocabulary **don't ask me** at ASK

go for sb/sth
to like or admire someone or something ◆ *I don't go for movies with lots of violence.* ◆ *My mom likes pop music, but her mother would never have gone for stuff like that.* ◆ Related vocabulary **sth goes for sb/sth else** at GOES

go for sth
1 to try to have or achieve something ◆ *He'll be going for his third Olympic gold medal.*
2 to choose something ◆ *Offered the choice between a higher salary and*

more vacation time, which would you go for? ♦ People who always bought a small car are now going for small trucks.

go for it
to do what you need to without additional thought ♦ I always have a strategy when I race, but Fran just goes for it. ♦ She shouldn't worry so much, she should just go for it.

go from bad to worse
to become even more difficult or unpleasant ♦ The Tigers lost their first game, 25 to 0, and then things went from bad to worse the following week when they lost by 38 points.

go haywire
to behave or work in a crazy or disorderly way ♦ The system went haywire, and they charged her 71 times for a $50 check. ♦ She arrived at work early, hoping to get a lot done, but within minutes things went haywire.

> ORIGIN: based on the idea that something is in such bad condition that it has to be held together with **haywire** (= wire used to tie together dried grasses)

go in for *sth*
to do something as a regular activity ♦ In Victorian times, audiences went in for very large, elaborate performances. ♦ Most girls her age like to spend time in shopping malls, but Amanda doesn't go in for that.

go into *sth*
to discuss, describe, or explain the details of something ♦ The book goes into her personal life as well as her work.

go it alone
to do something without help from other people ♦ After two years as a member of the quartet, Sinatra decided to go it alone. ♦ Even countries cannot go it alone in the world today.

go live
1 to start to operate ♦ Switchboard's online service went live Tuesday. USAGE: used of a new system, especially a computer system
2 to be broadcast while it is happening ♦ Suddenly the program was interrupted and went live to the White House for the announcement that the president had died.

> ORIGIN: based on the literal meaning of **live** (= living, active)

go nowhere (fast)
to not progress ♦ This debate is going nowhere – we're no closer to a solution than we were when it started. ♦ Chloë's job at the health department was going nowhere fast.

go off
1 to explode or fire bullets ♦ We left the building just before the bomb went off. ♦ Fireworks were going off, signaling the end of the race. ♦ The gun went off near a whole bunch of kids.
2 to start to ring loudly or make a loud noise ♦ The alarm started going off in the middle of the night for no reason.

go on
1 to continue ♦ We can't go on living in such a small house. USAGE: sometimes used to encourage someone to continue: Go on, tell me what happened next!
2 to happen ♦ We had to make sure we understood what was going on. ♦ She wants to know everything that goes on in Europe.

go on (and on) about *sth*
to talk about something for too long or in a boring way ♦ He's forever going on about how he'll take on anyone who wants to challenge him. ♦ I can go on and on about football. USAGE: sometimes used with the verb **keep**: He kept on about the weather for more than five minutes.

go one better (than *sb/sth*)
to do more or be better than someone or something else; = **do one better (than *sb/sth*)** ♦ When her friend picked up a pair of those new spike-heeled boots, Shirley went one

better and ordered a custom-made pair. USAGE: sometimes used in the form **go someone or something one better**: *Her opponent made a strong statement against her, but she went him one better by proving him wrong.*

go out (with *sb*)
to have a romantic relationship with someone ◆ *How long have you been going out with him?* ◆ *My husband and I worry about what we are going to do when our daughter starts going out.*

go over
to be judged in a particular way ◆ *I think your speech went over very well.*

go over *sth*
1 to examine or look at something in a careful way ◆ *Remember to go over your essay to check for spelling mistakes.*
2 to study or explain something ◆ *Let's go over the rules before we begin.*

go overboard
to do or say too much because you are so enthusiastic ◆ *I think I went overboard in decorating my house for Christmas.* ◆ *It's OK to discuss business during dinner, but don't go overboard and hand out documents for your guests to read while they're eating.* ◆ Related vocabulary **overdo it** at OVERDO

ORIGIN: based on the literal meaning of **go overboard** (= to fall over a ship's side)

go postal
to suddenly become violent or angry ◆ *I don't think anybody is going to come in to work and go postal on me.*

ORIGIN: based on an event in which an employee of the US Postal Service shot and killed other workers

go straight
to stop doing things that are illegal or dishonest ◆ *About 75 percent of young offenders who graduate from the program go straight.*

go through
to be officially accepted or approved ◆ *We're hoping that the proposal for the new mall won't go through.*

go through with *sth*
to do something you planned or promised to do ◆ *I hoped he wasn't really going through with the plan.* ◆ *Had she known about the risks, she might not have gone through with the operation.* USAGE: usually said about something that is difficult or unpleasant

go under
to fail financially ◆ *Nothing could be done to keep his business from going under.*

ORIGIN: based on the literal meaning of **go under** (= to sink below the surface of some water)

go without (*sth*)
to manage to live despite not having or doing something ◆ *You think you can go without sleep, but you can't.* ◆ *Did you pay for health insurance on your own, or did you just go without?* ◆ Related vocabulary **do without (*sb/sth*)** at DO

go wrong
1 to make a mistake or a bad decision ◆ *With so many great players to choose from, there was no way I could go wrong.* ◆ *If you follow the signs to the park, you can't go wrong.* ◆ *You can't go wrong with the Italian restaurants in this neighborhood.*
2 to experience problems or have a bad result ◆ *I don't know what I would have done if anything had gone wrong.* ◆ *They tried to find out what went wrong with the science experiment.*
3 to start to behave very badly ◆ *He was a kid who went wrong, although he came from a very good family.* ◆

goat

Has something gone wrong with nature?
USAGE: often used for all three meanings in the form **something goes wrong with something**, as in the examples

good to go
ready for the situation ♦ *If it gets really hot, I bring a lot of water and wear light clothes and I'm good to go.*

have a go at *sb*
to criticize someone angrily ♦ *Andy decided to be quiet and let his critics have a go at him.*

have a go at *sth/doing sth*
to try to do something; = **take a crack at** *sth/doing sth* ♦ *Tyler is having a go at a career in music.* ♦ *Let me have a go at getting that window open.*

here you go esp. spoken, also **here you are**
this is for you; = **there you go** ♦ *Here you go. Have something to eat.*

here *sb* **goes again** esp. spoken
what someone is saying or doing is something they often say or do ♦ *When the news came on, I thought, here we go again, another story about kids and guns and schools.*

make a go of *sth*, also **make a go of it**
1 to try to succeed in an activity ♦ *It's almost impossible for anyone to make a go of this kind of thing.* ♦ *To make a go of it overseas, you have to respect the local culture and tradition.*
2 to try to make a relationship succeed ♦ *Marriage is a statement of two individuals saying, "We love each other and want to make a go of it."*

no go
it did not or will not happen; = **no dice** ♦ *She tried to get back to sleep, but no go, she was too wired.* ♦ *The town council said no go to the offer of a peace sculpture.*

on the go
1 very busy or active; = **on the move** ♦ *I'm always on the go and I just don't have the energy to cook a real meal.* USAGE: sometimes used in the form **someone on the go** (= a busy person): *This is a family on the go – Mom and Dad both coach their kids' basketball teams, volunteer in their kids' classrooms, and teach Bible class.*
2 while traveling ♦ *Cell phones are a simple and efficient way to send and receive e-mail on the go from almost anywhere.*

raring to go
to be ready and excited to begin doing something ♦ *The lawyers were raring to go Monday afternoon when the judge started the hearing.* USAGE: sometimes spelled **rarin' to go** to show how it is said: *Sometimes she'd wake up at five in the morning and was rarin' to go.*

there you go esp. spoken
1 this is for you; = **here you go** ♦ *"Let me have a tuna sandwich." "There you go."*
2 I have done what I said I would ♦ *Let me open the door for you. There you go.*
3 that is correct ♦ *Try hitting the backspace key – there you go.*

(*sth***) to go**
packed or wrapped to take with you ♦ *I'd like two cheeseburgers to go.* ♦ *The ads say these bars offer complete, balanced nutrition to go.*

goat

get *your* **goat**
to make you very annoyed or angry ♦ *The message on her answering machine is really annoying, and I think she leaves it on there just to get my goat.*

God

for God's sake rude slang, also **for God's sakes**
I am surprised or annoyed by this; = **for Christ's sake** ♦ *For God's sake, Eleanor, what happened to your hair?* ♦ *It's time we started worrying about educating our children,*

for God's sake. ♦ *At three-thirty in the morning, for God's sake, my dog decided to have her puppies.* USAGE: used for emphasis ♦ Related vocabulary **for crying out loud** at CRYING, **for goodness' sake** at GOODNESS, **for Pete's sake** at PETE

> ORIGIN: based on the literal meaning of **for God's sake** (= in the name of or for God)

God forbid
I hope it does not happen; = **heaven forbid** ♦ *If, God forbid, anything should happen to him I might not want to stay here.* USAGE: also used to suggest that someone would never do something: *God forbid they should help someone who isn't paying them for help.*

God rest sb's soul
I hope this person's spirit is at peace ♦ *I mean, Walt Disney – God rest his soul – has been dead for some time, but his presence is still so much a part of that company.* USAGE: said about someone who is dead

honest to God esp. spoken
this is really true; = **honest to goodness** ♦ *I didn't tell her about the party, honest to God!* USAGE: also used as a modifier: *It was an honest to God mix-up.*

play God
to make decisions that effect people's lives, health, or happiness ♦ *Doctors are forced to play God on a daily basis.* ♦ *Human cloning is further evidence that people want to play God.*

thank God esp. spoken
be pleased or happy ♦ *Thank God no one was in the way or on the sidewalk when the bus went out of control.* ♦ *Thank God for John Hopkins – he has been a friend when my family needed friends.* ♦ Related vocabulary **thank goodness** at GOODNESS, **thank heavens** at HEAVENS

(God) bless you See at BLESS
put the fear of God into sb See at FEAR
so help me (God) See at HELP

godmother
fairy godmother
someone who helps you solve your problems ♦ *These children, sent to school without lunch or lunch money and sometimes without shoes, were in need of a fairy godmother.* ♦ *If a fairy godmother offered most editors a single wish, it would probably be the ability to predict sales.*

> ORIGIN: based on a character in a **fairy tale** (= traditional story) who uses magic to help people

goes
as far as sth goes esp. spoken
to the degree something is considered or exists ♦ *As far as gun control goes, I think we definitely need to make some changes.* ♦ *Their action is encouraging as far as it goes.* ♦ Related vocabulary **as far as** at FAR, **as far as possible** at POSSIBLE

sth goes for sb/sth else
something is also true for someone or something else ♦ *Jordan is famous, but he's not comfortable in a crowd – the same goes for most movie stars and politicians.* ♦ *San Francisco should have a beautiful day on Friday, and that goes for Seattle and Portland, too.* ♦ Related vocabulary **go for sb/sth** at GO

sth goes to show (you)
something proves that something else is true ♦ *The website goes to show that almost anything can be marketed online.* USAGE: often preceded by **it (just)**: *"You can get a bigger car for twice the price, but it has the same features as the smaller one." "It just goes to show you – bigger might not necessarily be better."*

here goes
I will now do this ♦ *I owe you an apology and an explanation, so here goes.*

here goes nothing
I will now do this although it is unlikely to be successful ◆ *I've never tried sailing before. Here goes nothing.*

how goes it esp. spoken
are you well ◆ *"Hey, Ted, how goes it?"*

it goes without saying
it should be generally understood or accepted ◆ *It goes without saying that you will improve your skills with practice.* USAGE: sometimes used in the form **that goes without saying**

going

have *sth* going for *you/it*
to have an advantage ◆ *She should be more confident because she has a lot going for her.* ◆ *It seems like you've got a lot of good things going for you.* USAGE: sometimes used in the form **have nothing going for you or it**: *That movie has nothing going for it except some nice scenery.*

(still) going strong
to continue to be successful, healthy, or working well ◆ *Our club was founded over 100 years ago, and it's still going strong.* USAGE: usually used after the verb **be**, as in the example

when the going gets tough, *also* when the going gets rough
when a situation becomes difficult or unpleasant ◆ *I run the farm on my own, but a local boy helps me out when the going gets tough.* USAGE: sometimes used in the form **if the going gets tough** and sometimes followed by **the tough get going** or, for a humorous effect, **the tough go shopping**: *When Anna gets upset, she goes out and buys something – you know, when the going gets tough, the tough go shopping.*

gold

strike gold
1 to become rich, happy, or successful ◆ *The actor has struck gold with his latest movie.*
2 to win a sports competition ◆ *She expects to strike gold in the world championship.*

> ORIGIN: based on the literal meaning of **strike gold** (= to find gold in the ground)

good as new

"Here's your bear, just as good as new."

good

a good
this much or more of a specific amount ♦ *It's a good half hour's walk to the stadium from here.*

a good many
a lot of ♦ *There were a good many people at the concert.*

as good as
almost or nearly ♦ *According to him, the report is as good as done.* ♦ *She owes me an apology – she as good as called me a liar.*

(as) good as new
in very good condition ♦ *There's a woman in Georgia who can take your favorite old toys or dolls and make them almost as good as new.* USAGE: refers either to something that has been cared for very well or that has been recently repaired

for good
permanently or forever ♦ *Now she says she's leaving him for good.*

good and
completely ♦ *She won't drink coffee if it's not good and hot.*

good for *you* esp. spoken
I am pleased about someone's success or good luck ♦ *"I told him I wasn't going to get involved." "Good for you."* ♦ *"He's started jogging again." "Good for him."* USAGE: usually said as a reaction to what someone has said

no good, *also* **not any good**
not very useful or effective ♦ *It's no good trying to change his beliefs.* ♦ *This little handgun isn't any good beyond ten yards.* USAGE: sometimes used in the form **not much good**: *I'm not much good at explaining math problems.*

too good to be true
not to be believed or likely to be real ♦ *They told me I'd be going on business trips to Europe, but it sounded too good to be true.*

up to no good
doing something bad ♦ *In movies or on television, a man who pulls out a cigar is up to no good.*

goodbye

you* can kiss *sth* goodbye**, *also **you* can say goodbye to *sth
you will not get something back ♦ *If you don't close your purse, you can kiss that money goodbye.* ♦ *If we allow these regulations to become law, you can kiss sidewalk food carts goodbye.* ♦ *You can say goodbye to your job if we don't get that contract.*

> ORIGIN: based on the literal meaning of **kiss someone goodbye** (= to press your lips against someone else's when you are leaving them)

goodness

for goodness' sake esp. spoken, *also* **for goodness sakes**
I am surprised or annoyed by this; = **for Pete's sake** ♦ *For goodness' sake, Harry, what are you doing at this time of night?* ♦ *Well, for goodness sakes, why didn't you tell me that earlier so I could have changed my plans?* USAGE: used for emphasis and often used instead of the more offensive idioms **for God's sake** and **for Christ's sake** ♦ Related vocabulary **for crying out loud** at CRYING

honest to goodness esp. spoken
this is really true; = **honest to God** ♦ *I'll be there on Tuesday, honest to goodness!*

thank goodness esp. spoken
I am pleased or happy; = **thank heavens** ♦ *My husband cleans the barn every day, thank goodness.* USAGE: often used instead of the more offensive idiom **thank God** ♦ Related vocabulary **thank God** at GOD

goods

deliver the goods
to do what someone hopes you will do ♦ *She hired a songwriter who has written several hit tunes and he delivered the goods for her.* USAGE: sometimes used in the form **come**

goof

up with the goods: *We'll have to replace him if he can't come up with the goods.*

get the goods on *sb* slang
to get or have proof that someone has done something wrong ♦ *For months, the cops were trying to get the goods on a drug dealer who lives down the street.* USAGE: sometimes used in the form **have the goods on someone**: *Look, Stan, you may think you have the goods on me, but you don't.*

have the goods
to be skilled ♦ *Dave Frank and the Blues Stompers are worth hearing – Dave's got the goods, and the band keeps up.*

goof

goof off
to avoid work ♦ *She spent most of the school day goofing off with her friends.*

goof on *sb*
to make jokes about someone ♦ *She doesn't goof on old people, but her characters are certainly older and very odd.* ♦ Related vocabulary **make fun of** *sb/sth* at FUN

gorgeous

drop-dead gorgeous
extremely beautiful ♦ *Some of her neighbors describe Eva as drop-dead gorgeous.*

gospel

take *sth* **as gospel**, *also* **accept** *sth* **as gospel**
to believe that something is certainly true ♦ *His opinions on international issues are taken as gospel by his colleagues.*

> ORIGIN: from the literal meaning of **gospel** (= one of the books in the Bible that tell the story of Jesus's life)

got

got it bad
to be very much in love ♦ *I played the message again just to hear her voice and thought, boy, I've got it bad.*

grabs

up for grabs
available to anyone who wants to compete for it ♦ *The state's senate seat will be up for grabs in the next election.*

grace

fall from grace
to lose your reputation or rank ♦ *After 12 years in power, the party has fallen from grace with voters.* USAGE: often used as a noun phrase: *His fall from grace began when FBI agents searched his home.*

> ORIGIN: based on the literal meaning of **fall from grace** (= to lose the approval and protection of God), which happened to Adam and Eve in the Bible

graces

in *sb*'s **good graces** slightly formal, *also* **in the good graces of** *sb*
benefiting from someone's good opinion ♦ *Marj would do just about anything to keep in Vinnie's good graces.*

grade

make the grade
to be good enough ♦ *An excuse like "I didn't call because I couldn't find your number" doesn't make the grade for most women.*

grain

go against the grain
to do something that is the opposite of what is usually done ♦ *It's not easy to go against the grain and buy stocks when others are selling them.* USAGE: sometimes used with verbs other than **go**: *The changes will certainly rub against the grain here.*

> ORIGIN: from the act of cutting wood **against the grain** (= in the direction opposite to the direction in which the fibers in the wood lie)

take *sth* with a grain of salt
to consider something to be not completely true or right ◆ *I've read the article, which I take with a grain of salt.* ◆ Related vocabulary **hard to swallow** at SWALLOW

> ORIGIN: based on the idea that food tastes better and is easier to swallow if you add a little salt

grapevine
hear *sth* through the grapevine
to hear news from someone who heard that news from someone else ◆ *I heard through the grapevine that she was pregnant, but I don't know anything more.*

grave
dig *your* own grave
to do something stupid that will hurt you later ◆ *Martinez dug his own grave when he admitted signing a false name on bank documents.*

spin in *sb*'s grave
to be shocked and upset by what someone has done ◆ *Hoch said the place was like a cow pasture, which no doubt had his grandmother spinning in her grave.* USAGE: also used in the forms **turn over in someone's grave** and **roll over in someone's grave** ◆ used to show that if someone already dead were present, they would be upset

green light
give *sb/sth* the green light, also **give the green light to *sb/sth***
to give permission for something to happen ◆ *She's waiting for her doctor to give her the green light to play in Saturday's game.* USAGE: also used in the form **give a green light**: *The House of Representatives gave a green light to oil exploration off the East Coast.*

grief
come to grief slightly formal
to end badly ◆ *His career as a lawyer came to grief after he became involved with gamblers.*

good grief esp. spoken
I am very surprised ◆ *"I have four computers at home" "Good grief. What do you do with them all?"* USAGE: often used humorously, when someone pretends that a situation is more serious than it really is: *Good grief, look at all this food! Are you feeding an army?*

grin
grin and bear it
to accept something unpleasant with good humor ◆ *Bad things happen and you just have to learn to grin and bear it.*

grip
get a grip (on *yourself*) esp. spoken
to control your emotions ◆ *I know it's hard, but get a grip on yourself and tell me what you saw.* ◆ *Oh, get a grip, Tess! It's really not as bad as you think.*

get a grip (on *sth*)
to understand how to deal with something ◆ *The program will have helpful tips on how to get a grip on your finances.* ◆ *Something is obviously not right in our organization, and we must get a grip on the problem.*

in the grip of *sth*
controlled by something ◆ *The country was in the grip of a continuing and deep depression.* ◆ *She sways and stomps and even cries when she's in the grip of her music-making.*

lose *your/its* grip
to be unable to control something ◆ *Changes in your body can make you feel like you're losing your grip.* ◆ *For many years now the old political parties have been losing their grip on the South.* ◆ Related vocabulary **lose it** at LOSE

grips
come to grips with *sth*
to make an effort to understand and deal with a problem or situation ◆ *The whole community is struggling*

grit

to come to grips with these kids' deaths. ♦ Related vocabulary **come to terms with** *sth* at TERMS

grit

grit *your* teeth
to decide to deal with an unpleasant or difficult situation ♦ *You may as well grit your teeth and accept that air travel is going to get worse before it gets better.*

> ORIGIN: based on the literal meaning of **grit your teeth** (= to press your teeth tightly together)

groove

get *your* groove on
to enjoy yourself by dancing ♦ *Expect to get your groove on to Jeanne O's smooth, soulful sound.*

in the groove
doing something easily and well ♦ *I haven't played in a month, but with a few more practices I'll be right back in the groove.*

gross

gross *sb* out, *also* **gross out *sb***
to make someone uncomfortable because it is very unpleasant ♦ *I could only watch part of the movie because it really grossed me out.*

ground

break (new) ground
to do something that has never been done before ♦ *Movie makers have broken ground in this film with their use of computer-generated special effects.*

> ORIGIN: based on the literal meaning of **break ground** (= to dig up land so you can plant crops or build something)

cover ground
to examine subjects or discuss ideas ♦ *Much of the book covers ground that will be familiar to Unix programmers.*

> ORIGIN: based on the literal meaning of **cover ground** (= to move across an area)

from the ground up
starting with nothing ♦ *The company was built from the ground up by two very creative people.*

gain ground
to become more successful ♦ *The United States is gaining ground as a cotton producer.* ♦ Opposite **lose ground**

gain ground on *sb/sth*
to get a bigger share compared to others ♦ *The company's software business is gaining ground on its biggest competitor.* ♦ Opposite **lose ground to *sb/sth***

> ORIGIN: based on the military meaning of **gain ground** (= to advance and get control of an area from an enemy)

get *sth* off the ground
to start ♦ *Casey and his friend tried to start a band, but it never got off the ground.* ♦ *A lot more money will be needed to get this project off the ground.*

> ORIGIN: based on the idea of an aircraft **getting off the ground** (= starting a flight)

hit the ground running
to be ready to work immediately on a new activity ♦ *His previous experience will allow him to hit the ground running when he takes over the Commerce Department.*

lose ground
1 to become less successful ♦ *The school allows young people to continue their education and not lose ground while in jail.*
2 to become less valuable ♦ *Stocks lost ground today despite good economic news.* ♦ Opposite **gain ground**

lose ground to *sb/sth*
to fail to maintain a share of something compared to others ♦ *Good Mexican restaurants are losing ground to less expensive, more informal places that have opened all over*

the city. ♦ Opposite **gain ground on** *sb/sth*

> ORIGIN: based on the military meaning of **lose ground** (= to move back and allow an enemy to get control of an area)

on dangerous ground
likely to cause offense ♦ *I know I'm on dangerous ground here, but it is a fact that some women do not find motherhood to be a magical experience.*

on shaky ground
not supported very well ♦ *Despite high retail prices and growing demand, the beef industry is still on shaky ground.*

prepare the ground for *sth*
to make conditions ready for something to happen in the future ♦ *These experiments prepared the ground for the development of sound-recording technology.* USAGE: often used in a political context: *Even if she is preparing the ground to run for governor, the senator will probably stay in the Senate.*

> ORIGIN: based on the literal meaning of **prepare the ground** (= to make land ready for planting crops)

run *sth* **into the ground**
1 to cause something to become less successful ♦ *Unless she gets some help, she will probably run her business into the ground.*
2 to use something so much that it does not work any more ♦ *I gave that car to my son and he ran it into the ground.* ♦ *It was a funny joke the first time he told it, but he ran it into the ground.*

run *yourself* **into the ground**
to do so much you become unable to do anything well ♦ *He'll run himself into the ground if he keeps working at this pace.* USAGE: also used with other verbs: *I tend to work myself into the ground.*

stand *your* **ground,** *also* **hold** *your* **ground**
to refuse to do what someone else wants ♦ *While others urged him to try to rescue the peace process, he's been insisting he'll stand his ground.*

> ORIGIN: based on the literal meaning of **stand your ground** (= to refuse to move back during a fight)

ground floor

(get) in on the ground floor
to become involved in something from its beginning ♦ *Can someone tell me how you get in on the ground floor of a money-making deal like that?*

grow

grow on *you*
to become increasingly liked or appreciated by you ♦ *At first the show seemed kind of weird, but it grew on us.*

grow out of *sth*
1 to develop from something ♦ *His book grew out of a trip to South America as a member of a government commission.*
2 to become too old to be interested in something ♦ *Vinnie did a lot of stupid stuff in high school, but I always thought he'd grow out of it.*

> ORIGIN: based on the literal meaning of **grow out of your clothes** (= to become too big to fit into your clothes)

grow up
to stop behaving like a child ♦ *Kayo says we ought to grow up and stop complaining.* USAGE: often used as an order: *Why were you guys wildly celebrating after scoring one goal? Grow up.* ♦ Related vocabulary **come of age** at AGE

> ORIGIN: based on the literal meaning of **grow up** (= to change from being a child to being an adult)

guard

catch *sb* off guard
to surprise someone ♦ *One of the larger airlines caught the competition off guard yesterday by announcing a cut in fares.*

drop *your* guard, *also* **lower *your* guard**
to stop being careful about sharing your ideas or feelings ♦ *Once he knew I wasn't a journalist, he dropped his guard and even let me take a photograph of him.*

on *your* guard
to be careful and aware because a situation might be dangerous ♦ *I resent this attitude that you can't trust anybody, that you always have to be on your guard.*

guess

guess what esp. spoken
this will surprise you ♦ *I want more for my son than a career running a photocopying machine, and guess what – so does my son.* USAGE: often said for emphasis before telling someone something that is not really surprising at all

I guess so esp. spoken
probably or possibly ♦ *"Are you ready to leave?" "Yeah, I guess so."* USAGE: said instead of saying **yes** to suggest you are not completely sure

***sth* is anyone's guess**, *also* ***sth* is anybody's guess**
no one knows the answer ♦ *How the lawsuit will turn out is anybody's guess.* ♦ *At that point, whether he was dead or alive was anyone's guess.*

your guess is as good as mine esp. spoken
I do not know the answer to that question ♦ *If you want to know why she left me, well, your guess is as good as mine.*

guessing

keep *sb* guessing
to not let someone know what will happen next ♦ *Right up to the last minute the movie keeps you guessing about whether the astronauts will make it home.*

guest

be my guest esp. spoken
I do not mind ♦ *If you want to add an exclamation point to that sentence, please be my guest.* USAGE: often used to answer a request: *"May I cut in?" she asked. "Be my guest," Angelo replied.*

gum

gum up *sth*, *also*, **gum *sth* up**
to cause something to stop working well ♦ *Don't send any attachments or pictures, because they tend to gum up my computer.* ♦ Related vocabulary **gum up the works** at WORKS

> ORIGIN: based on the idea of getting **gum** (= a sticky substance) in a machine

walk and chew gum (at the same time)
to be able to do more than one thing at a time ♦ *Officials say they have to plan for all kinds of possibilities, that they have to be able to walk and chew gum at the same time.*

gun

gun down *sb*, *also* **gun *sb* down**
to shoot someone ♦ *He was the second major rap star to have been gunned down in the last six months.*

hold a gun to *sb*'s head, *also* **put a gun to *sb*'s head**
to use threats to get what you want ♦ *No one held a gun to her head and made her live with the guy – she made that bad decision all on her own.*

jump the gun
to do something before it should be done ♦ *We do not want to jump the gun by making a statement about what caused the explosion before the investigation is completed.*

> ORIGIN: based on the literal meaning of **jump the gun** (= to begin to run a race before the gun that signals the start has been shot)

under the gun
to feel pressure to do something ◆ *Al is under the gun to decide whether to move to Texas with his company.*

> ORIGIN: based on the idea of pointing a gun at someone to make them do something

gunning
gunning for *sth*
trying to achieve something ◆ *Students gunning for admission to one of the top colleges often believe their test scores are the most important thing.*

gunning for *sb*
trying to hurt or defeat someone ◆ *Now that we're the champions, everybody's going to be gunning for us.*

> ORIGIN: based on the literal meaning of **gunning for someone** (= to try to find someone so you can shoot them)

guns
go great guns
to be very successful ◆ *I'm not worried about our company's future – we're going great guns, and I expect it to continue.* USAGE: usually used in the form **going great guns**

stick to *your* **guns**
to refuse to change your beliefs or actions ◆ *My parents want me to study accounting, but I'm sticking to my guns and majoring in philosophy.*

> ORIGIN: based on the military meaning of **stick to your guns** (= to continue shooting at an enemy although it puts you in great danger)

gut
bust a gut slang
1 to work very hard to achieve something ◆ *It's kind of sad to see these kids bust a gut chasing a dream that will never succeed.*
2 to laugh very energetically ◆ *I busted a gut reading that essay.*

> ORIGIN: based on the idea that extremely hard physical work or laughter could damage your **gut** (= stomach)

go with *your* **gut**
to trust your feelings when deciding what to do ◆ *He often goes with his gut in making important decisions.*

guts
hate *sb's* **guts** esp. spoken
to dislike someone very much ◆ *I don't think you should hate my guts just because I like to hunt.*

spill *your* **guts**
to tell secret or personal information ◆ *She thinks you should share such things only with your family, and not spill your guts to every stranger you see.*

H, h

habit
kick the habit
to stop smoking cigarettes ♦ *Researchers said smokers who kicked the habit would have much less chance of developing cancer.* USAGE: sometimes used about other bad habits: *He sort of let drugs take over his life, and made only occasional efforts to kick the habit.*

hack
not hack it
to be unable to work or deal with something effectively ♦ *Most people think he just can't hack it in this business anymore.*

hackles
raise *your* hackles
to annoy someone ♦ *Jim could raise her hackles quickly, but she enjoyed being with him anyway.* ♦ Related vocabulary **make *your* hair stand on end** at HAIR

> ORIGIN: based on the literal meaning of **hackles** (= the hairs on the back of a dog's neck that stick up when the dog fears something)

had
have (just about) had it esp. spoken
1 to not be willing or able to continue doing something ♦ *We've been to three museums today and I've just about had it.*
2 to fail to work ♦ *The vacuum cleaner just quit – I think it's had it.* USAGE: usually said of something the no longer works because of too much use

have had it with *sb/sth* esp. spoken
to not be willing to continue to deal with someone or something ♦ *After eight years in office, he said he had had it with reporters.* USAGE: sometimes used with **up to here** for emphasis: *I've had it up to here with his constant complaining.*

been had esp. spoken See at BEEN

had better See at BETTER

hail
hail from *somewhere*
to come from a place ♦ *Both John and Liza hail from South Carolina.*

kick the habit

It wasn't easy, but Mike finally kicked the habit.

USAGE: sometimes used in referring to someone's background: *Many of our students hail from poor backgrounds.*

hair

let *your* hair down
to relax and do what you want ◆ *The party gives you a chance to let your hair down at the end of the week.*

make *your* hair stand on end, *also* **make *your* hair stand up on the back of your neck**
to cause you to be very frightened ◆ *Massey's detailed account of the battle made my hair stand on end.* USAGE: sometimes used in the form **feel your hair stand on end** (= to recognize you are very frightened): *I could feel the hair stand up on the back of my neck at the thought of crossing that old bridge.* ◆ Related vocabulary **raise *your* hackles** at HACKLES, **send shivers down *your* spine** at SHIVERS

tear *your* hair (out) esp. spoken, *also* **pull *your* hair out**
to be extremely worried or upset about something ◆ *I got my new tax bill and decided I could tear my hair or move, so I've decided to sell and move.* ◆ *Companies are pulling their hair out trying to decide how to deal with these new regulations.*

the hair of the dog (that bit you)
an alcoholic drink taken to make you feel better after drinking too much alcohol the night before ◆ *Paul offered me the hair of the dog, but I couldn't stand the thought of drinking any more.*

> ORIGIN: based on the idea that if you were bitten by a crazy dog, the injury would heal if hair from the dog were put on it

hairs

split hairs
to argue about very small differences or unimportant details ◆ *It's splitting hairs to tell people that they cannot lie but it is all right if they exaggerate.*

half

sth and a half
a great deal more than something ◆ *She was trouble and a half, an unpredictable child you'd have to watch all the time.*

getting there is half the fun
what happens before doing something is a large part of what makes that thing enjoyable ◆ *If you like model railroads, getting there is half the fun when you design and build your own layout.* USAGE: also used in the form **half the fun** (= what makes something enjoyable): *Half the fun of eating out is not having any dishes to wash.*

half a loaf
less than what is wanted or is right ◆ *I didn't get everything I wanted in my contract but decided to accept half a loaf and not fight it.* USAGE: the full form of this idiom is **half a loaf is better than none** (= getting less than what you wanted is better than getting nothing): *The new ferry service operates only on weekends, but half a loaf is better than none.* ◆ Related vocabulary **see the glass (as) half full** at GLASS

> ORIGIN: based on the idea that it is better to have some bread to eat than none at all

half the battle
a part of the effort or work needed ◆ *With so many search engines on the Web, deciding which is the best one is half the battle.* ◆ *Half the battle was simply convincing my mother that she couldn't be alone any more.* USAGE: sometimes used in the form **half the battle is won**: *If you know where to look for the information, half the battle is won.*

have half a mind to *do sth*
to consider possibly doing something ◆ *He had half a mind to go home, but most likely no one would*

be there until much later. ◆ Related vocabulary **have in mind** *sb/sth* at MIND

how the other half lives
the kind of existence other people who have much more or much less money ◆ *A visit to this largely Hispanic neighborhood will give the senator an idea of how the other half lives.* ◆ *Well-educated social workers know all too well how the other half lives in desperately poor circumstances.*

not half bad esp. spoken
almost good ◆ *He didn't look half bad by the time he'd had a bath and put on clean clothes.* ◆ Related vocabulary **not bad** at BAD

not the half of it
not the most important part of something ◆ *The badges and camping weren't the half of it – it was the wonderful uniform that made me want to join!*

halt

call a halt (to *sth*)
to stop something ◆ *When the rain got very heavy, the referees called a halt to the game.*

grind to a halt
to slowly come to a stop ◆ *Traffic on the interstate almost ground to a halt today because it was so foggy.* ◆ *The strike has caused production of new cars to grind to a halt.*

halves

do *sth* by halves
to do something without enthusiasm or not completely ◆ *He did not do things by halves, and so the rundown farm became a beautiful country estate.* USAGE: usually used in the negative forms **never do something by halves** or **not do something by halves**, as in the example

ham

ham it up
to show expressions or emotions more obviously than is realistic ◆ *Here's a picture of Philip hamming it up for grandma when he was only three.* USAGE: usually said about expressions made to amuse others

> ORIGIN: based on the literal meaning of **ham** (= an actor who performs with very obvious emotions and expressions)

hammer

hammer home *sth*, also hammer *sth* home
to keep repeating an idea or opinion so it is understood ◆ *Politicians seem to think voters won't understand even a simple message unless it is hammered home in speech after speech.* ◆ Related vocabulary **bring *sth* home (to *sb*)** at BRING, **drill *sth* into *sb*** at DRILL

> ORIGIN: based on the meaning of **hammer home a nail** (= to hit a nail deep into the wood)

hammer out *sth*, also hammer *sth* out
to create an agreement or solution to a problem ◆ *After months of just talk, we have begun to hammer out a deal which will join our two companies.* ◆ *We'd been arguing about the issue for weeks, so the four of us got together to hammer it out.*

hand

at first hand
from seeing or experiencing directly ◆ *For Carter, the visit was a chance to see at first hand the life and work of someone he admired.*

at hand
happening or present at this time ◆ *The space shuttle's crew must stay completely focused on the task at hand.* ◆ *The list includes 21 legal cases, but none of them deal with the issue at hand.*

> ORIGIN: from the literal meaning of **at hand** (= easily reached)

bite the hand that feeds *you*
to severely criticize the person or organization that helps you or pays

you ◆ *It is unwise to bite the hand that feeds you, but TV journalists need to tell the truth about the news business.*

(but) on the other (hand)
the second thing to consider ◆ *You say you're lonely and bored, but on the other hand, you never go out anywhere!* ◆ *There has always been a struggle between the reformers on the one hand and the conservatives on the other.* USAGE: often in two parts – **on the one hand** followed by **but on the other hand** (= there are two things to be considered): *On the one hand, I'm delighted my work won the prize, but on the other hand, I know I could have done it better.*

by hand
without the help of a machine ◆ *If calculators are permitted, we have no idea whether or not students can compute by hand.* ◆ *My dad and I used to split logs by hand, but now we rent a log splitter.*

force *sb's* **hand**
to make someone do something before they are ready ◆ *Information dug up in the investigation forced the president's hand, and he resigned much sooner than anyone expected.*

give *sb* **a hand**, also **give a hand to** *sb*
to help someone ◆ *If you have any trouble with your homework, I'll be glad to give you a hand.* ◆ *She tries to give a hand to those in need of help.*

go hand in hand
to be present together ◆ *I thought ability in math and music were supposed to go hand in hand, but Tyler's much better in music than math.*

hand down *sth*, also **hand** *sth* **down**
1 to give something to a younger member of a family ◆ *Fewer and fewer small farms are handed down from one generation to the next.* ◆ *My grandfather handed his toy trains down to my father.* USAGE: sometimes said about people who are not related: *He believes that confidence cannot be handed down from your coach or anyone else.*
2 slightly formal ◆ to announce a decision in a trial ◆ *After a three-month trial, the jury handed down a guilty verdict.* ◆ Related vocabulary **hands down** at HANDS

ORIGIN: both meanings come from the idea of someone older or in authority literally handing something to someone smaller or less important

hand out *sth*
to give something to each person present ◆ *Would you please hand out the balloons to the children?*

hand over *sb/sth*, also **hand** *sb/sth* **over**
to give someone or something to someone else ◆ *The prisoners were handed over to the marshals to be taken to another jail to serve their sentences.* ◆ *The old man handed his passport over.*

hand over fist
quickly and continuously ◆ *A few years ago, those people made money hand over fist.* ◆ *Developers are putting up cheap new houses hand over fist in our town.*

have a hand in *doing sth*
to take part in an activity ◆ *We don't put our label on anything unless we have a hand in designing and producing it.*

in hand
1 controlled ◆ *They seemed to have the game in hand when they scored three goals.* USAGE: also used with **take**: *I think the state failed to take the situation in hand.*
2 immediately available; = **on hand** ◆ *We have about 6,000 applications in hand for about 200 new positions.*

keep *your* **hand in (***sth***)**
to continue to be involved in something ◆ *Rick turned the business over*

to his son, but he comes in Fridays to keep his hand in.

lay a hand on *sb*
to hurt someone ♦ *He claimed he would never once lay a hand on them.*

lend a (helping) hand, *also* **lend** *sb* **a hand**
to help do something ♦ *Jay expected his children to lend a hand where they were needed.*

on hand
immediately available; = **in hand** ♦ *Ms. Sharp will be on hand to answer questions later about the film.* ♦ *The two cosmonauts have seven hours of oxygen on hand, but the job should take only four hours.*

on the one hand
the first thing to consider is ♦ *On the one hand, I'd like more money, but I don't want to work extra hours.* USAGE: often followed by **but on the other (hand)** as a second consideration different from the first (even when **on the one hand** has not been used): *I like classical music, but on the other hand, my husband loves jazz.*

out of hand
1 not controlled ♦ *Our use of credit cards was out of hand for a while, but then we just stopped using them and paid cash.* USAGE: often used in the form **got out of hand**: *The party got out of hand, and neighbors called the police.*
2 without any more thought ♦ *They were forced to do the sort of work that anyone who wasn't a prisoner would have rejected out of hand.* USAGE: often used in the form **dismissed out of hand**: *My idea was dismissed out of hand.*

overplay *your* **hand**
to do more than you should ♦ *I think people did want change, but the mayor may have overplayed his hand by making so many changes so quickly.*

raise *your* **hand against** *sb*
to fight someone ♦ *He was horrified when the situation became so bad that one neighbor could raise a hand against another.*

shake *sb's* **hand**
to greet someone by taking their hand in your own and moving it up and down a little ♦ *The Texas coach shook my dad's hand and said he had wanted to meet him for a long time.* USAGE: sometimes used as a way to express pleasure at someone's success and often said but not actually done: *Admiral, we shake your hand for a job well done.*

tip *your* **hand**, *also* **show** *your* **hand**
to let other people know what you are planning to do ♦ *Some people think Smith will announce today that he's quitting, but he certainly didn't tip his hand at yesterday's meeting.*

> ORIGIN: based on the literal meaning of **tip** or **show your cards** (= intentionally or unintentionally let others see the cards you hold in your hand in a card game)

try *your* **hand at** *sth*
to attempt to do something ♦ *Goodwin worked as a journalist, and he also tried his hand at writing fiction for a time.*

turn *your* **hand to** *sth*
to begin working on something ♦ *After finishing the book, he couldn't wait to turn his hand to building his sailboat.*

wait on *sb* **hand and foot**
to do everything for another person ♦ *You should do some of the work around here instead of being waited on hand and foot all the time.* USAGE: often used as a negative remark about someone thought of as unwilling to work ♦ Related vocabulary **wait on** *sb* at WAIT

do sth **with one hand tied behind**

hands

your back, *also do sth* with one arm tied behind *your* back
to do something very easily; = ***do sth* with *your* eyes closed** ◆ *Cleaning your bike chain is so simple a chimp could do it with one hand tied behind its back.*

work hand in glove with *sb/sth*
to do something in close combination with someone or something else ◆ *The computer chips are designed to work hand in glove with this new microprocessor.* USAGE: sometimes used in the form **go hand in glove** (= to be closely related): *Researchers believe that mental well-being and physical strength go hand in glove.*

a bird in the hand See at BIRD
hat in hand See at HAT
have (got) to hand it to *sb* See at HAVE
have the upper hand See at UPPER HAND
in the palm of *your* hand See at PALM
know *sth* like the back of *your* hand See at BACK

handle

fly off the handle
to get very angry; = **fly into a rage** ◆ *When we make mistakes, he brings it to our attention, but he doesn't fly off the handle like he used to.*

get a handle on *sth*
to understand something ◆ *We need to get a handle on what caused the fire and what can be done to prevent another one.*

too hot to handle
too dangerous or difficult to deal with ◆ *Certain subjects are still too hot to handle on television shows.*

handle *sb* with kid gloves See at KID GLOVES

hands

at the hands of *sb*, *also* **at *sb's* hands**
because of someone's actions ◆ *It looked as if the Sparks would suffer defeat at the hands of their rivals, the Liberty.* ◆ *Since June, two young people who were under arrest have died at the hands of the police.* ◆ *The process has suffered badly at their hands.*

change hands
to be moved from one owner to another ◆ *Today a record number of shares changed hands on the stock market.* ◆ *Over two centuries, this beautiful city on the border between the two countries changed hands at least four times.*

fall into *sb's* hands
to be caught or controlled by someone ◆ *The first Canadian soldier fell into enemy hands in the autumn of 1914 and was a prisoner of war for three years.* ◆ *There is great concern that such dangerous weapons might fall into rebel hands.* USAGE: sometimes used in the form **fall into the wrong hands**: *Guard your secrets to be sure they don't fall into the wrong hands.*

get *your* hands dirty, *also* **dirty *your* hands**
to involve yourself in doing work that is basic to something ◆ *Erin likes to get her hands dirty by altering the computer code to make it run the way she wants it to.* ◆ *She'll organize the event, but she doesn't like to get her hands dirty by selling tickets.* ◆ Opposite **keep *your* hands clean**

get *your* hands on *sb*, *also* **lay *your* hands on *sb***
1 to work with someone ◆ *"I would love to get my hands on somebody like that," said Jones, whose company teaches politicians how to present themselves on TV.*
2 to punish someone severely ◆ *You wait till I get my hands on you, young man – you'll be sorry you ever heard of cigarettes!*

hands

get *your* hands on *sth*, *also* **lay *your* hands on *sth***
to obtain something ◆ *I bought all the mystery videos that I could get my hands on.* ◆ *As a kid I read anything I could lay my hands on.*

***your* hands are tied**
you are not free to act ◆ *Some of my students are failing, but my hands are tied by their parents, who can't admit their kids need extra help.*
USAGE: sometimes used in the form **something has tied someone's hands**: *The new rules have tied his hands.*

hands down
very easily ◆ *The last time we played tennis he beat me hands down.* ◆ *That leader is hands down the biggest threat to peace in the region.*
USAGE: often used in the form **win something hands down**: *If there were an award for bad luck, you'd win it hands down.* ◆ Related vocabulary **hand down *sth*** at HAND

have *your* hands full
to be very busy ◆ *She has her hands full raising their eight children.* ◆ *The new government will have its hands full dealing with all the problems that face it.*

have *sb/sth* on *your* hands
to be responsible for someone or something ◆ *If the president doesn't take an interest in the economy, he could well have an economic disaster on his hands.* ◆ *The coach was a little surprised to have this tall, talented athlete on her hands.* ◆ Related vocabulary **have blood on *your* hands** at BLOOD

in good hands, *also* **in safe hands**
managed or cared for with great attention ◆ *I'm just glad to know that our money's in such good hands.* ◆ *Nothing gives parents greater comfort than knowing their children are in safe hands.*

in the hands of *sb*, *also* **in *sb's* hands**
held and controlled by someone ◆ *The nation's wealth is increasingly in the hands of very, very few people.* ◆ *The paper published lists of all the prisoners who died in enemy hands.*

join hands (with *sb*)
to unite with other people or groups ◆ *Many people are ready to join hands to improve health care around the world.*

> ORIGIN: based on the literal meaning of **join hands** (= to hold the hand of the person next to you, connecting all of the people in a group)

keep *your* hands clean, *also* **have clean hands**
to avoid becoming involved in something, esp. immoral or illegal ◆ *I do not see how anyone working with such corrupt and greedy people could have clean hands.* ◆ Opposite **get *your* hands dirty**

keep *your* hands off *sth*
to not touch or become involved with something ◆ *It's a wilderness area, and the oil companies should keep their hands off it.* USAGE: sometimes used as an order: *Hands off, Buddy. That's my beer.*

out of *your* hands, *also* **out of the hands of *sb***
not under your control ◆ *Decisions about how the money is spent are totally out of our hands.* ◆ *The new gun law is designed to keep automatic weapons out of the hands of the wrong people.*

play into the hands of *sb*, *also* **play into *sb's* hands**
to give someone an advantage ◆ *If this information is made public, it will play into the hands of people who are demanding an investigation of the police.* USAGE: usually an advantage one person believes another should not have

shake hands
to greet or say goodbye by briefly joining hands with someone and moving them slightly up and down ◆ *On the way out, the president*

stopped to shake hands with many in the audience.

sit on *your* **hands**
to take no action ♦ *Many companies are sitting on their hands, unable to decide which of the new technologies for linking computers is the smartest choice.*

take *sth* **into** *your* **own hands**
to deal with something yourself ♦ *Many people are starting to take privacy protection into their own hands.* ♦ *Mike's mother wouldn't call the doctor, so Mike took matters into his own hands and did it for her.* ♦ Related vocabulary **take the law into** *your* **own hands** at LAW

take *sb/sth* **off** *sb's* **hands**
to take control or ownership of something ♦ *Ross was willing to take the merchandise off their hands but at a very low price.* ♦ *When we deliver your new refrigerator, we'll take the old one off your hands.*

throw up *your* **hands**
to stop trying to do something because it is too difficult ♦ *Instead of throwing up our hands, we found a way to fix this thing.*

wash *your* **hands of** *sb/sth*
to end all involvement with someone or something ♦ *Phil seemed cold and distant, and now she was very afraid that he would wash his hands of her.* ♦ *You can't just wash your hands of the problem of homelessness.*

wring *your* **hands**
to worry about something but not do anything about it ♦ *It's too bad your grades have dropped, but if you just wring your hands over it, nothing will improve.*

have blood on *your* **hands** See at BLOOD
putty in *your* **hands** See at PUTTY
take *your* **life into** *your* **hands** See at LIFE
take the law into *your* **own hands** See at LAW
time on *your* **hands** See at TIME

hang

get the hang of *sth*
to learn how to do something ♦ *I wasn't especially interested and never did get the hang of that stupid violin.*

hang around
1 to stay in a place ♦ *I don't like to hang around here after dark.* ♦ *He had stupidly hung around – just to see what the cops were doing – and ended up being arrested!*
2 to be with another person ♦ *I hate hanging around with her in the mall. It's so boring!*
3 to not go away ♦ *The flu can hang around for almost a month.* USAGE: usually said about a medical condition, as in the example

hang back
to wait before doing something ♦ *We opened our office at a time when other businesses hung back because of bad economic conditions.*

hang in there
to continue despite difficulties ♦ *Our store isn't making a ton of money, but we're hanging in there.* ♦ *Parents of teenagers shouldn't be too strict or too easy – they just need to hang in there and wait.*

hang it up
to stop doing something ♦ *If you weigh less than 250 pounds and want to play football, you might as well hang it up.* ♦ Related vocabulary **give up** at GIVE

> ORIGIN: from the idea of hanging up your clothing or equipment when you are finished using it

hang on
1 to hold on tightly ♦ *Firefighters used to hang on to the back of the fire truck as it raced to a fire.*
2 to wait ♦ *Excuse me, wait a minute! Verna, can you hang on just a second? I'll be right back.* USAGE: often used when you are talking on the telephone
3 to continue despite appearing as

happens

if the end is near ♦ *That awful show has hung on for yet another year, although we can't imagine why or how.*

hang onto, *also* **hang on to**
to keep something ♦ *Our team was just trying to hang onto the lead.* ♦ *I'm going to hang on to the car I've got for a few years – it's almost four years old, but it's still in great shape.*

hang *sb* **out to dry**
to not support or help someone ♦ *After losing the election, the party is going to hang him out to dry.*

> ORIGIN: based on the practice of hanging an animal that has been killed in a tree so its meat can dry

hang out with *sb*
to spend time with someone ♦ *I don't have much free time now and almost never get to just hang out with my friends.*

hang tough
to refuse to change your actions or opinions ♦ *The president is hanging tough on his programs and will not even discuss a compromise with leaders of Congress.*

hang up
to end a telephone connection ♦ *I can't think of his name, but it'll come to me as soon as we hang up.*

hang up on *sb*
to end a telephone conversation before it is finished ♦ *I've learned to hang up on people who call to sell me insurance and stuff.*

hang by a thread See at THREAD
hang *your* **hat on** *sth* See at HAT
hang *your* **head** See at HEAD
hang in the balance See at BALANCE
hang on (*sb's***) every word** See at WORD
let it all hang out See at LET

happens

it just so happens (that)
surprisingly ♦ *It just so happens that my daughter lives in Mexico, and I do know a bit about the situation there.* USAGE: said about an unexpected or unlikely fact

hardball

play hardball
to behave in an unpleasant, threatening way so that you get what you want ♦ *Some of these religious groups play hardball with those who leave the faith.* ♦ Related vocabulary
go for the jugular at JUGULAR

> ORIGIN: based on the literal meaning of **hardball** (= the game of baseball, which is played with a small, hard ball)

hark

hark back to *sth*
to be similar to something from the past ♦ *His music harks back to Elvis Presley and other 1950s influences.*

harm

do more harm than good
to be damaging rather than helpful ♦ *Giving children too much freedom often does more harm than good.* USAGE: usually said about things that are intended to be helpful but do not have a good result

no harm, no foul
there is no problem if no serious damage was done ♦ *In his excitement, he deleted all the files, but they were restored later from a backup copy – no harm, no foul.*

> ORIGIN: from the use of this phrase in basketball (= a sport) to say that if an action that is against the rules has no effect on the results of the game, there should be no **foul** (= punishment)

harp

harp on *sth*
to repeat something many times in an annoying way ♦ *I'm tired of people who keep harping on what is wrong with the country.* USAGE: said especially about complaints

hash

hash out *sth*, *also* **hash** *sth* **out**
to talk about something in order to reach agreement about it ◆ *The talks continued on Sunday, with the two sides trying to hash out the details of an agreement.*

hat

hang *your* **hat on** *sth*
1 to depend on something ◆ *The company's earnings were up 70% last year, but I don't think you can hang your hat on that kind of growth.*
2 to believe something ◆ *It's hard to hang your hat on a lack of money as the real reason they didn't take the trip.*

hat in hand, *also* **cap in hand**
with an attitude of respect for someone powerful ◆ *The Secretary of Defense must go to Congress, hat in hand, to get approval to close military bases.* USAGE: said about someone who is hoping to get something they want

ORIGIN: based on the custom of men removing their hats to show respect, and on the idea that people beg (= ask for money) by holding out a hat

pass the hat
to ask a group of people to give money ◆ *Our group has tried passing the hat, and they've had auctions and done various things to raise funds.* USAGE: usually said about money that is given to help pay for something or to reward someone

ORIGIN: based on the literal meaning of **passing a hat** (= asking people to put money in a hat that is handed from one person to another)

take *your* **hat off to** *sb*
to express your admiration and respect what someone has done ◆ *I think you have to take your hat off to him for all that he has accomplished.*

ORIGIN: based on the custom of men removing their hats to show respect for someone

throw *your* **hat in the ring**
to announce that you intend to compete for something, esp. a political position ◆ *At today's news conference, the congressman officially threw his hat in the ring and began his campaign for the Senate.*

hatchet

bury the hatchet
to agree that you will forget about arguments and disagreements with someone ◆ *The two teammates hope to bury the hatchet long enough to win the championship.*

ORIGIN: based on the custom of literally **burying a hatchet** (= cutting tool with a small handle) as a symbol of peace between Native American tribes (= groups of people)

hats

hats off to *sb*
I admire you ◆ *This new car has the most unusual design on the road, and for that I say hats off to the designers.*

haul

for the long haul
for a long period of time; = **over the long term** ◆ *Before you invest in Internet stocks, be sure you can afford to invest for the long haul.* USAGE: also used in the form **over the long haul** (= during a long period of time): *It's possible, over the long haul, to see changes in the populations of these birds.*

haul *sb* **into** *somewhere*
to use or threaten force to make someone go somewhere ◆ *He was hauled into court and fined ten dollars for not putting his garbage in sealed bags.*

have

and what have you
and other similar things ◆ *All the women are dressed like men, with white shirts and ties and what have you.* ◆ *Everyone in the family was invited, including cousins, second cousins, and what have you.*

have *sth* down pat
to learn something so well that you do not have to think about how to do or say it ◆ *Bud had his answers down pat, but he knew there could be some questions on the test that he hadn't thought of.*

have (got) it made
1 to be able to relax and not have to worry about work or other problems ◆ *If you were assigned to the Kansas City office, you had it made.* **2** to be rich and successful ◆ *Instead of inviting speakers who have it made, wouldn't students rather hear speakers more like themselves?* ◆ Related vocabulary **make it** 2 at MAKE

have (got) to hand it to *sb*
to recognize that someone deserves respect for what they did ◆ *You have to hand it to her – she turned that company around and made it profitable.*

have (got) what it takes
to have the qualities or character needed to achieve something ◆ *Every one of these guys thinks he has what it takes to get to the White House.* ◆ Related vocabulary **what it takes** at TAKES

have it coming
to deserve something ◆ *We worked so hard to make the business succeed that I think we have it coming.* USAGE: often said about someone who deserves something bad: *The jury felt the guy had it coming, so they didn't convict her of attacking him.*

have it in *you*
to possess a particular ability ◆ *His speech was really funny – we didn't know he had it in him.*

have it in for *sb*
to be determined to harm or criticize someone ◆ *As one of the first women on the police force, she felt some of the men had it in for her.*

have it out (with *sb*)
to argue or fight with someone because they have done something that made you angry ◆ *Demonstrators had it out with police in South Korea and Turkey, and several people were injured.* ◆ *Johnny had it out with Richie in the bar and we all got thrown out in the end.*

have nothing to do with *sb/sth*
to not involve someone or something ◆ *This argument has nothing to do with me.* ◆ *Most of the provisions of the new law have nothing to do with terrorism.* ◆ *She's from a small town, but that has nothing to do with it, I think.*

have something to prove
to need to show that you can succeed when people expect you to fail ◆ *After two dismal seasons, the players on this team feel they have something to prove.* USAGE: also used in the negative form **have nothing to prove** or **not have anything to prove** (= to have no reason to persuade others you can succeed, because you have already succeeded): *He was as famous as he wanted to be, and felt he no longer had anything to prove.*

have *sth* to spare
to have something available to use ◆ *I'm doing a survey and I wonder if you have five minutes to spare.*

have to do with *sb/sth*
to deal with something or someone ◆ *My question has to do with last week's assignment.*

have *sth* to show for *sth*
to be the result of your effort ◆ *She tried her best to make the business work, but now all she had to show for her effort was a huge debt.*

havoc

play havoc with *sth*
1 to cause someone to have trouble doing something ◆ *Strong winds played havoc with her golf game.*
2 to damage something ◆ *Stormy conditions played havoc with the fishing.*

wreak havoc
to cause a lot of trouble or damage ◆ *Storms wreaked havoc on both coasts of the United States.* USAGE: often used with **on**: *Strikes have wreaked havoc on businesses here.*

hawk

watch *sb* **like a hawk**
to look at someone very carefully ◆ *She had a horrible boss who watched everyone like a hawk.* USAGE: usually said about someone who looks for people to do something wrong

> ORIGIN: based on the idea that a **hawk** (= type of bird) can see small objects from great distances

hay

hit the hay
to get into bed; = **hit the sack** ◆ *It was time to hit the hay and drift off to sleep.*

make hay
to use an opportunity to get the most benefit ◆ *Critics continue to make hay over the president's lack of self-discipline.* USAGE: usually said about a competitive situation

head

a head of steam
energy to quickly make progress ◆ *There's no question, though, that the drive to stop capital punishment has picked up a head of steam.*

> ORIGIN: based on the literal meaning of **a head of steam** (= the pressure that is needed in the engine of an old-fashioned steam train to make it start moving)

sth **comes into** *your* **head**
you think or remember something ◆ *It just came into my head that I should give my money away and throw myself on God's mercy.* USAGE: sometimes used in the form **the first thing that comes into your head** (= the first thing you think of): *Mrs. Winn said the first thing that came into her head.*

come to a head
to reach a stage in a difficult situation when someone takes a strong action to deal with it ◆ *The crisis came to a head when the teachers' union threatened to sue the city.*

(from) head to toe, also **(from) head to foot**
completely; = **(from) top to toe** ◆ *Each person was scrubbed head to toe with antibacterial soap.* ◆ *She was tall and thin, and dressed head to toe in black.*

get it into *your* **head**, also **get** *sth* **into** *your* **head**
to begin to think that something is true ◆ *Charles somehow got it into his head that I was an athlete.* ◆ *She got the notion into her head that we should buy the place.*

go head to head
to compete directly ◆ *The two most popular TV shows are going head to head every Saturday night.*

> ORIGIN: based on the idea that in a fight, the heads of the fighters are very close

go over *sb's* **head**
1 to deal with someone at a higher level ◆ *I would occasionally go over my manager's head to complain to the top financial officer.*
2 to fail to understand something ◆ *She was being sarcastic, but he took her seriously – the joke totally went over his head.*

go to *your* **head**
to make you believe that you are more important than you really are ◆ *You won the poetry prize, but you won't let it go to your head, will you?*

hang *your* head
to be ashamed ◆ *Though our team lost, it played well and had no need to hang its head.*

have a good head on *your* shoulders
to be intelligent ◆ *She doesn't do well in school, but I think she has a good head on her shoulders.*

have a head for *sth*
to have a natural ability to do something well ◆ *I never had a head for music.*

have *sth* hanging over *your* head
to be worried about something you have to do ◆ *I hate having all those bills hanging over my head.*

have *your* head screwed on right, *also* **have *your* head screwed on straight**
to have good judgment ◆ *If you have your head screwed on right, you don't complain when you have to work overtime.*

head and shoulders above *sb/sth*
much better than other similar people or things ◆ *Chicago's basketball team may be the oldest, but it is still head and shoulders above the rest of the league.*

head *sb/sth* off, *also* **head off *sb/sth***
to stop the movement of people or animals by getting in front of them ◆ *The horses broke into a gallop, and Pete yelled for Jack to head them off.*

head off *sth*, *also* **head *sth* off**
to avoid something bad by doing something now ◆ *The UN Security Council is hoping to head off further violence.*

head off to *somewhere*
to go somewhere ◆ *While Marianne heads off to work each morning, Keith takes care of the kids.*

head over heels (in love)
to be in love with someone very much ◆ *It's obvious that they're head over heels in love with each other.* USAGE: often used with **fall** to describe the beginning of a relationship: *They met at a nightclub and instantly fell head over heels for one another.*

hide *your* head in the sand, *also* **stick *your* head in the sand**
to refuse to think about an unpleasant situation ◆ *Teachers can't just hide their heads in the sand and not try to find out why students aren't doing better.* USAGE: also used with **bury** and other verbs: *All Olivia wanted to do was bury her head in the sand and forget everything.*

hold *your* head high
to show that you are not ashamed of your efforts ◆ *As long you play the best tennis you're capable of, you can hold your head high.*

in over *your* head
involved in a situation that is too difficult for you to deal with ◆ *Historians say that as president, Harding was a man who was in over his head.*

keep *your* head
to be calm despite danger or difficulty; = **keep *your* cool** ◆ *When Lisa collapsed he kept his head and tried to revive her, but nothing worked.* ◆ Opposite **lose *your* head**

keep *your* head down
to do or say as little as possible in order to avoid attention ◆ *I think a lot of people keep their head down when they start a new job.*

lose *your* head
to not have control of your emotions ◆ *I was so frightened, I lost my head completely.* ◆ *She had lost her head over a man once before.* ◆ Opposite **keep *your* head**

need (to have) *your* head examined
you have done something that will make others think you stupid or strange ◆ *Anyone who pays that much for a pair of jeans needs to have her head examined.* USAGE: usually used as a humorous criticism

rear its (ugly) head
to become a problem that has to be dealt with ◆ *It was in the 1970s that the problem of violent soccer fans first reared its head in Britain.*

scratch *your* head
to have difficulty understanding something ◆ *A lot of people must be scratching their heads and trying to figure out what happened.*

shake *your* head
to move your head from side to side as a way of saying no or to express disagreement ◆ *Asked if she wanted any more to eat, Judith shook her head.*

take it into *your* head to *do sth*
to decide to do something ◆ *Uncle Julian might take it into his head to say almost anything.* USAGE: usually said about doing something silly or surprising

turn *sth* on its head, *also* **stand *sth* on its head**
1 to use something in a completely wrong way ◆ *The basic problem is that your report turns history on its head.*
2 to change something completely ◆ *I really hope that doctors and nurses can pull together and turn the system on its head.* ◆ Related vocabulary **turn *sth* inside out** at INSIDE, **turn sth upside down** at UPSIDE

a roof over *your* head See at ROOF

***your* eyes pop out of *your* head**
See at EYES

hit the nail on the head See at NAIL

hold a gun to *sb's* head See at GUN

off the top of *your* head See at TOP

headlines

make (the) headlines, *also* **hit the headlines**
to become an important news story ◆ *Stephen King made headlines by electronically distributing his novella.* ◆ *The group made the head-lines for supporting Fox in his successful bid for Mexico's presidency.*

heads

give *sb* a heads up
to give someone information or a warning ◆ *I wanted to give you a heads up that I'll be sending you the revised form for your approval.* USAGE: sometimes used in the form **get a heads up**: *They promised we'd get a heads up on the new proposal tomorrow.*

heads up *esp.* spoken
look up because something may hit you USAGE: often shouted as a warning: *Heads up! Watch out for the baseball!*

make heads or tails (out) of *sth*
to understand something ◆ *The way the document was worded was incredibly complicated – no one could make heads or tails out of it.* USAGE: almost always used in the negative

put *your* heads together
to share ideas in trying to solve a problem ◆ *If we can put our heads together we'll figure out a way to deal with this.*

turn heads
to be so interesting or attractive that people turn to look ◆ *Williams has the kind of beauty that turns heads wherever she goes.*

headway

make headway
to achieve progress ◆ *We hope scientists are able to continue to make headway against cancer.*

heap

heap *sth* on *sb*/*sth*
to express a strong opinion about someone or something ◆ *Other leaders heaped praise on the president at the meeting.* USAGE: often **heap scorn on someone or something** (= to express a strong lack of respect): *He heaped scorn on those who thought the plan would work.*

hear

hear sb out
to listen to someone until they have finished ♦ *Everyone in that room was angry when I got there, but except for one person, they all stayed to hear me out.* USAGE: sometimes used as a request: *"Can we end this discussion and get back to work?" "Hear me out, please – I want to be sure you understand my point."*

hear *yourself* think
to be able to think ♦ *The music was so loud I could hardly hear myself think.* USAGE: usually used in the negative, as in the example

***you* could hear a pin drop** See at PIN

hear the last of *sb/sth* See at LAST

hear *sth* through the grapevine See at GRAPEVINE

never hear the end of it See at END

heart

sb after *your* own heart
someone who is similar to you ♦ *I was delighted by your comments about vocabulary and grammar – you're clearly a man after my own heart.* USAGE: sometimes used in the form **a something after your own heart**: *She's a cook after my own heart.*

a heart of gold
a kind and generous character ♦ *He plays the part of a tough cop with a heart of gold.* ♦ Opposite **a heart of stone**

a heart of stone
an unfriendly and unkind character ♦ *The sad condition of these refugees would move a heart of stone to sympathy.* ♦ Opposite **a heart of gold**

at heart
1 as what someone cares about the most ♦ *Your academic adviser should have your best interests at heart.* ♦ *I'm an English teacher at heart but also a writer.* **2** in the most basic way ♦ *He was at heart a conservative man.*

bless *your* heart esp. spoken
you are a good person ♦ *"I changed the whole engine in one of my sons' trucks." "Well, bless your heart."* USAGE: also used to wish someone good health or good luck: *"I spent most of the day Sunday in the emergency room, and I just got home last night." "Oh, bless your heart."*

break *your* heart
to make you very sad ♦ *If their father knew his sons were selling the company, it would have broken his heart.*

by heart
exactly and from memory ♦ *You know the telephone number by heart, don't you?* USAGE: often used with **know**, **learn**, **recite**, and **play**: *I studied piano for two years, and all I learned to play by heart was "Twinkle Twinkle Little Star."*

close to *your* heart, also **dear to *your* heart**
of great importance to you ♦ *The issue of race is one that is close to his heart.*

eat *your* heart out esp. spoken
you should be sorry for the choices you have made ♦ *I thought I'd become famous, and I could say "Eat your heart out" to every girl I'd ever gone out with.* USAGE: usually said as if it were an order, as in the example

from the heart
in a sincere manner ♦ *My job is to get these people to sing from the heart.* ♦ *This is generosity that comes from the heart, and that's what makes it valuable.*

harden *your* heart slightly formal
to make yourself stop feeling kindness and sympathy ♦ *He found it difficult to harden his heart completely against his old colleague.*

have a heart
to show kindness and sympathy ♦ *I can't teach somebody to have a heart.*

heart

have *your* heart set on *sth*, also **set *your* heart on *sth***
to want something very much ◆ *She's got her heart set on dance lessons.*

***your* heart bleeds (for *sb*)**
you feel sadness and sympathy for someone ◆ *When my little girl cries in the night, my heart bleeds.*

your* heart goes out to *sb
you feel sympathy for someone ◆ *My heart goes out to the families of those who died in the accident.*

***sb's* heart is in the right place** esp. spoken
someone has only good intentions ◆ *He isn't a good judge of other people, but his heart is in the right place.*

***your* heart isn't in it**
you do not feel something is exciting or interesting enough to do ◆ *I tried to do some writing, but my heart wasn't in it.* USAGE: sometimes used in the form **your heart isn't in something**: *His heart isn't in supervising people.* ◆ Related vocabulary **not have the stomach (for *sth*)** at STOMACH

***your* heart out**
to an extreme degree ◆ *The child cried her heart out after finding her beautiful snowman melted by the sun.* ◆ *I'd go to my room and sing my heart out to forget that people made fun of me.*

***your* heart sinks**
you become discouraged or disappointed ◆ *My heart sank when I opened the letter and realized I had not been accepted into graduate school.*

***your* heart skips a beat**, also ***your* heart stands still**
you are suddenly surprised, excited, or frightened ◆ *Ben walked into the room and her heart skipped a beat.* ◆ *When the shark came toward us, my heart stood still.*

in *your* heart of hearts
if your true thoughts and feelings were known ◆ *In his heart of hearts, I don't think he wants to win this election.*

lose heart
to stop believing that you can succeed ◆ *When the other troops failed to arrive, the men lost heart and surrendered.*

lose *your* heart (to *sb/sth*)
to fall in love ◆ *I lost my heart to*

lose your heart

He lost his heart to Caroline the minute he saw her.

hearts

airplanes when I was eight years old, and I've wanted to be a pilot ever since.

not have the heart (to *do sth*), *also* **not have the heart (for *sth*)**
to lack the desire or strength to do something ♦ *I didn't have the heart to tell him his injury would prevent him from playing football.* USAGE: sometimes used in the form **have the heart to do something** (= be able to do something): *How could we have the heart to disappoint Mom?* ♦ Related vocabulary **not have the stomach (for *sth*)** at STOMACH

open *your* heart
to show or tell your true feelings and thoughts ♦ *It is easier to open my heart to Dad in a letter than to speak to him face to face.*

put *your* heart (and soul) into *sth*, *also* **pour *your* heart (and soul) into *sth***
to do something with all of your energy and interest ♦ *He wanted the restaurant to be a success and really put his heart into it.*

sick at heart
very sad, unhappy, or upset ♦ *She was sick at heart, knowing that he was putting himself in great danger.*

steal *sb's* heart
to cause someone to love you ♦ *He married the beautiful singer who stole his heart while singing the blues.*

take heart
to feel encouraged ♦ *The entire world should take heart that progress is being made in the effort to eliminate this disease.*

take *sth* to heart
to consider something very seriously ♦ *Everything he said is true, and I hope people will take it to heart.*

tear *your* heart out
to make you very sad ♦ *Your article on the death of those students tore my heart out.*

to *your* heart's content
as much as you want ♦ *You can take over the kitchen and cook to your heart's content.*

wear *your* heart on *your* sleeve
to show your feelings, esp. your love for someone ♦ *You always know where John stands because he wears his heart on his sleeve.* ♦ Related vocabulary **wear *sth* on *your* sleeve** at SLEEVE

a change of heart See at CHANGE

from the bottom of *your* heart See at BOTTOM

hearts

the hearts and minds of *sb*
the complete support of a group of people ♦ *I thought the president could have done a better job of reaching the hearts and minds of the American people in his speech on television yesterday.*

heartstrings

tug at *your* heartstrings, *also* **pull on *your* heartstrings**
to cause strong feelings of affection or sympathy ♦ *He looked into his son's smiling eyes and felt a tug on his heartstrings.* USAGE: sometimes used with other verbs: *The stories he told plucked at your heartstrings.*

heat

heat up (*sth*), *also* **heat *sth* up**
to become more active ♦ *Although nothing is happening right now, business will likely heat up in September after vacation season.* ♦ *Her report has heated up debate on how the president should behave.*

in the heat of *sth*
while there is much activity and strong emotions ♦ *Sometimes in the heat of an election campaign a candidate makes a mistake.* USAGE: sometimes used in the form **in the heat of the moment** (= while experiencing strong emotions): *His remarks were made in the heat of the moment.*

turn up the heat
to increase the amount of pressure, activity, or effort ♦ *Citizen groups say they will turn up the heat on the governor to sign the education bill.* ♦ *Newspapers need to turn up the heat and pursue more stories about women in business.*

heaven
heaven forbid
I hope it does not happen; = **God forbid** ♦ *If he ever – heaven forbid – has to go through anything like that again, at least he'll know what to do.* USAGE: also used to suggest that others oppose the reasonable thing being mentioned: *It's OK to prevent tooth decay, but heaven forbid that we try to prevent people from becoming addicted to drugs.*

heaven on earth
something extremely good ♦ *Brian's parties are heaven on earth – the food is marvelous and the company is terrific.*

in heaven's name
of all possible things ♦ *What in heaven's name are we doing here?* USAGE: usually used with **why, what, where,** or **how**

move heaven and earth (to *do sth*)
to do everything possible to achieve a result ♦ *I have instructed police to move heaven and earth to find whoever is responsible for this terrible crime.*

a match made in heaven See at MATCH

a marriage made in heaven See at MARRIAGE

manna from heaven See at MANNA

heavens
thank heavens
I am pleased or happy; = **thank goodness** ♦ *Thank heavens that I began my career when there were a lot of jobs available.* ♦ Related vocabulary **thank God** at GOD

heck
> USAGE
> People use **heck** to avoid using idioms that include the word **hell**, which is sometimes considered offensive.

a heck of a *sb/sth*
a surprisingly good person or thing; = **a hell of a *sb/sth*** ♦ *It's a heck of a deal from a business standpoint.* ♦ *He's a great teacher, and besides that, he's a heck of a nice guy.*

a heck of a *sth*
a very difficult activity or bad thing; = **a hell of a *sth*** ♦ *We have a heck of a time putting the day's news into a half-hour program.* ♦ *That was a heck of a present – why would anyone think you wanted such an ugly painting?*

a heck of a lot of *sth*
a large amount of something; = **a hell of a lot of *sth*** ♦ *You've spent a heck of a lot of money on that thing.*

(just) for the heck of it esp. spoken
without having any particular reason or purpose; = **(just) for the hell of it** ♦ *Let me explain this another way, just for the heck of it.*

heel
bring *sb* to heel slightly formal
to force someone to obey you ♦ *Western politicians opposed the president's effort to bring the Supreme Court to heel.*

> ORIGIN: based on the literal meaning of **bring to heel** (= to order a dog to walk close behind you)

turn on *your* heel
to leave quickly and suddenly ♦ *She turned on her heel and went back to her room.*

> ORIGIN: based on the idea that you could quickly change the direction in which you are moving by literally turning on your heel

heels

cool *your* heels
to wait or to be kept waiting ◆ *Fans of the band were forced to cool their heels outside the theater for 90 minutes.*

dig in *your* heels, *also* **dig *your* heels in**
to refuse to change what you believe is right or what you want to happen ◆ *Be firm on important issues, but do not dig in your heels at every opportunity.*

drag *your/its* heels
to do something slowly because you do not want to do it; = **drag *your/its* feet** ◆ *When they told us they wanted to put computers in our classrooms, we dragged our heels a little bit.*

(hard) on the heels of *sth*
close behind or soon after something ◆ *The fighting came on the heels of even deadlier combat in a village ten miles to the north.* USAGE: usually used with the verbs **come** or **follow** and also used in the forms **close on the heels of something** or **hot on the heels of something**: *The manager's resignation followed close on the heels of the hiring of a new chairman.*

hot on *your* heels, *also* **close on *your* heels**
1 following directly behind someone ◆ *She headed inside the house with her brother hot on her heels.* ◆ Related vocabulary **in hot pursuit (of *sb/sth*)** at PURSUIT
2 very near to someone in rank ◆ *They know we're hard on their heels and that they've got to win their next three games to make the playoffs.*

kick up *your* heels
to do things that you enjoy ◆ *In spring people dash outdoors to kick up their heels and join in their favorite sports.*

height

the height of *sth*
1 the period when something is strongest ◆ *In 1955, he was at the height of his fame.* ◆ *The constitution was drawn up at the height of military rule.*
2 the greatest amount of something ◆ *It's the height of arrogance to feel you need to convert someone to your own religion.*

hell

> USAGE
> Some people are upset by use of the word **hell** although it is used in most types of writing, on radio and TV, and in ordinary speech.

a hell of a *sb/sth*, *also* **one hell of a *sb/sth***
a surprisingly good person or thing; = **a heck of a *sb/sth*** ◆ *That was a hell of a show – great acting, amazing special effects, and a terrific ending.* ◆ *He's one hell of a guy.* USAGE: sometimes written as **helluva**: *We're going to have a helluva football team this year!*

a hell of a *sth*, *also* **one hell of a *sth***
a very difficult activity or bad thing; = **a heck of a *sth*** ◆ *We had a hell of a time getting home last night.* ◆ *Isn't this a hell of a mess?*

a hell of a lot of *sth*
a large amount of something; = **a heck of a lot of *sth*** ◆ *We've got a hell of a lot of books – do you think we should try to get rid of some of them?*

a living hell, *also* **hell on earth**
an extremely unpleasant place or experience ◆ *She worked as a substitute teacher in a living hell of a public high school.*

(all) hell breaks loose
great confusion and excitement suddenly develops ◆ *All hell broke loose when the mayor proposed a 10% pay cut for city employees.* ◆

hell

Related vocabulary **break loose** at BREAK

as hell
in an extreme way ◆ *It makes people mad as hell when you print stories like that.* USAGE: used for emphasis after adjectives like **mad**, **angry**, and **frustrated**

beat the hell out of *sb*
1 to hit someone hard and repeatedly ◆ *Bill beat the hell out of me after we started arguing over a girl.*
2 to completely defeat someone ◆ *It's a thrill to beat the hell out of another team in front of 20,000 screaming fans.* ◆ Related vocabulary **(it) beats me** at BEATS

beat the hell out of *sth*
to be much better than something ◆ *It wasn't much of a plan, but it beat the hell out of sitting around the office waiting for something to happen.*

come hell or high water
whatever happens; = **come what may** ◆ *I'm leaving the office tonight at five o'clock, come hell or high water.* USAGE: the same meaning can be also expressed by **at (the very) least**, **either way**, **in any case**, and **in any event**

sb/sth from hell slang
someone or something with very unpleasant characteristics ◆ *It was the airport from hell.*

get the hell out of *somewhere*
to leave or move quickly ◆ *She told them to get the hell out of her house.* USAGE: sometimes used as an order: *Get the hell out of my way!*

give *sb* **hell**
1 to speak to someone in a very angry way ◆ *My wife's giving me hell for not selling the farm.*
2 to cause someone pain or difficulty ◆ *These new shoes are giving me hell.*

go to hell rude slang
stop annoying me, I do not want to deal with you any more; = **go to the devil** ◆ *Anybody who objects to what I've done can just go to hell.*

go to hell (in a handbasket)
to become worse in quality or character; = **go to the dogs** ◆ *The roads in this part of the country are going to hell in a handbasket.* ◆ Related vocabulary **go to pot** at POT

> ORIGIN: based on the idea of being carried to **hell** (= a place for punishment after life) in a **handbasket** (= a small container with a handle)

hell on wheels
extremely difficult ◆ *He's going to be hell on wheels to deal with.*

hell to pay
serious problems ◆ *There will be hell to pay when you get back home.* USAGE: used to describe the result of an action

(just) for the hell of it esp. spoken
without having any particular reason or purpose; = **(just) for the heck of it** ◆ *Just for the hell of it, I bought tickets to tonight's concert.*

like hell
1 very much ◆ *It was raining like hell.*
2 very badly ◆ *My shoulder hurt like hell.*
3 it is not true or it will not happen ◆ *You want me to apologize? Like hell I will!*

put *sb* **through hell**
to make someone suffer ◆ *He didn't understand the people he worked with or care whether he put us through hell.*

raise hell
1 to behave in a way that is not controlled ◆ *He never skipped classes or got into fights or raised hell.*
2 to loudly argue or make demands ◆ *I've been calling them every day, raising hell about it, but they told me I may have to wait until Thursday to get the software.*

scare the hell out of *you*
to make you feel extremely fright-

helm

ened; = **scare *you* to death** ◆ *His idea of fun scares the hell out of me.* ◆ Related vocabulary **scare the pants off *you*** at PANTS

see *sb* in hell before *doing sth* rude slang, *also* **see *sb* in hell first** to never do something ◆ *I'll see you in hell before I'll answer your questions.*

sure as hell
surely ◆ *He may not be a college graduate, but he sure as hell knows how to run a business.*

to hell with *sb*/*sth*, *also* **the hell with *sb*/*sth***
I do not care about someone or something ◆ *She didn't seem to care about me, and I was ready to say to hell with her and walk out.* ◆ *He's a man who expects to get things done, and to hell with what the rest of the world thinks.*

until hell freezes over, *also* **till hell freezes over**
forever ◆ *I will fight for these children till hell freezes over.* USAGE: also used in the form **when hell freezes over** (= never): *They said they would get back together when hell freezes over.*

> ORIGIN: based on the idea that **hell** (= a very hot place where people are punished forever) can never freeze

what the hell esp. spoken
why not ◆ *I wasn't going to go but then I thought, what the hell.*

like a bat out of hell See at BAT

not have a (snowball's) chance in hell See at CHANCE

helm

at the helm (of *sth*) slightly formal
in control ◆ *He resigned and left the company last July after two years at the helm.*

> ORIGIN: based on the literal meaning of **helm** (= the handle or wheel that controls the direction in which a ship travels)

help

can't help *sth*, *also* **cannot help *sth***
to not be able to control or stop something ◆ *A lot of kids daydream in school. They just can't help it.* USAGE: sometimes used in the form **can't help but do something**: *I couldn't help but notice that the table is a bit wobbly.*

(not) if *you* can help it
when you are able to prevent it ◆ *No one sails at this time of year if they can help it.*

so help me (God)
this is the truth ◆ *That was one of the most frightening sights of my life, so help me.* ◆ *You look at me when I'm talking to you or, so help me God, I'll hit you.* USAGE: used for very strong emphasis, as in the examples

hem

hem and haw
to pause a lot and avoid saying something directly ◆ *When asked what kind of woman he was looking for, he hemmed and hawed and finally admitted he was looking for a party girl.*

hem in *sb*/*sth*, *also* **hem *sb*/*sth* in**
to surround someone or something ◆ *They found themselves hemmed in by the crowd.* ◆ *The building was hemmed in by high walls.*

here

here and there
in different places ◆ *Towns are scattered here and there across this region of the country.*

here's to *sb* esp. spoken
this is in honor of someone ◆ *So here's to you, Dave – happy fifteenth anniversary, and another fifteen more.* USAGE: often said when making a **toast** (= a short speech honoring someone and followed by everyone present having a drink)

(right) here and now
in this place at this time ◆ *People*

will remember us because we're going to make a deal, not tomorrow or next week but right here and now. ◆ Related vocabulary **then and there** at THEN

the here and now
the present ◆ *Jazz and hip-hop and gospel talk about the here and now in a way that everyone can understand.*

from there to here See at THERE

here *you* go See at GO

here goes nothing See at GOES

here today, gone tomorrow See at TODAY

look here See at LOOK

neither here nor there See at NEITHER

same here See at SAME

high

high and mighty
as if you are more important than other people ◆ *The members of the club all act high and mighty.*

on high
1 in the air ◆ *The runner turned into our street holding her flag on high.* USAGE: often with **from**: *You can hire a boat to explore the swamps, where monkeys chatter at you from on high.*
2 someone in a position of authority ◆ *The boss said that the new rules came from on high.*
3 in heaven ◆ *The angels on high sang His praises.*

high horse

get off *your* high horse
to stop acting as if you are better or more intelligent than other people ◆ *He never got off his high horse long enough to consider how insulting his words were to many immigrants.* USAGE: also used in the forms **knock someone off their high horse** and **fall off your high horse**

get on *your* high horse
to act as if you are better or more intelligent than other people ◆ *We can't get on our high horse and judge other countries by our own standards.*

high time

it is high time, *also* **it's high time**
it should have happened a long time ago ◆ *It was high time someone invited me to lunch.* ◆ *It's high time you got that bad knee of yours looked at by a doctor!* ◆ Related vocabulary **(it's) about time** at TIME, **at (long) last** at LAST

highways

highways and byways slightly formal
large and small roads ◆ *The two friends traveled America's highways and byways from New Hampshire to California.*

hike

take a hike
to leave; = **take a walk** ◆ *He told them, politely but firmly, to take a hike.* USAGE: sometimes used as an order: *I don't want to hear your excuses, Grady – just take a hike.*

hill

amount to a hill of beans
to be of little importance ◆ *You are making yourself miserable over something that amounts to a hill of beans.*

over the hill
no longer able to do something at an acceptable level because of age; = **past *your/its* prime** ◆ *Some judges who are 75 may be over the hill, but others still have energy galore.*

hills

as old as the hills
ancient ◆ *Some of these rituals are as old as the hills.*

hilt

to the hilt
as much as possible ◆ *We're already being taxed to the hilt.*

> ORIGIN: based on the idea of pushing a sword into something **to the hilt** (= as far as its handle)

hinge

hinge on *sth*, *also* **hinge upon** *sth*
to depend on something ♦ *The case hinged on whether the jury believed the accused thief or the two witnesses.*

> ORIGIN: based on the idea that a door is attached to its frame by a **hinge** (= folding device)

hint

drop a hint
to suggest something indirectly to someone ♦ *I was hoping to see her again, so I dropped a hint, saying I wasn't doing anything this weekend.*

take a hint, *also* **take the hint**
to understand or do something that is communicated indirectly ♦ *I can take a hint – if you don't want to talk about it, that's OK with me.* ♦ *"Weren't you going to check your messages?" she asked. I took the hint and left.*

hip

joined at the hip
1 very closely connected ♦ *The two companies have been joined at the hip since their founders went camping together a hundred years ago.*
2 together ♦ *The new law would keep unhappy couples joined at the hip for the sake of their children.*

shoot from the hip
to react quickly without considering the possible effects ♦ *He works slowly and methodically while she jumps quickly into projects and shoots from the hip, but they make a good team.*

history

go down in history
to be recorded in a particular way ♦ *I think that, in the end, this will go down in history as a very important project.* USAGE: sometimes used in the form **go down in the annals of history** or **go down in the history books**: *He hopes to go down in the history books as a man of vision who brought the country together.* ♦ Related vocabulary **go down as** *sth* at GO

history in the making
something very important that is happening now ♦ *The broadcast gave a vivid account of medical history in the making.*

make history
to do something important that will be remembered for a long time ♦ *Faulkner made history Wednesday when she became the first woman to register for classes at the all-male college.* USAGE: often said about something that has not been done before ♦ Related vocabulary **go down as** *sth* at GO

the rest is history See at REST

hit

hit back
to react to something bad by doing something bad ♦ *The attorney general hit back at critics who have questioned her handling of the crisis.* ♦ *We imposed import duties on their goods, and they hit back with tariffs on our products.*

> ORIGIN: based on the idea of literally hitting someone who has hit you

hit home
to be understood completely and have a strong effect; = **strike home** ♦ *The president's message seemed to hit home with most people who watched him on TV.* ♦ Related vocabulary **come home (to** *sb***)** at COME

hit it off (with *sb***)**
to be friendly with each other immediately ♦ *She hit it off with Dean and soon the two of them set out on a cross-country adventure.* ♦ *We hit it off beautifully – we liked all the same things, and we liked each other a lot.*

hit on *sb* slang
to clearly show that you are sexu-

ally attracted to someone ◆ *Pete doesn't even realize half the time when girls are hitting on him.* ◆ Related vocabulary **come on to sb** at COME

hit on sth, *also* **hit upon sth**
1 to discover or think of something new ◆ *Adams and her record producer hit on a jazzy, sophisticated style.*
2 to mention something briefly ◆ *I just called to make sure that we hit on everything you need when we met yesterday.*

hit or miss, *also* **hit and miss**
not planned carefully and as likely to be bad as to be good ◆ *Hiring has often been hit or miss – we never really knew whether a person was qualified until after they started working here.*

hit sb up slang, *also* **hit up sb**
to ask someone for something, esp. money ◆ *He tried to hit me up for some cigarettes.* ◆ *What about hitting up your daddy for a loan?*

hock

in hock
having a debt ◆ *Middle-class consumers are deep in hock and worried about their jobs.*

hog

go whole hog
to do something as completely as possible ◆ *We decided the only way we could afford vacations is to go camping, so we went whole hog and got the tents and sleeping bags and everything else.*

live high on the hog, *also* **live high off the hog**
to live in great comfort with a lot of money ◆ *Gardner, who made only $8,000 last year, has definitely not been living high on the hog.* ◆ Related vocabulary **live it up** at LIVE

> ORIGIN: based on the idea that better quality meat is found on the upper parts of a **hog** (= pig)

hold

get hold of sb
to communicate with someone; = **get ahold of sb** ◆ *He said he planned to call Mom this week, so I thought he'd get hold of her sooner or later.*

get hold of sth
to obtain something; = **get ahold of sth** ◆ *I think it should be harder for a criminal to get hold of a gun.* ◆ *Nothing was done by officials until the press got hold of the story.*

hold sth against sb
to have a bad opinion about someone because of something they did ◆ *I understand that your car isn't working, but please don't hold it against me personally – I didn't build your car.*

hold sth back, *also* **hold back sth**
to keep something secret ◆ *They talk about everything and hold back nothing.*

hold back (from *doing sth*)
to avoid doing something ◆ *Unable to hold back, we screamed with laughter.* ◆ *We were worried about viewers' reactions, so we held back from broadcasting the show.*

hold down sth, *also* **hold sth down**
to succeed in keeping something ◆ *He's never been able to hold down a steady job.* ◆ *The film held down second place in the top five movies over the last weekend.*

hold forth
to talk for a long time on a subject ◆ *She held forth for half an hour on the stupidity of TV reality shows.*

hold it
to stop doing something or to wait before continuing ◆ *Hold it! You're putting too much pepper in the stew.*
USAGE: usually used as an order, as in the example

hold off (*sth*), *also* **hold (*sth*) off**
to delay something ◆ *They're hoping to hold off surgery until he's stronger.* ◆ *I hope the rain holds off until we get home.*

hold

hold on esp. spoken
1 to wait for someone ◆ *Tell them to hold on, I'll be there in a minute.* USAGE: often used to tell someone to wait for someone else to answer the telephone: *Please hold on, he's on another line.*
2 to wait for something ◆ *Try to hold on while I go and get some help.* USAGE: usually used to tell someone they must wait although it is difficult to do so

hold onto *sth*, also **hold on to** *sth*
to continue to keep something ◆ *She might be better off holding onto her old computer for a year or two.* ◆ *The way to prevent fear from becoming panic is to hold onto your good sense.* ◆ *The team held on to first place with a 4–3 win last night.*

hold out
1 to continue to defend yourself without being defeated ◆ *The city won't be able to hold out much longer against the bombing attacks.*
2 to continue to demand something in a determined way ◆ *The factory workers are holding out for a pay increase.*
3 to continue to be enough ◆ *How much longer will our food supplies hold out?*

hold out *sth*
to offer the possibility that something will happen ◆ *We don't hold out much hope of finding more survivors.* ◆ *Our supervisor held out the possibility that he would return to work next month.* USAGE: often used with **not** as in the first example

hold out on *sb*
to refuse to give help or information to someone ◆ *I discovered that she had been holding out on me all these years, not telling me the secret ingredient in her pies.*

hold *sb* **over**, also **hold over** *sb*
to prevent someone from leaving ◆ *The authorities held the couple over for two days.* ◆ *Harold Anderson and his accordion act have been held over until March 13th.*

hold *sth* **over**, also **hold over** *sth*
to delay something ◆ *I'd like to hold the presentation over until next week.* ◆ *Several flights were held over because of the storm.*

hold *your/its* **own**
to prove that you or something is as good as others ◆ *She can hold her own in any debate on religion.* ◆ *Our cotton shirts can hold their own against shirts costing $40 or more.* USAGE: often said about a competitive situation

hold *sb* **to** *sth*
to make someone act on a promise or agreement ◆ *They're holding him to the exact terms of the contract.*

hold up
1 to continue to operate or be able to do things ◆ *I hope the spare tire holds up until we can get to a garage.* ◆ *She is holding up well despite her financial problems.*
2 to continue to seem true after being carefully examined ◆ *The evidence may not hold up in court.* ◆ Related vocabulary **not hold water** at WATER

hold up *sb/sth*, also **hold** *sb/sth* **up**
1 to try to steal from a person or place by using violence ◆ *Two masked men held up the grocery store on my block.* ◆ *They held her up at gunpoint.* ◆ Related vocabulary **stick up** *sb/sth* at STICK
2 to delay someone or something ◆ *Traffic was held up for several hours by the accident.* ◆ *Sorry to hold you up, but my train was late.*
3 to offer someone or something as an example ◆ *Her parents always held her sister up as the kind of person she should be.*

hold with (doing) *sth*
to agree with or support something ◆ *He married a woman who didn't hold with gambling.* USAGE: often

used in the form **not hold with (doing) something**: *I don't hold with the idea that I was rebellious as a child.*

on hold
1 intentionally delayed ♦ *The space launch is on hold until the weather clears.* USAGE: often used in the form **be on hold**, as in the example
2 connected but waiting to speak to someone on the telephone ♦ *Her line was busy, so the operator put me on hold.* USAGE: often used in the form **put someone on hold**, as in the example

holds

no holds barred
no limits or controls ♦ *This is comedy with no holds barred, and it may offend some viewers.* ♦ *I like nothing better than a fight with no holds barred.*

hole

hole up (*somewhere*)
to stay in a hidden place ♦ *While writing his book, he holed up for a year in a cabin in the woods.*

in the hole
owing money ♦ *We're in the hole – every year our revenues grow more slowly than our costs.* USAGE: often used after an amount of money: *He's $500 in the hole after buying his car.*

put *sb/sth* in a hole
to cause a difficult situation for someone or something ♦ *Whitson gave up home runs to Palmeiro and Bonilla that put Cleveland in a hole.* ♦ *I campaigned against two opponents from this state, and I think it put me in a hole.* ♦ Related vocabulary **in a bind** at BIND, **in a tight spot** at SPOT

holes

full of holes
including many faults ♦ *Experts say the scientists' research is full of holes and unrealistic assumptions.* ♦ *Their stories are so full of holes that anyone who knows the facts can see right through them.*

pick holes in *sth*
to find mistakes in something someone has done or said ♦ *We send the articles out and let other scientists in the same area of study try their best to pick holes in your research.*

home

a home away from home
a place where you feel as comfortable as you do in your own home ♦ *I visit Chicago so often, it's become a home away from home for me.*

at home
comfortable and relaxed ♦ *She's beginning to feel at home in her new job.* ♦ *He is equally at home with people his own age or with his older brother's friends.* USAGE: sometimes used in the form **make yourself at home**: *Sit down and make yourself at home while I get you some coffee.*

home free
sure of success because you have finished the most difficult part ♦ *Once you get past the essay questions on the test, you're home free.*

home in (on *sth*)
1 to aim for and move directly toward something ♦ *When he questioned the witness, the lawyer homed in on him like a laser.* ♦ *The missile homed in on the ship.*
2 to aim your attention toward something ♦ *The report homed in on the faulty wiring that might have caused the fire.*

bring home the bacon See at BACON

bring *sth* home (to *sb*) See at BRING

close to home See at CLOSE

come home to *sb* See at COME

come home to roost See at COME

eat *sb* out of house and home See at HOUSE

hammer home (*sth*) See at HAMMER

home run

hit home See at HIT

nothing to write home about See at WRITE

strike home See at STRIKE

until the cows come home See at COWS

home run

hit a home run
to succeed with something ◆ *We felt our band hit a home run that night – it was the best performance we ever gave.*

> ORIGIN: based on the literal meaning of **home run** (= a play in baseball in which the person hitting the ball scores)

homework

do *your* homework
to learn everything you need to know before doing something ◆ *If you had done your homework, you would have known it was a silly question to ask.*

honor

on *your* honor
1 without being watched to see if you behave in the right way ◆ *We ask people, on their honor, to avoid leaving garbage at the campsite.*
2 with a serious promise ◆ *She swore on her honor that she'd finish the assignment.*

honors

do the honors
to perform social duties at an event ◆ *Jerry, I need to go into the kitchen for a moment, so why don't you do the honors and get Carol a drink?* USAGE: usually said about serving food and drinks or greeting and introducing guests

hoof

hoof it
to walk ◆ *My car was being repaired, so I decided to hoof it to the train station.*

hook

by hook or by crook
using any method possible ◆ *Templeton was recruited to obtain the formula by hook or by crook.*

hook, line, and sinker
completely ◆ *The public isn't swallowing the administration's policies hook, line, and sinker.* ◆ *They made up such a good story that we fell for it hook, line, and sinker.* USAGE: often used in the forms **fall for something hook, line, and sinker** or **swallow something hook, line, and sinker** (= to be tricked into believing something without any doubts)

> ORIGIN: based on the idea of a fish so hungry it swallows the **hook** (= the part that catches the fish), the **line** (= the string) and the **sinker** (= a weight attached to the line to keep it under water)

hook up (with *sb*)
to meet someone and spend time together ◆ *I was traveling alone, but then I hooked up with another woman about my age.*

off the hook
having avoided a difficult situation ◆ *He's just happy to be off the hook on that harassment charge.* USAGE: often used with the verbs **get** or **let**: *She got him off the hook by lending him her class notes.*

ring off the hook
to receive an extremely large number of telephone calls ◆ *The box office phones were ringing off the hook all day.*

> ORIGIN: based on the idea of having the telephone ring so much it causes the part you hold in your hand to fall off the part it rests on

hooky

play hooky
to stay away from school without permission ◆ *Any kid who's not in school at this time of day must be playing hooky.* USAGE: sometimes

refers to staying away from a job or avoiding a duty: *I decided to play hooky from work so I could go to the ballgame.*

hoops
jump through hoops
to do a lot of extra things so you can have or do something you want ◆ *The company is jumping through hoops these days to try to please advertisers.*

shoot hoops
to play the game of basketball ◆ *Sometimes we stopped off at the gym after school and shot some hoops.*

ORIGIN: based on the basketball meaning of **hoop** (= a high metal ring through which a ball is thrown to score points)

hoot
not give a hoot, *also* **not give two hoots**
to not care about something at all ◆ *I don't give a hoot about her opinion of my housekeeping.*

hop
hop to it
to hurry ◆ *If we're going to meet them for breakfast we'd better hop to it.*

hopes
get *sb's* hopes up
to make someone think that what they want is going to happen ◆ *If we can't afford the trip then we shouldn't get the children's hopes up.* USAGE: usually said when something is not likely to happen

in hopes of *doing sth*
with the intention of influencing something in the future that you do not control directly ◆ *McDougall is cooperating with police in hopes of reducing his sentence.* USAGE: also used in the form **in hopes that something will happen**: *The agency sued the farmer in hopes that other growers would obey the government's demands.*

pin *your* hopes on *sb/sth*
to depend on someone or something for a successful result ◆ *The party is pinning its hopes on its new leader, who is young, good-looking, and very popular.* ◆ *Scientists are pinning their hopes on the high-tech laboratory.* USAGE: usually said when it is not certain whether something will happen or succeed

hopped
hopped up
very active and excited ◆ *The union is hopped up about rumors that some of these jobs may be eliminated.* USAGE: often used to describe someone who is influenced by drugs: *I was pretty hopped up on coffee.* ◆ *I don't want some guy hopped up on drugs next to me working on a machine.*

horizon
on the horizon
likely to happen or appear soon ◆ *There are no new drugs on the horizon to treat this disease.* ◆ Related vocabulary **a cloud on the horizon** at CLOUD

ORIGIN: based on the literal meaning of **horizon** (= the place in the distance where the earth and sky seem to meet)

horn
horn in (on *sb/sth*)
to interrupt or try to become involved when you are not welcome ◆ *George worried that his brother would try to horn in on the company's success.* ◆ Related vocabulary **in on *sth*** at IN, **let *sb* in on *sth*** at LET

horns
lock horns (with *sb*)
to argue with someone in a very determined way ◆ *In her new movie she plays a middle-aged college*

horse

lock horns

The two sides locked horns over the terms of the new contract.

student who locks horns with her professor.

> ORIGIN: based on the literal meaning of two fighting animals such as deer whose horns lock together

on the horns of a dilemma
unable to decide between two things because either could bring bad results ♦ *Nonprofit groups are often caught on the horns of a dilemma – they have to satisfy their donors, but at the same time, they need to attract new donors.*

horse

beat a dead horse
to waste time doing something that has already been attempted ♦ *Do you think it's worth sending my manuscript to other publishers or I am just beating a dead horse?*

eat like a horse
to eat large amounts of food often ♦ *I eat like a horse, but I eat healthy food.*

horse around
to be active in a silly way ♦ *Stop horsing around and pay attention to your father!*

look a gift horse in the mouth
to criticize or refuse to take something that has been offered to you ♦ *I know the car's not in great condition, but you shouldn't look a gift horse in the mouth.* USAGE: usually follows **never** or **not**, as in the example

> ORIGIN: based on the idea that you can discover a lot about a horse's condition by looking at its teeth

get on *your* high horse See at HIGH HORSE

get off *your* high horse See at HIGH HORSE

(put) the cart before the horse See at CART

(straight) from the horse's mouth See at MOUTH

horses

hold *your* horses
wait ♦ *Hold your horses, Colin, I'm working as fast as I can!* USAGE: usu-

ally used as an instruction, as in the example

hot
hot and bothered
angry and excited ♦ *Dad gets all hot and bothered if someone parks in his parking space.*
hot and heavy
full of very strong feelings ♦ *The argument is still going hot and heavy about whether genetically modified foods are safe to eat.*

hotcakes
sell like hotcakes, *also* **sell like hot cakes**
to sell quickly and in large numbers ♦ *Since word got out about the Perry case, the book has been selling like hot cakes.*

hots
have the hots for *sb* slang
to be strongly sexually attracted to someone ♦ *He's got the hots for that new girl Libby.* USAGE: sometimes used in a humorous way that is not sexual: *Consumers have the hots for DSL Internet connections.*

hour
on the hour
at the time an hour begins ♦ *Buses pull out every hour on the hour.*

house
a house of cards
an organization or a plan that is very weak and can easily be destroyed ♦ *Their partners began to suspect that the company was a financial house of cards.*

> ORIGIN: based on the literal meaning of **house of cards** (= a small structure made of playing cards)

bring the house down, *also* **bring down the house**
to entertain people very successfully, so that they laugh or clap for a long time ♦ *The clown sang a duet with the talking horse, which brought the house down every night.*

eat *sb* out of house and home
to eat a large amount of food in someone's home ♦ *The boys have only been back two days and they've already eaten me out of house and home.*

in the house esp. spoken
present ♦ *This is Sam Perkins in the house with all your favorite tunes.*

keep house
to clean, wash clothes, cook, and do other similar jobs in a home ♦ *His cousin Ella lived there and kept house for both of them.*

on the house
without asking for money ♦ *We had to wait for a table so they gave us all drinks on the house.* USAGE: said about food, drink, or services offered by a hotel, restaurant, or bar

put *your* (own) house in order, *also* **get *your* (own) house in order**
to solve your own problems ♦ *You should put your own house in order before you start giving me advice.* USAGE: usually said about someone who has many problems but criticizes others for not taking care of their problems ♦ Related vocabulary **have *your* ducks in a row** at DUCKS

housekeeping
set up housekeeping
to start living in a place ♦ *After a honeymoon in Georgia, the newlyweds set up housekeeping in Washington.* USAGE: often said about two people who are just starting to live together ♦ Related vocabulary **shack up (with *sb*)** at SHACK

how
and how esp. spoken
I agree very strongly ♦ *"That was a great game last night." "And how!"* USAGE: usually used as a separate sentence, as in the example

how about *sb/sth* esp. spoken
I am surprised by someone or something ♦ *How about that guy who was arrested for riding his bicycle on the*

huff

expressway? USAGE: usually intended to get someone to say what they think

how about *sth/doing sth* esp. spoken

I suggest this ♦ *"What time should I pick you up?" "How about five o'clock?"* ♦ *How about going for a drink after work?*

how come esp. spoken

why do or why have ♦ *How come birds fly south in the winter?* ♦ *How come you got invited and I didn't?* USAGE: usually used to introduce a question, but also used to react to a statement: *"I haven't watched a football game all year." "How come?"*

how so esp. spoken

please explain what you mean ♦ *"I thought her answers didn't make sense." "How so?"*

how's that esp. spoken

1 I do not understand ♦ *"What time do you close?" "How's that?"*
2 why ♦ *"I'm glad I don't work in a store." "How's that?" "Because I wouldn't want to have to deal with customers all day."* ♦ *"If you were planning on looking at the place today, you may be disappointed." "How's that?"*

how's that for *doing sth*

this is an excellent example of doing something ♦ *After losing his old business, he started a new one that has five movies in production right now – how's that for ending up OK?*

how dare you *do sth* See at DARE

how goes it See at GOES

how the land lies See at LAND

how the other half lives See at HALF

no matter how *you* slice See at MATTER

huff

huff and puff

1 to breathe in a noisy manner ♦ *He was on the top of the hill long before I came up huffing and puffing behind him.*
2 to complain ♦ *The owners will huff and puff about their financial problems and then not do anything to solve them.*

hump

over the hump

past the most difficult or dangerous part of something ♦ *I hope power companies will have enough electricity to get over the hump of seasonal demand.* ♦ *The other team got off to a big lead at the start, and we just couldn't quite get over the hump.*

hung

hung over

feeling ill from drinking too much alcohol ♦ *I was so hung over that I couldn't even get out of bed.*

hung up on *sb*

in love with someone in a foolish way ♦ *Jeff's hung up on that actress he met at the party.*

hung up on *sth*

stopped from making progress by something you think is very important ♦ *We got hung up on the planning and forgot that we were supposed to produce something.*

hunker

hunker down

to stay in a place or situation ♦ *Members of Congress were hunkered down for weeks of debate on the issue.* ♦ *It had been raining since early morning, a perfect day to hunker down behind the computer and get some work done.*

hurry

hurry up and *do sth*

to do something very soon ♦ *All I wanted was for these very boring people to hurry up and leave.* ♦ *Smokers should consider the illnesses that could lie ahead if they don't hurry up and quit.*

hurry up and wait

to prepare quickly for an activity

hurt

it doesn't hurt to *do sth*, *also* **it doesn't hurt to *have sth***
it is an advantage to do or have something ◆ *It doesn't hurt to take a look at what you've done and see if it could be improved.* ◆ *It doesn't hurt to have a group of talented, educated people living in your community.* USAGE: also used in the forms **it couldn't hurt**, **it wouldn't hurt**, or **it can't hurt**, or in the form of a question, **would it hurt**, all with the meaning that doing or having something would be an advantage

hush

hush *sb* up, *also* **hush up *sb***
to not let someone talk about something ◆ *She knew about the defects, and company officials tried to hush her up.*

hush *sth* up, *also* **hush up *sth***
to not let something become known ◆ *She could have died ten years ago, and the news was hushed up.* ◆ *They made a great effort to hush things up and maintain order.*

hustle

hustle and bustle
energy and excitement ◆ *Some folks delight in the hustle and bustle of holiday shopping.*

I, i

ice

break the ice
to start a conversation with someone you have not met before ◆ *I never know how to break the ice with someone I've just met at a party.*

on thin ice
in an uncertain condition ◆ *My brother was already on thin ice with the coach when he injured his knee.*
USAGE: often appears as **skating** or **walking on thin ice** (= taking a big risk): *They knew that by publishing the article they were skating on thin ice.*

put *sth* on ice
to delay something ◆ *Both projects have been put on ice until they can be paid for.*

icing

icing on the cake
something good that is added to another good thing ◆ *He was delighted to have his story published – getting paid for it was just icing on the cake.*

idea

float an idea
to suggest something informally to see if people accept it or are interested in it ◆ *The mayor originally floated the idea, and it was quickly taken up by a number of city agencies.* ◆ Related vocabulary **test the waters** at WATERS

not have the faintest idea, also **not have the foggiest idea**
to not know anything at all about something; = **not have the foggiest notion** ◆ *I didn't have the faintest idea where I was or which way I was going – I simply knew I had to get away.* ◆ *These people don't have the foggiest idea what America's really like.* USAGE: also used in the forms **I have no idea** and **I haven't the slightest idea**

identify

identify with *sb*
to understand and feel sympathy for someone; = **relate to *sb*** ◆ *Ordinary people can identify with him in many ways, mainly because he talks to voters like an ordinary person.*

identify with *sth*
to feel that you understand a situation; = **relate to *sth*** ◆ *So, they've run out of money? I can identify with that!*

if

if I were you
putting myself in your situation ◆ *Oh, I wouldn't listen to that nonsense if I were you.*

if only
if this situation had been different in this way ◆ *If only she had listened to me, she wouldn't be in this mess.* ◆ *He could have made a very beautiful bookcase, if only he had the time.*
USAGE: used to express disappointment about a result

if you will esp. spoken
this is one way of saying this ◆ *Someone recovering from a serious accident often goes through a period of emotional numbness, if you will.* ◆ *Well, a dictionary describes words but doesn't make laws, if you will, about their use.* ◆ Related vocabulary **in a manner of speaking** at MANNER, **in other words** at WORDS, **so to speak** at SPEAK

ifs

no ifs, ands, or buts esp. spoken
without excuses or doubts ◆ *If they catch you stealing, you're fired on the spot – no ifs, ands, or buts about it.*

imbue

imbue *sb/sth* with *sth*
to fill someone or something with a particular quality or feeling ◆ *Her poetry was imbued with a love of the*

outdoors. ✦ *They seemed more interested in enriching themselves than in imbuing people with the spirit of God.*

in

in and of itself
without considering anything else ✦ *Any step we can take to end the conflict and save lives is important in and of itself.* USAGE: sometimes used in the form **in and of themselves**: *Lower interest rates in and of themselves don't mean much for stock prices.*

in on *sth*
doing something with others ✦ *I wasn't in on planning the party.* USAGE: often used in the form **get in on something**: *Let's go! Don't you want to get in on the fun?* ✦ Related vocabulary **horn in (on sb/sth)** at HORN, **let sb in on sth** at LET

inch

every inch of *somewhere*
all of a place ✦ *Cassandra knows every inch of Boston.* ✦ *A layer of grease covered every inch of the engine room.*

every inch the *sth*, also every inch a *sth*
completely like something ✦ *He looked every inch the slick, city businessman.* ✦ *From his white running shoes to his baseball cap, he looks every inch a Californian.* USAGE: used with verbs like **look**, **seem**, and **be**

give an inch
to agree to part of what someone wants or says ✦ *My ex-husband never gave an inch on anything we disagreed about, even when I was right.*

ORIGIN: based on the saying **give someone an inch and they'll take a mile** (= if you agree to part of what someone wants they will get all of what they want)

within an inch of *your/its* life
nearly completely ✦ *Caroline hoped the information she had would frighten Mr. Mott within an inch of his life.*

influence

under the influence
feeling the effect of alcohol or drugs ✦ *Were you serious last night about wanting a baby or did you say it because you were under the influence?* ✦ *If you are caught driving under the influence, you can lose your license.*

initiative

take the initiative
to be the first one to do something ✦ *She wanted to move, to take the initiative, to give him a big hug.* USAGE: often said about an effort to solve a problem: *Parents need to take the initiative with their children's after-school programs.*

inquire

inquire into *sth*
to try to discover the facts or truth of something ✦ *She thought the committee had no right to inquire into her politics.* ✦ Related vocabulary **look into sth** at LOOK

ins

the ins and outs of *sth*
the details or facts about something ✦ *In a matter of weeks we all became experts in the ins and outs of airline security.* ✦ *Hong was still learning the ins and outs of the North American market.*

inside

know *sth* inside out
to know everything about something ✦ *I know this machine inside out.*

turn *sth* inside out
to change something completely; = **turn *sth* upside down** ✦ *It's as if everything I thought I knew about my family has been turned inside*

inside track

out. ♦ Related vocabulary **turn *sth* on its head** at HEAD

> ORIGIN: based on the literal meaning of **turn something inside out** (= put the inside part of something on the outside)

inside track
have the inside track
to have an advantage in a competitive situation ♦ *Of the three advisors, Maddie may have the inside track because her personality fits perfectly with the president's.* ♦ *In this year's election, we've got the inside track, and the horse on the inside track is me.*

> ORIGIN: based on the **inside curve** of the track for horse races, which is not as long as the outer part and gives an advantage to the horse running in that position

insult
add insult to injury
to make a bad situation worse ♦ *The airline charged me extra for checking in a bike and then added insult to injury by charging me for a box to pack it in.*

intent
intent on *doing sth*
determined to do something ♦ *She seems intent on specializing in family law.*

intents
for all intents and purposes, *also* **to all intents and purposes**
almost completely; = **pretty much** ♦ *Escape from that prison was, for all intents and purposes, impossible.* ♦ *A licensed physician's assistant is to all intents and purposes a doctor.*

interference
run interference
to turn attention away from something ♦ *She wanted a minute alone with him to say goodbye, so her sister ran interference for her with the other guests.* ♦ *Buddy ran interference with his parents to keep them from finding out that Tom was a bit drunk.*

interim
in the interim
during this period ♦ *It's been five years since the band released a new album, but in the interim they've been touring a lot.*

iron
iron out *sth*, *also* **iron *sth* out**
to solve all problems that are still left ♦ *The two sides need to keep talking until they iron out their differences.*

> ORIGIN: based on the literal meaning of **iron out** small folds in cloth (= to use a small, heated device to make cloth smooth)

pump iron
to use special equipment to strengthen your muscles ♦ *The ads show people of all ages pumping iron.*

strike while the iron is hot
take action immediately in order to have a better chance of success ♦ *When you have a customer on the phone, strike while the iron is hot by offering special discounts on certain items.*

irons
several irons in the fire
a number of jobs or possibilities available at the same time ♦ *Job counselors recommend keeping several irons in the fire when you're looking for work.* USAGE: also used in the forms **a lot of** or **many irons in the fire**

irregardless
irregardless of *sth* esp. spoken
without being influenced by something; = **regardless of *sth*** ♦ *If you come to this country and commit a crime, I think that irregardless of whether you're now a citizen, you should be deported.* USAGE: not considered standard English

tickle the ivories

Bridget just loves to tickle the ivories.

is

as it is esp. spoken
actually ♦ *Our children are overscheduled and overworked as it is.*

that is (to say)
what I really mean is ♦ *I should be at the airport by seven, that is, unless there's a lot of traffic.*

issue

at issue slightly formal
1 not decided ♦ *At issue is whether Linda broke state law by secretly tapping conversations.*
2 in disagreement ♦ *What is at issue is how the organization spends its money.*

take issue with *sb*
to disagree with someone or something ♦ *I take issue with people who say it is unpatriotic to criticize our government.* ♦ *Thorogood took issue with the story that he had a drinking problem, calling it a nasty rumor.*

it

with it slang
aware of popular ideas and fashions ♦ *She always prided herself on being with it.*

ivories

tickle the ivories
to play the piano ♦ *She writes and produces her own music, and also tickles the ivories on her new album.*
USAGE: usually refers to playing the piano informally rather than in a concert

ORIGIN: from the literal meaning of **ivories** (= piano keys)

J, j

jack
jacked up on *sth*
made very excited and enthusiastic ♦ *My kids love to spend an afternoon at the video arcade with hundreds of other screaming kids jacked up on cola and pizza.*

jack up *sth*, also **jack** *sth* **up**
to increase something steeply ♦ *Credit card companies have jacked up interest rates on most of their accounts.* ♦ *The company decided to jack up the amount of protein in its animal feed.*

> ORIGIN: based on the literal meaning of **jack up something** (= to raise something using a special device called a jack)

jackpot
hit the jackpot
to succeed ♦ *I think we hit the jackpot with our ad campaign because our sales have nearly doubled.*

> ORIGIN: based on the meaning of **jackpot** (= a large amount of money you can win in a game)

jaw
***your* jaw drops**
to show great surprise ♦ *My jaw dropped when I heard she'd been admitted to Harvard.*

jazz
jazz up *sth*, also **jazz** *sth* **up**
to make something more interesting, exciting, or stylish ♦ *She uses a basic recipe and jazzes it up with chocolate chips, apples, or bananas.* ♦ *My daughters think I should jazz up my wardrobe.*

jeopardy
in jeopardy
in danger ♦ *It worries me that the money for these projects is in jeopardy, and I wonder what we will do if there is no money.* ♦ *Fiona's injury put her basketball career in jeopardy.*

jerk
jerk *sb* **around**
to deceive someone about whether or not you intend to do something ♦ *They've been jerking us around for a long time, first by not offering us a contract or then by saying they won't sign one.*

jerk off rude slang
to rub your sex organs with your hand ♦ *The only naked male I saw before I got married was a farm worker jerking off in a barn.*

jest
in jest
as a joke ♦ *He called me stupid, then said it was all in jest and he felt really bad about it.*

jewel
the jewel in the crown
the best or most valuable thing in a group ♦ *This college is the jewel in the crown of the city's university.*

job
fall down on the job
to fail to do something that you were expected to do ♦ *Someone fell down on the job and didn't catch the obvious mistakes in the ad.*

do the job
to achieve the desired result; = **do the trick** ♦ *I needed to tie the two parts together and an old stocking did the job perfectly.* USAGE: an object, tool, or other thing, but not a person, is what does the job

on the job
1 while working ♦ *Glass is always checking his workers to be sure they're wearing hard-hats on the job.*
2 ready and able to work ♦ *Just put the CD into the slot, click "Install" and the program will install itself*

join

join in
to take part with others in an activity ◆ *We play touch football on Saturdays if the weather is good, so bring sneakers with you and join in.*

join up
to become a member of the military ◆ *Levy joined up in World War II, received his citizenship and ended up a corporal in the combat engineers.*

joined at the hip See at HIP

join hands (with *sb***)** See at HANDS

join the ranks of *sth* See at RANKS

joke

no joke
a serious matter ◆ *It's no joke when a virus eats your computer files.* ◆ Related vocabulary **no laughing matter** at MATTER

play a joke (on *sb***)**
to do something that makes someone look foolish ◆ *Richard called and said I had won ten thousand dollars, and it took me a second to realize he was playing a joke on me.*

take a joke
to accept it with good humor when others make fun of you ◆ *He has a great sense of humor and isn't so self-important that he can't take a joke.* USAGE: usually used in the negative

Joneses

keep up with the Joneses
to have all the same things as other people to avoid looking poor or old-fashioned ◆ *In this neighborhood, keeping up with the Joneses has become an art form.*

joy

jump for joy
to show great happiness or excitement ◆ *The blood tests so far show my mother doesn't have cancer, but it's still too early to jump for joy because she has to have more tests.*

judgment

against *your* **better judgment**
not the best decision you believe you could make ◆ *I wasn't surprised when Scott's business failed because I had lent him the money for it against my better judgment.*

pass judgment on *sb/sth*
to express a strong opinion about someone or something ◆ *Don't pass judgment on the exhibit until you've seen it for yourself.* USAGE: the opinion is usually not likely to be changed

sit in judgment (of *sb***)**
1 to decide whether someone is guilty or not guilty of something ◆ *The men and women who sit in judgment of the bomber can decide whether or not he is put to death for his crime.*
2 to decide whether someone is good or bad ◆ *There is a committee that sits in judgment of every job applicant, and they can be very harsh.* USAGE: sometimes used to suggest that someone sitting in judgment should not be: *How can they sit in judgment of anyone when they have so little experience?*

sit in judgment (of *sth***)**
to decide whether something is good or bad ◆ *I should probably not be allowed to sit in judgment of movies made for teens.*

jugular

go for the jugular
to attack fiercely in order to have no doubt about winning ◆ *He was a politician known as someone who went for the jugular of his opponent.* ◆ Related vocabulary **play hardball** at HARDBALL

> ORIGIN: from the idea that an animal often kills another animal by biting the **jugular vein** (= tube that carries blood) in the neck, causing the animal to bleed to death quickly

juice

juice up *sth*, *also* **juice** *sth* **up**
to make something more interesting or exciting ◆ *The team's new forward has juiced up their games with fast passing and running.* ◆ *She finds songs no one remembers and juices them up with modern rhythms.*

jump

get a jump on *sb/sth*, *also* **get the jump on** *sb/sth*
to get an advantage over other people by doing something before they do ◆ *Job listings are updated continuously on our website, so you can get a jump on your competition.*

jump all over *sb*, *also* **jump on** *sb*
to criticize someone severely ◆ *I know that some lawyers will jump all over me for agreeing with the prosecutors.*

jump at *sth*
to quickly and eagerly accept an opportunity; = **leap at** *sth* ◆ *She jumped at every invitation she got to speak about her discovery.* USAGE: often used in the form **jump at the chance**: *She jumped at the chance to go to Paris.*

jump in
to become involved in something very quickly ◆ *I made a big mistake when I jumped in the middle of the discussion.* ◆ Related vocabulary **jump in with both feet** at FEET

jury

the jury is still out
no decision has been made, esp. because information is lacking ◆ *The jury is still out on whether those particular chemicals pose a threat to public health.*

just

just now
a short time ago ◆ *I came from a meeting just now where the governor said he would veto the proposed law.*

just so
very ◆ *The salmon is just so beautifully pink when it's fresh.* ◆ *I love being in Europe because the way of life there is just so pleasant.*

would just as soon
to prefer to ◆ *I'd just as soon work at home and not have the hassle of the subway every morning.*

justice

do justice to *sb/sth*, *also* **do** *sb/sth* **justice**
to treat or present someone or something fairly and accurately ◆ *He supports his case with very technical information and it is impossible to do justice to it here.* ◆ *To do them justice, George and Nell did all they could to keep the puppet theater going.*

K, k

kaboodle
the whole kaboodle See **the whole kit and caboodle** at KIT

keel
keel over
1 to fall down suddenly because of illness or weakness ◆ *Working outside in this heat, she was afraid someone would keel over.*
2 *slang* ◆ to die suddenly ◆ *The old man simply keeled over on the sidewalk from a heart attack, I suppose.*

> ORIGIN: based on the idea of a boat that **keels over** (= turns over) with its **keel** (= bottom) up

keep
keep abreast of *sth*
to have the most recent information about something; = **stay abreast of** *sth* ◆ *This new service helps doctors keep abreast of the newest drugs available.*

keep after *sb/sth*
to continually remind someone to do something ◆ *She kept after her former husband's lawyer with letters and phone calls but still didn't receive a response.*

keep at *sth*
to continue to do something ◆ *It wasn't easy to learn to skate, but I kept at it, and finally I could skate decently enough.*

keep *sb* down
1 to make someone discouraged ◆ *The loss of his job has really kept him down.*
2 to not advance someone ◆ *Why would someone so capable be kept down by his superiors?*

keep *sth* down, *also* keep down *sth*
1 to not vomit food or liquid ◆ *I was sick most of the day and couldn't keep anything down.*
2 to prevent something from increasing ◆ *We need to keep down our costs.*

keep (*you*) from *doing sth*
to prevent you from doing something ◆ *We couldn't keep ourselves from laughing.* ◆ *Even the mounting phone bills didn't keep him from calling her twice a day.*

keep *sth* from *you*
to prevent you from learning about something ◆ *He's seriously ill, and I don't think it's right to keep it from the children.*

keep *you* guessing
to cause you to be uncertain ◆ *I really enjoy a good mystery story that keeps me guessing the whole time.*

keep it down
to make less noise ◆ *Is it possible for you boys to keep it down?*

keep *you* posted
to make sure you know what is happening ◆ *The doctors kept me posted about her condition.* USAGE: usually refers to a situation that is quickly changing

keep quiet (about *sth*)
to not talk about something ◆ *You know you can trust me to keep quiet.* ◆ *The governor has kept quiet about raising taxes.*

keep to *sth*
1 to continue to do something ◆ *They keep wondering how she keeps to a schedule of 200 concerts a year at her age.*
2 to continue to follow something ◆ *It is difficult to keep to your beliefs.*

keep to *yourself*
to often avoid other people ◆ *He kept to himself and remained a mystery to his neighbors.*

keep *sth* to *yourself*
to not tell anyone something ◆ *He kept his business completely to himself, and even his wife didn't know he was a spy all those years.*

keeping

keep up (with *sb/sth*)
1 to stay level or equal with someone or something ◆ *I'm too old or too tired and I just can't keep up.* ◆ *The little boy tried very hard to keep up with his older brother's accomplishments.*
2 to move as quickly as someone else ◆ *I have short legs, and I almost had to run to keep up.*

keep *sb* up, *also* keep up *sb*
to cause someone to stay awake ◆ *I hope I'm not keeping you up.* ◆ *You're making so much noise, you're going to keep up the whole neighborhood!*

keep up *sth*, *also* keep *sth* up
to continue to do or have something ◆ *Keep up the good work.* ◆ *Even though he lost his job, they managed to keep up an expensive lifestyle.* ◆ *I have a great relationship with my children now, and I'm doing my best to keep that up.*

keeping

in keeping with *sth* slightly formal
1 because of something ◆ *There will be no flowers at the funeral, in keeping with the family's wishes.*
2 suited to something ◆ *The new windows are in keeping with the colonial style of the house.*

keeps

for keeps
yours forever ◆ *When I give someone a present, it's for keeps.*

play for keeps
to do something with very serious concern about the results ◆ *These bargaining sessions are most difficult because both sides are playing for keeps.* ◆ *In many New York publishing houses, softball is played for keeps.*

keyed

keyed up
nervous or excited ◆ *The interview went well today but now I'm too keyed up to sleep.*

kibosh

put the kibosh on *sth*
to prevent an activity from happening ◆ *They had planned a two-day, 150-mile bike ride but bad weather put the kibosh on it.*

kick

a kick in the butt, *also* a kick in the pants
forceful encouragement to do something ◆ *She knows when we need a kick in the butt to get this done right.* ◆ *Luckily, you can add memory and give your computer a real kick in the pants without spending a ton of money.* ◆ Related vocabulary **a pat on the back** at PAT

get a kick out of *sth* esp. spoken
to enjoy something very much; = **get a charge out of *sth*** ◆ *This book is just the kind you like and you'll get a real kick out of it.*

kick *yourself*
to be annoyed with yourself ◆ *I could have kicked myself when I realized that all that work was a complete waste of time.*

kick around
to exist ◆ *She is one of the most creative people kicking around advertising today.*

kick *sb* around, *also* kick around *sb*
to treat someone badly ◆ *When his boss didn't promote him, he felt as if he'd been kicked around long enough, and he finally quit.* ◆ *He represents every big guy that's ever kicked around a little guy.*

kick *sth* around, *also* kick around *sth*
to discuss something ◆ *I don't know who will be on the committee, but we've kicked a lot of names around.* ◆ *Black intellectuals have been kicking around the idea since the beginning of the twentieth century.*

kick back
1 to do less ◆ *It's time to kick back and relax.*
2 to return something ◆ *My editor*

kicked back the first draft of the article and asked me to make some changes. ♦ Related vocabulary **let yourself go**, at LET

kick in
1 to start operating or happening ♦ *We still don't know why the emergency generator failed to kick in when the power failed.*
2 to provide money ♦ *The mayor persuaded local firms to kick in the money to start the scholarship fund.*

kick off *sth*
to begin something ♦ *We like to kick off the summer by having friends over for a barbecue.*

kick *sb* off *sth* slang
to force someone to leave a group ♦ *Fred was difficult to work with and finally we kicked him off the planning committee.* ♦ *He was kicked off the team.*

kick *sb* out (of *somewhere*) slang
to tell someone to leave a place ♦ *They kicked us out of the gym because it was needed for a basketball game.* ♦ *When the principal caught Lisa smoking in the bathroom, she was kicked out.* USAGE: usually someone is **kicked out** for doing something wrong, as in the second example

kick ass See at ASS
kick butt See at BUTT
kick the bucket See at BUCKET
kick the habit See at HABIT
kick up a stink See at STINK
kick up *your* heels See at HEELS

kid

kid around
to joke with someone ♦ *At the end of the show, the dancers kidded around with the audience and tried to get them to dance.*

the new kid on the block
a recent arrival ♦ *The Internet is still the new kid on the block in communications technologies.*

kidding
***you* have got to be kidding** esp. spoken, *also* ***you* must be kidding**
I am very surprised and cannot believe you are serious ♦ *You want me to drive into the city in this rain? You've got to be kidding.*

no kidding esp. spoken
really or honestly ♦ *No kidding, there must have been at least twenty thousand people at the festival.*

kid gloves
treat *sb* with kid gloves, *also* **handle *sb* with kid gloves**
to deal with someone very gently or carefully ♦ *While he treated writers with kid gloves, he was unpleasant to everyone else.*

> ORIGIN: based on the literal meaning of **kid gloves** (= gloves made of very soft, smooth leather)

kill

in for the kill
intending the complete destruction of someone or something ♦ *The president promised not to raise taxes, and now that they've been raised, his political enemies are moving in for the kill.* USAGE: used with **move**, **close**, **swoop**, and other verbs meaning move

> ORIGIN: based on the literal meaning of **in for the kill** (= involved in the death of an animal)

dressed to kill See at DRESSED
kill time See at TIME
kill two birds with one stone See at BIRDS
kill *sb* with kindness See at KINDNESS

killing

make a killing
to quickly earn a lot of money ♦ *Street vendors should make a killing today selling souvenirs.*

kilter

out of kilter
1 not working well or not in good condition; = **out of whack** ♦ *Going just one night without sleep throws me out of kilter for a couple of days afterward.* ♦ *She wasn't behaving normally – her sense of humor was out of kilter.*
2 not matching; = **out of whack** ♦ *His fancy new home seems slightly out of kilter with his plain, quiet image.*

kind

in kind
with the same thing ♦ *It was a nasty letter, but I will not respond in kind.*

> ORIGIN: based on **payment in kind** (= paying for something with food or things or work rather than money)

kind of
to some degree; = **sort of** ♦ *I try to dress kind of nicely for work.* ♦ *I guess I kind of forget to thank her for all she does for me.*

one of a kind
the only item of a particular type ♦ *He was an extraordinary person – absolutely one of a kind.*

two of a kind
very similar; = **(like) two peas in a pod** ♦ *Where books are concerned, Tyler and Chloë are two of a kind.*

kindly

not take kindly to sb/sth
to not be pleased by someone or something ♦ *He did not take kindly to instruction or advice.* ♦ *Society did not take kindly to women who wanted a career in those days.*

kindness

kill sb with kindness
to get what you want by being very kind to another person ♦ *While most coaches can be very tough, ours kills his players with kindness.*

kiss

kiss and make up
to become friendly again after arguing ♦ *Why can't we kiss and make up? I don't want us to be angry.*

kiss and tell
to publicly discuss private information about someone you know well

one of a kind

These chess pieces are one of a kind, each set carved and painted by hand.

♦ She doesn't kiss and tell, not even in her new memoir. USAGE: often said about published information about someone famous

kiss *sth* goodbye, *also* **kiss goodbye *sth***
1 to lose something ♦ *If you lend him money, you should just kiss it goodbye.*
2 to end something ♦ *We began to argue all the time, so I kissed another relationship goodbye.* ♦ *You can kiss goodbye any hopes you had of winning the lottery.*

kiss off
go away ♦ *She finally decided to tell her boss to kiss off.*

kiss off *sb/sth* slang, *also* **kiss *sb/sth* off**
to get rid of someone or something ♦ *The company plans to kiss off three thousand employees next month.* ♦ *If you raise prices, you'll just be kissing your customers off.*

kit

the whole kit and caboodle, *also* **the whole kit 'n' caboodle**
everything ♦ *We had to pack up the whole kit and caboodle before the movers arrived.* USAGE: also used in the shorter forms **the whole kit** or **the whole caboodle**, and sometimes spelled **kaboodle**

kitchen sink

everything but the kitchen sink
almost all that you can imagine of something ♦ *Here's a website that simply has everything but the kitchen sink.*

ORIGIN: based on the idea that if you brought many things to someone, a kitchen sink is one of the last things you would bring because it is difficult to move

knee

at *sb's* knee
from someone older when you were young ♦ *His father was a programmer in the early days of computers,* *and Briggs learned all about them at his dad's knee.*

ORIGIN: based on the idea of a child standing next to or being the height of someone's knee

on bended knee
like a servant ♦ *The governors have to ask on bended knee for more money from Washington to pay for increased security.*

knees

bring *you/sth* to *your/its* knees
to defeat or stop someone or something ♦ *Severe oil shortages could bring our economy to its knees.* ♦ *They played a great game and brought our local basketball champs to their knees.*

on *your/its* knees
not operating well ♦ *Many retail stores are already on their knees and some might have to close.*

knife

twist the knife, *also* **turn the knife**
to do or say something to make a situation worse ♦ *He caused McCarthy to make a fool of himself, and then twisted the knife by asking, "Have you no decency, sir?"* USAGE: also used in the form **a twist of the knife**: *When discussing the union, even when he starts by saying positive things George can never resist a twist of the knife.*

under the knife
having a medical operation ♦ *I wouldn't go under the knife just to improve my appearance.* USAGE: most often used with the verbs **go** or **be**, as in the example

knight

a knight in shining armor
someone who helps you when you are in a difficult situation ♦ *She was looking for a knight in shining armor who might save her from*

knock

her boring life. USAGE: usually said by a woman about a man

> ORIGIN: in medieval times (= 500 to 1500 C.E.), knights were soldiers on horses who were also supposed to help and protect women

knock

knock *sb* dead
to do something so well or look so attractive, other people admire you a lot ◆ *Whenever Ella sang at a small club, she knocked 'em dead.*

knock *sth* down, *also* **knock down *sth***
1 to show that an idea or opinion is completely wrong ◆ *He knocked down my business plan, saying I couldn't raise the money to do it.* ◆ *Every time I make a suggestion, you knock it down.*
2 to reduce the price of something or the amount you want for something ◆ *He usually charges $50, but he knocked it down to $40.* ◆ *He wanted $300 for the ring, but we got him to knock down the price.*

> ORIGIN: based on the literal meaning of **knock something down** (= to cause a structure to fall)

knock it off esp. spoken
to stop doing something that annoys you ◆ *The boys were making too much noise, so I told them to knock it off.* USAGE: usually used as an order: *Knock it off! I'm tired of your teasing.*

knock off (*sth*)
to stop work for a time ◆ *When do you knock off for the day?* ◆ *We knocked off work at six o'clock.*

knock *sth* off, *also* **knock off *sth***
1 to subtract a certain amount from the price of an item ◆ *The manager knocked two bucks off because the dress had a button missing.* ◆ *If you knock off five dollars, I'd consider buying it.*
2 to produce something quickly and easily ◆ *He can usually knock off a short story in just a few days.*

knock *sb* out, *also* **knock out *sb***
1 to hit someone so that they become unconscious ◆ *His fall from the ladder knocked him out.*
2 to cause someone to go to sleep ◆ *I didn't realize those pills would knock me out.*
3 to remove someone from a competition ◆ *A loss in today's game will knock us out of the playoffs.*

knock *sb*/*yourself* out
to make someone very tired ◆ *Pat has really knocked herself out cooking this dinner.* ◆ *All that shopping has knocked me out!*

knock *sth* out, *also* **knock out *sth***
1 to destroy something ◆ *Enemy aircraft have knocked out 25 tanks.*
2 to cause something to stop working ◆ *The lightning knocked out our electricity.*

knock *sb* up slang, *also* **knock up *sb***
to make a woman pregnant ◆ *The rumor was that he'd knocked up two women in the town.*

knock yourself out
please begin doing it ◆ *If you want to make hotel and airline and car reservations and take care of everything, well, then, knock yourself out.* USAGE: usually said to show you are unhappy with someone who has complained about your efforts

knock *sb* off *their* feet See at FEET
knock (on) wood See at WOOD
knock *your* socks off See at SOCKS

knot

tie the knot
to get married ◆ *She's planning to tie the knot with her German boyfriend next June.*

knots

tie *sb* (up) in knots, *also* **tie *sb* into knots**
to cause someone to become very confused or worried ◆ *They tied themselves up in knots over the seat-*

ing arrangements for the party. ◆ The possibility of layoffs in Joe's department has tied him into knots.

know

before *you* know it
surprisingly quickly; = **before you can say *sth*** ◆ *I saw a rabbit in the field, but it was gone before I knew it.*

(do you) know something esp. spoken
are you aware of something ◆ *You know something? Drinking and driving don't mix!* ◆ *Know something? I'm pretty disgusted with you!*

in the know
having more information about something than most other people ◆ *People in the know go there for the best skiing in the east.*

know *sth* backwards and forwards, *also* **know *sth* inside out**
to be extremely well informed about something ◆ *After 30 years in the fashion business, she knows it backwards and forwards.* ◆ *He knows New York inside out.* ◆ Related vocabulary **know *sth* like the back of *your* hand** at BACK

know best
to have opinions that should be accepted and respected ◆ *Mom knows best when it comes to judging a person's character.* USAGE: used to suggest that such opinions are based on greater knowledge and experience than other people have

know better (than to *do sth*)
1 to be wise enough to behave in a more responsible or acceptable way ◆ *It was a stupid thing to do, and I thought she knew better.* ◆ *You know better than to interrupt when someone else is talking.* USAGE: sometimes used in the form **not know any better**: *Doesn't she know any better than to wear jeans to a place like this?*
2 to be wise enough to know that you should not believe someone or something ◆ *The guy who was try-*

ing to sell us the car said it was in great condition, but I knew better.

know different, *also* **know otherwise**
to realize that certain information or an opinion is not correct ◆ *Some people might say the job is easy, but I know different.*

know of *sb/sth*
to have information about someone or something ◆ *Do you know of a way to remove this stain?* ◆ *We've never met, but I certainly know of him.* USAGE: also used in the spoken phrase **not that I know of** (= I do not know): *"Is he home yet?" "Not that I know of."*

know what *you* are doing
to have the necessary knowledge or experience to do something ◆ *Mountain climbing is a dangerous sport, so I hope he knows what he's doing.*

know what *you* are talking about
to speak in an informed way because of your experience or education ◆ *He doesn't know what he's talking about. He's never even been to Alaska.*

know where *you* stand
1 to be certain of what someone thinks ◆ *He didn't even send me a birthday card, so now I know where I stand.*
2 to be certain of your position ◆ *In the old days, the editor was the dictator, and all the employees knew where they stood.*

not know if *you* are coming or going, *also* **not know whether *you* are coming or going**
to be confused or unable to control something that is happening to you ◆ *I am so busy packing everything to move, I don't know if I'm coming or going. It's scary.*

not know what hit *you*
to be shocked and confused by something surprising ◆ *When Nancy said she wanted a divorce, I*

knuckle

didn't know what hit me. USAGE: usually said about something bad, and often used in the form **before someone knows what hit them**: *We'll have the handcuffs on them before they know what hit them.*

not know where to turn, *also* **not know which way to turn**
to not know what to do ◆ *I was at a time in my life when I had no money and didn't know where to turn.*

not know whether to laugh or cry
to be very upset by something ridiculous ◆ *When they announced that my flight was delayed for ten hours, I didn't know whether to laugh or cry.*

what do you know esp. spoken
this is surprising ◆ *What do you know! Joan has quit her job and moved to Mexico.* USAGE: often used humorously to mean you are not surprised: *Well, what do you know – the Raiders lost again.*

you know esp. spoken
you understand ◆ *She was cleaning, you know, when the police called to tell her about the accident.* USAGE: usually used to be sure someone is listening carefully and agrees with what you are saying: *It didn't have to happen that way, you know?*

knuckle

knuckle down
to work hard ◆ *You're going to have to knuckle down to improve your grades if you want to get into a good college.* ◆ *Volunteers really knuckled down and cleaned up the town after the storm.*

knuckle under (to *sb/sth*)
to accept unwillingly what someone or something demands ◆ *We want to reach an agreement, but we won't knuckle under to their demands.* ◆ Related vocabulary **give in (to *sb/sth*)** at GIVE

L, l

labor
a labor of love
work that you do because it brings you great pleasure ♦ *Most of Earl's businesses make money, but this one is just a labor of love.*

lag
lag behind (*sb/sth*)
to not be at the level that someone or something else has already achieved ♦ *The pay for government workers lags behind the pay for workers in private industry.* ♦ *He lagged far behind his classmates in reading and math skills.*

> ORIGIN: based on the literal meaning of **lag behind** (= to not walk as quickly as your companions)

lam
on the lam
moving from place to place to avoid being found or caught ♦ *She got in trouble in the '70s and was captured after 23 years on the lam.* USAGE: usually said about someone who is avoiding the police ♦ Related vocabulary **on the run** at RUN

land
how the land lies
the way a situation has been arranged or has developed; = **the lay of the land** ♦ *After a few days on the job, I began to understand how the land lies and which people would be helpful.*

land of milk and honey
an imaginary place where there is more than enough of everything ♦ *She came to the United States thinking it was the land of milk and honey.*

> ORIGIN: from the Bible story in which the Lord promises to bring the Israelites out of Egypt and into a land flowing with milk and honey

land on *your* feet See at FEET

language
speak the same language, *also* **speak *sb's* language**
to share similar beliefs and opinions ♦ *Environmentalists and developers don't speak the same language.* ♦ *When we got down to planning where to go on our trip, I was glad we spoke the same language.*

lap
fall into *your* lap, *also* **drop into *your* lap**
to come to you without you making any effort ♦ *You can't expect the ideal job to just fall into your lap – you've got to go out there and look for it.*

lap up *sth*, *also* **lap *sth* up
1 to enjoy something very much ♦ *My dogs lap up whatever attention I can give them.* ♦ Related vocabulary **eat it up** at EAT
2 to believe what is said or written without knowing or caring if it is true ♦ *Even if you're lying, there's always someone who will lap it up because most people want to believe you.*

> ORIGIN: based on the literal meaning of **lap up** (= to eat with great enthusiasm)

large
at large
1 most of ♦ *The public at large doesn't take the problem seriously.* ♦ Related vocabulary **in general** at GENERAL
2 not in prison ♦ *Police arrested one man, but the other suspects in the robbery are still at large.*

by and large
mostly or generally; = **for the most part** ♦ *By and large, the people I'm talking about are Internet users.* ♦ *There are a few things that I don't like about my job, but by and large it's just fine.*

in large part See at PART
larger than life See at LIFE
living large See at LIVING
loom large See at LOOM
writ large See at WRIT

lash
lash out (at *sb/sth*)
to angrily criticize someone or something ◆ *The mayor often lashes out at people who don't agree with him.* USAGE: usually criticism of an opinion or statement

last
at (long) last
after much delay ◆ *The line of traffic began to move at last.* ◆ Related vocabulary **(it's) about time** at TIME, **it is high time** at HIGH TIME

before last
before the most recent ◆ *The year before last, we moved to the farm.* USAGE: used with periods of time, such as **the day, the night, the week, the month, the year**

hear the last of *sb/sth*, also see **the last of *sb/sth***
to not have to deal with someone or something again ◆ *It's uncertain whether we've heard the last of the harassment case.* ◆ *Few believe Northern Ireland has seen the last of its troubles.*

last but not least
important, despite being mentioned at the end ◆ *The mall has sports and shoe and clothing stores and, last but not least, plenty of terrific places to eat.*

breathe your last See at BREATHE
every last See at EVERY
have the last laugh See at LAUGH
on its last legs See at LEGS
the last minute See at MINUTE
the last word in *sth* See at WORD

latch
latch onto *sb/sth*
to become closely connected to someone or something ◆ *I knew she would be perfect in the film, so I latched onto her like a magnet.* ◆ *More and more countries latched onto computer technology as an important tool for development.*

late
of late slightly formal
recently ◆ *She hasn't been feeling well of late.*

a day late and a dollar short See at DAY

better late than never See at BETTER

late in the day See at DAY
too little, too late See at LITTLE

latest
at the latest
no later than a particular time ◆ *We expect to reach Rome by Wednesday at the latest.* USAGE: used after the time or day

laugh
a laugh a minute
very funny and entertaining ◆ *Paul's clever screenplay makes this new comedy a laugh a minute.* USAGE: often used humorously to mean the opposite: *Any meeting with a school principal has to be a laugh a minute.*

have the last laugh
to succeed when others thought you would not ◆ *The company fired her last year but she had the last laugh because she was hired by their main rival at twice the salary.* USAGE: sometimes used with **get**: *She said I'd never make it to college, but I got the last laugh.*

laugh at *sb*
to ridicule someone ◆ *A lot of kids laughed at me because of the way I dressed, but it never bothered me.*

laugh at *sth*
to show you think something is ridiculous ◆ *Cynthia laughs at the suggestion she's doing this job for the money.*

laugh off *sth*, *also* **laugh** *sth* **off**
to act as if something is not important to you ♦ *It's not easy to laugh off an insult.* ♦ *She criticizes his work constantly but he doesn't get angry, he just laughs it off.*

laugh all the way to the bank See at WAY

no laughing matter See at MATTER

not know whether to laugh or cry See at KNOW

launch

launch into *sb*
to criticize someone severely ♦ *He launched into me for not having called or e-mailed in a long time.*

launch into *sth*
to start something with energy or enthusiasm ♦ *She launched into the song as if she couldn't hold herself back.* ♦ *He launched into an attack on all the people who had laughed at his idea.*

laurels

rest on *your* **laurels**
to be so satisfied with your achievements that you make no effort to improve ♦ *Even though you did well on all your exams, you can't simply rest on your laurels.*

ORIGIN: based on the literal meaning of **laurels** (= a ring of leaves worn on the head in ancient times as a symbol of victory)

law

above the law
not having to obey laws or rules ♦ *Football players can't be above the law just because they are so valuable to team owners.*

a law unto *yourself*
a person who does things differently and ignores the usual rules ♦ *The male characters in her novels are usually attractive, powerful, and dangerous – a law unto themselves.*

lay down the law
to tell people what they must do, without caring about their opinions ♦ *I'm not going to let some new guy come into my office and start laying down the law.* ♦ *Riley laid down the law, telling his players, "We're going to play the game my way."* ♦ Related vocabulary **read** *sb* **the riot act** at RIOT ACT

take the law into *your* **own hands**
to do something illegal in order to punish someone ♦ *Her mother took the law into her own hands when she heard that her child had been abused.* ♦ *She decided to take the law into her own hands and rescue the dog from its owner, who beat it.* USAGE: usually said about someone who does something because they believe that the authorities will not take action ♦ Related vocabulary **take** *sth* **into** *your* **own hands** at HANDS

in the eyes of the law See at EYES

on the wrong side of the law See at SIDE

the long arm of the law See at ARM

sb's **word is law** See at WORD

lay

lay aside *sth*, *also* **lay** *sth* **aside**
to ignore something or decide that it is not important ♦ *Our neighbors laid aside their personal safety to help us save our animals from the fire.* ♦ Related vocabulary **set aside** *sth* 2 at SET

lay bare *sth* slightly formal, *also* **lay** *sth* **bare**
to make something obvious that was not known before ♦ *Her story lays bare the conflicts between two ambitious brothers.* ♦ *The trial was the first to lay bare the secrets of the organization.* ♦ Related vocabulary **bare** *your* **soul** at SOUL

lay down *sth*, *also* **lay** *sth* **down**
to say or write something plainly ♦ *The coach laid down the rules for all*

team members, including being at every practice and getting eight hours sleep. ◆ Related vocabulary **set down** *sth* at SET

lay into *sb*
to attack someone physically or with words ◆ *First the two kids just yelled but soon they laid into each other with hard punches.* ◆ *My sister really laid into me for borrowing her dress without asking first.*

lay into *sth*
to eat something quickly and with pleasure ◆ *Both hikers laid into a huge dinner with great enthusiasm.*

lay *sb* **low**
to make someone weak or extremely sad ◆ *The death of her father really laid her low.* ◆ *Paul was laid low by the flu for about a week.*

lay off (*sth***)**
to stop doing or using something ◆ *She usually runs several miles every day but lays off in the hot weather.*

lay *sb* **off**, *also* **lay off** *sb*
to force a worker to give up a job, usually because of high costs or other business reasons ◆ *She was laid off along with many others when the company moved to California.* ◆ *Our choices are to lay off ten workers, or raise our prices by 10%.*

lay *sth* **on** *sb*
to blame someone for something; = **lay** *sth* **at** *sb***'s door** ◆ *Don't lay that on me! I wasn't even there when it happened.*

lay *sb/sth* **open (to** *sth***)**
1 to put someone or something in a position where there is risk or danger ◆ *The Senator's remarks were thoughtless and laid him open to criticism.*
2 to create an opportunity ◆ *A string of victories laid the way open for our track team to compete in the regional championship.* ◆ Related vocabulary **pave the way for** *sb/sth* at WAY

lay out *sth*, *also* **lay** *sth* **out**
1 to plan or explain something very carefully and in great detail ◆ *Plans for the ceremony were laid out so well that everyone knew what they were to do.* ◆ *Let's review the points one more time before we lay them out for the press.*
2 to spend money ◆ *I can't believe he laid out $100 for flowers and $150 for two bottles of wine!* USAGE: often the amount of money seems like too much
3 to arrange something ◆ *First the pictures are approved by the editor, then the designer lays them out on pages.*

lay over
to stop or have to stay in a place when you are traveling ◆ *He laid over with a German family living in the area.* ◆ *People were getting laid over in Dallas because of the floods in Houston.*

lay *sb* **up**
to force someone to stay in bed or do very little ◆ *She's been laid up with the flu for a week.* ◆ *The accident laid him up with a broken leg.*

the lay of the land
the way a situation has been arranged or has developed; = **how the land lies** ◆ *If you see them together, you don't have to be a detective to understand the lay of the land.*

lead

lead *sb* **astray**
1 to influence someone in a negative way ◆ *Parents always worry that certain friends will lead their children astray.*
2 to cause someone to make a mistake ◆ *The police were led astray by some false information.* ◆ Related vocabulary **go astray** at GO

lead off (*sth***)**, *also* **lead** *sth* **off**
to begin something ◆ *The shootings led off a month-long gang war in the city.* ◆ *He led off the fourth inning*

with a home run. ◆ *I'd like to lead the evening off with a poem.*

lead *sb* on
to deceive someone in order to get what you want from them ◆ *She led him on for five months while she was going out with another guy.* ◆ Related vocabulary **toy with *sb*** at TOY

lead a double life See at LIFE

lead *sb* by the nose See at NOSE

lead *sb* down the garden path See at GARDEN PATH

lead the pack See at PACK

lead the way See at WAY

leaf

leaf through *sth*
to turn pages, briefly looking at them ◆ *We leafed through some old photo albums.* ◆ *The detective leafed through some papers on the desk, looking for clues to my father's disappearance.*

take a leaf out of *sb*'s book
to copy something that someone else has done ◆ *I should take a leaf out of Robert's book and start coming in at ten every morning – maybe then the boss will notice me!*

turn over a new leaf
to start behaving in a different way ◆ *Apparently he's turned over a new leaf and he's not drinking any more.* USAGE: usually suggesting an improvement in behavior ◆ Related vocabulary **turn the page** at PAGE

league

in league with *sb*
agreeing to do something with someone else ◆ *The accountant and the chairman were in league to hide the company's debts.* ◆ *I believe my children are in league with the devil!* USAGE: often said about an activity that is not completely legal or approved of

in the same league (as *sb/sth*), *also* **in the same league (with *sb/sth*)**
having qualities or achievements similar to someone or something else ◆ *The new foundation will be giving away $55 million a year, putting it in the same league as other well-known charities.* ◆ *You don't often get to hear two symphony orchestras that are in the same league within a single week.* USAGE: often used in the form **not in the same league**: *He's made a lot of money, but his net worth is not in the same league as that computer guy's.*

out of *your* league
1 doing something you are not prepared for ◆ *She was clearly out of her league, suddenly forced to finish a project she knew little about.*
2 not right for you ◆ *I think an expensive car is a little out of your league right now, don't you?*

leak

take a leak rude slang
to excrete urine ◆ *He could see the truck driver with his back to them, taking a leak against an old tree.* USAGE: usually said about men or boys, but sometimes said about an animal: *The dog ran under the trees and took a leak.*

lean

lean on *sb/sth*
1 to depend on someone or something ◆ *The children leaned on each other for help and comfort.* ◆ *Verplank leaned on his experience as a waiter to figure out how to behave when he met the prince.*
2 to put pressure on someone or something to get what you want ◆ *The Spanish teacher had to lean on the school principal to get new textbooks for the class.*

lean over backwards
to try very hard; = **bend over backwards** ◆ *She and her staff will lean over backwards to see that you are satisfied with their services.* USAGE: usually used to describe efforts to help or please someone ◆ Related vocabulary **fall all over *yourself* (to *do sth*)** at FALL

leap

leap at *sth*
to quickly and eagerly accept an opportunity; = **jump at** *sth* ♦ *I would leap at an opportunity to work for that organization.* USAGE: often used in the form **leap at the chance**: *I leaped at the chance to visit India.*

leaps

grow by leaps and bounds
to become larger quickly ♦ *Since we had that good rain, my tomatoes have grown by leaps and bounds.* ♦ *That boy has grown by leaps and bounds this year.*

lease

a new lease on life, *also* **a new lease of life**
an opportunity to be successful or happy after having experienced a series of difficulties ♦ *The heart operation was a complete success and has given her a new lease on life.*

leash

keep *sb* **on a tight leash**, *also* **keep** *sb* **on a short leash**
to allow someone very little freedom to do what they want ♦ *He doesn't go out with the guys much now that his girlfriend is around to keep him on a tight leash.* USAGE: sometimes used with **have**: *The police will have a tight leash on all the suspects until the trial.*

> ORIGIN: based on the literal meaning of **leash** (= a length of rope or leather used to prevent a dog or other animal from getting away)

least

at (the very) least
1 not less than ♦ *At least 73,000 homes are without power in the Atlanta area.* ♦ *The repair will cost $100 at the very least.* USAGE: always used with a particular amount or measure: *At the least, the room is 30 feet long.*
2 more exactly; = **at any rate** ♦ *I can handle it – at least, I think I can.* ♦ *The car was damaged, but at least no one was hurt.* USAGE: often used to make a statement sound less strong
3 whatever happens ♦ *At least Josh tried to apologize.* ♦ *At the very least, you should call to tell me that you've arrived there safely.* USAGE: the same meaning can be also expressed by **come hell or high water, come what may, either way, in any case**, and **in any event**

least of all
especially not ♦ *No one believed her, least of all me.*

not in the least
not in any way; = **not in the slightest** ♦ *"Is he bothering you?" "Not in the least."*

the least *you* **can do**, *also* **the least** *you* **could do**
something you should do ♦ *If Bob wants to apologize, the least you can do is listen.*

last but not least See at LAST

the path of least resistance See at PATH

to say the least See at SAY

leave

leave *sb* **alone**
to not annoy or interrupt someone; = **let** *sb* **alone** ♦ *If you just leave her alone she'll do the job right.*

leave *sth* **alone**
to not touch or be involved with something ♦ *Leave the bite alone and don't scratch it.*

leave *sb* **hanging**
to keep someone waiting for a decision or answer; = **(leave** *sb* **to) twist in the wind** ♦ *I was left hanging for three weeks before I got a call offering me the job.*

leave *sth* **hanging**
to delay making a decision about something ♦ *We don't know if we can buy the house yet because the bank left our loan application hanging.* ♦ Related vocabulary **up in the air** at AIR

leave *you* high and dry
to leave you alone and without any help ◆ *We were left high and dry, without any money or credit cards.*

leave it at that
to say or do no more about something ◆ *I've simply decided to quit – let's leave it at that.*

leave off (*doing sth*)
to stop doing something ◆ *Mr. Summers finally left off talking and returned to his seat.* ◆ *We'll pick up the story where we left off yesterday.*

leave off *sth*
to forget or omit something ◆ *All the names beginning with "R" were left off the list.*

leave *sth* open, also **leave open *sth***
to keep something available ◆ *I've left the evening of the 12th open, just in case you want to go out to dinner.* ◆ *We still have plenty of alternatives left open to us.* ◆ Related vocabulary **leave open the possibility of *sth*/*doing sth*** at POSSIBILITY

leave out *sb*/*sth*
to omit someone or something ◆ *You left out the best parts of the story.* ◆ *How many friends did you have to leave out of the guest list for the wedding?*

leave something to be desired
to be not very good or not as good as you would like; = **leave a lot to be desired** ◆ *And if you think my driving leaves something to be desired, his driving is even worse!*

leave well enough alone
to allow something to stay as it is because doing more would not improve it ◆ *I thought about rewriting the letter, but I decided to leave well enough alone.*

take leave, also **take a leave (of absence)**
to use time permitted to be away from work ◆ *For the first time fathers are allowed to take leave to care for new babies or for seriously ill children.* ◆ *Employees must tell employers ahead of time that they plan to take a leave under the Family and Medical Leave Act.*

take *your* leave
to go away from a gathering ◆ *Barlow could only manage a few brief words before taking his leave of this group of happy supporters.*

left

left and right
everywhere, without any plan or pattern ◆ *People are complaining left and right about the new parking regulations.*

left field

(way) out in left field
not effective, useful, or likely ◆ *Some of these ideas are from out in left field, and I can't imagine where my students get them from.*

out of left field
not expected or prepared for ◆ *A fierce storm came out of left field and surprised everyone.*

leg

a leg up (on *sb*/*sth*)
an advantage over someone or something ◆ *The new rules give businesses here a leg up on competition from other countries.*

not have a leg to stand on
to have no support for your position ◆ *The company settled the lawsuit because they did not have a leg to stand on.*

pull *sb*'s leg
to tell someone something that is not true as a way of joking with them ◆ *Is he really angry with me or do you think he's just pulling my leg?*

legs

have legs
to continue to be of interest ◆ *This latest scandal has legs – you'll probably still be reading about it in a year's time.*

on its last legs
about to stop working ◆ *We've had*

leisure 218

the same vacuum cleaner for twenty years now and it's on its last legs.

stretch *your* legs
to move around after having to be in one place or position for a long time ◆ *We drove there in five hours, including a couple of stops to stretch our legs.*

leisure

at (your) leisure
when you want to or are not busy; = **at *your* convenience** ◆ *Make a video of the program and then you can watch it at your leisure.* ◆ *Understanding what must be done now and what can be done at leisure is an important skill to learn.*

lend

lend itself to *sth*
to be good for a particular use ◆ *It was surprising how well her book lent itself to being turned into a film.*

lend a (helping) hand See at HAND

lend an ear to *sb/sth* See at EAR

length

keep *sb/sth* at arm's length, *also* **hold *sb/sth* at arm's length**
to avoid becoming connected with someone or something ◆ *We proposed a tax break for companies that treat their workers well, but lawmakers are keeping the idea at arm's length for now.* ◆ *She doesn't talk much about it because she needs to hold these painful experiences at arm's length.* ◆ Related vocabulary **keep *your* distance (from *sb/sth*)** at DISTANCE

> ORIGIN: from the literal meaning of **at arm's length** (= away from you by a distance equal to the length of your arm)

at length
1 for a long time ◆ *We have discussed at length the events that led to his suspension.*
2 after a period of time ◆ *At length, Nick realized that she was listening to the music more than she was listening to him.*

keep someone at arm's length

Aides like to keep anyone who opposes the mayor at arm's length.

lengths

go to great lengths to *do sth*
to try very hard to achieve a result ◆ *This champion marathon runner is going to great lengths to help needy children.* ◆ *Both sides have gone to great lengths to emphasize areas of similarity in their proposals.* ◆ Related vocabulary **take (great) pains to** *do sth* at PAINS

less

less than *sth*
not something ◆ *The weekend was less than wonderful, but parts of it were pretty good.* ◆ *The result was less than thrilling television – you could even call it boring.* USAGE: used to describe a quality you had expected or hoped for

no less
this is surprising to me, and must surprise you too ◆ *I happen to own the very same sweater – and in green, no less.* ◆ *They lost the first two games in a best-of-five series, and on their home field, no less.*

no less than *sb/sth*
this very important person or organization ◆ *Carroll is the most entertaining talk-show host on TV – no less than "Entertainment Weekly" said so.* ◆ *Almost two dozen representatives flew in for meetings with top officials, including no less than the country's president.*

nothing less than *sth*
strongly showing this quality; = **nothing short of** *sth* ◆ *The violinist's playing is nothing less than magnificent.* USAGE: used to emphasize the quality mentioned

sb **couldn't care less** See at CARE

more or less See at MORE

much less See at MUCH

lesser

the lesser of two evils
the less unpleasant of two choices, neither of which are good ◆ *Sometimes I don't like either of the candidates, so I just try to choose the lesser of the two evils.* USAGE: sometimes used in the form **a lesser evil**: *I don't like her, I just think of her as the lesser evil.*

lesson

learn a/your lesson
to understand something because of an unpleasant experience ◆ *We learned a lesson from last year's failure to reform health care.* ◆ *You hope that prisoners will say, "I don't want to end up back in jail again – I've learned my lesson."*

teach (*sb***) a lesson**, *also* **teach a lesson to** *sb*
to show what should not be done ◆ *You would think that losing her job because she took too much time off would have taught her a lesson, but it's happened again!* ◆ *He had this idea that the government is evil and must be taught a lesson, so he blew up a government office.*

let

let alone *do sth*
and to an even greater degree do something ◆ *We were trapped in a situation you can barely imagine, let alone understand.* USAGE: used to emphasize the extreme character of something ◆ Related vocabulary **not to mention** *sb/sth* at MENTION

let *sb* **alone**
to not annoy or interrupt someone; = **leave** *sb* **alone** ◆ *I tried to keep my promise not to call her, to let her alone to think, but finally I needed to talk to her.*

let *sb/sth* **be**
to not change anything related to someone or something ◆ *As long as no one complains about the clubs, the authorities let them be.*

let *sb* **down**
to disappoint someone, usually by not doing something ◆ *I know it's silly, but I feel like everyone lets me down when I really need help.*

let fly (with) *sth*, *also* **let** *sth* **fly**
1 to throw something or shoot

something from a weapon ◆ *Police officers let fly canisters of tear gas.* ◆ *The guy in the leather jacket was leaping over the counter when I let fly with a soda bottle.*
2 to express yourself in a way that will excite or anger others ◆ *If you disagree with the officials, it's bad form to let fly with four-letter words.* ◆ *When she got together with her friends, they would let fly all their innermost secrets.*

let (*sth*) go
1 to stop having something ◆ *Even though these stocks are now worthless, I can't let them go.*
2 to stop trying to control something ◆ *Once it's published, you can say you should have done this or that, but it's too late – you have to let it go.* ◆ *She kept doing the scene over until she finally let everything go, and then she did it perfectly.* ◆ *Family members have to learn to let go when someone is dying.*
3 to not take action ◆ *Some of the pictures were out of focus, but I let it go, thinking it might have been my fault and not the developers.*

let go (of *sb/sth*), *also* **let *sb/sth* go**
to stop holding someone or something ◆ *The little boy let go of the string and his balloon drifted high above the trees.* ◆ *He was holding onto the hand of his boss's wife, and even when his boss walked in he didn't let go.*

ORIGIN: based on the literal meaning of **let someone or something go** (= to stop preventing someone or something from leaving)

let *sb* go, *also* **let go *sb***
to end someone's employment ◆ *It was too bad that we had to let him go.* ◆ *The company has let go about 70 contract engineers.*

let *yourself* go
1 to behave in a relaxed and free manner ◆ *I got out on the dance floor* *and just let myself go.* ◆ Related vocabulary **kick back** at KICK
2 to take less care of your appearance ◆ *He's gained a lot of weight lately, and kind of let himself go.*

let *sb* have it
to attack someone physically or with words ◆ *When Joe got home late, Ann really let him have it.*

let *sb* in on *sth*
to tell someone a secret ◆ *Bill, could you let me in on your techniques for getting along with girls?* ◆ *The plan was so well guarded they only let three people in on it.* ◆ Related vocabulary **horn in (on *sb/sth*)** at HORN, **in on *sth*** at IN

let it all hang out
to do something enthusiastically and without fear of the results ◆ *Now you can let it all hang out online at the angry.org website.* ◆ *We have nothing to lose – we just have to play more relaxed and let it all hang out.*

let it be known
to inform people about something ◆ *He let it be known that he was available for the job.*

let it rip, *also* **let her rip**
1 to make a vehicle or machine move very fast ◆ *He would get up early Sunday mornings, fire up the lawnmower, and let her rip.* USAGE: the pronoun **her** is often used to refer to a machine
2 to do something with energy and enthusiasm ◆ *Hendrix would walk into a recording studio, turn on his amp, and let it rip while the tape recorder rolled.*

let *sb* off
to not punish someone ◆ *The judge let the boys off because they hadn't ever been in trouble before.* ◆ Related vocabulary **off the hook** at HOOK

let *sb* off easy
1 to give someone a light punishment ◆ *Stern let Robbins off easy, suspending him for just three games.*
2 to demand less effort from some-

one ♦ *She laughed at the suggestion that people are letting her off easy now that she is 81.*

let on
to allow other people to know about something ♦ *He wasn't going to let on that there was any crisis in his family.* USAGE: usually said about something you want to be a secret

let out
to end or be finished ♦ *Classes let out at 4:15.* USAGE: said about meetings, classes, performances, and other events that groups of people leave at a particular time

let out *sth*, *also* **let *sth* out**
1 to suddenly make a sound ♦ *Elena let out an ear-splitting scream as her brother, Julio, disappeared over the wall.* USAGE: often said about laughing or shouting
2 to make a piece of clothing larger ♦ *Can this skirt be let out at the side?*
3 to make something known ♦ *If anyone lets out this information, they will face immediate punishment.*

let *sb/sth* slide
to not do anything about someone or something ♦ *She misbehaved a bit when she got here, and I let her slide because she was in a strange city.* ♦ *It's easy to let exercise slide when you feel bad, but that's when you need it the most.* USAGE: often used in the form **let it slide**: *Kids don't like practicing because of the repetition, and some coaches tend to let it slide.*

let *sth* slip, *also* **let slip *sth***
to say something that you intended to keep secret ♦ *She doesn't like to tell people what she's doing, but sometimes she'll let something slip.* ♦ *From time to time, Alex lets slip an ugly comment about his colleagues.* USAGE: also used in the form **let it slip**: *Pam let it slip that I'm not going to be promoted.*

let up
to stop ♦ *The action and special effects never let up long enough for you to realize how stupid the movie actually is.* USAGE: often used in the form **not let up**: *The heat didn't let up until the weekend.*

let up on *sb*
to make less of an effort to get someone to do something ♦ *Teachers let up on us when we were seniors, probably figuring they'd taught us as much as we'd ever learn.* USAGE: often used in the form **not let up on someone**: *The police said they would not let up on drug dealers.*

let up on *sth*
to make less of an effort to do something ♦ *NASA eventually let up on trying to convince the public that every astronaut was happily married.*

let's

let's see esp. spoken
1 I am thinking about this ♦ *"Do you have any idea how many people will be there?" "Well, let's see – I don't think I could put a number on it."* USAGE: used in conversation when you are not sure what to say next
2 I want to discover ♦ *Let's see how much you want to win this event.* ♦ *Now that we know what your interests are, let's see if we can match you to a job that you'd like.*

letter

to the letter
completely or exactly ♦ *I followed the instructions to the letter but I still couldn't put the fan together.*

level

level off
to stop increasing or being reduced ♦ *The price of gas has finally leveled off after going up for several months.* ♦ *Television ratings had leveled off and then dropped slightly.*

level with *sb*
to tell someone the truth ♦ *If our leaders don't level with us, we lose faith in our government.* USAGE: usually said about information that may be unpleasant

liberties

on the level
honest or true ◆ *We are there when the inspections are done, so we know that everything is on the level.*

do *your* (level) best See at BEST

level the playing field See at PLAYING FIELD

liberties

take liberties (with *sb*)
to be friendly with another person for your own benefit ◆ *The head of our department believed that everyone there would take liberties with her if she let them.*

take liberties with *sth*
to change something to suit your needs, esp. when writing a story or book ◆ *The play takes liberties with history, but it brings to life the people from so long ago.*

liberty

at liberty
able or allowed to do something ◆ *I'm not at liberty to discuss this with you.* USAGE: often used in a negative statement, as in the example

take the liberty of *doing sth*
to do something without first getting someone's approval ◆ *I've taken the liberty of reserving a seat for you on tomorrow morning's flight to New York.*

licking

take a licking
to be defeated or very strongly criticized ◆ *Their latest album took a licking from the critics, but it's selling well anyway.* ◆ Related vocabulary **take a beating** at BEATING

lid

> ORIGIN
> These idioms are based on the idea that you can see what is in a container when a **lid** (=cover) is off and not see what is in it when a lid is on.

blow the lid off (*sth*)
to make public something that was previously not known or was hidden ◆ *He blew the lid off modern photography by publishing gritty, realistic pictures at a time when most photos showed a clean, happy world.* USAGE: sometimes used with other verbs meaning "remove": *Her novel tore the lid off small-town life.*

keep a lid on (*sth*)
to maintain control over something ◆ *His forces kept a lid on unrest for nearly eight years.*

put a lid on (*sth*)
to stop something from increasing ◆ *The mayor wants to put a lid on spending.* ◆ *Diplomats hope to put a lid on rising tensions between the two countries.* USAGE: sometimes used in the form **put a lid on it** (= stop complaining): *Put a lid on it, Jeff, would you please?*

lie

give the lie to *sth* slightly formal
to show that something is not true ◆ *He did not go into hiding, which gave the lie to the statement that he could not be found for an interview.* USAGE: also used in the form **give the lie to someone** (= to show that someone has not been telling the truth): *The latest soil tests give the lie to officials who say that the area is not contaminated.*

lie behind *sth*
to explain or be the reason for something ◆ *I wonder what lay behind his decision to quit school.*

lie low
to hide so you will not be caught by someone ◆ *All we could think to do was to get into the woods – any woods – as fast as possible and just lie low.* USAGE: often confused in form with **lay someone low** (= to weaken someone) ◆ Related vocabulary **lie in wait** at WAIT

live a lie
to spend your life as someone else ◆ *For all of his adult life, he lived a lie and didn't confess even to his family that he was a spy.*

how the land lies See at LAND

lie in state See at STATE
lie in wait See at WAIT
lie through *your* teeth See at TEETH

lieu
in lieu of
instead of ◆ *The teachers have accepted longer workdays in lieu of a pay cut.* USAGE: often used in newspaper articles announcing someone's death: *In lieu of flowers, please send donations to the Cancer Society.*

life
bet *your* life
to be certain that something will happen or be true ◆ *You bet your life there are a lot of politicians who are more interested in getting elected than they are in solving problems.*

breathe (new) life into *sth*
to bring ideas and energy to something ◆ *Changes in the performance have breathed new life into a show that seemed ready to close.* ◆ *He has promised to breathe new life into the organization.*

bring *sb/sth* to life
to make something exciting and interesting ◆ *Large, colorful illustrations bring to life the classic story of Snow White.*

for the life of *you*
to any degree at all ◆ *She couldn't pronounce it for the life of her.* ◆ *For the life of me, I can't figure out why somebody would want to spend so much time watching TV.* USAGE: usually used to emphasize negative statements, as in the examples

get a life
1 to have fun ◆ *With the time you save, you could learn Italian, paint your basement, even get a life.* ◆ Related vocabulary **lighten up** at LIGHTEN
2 to do something different ◆ *He needs to leave home and get a job – in short, he needs to get a life.* USAGE: often used as an instruction to someone who complains: *They're always telling me I shouldn't make fun of people, and I just tell them, "Grow up, you know, get a life."*

hold on for dear life
to use a lot of effort to keep something ◆ *With so few jobs available, workers are holding on for dear life to the jobs they already have.*

larger than life, *also* **bigger than life**
more interesting and more exciting than an ordinary person or thing ◆ *He may not live like a rock star, but in the eyes of his fans he's larger than life.* ◆ *You have to be bigger than life to make it in Times Square, and this restaurant wasn't.*

lay down *your* life slightly formal
to die ◆ *I hope you will never be asked to lay down your lives for your principles.*

lead a double life
to have a second, secret life that is usually not socially acceptable ◆ *The investigation uncovered details of Boley's double life, including secret bank accounts and a private post office box.* USAGE: also used with the verb **live**: *Nobody in France seemed to really care that he lived a double life.*

life after *sth*
a return to a normal existence after doing something unusual ◆ *These athletes may find it hard to believe that there's life after winning a gold medal, but there is.*

> ORIGIN: based on the literal meaning of **life after death** (= the belief that a person continues to live in some form after they die)

life and limb
continued existence or serious injury ◆ *These skiers risk life and limb every day for the thrill of a super-fast downhill run.* ◆ *The storms across the west are posing a threat to life and limb.* USAGE: used when talking about situations in which someone

could die or be injured, as in the examples

life in the fast lane
an exciting, active style of living that usually involves great wealth ♦ *When Ashmead decided that life in the fast lane wasn't much fun anymore, he turned his attention to another kind of business.* ♦ Related vocabulary **in the fast lane** at FAST LANE, **on the fast track** at FAST TRACK

> ORIGIN: based on the **fast lane** of a highway, where cars drive faster than other cars on the road

not for the life of me
no matter how hard you try ♦ *I knew I had met her before, only I couldn't for the life of me remember where or when.*

put *your* life on the line
to risk dying ♦ *Why would a man with a wife and three children put his life on the line for one of his coworkers?*

spring to life
1 to suddenly become active ♦ *I was standing on the golf course when the sprinkler system sprang to life without warning.*
2 to begin existing ♦ *The company sprang to life in 1939 as a manufacturer of testing instruments.*

take *your* life in *your* hands
to do something very dangerous ♦ *I think you take your life in your hands every time you get on a plane.*

take on a life of *its* own
to no longer be controlled by anyone ♦ *Once an earthquake starts, it takes on a life of its own.* ♦ *Someone imagined it, and the idea took on a life of its own.*

that's life, *also* **such is life**
this is the way things are ♦ *I'm disappointed that I won't be allowed to compete, but that's life.* ♦ *I went to two afternoon sessions and then I had to leave, which was a shame, but such is life.* USAGE: used to show that you have to accept things as they are

the life of the party
someone who makes everyone enjoy things more ♦ *She was the one who was always smiling in pictures, the one who was the life of the party.*

a matter of life and death See at MATTER

a new lease on life See at LEASE

a way of life See at WAY

have the time of *your* life See at TIME

the story of *sb's* life See at STORY

within an inch of *your/its* life See at INCH

light

bring *sth* to light, *also* **bring to light *sth***
to make something known ♦ *Her books brought to light women's contributions to society across the centuries.*

come to light
to become known ♦ *Four soldiers have faced charges since the scandal came to light last fall.*

in a good light
positively ♦ *Most voters see him in a good light but think he could have done more for the city.*

in (the) light of *sth*
for the reason given ♦ *In light of how much our own costs have gone up, we have to raise prices to our customers.* ♦ Related vocabulary **in view of *sth*** at VIEW

light up
to look happy ♦ *Grandma's eyes would light up when she started talking about her younger days.*

light up *sth*/somewhere
to add excitement to a place or thing ♦ *She was one of those people who would light up a room.* ♦ *Her personality doesn't exactly light up a television screen – in fact, she's painfully shy.*

make light of *sth*
to act as if something is not serious

or important ◆ *I tried to make light of his fear, but the look on his face made that impossible.*

out like a light
in a deep sleep or unconscious ◆ *Stu was out like a light, so I threw a blanket on him and turned out the light.*

see the light
to completely understand something ◆ *Personal stories help people see the light on complex social issues.*

see the light of day
to be made available or be known about ◆ *The company agreed the ad was an embarrassment and promised it would never again see the light of day.*

shed light on *sth*, also throw light on *sth*
to make something clearer ◆ *Experts hope the plane's flight recorders will shed light on the cause of the crash.* ◆ *The latest study could throw light on why older people are the only ones affected.* ◆ Related vocabulary **put a spotlight on *sb/sth*** at SPOTLIGHT

(the) light at the end of the tunnel
the end of a difficult period or job ◆ *At this point, there is no light at the end of the tunnel because we have to start over.* ◆ *Once I could see light at the end of the tunnel, writing the last part of the book wasn't so hard.*

light a fire under *sb* See at FIRE
make light of *sth* See at MAKE
***your* name in lights** See at NAME
travel light See at TRAVEL

lighten

lighten up
to be less serious about something ◆ *People are usually relieved when they're given a chance to lighten up.* USAGE: often used as an order: *When she complained that these people were being treated badly, he told her, "Lighten up."* ◆ Related vocabulary **get a life** 1 at LIFE

lighten *your* load See at LOAD

like

and the like
and similar things ◆ *The club has courts for tennis and badminton and the like.* ◆ *A new edition of any book should incorporate major changes – an added chapter, a revised conclusion, overall updating, and the like.*

as like as not See **as likely as not** at LIKELY

likelihood

in all likelihood
I think this is true or will happen; = **in all probability** ◆ *Excuses for not attending will be offered and in all likelihood will be accepted by the hosts.*

likely

as likely as not
probably; = **as like as not** ◆ *She didn't usually work all night, but she was as likely as not to be at the lab at any given time.*

likes

the likes of *sb/sth*
someone or something as good as someone or something else ◆ *We haven't seen the likes of Muhammad Ali since he retired from the ring.* ◆ *They're not competing against the likes of you or me but real, first-class, serious athletes.*

limb

out on a limb
in a situation where you lack support ◆ *He was pretty far out on a limb when he predicted the future of the industry two years ago.* USAGE: often used with **go**: *I'll go out on a limb and pick the Panthers to win on Sunday.*

tear *sb* limb from limb
to attack someone violently ◆ *I'm sure she'd tear the guy limb from limb for what he's done.*

> ORIGIN: based on the literal meaning of **tear someone limb from limb** (= to pull someone's arms and legs off)

line

line

along the line *esp. spoken*
during the time while something is happening or being done ◆ *Somewhere along the line we must have made a few right decisions.* ◆ *All along the line we missed chances to patch up our quarrel.*

bring *sth* into line
to make one thing like another ◆ *These increases will bring city teachers' salaries into line with teachers' pay throughout the area.*

cross the line
1 to change from being acceptable to being unacceptable ◆ *I thought the jokes crossed the line and were basically embarrassing.*
2 to do something wrong ◆ *If you steal someone's idea, you have absolutely crossed the line.*

down the line *esp. spoken*
in the future; = **down the road** ◆ *Waiting even a year to put money into your retirement account can make a big difference down the line.*

draw a line in the sand, *also* **draw the line in the sand**
to say that a particular idea or activity will not be supported or accepted ◆ *The president has drawn a line in the sand, which means that if the foreign troops are not removed, they will be attacked.*

> ORIGIN: based on the idea of literally making a mark in sand to show someone they cannot move across it

draw the line
to separate one thing from another ◆ *It's not clear where this author draws the line between fact and fiction.*

draw the line at *doing sth*, *also* **draw the line on *doing sth***
to decide you will not do something ◆ *I love vampires, but I draw the line at attending some silly Dracula convention.* ◆ *Where to draw the line on treatment for people who are dying is a decision made by patients, their families and their doctors.* USAGE: often used to say you will not do something because you think it is wrong: *I'm a loyal employee, but I draw the line when I am asked to do something I think is wrong.*

drop *sb* a line
to send a short letter to someone ◆ *We really do like hearing from you, so drop us a line and let us know how you are.*

fall into line, *also* **fall in line**
to do something similar ◆ *Once we bring out a CD-ROM version, all our competitors will fall into line.* ◆ *If students see that everyone else in school is wearing a uniform, they tend to fall in line and wear one, too.*

get a line on *sb/sth*
to get information about someone or something ◆ *It sounds like you've already got a line on where the problem is.*

hold the line (on *sth*)
to not reduce or increase something ◆ *Businesses are holding the line on hiring and spending plans because of uncertainty about the economy.*

in line for *sth*
to be likely to get something ◆ *Waxman would be in line for the job if Rawson resigns.*

in line with *sth*
similar to something ◆ *The company's profits were in line with what was expected.*

in the line of duty
while doing what was expected in a particular job ◆ *A police officer was killed in the line of duty while chasing a suspect.* USAGE: mostly used about police and others who do dangerous work

in the line of fire
in a situation in which you may be severely criticized ◆ *Maria was willing to place herself in the line of fire and accept the blame if the music festival failed.* ◆ Related vocabulary **on the firing line** at FIRING LINE

ORIGIN: based on the literal military meaning of **in the line of fire** (= in the place where bullets are being shot)

lay it on the line
to be completely honest ♦ *Dad really laid it on the line and told me I couldn't use the car unless all my grades went up.*

line up *sth*, *also* **line** *sth* **up**
to organize or arrange for something to be done ♦ *Lee had already lined up a good lawyer to handle his case.* ♦ *I'll try to line something up for Saturday – maybe we could go to the museum.*

ORIGIN: based on the literal meaning of **line up** (= to form a line)

on the line
1 at risk of failing or being harmed ♦ *There's a lot of pride on the line when your book is published.*
2 speaking on the telephone ♦ *I asked to speak to Tyler, but Tyler's mom came on the line instead.*

out of line
completely unacceptable ♦ *Some members of Congress said the decision to send in troops was completely out of line.* ♦ *She's trying to sell the house for about $250,000, but that price is way out of line for this part of town.* USAGE: often used with **get** and **step**: *When a student steps out of line, someone should do something about it.*

over the line
beyond what is accepted ♦ *After visiting a number of bars, a handful of navy pilots went completely over the line and were picked up by police.* USAGE: often used with **step**: *Mister, you stepped over the line by saying that!*

put it on the line
to risk failure ♦ *Athletes put it on the line every day – in sports, you don't get to do something over.* USAGE: often used in the form **put something on the line**: *The lawyer put his reputation on the line when he agreed to defend this man.*

sign on the dotted line
to formally agree to something ♦ *We signed on the dotted line Wednesday and will move into our new house next week.*

ORIGIN: from the lines on a legal document where a person signs their name to show they agree to it

toe the line
to do what you are ordered or expected to do ♦ *Not everyone was happy with the plan, but most of us toed the line.* USAGE: sometimes used with a noun describing whose orders are being followed: *They promised to toe the party line and vote with the leadership.*

walk a thin line (between *sth***)**, *also* **walk a fine line (between** *sth***)**
to balance two competing ideas or groups ♦ *The diplomats knew they had to walk a fine line between the rebel groups and the government.*

the end of the line See at END

hook, line, and sinker See at HOOK

line *your* **(own) pockets** See at POCKETS

on the firing line See at FIRING LINE

on the front line of *sth* See at FRONT LINE

put *your* **life on the line** See at LIFE

(the) top of the line See at TOP

lines

along the lines of *sth*
similar to something ♦ *I think my point is very much along the lines of things that I heard Steve and Ana suggest.*

along those lines, *also* **along these lines**
1 of a similar quality or type ♦ *I want to buy an SUV or something along those lines.*

lips

on everyone's lips

Now that they're dating again, there's just one question on everyone's lips.

2 in this way ♦ *What evidence do we have that Adams is willing to sign an agreement along these lines?*

read between the lines
to find a hidden meaning in something said or written ♦ *The report doesn't criticize the research directly, but you can read between the lines that the review committee wasn't impressed.* USAGE: sometimes used without the verb: *Leo read Melodie's letter again, hoping for some hidden message between the lines.*

draw (the) battle lines See at BATTLE

on the front lines of *sth* See at FRONT LINE

lips

your lips are sealed
you will not talk about something ♦ *He acts like he wants you to ask what happened, and then if you do ask, he tells you his lips are sealed.*

on everyone's lips
being talked about by many people ♦ *He hasn't answered the question on everyone's lips – how is his health?*

smack *your* lips
to show excitement or satisfaction ♦ *Planners began smacking their lips at the thought of all that farmland to build on.*

> ORIGIN: from the sound made when you quickly move your lips together and apart to show you are hungry or that you like something

liquor

not hold *your* liquor
to not be able to drink alcohol without showing any effects ♦ *Scott didn't hold his liquor very well – he'd either fall asleep or sit silently and sadly after a couple of drinks.* USAGE: the opposite meaning is expressed by **hold your liquor**: *Now there's a gang that can hold their liquor!*

little

little by little
in small amounts; = **bit by bit** ♦ *I started out with some basic hand tools and little by little added some power tools, a good sander, and a drill.*

too little, too late
not enough and not given soon enough to be useful ♦ *Financial help for food pantries and soup kitchens may be too little, too late.*

live

live and breathe *sth*
to be extremely interested in something ♦ *I found it hard to discuss the poems, since I did not live and breathe poetry like many of my classmates did.*

live and let live
to accept other people as they are, although they may have a different way of life ♦ *I firmly believe in live and let live, and if people don't rob, cheat or beat their wives, I have no complaints.*

live dangerously
to not worry about the risks involved in your actions ♦ *She always felt a powerful attraction to men who lived dangerously.* ♦ Related vocabulary **(live) on the edge** 1 at EDGE

live down *sth*, *also* **live** *sth* **down**
to do well so that others forget something bad you said or did ♦ *Ken is still trying to live down his comment that most of what's on the Web now is crap.* ♦ *After the way she behaved at the office party, I don't think she'll ever be able to live it down.*

live for *sth*
to enjoy doing one thing more than anything else ♦ *You live for your sport or your work or your family and most other things you simply enjoy.*

live it up
to enjoy yourself completely without worrying about anything ♦ *They took a six-week holiday and lived it up in the Caribbean.* ♦ Related vocabulary **live high on the hog** at HOG

live up to *sth*
to be as good as you said or thought something would be ♦ *Analysts are concerned that corporate profits will not live up to expectations and could cause stock prices to fall.* ♦ *The game fails to live up to the excitement promised on its box.*

live with *sth*
to accept something that is not exactly what you wanted ♦ *I'm not earning much money, but I guess we're just going to have to live with it.* ♦ *This agreement isn't perfect but it's something I can live with.*

go live See at GO
live a lie See at LIE
live by *your* **wits** See at WITS
live high on the hog See at HOG
live in sin See at SIN
live in the past See at PAST
(live) on the edge See at EDGE

lived

you **haven't lived until** *sth* esp. spoken, *also you* **haven't lived till** *sth*
you will be sorry if you do not try this ♦ *You haven't lived until you've got a personal trainer to work out with.*

liven

liven *sth* **up**, *also* **liven up** *sth*
to make something more interesting or attractive ♦ *There was a live band at the party, and that really livened things up.* ♦ *A colored shirt can certainly liven up an outfit.*

living

in living memory, *also* **within living memory**
able to be remembered by people who are alive now ♦ *Water levels on the Mississippi River haven't been this high in living memory.*

living large
able to pay for and enjoying a very expensive style of living ♦ *Vacations in the hot spots, a huge apartment in the city, cars, servants – that's my idea of living large!*

lo

lo and behold
look or what a surprise ◆ *Carine tried her luck at the lottery and, lo and behold, won $1,500 last month.* USAGE: used as an exclamation: *Lo and behold! You did come after all!*

load

a load of *sth* esp. spoken
much of something ◆ *She's a good student and has a load of friends.* ◆ Related vocabulary **loads of *sth*** at LOADS

a load of crap rude slang, *also* a load of shit
nonsense ◆ *So, according to you, classical physics is a load of crap.* USAGE: often used to react to what someone else has said: *"What a load of crap – I love her and I always will."*

a load off *your* mind
a big problem you do not have to worry about any more ◆ *Finally getting a job was a huge load off my mind.* USAGE: sometimes used with **real**: *I'm so relieved I don't have to give a speech – it's a real load off my mind.*

get a load of *sth* esp. spoken
look at something that is very surprising or attractive ◆ *Get a load of the lies in their press release!* ◆ *Get a load of that dress! It's beautiful!*

lighten *your* load, *also* lighten the load
to make something easier for you to deal with ◆ *Every kind of helper, from eye doctors to massage therapists, volunteered time to lighten the rescue workers' load.*

loads

loads of *sth*
much or many things ◆ *Wadsworth received loads of support from other teachers and parents.* ◆ *I've heard that story from loads of different people.* ◆ *I've collected loads of stuff for my scrapbook.* ◆ Related vocabulary **a load of *sth*** at LOAD

lock

lock in *sth*, *also* lock into *sth*
to be unable to change a condition ◆ *A large percentage of these groups remain locked in poverty.* ◆ *The two countries are locked in a dispute over the islands off the northern coast.*

lock, stock, and barrel
taking or including everything ◆ *The soldiers received orders that they were to move, lock, stock and barrel, some 600 miles west.*

under lock and key
in a safe, protected place ◆ *The old man keeps such documents under lock and key.*

log

log on, *also* log in
to open a computer system so that it can be used ◆ *As a graduate student, Erin often logged on to the system from home around midnight.* ◆ *Internet companies are trying to help business travelers log in while they're on the road.*

log off, *also* log out
to stop using a computer system ◆ *When the file transfer is complete, you can log off the Web and launch your print program.*

sleep like a log
to sleep very well ◆ *With a full stomach and a warm blanket, I slept like a log.*

(as) easy as falling off a log See (as) easy as pie at PIE

loggerheads

at loggerheads
strongly disagreeing ◆ *The two sides are still at loggerheads on how big the workers' pay increase will be.*

long

as long as, *also* so long as
if ◆ *My roses grow well as long as they have just enough water and plenty of plant food.* ◆ *Promoting a product before it is available is a good idea, so long as you are certain it will be available soon.*

before long
soon ♦ *I think we'll be finished with this before long.*

long on *sth* **(and short on** *sth else***)**
having a lot of one quality and not enough of another ♦ *The story is a slow-moving mystery that's long on atmosphere and short on tension.* ♦ Related vocabulary **short on** *sth* **(and long on** *sth else***)** at SHORT

so long
1 a very long time ♦ *I haven't seen him in so long.*
2 goodbye ♦ *So long, see you tomorrow.* ♦ *If he didn't want to see her anymore, would he be able to tell her so long?* USAGE: usually used in a friendly way

the long and the short of it
the truth of the matter ♦ *The long and the short of it is that physical activity is extremely good for your health!*

look

look after *sb/sth*
to be responsible for someone or something ♦ *A neighbor will look after the dogs while we're away.* ♦ Related vocabulary **take care of** *sb/sth* at CARE

look ahead
to think about the future ♦ *We need to look ahead as much as five years to make realistic plans.*

look askance at *sb/sth* slightly formal, *also* **look at** *sb/sth* **askance**
to consider someone or something in a disapproving way ♦ *The courts have tended to look askance at many of these claims.* ♦ *Our teachers looked at us askance.*

look back
to think of or remember what has happened in the past ♦ *We raised three kids and worked full-time – sometimes I look back and wonder how we did it.* USAGE: often used with **at** or **on**: *Now we look back at the late 1940s as the good old days.*

look down on *sb/sth*
to consider someone or something as not important or of value; = **look down** *your* **nose at** *sb/sth* ♦ *"A lot of people look down on us because we're homeless," she says.*

look for *sth*
to expect something ♦ *We're looking for snow in the Great Lakes on Tuesday.*

> ORIGIN: based on the literal meaning of **look for something** (= to search for something)

look forward to *sth*
to be pleased or excited because something is going to happen ♦ *I'm looking forward to my trip to Berlin and Paris.*

look here esp. spoken
listen to what I am going to say ♦ *Look here, what kind of fool do you take me for?* USAGE: usually used to show that you are angry or annoyed

look in on *sb*
to visit someone briefly ♦ *The doctor said he'd look in on you tomorrow.*

look into *sth*
to try to find out about something ♦ *A federal grand jury is looking into the charges of misconduct.* ♦ Related vocabulary **inquire into** *sth* at INQUIRE

look like *sth* esp. spoken
to seem likely that something will happen ♦ *It looks like the unusually warm weather we've been having may be coming to an end.*

look out
to watch what is happening and be careful ♦ *But when the ice suddenly breaks, look out.* USAGE: often used as an instruction: *Someone shouted, "Look out, he's got a gun!"* ♦ Related vocabulary **watch out** at WATCH

look out for *sb/sth*
1 to feel responsibility for someone or something; = **watch out for** *sb/sth* ♦ *I have a network of neigh-*

looking

bors who look out for each other and support each other.
2 to be aware of the existence of someone or something ◆ *Everybody thought I'd win, but I kept telling them to look out for Walter, too.* ◆ *Look out for a small amount of extremely vulgar language in the middle of the movie.*

look *sb* over, *also* **look *sb* up and down**
to examine someone very carefully ◆ *She looked him over, noticing his bruised face and dirty jacket.* ◆ *The old man remained silent for a moment while he continued to look John up and down.*

look *sth* over, *also* **look over *sth***
to examine something carefully ◆ *Epstein poked through the stuff inside, carefully picking each thing up and looking it over from all angles.* ◆ *She had her own lawyer look over the agreement.*

look right through *sb*
to behave as if you do not see someone ◆ *He tried to engage the woman next to him in conversation, but she looked right through him.* USAGE: usually said of someone who is trying to ignore someone else

look to *do sth*
to expect or plan to do something ◆ *In the following year, Columbia looked to expand its operations in either film or radio.*

look to be *sth*
to have this appearance or characteristic ◆ *The waitress was a young woman who looked to be 20 or so.* ◆ *Her moves look to be much easier and more relaxed than in the past.*

look to *sb/sth* for *sth*
to expect someone or something to provide information or help ◆ *They look to us for answers, but we have none.*

look *sb* up, *also* **look up *sb***
to visit someone ◆ *Look me up the next time you're in Los Angeles.* ◆ *I hope you'll look up my niece while you're in Pittsburgh.*

look *sth* up, *also* **look up *sth***
to check a fact or get information about something ◆ *If you don't know the meaning of the word, look it up in your dictionary.* ◆ *The research involved looking up how my opponent voted.*

look upon *sb/sth* as *sth*, *also* **look on *sb/sth* as *sth***
to consider someone or something in a particular way ◆ *Although she was actually not related to us, we all looked upon her as an aunt.* ◆ *I look upon education as an investment in the future.* USAGE: often used in the form **looked upon as**: *He was looked upon as an upper-class snob.*

look up to *sb*
to admire and respect someone ◆ *He was older and more experienced, and I looked up to him.*

not much to look at
not attractive ◆ *The school dormitories weren't much to look at – just concrete blocks with windows.*

take a long hard look at *sth*
to examine something carefully ◆ *I think they ought to take a long hard look at who is allowed to carry a gun.* USAGE: usually said about something that should be improved in the future

look a gift horse in the mouth See at HORSE

look down *your* nose at *sb/sth* See at NOSE

look for trouble See at TROUBLE

look high and low (for *sth*) See **search high and low (for *sth*)** at SEARCH

look the part See at PART

look the other way See at WAY

looking

looking up
getting better or improving ◆ *Things are certainly looking up now that the tourists are coming back.* USAGE: often used humorously in

the phrase **things are looking up** when a situation is not good: *Well, we're out of food but at least we've got a bottle of wine – things are looking up!*

loom

loom large
to be important ◆ *Car trips loom large in my family's history.* USAGE: often said of something that causes worry: *The threat of tragic events loomed large over a whaling voyage.*

loop

in the loop
having knowledge of and involvement in something ◆ *Is Congress fully in the loop on issues of national security?* ◆ *Watkins didn't go out of his way to keep his employees in the loop.* ◆ Opposite **out of the loop** ◆ Related vocabulary **in the picture** at PICTURE

out of the loop
not having knowledge of or involvement in something ◆ *A few people at the top knew what was going on, but everybody else was out of the loop.* ◆ Opposite **in the loop** ◆ Related vocabulary **out of the picture** at PICTURE

throw sb for a loop
to upset someone unexpectedly and severely ◆ *Seeing an accident on the road always throws me for a loop.*

loose

on the loose
free to move about and dangerous ◆ *Police warned that a serial killer is on the loose in the northwest.*

(all) hell break loose See at HELL
at loose ends See at ENDS
break loose See at BREAK
cut loose See at CUT
cut sb/sth loose See at CUT
play fast and loose with sth See at PLAY
turn sb/sth loose See at TURN

loosen

loosen up (sb), also loosen sb up
to behave in a relaxed, informal way ◆ *Slowly she began to loosen up and, by the second semester, she was making friends with her classmates.* ◆ *The question was supposed to loosen people up and chase away their anxieties.*

loosen your tongue See at TONGUE

lord

lord it over sb
to behave as if you are better than someone else ◆ *Unfortunately, some senior faculty have a habit of lording it over younger professors.*

lose

lose yourself (in sth)
to stop worrying about yourself by giving attention to something else ◆ *Out on the golf course, you can lose yourself and forget everything else in the world.* ◆ *You can reduce stress by losing yourself in the pages of a good book.*

lose it
to become very angry ◆ *He was afraid he was going to lose it, so he cut the meeting short.* ◆ Related vocabulary **lose your/its grip** at GRIP

lose out (on sth)
to fail to get something desired, esp. in a competitive situation ◆ *We're losing out on major economic opportunities that would be good for the whole city.* ◆ *If we don't act quickly, we'll lose out.*

loss

at a loss
unable to know how to act or what to do ◆ *He felt totally at a loss about how to proceed with the making of a dictionary.*

at a loss for words
unable to think of something to say; = **lost for words** ◆ *If I was alone with her, I'd feel at a loss for words.* USAGE: usually this happens because you are surprised

losses

cut *your* losses
to stop wasting time or money on something by ending your connection to it ♦ *When a project is failing, you've got to learn to cut your losses and move on.*

lost

lost on *you*
not understood by you ♦ *Civilization developed because ideas and technology were exchanged between cultures – a truth that is lost on many of us.* USAGE: often used in the form **not lost on someone** (= clearly understood by someone): *Increased airport security is now a fact of life, something not lost on passengers who put up with long delays.*

lost without *sb/sth*
unable to work in the usual way because something is not available ♦ *I'm lost without my cell phone.* ♦ *I'd be lost without you, honey.*

get lost See at GET
lost for words See at WORDS
lost in the shuffle See at SHUFFLE
lost in thought See at THOUGHT
no love lost See at LOVE
make up for lost time See at TIME

lot

cast *your* lot with *sb/sth*
to choose to share in whatever happens to another person or a group ♦ *If I'm going to cast my lot with this team, I'm going to try to make them as good as possible any way I can.*

ORIGIN: based on the literal meaning of **cast your lot** (= to throw dice or other objects as a way of deciding what will happen)

have a lot to answer for
to have much of the responsibility for a situation ♦ *The owners forced a strike, but the workers have a lot to answer for, too.* ♦ Related vocabulary **answer for *sth*** at ANSWER

leave a lot to be desired
to be not very good, or not as good as you would like; = **leave something to be desired** ♦ *My tennis game is improving, but my backhand still leaves a lot to be desired.*

quite a lot esp. spoken
a large number or amount ♦ *We've had quite a lot of rain this year.*

a heck of a lot of *sth* See at HECK
the best of the lot See at BEST
say a lot about *sth* See at SAY

loud

loud and clear
in a way that is easy to understand ♦ *Major airlines are saying loud and clear that passengers are limited to two carry-on items.* USAGE: often used to say that a **message** is understood: *Our message came through loud and clear in that ad.*

ORIGIN: based on the literal use of **loud and clear** to describe an easily understood radio or telephone communication

love

fall in love (with *sb*)
to begin to love someone ♦ *The movie tells the story of a country doctor who falls in love with a beautiful waitress.* ♦ *I was thinking about falling in love for the first time and trying to remember my first boyfriend.*

fall in love (with *sth*)
to become strongly attracted to a place, activity, or thing ♦ *We spent three weeks in Georgetown and absolutely fell in love with it.* ♦ *I test drove the car and I just fell in love.*

love at first sight
an immediate, strong attraction for someone you just met ♦ *She took an immediate liking to him – it was love at first sight.*

make love
to have sex ♦ *They'd swum, they'd danced, they'd walked barefoot along a starlit beach and made love as if there was no tomorrow.*

no love lost
no feelings of respect, admiration, or affection ◆ *They had a curious relationship – there was no love lost there.* USAGE: often used with **between**: *There's no love lost between Morris and his publisher.*

send *your* **love to** *sb*, *also* **send** *sb* *your* **love**
to give a message of affection from you to someone else ◆ *Maggie asked me to send her love to you and the boys.*

head over heels (in love) See at HEAD

love *sb* **to death** See at DEATH

lowest

the lowest of the low
a person or organization that has no moral standards ◆ *Anyone who would trick poor people into giving him their money has got to be the lowest of the low.* USAGE: used to show you strongly disapprove of someone

luck

down on *your* **luck**
suffering because a lot of bad things are happening to you ◆ *For a while they were homeless, living in a shelter for families down on their luck.* USAGE: usually said about someone who has no work or money

in luck
experiencing a surprisingly good situation ◆ *Judy arrived for work very late, but she was in luck, as the boss was out that day.*

luck into *sth*
to get or find something good by chance ◆ *The flight was pretty empty, and the passenger across from me lucked into three seats to himself.*

luck out
to be in an unusually good situation ◆ *She lucked out, investing at just the right time to make a lot of money.*

no such luck esp. spoken
the situation or event did not develop as you hoped it would ◆ *I believed that was the end of the conversation, but no such luck – he just kept on talking.*

out of luck
not having an opportunity or situation you want ◆ *This type of racing bike only comes in large sizes, so if you're a short person, you're out of luck.*

push *your* **luck**, *also* **press** *your* **luck**
to expect good things to continue to happen because they have in the past ◆ *I was fortunate to survive the crash, and there was no point pushing my luck by continuing to race.* USAGE: often used in the phrase **don't push your luck**: *We've given you a lot of time off recently, but don't push your luck.*

the luck of the draw
completely the result of chance ◆ *You can't choose whom you play against. It's just the luck of the draw.*

> ORIGIN: based on a literal meaning of **a draw** (= a competition in which you win if the number on your ticket is chosen)

tough luck esp. spoken
I do not have any sympathy for your problems ◆ *Anyone who misses three classes will fail, and if you don't like it, tough luck!* USAGE: sometimes used to say you are sorry that someone is having problems: *If a beggar approached us, she would murmur "tough luck" and give him a few coins.* ◆ Related vocabulary **tough shit** at SHIT

try *your* **luck**
to attempt something that may or may not succeed ◆ *Hundreds of fishermen had shown up early at the lake to try their luck.*

a stroke of luck See at STROKE

lull

lull *you* **into** *sth/doing sth*
to make you feel calm or safe when it is not reasonable to feel this way ◆ *His confidence lulled me into thinking things were somehow going to*

lump

leave someone in the lurch

Commuters were left in the lurch when the train line was shut down.

work out. USAGE: often used with the phrase **a false sense of security** (= a feeling that everything is under control when it really is not): *Don't let the computer lull you into a false sense of security – there are still lots of ways for you to make mistakes.*

the lull before the storm See **the calm before the storm** at CALM

lump

a lump in *your* throat
a strong feeling of emotion that makes speaking difficult ♦ *He still couldn't watch the video without getting a lump in his throat, and he wasn't the only one.*

lumps

take *your* lumps
to experience and accept difficulties as part of doing something ♦ *When unemployment increased, the Midwest took its lumps earlier than the East, but recovered faster.*

ORIGIN: based on the idea of a fighter being able to **take lumps** (= accept swelling in parts of the body)

lunch

out to lunch
1 not giving your attention to what you are doing ♦ *Their team is so good, they'd have to be totally out to lunch for us to win a game.*
2 lacking good mental judgment ♦ *She's clearly an idiot, and even a five year old should be able to tell she's out to lunch.*

ORIGIN: based on the literal meaning of **out to lunch** (= away from your place of business because you are eating lunch)

lurch

leave *sb* in the lurch, *also* **leave *sb* in a lurch**
to cause someone to be in a situation in which they do not have what they need ♦ *Her ex-husband didn't want to deal with the kids, so she was left in the lurch.* ♦ *Factories here that rely on parts from overseas were suddenly left in the lurch when imports were suspended.*

Study Section

Idioms are often unusual groups of words that have an unexpected meaning. But some idioms share particular words or patterns of words that make their meanings more easily expected.

Focus on form

These idioms that are built around prepositions, conjunctions, and other function words are described.

about	238
and	239
around	240
as . . . as . . .	241
at	242
by	243
something by *something*	244
in a	244
in (the)	245
in your	246
like	247
on (a)	248
on the /on your	249
over	251
quite a	252
so	253
idioms of repetition	254

Phrases with a purpose

These idioms share a purpose rather than a meaning and are used to react to situations and to express emotions.

idioms of reaction	255
expressions of surprise, anger, saisfaction, or attitude	256

The human body

This groups of idioms use the words *eyes*, *ears*, or *nose* and *heart*, *stomach*, or *teeth* in phrases that describe awareness, understanding, and other features of the human condition.

sense organs	257
body parts	258

FOCUS ON FORM

about

About is most frequently used to connect an adjective, verb, or phrase with a situation or person:

crazy about **sb/sth** to like or love someone or something very much

forget about **sth** do not expect something

know what **you** *are talking about* to speak in an informed way because of your experience or education

no two ways about it there is no doubt about something

say a lot about **sth** to show or express something

see about **sb/sth** to get information about someone or something

think twice (about **sth***)* to consider something more carefully

what about **sb/sth** can you explain or give your opinion about someone or something

Sometimes *about* is used with special emphasis with this meaning, especially in speech and in slang expressions:

forget about it do not even ask about it

tell me about it I have had the same experience

give a damn (about **sb/sth***)* to be interested or involved

not give a damn (about **sb/sth***)* to not be interested in someone or something

About is also used after a verb in expressions that tell someone to do something or suggest how something is done:

go about **your** *business* to do what you usually do

*go about (***sth/doing sth***)* to do something

set about **sth/doing sth** to begin to do or deal with something

About is also used to mean "around or in the area of someone or something":

cast about (for **sth***)* to try to find something

have **your** *wits about* **you** to be able to think clearly

Sometimes *about* is used to mean "enough":

it's about time this should have happened long ago

and

And is used in many idioms to connect two similar things or activities, usually to emphasize a quality or condition:

alive and well involved or active

bright and early very early in the morning

crash and burn to fail suddenly and completely

far and wide many places

free and clear without debt or legal claims

high and mighty as if you are more important than other people

hot and heavy full of very strong feelings

loud and clear in a way that is easy to understand

pure and simple plainly, and without having to say anything else

safe and sound not hurt

signed and sealed having official approval

smoke and mirrors something that is meant to confuse or deceive people

Sometimes the two words connected sound alike, as if they were part of a poem:

fair and square honestly

wear and tear damage from work or use

wheeling and dealing looking for and using a good opportunity

wine and dine sb to entertain someone expensively

Sometimes *and* connects two opposite things:

a carrot and stick (approach) rewards and punishments that influence someone's behavior

black and white a very clear choice that causes no confusion

blow hot and cold to be enthusiastic one moment and not interested the next

give and take the exchange of some of what you want for some of what someone else wants

pros and cons advantages and disadvantages

through thick and thin including both bad and good times

And is also used after a verb to show progress in a relationship or to emphasize a particular type of action:

kiss and make up to become friendly again after arguing

kiss and tell to publicly discuss private information about someone you know well

play fast and loose with sth to treat something without enough care or attention

Study Section

around

A number of verbs use *around* in one of its basic meanings to suggest the movement or existence of a person or thing:

come around to visit

hang around to stay in a place

kick around to exist

run around to go from place to place

send around sth to cause something to be seen by a number of different people

show sb *around* **somewhere** to lead someone through a place

A surprisingly large number of idioms formed with a verb and *around*, some of them slang, refer to silly behavior, wasting time, or having sex:

fool around to waste time doing something without a particular purpose

fool around with sb to have sex with someone other than your husband, wife, or usual sexual partner

fool around with sth to amuse yourself by doing or saying something that is likely to cause trouble

horse around to be active in a silly way

mess around to waste time doing something without a particular purpose

mess around with sb to have sex with someone other than your husband, wife, or usual sexual partner

play around **1** to have a sexual relationship with someone not your husband, wife, or partner **2** to behave in a silly way

screw around (with sb*)* **1** to annoy someone by wasting their time **2** to have sex with someone who is not your regular partner

screw around (with sth*)* to waste time

sleep around to have sex with a lot of different people

Less often, *around* is used about friendly relationships:

pal around (with sb*)* to spend time doing things you enjoy with someone you like

run around with sb to spend a lot of time with someone

Around is also used with verbs to mean "to consider or talk about something":

bat around sth to discuss an idea or opinion

beat around the bush to avoid talking about what is important

come around (to sth*)* to change your opinion of something

get around sth to find a way to avoid a problem

kick sth *around* to discuss something

play around with sth to experiment with something

toss around sth to consider or think about something

Focus on form

as . . . as . . .

Many idioms take the form *as (something) as (something else)*, in which two things are compared, often a quality with a physical object, and usually to emphasize the strength of the quality. In almost every case, the first *as* may be omitted.

> *as American as apple pie* having qualities that are thought to be typical of the US or of the people of the US
>
> *(as) cool as a cucumber* very calm and in control of your emotions
>
> *(as) happy as a clam* very happy
>
> *(as) dead as a doornail* obviously dead
>
> *(as) easy as pie* very easy
>
> *(as) nutty as a fruitcake* crazy
>
> *as old as the hills* ancient
>
> *(as) plain as day* easy to see or understand
>
> *(as) right as rain* feeling well
>
> *(as) sharp as a tack* very intelligent
>
> *(as) strong as an ox* very strong
>
> *(as) tough as nails* strong and determined

There are a few very common idioms consisting simply of *as*, an adjective or adverb, and a second *as*. The part of the comparison after the second *as* may be a single word, but is frequently a clause. These basic, three-word idioms sometimes become part of longer idioms, and in that case, *so* may be used instead of the first *as*:

> *as far as* to the degree that
>
> *as far as* **you** *are concerned* in your opinion
>
> *as far as* **sth** *goes* to the degree something is considered or exists
>
> *as far as possible* if you can
>
> *as far as I can see* in the way that I understand
>
> *as good as* almost or nearly
>
> *(as) good as new* in very good condition
>
> *as likely as not* probably
>
> *as soon as* when
>
> *give as good as* **you** *get* to treat people the same way they treat you
>
> *your guess is as good as mine* I do not know the answer to that question

The *as . . . as* form is also very common in many phrases apart from idioms, such as *as long as*, *as much as*, and *as simple as*.

at

Many idioms are formed with *at* and a noun or adjective. In some of these idioms, *at* is used to mean "having the qualities of":

at home comfortable and relaxed

at sea confused

In other idioms, *at* is used to mean "experiencing":

at ease relaxed and comfortable

at leisure when you want to or are not busy

at odds (with sb/sth*)* in disagreement

Sometimes, *at* is used before a superlative (= the form of an adjective used to show that a quality is the most it can be):

at best in the most satisfactory conditions

at (the very) least not less than

at (the) most no more than

at worst in the least satisfactory conditions

Here are the other idioms in this dictionary formed with at and a noun or adjective:

at all to any degree

at hand happening or present at this time

at heart as what someone cares about the most

at issue not decided

at it doing something

at large most of

at (long) last after much delay

at liberty able or allowed to do something

at loggerheads strongly disagreeing

at once immediately

at present now

at stake in danger of being lost

at that because of what was said or done

at will at any time or in any way you want

by

By, followed by a noun, appears in many idioms, usually expressing how or why something happens:

by definition because of the nature of someone or something

by degrees in small stages

by dint of sth as a result of or because of something

by heart exactly and from memory

by hook or by crook using any method possible

by mistake without intending to

by rote automatically and without thinking

by the same token because of this same situation or condition

by virtue of sth because of something

fly by the seat of your pants to do something difficult without the necessary experience or ability

grow by leaps and bounds to become quickly larger

hang by a thread to be in danger of having something unlucky or bad happen

know sb/sth *by sight* to recognize someone or something

live by your *wits* to exist by taking advantage of any opportunity you have

lead sb *by the nose* to control someone so that they do exactly what you want them to do

not by any stretch (of the imagination) even if you try, it is still difficult to accept

take sb/sth *by storm* to be suddenly and extremely successful

take (sb) *by surprise* to do something not expected

In some idioms, *by* refers to an amount or a difference between two amounts:

by a mile by a large number, distance, or amount

by far to a great degree

by the dozen in large numbers

not by a long shot not at all

By is also used as part of a few phrasal verbs with the meaning "giving support":

stand by sb/sth to support someone or something

stick by sb/sth to support someone or something

swear by sth to strongly believe in something

Finally, *by* appears in these common idioms, which are often spoken:

by all means certainly

by the way in addition but of less importance

Study Section

something by *something*

By can be used to connect almost any period of time with the same word to refer to those periods of time going past:

day by day every day
month by month every month
week by week every week
year by year every year

Similarly, *by* is used between pairs of other words to suggest a gradual but regular process:

bit by bit in small amounts
little by little in small amounts
one by one one person or thing following another in order
step by step gradually or slowly

By is used in the following idiom to show that two people or things are close together:

cheek by jowl very close together

in a

A number of idioms take the form *in a (something)*, usually referring to being in a particular condition or situation, often one that is difficult or frightening:

in a bad way having difficulties
in a bind forced to deal with a difficult situation
in a cold sweat very frightened or worried
in a fog confused or not aware
in a pickle experiencing a difficult situation
in a quandary not knowing what to do
in a tight spot in a difficult situation

This form is also used in these short expressions that manage to say a lot with a few words

in a pinch if necessary
in a row in a series without interruption
in a sense considering a situation in a particular way
in a vacuum without any connection to other people or events
in a way considered in this manner

It is also sometimes used in comparisons with different situations:

a needle in a haystack something extremely hard to find
a pig in a poke something that you buy without knowing if it is good or not
in a nutshell very briefly
(like) two peas in a pod very similar
a square peg (in a round hole) someone who is different from most people of the same age and situation

Focus on form

in (the)

Many idioms take the form *in the*, or sometimes simply *in*, followed by a noun, often with the meaning of being able to do or begin something in a confident way:

- **back in the game** active again
- **in gear** working well
- **in hand** controlled
- **in place** ready for use
- **in the can** completed and ready to be shown
- **in the cards** very likely to happen
- **in the catbird seat** in a position of power or influence
- **in the fast lane** doing things that will lead to success
- **in the loop** having knowledge of and involvement in something
- **in the right place at the right time** lucky to be somewhere
- sb **is in business** someone is able to begin doing something

Since the language of idioms represents life realistically, at least as many idioms similar in form to those above have negative meanings. These idioms are about not being able to do something or about being disappointed or in trouble:

- ***a fly in the ointment*** someone or something that spoils a good situation
- ***a slap in the face*** an insult
- ***caught in the middle*** to experience the influence of opposing groups in a disagreement
- ***dead in the water*** without any chance for success
- ***in the dumps*** not successful
- ***in the hole*** owing money
- ***in the line of fire*** in a situation in which you may be severely criticized
- ***in the wrong place (at the wrong time)*** unlucky to be somewhere
- ***keep*** sb ***in the dark*** to not tell someone about something
- ***leave*** sb/sth ***in the dust*** to replace someone or something with something new
- ***leave*** sb ***in the lurch*** to cause someone to be in a situation in which they do not have what they need
- ***lost in the shuffle*** ignored or forgotten
- ***pie in the sky*** something good that is unlikely to happen
- ***whistling in the dark*** to be confident about something although you have no good reason to be confident

Study Section

in your

A large number of idioms with *in* are used in a personal way and take the form of a verb followed by *in your (something)*. Many of these have to do with feelings or attitudes that are often not expressed:

feel sth *in your bones* to know something is true, even though it cannot be proved

have butterflies in your stomach to feel very nervous

sb's *heart is in the right place* someone has only good intentions

leave a bad taste in your *mouth* to cause an unpleasant memory

stick in your *craw* to be unacceptable and therefore annoying to you

stick in your *mind* to have a strong effect on you, so that you remember

spin in sb's *grave* to be shocked and upset by what someone has done

tie sb *(up) in knots* to cause someone to become very confused or worried

A few others with similar meanings omit the verb:

a gleam in your *eye* something that is thought about or planned but not yet started

a lump in your *throat* a strong feeling of emotion that makes speaking difficult

in your *heart of hearts* if your true thoughts and feelings were known

Some other idioms introduced by a verb have different meanings:

born with a silver spoon in your *mouth* to have opportunities that you did not earn but that you have from the influence of your family

have your *day in court* to have the opportunity to make a complaint publicly and to have it judged fairly

put all your *eggs in one basket* to risk your money or your reputation in support of one idea or plan

shoot yourself in the foot to do or say something that causes problems for you

stare you in the face to be obvious

stop (dead) in your *tracks* to suddenly stop moving or doing something

the ball is in your *court* you need to react or answer

until you *are blue in the face* for a long time

A very few idioms, like *a lump in your throat* above, take the form *(noun) in your (something)*:

a feather in your *cap* an achievement that you can be proud of

putty in your *hands* willing to do anything you want

Other idioms consist of *in your (something)*. These usually have more immediate force, and are often spoken:

in your *face* rudely annoying you

in your *right mind* thinking clearly and able to make good decisions

in your *sights* in a situation in which you will attack

Focus on form

like

Like is used in many idioms as a preposition before a noun to make a comparison with something that is not related at all to the subject being discussed, but adds emphasis to the statement you are making. Because the meaning of the idiom and the meaning of the actual words you are using are very different, often in a surprising way, this type of idiom adds variety to language and, if not used too often, can make it more interesting. Here are some idioms using such comparisons:

(come up) smelling like a rose to end something positively or as a winner

eat like a horse to eat large amounts of food often

fit (you) like a glove to be perfectly suited to you

(hit you) like a ton of bricks to shock you so much that you do not know how to react

like a bolt from the blue suddenly and unexpectedly

like a dream so well or so good that it cannot quite be believed

like a shot very quickly and eagerly

like clockwork at regular times

like nobody's business very quickly, very easily, or very well

sell like hotcakes to sell quickly and in large numbers

sleep like a log to sleep very well

stick out like a sore thumb to be easily noticed as different

watch sb *like a hawk* to look at someone very carefully

work like a charm to operate perfectly

In some *like* idioms, the comparison is with something to be avoided, in order to show how extremely bad or unpleasant something is:

avoid sb/sth *like the plague* to keep far away from someone or something

like pulling teeth extremely difficult

Like is also used informally in speech before phrases and clauses in a way that would not be considered good grammar if written. In these idioms, *like* is used as a conjunction:

feel like sth to seem likely to do something

like I said as I mentioned before

look like sth to seem likely that something will happen

like there's no tomorrow quickly and eagerly, without thinking

tell it like it is to describe a situation honestly without avoiding any unpleasant details

In two idioms also commonly used in speech, *like* comes before an adjective and has the meaning "very" or "very much":

like crazy **1** a lot **2** very quickly

like mad **1** a lot **2** very quickly

Study Section

on (a)

A number of idioms take the form *on*, followed immediately by a noun or noun phrase, often referring to a particular condition that someone or something is in:

    dead on arrival without any chance for success

    firing on all cylinders operating as powerfully and effectively as possible

    heaven on earth something extremely good

    hell on wheels extremely difficult

    on borrowed time not likely to be active or working much longer

    on call available and ready to work or do something at any time

    on cloud nine very happy

    on dangerous ground likely to cause offense

    on edge nervous or worried

    on hand immediately available

    on paper possibly

    on shaky ground not supported very well

    on thin ice in an uncertain condition

    on top of sth aware of or in control of a situation

    (right) on cue as if planned to happen exactly at that moment

    (right) on target correct or accurate

    running on empty lacking energy or enthusiasm

    walk on air to be very happy

    walk on eggshells to try very hard not to upset someone or something

A few short idioms in this form have special meanings and do not fit this pattern:

    on earth in any conditions

    on sight as soon as someone or something is seen

    on time when expected or scheduled

There are fewer idioms having the form *on a (something)*. Some of these idioms include the basic meaning of *on* (= physically close to or touching something, usually from above), as in these:

    out on a limb in a situation where you lack support

    put sb/sth ***on a pedestal*** to behave as if one person is more important than others

    stop on a dime to end movement very quickly

Others are not so literal:

    keep sb ***on a tight leash*** to allow someone very little freedom to do what they want

    (off) on a tangent suddenly dealing with a completely different matter

    on a roll experiencing a period of success or good luck

Focus on form

Although many verb phrases include *on*, a few slang or informal expressions in particular use *on* with special emphasis:

hit on **sb** to clearly show that you are sexually attracted to someone

lay **sth** *on* **sb** to blame someone for something

right on exactly right or correct

tell on **sb** to give information about bad behavior to someone in authority

turn **sb** *on* to cause someone to feel excited and very interested

on the/on your

A very common pattern of idioms takes the form of *on the* followed by a noun. Some of these idioms include the basic meaning of *on* (= physically close to or touching something, usually from above). Many other idioms do not have such a literal meaning. Compare, for example, the following two:

a fly on the wall someone who can secretly see or hear what happens

on the fly in a hurry

In the first, the image is of a fly actually on a wall. In the second, *on* has no such meaning. Here are some other idioms in which *on* has much of its literal meaning:

a cloud on the horizon a problem or difficulty that is likely to happen in the future

a pat on the back praise

a slap on the wrist a gentle warning or light punishment

your *feet on the ground* a realistic understanding of your own ideas, actions, and decisions

(get) in on the ground floor to become involved in something from its beginning

hit the nail on the head to be right about something

keep you *on the edge of* your *seat* to make you very excited or nervous because of uncertainty

on the cutting edge (of sth*)* in front of others with what is new

on the right track doing something correctly or well

on the wrong track not correct about something

put (all) your *cards on the table* to truthfully explain what you know or think

put sb *on the shelf* to cause someone not to be available

put sth *on the shelf* to delay something

step on the gas to hurry in order to get something done quickly

the icing on the cake something good that is added to another good thing

the shoe is on the other foot the situation is now the opposite of what it was before

Here are some other idioms in which *on* is not used with its literal meaning:

(hard) on the heels of **sth** close behind or soon after something

keep* your *eye on the ball to give your compete attention to what you are doing or want to achieve

live high on the hog to live in great comfort with a lot of money

(live) on the edge to be in an uncertain situation or one that could cause harm

on the air broadcasting

on the case doing what needs to be done

on the face of it when first considered

on the go very busy or active

on the job while working

on the line at risk of failing or being harmed

on the make trying forcefully to succeed

on the mend getting better after an illness, injury, or a bad period

on the move very busy or active

on the run avoiding being found

on the side in addition to your regular job or activities

on the spot in the place where something has just happened

on the spur of the moment without any planning

put* sth *on the map to make something famous

(right) on the money exactly right or correct

slow on the uptake not able to understand something quickly

Some idioms with *on* are used in a more personal way and take the form of a verb followed by *on your (something)*. Most of these have to do with something you have just done or are about to do:

have blood on* your *hands to be responsible for violent injuries or deaths

land on* your *feet to be in good or improved condition after a difficult experience

turn on* your *heel to leave quickly and suddenly

Idioms without a verb have a wider range of meanings, dealing with attitudes as well as actions:

a chip on* your *shoulder a tendency to be easily angered or upset

a monkey on* your *back a serious problem that you cannot forget

have egg on* your *face to be embarrassed

on* your *side helping you or giving you an advantage

on* your *toes aware and energetic

Focus on form

over

Over is a part of many verb phrases, often with the meaning of going past or beyond something, or happening for a longer time:

blow over to be forgotten because something else happens

get over sth to feel better after an illness or bad experience

lay over to stop or have to in a place when you are traveling

pass over sb/sth to ignore someone or something

skip over sb/sth to omit or not choose someone or something

sleep over to stay the night in someone else's home

spill over to reach or influence a larger area

stay over to spend one or more nights in a place away from home

stop over to stay at a place briefly on the way to somewhere else

tide sb *over* to supply someone with something they need for a short period

Over has this literal meaning in some idioms without verbs:

over the edge into a condition of extreme emotional or mental suffering

over the hill no longer able to do something at an acceptable level because of age

over the hump past the most difficult or dangerous part of something

over the line beyond what is accepted

over the top too extreme

In some verb phrases, *over* has the meaning of moving in a particular direction:

double over to suddenly bend forward and down, usually because of pain or laughter

keel over to fall down suddenly because of illness or weakness

move over to stop having a job, rank, or condition

pull over to move a vehicle to the side of a road and stop

In the following expressions, *over* refers to doing something in a slow and careful way:

go over sth to examine or look at something in a careful way

mull over sth to think carefully about something for a period of time

pick over sth to examine a group of things carefully

pore over sth to look at and carefully study a document

puzzle over sth to give a lot of attention and thought to something

talk sth *over* to discuss something

think sth *over* to consider something carefully

quite a

One of the ways to express the idea of a lot or a large number of something is to say *quite a something*:

quite a change something very different

quite a ways a long distance

quite a while a long time

Idioms that mean simply a large number or amount, unlike the ones given above, are often used before *of something*:

quite a bit a large number or amount *We had quite a bit of time before the movie, so we went for a walk.*

quite a lot a large number or amount *Sheila has quite a lot of friends.*

These idioms may also be used by themselves, usually in answer to a question:

"Do we have much time before the show?" "Oh, yes, quite a bit."

"Did the professor assign much to read?" "Unfortunately, quite a lot."

An idiom that can refer only to a large number can appear before a plural noun, or, in answer to a question, by itself:

quite a few a large number *There were quite a few people waiting in line to see the show.* ◆ *"Do we have any Christmas cards left over from last year?" "Actually, quite a few."*

Apart from idioms, you can use *quite a something* in many other expressions when you want to emphasize how big, severe, unusual, or good something was: *That was quite a storm!* (= it was a very severe storm) ◆ *That was quite a party!* (= that was a great party) ◆ *It was quite a hard exam.* (= it was an unusually hard exam) ◆ *It's quite a long drive from here to San Francisco.* (= it's a very long drive to San Francisco)

Before a vowel, *quite a* becomes *quite an*:

He's quite an impressive speaker. (= he is a very good speaker)

so

So is used in many idioms to refer to a situation in which something is happening or developing and has reached a particular stage:

go so far as to do sth to be extreme in talking about or doing something

so far, so good at this stage of the process it is satisfactory

so long as if

so long a very long time

so much to such a great degree

so much the better it will be more satisfactory

very much so to a great degree

So can also mean that something is certain or is true, or refer to a particular amount of something:

in so many words directly or very clearly

it just so happens (that) surprisingly

so be it nothing can be done about this

so help me (God) this is the truth

so much for sth that is the end of something

In some idioms, *so* is used to refer you to someone or something. In these expressions, *as* may also be used:

so far as you *are concerned* in your opinion

so far as sth *is concerned* in considering something

So also appears in these idioms:

every so often sometimes

or so approximately

so long goodbye

so much as but rather

so and so someone whose name is not known or said

so to speak this is one way to say it

so what it does not seem important

idioms of repetition

Many idioms that repeat the same word show a continuing or repeated action, or deal with time in some way:

again and again many times

and so forth and other similar things

around and around in a circle

by and by soon

day after day repeatedly for many days

day in, day out one day after another

from time to time sometimes

more and more an increasing number of

on and on for a long time without stopping

over and over (again) many times

time after time on repeated occasions

time and (time) again very often

year in, year out every year for a long time

Used with the same meaning, *and* sometimes connects two opposites that are closely related and often used together:

damned if you *do and damned if* you *don't* criticized whatever you decide

day and night all the time

(every) now and then sometimes

here and there in different places

left and right everywhere, without any plan or pattern

to and fro in one direction and then in the opposite direction

ups and downs the mixture of good and bad things that happen

And can connect the same or closely related words to show that something is complete or extreme:

neck and neck very close or equal

raining cats and dogs to be raining in great amounts

the be-all and end-all the best or most important thing

the ins and outs of sth the details or facts about something

through and through completely

toss and turn to be unable to sleep because of worrying

well and truly completely

PHRASES WITH A PURPOSE

idioms of reaction

When a person wants to react to something that someone else has done, either something good or something bad, they have a number of expressions to choose from.

If someone has done something helpful, you will be likely to use a polite expression like *thank you* or *thanks*, which is a way of showing your appreciation. When someone thanks you for something you have done for them, it is polite to say *you're welcome*. A more formal expression, not so often used, is *don't mention it*. Far more common today, especially among younger people, is the informal expression *no problem*, which also has other uses.

No problem is also used with the meaning of agreeing to do something that you have been asked to do. The intention is to tell the person asking you that they have not caused you any difficulty because what you have been asked to do is easy or unimportant, and not worth worrying about:

> "Can you pick up Sophie when she gets out of school today?" "Sure, no problem."

No problem is also used in situations where someone might think you are annoyed or angry about something they have done, and you want them to know that you are not annoyed:

> "I'm sorry, I dialed the wrong number." "No problem."

OK is used in answer to a variety of questions, including each of the three situations given above for *no problem*. The basic meaning of *OK* is Yes, I agree, but it is also very commonly used as a way of reacting to a greeting, meaning you are doing well, or as well as you can expect to do.

> "How are you today?" "I'm OK, how about you?"

Other, less pleasant ways to react are also available:

> ***dream on*** what you want will not happen

This idiom might be used when someone has said something that you think is very unlikely ever to happen:

> "I tried out for the leading part and I just know I'll get it!" "Dream on!"

More rude expressions are sometimes used by those who want to show their anger or annoyance at someone:

> ***tough luck*** I have no sympathy for your problems

Sometimes *tough* is used alone when answering someone.

> *He asked the police if he could say good-bye to his wife before he was taken away to prison, but they said, "Tough" and put him in the car.*

Similar in meaning is this expression:

> ***no dice*** this result did not or will not happen *The Giants could have made it an exciting ballgame, but no dice, they didn't even score.*

expressions of surprise, anger, satisfaction, or attitude

Some idioms that are usually spoken with emphasis provide the speaker with a way to express certain strong emotions or to show attitudes, but do not have much meaning apart from the emotions or attitudes they express. Some of these idioms are slang. Among the emotions they express are surprise:

holy cow what a surprise

holy smoke what a surprise

boy oh boy I am excited or surprised to say

no kidding really or honestly

what do you know this is surprising

Others express annoyance or anger. Some are or are based on a form of swearing:

for Christ's sake rude slang I am surprised or annoyed by this

for God's sake rude slang I am surprised or annoyed by this

for goodness sake I am surprised or annoyed by this

for Pete's sake I am surprised or annoyed by this

Others express satisfaction that something bad has not happened:

thank God be pleased or happy

thank goodness I am pleased or happy

thank heavens I am pleased or happy

Others are used to strengthen the force of an opinion or emotion:

as hell in an extreme way

like hell 1 very much 2 very badly

Some express an attitude, such as not caring:

what the hell why not

This common expression is used to make sure that what you have said has been listened to or understood:

you know you understand

THE HUMAN BODY

sense organs

Not surprisingly, idioms including the eyes, ears, and nose have to do with being able to see, hear, and smell. But they include other meanings as well. *Eye* and *eyes* often follow a verb, especially *keep*, with the meaning of to watch or give your attention to something:

catch **sb's** *eye* to attract someone's attention

have **your** *eye on* **sb** to watch someone carefully

keep **your** *eyes peeled (for* **sth***)* to watch carefully for someone or something

keep an eye on **sb/sth** to watch or give your attention to someone or something

keep **your** *eye on the ball* to give complete attention to what you are doing or want to achieve

keep one eye on **sth/sb** to give part of your attention to one person or thing

Sometimes the emphasis, both for *eyes* and *ears*, is on giving your full attention to someone or something because you are very interested in them:

all eyes with a lot of interest in something or someone you see

all ears very eager to listen to what someone is going to say

all eyes are on **sb/sth** everyone is watching someone or something

only have eyes for **sb/sth** to be interested in just one person or thing

Sometimes *eyes* and *ears* emphasize awareness rather than interest:

have **your** *ear to the ground* to watch and listen carefully to what is happening around you

hit **you** *(right) between the eyes* to be very easy to notice

with **your** *eyes (wide) open* understanding the true character of someone or something

Idioms with *nose* often make use of the fact that the nose is the most forward part of the face:

follow **your** *nose* to move forward

keep **your** *nose out of* **sth** to not become involved in something

lead **sb** *by the nose* to control someone so that they do exactly what you want them to do

poke **your** *nose into* **sth** to try to discover things that do not involve you

under **your** *nose* obvious or not hidden

Nose is also used in idioms dealing with social relationships:

look down **your** *nose at* **sb/sth** to consider someone or something as not important or of value

thumb **your** *nose at* **sb/sth** to show that you do not respect someone or something

turn up **your** *nose at* **sth** to not like something because you think it is not good enough for you

body parts – heart, stomach, and teeth

Most idioms containing *heart* have to do with the emotions, since the heart has traditionally been considered the origin of feelings, as seen in these examples:

> ***break* your *heart*** to make you very sad
>
> ***eat your heart out*** you should be sorry for the choices you have made
>
> ***from the heart*** in a sincere manner
>
> ***in* your *heart of hearts*** if your true thoughts and feelings were known
>
> ***open your heart*** to show or tell your true feelings and thoughts
>
> ***sick at heart*** very sad, unhappy, or upset

Of the many emotions *heart* can be used to suggest, love or strong affection is common:

> ***close to* your *heart*** of great importance to you
>
> ***lose* your *heart (to* sb/sth*)*** to fall in love
>
> ***steal* sb's *heart*** to cause someone to love you
>
> ***wear* your *heart on* your *sleeve*** to show your feelings, esp. your love for someone

But kindness and sympathy are also common:

> ***a heart of gold*** a kind and generous character
>
> ***a heart of stone*** an unfriendly and unkind character
>
> ***harden your heart*** to make yourself stop feeling kindness and sympathy
>
> **your *heart bleeds (for* sb*)*** you feel sadness and sympathy for someone
>
> **your *heart goes out to* sb** you feel sympathy for someone

Heart, as well as *stomach*, can be used to mean determination or purpose:

> ***have* your *heart set on* sth** to want something very much
>
> **your *heart sinks*** you become discouraged or disappointed
>
> ***lose heart*** to stop believing that you can succeed
>
> ***not have the heart (to* do sth*)*** to lack the desire or strength to do something
>
> ***not have the stomach (for* sth*)*** to not feel strong or brave enough to do something unpleasant
>
> ***a strong stomach*** the ability not to be upset by unpleasant things

Teeth is used, often after a verb, to mean strength or energy:

> ***grit* your *teeth*** to deal with something in a determined way
>
> ***put teeth into* sth** to make a law or rule effective
>
> ***sink* your *teeth into* sth** to start to do something with a lot of energy or enthusiasm

Teeth is also used in idioms to show the difficulty of doing something:

> ***in the teeth of* sth** while experiencing something difficult
>
> ***like pulling teeth*** extremely difficult

M, m

mad
like mad
1 a lot; = **like crazy** ♦ *The competition is growing like mad in this field.*
2 very quickly; = **like crazy** ♦ *My poor heart is beating like mad.*
mad about *sb/sth*
to like or love someone or something very much; = **crazy about** *sb/sth* ♦ *I was mad about animals and ignored everything else until I was about eleven.*

> ORIGIN: based on the literal meaning of **mad** (= crazy)

made
made for each other
perfectly matched ♦ *Those cool drinks and that hot, spicy food seem to have been made for each other.* ♦ *They are truly in love, and all of their friends thought they were made for each other.*
a marriage made in heaven See at MARRIAGE
a match made in heaven See at MATCH
have (got) it made See at HAVE
tailor-made for *sb/sth* See at TAILOR-MADE

magic
work *your/its* **magic**
to achieve a positive result ♦ *Can the Austrian men win, or will the Americans work their magic at the Olympics?* ♦ *You have to sit back and let the images in Ozu's films work their magic.*
wave a magic wand See at WAND

main
in the main slightly formal
mostly ♦ *Major crime seems to be, in the main, caused by drugs and poverty.*

make
make a *sth* **of it**
to spend all of a particular amount of time on an activity ♦ *You can easily make a day of it just by going to museums.* USAGE: used only with periods of time, especially **day** or **night**, and usually used to talk about spending time doing something entertaining

make as if to *do sth*
to behave in a way that seems to show you will do something ♦ *She made as if to run away, then stopped and stood still.*

make believe
to pretend ♦ *Claude made believe he hadn't heard what she said.*

make do
to use what is available although it is not everything you need ♦ *She's a mother of three who struggles to make do on very little money.* ♦ *The storm knocked down power lines, and we had to make do without electricity.*

make for *sth*
1 to result in or cause something ♦ *Having so much music, dance, and drama available makes for a great cultural experience.*
2 to move toward something ♦ *Joe was ready to make for the back door.*

make good
to become successful ♦ *He was represented as the local boy who made good in Hollywood.*

make good *sb's sth*
to succeed in doing something difficult ♦ *She made good her escape from the hospital.*

make good on *sth*
to do what you have said you would do ♦ *I told them they would have a great time, and I want to make good on my promise.* ♦ *My dad made good on his threat to cut off our Internet service.*

make it
1 to arrive at a place or go to an event ♦ *She made it to the airport*

just in time to catch her plane. ♦ *We're having a party on Saturday – can you make it?*
2 to be successful ♦ *Now that she's got her own home, she feels as if she's really made it.* ♦ *Trying to make it as an actor is tough.* ♦ Related vocabulary **have (got) it made 2** at HAVE
3 to stay alive ♦ *She was losing so much blood, I really thought she wasn't going to make it.*

make it big
to be successful and famous ♦ *It was obvious to everyone that Tom had the potential to make it big in the movies.*

make it up to *sb*
1 to do something good for someone because you upset them ♦ *I know I disappointed him, but I promised to make it up to him.*
2 to do something good for someone because they did something good for you ♦ *She had always been there for him, and he didn't know how he could ever make it up to her.*

make it with *sb* slang
to have sex with someone ♦ *These college boys were hoping to make it with someone older than them.*

make light of *sth*
to talk or behave as if something is not serious or important ♦ *I don't mean to make light of the fact that this was a horrible crime.*

make off with *sth*
to steal something ♦ *Someone broke into the vehicle last night and made off with three sculptures worth about $600,000.*

make or break *sth*
to cause something to succeed or fail ♦ *His opinion could make or break a Broadway play.*

make out
1 to achieve a particular level of success ♦ *I know you've just started college and I wondered how you are making out.* ♦ *It was hard at first, but now I'm making out OK.*
2 slang ♦ to kiss and touch someone in a sexual way ♦ *Esther was making out with her boyfriend in the library the other day.*

make out *sb*, *also* **make** *sb* **out**
to see someone ♦ *It was getting dark, but I could make out two people in the distance.*

make out *sth*, *also* **make** *sth* **out**
1 to hear or understand something ♦ *With all the traffic noise, I couldn't make out a single word she said.*
2 to write information on a form or document ♦ *I just made out my application for a new credit card.*

make *sb* **out to be** *sth*
to represent someone as being something ♦ *He was not the monster that everyone made him out to be.*

make over *sb/sth*, *also* **make** *sb/sth* **over**
to improve the way someone or something looks ♦ *For the first time since it was built we will be making over the entire building.*

make ready to *do sth*
to prepare to do something ♦ *He made ready to jump in the water and swim to shore as soon as the boat neared the beach.*

make *you* **sick**
to cause you to feel disgust ♦ *It makes me sick to think of how many people are destroying themselves with drugs.*

make something of *yourself*, *also* **make something of** *your* **life**
to achieve success ♦ *I want to make something of myself so that my family will be proud of me.* ♦ *She worked hard in school, hoping she could make something of her life.*

make something out of nothing, *also* **make something (out) of it**
to say that something is a problem when it is not ♦ *You seem to think I'm making something out of nothing, but I think these letters are important.* USAGE: often used to ask someone if they want to disagree or fight about something: *Yeah, I like*

Lee's movies – you want to make something of it?

make *sth* **stick**
to cause something to be accepted or agreed to ◆ *Investigators didn't have the evidence to make the charges stick.* ◆ *Workers got a good agreement and made it stick by threatening another costly strike.*

make that *sth* esp. spoken, *also* **make it** *sth*
I want to change what I just said to something else ◆ *We'll be there at 7:30 – no, better make that 8 o'clock.* ◆ *Luxury products are usually gold – uh, make it platinum.*

make up
to become friendly again after having an argument or disagreement ◆ *It took us a while to make up after the fight we had last Sunday.*

make up *sth*
1 to form part or all of a group ◆ *Women made up about 28 percent of the students earning a master's degree that year.*
2 to add to an amount of money to reach a total ◆ *We're $5 short, but I'll make up the difference.* ◆ *We'll have to try to make up the shortfall by cutting costs.*

make up *sth*, *also* **make** *sth* **up**
1 to invent a story or an excuse ◆ *He made up a story to explain why he was late for work.* ◆ *I don't know how a computer works, but I could make something up.*
2 to use time later to do something you did not do when it was scheduled ◆ *She'll have to make up the exam next Wednesday.* ◆ *I take an extra fifteen minutes for lunch and I make it up at the end of the day.*

make up for *sth*
1 to take the place of something ◆ *She's a popular girl whose lively spirit makes up for her slight speech problem.*
2 to help you deal with something ◆ *The court awarded them two million dollars to make up for their pain and suffering.*

on the make
trying forcefully to succeed ◆ *The movie is about a businessman on the make who starts stealing company funds.* ◆ *New York is a city on the make, a place of energy and speed.*
USAGE: sometimes said about someone who is trying very hard to have sex with others: *He was a man on the make, ready to pursue any woman who crossed his path.*

what do you make of *sb/sth*
what is your opinion about someone or something ◆ *What do you make of the new guy in the mailroom?* ◆ *What do you make of the report that terrorists are planning another attack?*

what makes *sb* **tick**
the reasons why someone behaves the way they do ◆ *The admiral was interested in people, what made them tick and what influenced their behavior.*

making

in the making
1 being created ◆ *Her novel was ten years in the making, and not very successful.*
2 in the process of happening ◆ *It became clear that this was a disaster in the making and we had no way of coping with it.*

of *your* **own making**
caused by your own mistakes ◆ *He blames everybody else instead of admitting that this is a problem of his own making.*

history in the making See at HISTORY

makings

have (all) the makings of *sth*
to seem likely to develop into something ◆ *I think we have the makings of a good team this year.* ◆ *This story has all the makings of a first-class scandal.*

man

man

a man of few words
a man who speaks only when necessary ◆ *He was respected as a man of few words and significant actions.*

a man of his word
a man who tells the truth and keeps promises ◆ *He's always been a man of his word, that I must say.*

every man for himself
each person here should do what is best for themselves ◆ *In the world of politics, it's every man for himself.* USAGE: usually used with **it's**, as in the example

man enough to *do sth*
someone with a strong enough character to do something ◆ *I appreciate you being man enough to tell me what happened.* USAGE: usually said about doing something difficult or unpleasant

the man on the street, *also* **the man in the street**
an ordinary man ◆ *Maybe the man on the street doesn't think this problem is very important.* ◆ Related vocabulary **the woman on the street** at WOMAN

to a man
including everyone ◆ *They supported him to a man.*

your own man See *your* **own person** at PERSON

manna

manna from heaven
something very good that you did not expect ◆ *Employees are enjoying manna from heaven in the form of year-end bonuses.*

manner

in a manner of speaking
this is one way to say it; = **so to speak** ◆ *"We should go south." "So that means I should turn left?" "In a manner of speaking, yes."* ◆ *She was, in a manner of speaking, not at her best – in fact, she was exhausted and had the flu.* USAGE: sometimes used to suggest that something unpleasant is being described in a more pleasant way ◆ Related vocabulary **if you will** at IF, **in other words** at WORDS

many

many a *sb/sth* slightly formal
a large number of people or things ◆ *Bad weather has brought many a farmer to the brink of disaster over the past decade.* USAGE: used before a singular noun

map

fall off the map, *also* **drop off the map**
to stop being known or considered ◆ *That team played in the World Series for three or four years in a row, but then they dropped off the map.*

map out *sth*, *also* **map** *sth* **out**
to decide in detail how something will be done ◆ *She is mapping out lesson plans for teachers who work with below-average readers.* ◆ *When we mapped it out before we began this project, we thought we would be finished by now.*

> ORIGIN: based on the literal meaning of **map out** (= to use a map to plan a trip)

put *sth* **on the map**
to make something famous ◆ *The Macintosh operating system put Apple computers on the map.*

wipe *somewhere* **off the map**
to cause a place to stop existing ◆ *The flood of 1965 almost wiped the town off the map.*

marbles

lose *your* **marbles**
to start forgetting things, behaving strangely, or becoming mentally ill ◆ *I haven't lost my marbles yet.* ◆ *She's begun to lose her marbles, and there's nothing we can do.*

mark

hit the mark
to be correct or accurate ◆ *The writer hit the mark in saying that*

market

map out something

We haven't finished mapping out the conference schedule.

the military contributes $400,000 a month to the local economy.

leave *your/its* **mark (on** *sb/sth***)**, *also* **leave a mark (on** *sb/sth***)**
to have an effect that changes someone or something ♦ *Another storm left its mark on California, knocking down trees and power lines across the state.* USAGE: often used in the phrase **leave your mark on the world** (= to be successful or famous): *I hope to leave my mark on the world through my music.*

make *your* **mark**, *also* **make a mark**
to be successful or famous ♦ *She played several sports in school, but it was in basketball that she made her mark.*

mark down *sth*, *also* **mark** *sth* **down**
to reduce the price of something ♦ *The machine, originally priced at $50, was marked down to $37.50.* ♦ *If it doesn't sell at full price, we'll have to mark it down.*

mark up *sth*, *also* **mark** *sth* **up**
1 to make changes, notes, and corrections on a document ♦ *Could you tell me what changes have been made so I can mark up my copy?* ♦ *Take the papers home with you, mark them up, and then bring them in tomorrow and we can discuss them.*
2 to increase the price of something ♦ *Farmers have marked up milk prices to cover their costs.* ♦ *I can't believe you marked it up by 400%.*

off the mark, *also* **wide of the mark**
wrong or not accurate ♦ *They said the course would be easy but that turned out to be way off the mark.* USAGE: sometimes used in the phrase **not far off the mark** (= almost right): *If you guessed he was jealous, you would not be far off the mark.*

mark my words See at WORDS
mark time See at TIME
up to the mark See **up to par** at PAR

market

corner the market, *also* **have a corner on the market**
to control the supply or sale of a particular product ♦ *The company*

marriage

tried to corner the market on several types of computer software.

in the market for *sth*
interested in buying something ◆ *I'm not in the market for a car at the moment.*

on the market
for sale ◆ *We put our house on the market last spring.*

play the market
to try to earn money by buying and selling shares in companies ◆ *These traders are people who play the market for profit.*

marriage

a marriage made in heaven
a perfect combination of two people or things; = **a match made in heaven** ◆ *He calls the deal between the two companies a marriage made in heaven.*

mat

go to the mat (for *sb/sth*)
to support someone or something very strongly ◆ *When he believes in a project, he's willing to go to the mat for it.*

match

a match made in heaven
a perfect combination of two people or things; = **a marriage made in heaven** ◆ *They needed a Spanish teacher as badly as Hayes needed a job, so you could say it was a match made in heaven.*

match up (against *sb*)
to have a chance to win in a competition against someone ◆ *He was nominated because he matched up better against the governor.* ◆ *With our team's experience, I think we match up well.*

meet *your* match
to find someone equal to you in some way ◆ *Martina finally met her match on the tennis court today and lost, three sets to two.*

mix and match See at MIX

matter

a matter of *doing sth*
something that needs to be done ◆ *Staying healthy as you age is often a matter of avoiding weight gain.*

a matter of *sth*
an amount that can be measured ◆ *The guards will react to an alarm call within a matter of minutes.* ◆ *We were off our course by a matter of ten to twenty miles to the west.*

a matter of life and death
something that is very important or serious ◆ *Don't disturb me unless it's matter of life and death.*

a matter of opinion
the particular belief that someone has about something ◆ *Whether the situation has improved is not a matter of opinion – things are much worse than they were before.*

a matter of record
a fact recorded in writing ◆ *The judgment of the court is a matter of record.*

a matter of time
sure to happen at some time in the future ◆ *If she wins next year's congressional race, it seems only a matter of time before she ends up running for the Senate.* USAGE: usually used with **only** or **just**: *It's just a matter of time before prices for the newest computer come down.*

as a matter of course
naturally or automatically ◆ *Many pet owners lavish affection on their animals as a matter of course.*

as a matter of fact esp. spoken
actually; = **in (point of) fact** ◆ *I did vote for her, as a matter of fact.* USAGE: used to emphasize the truth of what you are saying ◆ Related vocabulary **in reality** at REALITY, **in truth** at TRUTH

for that matter
to the degree that something is considered ◆ *I don't know why she wanted to fly to Salt Lake City in this weather, or why she wanted to fly at all for that matter.* ◆ Related vocab-

ulary **so far as** *sth* **is concerned** at CONCERNED

no laughing matter
something serious that people should not make jokes about ◆ *A wound on your foot is no laughing matter when you're a diabetic.* ◆ Related vocabulary **no joke** at JOKE

no matter
1 without considering ◆ *He will do anything, no matter how unfair, to win an election.* USAGE: usually followed by **how**, as in the example, or by **who**, **what**, or **which**: *He'll say what he thinks, no matter who you are.* ◆ *She goes out running no matter what the weather is like.*
2 esp. spoken ◆ it is not important ◆ *You never thought about it, did you? Well, no matter.*

no matter how you slice it esp. spoken
in whatever way you consider this; = **any way you slice it** ◆ *No matter how you slice it, graduate school is expensive.*

no matter what
whatever the conditions are ◆ *Gun-control laws won't stop crime because I think the criminals will get guns no matter what.*

mind over matter See at MIND

max

max (*yourself*) out
to reach a limit ◆ *By Christmas our credit cards were maxed out.* ◆ *This great athlete hasn't maxed herself out – yet.*

> ORIGIN: based on the literal meaning of **maximum** (= the greatest amount possible)

to the max
to the highest degree or level ◆ *She does what she wants, living her life to the max and enjoying every moment.*

may

***you* may as well (*do sth*)**
there is no reason you should not do something; = ***you* might as well (*do sth*)** ◆ *If you want to buy stocks, you may as well do it now, when the prices are low.*

be that as it may See at BE
come what may See at COME
let the chips fall (where they may) See at CHIPS

me

me neither esp. spoken
I also would not ◆ *"I'd never go there alone at night." "Me neither."* USAGE: used to agree with a negative statement

me, too esp. spoken
and I am also ◆ *"I'm crazy about history." "Yeah, me, too."* USAGE: used to say that you agree with something

mean

mean well
to intend to be helpful ◆ *He's a good person, and I know he means well.*

no mean *sth*
not something small or unimportant ◆ *Getting the job finished so quickly was no mean achievement.*

mean business See at BUSINESS

means

a means to an end
something done to achieve something else ◆ *You may get tired of regular physical exercise, but it's simply a means to an end.*

beyond *your* means, *also* **beyond the means of *sb***
too expensive for you ◆ *We bought a retirement home, but at first the repair work was beyond our means.* ◆ Opposite **within *your* means**

by all means
certainly ◆ *If you can find a use for this old computer, by all means keep it.*

by no means slightly formal, *also* **not by any means**
not in any way ◆ *This is by no means a terrible film.* ◆ *We are by no means finished yet.* USAGE: usually used to

disagree with someone who might have an opposite opinion

within *your* means
without spending more than the money you have ♦ *We need to reduce spending and live within our means.* ♦ Opposite **beyond *your* means**

ways and means See at WAYS

meantime

in the meantime
while something else is happening or until something else happens; = **in the meanwhile** ♦ *A new school is being built, but in the meantime this school building remains seriously overcrowded.*

meanwhile

in the meanwhile
while something else is happening or until something else happens; = **in the meantime** ♦ *You go back to school to learn a new trade and hope you can keep the family together in the meanwhile.*

measure

beyond measure slightly formal
to an extremely high degree ♦ *Our religious faith improved our lives beyond measure.*

for good measure
in addition to something else already said or done ♦ *He wrote a great article, and for good measure took the photograph used for the magazine cover.*

measure up (to *sb/sth*)
to reach a standard that is as good as someone or something else ♦ *The math skills of the majority of children in this school measure up to the national standards.* USAGE: often used in a negative way: *They didn't measure up so I couldn't hire them.* ♦ *Too often computer software fails to measure up to expectations.*

take the measure of *sb/sth* slightly formal
to make a judgment or form an opinion about someone or something ♦ *She quietly observed him,* *taking the measure of this man she had heard so much about.*

meet

meet *sb* halfway
to do some of what someone asks you to do ♦ *He's put forward some good proposals for settling the strike, but the other side has not been willing to meet him halfway.* USAGE: often said about an attempt to reach an agreement about something ♦ Related vocabulary **split the difference** 1 at DIFFERENCE

meet up (with *sb*)
to see and talk to someone familiar or someone you do not know ♦ *Let's meet up for drinks after work.* ♦ *I met up with a couple of Australians on the train.* USAGE: refers to seeing someone either intentionally or unexpectedly

meet with *sth* slightly formal
to experience something, esp. something unpleasant ♦ *The proposal for the new highway met with harsh criticism.* USAGE: often used of a negative reaction

make ends meet See at ENDS

meet *your* match See at MATCH

never the twain shall meet See at TWAIN

meeting

a meeting of the minds slightly formal
a situation in which people find that they have similar ideas and opinions ♦ *There was a true meeting of minds between the two leaders during the six-hour talks.*

mellow

mellow out
to become more relaxed ♦ *I used to get upset about my golf game, but now I've mellowed out a little bit and it doesn't bother me so much.*

melt

melt away
to disappear ♦ *The polls show him with a big lead now, but his support*

could melt away before the election.
USAGE: sometimes used in the form **melt something away**: *She put on some music that's meant to melt your tension away.*

melt in *your* mouth See at MOUTH

memory

commit to memory *sth*, *also* **commit *sth* to memory**
to study something in order to make yourself remember it ◆ *If you want to learn a language well, you have to commit to memory long lists of vocabulary and grammatical rules.* ◆ *The boys read the holy book several times, committing it to memory.*

if memory serves
if I am remembering correctly ◆ *If memory serves, there will be flags and parades for the Olympic opening ceremonies.*

in memory of *sb*, *also* **in *sb's* memory**
in order to honor someone who has died and to help people remember them ◆ *A service was held in memory of the earthquake victims.* ◆ *Donations can be made to the Heart Association in Diane's memory.*

jog *your* memory
to cause you to remember something ◆ *I use the photos to remind me of what I've seen, to jog my memory.*

refresh *your* memory
to help you to remember something ◆ *McNamara has refreshed his memory by listening to a tape recording of the meeting.* USAGE: often used by lawyers when asking questions in a trial: *"Will this photograph I now show you refresh your memory?"*

memory lane

down memory lane
in your memory of the pleasures of past events ◆ *For older people, visiting the old-fashioned stores in the town was a trip down memory lane.*

men

separate the men from the boys
to show which people in a group can do something difficult and which people cannot ◆ *The five-day camping trip next month should separate the men from the boys!*

mend

on the mend
getting better after an illness, injury, or a bad period ◆ *He's on the mend and walking a mile a day after a mild heart attack.* ◆ *With fewer people out of work, the economy is clearly on the mend.*

mend (*your*) fences See at FENCES

mend *your* ways See at WAYS

mention

don't mention it
it was no trouble ◆ *"Thanks for lending me your bicycle." "Don't mention it!"* USAGE: used as a polite answer after someone has thanked you for something

mention (*sb/sth*) in passing
to refer to someone or something briefly while talking about something else ◆ *During the interview, she mentioned in passing that her father had also been involved in publishing.*

not to mention *sb/sth*
and also someone or something else ◆ *Gaining weight didn't help her health, not to mention the high blood pressure that ran in her family.* ◆ *They don't have any of the players from that championship team anymore, not to mention manager Casey Stengel.* USAGE: used to add emphasis to what you are saying ◆ Related vocabulary **let alone do *sth*** at LET, **to say nothing of *sb/sth*** at SAY

mercy

at the mercy of *sb/sth*, *also* **at *sb's/sth's* mercy**
unable to protect yourself from someone or something ◆ *The entire movie business is at the mercy of teenage moviegoers.* ◆ *If you're not legally employed, you're at your employer's mercy.*

merits

on its (own) merits
based on considering which person or thing has the best qualities ◆ *Judge the product on its own merits and not on any advertising claims.*

on the merits
based on the qualities of someone or something, or on the facts of a situation ◆ *The mayor makes job appointments only on the merits.* USAGE: used especially in legal decisions: *His pardon was granted solely on the merits.*

mess

a mess of *sth*
a lot of something ◆ *The fridge door is a mess of notes, schedules, and magnets.* ◆ *The practice field was a mess of weeds and dirt.*

make a mess of *sth*
1 to spoil something or do it very badly ◆ *Our bank seems to have made a mess of our loan documents.*
2 to cause a lot of damage to a place ◆ *Violent storms are making a mess of the Midwest.*

mess around
to waste time doing something without a particular purpose; = **fool around** ◆ *The kids were just messing around at the mall.* USAGE: often used in the **not mess around** (= to act with a serious purpose): *Being a federal agent on the track of terrorists, Matt doesn't mess around.*

mess around with *sb*
1 to treat someone badly ◆ *He was always messing around with her, and she was right to leave him.*
2 to have sex with someone other than your husband, wife, or usual sexual partner; = **fool around with** *sb* ◆ *She found out that her husband was messing around with her best friend.*

mess around with *sth*
to amuse yourself by doing or saying something that is likely to cause trouble; = **fool around with** *sth* ◆ *I don't know if I'm dealing with a 14-year-old messing around with a computer or if I'm dealing with organized crime.*

mess *sb* **up**, *also* **mess up** *sb*
to cause someone emotional problems ◆ *I don't want to mess her up any more than she already is, I decided to leave her alone.* ◆ *He's so messed up.* ◆ *Having just one parent has been known to mess up a kid.*

mess *sth* **up**, *also* **mess up** *sth*
1 to do something badly or make mistakes ◆ *I really messed up my chemistry exam.* ◆ *We had a chance to win the game, but we messed it up.* USAGE: sometimes used in the form **mess up on something**: *I messed up on my driving test.*
2 to break, damage, or spoil something ◆ *She worries that X-rays could mess up her laptop's hard drive.* ◆ *I messed up my ankle playing touch football.* ◆ *Most of kids at the party were well behaved, but there's always a few who mess things up.*

mess with *sb*
to annoy, worry, or cause problems for someone ◆ *I'm tired of people messing with me and not telling me the truth.* USAGE: often used with **not**: *You don't want to mess with this guy.* ◆ Related vocabulary **fool with** *sb* at FOOL

mess with *sth*
1 to become involved with something dangerous ◆ *He admitted that he had messed with drugs as a teen.* ◆ *You wouldn't want to mess with a truckload of mail that might be contaminated.*
2 to change something in a way that is likely to cause harm ◆ *Crime really messes with the quality of life in a community.* ◆ *Don't mess with funding for education programs that have a direct impact on student learning.*
3 to take apart or fix something complicated esp. in order to learn more about how it works ◆ *I enjoy messing with computers the way*

some folks get pleasure from rebuilding old cars. ♦ Related vocabulary **fiddle with sth** at FIDDLE, **fool with sth** at FOOL, **fuss with sth** at FUSS

message
get the message
to understand what someone is trying to tell you, although they do not say it directly ♦ *Next time he calls, tell him you're busy for the next three months – he'll get the message.*

send a message
to do something that is likely to influence someone's attitudes or behavior; = **send a signal** ♦ *The arrests of several well-known people in the area sends a message that no one is immune from the law, not even the famous.* ♦ *The fact that nothing is done to help the homeless sends a message that we don't care.* USAGE: said about actions whether they are intentional or not

mete
mete out sth slightly formal
to give or order a punishment ♦ *The jail sentences meted out to drug traffickers were considered too light by US officials.*

mettle
prove *your* mettle slightly formal, also **show *your* mettle**
to show that you are brave and have a strong character ♦ *As a reporter, she certainly proved her mettle working in the midst of a war zone.*

microscope
under a microscope, also **under the microscope**
in a way that something can be examined carefully ♦ *The new law allows the president to hold every item of spending under a microscope.*

> ORIGIN: from the literal meaning of **microscope** (= a device used for scientific study that makes very small objects look larger)

middle
caught in the middle
to experience the influence of opposing groups in a disagreement; = **caught in the crossfire** ♦ *My mother and sister are always yelling*

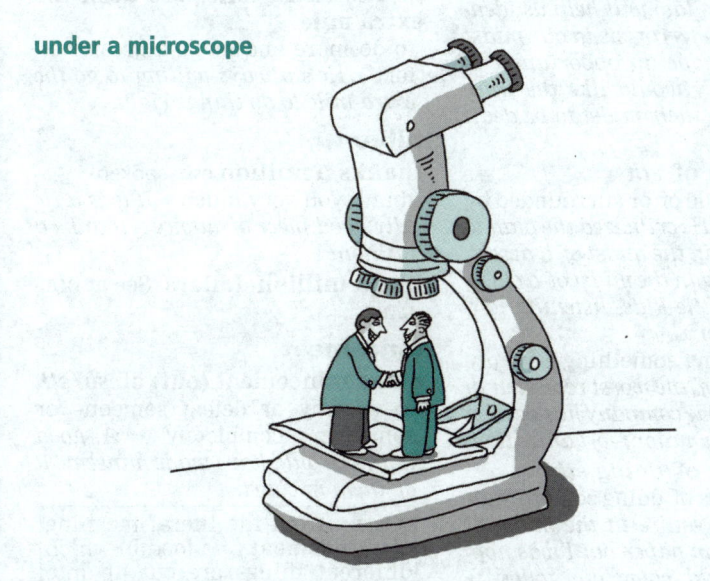

under a microscope

Their business relationship has been put under a microscope.

at each other, and I find myself caught in the middle. ♦ Related vocabulary **in the cross hairs** at CROSS HAIRS

in the middle of *sth/doing sth*
busy doing something ♦ *We were in the middle of supper when we heard the news.* ♦ *When she called, I was in the middle of giving the baby a bath.*

(out) in the middle of nowhere
in a place that is far away from where most people live ♦ *We spent a wonderful year living on a farm in the middle of nowhere.*

midnight

burning the midnight oil
working very long hours, often into the night ♦ *What doctors do know is that burning the midnight oil is bad for your health.*

ORIGIN: from the use of oil to provide light before the invention of electricity

midst

in *sb's* **midst**
existing in or among a group of people ♦ *This law will help us identify and catch terrorists in our midst before they have an opportunity to strike.* ♦ *They would like the troublemakers in their midst to be dealt with.*

in the midst of *sth*
1 in the middle of or surrounded by something ♦ *He criticized the plan to build homes in the midst of a desert.* ♦ *I was sitting in the midst of a classroom with little kids, listening to a children's story.*
2 experiencing something ♦ *We are in the midst of the worst recession in ten years.* ♦ *The company has been in the midst of a major reorganization.*

in the midst of *doing sth*
in the process of doing something ♦ *I know that you're in the midst of writing a term paper but I was hoping you could come out today.* ♦ *People in the midst of moving would*

benefit from the information given on the website.

might

you might as well (*do sth*)
there is no reason you should not do something; = *you* **may as well** (*do sth*) ♦ *Since you have to wait, you might as well sit down and relax.*

mile

a mile away
very easily ♦ *His accent is so strong, you can tell a mile away he's from Brooklyn.* ♦ *He had that mad-at-the-world attitude that you could spot a mile away.*

a mile a minute
very quickly ♦ *Mike was very excited and talking a mile a minute.*

ORIGIN: the speed of going a mile in a minute, or 60 miles an hour, at one time was considered extremely fast

by a mile
by a large number, distance, or amount ♦ *It's the biggest football club in Brazil by a mile.*

go the extra mile, *also* **walk the extra mile**
to do more and make a greater effort ♦ *He's always willing to go the extra mile to do things right.*

million

thanks a million esp. spoken
thank you very much ♦ *It was a really good piece of advice – thanks a million!*

like a million dollars See at DOLLARS

mincemeat

make mincemeat (out) of *sb/sth*
to destroy or defeat someone or something completely ♦ *A good lawyer would have made mincemeat of them in court.*

ORIGIN: from the literal meaning of **mincemeat** (= a food in which different things are cut up into very small pieces)

mind

a mind of *your* own
the ability to act or think independently ◆ *I advised her to take the job offer, but she has a mind of her own, so I don't know what she'll decide.* USAGE: sometimes used humorously of things that are not alive to suggest that they can think or act: *My hair seems to have a mind of its own this morning.*

blow *your* mind
to surprise or excite you, or cause you to be extremely interested ◆ *The first time I heard this band, they just blew my mind, and I've been a fan ever since.* ◆ Related vocabulary **blow sb away** 1 at BLOW, **knock sb off *their* feet** at FEET

boggle the mind, *also* **boggle *your* mind**
to shock or surprise you ◆ *He has a record of arrests for shoplifting that boggles the mind.* ◆ *It just boggles my mind how many people think they're the only ones who are having a hard time.*

bored out of your mind
extremely bored ◆ *Jeanne moved to a small town in New York State, and she was bored out of her mind.* USAGE: also used with other adjectives: *I think he was scared out of his mind.*

bring to mind sb/sth, *also* **bring sb/sth to mind**
to cause you to think of someone or something ◆ *Something about her face brings to mind my first-grade teacher.* ◆ *My daughter said the story brought her relationship with me to mind.* USAGE: also used in the form **call to mind**: *He asked how I knew and I couldn't call it to mind at the time.* ◆ Related vocabulary **bring back sth** at BRING

change *your* mind
to have a different opinion or intention than you had before ◆ *If you don't buy the painting now, he may change his mind and refuse to sell it.* ◆ *After the interview I completely changed my mind about her abilities.*

come to mind
to enter or appear in your thoughts ◆ *Mention fashion and Kate's name comes to mind.* ◆ *As he spoke, the powerful voice of Dr. Martin Luther King, Jr., came to mind.*

cross *your* mind
to come into your thoughts as a possibility ◆ *It never crossed my mind that George might be lying.*

do you mind esp. spoken
1 what you are doing annoys or upsets me ◆ *Do you mind? That's my brother you're talking about!*
2 will you be upset ◆ *I'm going to ask you a personal question, John, do you mind?*

get *your* mind around sth
to succeed in understanding something difficult or strange ◆ *I still can't get my mind around the cruel things she said last night.* ◆ Related vocabulary **get *your* arms around sth** at ARMS

get sth out of *your* mind, *also* **put sth out of *your* mind**
to stop thinking about something ◆ *I can't get that image out of my mind.* ◆ *If you're afraid of flying, you have to put that fear out of your mind.*

have in mind sb/sth, *also* **have sb/sth in mind**
to think about someone or something as being right for a particular situation ◆ *What job did the president have in mind for the former senator?* ◆ *The costumes were exactly what he had in mind.* ◆ *She would say only that they had ambitious projects in mind.* ◆ Related vocabulary **have half a mind to do sth** at HALF

in *your* right mind
thinking clearly and able to make good decisions ◆ *We don't believe any woman in her right mind would*

harm her child. ♦ Opposite **out of your mind**

keep an open mind, *also* **have an open mind**

to wait until you know all the facts before having an opinion or making a judgment ♦ *A history major, Aimee is keeping an open mind as she applies for jobs in many different fields.* USAGE: also used in the form **with an open mind** (= without having made a judgment): *Mom says he's acting strangely, but when I see him I'm going with an open mind.*

keep *sth* in mind, *also* **keep in mind *sth***

to remember a piece of information when you are doing something or thinking about a matter ♦ *We will only have 20 minutes to argue our position – you must keep that in mind.* ♦ *If you can help them, fine, but keep in mind that our policy is, no special deals.* USAGE: also used in the form **bear something in mind**: *Bearing in mind that she's had so little experience, I thought she did very well.*

keep *sb* in mind

to remember that someone is available ♦ *Please keep me in mind if any new projects come up.*

lose *your* mind

to become crazy ♦ *He was not the only prisoner to lose his mind.* ♦ *Taking a child on a bike without a helmet – have you completely lost your mind?*

make up *your* mind, *also* **make *your* mind up**

to decide something, esp. what to do ♦ *She's made up her mind to take dancing lessons.* ♦ *Once you've made your mind up, there's no turning back.*

***your* mind goes blank**

you cannot think of anything to say ♦ *They asked me about my experience and my mind just went blank.*

mind over matter

thought is stronger than physical things ♦ *Curing cancer may not be a question of mind over matter, but your attitude is important.*

never mind (*sb/sth*)

do not worry about someone or something ♦ *"I lost that wallet you gave me." "Well, never mind, I can always buy you another one."* ♦ *Never mind Susan – she can get a ride home with someone else.* ♦ Related vocabulary **skip it** at SKIP

never mind *sth*

without considering something ♦ *Top executive salaries are huge, never mind that ordinary employees are having their pensions cut.*

of a mind to *do sth*, *also* **have a mind to *do sth***

to feel likely to do something ♦ *In those days, no one was of a mind to worry if you had to walk six miles to school.* ♦ *I can put you up for the night, if you've a mind to stay.*

of one mind, *also* **of the same mind**

in agreement ♦ *We're of one mind on most political issues.*

on *your* mind

in your thoughts, esp. because you are worried ♦ *I'm sorry if I've been a bit irritable recently but I've got a lot on my mind.*

out of *your* mind

crazy ♦ *You'd have to be out of your mind to reject an offer like that.* ♦ *Blanche thought she was going out of her mind.* USAGE: often followed by **with**: *We were out of our minds with fear.* ♦ Opposite **in *your* right mind**

put *sb's* mind at ease, *also* **set *sb's* mind at ease**

to cause someone to stop worrying ♦ *He chose his words carefully to put his mother's mind at ease.* USAGE: also used in the forms **put someone's mind at rest** and **set someone's mind at rest**: *To put his mind at rest, I offered to make one final check.*

put *your* mind to it, *also* **set *your* mind to it**
to put all your attention and effort into doing something ♦ *If you put your mind to it, you could have the job finished in an afternoon.*

put *sb/sth* out of *your* mind, *also* **get *sb/sth* out of *your* mind**
to stop thinking about someone or something ♦ *Karen can't put the burglary out of her mind.*

read *your* mind
to guess what you are thinking without being told ♦ *I was looking at the books, trying to choose, when Shirley apparently read my mind and handed me the one I wanted.*

slip *your* mind
to be forgotten ♦ *I meant to tell her that Nick had phoned, but it completely slipped my mind.*

speak *your* mind
to say exactly what you think or feel ♦ *She's not afraid to speak her mind, even if it upsets people.*

spring to mind
to appear suddenly or immediately in your thoughts ♦ *That's not a publisher that springs to mind when you mention quality fiction.*

stick in *your* mind
to have a strong effect on you, so that you remember ♦ *She had one of those faces that sticks in your mind.*

take *your* mind off *sb/sth*
to cause you to stop thinking about who or what is causing worry ♦ *That's the good thing about helping other people – it takes your mind off your own problems.*

the mind boggles
it is very difficult to understand or imagine ♦ *The mind boggles at the thought of what you could do with all that money.*

to my mind
in my opinion ♦ *He's got red walls and a green carpet which, to my mind, look awful.* USAGE: sometimes used in the form **to someone's mind**: *The professor made a com-* *ment about her appearance that, to her mind, was not appropriate.*

minds

of two minds (about *sth*)
unable to decide about something ♦ *We are of two minds about whether to take this information to the police or just forget it.*

minute

in a New York minute
very quickly ♦ *I would sell that car in a New York minute if the right offer came along.*

> ORIGIN: based on the idea that everything happens more quickly in New York City

in just a minute *esp.* spoken
after a little while; = **in just a moment** ♦ *She'll be downstairs in just a minute.*

just a minute *esp.* spoken
wait a short period of time; = **just a moment** ♦ *Just a minute, I'm not finished talking.* USAGE: also used in the form **just a second**: *Just a second, let me check the batteries first.*

the last minute
the last possible opportunity for doing something ♦ *He always waits until the last minute to shop for presents.* USAGE: used with **until** or **till**, as in the example, or with **at**: *At the last minute, we found our tickets.*

the minute (that)
as soon as ♦ *The minute I saw him, I knew something was wrong.*

up to the minute
the most recent ♦ *Now coverage of the news on the Internet is up to the minute.*

wait a minute *esp.* spoken
I have just thought of something important; = **wait a second** ♦ *Wait a minute, what did you say her aunt's name was?* USAGE: used to interrupt someone

a laugh a minute See at LAUGH
a mile a minute See at MILE

misery

misery

put *sb/sth* out of *their/its* misery
1 to kill an animal or person because they are in extreme pain ◆ *The horse's leg was badly broken, and the kindest thing was to put it out of its misery.* ◆ *Badly wounded himself, he put a gun in his buddy's hand and asked his friend to put him out of his misery.*
2 to end someone's worry or something's suffering ◆ *I thought I'd call her with the test results today and put her out of her misery.* ◆ *Business was so bad, they considered bankruptcy to put the company out of its misery.*

miss

miss out (on *sth*)
to fail to use or enjoy an opportunity ◆ *Other people my age are married and have families, and I am beginning to feel I am missing out.* ◆ *We missed out on a chance to get a cheaper mortgage.*

you can't miss it esp. spoken
it is very easy to find ◆ *To get to the church, go to the next traffic light and make a left – you can't miss it.*

hit or miss See at HIT
miss the boat See at BOAT
miss the point See at POINT
not miss a beat See at BEAT

mistake

by mistake
without intending to ◆ *I'm sorry – I dialed your number by mistake.*

make no mistake (about it)
do not imagine that I am wrong ◆ *Make no mistake, any violence against an individual is an act of terror.* ◆ *They are in control of the business, make no mistake about it.*

mistake *sb/sth* for *sb/sth*
to think that a person or thing is really someone or something else ◆ *The prison buildings could almost be mistaken for a college campus.*

mix

mix and match
to combine things that are not related ◆ *You can mix and match desks, bookcases, and other office furniture to fit your needs.*

mix it up
1 to compete in an active, physical way ◆ *Shaffer was aggressive and didn't mind mixing it up when she had to.*
2 to argue or exchange criticisms ◆ *She was a top TV news reporter, and she could mix it up with anyone, no matter how important they were.*

mix up *sb/sth*, also mix *sb/sth* up
to confuse one person or thing with another ◆ *Mrs. Albert was always mixing up the two boys even though they didn't look very much alike.* ◆ *I mixed the appointment up and went for a haircut on the wrong day.*

mix *sth* up, also mix up *sth*
to put something in the wrong order or place ◆ *If you mix the photos up in these envelopes I'll never find them.*

mockery

make a mockery of *sth*
to make something seem stupid or without value ◆ *The film makes a mockery of a serious illness.* ◆ *Spending in the last election made a mockery of campaign finance laws.*

mold

break the mold
to do something differently, after it has been done in the same way for a long time ◆ *She was the woman who broke the mold and brought new energy to the role of First Lady.*

moment

at the moment
now ◆ *At the moment I'm living with my parents.* USAGE: often used to suggest that the situation may change soon: *At the moment the flood is receding, but more rain is expected tonight.*

for the moment
at this time; = **for the time being** ♦ *For the moment, he was alone in a his hotel room.* ♦ Related vocabulary **for the present** at PRESENT

in just a moment esp. spoken
after a little while; = **in just a minute** ♦ *We'll be back with more news in just a moment.*

just a moment
wait a short period of time; = **just a minute** ♦ *Just a moment, don't be in such a hurry.*

of the moment
popular or important now ♦ *The weather has become India's biggest enemy of the moment.*

(there is) never a dull moment
something interesting is always happening ♦ *One thing about an ice show – there's never a dull moment.*

at a moment's notice See at NOTICE

in the heat of the moment See at HEAT

on the spur of the moment See at SPUR

moments

have *your* moments
to be partly successful ♦ *This movie's not as good as her last one, but it has its moments.*

money

for my money
in my opinion ♦ *That guy writes mysteries that, for my money, are a million times better than anyone else's.*

get *your* money's worth esp. spoken
to receive good value for the amount you have paid ♦ *When I see how much I spend on repairs, I wonder if I got my money's worth with this car.*

have money to burn
to have a lot of money that you can spend any way you want ♦ *Even though they have money to burn, she didn't really enjoy spending it.*

in the money
wealthy ♦ *Many people believe if they become lawyers, they'll really be in the money.*

money is no object
how much something costs is not important ♦ *If money was no object, what sort of a house would you live in?*

money talks
money can influence what is done or how it is done ♦ *He was a fool to take the job, but money talks, so of course he took it.*

put *your* money where *your* mouth is
to do something rather than to just talk about it ♦ *I finally realized that I should stop complaining about the people who run our town, put my money where my mouth is, and run for office.* USAGE: sometimes used in the form **put its money where its mouth is**: *Congress needs to put its money where its mouth is and really support energy conservation.*

(right) on the money
exactly right or correct; = **right on** ♦ *You were right on the money when you said that I would really like that book.*

throw good money after bad, also **pour good money after bad**
to spend more money on something that has already failed ♦ *If you try to fix that car, you'll simply be throwing good money after bad.* ♦ *There's got to be a better way to save our children than pouring good money after bad into government agencies.*

throw money at *sth*
to spend money in the belief that money alone will solve a problem ♦ *Many people agree that throwing money at education has not produced great results.*

give *you* a run for *your* money
See at RUN

monkey

a monkey on *your* back
a serious problem that you cannot

monkey wrench

forget ♦ *When you know you have to do everything perfectly, it puts a giant monkey on your back.* USAGE: also used in the form **get the monkey off your back** (= to end a problem): *By winning the championship, this team has finally got the monkey off its back.*

> ORIGIN: based on an earlier meaning of **a monkey on your back** (= a habit of using an illegal drug)

monkey (around) with *sth*
to adjust something ♦ *It seems like any time they monkey with taxes, wealthy people benefit the most.* USAGE: usually said about an effort to fix or improve something, especially an effort that does not succeed

monkey wrench
throw a monkey wrench into *sth*
to cause something to fail ♦ *We keep trying to get together, but her crazy schedule keeps throwing a monkey wrench into our plans.*

month
month after month
repeatedly for many months ♦ *You have to pay for Internet access month after month.* ♦ Related vocabulary **day after day** at DAY, **week after week** at WEEK, **year after year** at YEAR

month by month
every month ♦ *I look at my bank statements month by month, and I can tell you to the penny how much we spend.* ♦ Related vocabulary **day by day** at DAY, **week by week** at WEEK, **year by year** at YEAR

moon
once in a blue moon esp. spoken
almost never ♦ *Once in a blue moon I'll have a beer with friends, but it's not my regular drink.*

> ORIGIN: based on the informal phrase **blue moon** (= the second time in one month that you can see the full disk of the moon)

over the moon
extremely pleased and happy ♦ *When he sent me flowers and a note, I was over the moon.*

mop
mop up (*sth***)**, *also* **mop** *sth* **up**
1 to complete something ♦ *The fire*

monkey around

I hate it when he monkeys around with my computer.

wasn't completely out, and we should have stayed and mopped it up.
2 to rid an area of an enemy ♦ *Army troops were mopping up the last of the rebel fighters.*
3 to remove what has been damaged by a storm or other violent event ♦ *California has just started to mop up after two storms blasted the state.*
4 to remove the results of a problem ♦ *Altman's department was in charge of mopping up the banking scandal.*

mop up *sb*, *also* **mop** *sb* **up**
to defeat someone ♦ *The vice president mopped up his opponent in a televised debate.* ♦ *Everyone says he's a great fighter, but Ali could have mopped him up in a second.*

more

more and more
1 an increasing number of ♦ *More and more people realize there's a pollution problem in more and more places.*
2 increasingly ♦ *The fans grew more and more unfriendly as the game went on.*

more like it
1 more accurate or true ♦ *Chris said he was fascinated with her – "madly in love" is more like it.* ♦ *They sit there thinking – maybe hoping might be more like it – that I can do something for them.*
2 an improvement ♦ *"She thinks business may be better next year." "Now that's more like it."*

more often than not esp. spoken
usually ♦ *In winter the days are very short, and more often than not you're driving with your headlights on.*

more or less
1 approximately ♦ *The box weighs 50 pounds, more or less.* ♦ *Each of the calls was more or less 10 minutes long.*
2 to some degree ♦ *This room is* more or less an extra – *we don't really need it.*

the more the merrier
additional people will make something better ♦ *"Do you mind if I invite my sister and her family?" "Why not? The more the merrier."*

the more *one thing happens* **the more** *another thing happens*
as one thing happens repeatedly, something else happens or becomes likely ♦ *The more Sheri thought about this, the more sense it made.* USAGE: also used in other similar forms: *The more you think about not eating, the hungrier you get.* ♦ the opposite meaning is expressed by **the more one thing happens, the less something else happens**: *The more time goes by, the less we seem to have achieved.*

most

at (the) most
no more than ♦ *We have at most a week to get the report ready.* ♦ *The dog weighs only 20 pounds at the most.* ♦ *At the most they probably spend five hours a week in their class.*

make the most of *sth*
to use or enjoy something as much as possible ♦ *We're only in Paris for a day so let's make the most of it.*

mother

the mother of all *sth*
an extreme example of something ♦ *Donny's car crash was the mother of all crashes.* ♦ *Hundreds will travel to Stonehenge, the mother of all places to celebrate the longest day of the year.*

motion

set *sth* **in motion**, *also* **set in motion** *sth*
to start a process ♦ *The recommendation could set in motion the largest cleanup in US history.* USAGE: also used in the form **put something in motion**: *Louisiana already has*

an emergency response plan, which Foster put in motion shortly after the attacks.

> ORIGIN: based on the literal meaning of **set something in motion** (= to make something move)

motions
go through the motions
to do something without believing it is important ♦ *After his wife died, he went through the motions of living, without feeling much of anything.*

mountain
make a mountain out of a molehill, *also* **make a molehill into a mountain**
to cause something simple to seem much more difficult or important ♦ *McAleer knows there's a mistake in the book and promised to correct it, but Rosen continues to complain about it – she's really trying to make a mountain out of a molehill.* ♦ *Clever lawyers can make a molehill into a mountain.* USAGE: sometimes used in the form **make a molehill out of a mountain** (= to cause something difficult to be much easier): *By dividing up a big assignment and working on it a little bit every day, you can make a molehill out of a mountain.* ♦ Related vocabulary **blow *sth* out of (all) proportion** at PROPORTION, **make a production (out) of *sth*** at PRODUCTION

mountains
move mountains
to achieve something difficult ♦ *Voters in his district have always recognized their representative's ability to move mountains.*

mouth
foam at the mouth
1 to be uncontrollably excited ♦ *The band's high-energy music left the crowd foaming at the mouth for more.*
2 to be uncontrollably angry ♦ *And there was my mom, still foaming at the mouth, still shouting at my brother.*

> ORIGIN: based on the literal meaning of **foam at the mouth** (= to have an illness that causes liquid and bubbles to collect around the mouth)

keep *your* mouth shut, *also* **shut *your* mouth**
to say nothing ♦ *I just keep my mouth shut and do my job, and I only offer an opinion if someone asks me for one.* ♦ *It's important to be a good listener, and that means you shut your mouth and let her talk.*

make *your* mouth water
to feel pleasure at the thought of something particularly beautiful or good ♦ *Such beauty is enough to make anyone's mouth water.*

> ORIGIN: based on the literal meaning of **make your mouth water** (= to cause your mouth to produce liquid when you see or think about food)

melt in *your* mouth
to be soft and creamy ♦ *The outside of the cake is just a little crisp and the center just melts in your mouth.*

mouth off
to complain or say what you think without showing respect for others ♦ *I hate it when celebrities mouth off about their loss of privacy.* ♦ *Mike has a reputation for mouthing off at the worst possible moments.*

open *your* mouth
to say something ♦ *Ms. Parker looks fragile, but as soon as she opens her mouth you know she's a tough, nononsense woman.*

run *your* mouth
to talk a lot ♦ *He was mean and angry and he just kept running his mouth.*

shoot *your* mouth off
to talk too much or without think-

ing about something ♦ *Don't go shooting your mouth off about how much money you're earning.*

(straight) from the horse's mouth
from someone who has the facts ♦ *"Are you sure she's leaving?" "Definitely, I heard it straight from the horse's mouth."*

move

get a move on
to hurry ♦ *Simon realized he'd have to get a move on if he was going to finish by 4 o'clock.* USAGE: sometimes used as an order: *Get a move on, Corey – you don't want to be late!*

make *your/its* move, also **make a move**
to do something to achieve a result ♦ *My father always waited to buy our Christmas tree, and I worried that by the time he made his move the best trees would be gone.* ♦ *The Federal Reserve made its move yesterday, cutting interest rates for the third time this year.* ♦ *Some of his advisors think he should make a move for the presidency soon.*

make a move on *sb* slang
to show someone you are sexually attracted to them ♦ *Farnsworth made a move on my sister when she was only 17.*

make no move
to do nothing ♦ *Mac made no move to help her.* ♦ *Although suspicion for the killing fell on the group, the police made no move against it.*

move away from *sth*
to change your ideas about something ♦ *He had moved away from the liberalism of his earlier heroes.*

move in on *sth*
to take control of a place or event ♦ *Drug dealers moved in on the cafe and scared away the customers.* ♦ *Commercial sponsors moved in on athletic competitions to sell their products.*

move on
to do something different ♦ *He wrote popular songs in the 1920s but moved on to become a producer of musicals in the 1940s.* ♦ *When someone dies, you need to go through certain rituals so you can finally move on.*

move over
to stop having a job, rank, or condition ♦ *Kurt said that it was time to move over and let younger players have a chance to play professionally.* ♦ *Move over "Star Wars" – "Titanic" is now the movie with the biggest earnings in North America.*

on the move
very busy or active; = **on the go** ♦ *Baby boomers don't accept the effects of aging – they want to stay on the move.*

moved to tears See at TEARS

move heaven and earth (to *do sth*) See at HEAVEN

move mountains See at MOUNTAINS

(when) the spirit moves *you* See at SPIRIT

mow

mow down *sb/sth*, also **mow *sb/sth* down**
to violently cause someone or something to fall ♦ *The car skidded along the side of the road and mowed down several mailboxes before coming to a stop.* ♦ *A young woman was mowed down in a public market by narcotics traffickers.*

> ORIGIN: based on the literal meaning of **mow down** (= to cut grasses or grains that fall over as they are cut)

much

as much as
1 this or almost this amount ♦ *These drugs can lead to as much as a 30 percent increase in sleep interruption.* **2** to the same degree as ♦ *People who live with this plant consider it a friend as much as a foe.*

as much as anything (else)
no less than other things ♦ *You need*

muck

to look at reliability and safety as much as anything when buying a car. ◆ *It was war, as much as anything else, that made an artist out of Westermann.*

make much of *sth*
to give a lot of importance to something ◆ *Curtis claimed to be one-eighth American Indian and made much of this in his political career.* ◆ *Her campaign made much of economic issues at the party convention.*

much less *do sth*
and do not even do this ◆ *When our headlights flashed, the deer barely blinked, much less moved.* ◆ *They can hardly keep their Internet site running, much less guard against hackers.*

so much
to such a great degree ◆ *She wanted to go with her mother so much, she ran after the car, crying, as it pulled away.*

so much as
1 but rather ◆ *I'm not looking at her so much as I am studying her hat.*
2 even ◆ *From outside, no one could see so much as a light on in the house.*

so much for *sth*
that is the end of something ◆ *He told me how his parents divorced, then said, "So much for the storybook romance."* ◆ *A bird hit my windshield, and I thought, so much for that bird.* USAGE: usually said about a disappointing end

so much so
to such a great degree ◆ *Computer games opened a new world, so much so you wonder what you used to do with your free time.* USAGE: often followed by a clause beginning with **that**: *The path was overgrown with grass, so much so that I could easily have missed it altogether.*

very much so esp. spoken
to a great degree ◆ *My father did inspire me, very much so.* ◆ *"So crime is a big concern where you live?" "Very much so."*

muck

muck around (with *sth*)
to do something without a serious purpose ◆ *Why was she mucking around in such a risky neighborhood?* ◆ *I kept working on this text until I thought it was good, and then I tried not to muck around with it anymore.*

muck *sth* up, *also* **muck up *sth***
to make a situation more confusing or difficult ◆ *Our leaders have demonstrated their great talent for mucking things up.* ◆ *Don't muck up our lives just because he was misbehaving.* ◆ Related vocabulary **muddy the waters** at WATERS

mud

(as) clear as mud
very difficult to understand ◆ *His traffic directions were as clear as mud.* USAGE: used to humorously explain that there was a problem ◆ Opposite **(as) plain as day** at DAY

muddle

muddle through (*sth*)
to continue despite confusion and difficulties ◆ *My grandparents muddled through droughts and crop failures and family crises.*

mull

mull over *sth*, *also* **mull *sth* over**
to think carefully about something for a period of time ◆ *She asked me what I thought about her idea, and I said I would have to mull it over.* ◆ *Bill mulled over the pros and cons of this job offer.*

multitude

hide a multitude of sins, *also* **cover a multitude of sins**
to prevent people from noticing something bad ◆ *I'm a messy eater, so I always wear black – it hides a multitude of sins.*

ORIGIN: based on the saying **love covers a multitude of sins** from the Bible

mum

mum's the word
do not tell anyone ♦ *I don't want to spoil the surprise for Tim, so please tell everyone that mum's the word.*

murder

get away with murder
to not be punished for bad behavior ♦ *It seems to me that kids these days really get away with murder in the classroom.*

scream bloody murder
to shout or to complain very loudly ♦ *Sometimes the baby screams bloody murder when we give her a bath.* ♦ *I'm so frustrated with the telephone company, I want to scream bloody murder.* USAGE: sometimes **holler bloody murder** and **yell bloody murder**, with the same meaning

muscle

muscle in on *sth*
to force a way into someone's business or other relationships in order to control them ♦ *Russell was the governor's closest friend, and he didn't like it when someone tried to muscle in on that relationship.* ♦ *These people pretended to be my friends, but they just wanted to muscle in on my life.*

muscles

flex *your* muscles
to use or increase your influence or power ♦ *He was a very successful movie actor, but he's decided to flex his muscles on the stage for a while.* USAGE: sometimes used with an adjective to show a particular kind of influence or power: *The attorney general is flexing his legal muscles to enforce gun control laws.*

ORIGIN: from the literal meaning of **flex your muscles** (= to tighten your muscles)

music

face the music
to accept responsibility for something you have done ♦ *Knight was returned to the US from Spain to face the music for his part in a robbery more than 20 years ago.*

music to *sb*'s ears
something pleasing to hear about ♦ *The decision to restore the old building is music to my ears.*

mustard

not cut the mustard
not satisfactory or right for the situation ♦ *Cutting taxes for the rich doesn't cut the mustard with most middle-class people.* USAGE: sometimes used in the form **cut the mustard**: *When you're a kid, you always think you have to prove that you can cut the mustard.* ♦ Related vocabulary **not cut it** at CUT

muster

pass muster
to be acceptable or satisfactory ♦ *The tortillas and tacos we offered for lunch today didn't pass muster with the students.*

ORIGIN: based on the military use of the phrase **pass muster** (= to gather soldiers in a group to show officers they are acceptably dressed and equipped)

mystery

a mystery to *you*
something that you do not understand ♦ *Why I'm telling you all this is a mystery to me.*

N, n

nail

hit the nail on the head
to be right about something ◆ *Mike hit the nail on the head when he said most people can use a computer without knowing how it works.*

nail *sth* down
to make something certain or final ◆ *My uncle has been meeting people all over the state to nail down support for his senate campaign.*

(a) nail in the coffin of *sth*, also **(a) nail in *sth's* coffin**
an action that will cause something to end ◆ *This report on the effects of smoking is another nail in the coffin of the tobacco industry.* ◆ *We thought the firings would put the final nail in the union's coffin, but in fact, the union has grown in size and importance.*

nails

(as) tough as nails, also **(as) hard as nails**
strong and determined ◆ *She is a warm and friendly person, but she is also as tough as nails.*

name

by the name (of)
known as ◆ *The teacher that I enjoyed the most in high school was a man by the name of Don Feinstein.* USAGE: sometimes used in the form **go by the name of**: *Francie goes by the name Franchita.*

clear *your* name
to prove you are not guilty of something ◆ *Mitch said the charges were completely untrue and promised he would clear his name.*

give *sth* a bad name
to cause a loss of respect for something ◆ *A few wild fans give soccer a bad name.*

in all but name
very like something that is called something different ◆ *He may call himself a liberal but he's actually a conservative in all but name.*

in name only
having a particular title without the power or duties that are a part of it ◆ *He was my father in name only – I never saw him while I was growing up.*

in the name of *sth*, also **in *sth's* name**
in order to do or become something ◆ *In the name of being cool and serious, people miss out on a lot of enjoyable stuff.* ◆ *Are we willing to be worked to death in the name of competition?*

in *sb's* name, also **in the name of *sb***
representing someone ◆ *She established a clinic in the name of her daughter, who died several years ago.* ◆ *A $5 million gift in Steve Perkins's name will be made to the University of Maine.* USAGE: sometimes used in the forms **in God's name** or **in heaven's name** for emphasis: *Why in God's name would you speak to a man like that?*

make a name for *yourself*, also **make *your* name**
to become well known and respected for doing something in particular ◆ *She would have done well in any sport, but Virginia ended up making a name for herself in soccer.* ◆ *The French director made his name in the 1980s with off-beat movies.*

your name in lights
to be famous and have your work recognized as especially important ◆ *He was never interested in seeing his name in lights – he was always too busy having fun.* USAGE: also used with **see**: *I want to see*

my name in lights for writing this book!

> ORIGIN: based on the brightly lit signs used to advertise the names of the most important actors in a show

the name of the game
the most important activity ◆ *The name of the game for many companies is to get the most work out of the fewest people.*

you name it
anything ◆ *There's plenty to do here – you can hike, bike, camp, canoe, you name it.* ◆ *As a messenger I've delivered classified documents, videotapes, bottles of liquor, candy, coffee makers, you name it.*

names
call *sb* names
to use rude or insulting words to describe someone ◆ *He was calling me names because he disagreed with something I'd written.*

name names
to say who is doing something bad or illegal ◆ *She swears she will never name names, even if she were offered a reward.*

napping
catch *you* napping
to be surprised by something that you have not given attention to ◆ *I was caught napping by the last storm, but this time I've already got batteries and flashlights and canned food on hand.*

native
go native
to become like the people who have lived in a place for a long time ◆ *Brian moved to Los Angeles seven years ago, and I think he's finally gone native.*

nature
let nature take its course
to allow something to happen naturally ◆ *Normally, the Parks Department lets nature take its course and doesn't replace dead trees, but this situation is different.*

(that's) the nature of the beast
this is the basic character of something ◆ *The place is wild and beautiful and also dangerous – that's the nature of the beast.* ◆ *People make progress but do not reach perfection because imperfection is the nature of the beast.*

naught
(all) for naught slightly formal
without achievement or result ◆ *Marge's time in jail wasn't all for naught – she earned a college degree while she was there.* USAGE: sometimes, in less formal use, **nothing** is substituted for **naught**: *I would hate to think that what we'd tried to do was all for nothing.*

> ORIGIN: based on the literal meaning of **naught** (= zero or nothing)

near
near and dear to *you*
very important to you ◆ *People usually give more attention to the things that are particularly near and dear to them.*

nearest
your nearest and dearest
your family ◆ *My wife and dozens of her nearest and dearest are from West Virginia.*

neck
breathe down *your* neck
to watch too closely what you do ◆ *The supervisor breathes down my neck all the time, trying to make sure I'm working hard enough.*

neck and neck
very close or equal ◆ *The two companies are neck and neck in the competition to win over customers.* USAGE: generally used to describe competitors, and often with

need

the verb **run**: *The two candidates are running neck and neck in the opinion polls.*

> ORIGIN: based on the meaning in horse racing of horse running **neck and neck** (= at the same speed with their heads and necks next to each other)

your neck of the woods
the area you come from or where you now live ◆ *If you're in our neck of the woods, we hope you'll come see us.* USAGE: often used in the form **this neck of the woods**: *It was a pretty small farm for this neck of the woods.*

risk your neck
to do something dangerous ◆ *We risked our necks to rescue you and all you can say is "Gee whiz"?*

stick your neck out, *also* **stick out your neck**
to take a risk ◆ *He's shown he's got the courage to stick his neck out to help people.*

up to your neck in sth
to be completely involved in something ◆ *I am up to my neck in assignments and exams at school.* ◆ *She said she knew nothing about the robbery, but I'm sure she's in it up to her neck.*

need

you don't need this esp. spoken
you refuse to deal with this ◆ *The first five minutes of that movie were so violent that I walked out – I don't need this.* ◆ Related vocabulary **who needs sth** at NEEDS

if need be
provided it is necessary ◆ *If need be, we'll rent a car.*

sth is all you need
that is something you do not want at all ◆ *"Do you still breed terriers?" "Heavens no! That's all I need."*

need I say more
you know what else would follow if I were to tell you more ◆ *This athlete has power, speed, and agility.*

Need I say more? ◆ *She is young, beautiful, clever, wealthy – need I say more?*

need (to have) your head examined See at HEAD

needle

a needle in a haystack
something extremely hard to find ◆ *It's pretty much a needle in a haystack because these fish are extremely hard to find.* USAGE: also used in the forms **look for a needle in a haystack** and **find a needle in a haystack**

> ORIGIN: based on the idea that it is to almost impossible to find a thin sewing needle in a haystack (= a very tall pile of dried grass)

needs

who needs sth esp. spoken
what was mentioned is not important or helpful ◆ *I wouldn't do it for the money – who needs money?* USAGE: often used in the forms **who needs it** or **who needs that**: *My wife suggested therapy, but I've always thought, therapy, who needs it?* ◆ *He never returned my phone calls – who needs that?* ◆ Related vocabulary **you don't need this** at NEED

neighborhood

(somewhere) in the neighborhood of sth
about or approximately ◆ *The size of the library is in the neighborhood of 5,000 books.* ◆ *We hope to get somewhere in the neighborhood of $150,000 for our house.* USAGE: used before a number and sometimes following **something**: *We've had something in the neighborhood of 80,000 hits on our website.*

neither

neither here nor there
not of any importance ◆ *Whether we take the train or drive is neither here nor there as far as I'm concerned.*

nerve

lose *your* nerve
to fear doing something ♦ *Jim lost his nerve and wouldn't try to ski down the hill.*

touch a (raw) nerve, *also* **hit a (raw) nerve**
to cause an emotional reaction ♦ *This film touched a nerve with many people who were already feeling very uneasy about the state of the world.* ♦ *Any talk of raising the cost of college tuition hits a raw nerve with students.*

nerves

get on *your* nerves
to annoy someone a lot ♦ *Sometimes watching TV really gets on my nerves because of all the commercials.*

nest

feather *your* (own) nest
to make a lot of money for yourself ♦ *While the CEO feathered his own nest, his company was firing employees by the hundreds.* USAGE: usually said about someone who takes unfair advantage of others ♦ Related vocabulary **line *your* (own) pockets** at POCKETS

leave the nest, *also* **fly the nest**
to move from your parents' home and live independently ♦ *Our kids have all left the nest and the house seems empty now.*

news

break the news
to make known new information ♦ *Detectives broke the news to Mrs. Allen that her husband's body had been identified.* USAGE: usually said about information that causes sadness or worry

(that's) news to *you*
something that you did not know ♦ *You say the jury found him guilty? That's news to me.* ♦ *The boss said it was news to him that some of the employees had shredded documents.* USAGE: usually said about something that surprises you

next

next to
almost ♦ *It is supposed to be next to impossible to escape from a high-tech, maximum security prison.*

next to nothing
very little ♦ *She knows next to nothing about politics.* ♦ *The town has done next to nothing about the parking problem.*

nick

(just) in the nick of time
at the last possible moment ♦ *A man walking his dog saw her fall into the river and pulled her out just in the nick of time.*

night

night after night
for several nights without interruption ♦ *The howling of the neighbors' dogs kept him awake night after night.*

night and day
all the time; = **day and night** ♦ *We worked night and day to finish the job in a month.*

in the dead of the night See at DEAD

nod

get the nod
to be approved or chosen for something ♦ *Martinez got the nod from the manager to be the starting pitcher in tomorrow's game.*

ORIGIN: based on the literal meaning of **nod** (= to move your head)

nod off
to go to sleep, esp. when not in bed or intending to sleep ♦ *I nodded off once or twice during the movie.*

noises

make noises about *sth*
to talk generally about something that you might do ♦ *Recently they have made noises about wanting to do a TV series together.*

none

none other than *sb/sth*
the very famous or important person or thing ◆ *The speech was given by none other than the vice president.* ◆ *The biggest surprise was that the false report was written by none other than the company's own legal department.* ◆ Related vocabulary **the one and only** at ONE

none too
not very ◆ *I gripped the back of his neck and, none too gently, gave his head a firm shake.*

bar none See at BAR

be none the wiser See at WISER

none of *your* **business** See at BUSINESS

none of the above See at ABOVE

none the worse (for *sth***)** See at WORSE

second to none See at SECOND

nook

every nook and cranny
every part of a place ◆ *Law books were stuffed into every nook and cranny of his office.*

follow your nose

nose

a nose for *sth*
a special ability to find or do something ◆ *Any good journalist has a nose for a good story.*

cut off *your* **nose to spite** *your* **face**
to hurt yourself in an effort to punish someone else ◆ *If you stay home because your ex-husband will be at the party, aren't you just cutting off your nose to spite your face?*

follow *your* **nose**
1 to move forward ◆ *I followed my nose down the narrow streets toward where I remembered seeing a metro station.*
2 to move in the direction of something you smell ◆ *I tried hiding that shoe in the closet, but my dog followed her nose right to it.*

keep *your* **nose clean**
to avoid trouble ◆ *If he kept his nose clean, he could look forward to being promoted to vice president.* ◆ *Since being released from prison, Tim has kept his nose clean.* ◆ Opposite **make waves** at WAVES ◆ Related vo-

He followed his nose to the kitchen.

cabulary **don't rock the boat** at BOAT

keep *your* **nose out of** *sth*
to not become involved in something ♦ *The two men worked together well and kept their noses out of each other's personal affairs.* USAGE: sometimes used in the form **keep your nose out of it** (= do not get involved in something): *I didn't ask for your help, so just keep your nose out of it.*

keep *your* **nose to the grindstone**
to work continuously ♦ *After a year of keeping your nose to the grindstone, you finally get away for that vacation you've dreamed about.* USAGE: sometimes used in the shortened form **nose to the grindstone**: *During the exam period, it was all nose to the grindstone.*

lead *sb* **by the nose**
to control someone so that they do exactly what you want them to do ♦ *He thinks she's perfect, and she leads him around by the nose.*

> ORIGIN: based on the way that a cow is sometimes led by rope attached to a ring in its nose

look down *your* **nose at** *sb/sth*
to consider someone or something as not important or of value; = **look down on** *sb/sth* ♦ *The regular staff looked down their noses at us freelancers.*

nose around
to try to discover information ♦ *Justice Department lawyers started nosing around after they received a complaint from a former employee.* ♦ Related vocabulary **sniff out** *sth* at SNIFF

your **nose is out of joint**
to feel upset or annoyed because you think you have not been treated well ♦ *You have to make everybody happy and be sure no one's nose is out of joint if you want people to work long hours on something special.* USAGE: also used in the plural form **noses out of joint**: *The kids' noses got out of joint because I told them their rooms were disgusting.*

pay through the nose
to pay too much for something ♦ *If you bring a car into the city, you have to pay through the nose for parking it.*

poke *your* **nose into** *sth*, also **stick** *your* **nose in** *sth*
to try to discover things that do not involve you ♦ *The government has no business poking its nose into people's personal lives.*

powder *your* **nose** esp. spoken
to use a public toilet ♦ *"I'm going to powder my nose," Vera said, following Elise out of the room.* USAGE: usually said by women

thumb *your* **nose at** *sb/sth*
to show that you do not respect someone or something ♦ *Many people feel that the company is thumbing its nose at the environment by reopening the mine.*

> ORIGIN: based on the literal meaning of **thumb your nose** (= to put your thumb to your nose as a rude sign)

turn *your* **nose up at** *sth*
to not like something because you think it is not good enough for you ♦ *In those days I turned my nose up at country music, but now I've come to like it.* USAGE: also used in the negative: *I never turn my nose up at homemade apple pie!*

under *your* **nose**
obvious or not hidden ♦ *Sorry it took me so long to see what was right under my nose.* USAGE: also used in the plural form **under your noses**: *She has been right under our noses all this time!*

it's no skin off *your* **nose** See at SKIN

not

not for nothing
for a good reason ♦ *Not for nothing is New York City called the fashion*

notch

capital of the world. ◆ Opposite **for nothing** at FOR

not *yourself*
to feel strange and not the way you usually feel ◆ *While I had to take that medicine, I felt as if I wasn't myself at all.*

notch

a notch below *sb/sth*
not quite as good as someone or something else ◆ *Fifty years ago, there were many big bands that were good, but they were a notch below the great ones.*

note

make a mental note
to make an effort to remember something ◆ *I made a mental note to call my mother tonight and ask her to meet me tomorrow for lunch.*

strike the right note
to say or do something that is suited to a particular occasion ◆ *Marjorie planned the party carefully because she wanted to strike the right note with her guests.*

take note (of *sb/sth*)
to give someone or something your attention; = **take notice (of *sb/sth*)** ◆ *Travelers who plan to leave next week should take note that there may be an airlines strike.*

notes

compare notes
to exchange information and opinions ◆ *We met at the coffee shop to compare notes on our new boss.* ◆ *The two sisters always compared notes.*

nothing

nothing but *sth*
1 only something ◆ *During spring vacation, he ate nothing but canned beans.* ◆ *The police were praised for showing nothing but the highest degree of professionalism.*
2 completely something ◆ *The story was nothing but lies.* ◆ *My car is nothing but trouble.*

nothing much
very little ◆ *I had nothing much to do that afternoon.*

nothing if not *sth*
this more than anything else ◆ *She is nothing if not ambitious.*

(there's) nothing to it
it is easy to do ◆ *You could paint the wall yourself. There's nothing to it.*

have nothing going for *you/it*
See **have *sth* going for *you/it*** at GOING

notice

at a moment's notice
almost immediately ◆ *Everyone was packed and ready to leave at a moment's notice.* ◆ Related vocabulary **at the drop of a hat** at DROP, **on the spur of the moment** at SPUR

give notice (to *sb*), *also* **give *sb* notice**
1 to warn your employer that you will stop working ◆ *Jones gave notice in October that he planned to leave at the end of the school year.*
2 to tell an employee that they will no longer be employed ◆ *The company didn't give its employees notice, they just sent everyone home and closed the plant.*

> ORIGIN: based on the literal meaning of **give notice** (= to give written or printed information)

on short notice, *also* **at short notice**
with little warning ◆ *It's hard to find someone to take care of the kids on short notice.*

sit up and take notice
to suddenly give something your attention ◆ *His election made even people who don't care about politics sit up and take notice.*

take notice (of *sb/sth*)
to give someone or something your attention; = **take note (of *sb/sth*)** ◆ *Voters are beginning to take notice of her as a serious candidate.* ◆ *Several professors took notice of her excellent grasp of the subject.*

notion

not have the foggiest notion
to not know anything at all about something; = **not have the faintest idea** ◆ *I don't have the foggiest notion what that book is about.*

now

(every) now and then, *also* **(every) now and again**
sometimes ◆ *We still meet for lunch now and then, but not as often as we used to.* ◆ *Every now and then I'll take the kids to the playground.* ◆ Related vocabulary **every so often** at EVERY, **(every) once in a while** at WHILE

(it's) now or never
you should do something immediately because you may not get another opportunity ◆ *Olympic athletes only get a chance to compete every four years, so it's now or never for me.*

just now See at JUST
now you're talking See at TALKING
(right) here and now See at HERE
the here and now See at HERE

nowhere

nowhere near
not in any way ◆ *It was a long list and it was nowhere near complete.* ◆ *The movie was nowhere near as bad as Erin said it was.* ◆ *Holzman was nowhere near the player Carey is.*
USAGE: used for emphasis

nowhere to be found
not able to be seen ◆ *There were several high-tech devices in the room, but the instructions were nowhere to be found.*

go nowhere (fast) See at GO
(out) in the middle of nowhere See at MIDDLE

number

do a number on *sb*/*sth*
to hurt or damage someone or something ◆ *Dairy foods do a number on my stomach.* ◆ *This case has really done a number on the judge – he looks much older than he did just a few months ago.*

have (got) *sb*'s number
to understand the way someone behaves ◆ *They've got our number – they play harder against us than anybody else.* ◆ *She seems to know exactly what people our age want – she definitely has our number.*

***sb*'s number is up**
someone is going to die ◆ *I don't worry about flying. I figure if your number's up, your number's up.*

nut

a tough nut (to crack), *also* **a hard nut (to crack)**
a difficult problem to solve ◆ *Unemployment is a tough nut.* ◆ *Overcoming local trade barriers is going to be a hard nut to crack.*

nutshell

in a nutshell
very briefly ◆ *The answer, in a nutshell, is no.*

O, o

oats
feel *your* oats
to have great confidence in your importance or ability ♦ *Workers are feeling their oats and demanding higher wages.*

occasion
on occasion
sometimes but not often ♦ *This is the sun belt, but we do get freezing weather here on occasion.*

rise to the occasion
to do what is needed at the time ♦ *When a crisis hits, will you rise to the occasion?* ♦ *She needed some help, so I rose to the occasion and volunteered my services.* ♦ Related vocabulary **rise to *sth*** at RISE

occur
occur to *you*
to come into your mind ♦ *Did it occur to you to call my apartment to see if I was there?* ♦ *It never occurred to me to ask where she'd been.* USAGE: often used in the form **not occur to you**: *It hadn't occurred to her that she would be expected to ride a bike.*

odds
against the odds, also **against all odds**
despite many difficulties ♦ *The team battled against the odds and won the championship in the final weekend.* ♦ *He should be famous given what he accomplished against the odds.*

> ORIGIN: based on the literal meaning of **odds** (= the likelihood of success expressed as a comparison of two numbers)

at odds (with *sb/sth*) slightly formal
in disagreement ♦ *Such behavior is clearly at odds with what civilized society expects.* ♦ *The two women were hopelessly at odds.*

off
off and on
sometimes but not regularly or continuously; = **on and off** ♦ *It's been drizzling off and on for most of the morning.* ♦ *I've been exercising kind of off and on for a while now.*

off and running
started and doing well ♦ *The company is off and running with its new cable television operation.* ♦ *The band played on a Monday night and broke the nightclub's attendance record, and after that they were off and running.*

off of *sb/sth* esp. spoken
from ♦ *We're interested in how much profit we could make off of a relationship with them.* ♦ *I got the pictures off of the Internet.*

offense
no offense
I do not mean to insult you ♦ *No offense, I just don't like parties.*

offing
in the offing
possible or likely to happen soon ♦ *There are signs that a hot new design may be in the offing.* ♦ *I really thought a big promotion was in the offing.*

old
of old slightly formal
in the past ♦ *Today's vegetables grow more quickly and efficiently than vegetables of old.* USAGE: used after the noun it describes, as in the example

the same old same old esp. spoken
something that has not changed ♦ *You walk through your old school, and it's the same old same old.* ♦ *This season hasn't been exactly the same old same old for the team, who are leading their division.* ♦ Related vo-

cabulary **it's the same old story** at STORY, **the same old thing** at THING
a chip off the old block See at CHIP
as old as the hills See at HILLS
for old times' sake See at SAKE
it's the same old story See at STORY
settle old scores See **settle a score** at SCORE
the same old thing See at THING

on
on and off
sometimes but not regularly or continuously; = **off and on** ◆ *I'll be around the rest of today on and off but I'll be gone next week.* ◆ *Cynthia has been here on and off since the project started.*
on and on, *also* **on and on and on**
for a long time without stopping ◆ *The noise outside my window just went on and on all morning.* USAGE: often used with **go,** as in the example

once
at once
1 immediately ◆ *They were told to leave the building at once.*
2 at the same time ◆ *Everything happened at once, so I didn't have time to ask for advice.*
once again, *also* **once more**
another time ◆ *I'll explain it once again, but please listen carefully this time.*
once and for all
completely and finally ◆ *I wish we could settle the matter once and for all.*
all at once See at ALL
(every) once in a while See at WHILE
once in a blue moon See at MOON
once upon a time See at TIME

once-over
give *sb/sth* the once-over
to quickly look at someone or something in order to make a judgment ◆ *The security guard gave me the once-over but didn't bother checking my pass.* ◆ *Can you give my list the once-over before I hand it in?*

one
at one with *sb/sth* slightly formal
1 in agreement with someone or something ◆ *I am completely at one with Michael on this decision.*
2 feeling comfortable with someone or something ◆ *Camping out in a tent, we were at one with nature.*
one after the other, *also* **one after another**
first one person or thing and then another, followed by more ◆ *The cornfields stretched for many miles, one after the other.* USAGE: often used with a noun immediately after **one**: *She ate one chocolate after the other until the box was empty.*
one and all slightly formal
everyone ◆ *And a good evening to one and all!*
one and only
only ◆ *This may be your one and only opportunity to meet her.*
one and the same
the same person or thing ◆ *The villain and hero look like different actors, but they're really one and the same.* ◆ *Art and science were almost one and the same until the Renaissance.*
one by one
one person or thing following another in order ◆ *The children filed out of the bus, one by one.*
one up (on *sb/sth*)
having an advantage that someone or something else does not have ◆ *Mary's just spent a year in Spain, so she's one up on the rest of her Spanish class.*
the one and only
the only person or thing of this type ◆ *And now we'll hear a song by the one and only Elvis Presley.* ◆ *This is the one and only website dedicated to French fries.* USAGE: used to empha-

size that there could not be another like this one ◆ Related vocabulary **none other than** *sb/sth* at NONE

only

only just
very recently ◆ *She's only just arrived in town.*

only too
very ◆ *She'd be only too happy to help you.* ◆ *We were only too aware of the risks involved in traveling there.*

open

open to *sth*
1 not protected from something ◆ *The decision to close the firehouse left the mayor open to criticism.*
2 willing to consider something ◆ *I'm open to any reasonable suggestion.*

open up
to talk in a free and honest way ◆ *I felt I couldn't open up to anybody, not even to my best friend.* USAGE: usually said about discussing your thoughts or feelings

open up (*sth***)**, *also* **open** *sth* **up**
to make something available ◆ *Two jobs have recently opened up in the sales department.* ◆ *Seniors can register for the class first, but then they open it up to everybody.*

(out) in the open, *also* **(out) into the open**
available for everyone to see or experience ◆ *I hope we can finally get our feelings out in the open.* ◆ *You need to bring the evidence out into the open.*

wide open
not yet decided ◆ *She's still in high school so her future is wide open.* ◆ *With only four points separating the top six teams, the championship is still wide open.*

openers

for openers
as a beginning; = **for starters** ◆ *For openers, we have a staff of 10 just to handle the billing.* ◆ Related vocabulary **to begin with** at BEGIN

opposed

as opposed to *sth*
in comparison with something ◆ *We should be stopping terrorists from operating, as opposed to chasing them after they've attacked.* ◆ *I like pro basketball, as opposed to the college game.*

options

keep *your* **options open**, *also* **leave** *your* **options open**
to wait before making a choice ◆ *I want to keep my options open, so I didn't sign the contract yet.*

order

in order
1 complete and correct ◆ *Make sure the legal documents are signed and in order.* ◆ *It looks like everything is in order.*
2 right for the occasion ◆ *Now that you're a college graduate, I think congratulations are in order!* ◆ *A speech seemed to be in order, but I wasn't sure what I should say.*
3 with the particular aim or purpose ◆ *Your bags will be searched in order that security can be maintained.* ◆ *He came home early in order to make some phone calls.*

in short order
very quickly ◆ *He was able to deal with the scheduling problems in short order.* ◆ *In short order, she became head waiter.*

on order
requested but not yet received ◆ *The lamp has been on order for several weeks.*

out of order
not working correctly ◆ *The copy machine is out of order and won't be repaired until tomorrow.*

the order of the day
an appropriate or common activity ◆ *When business is bad, cost-cutting is the order of the day.* ◆ *Sadly, cheating seems to be the order of the day.*

other

other than
not including ♦ *The form cannot be signed by anyone other than you.* ♦ *Other than a small mark on his right cheek, there is no way to tell him apart from his twin brother.*

out

out from under (*sth*)
no longer being controlled by something ♦ *They're struggling to get out from under a lot of debt.* USAGE: often used after **get**: *Unfortunately, more employers are trying to get out from under state regulations.*

out loud
clearly, so it can be heard by other people ♦ *My reaction to her suggestion was to laugh out loud.* ♦ *If you have something to say, you should say it out loud so the whole class can hear it.*

out of it
1 not aware of what is happening ♦ *After working all night, she was so out of it she didn't remember to feed the dog.* USAGE: usually refers to the effects of lack of sleep or the use of alcohol or drugs: *Man, were you out of it at the party last night.*
2 not included in what is happening ♦ *They all loved sports, and I didn't, so I felt really out of it.*

outs

on the outs
not friendly ♦ *Peter is on the outs with his father.* USAGE: usually said about people who are not friendly because of having had an argument or disagreement

outside

at the outside
no more than ♦ *We'll be ten minutes late at the outside.* USAGE: used to emphasize that the actual amount of time will be less than what was mentioned

outside of *sb/sth*
not including someone or something ♦ *I don't have any work experience, outside of a few summer jobs.* ♦ *Outside of my two cousins in California, I don't have many relatives.*

over

over and above *sth*
in addition to something ♦ *We spent $1000 on hotels, and that's over and above food and entertainment.*

over (and done) with
finished or completed ♦ *I had my wisdom tooth out yesterday morning, so that's over and done with.* ♦ *He skipped to the end of the chapter just to get it over with.* USAGE: usually refers to something bad or unpleasant

over and over (again)
many times; = **again and again** ♦ *Bad language can lose its effect when it's used over and over.* ♦ Related vocabulary **time after time** at TIME

overdo

overdo it
to do too much of something ♦ *You need to exercise every day, but don't overdo it.* ♦ *Everything is painted black, which may be overdoing it.* ♦ *There are always some students at parties who overdo it.* ♦ Related vocabulary **go overboard** at GO

overdrive

into overdrive
into a condition of hard work and effectiveness ♦ *The staff went into overdrive, trying to get the software ready for release on Monday.* ♦ *There are times when you think this show is going to shift into overdrive, but it never does.* USAGE: sometimes used in the form **in overdrive**: *Law enforcement agencies are in overdrive preparing for the summit meeting.*

owe

owe it to *sb* to *do sth*
to have a duty to do something for someone ♦ *We owe it to our students*

strong as an ox

"Ask him to lift that box – he's as strong as an ox!"

to figure out how we can help them get a education.

you owe it to yourself to do sth
you deserve to do something you want to do ◆ *After working so hard, you owe it to yourself to take a long vacation.*

own

on your own
1 without help from anyone else ◆ *He came from a wealthy family, but he wanted to succeed on his own.*
2 alone ◆ *When I first started living on my own, I spent a lot of time fixing up the house.*

own up (to sth)
to admit that you are to blame for something ◆ *If you want to be forgiven, you've got to own up to your mistakes.*

ox

(as) strong as an ox
very strong; = **(as) strong as a bull**
◆ *He's one of our best players – strong as an ox, with good speed and great hands.*

> ORIGIN: based on the idea that an **ox** (= male cow) is a very strong animal

P, p

pace

at a snail's pace
very slowly ♦ *The action moves at a snail's pace in this film, as if all the characters were asleep.*

ORIGIN: from the fact that a **snail** (= a small animal with a round shell) moves very slowly

keep pace (with *sb/sth*)
to stay at the same level as someone or something ♦ *We get regular pay raises that are supposed to keep pace with inflation.*

set the pace
to do something that establishes a standard ♦ *What institutions set the pace for TV news?* ♦ *Our company is setting the pace for flexibility and responsiveness in the industry.*

ORIGIN: based on the literal meaning of **set the pace** (= to establish the speed at which a group moves)

a change of pace See at CHANGE

paces

put *sb/sth* through *their* paces
to test the ability or skill of a person or system ♦ *This contest will really put you guys through your paces.* ♦ *Frank took the car for a drive through the mountains and really put it through its paces.*

pack

ahead of the pack
more successful than those you are competing against ♦ *In terms of raising money, Joe Anderson is way ahead of the pack.* ♦ *Of all the software I've tested, this product is ahead of the pack.*

lead the pack
to be first or best of a group ♦ *For the second week in a row, the new Star Wars movie leads the pack at the box office.*

pack it in
to stop doing an activity or job ♦ *After another 11-hour day of campaigning, Kerns is ready to pack it in.* ♦ *Most professional athletes want to pack it in before they lose their ability to play well.*

pack *sb* off, *also* **pack off *sb***
to send someone away ♦ *We packed the kids off to their grandparents for the weekend.*

pack them in, *also* **pack 'em in**
to attract many people ♦ *Her Friday night appearances at the club have been packing them in.*

pack up *sb*, *also* **pack *sb* up**
to prepare someone to leave by gathering all their possessions ♦ *When the teachers heard about a flood warning, they packed up the children and sent them home.*

pack a punch See at PUNCH
pack *your* bags See at BAGS

page

on the same page
thinking in a similar way ♦ *Louisa said she called the meeting to make sure everybody's on the same page.* USAGE: usually said about efforts made to solve a problem ♦ Related vocabulary **on the same wavelength** at WAVELENGTH

turn the page
to stop thinking about or dealing with something ♦ *When a patient dies, a doctor just has to turn the page and concentrate on the next patient.* ♦ Related vocabulary **turn over a new leaf** at LEAF

pain

a pain in the ass rude slang, *also* **a pain in the neck**
someone or something that is very annoying ♦ *He doesn't win cases – he just makes such a pain in the ass of himself that opponents give up.* ♦ *She acts like all the people she works with are a pain in the neck.* USAGE: also used in the forms **a pain in the**

pains

butt or **a pain in the backside:** *Watering the lawn is always a pain in the butt.*

on pain of *sth* slightly formal
at risk of experiencing something bad ♦ *She says she was asked to approve the report on pain of losing her job.*

pains

at pains to *do sth* slightly formal
making an effort to do something ♦ *The management was at pains to stress that there are no plans for closing the factory.* ♦ *He was at pains to show he does not favor the change.*

take (great) pains to *do sth*, also **go to (great) pains to** *do sth*
to try very hard to do something ♦ *We took great pains to insure that no one felt left out.* ♦ Related vocabulary **go to great lengths to** *do sth* at LENGTHS

pal

pal around (with *sb***)**
to spend time doing things you enjoy with someone you like ♦ *Jackie pals around with other students who also listen to rap music.*

pale

beyond the pale
not acceptable to most people ♦ *For most people, a discussion like this has been simply beyond the pale.*

> ORIGIN: based on a past meaning of **pale** (= an area in Ireland, Scotland, or France controlled by England), and the idea that places outside this area were dangerous for the English

pale in comparison (with *sth***)**
See at COMPARISON

pall

cast a pall over *sth*
to spoil something ♦ *Her illness cast a pall over the awards ceremony.*

> ORIGIN: from the literal meaning of a **pall** (= something, such as smoke or fog or dust in the air, that makes the sky dark)

palm

grease *sb's* **palm**, also **grease the palm of** *sb*
to give someone money to persuade them to do what you want ♦ *Some of those candidates spent money greasing the palms of local political bosses.*

in the palm of *your* **hand**
under your complete control ♦ *The audience was fascinated – he held them in the palm of his hand.*

palm off *sth*, also **palm** *sth* **off**
to trick or persuade someone to take something ♦ *They palmed off cheap wine at high prices by putting it in fancy bottles.* ♦ *She produced fake stamps and palmed them off as genuine.* ♦ Related vocabulary **fob** *sth* **off on** *sb* at FOB

pan

pan out
to happen or be successful ♦ *He was very creative, although not all his ideas have panned out.*

pander

pander to *sb*
to give someone what they want, although it may not be good or right for them ♦ *TV stations pander to viewers who don't seem to get enough of sex and violence.*

pander to *sth*
to accept or support something bad in order to get an advantage ♦ *He is the worst sort of politician, who panders to fear to win votes.*

Pandora's box

open (a) Pandora's box
to start something that causes many new and unexpected problems ♦ *They worry that any decision they make about testing will open a Pandora's box.* ♦ *What kind of Pandora's box do we open if we decide not arrest people who have committed a crime?*

> ORIGIN: based on an old Greek story in which a woman named Pandora opened a box containing all the troubles the world has experienced

panic button
push the panic button
to react to a situation with fear and confusion ◆ *Our coach isn't about to push the panic button just because we've lost two games in a row.* USAGE: sometimes used with other verbs that have a similar meaning, such as **press** and **hit**: *It's too early to hit the panic button, but our stocks lost half their value today.*

pants
caught with *your* pants down
in a situation that embarrasses you ◆ *My job was to get as much information as possible so that my boss would not be caught with her pants down.* USAGE: often said about situations you are not prepared for

scare the pants off *you*
to frighten you very much ◆ *Spiders scare the pants off me.* USAGE: also used with other verbs to emphasize an extreme reaction: *Sunbathing bores the pants off me.* ◆ *Hugh always beats the pants off me in tennis.* ◆ Related vocabulary **scare the hell out of *you*** at HELL, **scare *you* to death** at DEATH

wear the pants
to be the person in charge in a marriage or family ◆ *She has the best-paid job and she also wears the pants in the family.* USAGE: used to describe women, as in the example

> ORIGIN: based on the idea that men are traditionally in control and wear trousers

paper
on paper
possibly ◆ *On paper it looks like it could work, but I won't be convinced until I see it in operation.*

not worth the paper *sth* is printed on, *also* **not worth the paper *sth* is written on**
to have no value or importance ◆ *He's got a degree from an online university that's not worth the paper it's printed on.* ◆ *The landlord's promises were not worth the paper they were written on.*

paper over *sth*, *also* **paper *sth* over**
to solve a problem temporarily ◆ *They papered over their disagreements in order to end the meeting on a positive note.* ◆ *She has a solid record of bridging differences between groups, not just papering them over.*

par
on a par with *sb/sth*, *also* **on par with *sb/sth***
at the same level as someone or something ◆ *With their win today, the Rangers are now on a par with the Orioles in the team rankings.* ◆ Related vocabulary **up to scratch** at SCRATCH

par for the course
what should be expected because of past experience ◆ *The school budget is going to be cut again this year, but then that's par for the course.*

> ORIGIN: based on the literal meaning of **par for the course** (= the expected number of times a good player in golf will hit the ball to get it in all the holes)

up to par
at the usual or expected standard; = **up to the mark** ◆ *When your work is up to par we can review your salary again.* ◆ *Are your computer skills up to par?* USAGE: often used in the form **not up to par**: *She hasn't been up to par since the beginning of last week.* ◆ Related vocabulary **at (a) low ebb** at EBB

parade
rain on *sb's* parade
to spoil someone's plans or pleasure ◆ *I'm sorry to rain on your parade,*

but you're not allowed to have food or drinks in the theater.

parcel

parcel out *sth*, *also* **parcel** *sth* **out**
to give parts of something to different people ♦ *The bookkeeper spent yesterday parceling out the profits from the deal.* ♦ *The settlement is very small and I'm glad I'm not the one who has to parcel it out.*

pardon

pardon me, *also* **I beg your pardon**
1 please repeat what you just said ♦ *Pardon me – what did you say your name was?*
2 I am sorry for what I just did ♦ *Oh, I beg your pardon! I didn't see your foot there!*
3 May I please have your attention? ♦ *Pardon me, does this train go to Oakland?*
4 I do not agree with what you just said ♦ *Pardon me, but I think you've got it backwards.* ♦ Related vocabulary **excuse me** at EXCUSE
USAGE: in all cases, **I beg your pardon** is more formal than **pardon me**

part

a part to play
involvement that is necessary to do something ♦ *Engineers have an important part to play in any military operation.*

do *your* **part**
to do your share of an activity; = **do** *your* **bit** ♦ *We're doing our part by recycling everything we can, even plastic bags.* ♦ Related vocabulary **do** *your* **share** at SHARE

for *sb's* **part**
relating to or involving one particular person ♦ *For her part, Ms. Newman will leave the team and start up an independent project.*

for the most part
mostly or generally; = **by and large** ♦ *This town has always been considered safe, and for the most part, it still is.*

in large part slightly formal, *also* **in good part**
mostly ♦ *The film's power comes in large part from Epstein's excellent and realistic screenplay.*

look the part
to appear to be suited to a particular type of work ♦ *You'd never guess he was a security guard – he doesn't look the part at all.*

on the part of *sb*, *also* **on** *sb's* **part**
coming from someone ♦ *This insurance plan involves a bigger investment on the part of employers than most of them may be willing to make.* ♦ *It was a mistake on my part and I apologized for it.*

part and parcel (of *sth***)**
something that cannot be separated from a condition or activity ♦ *Being recognized on the street is part and parcel of being a celebrity.*

play *your* **part**
to do what you can do or should do ♦ *Local leaders played their part in making the festival a great success.*
USAGE: sometimes used in the form **play a part** (= to be involved): *I'm afraid that I also played a part in wrongly accusing her.*

take *sb's* **part**
to support someone in an argument or disagreement ♦ *For once, my brother took my part instead of attacking me.*

take part (in *sth***)**
to be actively involved in something ♦ *We haven't taken part in any of the family parties recently.*

the better part of *sth*, *also* **the best part of** *sth*
more than half of something ♦ *We waited for the better part of an hour, then called again.* USAGE: usually used with periods of time, as in the example

part company (with *sb***)** See at COMPANY

parting

parting of the ways
a separation of two things or people because of a disagreement ♦ *We came to a parting of the ways because of our different ideas about what should be done to move the company forward.* ♦ Related vocabulary **part company (with** *sb***)** 1 at COMPANY

party

the party is over, *also* **the party's over**
something successful has ended ♦ *The party is over for the Raiders, who were eliminated from the playoffs today.*

pass

make a pass at *sb*
to act toward someone in a way that shows a sexual interest in them ♦ *It seems as if those boys can't think of much more than fast cars and making passes at girls.*

pass along *sth* **(to** *sb***)**, *also* **pass** *sth* **along (to** *sb***)**
to give something to someone; = **pass** *sth* **on (to** *sb***)** ♦ *Reporters passed along the information as they heard it.* ♦ *If you don't want the book, you can pass it along to someone who does.* USAGE: also said about something given to younger people: *I wanted friends and family to be able to pass along some special memory about my father after his death.* ♦ *Women can also pass the gene along to their children.*

pass away, *also* **pass on**
to die ♦ *Both my parents passed away fairly young, and then my brothers and I lived with our uncle.*

pass for *sb/sth*
to appear to be someone or something else ♦ *A lot of what passes for humor these days is just anger expressed in the form of a joke.* ♦ *Although he's 35, he could still pass for a college student.*

pass off
to happen in a particular way ♦ *The ceremony passed off without a problem, with the baby sleeping through most of it.*

pass *sth* **off as** *sth*, *also* **pass off** *sth* **as** *sth*
to pretend that something is different from what it really is ♦ *Mother would never try to pass off supermarket cookies as homemade, would she?* ♦ *The senator passed his impolite language off as "the way we talk where I come from."*

pass *yourself* **off as** *sb*
to pretend that you are someone else ♦ *Maurice is trying to pass himself off as a journalist to get admitted to the press conference.*

pass *sth* **on (to** *sb***)**, *also* **pass on** *sth* **(to** *sb***)**
to give something to someone; = **pass along** *sth* **(to** *sb***)** ♦ *Companies almost always pass any increase in costs on to consumers.* ♦ *She had passed on some false information, but I'm sure she thought it was true.* USAGE: often said about something given to younger people: *I think it's wonderful that you have passed your interest in music on to your children.*

pass out
to become unconscious ♦ *A few people passed out from the heat.*

pass over *sb/sth*
to ignore someone or something ♦ *Thirty attorneys were passed over for promotion by the department.*

pass up *sth*, *also* **pass** *sth* **up**
to fail to take advantage of an opportunity ♦ *Phillips could never pass up a chance to tell you how much he hated lawyers.* ♦ *When they invited her to perform, I told her she shouldn't pass it up.*

mention (*sb/sth***) in passing** See at MENTION

pass judgment on *sb/sth* See at JUDGMENT

pass muster See at MUSTER

pass the buck See at BUCK
pass the hat See at HAT
pass the smell test See at TEST
pass the time See at TIME
pass the torch (to *sb***)** See at TORCH

past
live in the past
to react to conditions that existed long ago rather than those that exist now ◆ *He believes the unions cannot live in the past and must deal with the changes in society.*
a blast from the past See at BLAST
a thing of the past See at THING
not put it past *sb* See at PUT
past *your*/*its* **prime** See at PRIME

pasture
put *sb* **out to pasture**
to make someone stop working at their job because they are too old to be useful ◆ *At 62, he felt he was not ready to be put out to pasture.*

> ORIGIN: based on the tradition of keeping farm animals that are too old to work in a **pasture** (= land covered with grass)

pastures
greener pastures
a better situation ◆ *After a successful year, the young, ambitious coach was seeking greener pastures with another team.* ◆ *The survey finds many older residents are looking for greener pastures.*

pat
a pat on the back
praise; = **a slap on the back** ◆ *The White House gave her a pat on the back Thursday, when the president said she was a highly valued member of his staff.* ◆ Related vocabulary **a kick in the butt** at KICK
have *sth* **down pat** See at HAVE
stand pat See at STAND

patch
patch up *sth*, *also* **patch** *sth* **up**
to fix a relationship ◆ *Charles said they wanted to patch up any outstanding differences as soon as possible.* ◆ *Early in our marriage, we sometimes argued about money, but we always patched things up.*

path
beat a path to *sb's* **door**
to be very eager to see you ◆ *Whenever some ordinary guy wins a big lottery, the press beats a path to his door.*
cross *your* **path**
to happen to you ◆ *If you only write about whatever crosses your path each day, your writing may not be very interesting to most readers.*
off the beaten path
not known or popular with many people; = **off the beaten track** ◆ *She enjoyed going to foreign-language movies that were a little bit off the beaten path.*
the path of least resistance
the way that is the easiest ◆ *Thieves usually take the path of least resistance, taking the cars that are easiest to steal.*
lead *sb* **down the garden path** See at GARDEN
the straight and narrow (path) See at STRAIGHT

patience
try the patience of *sb*, *also* **try** *sb's* **patience**
to cause someone to become extremely annoyed ◆ *The judge told the lawyer that he was trying the patience of the court with his delaying tactics.*

pause
give *sb* **pause**, *also* **give pause to** *sb*
to cause someone to stop and think carefully ◆ *Surviving a serious car wreck is an experience that really gives you pause.*

pavement
pound the pavement
1 to look for a job ◆ *Mary had chil-*

dren to feed, so she kept pounding the pavement until she finally landed a job at a burger restaurant.
2 to look for money or support ◆ *She's been going out and pounding the pavement, raising money for research.* ◆ *Day after day, they pound the pavement, hoping to share a message about their religious faith.*

pay

pay *sb/sth* **back**, *also* **pay back** *sb/sth*
to return money that you have borrowed ◆ *I'll pay you back as soon as I get my next paycheck.* ◆ *I'll pay the money back on Friday.* ◆ *It will take years for him to pay back his student loans.*

pay down *sth*, *also* **pay** *sth* **down**
to reduce the total amount of money owed ◆ *If this trend continues, the government could start paying down the national debt.* ◆ *We've got a big mortgage on the house and want to pay it down as quickly as we can.* USAGE: most often used in connection with large debts

pay off
to result in success ◆ *I hope all this hard work pays off.*

pay off *sb*, *also* **pay** *sb* **off**
to give someone money illegally to get them to do what you want ◆ *The pair had paid off local police to protect their drug-selling operation.*

pay off *sth*, *also* **pay** *sth* **off**
to pay all of a debt ◆ *It took her six years to pay off her student loan.* ◆ *I guess I can afford a new car, but it's a lot of money and it's not easy to pay it off.*

pay out *sth*, *also* **pay** *sth* **out**
to spend money for expenses or costs ◆ *An important expense for the company is the amount it must pay out to managers.* ◆ *The federal government paid several billion out in emergency aid this year.*

pay up
to give the total amount that is owed or asked for ◆ *Some ballplayers charge fans $50 for autographs, and the fans pay up.* ◆ *He would surely have paid up if she had asked him for the money.*

pay dirt

hit pay dirt, *also* **strike pay dirt**
to succeed ◆ *He hit pay dirt with his next movie, which grossed $270 million worldwide.*

> ORIGIN: based on the literal meaning of **pay dirt** (= dirt that contains valuable metals)

peace

at peace with *sth/yourself*
feeling calm and relaxed about something or yourself ◆ *He appears to be at peace with the world these days.* ◆ *These are good times for Randy, a man at peace with himself and his career.*

keep the peace slightly formal
to prevent fighting or difficulties ◆ *The judge made her sign an agreement promising she would try to keep the peace with her husband for one year.* ◆ *Troops were sent in to keep the peace in the region.*

leave *sb/sth* **in peace**
to let someone or something stay as they are ◆ *He's hoping everyone will leave him in peace so he can work on his paintings.* ◆ *She thinks the wreck should be left in peace as a memorial.*

make *your* **peace with** *sb*
to stop arguing with someone ◆ *Melanie knew she had to go back into the house and make her peace with her parents.*

make *your* **peace with** *sth*
to accept something ◆ *He knows that he's really too old to play ball, and he's made his peace with that.*

peace of mind
a feeling of calm or not being worried ◆ *Worries disturbed my peace of mind enough to keep me from falling asleep.*

rest in peace
to be free from trouble ◆ *The late Mr.*

peas

Aspin, may he rest in peace, was a good friend to all of us. ◆ The girl is dead. Why can't you stop criticizing and let her rest in peace? USAGE: always used in reference to a dead person

peas
(like) two peas in a pod
very similar; = **two of a kind** ◆ We were two peas in a pod – we liked all the same things, and we did everything together.

pedal
(put) the pedal to the metal
to make something go forward or increase as fast as possible ◆ Ingrid put the pedal to the metal and finished writing her essay a day early ◆ Related vocabulary **floor it** at FLOOR.

> ORIGIN: based on the idea of pressing a car's gas **pedal** (= a flat piece that you control with your foot) all the way to the floor to make the car go as fast as possible

pedestal
put *sb/sth* on a pedestal
to behave as if one person is more important than others ◆ They put the local doctor on a pedestal, seldom questioning his word or his authority. ◆ Professional athletes are often put on a pedestal, and they forget that the fans pay their salaries. USAGE: the opposite meaning is expressed by **take** or **knock someone off their pedestal**: *You know something will happen that will knock her off her pedestal.*

peel
peel off, *also* peel away
to move away quickly ◆ The first of three attack jets suddenly peeled off to the right.

peg
a square peg (in a round hole)
someone who is different from most people of the same age and situation ◆ In high school she was definitely a square peg, but even if they didn't understand her, most kids admired her.

bring *sb/sth* down a peg (or two), *also* take *sb* down a peg (or two)
to show that someone or something is not as good as people think ◆ His arrogant behavior made some people want to see him brought down a peg. ◆ She uses her position to take other people down a peg or two.

two peas in a pod

Colin and his brother are two peas in a pod.

pen

put pen to paper, *also* **set pen to paper**
to write on paper ♦ *You can e-mail us, or, of course, you can always put pen to paper and send us a letter.*

penchant

a penchant for *sth*
a great liking for something ♦ *He had a penchant for luxury hotel suites, limousines, and high-priced meals.*

pencil

pencil *sb/sth* **in**, *also* **pencil in** *sb/sth*
to have a temporary plan to do something with someone ♦ *The team had penciled in Morton as a key player this season.* ♦ *I penciled you in for lunch next Thursday.*

ORIGIN: based on the idea that a pencil mark can easily be removed or changed

penny

a penny for your thoughts
I would like to know what you are thinking about ♦ *For several minutes they sat silently, then finally she looked at him and said, "A penny for your thoughts, Walter."*

penny wise and pound foolish
unwise because doing something small now would prevent much more trouble later ♦ *Education budget cuts are penny wise and pound foolish – public education is an investment in our future.*

people

of all people
more than anyone else ♦ *You, of all people, should understand the importance of historical analysis.* USAGE: also used to emphasize that the person named is surprising: *I guess the weirdest version of that song I've ever heard is by Frank Sinatra, of all people.* ♦ Related vocabulary **of all places** at PLACES, **of all things** at THINGS

pep

pep *sb/sth* **up**, *also* **pep up** *sb/sth*
to make someone or something more active or exciting ♦ *With her energy and enthusiasm, she may be able to pep up the company's sales.* ♦ *She was always busy trying either to pep someone up or calm someone down.*

perk

perk up *sth*, *also* **perk** *sth* **up**
to make something more interesting or active ♦ *Chopped prunes can really perk up a fruit salad.* ♦ *It's a pretty dull movie, though the supporting actors perk things up a little.* USAGE: sometimes used in the form **perk up your ears** (= to cause you to become interested): *A new book about using the Internet might not exactly perk up your ears.*

perk up (*sb***)**, *also* **perk** *sb* **up**
to make someone more active and interested ♦ *It was a clear summer day, and Nancy looked like she was beginning to perk up.* ♦ *His stay with Aunt Podie soon perked him up.*

perpetuity

in perpetuity slightly formal
forever ♦ *The land was given to the university in perpetuity.*

person

in person
physically ♦ *Though they chatted online, they'd never met in person.* ♦ *The actor looks even shorter in person than he does on the screen.*

on *your* **person** slightly formal
with you ♦ *Anderson was carrying $10,000 in cash on his person at the time.*

your **own person** esp. spoken
not very much influenced by other people ♦ *Scott is his own person, and he does what he wants to do.* USAGE: also used with **man** or **woman** instead of **person**: *Ben remains refreshingly his own man.* ♦ *Beth was her own woman, even back in high*

school. ◆ Related vocabulary **do your own thing** at THING

pertain

pertain to *sth* slightly formal
to have a connection with something ◆ *His organization wants to provide input to the county on issues pertaining to wildlife.*

petard

hoist with *your* **own petard**, also **hoist on** *your* **own petard**
to be harmed by something that was intended by you to harm someone else ◆ *The most enjoyable moment in any action film occurs when the villain is hoist with his own petard.*

> ORIGIN: based on the literal meaning of **hoist by your own petard** (= blown into the air by your own explosive device), an expression made popular in Shakespeare's play, "Hamlet"

Pete

for Pete's sake esp. spoken
I am annoyed or surprised by this; = **for goodness' sake** ◆ *She has a huge salary and gets a bonus, too – how much money does she need, for Pete's sake?* USAGE: used for emphasis and often used instead of the more offensive idioms **for God's sake** and **for Christ's sake** ◆ Related vocabulary **for crying out loud** at CRYING

peter

peter out
to be reduced gradually so that nothing is left ◆ *The road petered out completely, and there was no choice but to walk the rest of the way.* ◆ *The attacks petered out during the rainy season.*

phase

phase in *sth*, also **phase** *sth* **in**
to introduce something gradually in stages ◆ *The plan would phase in a pay raise for many state-government workers.* ◆ *They added too many stores at once instead of phasing them in over time.* ◆ Opposite **phase out** *sth*

phase out *sth*, also **phase** *sth* **out**
to gradually stop providing or using something ◆ *The city decided to phase out half-day kindergarten for 4-year-olds in the public schools.* ◆ Opposite **phase in (***sth***)**

pick

have *your* **pick of** *sth*
to be able to choose any one you want from a group of things ◆ *The president's daughter had her pick of the best colleges in America.*

pick and choose
to take only what you want from a group ◆ *You cannot pick and choose which rules to accept and which to ignore.*

pick *sb/sth* **apart**, also **pick apart** *sb/sth*
to find mistakes, weaknesses, or faults in someone or something ◆ *When new software is developed, the company sends out a test version and asks users to pick it apart.* ◆ *Lots of players are picked apart by their coaches, by the fans, and by the media.*

pick at *sth*
to eat food in small pieces and without enjoyment ◆ *He eats very little, picking at his food with his fork.*

pick *sb/sth* **off**, also **pick** *sb/sth* **off**
1 to kill or shoot one person or animal at a time ◆ *Snipers picked the soldiers off one by one.* ◆ *The birds in the nest were picked off by hawks.* **2** to select and attack or defeat a particular person or group ◆ *During the race I just picked off the runners ahead of me one at a time.* ◆ *We try to identify these criminal groups and pick their leaders off before they can cause too much trouble.* ◆ *The Republicans picked off Democrats in Oklahoma, Alabama, and Mississippi in the last election.*

pick on *sb*
to treat someone unfairly by criticizing or punishing them ◆ *What could have caused so many people to pick on him?* ◆ *My sister was always picked on at school.*

pick out *sb/sth*, *also* **pick** *sb/sth* **out**
1 to choose someone or something instead of others ◆ *The writer picked out certain things about the event that he thought were important.* ◆ *His boss picked him out for an assignment in Japan.*
2 to find someone or something in a group ◆ *The upgrade will increase the telescope's ability to pick out individual objects in space.* ◆ *He was so tall, it was easy to pick him out in the crowd.*

pick over *sth*, *also* **pick** *sth* **over**
to examine a group of things carefully ◆ *The boss picked over every word in Kelley's memo.* ◆ *She picked the strawberries over, selecting the largest ones.*

pick up
1 to increase in speed or amount ◆ *The wind really picked up this morning.* ◆ *Economic growth is expected to pick up next year.*
2 to improve ◆ *The team usually plays poorly in the first half, then picks up later in the game.*

pick *sb* **up**, *also* **pick up** *sb*
1 to get someone and bring them somewhere ◆ *I'll pick you up at the airport.* ◆ *I'm just waiting to pick up the kids.*
2 to get someone to play for your team ◆ *They made trades with several teams, and picked up Davis from the Reds.*
3 to meet someone you did not know and begin an informal and often sexual relationship with them ◆ *Is that the girl who picked him up at a bar last week?* ◆ *I was almost picked up by a 16-year-old last summer.*
4 to put someone under the control of the police ◆ *Police picked up 12 suspects in early-morning raids.* ◆ *The police pick them up, but the judges just let them go.*

pick *you* **up**
to make you happy ◆ *This is the kind of music that just picks you up.* ◆ *Seeing her always picked me up.*

pick up (*sth***)**
to answer the telephone ◆ *Her answering machine came on, and I yelled, "Pick up, Marie! Pick up the phone!"*

pick up *sth*
to earn points or a victory ◆ *McDowell picked up his first win in almost a year last night.* ◆ *Armstrong increased his lead in the race, picking up another 94 points.*

pick up *sth*, *also* **pick** *sth* **up**
1 to get something ◆ *Gwen picked up a cold on her trip.* ◆ *We need some milk, so I'll pick some up on the way home.*
2 to pay for something ◆ *Bob was going to pay for dinner, but I said no, I'll pick it up.* ◆ *He was hoping that his insurance would pick up most of those bills.*
3 to learn something ◆ *I was born up north, but I moved at such a young age that I picked up the southern ways real quick.* ◆ *She lived in Paris and picked the language up easily, soon speaking it like a native.*
4 to notice something ◆ *You'd have to know him extremely well to pick up details like that.* ◆ *We gave him a hint, but he failed to pick it up.*
5 to continue something ◆ *The TV series is over for this year, but the station plans to pick it up again next season.* ◆ *The network picked up Rogers's show in 1970.*
6 to receive sounds, pictures, or other information carried by energy waves ◆ *The microphone picked up much more noise than we expected.* ◆ *I could hear a voice, but my cell phone couldn't pick it up well enough for me to know who it was.*
7 to print or broadcast information that has been printed or broadcast somewhere else ◆ *The story first*

appeared in a Baltimore weekly, but was soon picked up by most of the nation's newspapers.

pick up on *sth* esp. spoken
1 to notice something ◆ *The evidence was there – I just didn't pick up on it.* **2** to continue talking about something previously said ◆ *Just to pick up on what Haley asked, I think the president clearly did get the message.*

take *your* **pick**
to choose what you want ◆ *The company offers family trips, learning vacations, beach getaways, or visits to historic sites – take your pick.*

pickle

in a pickle
experiencing a difficult situation ◆ *He thinks the media are responsible for his being in such a pickle.* USAGE: often used with a word describing the type of difficulty: *They are going to put themselves in a legal pickle.*

picture

get the picture
to understand a situation ◆ *The team won two, then lost three, then won two, then lost two, then won three – you get the picture?*

in the picture
to be involved in a situation ◆ *Strong thunderstorms and heavy rain are in the picture for the Southeast on Monday.* ◆ Related vocabulary **in the loop** at LOOP

out of the picture
to not be involved in a situation ◆ *With the national government out of the picture, local leaders will have to work out a solution.* ◆ Related vocabulary **out of the loop** at LOOP

paint a picture (of *sth***)**
to describe a situation in a particular way ◆ *The report paints a picture of a neighborhood in decline.* USAGE: often used with an adjective that describes the type of situation: *Doctors have begun to paint a grim picture of his condition.* ◆ *I don't want to paint too rosy a picture.*

the big picture, *also* **the whole picture**
the most important facts about a situation and the effects that it has on other things ◆ *Melissa's opinions don't take the big picture into account.* USAGE: often used after **look at**: *When you look at the big picture, a slight increase in unemployment is not significant.*

the picture of *sth*
a very good representation of a condition or an attitude ◆ *Except for a little arthritis, my mother is the picture of health.* ◆ *He seemed the picture of confidence.*

pie

(as) easy as pie
very easy ◆ *You make everything sound as easy as pie, George.* USAGE: used in the forms **(as) easy as 1-2-3** or **(as) easy as A, B, C** (= very easy to understand) and **(as) easy as falling off a log** (= very easy to do)

pie in the sky
something good that is unlikely to happen ◆ *Our leaders need to offer more than pie in the sky when they talk about political and social issues.*

piece

(all) of a piece slightly formal
sharing the same basic characteristics or ideas ◆ *Willner edited the music to make the different parts seem all of a piece.* USAGE: often followed by **with**: *His attitude toward imagination was very much of a piece with his attitude toward existence.*

a piece of cake
something very easy ◆ *Most parents know that dealing with a sick child makes everything else look like a piece of cake.* ◆ *Our team is strong, but it won't be a piece of cake to make it to the finals.*

a piece of the action
a share of the profits or advantages that come from an activity ♦ *He agreed to run the golf course for $15,000 a year and a piece of the action.*

a piece of the pie
a share in something ♦ *Each group needs money and is working hard for its own piece of the pie.*

> ORIGIN: based on the idea that something whole is like a **pie** (= a round, filled pastry) that can be divided

give sb a piece of *your* mind
to tell someone angrily that you disapprove of something they have done ♦ *There's the car that almost hit us this afternoon – I'm going to give those people a piece of my mind.*

in one piece
not injured or damaged ♦ *I'm glad the kids arrived home in one piece from school.*

> ORIGIN: based on the idea of an object that is not broken

piece together *sth*, *also* piece *sth* together
1 to combine many small details to give a complete description of something ♦ *In this account, Rawson tries to piece together the events leading up to the tragedy.* ♦ *I hadn't told anyone about it, though I suppose someone could have pieced it together.*
2 to combine small things to make something bigger ♦ *Peters pieced together night courses for five years to earn a college degree.* ♦ *We had to piece the money together to pay off our debts.*

> ORIGIN: from the idea of combining the parts of something to make a whole

say *your* piece, *also* speak *your* piece
to express your opinion about something, esp. something that you do not like ♦ *When the young man interrupted, the president stopped talking and let the man say his piece.*

pieces

go to pieces, *also* **fall to pieces**
to lose confidence in yourself and feel you have no control over events ♦ *After he and Edna divorced, Art went to pieces.* ♦ *His world fell to pieces in 1966 when civil war broke out in Nigeria.* ♦ Related vocabulary **fall apart 1** at FALL

pick up the pieces
to try to get back to an ordinary way of life after a very bad experience ♦ *Survivors of the mudslides are hoping to pick up the pieces of their shattered lives.* ♦ *When their parents died, the grandparents had to pick up the pieces and care for the children.*

pig

a pig in a poke
something that you buy without knowing if it is good or not ♦ *When you buy a used car, you may be getting a pig in a poke.*

> ORIGIN: based on an old meaning of **buy a pig in a poke** (= buy a pig in a bag), which you would buy without first seeing it

pig out
to eat a lot ♦ *Our kids dream of staying up late and pigging out on junk food.*

pike

come down the pike
to happen or appear ♦ *He's the worst writer to come down the pike in a long time.*

> ORIGIN: based on the literal meaning of **pike** (= a large road)

down the pike
in the future ♦ *She may do something else down the pike, but she won't be doing this.*

pile

pile up *sth*, *also* **pile** *sth* **up**
to increase something ◆ *Many civilians were killed – the evidence continues to pile up.* ◆ *The company piled up hundreds of millions of dollars of losses over the last year.* USAGE: usually used in passive forms: *Earnings began piling up from the sale of the new switches.*

pill

a bitter pill (to swallow)
an unpleasant situation that must be accepted ◆ *Losing the championship was a bitter pill to swallow for a team that was used to winning every year.* ◆ *Having his fate in the hands of others is a bitter pill for this proud man.*

pillar

a pillar of strength
someone who is emotionally very strong ◆ *Roger was a pillar of strength when my father died.*

pin

you could hear a pin drop
to be extremely quiet ◆ *The new sound-proof lab is so well designed, you can hear a pin drop.* ◆ *You could have heard a pin drop for a full minute after every song and then the audience would clap wildly.*

pin down *sb*, *also* **pin** *sb* **down**
1 to get specific information from someone ◆ *It is not easy to pin down a politician who won't even tell you if it's raining or snowing!* ◆ *We tried to pin him down on where the money would come from.*
2 to keep someone from being able to escape by shooting at them ◆ *For a time, the crew was pinned down by machine-gun fire.*
3 to hold someone by force so that they cannot move ◆ *Burns usually pinned down and then handcuffed his victims.* ◆ *I was pinned down by a wall that had fallen.* USAGE: when the object is a pronoun, it always follows **pin**: *Don't pin me down about my plans.*

pin down *sth*, *also* **pin** *sth* **down**
to discover the facts or exact details about something ◆ *The fire department is trying to pin down the cause of Wednesday's fire.* ◆ *So far we haven't pinned down a date.*

pin *sth* **on** *sb*
to blame someone for something ◆ *The accident can't be pinned on me, but I truly don't know how it happened.*

pin *sth* **on** *sth*
to depend on something for a particular result ◆ *We are all pinning our hopes on the new pipeline for a cleaner water supply.*

pinch

feel the pinch
to experience the effect of having less money ◆ *Consumers have felt the pinch of higher gasoline prices.*

in a pinch
if necessary ◆ *You should use lime juice, but in a pinch lemon is all right.*

pink

in the pink (of *sth***)**
very strong and operating well ◆ *It was almost a miracle that after his bout with pneumonia, he was back in the pink of health.* ◆ *These men are in the pink of condition, and the army wants to keep them that way.* ◆ *Our business is in the pink these days.*

pins

on pins and needles
worried or excited about something ◆ *I was on pins and needles until she called to say she had arrived in Istanbul.*

pipe

pipe up
to speak unexpectedly ◆ *"I want to be the first female president!" piped up one of the little girls.*

pipeline
in the pipeline
being developed ♦ *According to the studio, there are ten films in the pipeline ready for release next year.* ♦ Related vocabulary **in the works** at WORKS

piper
pay the piper
to accept the unpleasant results of something you have done; = **pay the price** ♦ *After fooling around for most of the semester, now he has to pay the piper and study over vacation.* ♦ *If you don't charge enough for your work, at some point you will have to pay the piper.*

piss
piss off rude slang
go away ♦ *Piss off, Chris, and stop flooding my e-mail with garbage!*

piss *you* off rude slang
to make you angry ♦ *It really pissed me off that they didn't help me out when I needed it.* ♦ *I think everyone is pissed off about the parking problem.*

pitch
pitch in
to help with others to get something done ♦ *As soon as we knew what a big job it was, Gwen and I just pitched in with the rest of the group.*

pity
have pity on *sb*
to do something out of sympathy that will help someone ♦ *An old man begged the soldiers to have pity on him and let him go.*

take pity on *sb*
to do something because you feel sympathy for someone ♦ *She stood there shivering until Claudia took pity on her and put her sweater around the child's shoulders.*

place
all over the place esp. spoken
1 everywhere ♦ *This city has beautiful parks all over the place.* ♦ *This summer there was a lot of rain and we had weeds all over the place.*

2 not well organized or carefully considered ♦ *You can't tell what Fred will do because his ideas are all over the place.*

as if *you* own the place, also **like *you* own the place**
showing too much confidence ♦ *They marched right in and started ordering us around as if they owned the place.*

fall into place, also **fall in place**
1 to become organized ♦ *Once Molly got a business loan, she hired a couple of people and very quickly things fell into place.*

2 to be correctly arranged ♦ *All the facts finally fell into place, and this allowed us to understand the problem.*

in place
1 ready for use ♦ *Certainly there are plans in place for a response to an attack.* ♦ Related vocabulary **at hand** at HAND

2 now in effect or being used ♦ *The new building code will replace the rules that are currently in place.*

in the first place
in the beginning ♦ *We should never have agreed to do this in the first place.*

in the right place at the right time
lucky to be somewhere ♦ *She was in the right place at the right time and got the apartment as soon as it became available.* ♦ Opposite **in the wrong place (at the wrong time)**

in the wrong place (at the wrong time)
unlucky to be somewhere ♦ *Cops say the kid who got shot was just in the wrong place at the wrong time.* ♦ *He was, simply, the wrong man in the wrong place and was very unhappy.* ♦ Opposite **in the right place at the right time**

places

know *your* place
to accept the behavior that is expected of you ◆ *Most women knew their place then, which was to take care of the kids and cook the meals.*

out of place
not comfortable or suitable for a particular situation ◆ *He is worried about his job and feels out of place in a large organization.* ◆ *The tree-lined streets of this city wouldn't be out of place in a small town.*

put *you* in *your* place
to let someone know that they are not as important as they think they are ◆ *He thinks he knows everything and needs to be put in his place.*

put *yourself* in *sb's* place
to imagine that you are someone else and have to do what they do ◆ *Now put yourself in the place of a policeman who is afraid and has to arrest a big guy with a knife.*

run in place, *also* **jog in place**
to move your legs as if you were running but without moving forward ◆ *To keep up your exercise program in winter, you can always run in place on a treadmill – or on the kitchen floor.*

take place
to happen ◆ *The meeting took place in the lawyers' office on October 20th.* ◆ *Not all engineering failures take place suddenly and dramatically.* USAGE: often **take place** suggests that something has happened at a particular time in a particular place

between a rock and a hard place
See at ROCK

***sb's* heart is in the right place**
See at HEART

place a premium on *sth* See at PREMIUM

places

change places, *also* **trade places**
to exchange positions with someone ◆ *He may be rich and famous, but I wouldn't change places with him, not even for a million dollars.* ◆ *The twins looked so alike, they would sometimes trade places and confuse their teachers.*

go places
to become very successful ◆ *The first time we heard her play the violin, we knew she would go places.*

of all places
somewhere you would not immediately think of ◆ *I always have lived in New York City and ended up going to school in Cornell, Iowa, of all places.* ◆ Related vocabulary **of all people** at PEOPLE, **of all things** at THINGS

friends in high places See at FRIENDS

plague

avoid *sb/sth* like the plague
to keep far away from someone or something ◆ *When he was in high school, he avoided girls like the plague.* USAGE: usually said about someone or something you fear or do not like

> ORIGIN: based on the literal meaning of **the plague** (= a disease that spreads quickly and kills great numbers of people)

plank

walk the plank
to have to leave your job ◆ *After he was caught stealing from the company, the treasurer was forced to walk the plank.*

> ORIGIN: based on the literal meaning of **walk the plank** (= to punish someone who worked on a ship by forcing them to walk off the end of a narrow board into the sea)

plate

a full plate
a lot of work to do or problems to deal with ◆ *Facing funding cuts and a lawsuit challenging the school's admissions policy, the university's new president has a full plate.*

a full plate

"I can't take on any more work – I've got a full plate already!"

step up to the plate
to take responsibility for doing something ◆ *It is time companies stepped up to the plate and made sure the meat they sell is safe to eat.* ◆ Related vocabulary **step in** at STEP

> ORIGIN: based on the baseball meaning of **step up to the plate** (= move into position to hit the ball)

platter

on a silver platter
without work or effort ◆ *The Internet provides huge quantities of information on a silver platter, but you don't know if it's accurate or true.*

play

bring *sth* into play
to use something ◆ *If they continue to ignore the treaty, then the military will surely be brought into play.*

come into play
to be involved ◆ *Oh, I'm sure personalities always come into play in situations like this.*

make a play for *sb*
to try to start a romantic relationship with someone ◆ *In the movie, she makes a play for her best friend's husband.*

play along (with *sb/sth*)
to seem to support or be friendly to someone or something ◆ *He knew that if he didn't play along with the reporters, they would write unpleasant stories about him.* ◆ *I don't really like their idea that much but for now, it is probably a good idea simply to play along.* ◆ Related vocabulary **go along (with *sb/sth*)** at GO, **play ball (with *sb*)** at BALL

play around
1 to have a sexual relationship with someone not your husband, wife, or partner ◆ *He played around with a number of women.*
2 to behave in a silly way ◆ *We have to quit playing around and get down to work.*

play around with *sth*
to experiment with something ◆ *We were playing around with various sauces to go with the fish.*

play at *sth*
to pretend to do something ◆ *The two men thought they might trick their guards by playing at sleep.*

play back *sth*, also play *sth* back
to show a film or listen to a something recorded earlier ◆ *I'm filming the race, so if we don't see it, we can always play back the videotape.* ◆ *Then you can edit the song on your computer and play it back.*

play ball slang
to agree to do what you have been told or encouraged to do ◆ *He was warned to keep his mouth shut and play ball, and that's pretty much what he did.* USAGE: often used to suggest that you do not approve of what you are told to do

play down *sth*, also play *sth* down
to try to make something seem less serious than it really is ◆ *He played down the seriousness of his condition because he didn't want anyone to worry.* ◆ *It's a sensitive issue, and they want to play it down until after the elections.*

play fast and loose with *sth*
to treat something without enough care or attention ◆ *The film is very entertaining even though it plays fast and loose with the historical facts.*

play hard to get
to pretend that you are less interested than you really are ◆ *Bill decided he would accept the job if it was offered rather than playing hard to get in the hope of being offered more money.* USAGE: often said about romantic relationships: *She said he was avoiding her, but maybe he was just playing hard to get.*

play it cool
to appear to be less interested in or excited than you really are ◆ *Hank played it cool and stood to the side while the president chatted with the other guests after the ceremony.*

play it safe
to avoid any risk ◆ *I like to play it safe with my investments.* ◆ *Once you have the ball, you can decide whether you want to be aggressive or play it safe.*

play on *sth*, also play upon *sth*
to use something for your own advantage ◆ *The news reports just seemed to play on people's emotions.*

play out *sth*, also play *itself* out
to go through a process ◆ *We're waiting to see how the debate about more education reform will play itself out in the weeks ahead.*

play up *sth*, also play *sth* up
to make something more easily noticed ◆ *The report plays up the benefits of the plan but doesn't say much about the costs.* ◆ *Instead of being defeated by her cancer treatment, she played it up, even showing off her bald head at work.* USAGE: often something is **played up** in order to gain an advantage

play up to *sb/sth*
to treat someone or something very well so they will like you ◆ *Politicians are always playing up to the media.* USAGE: often said about efforts to benefit from someone's position or importance

play with *sth*
to use something in a way that is not serious or careful ◆ *She's playing with a dangerous drug.* ◆ *The budget is just playing with numbers and doesn't make sense.*

playing field

level the playing field
to give everyone the same advantages or opportunities ◆ *It was an effort to level the playing field and achieve greater equality between the sexes.* ◆ *Government funding can level the playing field for political candidates without money.* ◆ Related vocabulary **have a fighting chance** at CHANCE

ORIGIN: based on a comparison with a sports competition played on a field that is not level, putting one side at a disadvantage

plot

the plot thickens
something has become more complicated or interesting ◆ *The plot thickens as police investigate dozens of deaths at a California hospital.*

plug

plug away (at *sth*)
to keep working in a determined way ◆ *He's experienced plenty of hard times, but Ed is still plugging away, playing several nights a week at a local jazz club.* ◆ *The powerful computer was plugging away at the problem for weeks.*

pull the plug (on *sth*)
to stop something from continuing ◆ *The judge is threatening to pull the plug on TV coverage of the trial.*

plump

plump for *sb/sth*
to support someone or something enthusiastically ◆ *Marcy had been writing campaign speeches and plumping for McCarthy since December.*

plunge

take the plunge
to decide to do something ◆ *Those women who took the plunge and ran for the state legislature enjoyed great success.* USAGE: usually said about doing something that involves some risk

ply

ply *sb* with *sth*
to give someone a lot of something ◆ *We were plied with coffee, doughnuts, and refreshments.* ◆ *He plied me with liquor, hoping to get me drunk.* USAGE: often used in the form **ply someone with questions** (= to ask someone a lot of questions): *Anxious to hear the latest news, they plied us with questions.*

ply *your* trade See at TRADE

pocket

in *sb's* pocket, also **in the pocket of *sb/sth***
under someone's control and influence ◆ *Industry leaders made the mistake of assuming they had the chairman in their pocket.*

pick *sb's* pocket
1 to steal from your pockets or bag without you noticing ◆ *Someone in the subway picked my pocket and got my wallet.*
2 to cheat someone ◆ *Her lawyer told her that he would look out for her interests and then proceeded to pick her pocket.*

pockets

line *your* (own) pockets
to make a lot of money for yourself ◆ *Allowing patients to sue will increase the cost of health insurance and line lawyers' pockets.* ◆ *He was using his position as an immigration official to line his pockets.* USAGE: usually said about a person who either makes money illegally or takes more than is fair or right ◆ Related vocabulary **feather *your* (own) nest** at NEST

point

at the point of *sth* slightly formal, also **on the point of *sth***
just before something is going to happen ◆ *I was so depressed I thought I was at the point of committing suicide.* ◆ *They were clearly at the point of saying, "Look, enough's enough."*

beside the point
not important ◆ *I can't think of anything that he and I agree on, but that's beside the point.* ◆ Opposite **to the point**

make a point of *doing sth*
to be certain to do something that you think is important ◆ *She makes a point of sending thank-you notes.*

miss the point
to fail to understand what is important about something ◆ *In case anyone missed the point of its weapons tests, the military practiced an island invasion the next month.*

not to put too fine a point on it
to mean exactly what is said ◆ *Her performance, not to put too fine a point on it, was terrible.*

point out *sth*, also point *sth* out
to show or talk about something so others will notice it ◆ *Angela pointed out some spelling errors in my paper.* ◆ *Researchers point out that fish contain a type of fat that is good for you.* ◆ *We didn't notice the spout of a whale until another passenger on the ship pointed it out.*

point up *sth*, also point *sth* up
to show something or make something clearer ◆ *The report points up the need for better public transportation.* ◆ *There are a lot of problems in society, and the trial is going to point that up.*

to the point
involving the most important idea ◆ *Her answer was short and to the point.* ◆ Opposite **beside the point**

a case in point See at CASE

in point of fact See at FACT

point the finger at *sb* See at FINGER

point the way See at WAY

points

score points
to do something that will make people like you ◆ *I don't think you'll score any points with your clients if you don't return their calls.* ◆ *Some reporters are so unpopular that politicians can score points by attacking them.*

pole

not touch *sth* with a ten-foot pole
to not want to become involved with something ◆ *If I were you, I wouldn't touch that job with a ten-foot pole.* USAGE: often used as a warning

polish

polish off *sth*, also polish *sth* off
to finish something quickly and easily ◆ *He polished off two burgers and a mountain of French fries.* ◆ *He was nearly finished with the report, and said he could polish it off in another hour or two.* USAGE: most often used about eating something: *He polished off entire pizzas.*

politics

play politics (with *sth*)
to make something into a political issue ◆ *She accused her opponent of playing politics with affirmative action in an attempt to divide the American people.* ◆ *Either we can play politics or we can take these studies seriously and make the changes we need to make.*

pony

pony up (*sth*)
to pay money ◆ *The price of gas increased and homeowners had to pony up more than anyone expected this winter.* ◆ Related vocabulary **come up with *sth*** at COME

pop

pop in
to visit suddenly and for a short time ◆ *I just popped in to wish her good luck.*

pop off
to complain angrily about something ◆ *Neal popped off in a nationally televised interview.* ◆ *Those owners are always popping off about the difficulty of competing against wealthy teams.*

pop up
to appear suddenly ◆ *After World War II, pizzerias popped up in every city in the nation.*

pore

pore over *sth*
to look at and carefully study a document ◆ *She spends a lot of time poring over the historical records of the church.*

possibility
leave open the possibility of sth/doing sth
to not prevent something from happening ◆ *The spokesman left open the possibility of another meeting before the Israeli leader left Washington.* USAGE: also used with **that**: *His retirement leaves open the possibility that a new judge will be appointed this year.* ◆ Related vocabulary **leave sth open** at LEAVE

possible
as far as possible, *also* **so far as possible**
if you can ◆ *You should avoid that topic as far as possible.* ◆ Related vocabulary **as far as** at FAR, **as far as sth goes** at GOES

as soon as possible
in the least amount of time there can be ◆ *We need an ambulance as soon as possible! Someone has been hurt!* ◆ Related vocabulary **as soon as** at SOON

possum
play possum
to pretend to be dead or sleeping ◆ *His younger sister jumped on him because she knew he was just playing possum.* USAGE: usually done so that someone will not annoy or attack you

> ORIGIN: from the habit of a **possum** (= or opossum, a small wild animal) of not moving when in danger

postal
go postal See at GO

pot
go to pot
to become worse or be spoiled because of a lack of care or effort ◆ *My diet has gone to pot since the holidays.* ◆ Related vocabulary **go to hell in a handbasket** at HELL, **go to the dogs** at DOGS

into the pot
among various things being considered or discussed ◆ *Does anyone have ideas or suggestions they want to throw into the pot?*

the pot calling the kettle black
a situation in which one person criticizes another for a fault they have themselves ◆ *Ernie accused me of being selfish. Talk about the pot calling the kettle black!*

pound
pound out sth, *also* **pound sth out**
to produce something quickly and with a lot of energy ◆ *I'm able to pound out at least three articles every week.* ◆ *He pounded out a couple of tunes on the old piano.* USAGE: often used to suggest that something was not produced carefully or correctly

powder
keep *your* powder dry
to be ready to do something if necessary ◆ *We're not ready to start buying yet. We'll keep our powder dry until we think prices are as low as they'll go.*

> ORIGIN: from the idea that **gunpowder** (= an explosive substance in the form of a powder) will not explode if it is wet

power
more power to sb/sth esp. spoken
someone or something has my support and encouragement ◆ *If they can make this city work, more power to them.* ◆ *I didn't know what I wanted to do after high school, so more power to you for knowing what you want.*

the power behind the throne
someone without an official job who secretly controls an organization or government ◆ *The chairman's daughter was the power behind the throne for several years before he died.*

powers
the powers that be
the people who have authority or

practice

control over others ♦ *I wanted to be a driver in the army, but the powers that be decided I should be a typist.* ♦ *Anytime athletes take a political stance, they're guaranteed to get a reaction from the powers that be.*

practice

in practice
1 actually ♦ *In theory, the license fee is only $5 but, because other costs get added on, in practice it is more like $20.* ♦ Opposite **in theory** at THEORY
2 prepared ♦ *It must have been six years since I took a girl out, and I wasn't in practice for the dating game.* ♦ Opposite **out of practice**

make a practice of *doing sth*
to do something regularly or as a habit ♦ *I don't make a practice of recommending restaurants, but this one is really special.*

out of practice
not prepared ♦ *When I take time off from work, I get out of practice and have trouble getting up in the morning.* ♦ Opposite **in practice** 2

practice what *you* **preach**
to behave the way you tell other people to behave ♦ *Other countries need to see that we practice what we preach when it comes to human rights.* ♦ *I practice what I preach in that I exercise almost every day.*

praise

damn (*sb/sth***) with faint praise**
to show only slight approval for someone or something ♦ *By qualifying his support, you could argue he was damning these leaders with faint praise.* ♦ *Maybe I'm damning them with faint praise, but the Yankees are easier to like than the Atlanta Braves in this series.*

praises

sing *sb's/sth's* **praises**, *also* **sing the praises of** *sb/sth*
to praise someone or something with enthusiasm ♦ *I hate the city, but my sister is always singing its praises.*

sing someone's praises

The committee was singing her praises as a writer, teacher, and creative thinker.

prayer
not have a prayer
to have no chance ♦ *With an injured ankle, he doesn't have a prayer of winning the race.* USAGE: sometimes used without **not**: *Do we have a prayer of convincing him to go?*

premium
at a premium
1 not easy to get ♦ *During the negotiations, sleep was at a premium.* USAGE: usually said about something that is highly valued because it is hard to get
2 for a higher price ♦ *It's possible to get a large apartment, but only at a premium.*

put a premium on *sth*, *also* **place a premium on *sth***
to consider something important or valuable ♦ *Busy shoppers put a premium on finding everything they need in one big store.*

presence
make *your* presence felt
to have a strong effect on other people or on a situation ♦ *Hockney made his presence felt in the New York art world shortly after he arrived there.* ♦ *The rebels have already made their bloody presence felt during the election campaign.*

present
at present
now ♦ *There are at present about 2500 employees in our company.*

for the present
now, although probably not for long ♦ *For the present, these puzzling crimes remain unsolved.* Related vocabulary **for the moment** at MOMENT, **for the time being** at TIME

press
hot off the press
just printed ♦ *Steele's latest novel about family and friendship is hot off the press.*

press on, *also* **press ahead**
to continue to go forward; = **push on** ♦ *We pressed on toward the town even though we were both so tired we could barely walk.*

press on (with *sth*), *also* **press ahead (with *sth*)**
to continue to do something in a determined way ♦ *He said his comments were meant as a joke, but the Miss America Organization pressed on with its lawsuit.* ♦ *The construction firm pressed ahead with plans to build the skyscraper.*

press *sb* into service See at SERVICE
press *your* luck See at LUCK
press the flesh See at FLESH

pressure
put pressure on *sb*/*sth*
to influence someone or something strongly, usually intentionally ♦ *He's putting pressure on me to change my mind.* ♦ *New companies are putting pressure on established firms to lower their prices.*

pretty
pretty much, *also* **pretty well**
almost completely; = **for all intents and purposes** ♦ *I've pretty much finished packing.* ♦ *All our kids are pretty well grown up now and one is already in college.* USAGE: also used in the form **pretty nearly**: *He's pretty nearly always right about cars.*

not a pretty sight See at SIGHT
sitting pretty See at SITTING

prevail
prevail on *sb* (to do *sth*), *also* **prevail upon *sb* (to do *sth*)**
to persuade someone to do something ♦ *My father prevailed on some friends to let us stay with them for a few days.* ♦ *The TV network prevailed upon the organizers of the track and field championships to schedule the 100-meter final for Sunday afternoon.*

prey

fall prey to *sb/sth*
to be harmed by someone or something ♦ *We worry that our children will fall prey to the influence of bad kids.* ♦ *Patients may fall prey to dishonest salespeople who say they can cure their pain.* USAGE: sometimes used with verbs other than **fall**: *These people are prey to superstition, disease, and hunger.*

prey on *sth*, *also* **prey upon** *sth*
to kill an animal in order to eat it ♦ *Spiders prey on small flies and other insects.* ♦ *Seals often prey upon the same fish people are trying to catch.* USAGE: said about animals that kill other animals for food

prey on *sb*, *also* **prey upon** *sb*
1 to commit a crime against someone ♦ *Police are looking for street criminals who prey on tourists.* ♦ *Gangs that prey upon small business owners in the city's Chinatown may be spreading to the suburbs.*
2 to have an effect on someone ♦ *Guilt preyed on him for years after the accident.* USAGE: sometimes said about something that has an effect on people's emotions: *The ads prey on our fear of being alone.*

price

at any price
no matter how difficult; = **at any cost** ♦ *They wanted to find out the truth at any price.* ♦ Related vocabulary **at all costs** at COSTS

come at a price
to include disadvantages in order to get what you want ♦ *The company's success was made possible by the country's rulers, but their support comes at a price.* USAGE: sometimes used without **come**: *Following the recommendation would have increased teamwork, but at a price.*

for a price, *also* **at a price**
for a lot of money ♦ *She'll do any kind of redecorating you need, for a price.* ♦ *They will do custom software programming, but at a price.*

pay the price, *also* **pay a price**
to accept the unpleasant results of something; = **pay the piper** ♦ *He achieved great fame in his later years, but he certainly paid the price.* ♦ *Professional athletes often pay a price for the beating their bodies have taken.*

put a price (tag) on *sth*
to say how much something costs ♦ *They finally put a price tag on the proposed renovations.* ♦ *You can't put a price on loyalty.*

pride

pride and joy
a person or thing that gives great pleasure and satisfaction ♦ *Her garden is her pride and joy.*

pride *yourself* **on** *sth*
to value a special ability that you have ♦ *He prides himself on his teaching.*

swallow *your* **pride**
to admit that you have been wrong about someone or something ♦ *He swallowed his pride and called his daughter to apologize.* ♦ *I swallowed my pride and asked for a second chance.* USAGE: often said about something that has embarrassed you

take pride (in *sb/sth***)**
to feel pleased about someone or what they have done ♦ *They take pride in their son's many accomplishments.* ♦ *He takes pride in the fact that he's never asked his parents for any money.*

prime

in *your/its* **prime**
in someone's or something's best, most successful, or most productive stage ♦ *She retired in her prime, but continued working part-time as a consultant.* ♦ *Though the magazine was in its prime, it stopped publication when the chief editor quit.* USAGE: often used in the form **in the prime of (your) life**: *The members*

of our squadron were in the prime of life.

past *your/its* prime
no longer able to do something at an acceptable level because of age; = **over the hill** ♦ *The dancer was past her prime, though she performed occasionally as a guest artist.*

principle
in principle
as a general idea, theory, or belief ♦ *Members of both parties agreed in principle that some federal dollars should be used to improve election systems.* USAGE: said about something done without considering details or special situations ♦ Related vocabulary **in theory** at THEORY

on principle, *also* **as a matter of principle**
according to a moral rule or personal belief ♦ *He opposed the death penalty on principle.*

print
in print
in a published form ♦ *This is the first time that I've seen his speeches in print.* ♦ *The biography generated a lot of interest and now all her novels are back in print.* ♦ Opposite **out of print**

out of print
no longer available in published form ♦ *I'm afraid you can't order that book – it's out of print.* ♦ Opposite **in print**

read the small print See **read the fine print** at FINE PRINT

prisoners
take no prisoners
to be extremely determined to get what you want ♦ *In the big games against the best players, he takes no prisoners.* USAGE: said about someone who is not worried about anyone's opinions of their actions

probability
in all probability slightly formal
I think this is true or will happen; = **in all likelihood** ♦ *This is a minimum estimate, but in all probability an accurate one.*

problem
no problem esp. spoken
1 I can easily do what you have asked ♦ *You can just call and say "I need a babysitter tonight" and we'll send one out, no problem.*
2 I am not upset by this ♦ *"I'm sorry, but we need to go home now." "No problem."*
3 I was happy to do it; = **you're welcome** ♦ *"I put some lettuce and tomato on the sandwich." "Oh, thank you." "No problem."* USAGE: usually said in answer to **thank you**

work the problem
to actively try different solutions ♦ *The mayor has named a committee to work the problem of downtown parking.*

process
in the process of *doing sth*
having begun but not yet finished doing something ♦ *Many countries in the region are in the process of becoming more democratic.* ♦ Related vocabulary **in progress** at PROGRESS

production
make a production (out) of *sth*
to make something seem more complicated or difficult than it is ♦ *It's only a couple of hours' work. Do you have to make such a production of it?* ♦ Related vocabulary **blow *sth* out of (all) proportion** at PROPORTION, **make a mountain out of a molehill** at MOUNTAIN

profile
keep a low profile, *also* **maintain a low profile**
to behave in a way that does not attract attention ♦ *The local people are not always pleasant to strangers, who are warned to keep a low profile while visiting.*

profit

turn a profit
to earn more money than you spend ◆ *He's been in business five years but has yet to turn a profit.*

program

get with the program
to make more effort to do what is needed now ◆ *There is increasing pressure on the Senate to get with the program and pass the tax-cut bill.* ◆ *We're all ready to go – come on, Dad, get with the program.*

progress

in progress
happening or being done now, but not finished ◆ *The show was already in progress when I turned it on.* ◆ Related vocabulary **in the process of** *doing sth* at PROCESS

promise

hold promise
to be likely to succeed ◆ *The new drug holds promise for helping to control addiction.*

promises

promises, promises esp. spoken
you will probably not do what you say you will do ◆ *"When I get my check I'll buy you a new coat." "Promises, promises!"*

proof

the proof of the pudding (is in the eating)
the way to judge something is by its results ◆ *Economic growth is the proof of the pudding for the president's tax and budget plans.*

proportion

blow *sth* out of (all) proportion
to make something seem more important than it actually is ◆ *I thought the picture of him wearing a dress was pretty funny, but the local newspapers blew it out of all proportion.* USAGE: often used with other adverbs to make a stronger statement: *This case has been blown totally out of proportion.* ◆ *She blew the figures way out of proportion.* ◆ Related vocabulary **make a mountain out of a molehill** at MOUNTAIN, **make a production (out) of** *sth* at PRODUCTION

props

give props to *sb* slang
to express your respect for someone ◆ *We would like to give props to all of the people who have contributed to the making of this website.*

> ORIGIN: **props** is a short form of **proper respect** (= the respect someone deserves)

pros

pros and cons
advantages and disadvantages ◆ *We've been discussing the pros and cons of buying a house.*

protest

protest too much
to say something so often that people doubt you are sincere ◆ *He constantly denies that the book is based on his boss, but does he protest too much?*

> ORIGIN: based on "Methinks the lady doth protest too much," a line from the play "Hamlet" by William Shakespeare

proud

do *sb* proud
1 to feel very pleased about someone because they have done something well ◆ *Once again, the armed forces have done us proud.*
2 to treat a visitor or guest very well ◆ *Rosemary did us proud with such a lovely lunch.*

prove

prove out *sth*, also **prove *sth* out**
to show that something is true ◆ *Of the many accusations against her, only two ever proved out.* ◆ *I think there was better safety when there were more controls on the industry,*

but I don't know if the accident rates will prove that out or not.

have something to prove See at HAVE

prove *your* **mettle** See at METTLE

provide

provide for *sb*
to give someone the things they need to live ◆ *Former prisoners must learn to provide for themselves once they get out of jail.* ◆ *She's struggling to provide for her family and pay her bills.*

provide for *sth*
1 to take care of a need ◆ *After you cross the border you will have to provide for your own security.* ◆ *The shape of the tank is designed to provide for water circulation.*
2 to allow something ◆ *The permit will provide for a 30-day hunt beginning in late November.*

prowl

on the prowl
1 actively looking for a romantic or sexual partner ◆ *Divorce isn't the only subject to avoid when you're on the prowl.*
2 actively trying to achieve something ◆ *Officials see the country as a competitor that's on the prowl to grab every export market within reach.*

> ORIGIN: based on the literal meaning of **prowl** (= to move quietly while hunting)

p's

mind *your* **p's and q's**, *also* **watch** *your* **p's and q's**
to pay close attention to small details ◆ *There had been two recent security problems in the company and everyone should mind their p's and q's.*

psych

psych out *sb*, *also* **psych** *sb* **out**
to make someone believe that they will fail ◆ *Our strategy is to psych out the other team before the game begins.* ◆ *She failed the test after psyching herself out, thinking how important it was for her future.*

psych *sb* **up**, *also* **psych up** *sb*
to make someone enthusiastic about something they will do ◆ *The children were so psyched up about the trip that they could hardly sleep.* ◆ *Tim was psyching himself up to run the 26.2-mile course.* USAGE: sometimes used without **up**: *Willa is really psyched, and hopefully that will get the others excited.*

public

go public
to become a company in which anyone can invest ◆ *It's the latest Internet company to go public and then immediately go bankrupt.*

go public (with *sth***)**
to make something known that was secret before ◆ *If she goes public with her story, the school's reputation will suffer.*

in the public eye See at EYE

pull

pull a fast one (on *sb***)**
to deceive or trick someone ◆ *Most people would never suspect that you'd even think of pulling a fast one on them.*

pull apart *sth*, *also* **pull** *sth* **apart**
to examine all the parts of something in order to understand it ◆ *We spent the afternoon pulling apart the figures supplied by the research team.*

pull back (from *sth***)**
to change to a less extreme way of thinking ◆ *The hijackers then pulled back from threats to blow up the ship and its 200 passengers.*

pull down *sth*, *also* **pull** *sth* **down**
1 to destroy a building ◆ *Many of those homes were pulled down to make way for new construction.* ◆ *They pulled my house down to build a QuickMart.*
2 to earn a large amount of money ◆ *She pulls down over $100,000 a*

pulp

year. ♦ *I don't know what he makes, but I know he's pulling it down.*
3 to get something ♦ *The play pulled down nominations for best play and best direction.* ♦ *The program lets you log onto the Web from any computer and pull your e-mail down.*

pull for *sb/sth*
to support someone or something ♦ *The crowd was clearly pulling for the home team.*

pull in
to arrive at a place ♦ *We got to the station just as his train was pulling in.* USAGE: used of vehicles or the people in them

pull in *sb/sth*, *also* **pull** *sb/sth* **in**
to attract things or people, esp. in large numbers ♦ *The new law is designed to pull in more imports from poor countries.* ♦ *The show has been pulling the crowds in since it opened.*

pull in *sth*, *also* **pull** *sth* **in**
to earn an amount of money ♦ *The film was a big hit this weekend, pulling in $11 million at the box office.* ♦ *The show pulled millions in, and still lost money.*

pull off *sth*, *also* **pull** *sth* **off**
to succeed in doing something difficult or unexpected ♦ *He won five straight games and pulled off one of the tournament's biggest upsets.* ♦ *I don't know how you pulled it off, but we're now $5,000 richer than we were yesterday.*

pull out
to leave a place ♦ *If everyone is ready, we can pull out by six in the morning.* USAGE: used of vehicles or the people in them

pull out (of *sth***)**
to stop being involved in something ♦ *She's considering a run for governor if Mr. Lamb pulls out of the race.*

pull over
to move a vehicle to the side of a road and stop ♦ *Roger pulled over so we could study the map.* ♦ *The bus pulled over to let the children off.*

pull *sb* **over**, *also* **pull over** *sb*
cause someone to stop their vehicle at the side of a road ♦ *Two highway patrol officers pulled him over after watching him weaving between lanes.* ♦ *They pulled over several drivers who went through the red light.*

pull through (*sth***)**
to experience difficulties and continue to live or succeed ♦ *I didn't think he'd survive, but he somehow pulled through.* ♦ *Those flowers can pull through a mild winter.* ♦ *We hope our experience will encourage them to pull through hard times.*

pull *sb/sth* **through (***sth***)**
to help someone or something through a difficult experience ♦ *She said her religious faith pulled her through this illness.*

pull together
to work as a group, esp. in order to achieve a result ♦ *Everyone on our street really pulled together after the fire.*

pull *yourself* **together**
to get control of your emotions and actions ♦ *He's finding it hard to pull himself together after the accident.*

pull up *sth*, *also* **pull** *sth* **up**
to get information from a computer ♦ *Police can now pull up your driving record on the computer in their car.* ♦ *He asked me for those files yesterday and I still haven't pulled them up.*

pulp

beat *sb* **to a pulp**
to seriously injure someone by hitting them hard ♦ *He was beaten to a pulp in a back street and left to die.*

pulse

quicken the pulse, *also* **quicken** *sb***'s pulse**
to cause excitement or interest ♦ *There's nothing in this book to quicken the pulse.*

your **finger on the pulse (of** *sth***)**
See at FINGER

pump

pump *sb* **up**, *also* **pump up** *sb*
to make someone very interested or enthusiastic ◆ *Our coach talks with every team member before a game, offering advice and trying to pump them up.* ◆ *Taylor's band came out and pumped up the crowd.*

pump up *sth*, *also* **pump** *sth* **up**
to make something appear to be bigger or more successful than it is ◆ *Opponents charged that the state treasurer pumped up the state's financial figures.* ◆ *We pumped the number of flights up to 500 in our report so everyone would think the airport was really busy.*

pump *sb/sth* **up**, *also* **pump up** *sb/sth*
to improve someone's or something's performance ◆ *Athletes can take drugs to pump themselves up, but there are huge risks involved.* ◆ *Everett hopes the new products will pump up corporate sales.*

pump iron See at IRON

punch

beat *sb* **to the punch**
to do something before someone else can do it ◆ *I wanted to give my mother a camera, but my brother beat me to the punch.*

> ORIGIN: from boxing, in which good fighters are quick to react by **punching** (= hitting) the other fighter before they are hit

pack a punch
to have a powerful effect or influence ◆ *For big flavor, a blend of cumin, chili powder, coriander, cayenne, and black pepper packs a punch.*

> ORIGIN: based on the literal meaning of **pack a punch** (= hit very hard)

punch in
to use a special machine to record the time you start working ◆ *If we punch in at 9 a.m., our actual start-*

ing time, the company automatically docks us 15 minutes.

punch in *sth*, *also* **punch** *sth* **in**
to enter information on a computer or other device by pressing keys ◆ *You punch in your code to get cash or your bank balance.* ◆ *Each door has a number pad, and for security you have to punch a number in to open the door.*

punch out
to use a special machine to record the time you stop working ◆ *Workers are kicking mud off their shoes and punching out at the construction trailer, weary after another 12-hour day.*

punch out *sth*, *also* **punch** *sth* **out**
1 to press buttons or keys on a computer or other device ◆ *In a panic, she grabbed her mobile phone and punched out 911.* ◆ *You'd hand a page to the operator and write the next one while he was punching the first page out.*
2 to press something hard to remove it from something larger of which it is a part ◆ *The ceiling panel was punched out so workers could reach the wires above it.* ◆ *First you have to cut along the lines of each piece with a razor blade, and then you can punch it out.*

punch out *sb/sth*, *also* **punch** *sb/sth* **out**
to hit someone or something ◆ *Barry lost his job for punching out his boss.* ◆ *He loved to hang out at local taverns and punch people out.*

punch a clock See at CLOCK

punches

pull no punches
to deal with something honestly without hiding anything ◆ *One congressional leader pulled no punches, saying "we have a recession."* ◆ *The 20-minute training video pulls no punches, showing chilling pictures of accident victims.* USAGE: often used in the form **not pull any punches**: *The television network*

isn't pulling any punches with the subject matter on its new show. ◆ Opposite **pull** *your/its* **punches**

pull *your/its* **punches**
to deal with something in a way that is not completely honest ◆ *I want you to tell me what you think, and don't pull your punches.* ◆ *The film pulls its punches by making a disaster seem romantic.* ◆ Opposite **pull no punches**

> ORIGIN: based on boxing, from the literal meaning of **pull your punches** (= to not hit the other fighter as hard as you can)

roll with the punches
to adjust to difficult events as they happen; = **roll with it** ◆ *She had to perform shortly after her brother died, but she rolled with the punches and put on a great show.*

> ORIGIN: based on boxing, from the literal meaning **roll with the punches** (= step back or to one side as you are being hit), so that you do not receive the full force of the attack

pure

pure and simple
plainly, and without having to say anything else ◆ *They closed the museum because, pure and simple, it cost too much to run.* ◆ *No one talked about issues or referred to facts – it was just gossip, pure and simple.*
USAGE: sometimes used in the form **purely and simply**: *It was purely and simply the most marvelous vacation.*

purpose

on purpose
intentionally ◆ *The idiot who set the fire on purpose is in jail, but that doesn't help the families who lost their homes.*

purposes

at cross purposes
in ways that are opposed to each other ◆ *The relief effort was charac-* *terized by a tendency to work at cross purposes instead of everyone working together.*

for all intents and purposes See at INTENTS

pursuit

in hot pursuit (of *sb/sth***)**
eagerly trying to get someone or something ◆ *Reporters set off in hot pursuit of the facts of the story.* ◆ *With border guards in hot pursuit, the boat sped away.* ◆ *The Yankees are in hot pursuit of a good left-handed pitcher.* ◆ Related vocabulary **hot on** *your* **heels** at HEELS

push

push (*sb***) around**, also **push around** *sb*
to threaten to hurt someone who is smaller or weaker ◆ *I feel like I'm in third grade and the fourth-grade bully is pushing me around and trying to steal my baseball cards.* ◆ *I was a lot skinnier then and could get pushed around.*

push for *sth*
to make a strong effort to get something or make something happen ◆ *The president is meeting with members of Congress to push for an increase in the minimum wage.*

push off
to leave ◆ *The settlers who pushed off for the far west opened the land for farming.*

push on
to continue to go forward; = **press on** ◆ *Although we needed to stop and rest, we decided to press on in order to reach the river by evening.*

when push comes to shove, also **if push comes to shove**
when all the easy solutions to a problem have not worked, and something must be done ◆ *Only a few people will really come through for you when push comes to shove.*

push *sb's* **buttons** See at BUTTONS
push *your* **luck** See at LUCK

push (the edge of) the envelope See at ENVELOPE

push the panic button See at PANIC BUTTON

put

hard put to *do sth*
finding something difficult to do ♦ *None of the family I was staying with spoke English and I was hard put to recall my high school French.* ♦ *You'd be hard put to find any other college students more deserving of the award.*

not put it past *sb*
to not be surprised if someone does something unacceptable ♦ *Jenny wouldn't put it past Jess to turn Lester in to the FBI and claim the reward.* ♦ *She had a great imagination, and I wouldn't put it past her to make the whole matter up.*

put aside *sth*, *also* **put** *sth* **aside**
1 to decide not to deal with something ♦ *Let's put aside our differences and enjoy the evening.*
2 to save something for later use, esp. money ♦ *We're putting aside $50 a week for our vacation.* ♦ *He puts some time aside each evening to read to his children.* ♦ Related vocabulary **set aside** *sth* 1 at SET

put away *sb*, *also* **put** *sb* **away**
1 to defeat someone ♦ *The Devils still have two more chances to put away the Flyers this season.*
2 to remove a criminal or mentally ill person from society ♦ *You have to put away the people who are so crazy that they are a danger to the rest of us.*

put away *sth*, *also* **put** *sth* **away**
1 to save or store something for future use ♦ *I found the box where I had put away the children's toys.* ♦ *When you finish using the lawn mower, put it away in the garage.*
2 to decide to forget or ignore something unpleasant; = **put** *sth* **behind you** ♦ *Nervous residents tried to put away their fears.*
3 to win something ♦ *Ella watched in amazement as Melissa simply walked to the net to put away an easy volley.*
4 to eat or drink a lot of something ♦ *He put away a whole apple pie in one sitting.* ♦ *I like to put away a few beers with my friends after work.*

put *sth* **behind** *sb/sth*
to support someone or something ♦ *When America declared war, Ford put his factories behind the war effort, making huge numbers of planes, trucks, and boats in his factories.* ♦ *My father put his reputation – and his money – behind the reform politicians.*

put *sth* **behind you**
to decide to forget or ignore something unpleasant; = **put away** *sth* ♦ *Frank, who survived the blast, says he still hasn't put the tragedy behind him.*

put *sth* **down**, *also* **put down** *sth*
1 to make a payment that is only part of the full cost ♦ *When we bought our first house, you really didn't have to put down anything.* ♦ *We had to put $500 down and paid the rest in installments.*
2 to write something on paper for others to read ♦ *We need to put something down that says this is what we plan to do and when we plan to do it.* ♦ *Marcia didn't know what to put down when asked to give the dates of the Middle Kingdom in Egypt.*
3 to force violence to stop ♦ *People asked why government troops weren't called in to put down the rioters.*
4 to stop doing something or using something ♦ *Once you start reading this book, you won't be able to put it down.* ♦ *They were ordered to put down their arms and surrender.*
5 to kill an animal medically; = **put** *sth* **to sleep** ♦ *The old dog couldn't walk and was in pain, so we had to have him put down.*

put *sb/sth* **down**, *also* **put down** *sb/sth*
to make someone or something ap-

put

pear foolish or unimportant ◆ *One critic put the author down by saying she wrote like a teenager, but in fact, she is an experienced lawyer.* ◆ *They never put down the competition in their ads.*

put forth
to do what is necessary to achieve something ◆ *The effort put forth by every employee of the town and every rescue worker was remarkable.*

put forth *sth*, also put *sth* forth
to offer something for consideration ◆ *We can put forth some guidelines for what you should write about in your essay.* ◆ *We tried to put something forth that's really sincere.*

put forward *sth*, also put *sth* forward
to offer for consideration ◆ *None of the ideas I put forward at the meeting have been accepted.* ◆ *He's still working on the report and plans to put it forward as soon as he finishes it.*

put in *sth*, also put *sth* in
to give something ◆ *Mary put in a lot of effort on this job.* ◆ *Why did you put so much of your own money in?*

put *sb* off, also put off *sb*
1 to cause someone to dislike someone or something ◆ *His appearance put people off.* ◆ *Her approach to the issues put off voters.*
2 to try to discourage someone by making them wait ◆ *He keeps asking me out, and I keep putting him off.* ◆ *I put off Eleanor, hoping she would find someone else to work with her on this.*

put off *sth*, also put *sth* off
to delay something ◆ *Something must be wrong because she's put off her wedding twice.* ◆ *Her vacation was scheduled to begin next week, and she was afraid she would have to put it off.*

put on *sth*, also put *sth* on
1 to pretend to feel something ◆ *I can't tell whether he's really upset or if he's just putting it on.* ◆ *He put on a good show of being angry, but he was really only joking.*
2 to add or increase something ◆ *I put on weight when I gave up smoking.*
3 to make a piece of equipment work ◆ *I put the heat on, but the car is still cold.* ◆ *Can you put on that great CD you played yesterday?*
4 to hold or produce an event ◆ *The second graders want to put on a play.*

put *sth* on *sth*
to add something to something else ◆ *Don't put dinner on your credit card – just pay cash.* ◆ *The school puts a lot of emphasis on music and art.*

put one over on *sb*, also put something over on *sb*
to deceive someone into believing something that is not true ◆ *He sometimes tries to put one over on us to stay home from school, but we're wise to his tricks.*

put *sb* out
to annoy, upset, or inconvenience someone ◆ *Would you be put out if we canceled our plans for dinner tomorrow?* ◆ *It always put him out when he was asked to wait while someone answered another call.*

put out *sth*, also put *sth* out
1 to make something, esp. information, publicly available ◆ *The organization has put out an excellent report on the treatment of political prisoners around the world.* ◆ *We have to put the word out that we need several more sales representatives.* ◆ *He's already put out 28 albums, and more are on the way.*
2 to stop something from burning or being used ◆ *Put out that cigarette!* ◆ *I have to put out the lights before I go to bed.* ◆ *When you leave the campgrounds, be sure to put all fires out.*
3 to spend money ◆ *You have to put out a lot of money when you buy a house.*

put *yourself* out for *sb/sth*
to make a special effort for someone or something ◆ *Grace had really put herself out to impress me with how good a cook she was.*

put *sth* right
to correct something to make it the way it should be; = **set *sth* right** ◆ *What did we do wrong? And how do we put it right?* USAGE: often used in the form **put things right**: *At the end, he got over his anger, and was determined to put things right.*

put *sb* through *sth*
1 to force someone to experience something unpleasant in order to help them ◆ *His teacher put him through six months of writing essays every day to improve his skills.*
2 to unintentionally cause someone to experience something painful ◆ *Elaine put her daughter through a kind of hell when she divorced the child's father.*

put *sb/yourself* through *sth*
to pay for someone or for yourself to go to school ◆ *I ended up putting my granddaughter through school.* ◆ *My father wasn't well and couldn't work, so all of us kids put ourselves through college.*

put *sb/sth* through, *also* **put through *sb/sth***
to arrange for a telephone call to be made to a place or person ◆ *The international operator put me through to London.* ◆ *Passengers could put through calls on their cell phones.*

put *sth* toward *sth*
to give money to pay for part of the cost of something ◆ *A local businessman has put $180,000 toward the creation of a model organic farm in upstate New York.* ◆ *Please put my deposit toward my hotel bill.* ◆ Related vocabulary **set aside *sth*** 1 at SET

put *sb* up, *also* **put up *sb***
to provide someone with a place to stay temporarily ◆ *Sally is kindly putting me up for the weekend.* ◆ *We can put up five people on the third floor.*

put up *sth*
to express your feelings about something ◆ *I'm not going to let them build a road here without putting up a fight.* ◆ *Jimmy always puts up a fuss at bedtime.*

put up *sth*, *also* **put *sth* up**
1 to pay or lend money ◆ *Seventy percent of the money was put up by the government.* ◆ *You have to put 10% of the mortgage up right away.*
2 to build a structure ◆ *We don't know what kind of memorial the city will put up.* ◆ *Did you see where they've put up a new hotel?* ◆ *They're planning to build a school, but I'm not sure where they plan to put it up.*

put up or shut up
either improve a bad situation or stop complaining about it ◆ *My father would not say, "Put up or shut up," but that's what he clearly meant.*

put *sb* up to *sth/doing sth*
to encourage someone to do something, esp. something wrong or not wise ◆ *My mom didn't believe I could think of doing anything on my own, so she wanted to know who put me up to staying out all night.* ◆ *Did you put your little sister up to pouring sugar all over the floor?*

put up with *sb/sth*
to be forced to experience someone or something that you do not like ◆ *I've had to put up with a long, cold winter all by myself.* ◆ *She said she was tired of his constant complaining and didn't want to put up with him anymore.*

to put it mildly
without making something seem as bad as it really is ◆ *The area is not very wealthy, to put it mildly – actually, it's pretty poor.*

putty

putty in *your* hands
willing to do anything you want ◆ *As soon as Jones realized he could*

get in trouble if they reported him, he became putty in their hands.

puzzle

puzzle out *sth*, *also* **puzzle** *sth* **out**
to study something in order to understand it ◆ *The reader shouldn't have to puzzle out what the writer means.* ◆ Related vocabulary **figure out** *sth* at FIGURE

puzzle over *sth*
to give a lot of attention and thought to something ◆ *I puzzled over those words, trying to understand their hidden message.* ◆ Related vocabulary **tease out** *sth* at TEASE

Q, q

quandary
in a quandary
not knowing what to do ♦ *Many parents are in a quandary about how much time their kids should spend on the Internet.*

quarters
in close quarters slightly formal, *also* **at close quarters**
in a small area together with others ♦ *Living in close quarters, college students frequently catch colds from each other.*

> ORIGIN: based on the literal meaning of **quarters** (= a place to live or stay)

question
beg the question
1 to cause a particular question to be asked ♦ *Cyber adventurers can even climb a mountain, which begs the question of how can someone at a keyboard take a hike?*
2 to fail to answer a particular question ♦ *Everyone agrees we have to cut spending, but this proposal begs the question, What do we cut?*

beyond question
not in doubt ♦ *His personal courage was beyond question.*

call into question *sth* slightly formal, *also* **call** *sth* **into question**
to cause doubt about something ♦ *The study calls into question how long the vaccine gives protection.*

in question
not very certain ♦ *Are you saying that the usefulness of this test is in question?* ♦ Opposite **without question**

out of the question
not possible ♦ *A trip to New Zealand is out of the question this year.*

pop the question
1 to ask someone to marry you ♦ *I remember he popped the question while we were eating ice cream.*
2 to ask about something that is very important ♦ *So then I pop the question, When do you expect this to happen?*

without question
certainly ♦ *The Lightning are the team that without question will be embarrassed in their opening game.* ♦ Opposite **in question**

questions
no questions asked
without providing additional information ♦ *If you have enough money, you can get a loan at the bank, no questions asked.* ♦ *There is a reward for the return of the violin, no questions asked.* USAGE: often used when you could not expect to get anything except by agreeing to this condition: *The police will pay $100 for every gun turned in, no questions asked.*

quote
quote unquote, *also* **quote**
named or described as ♦ *Even the quote unquote realistic movies don't show very realistic violence.* ♦ *In order to make some foods, quote, healthy, you end up cooking all the flavor out of them.* USAGE: often used to show doubt that something is true or exactly as it is described

R, r

rabbit

pull a rabbit out of *your* **hat**, *also* **pull a rabbit out of a hat**
to do something surprising ◆ *You didn't know how the story would end and then the author pulled a rabbit out of her hat, and it all made sense.* USAGE: sometimes used to describe a surprising solution to a problem: *The governor pulled a rabbit out of a hat by putting together a budget without increasing taxes.*

ORIGIN: based on the literal meaning of **pull a rabbit out of a hat**, which is often done as a magic trick

race

a race against time, *also* **a race against the clock**
an attempt to do something when there is little time to do it ◆ *It was a race against time as staff members tried to keep the struggling company open.* USAGE: sometimes used as a verb phrase: *The villagers raced against time to protect their town against the flood.*

races

off to the races
busy doing something ◆ *I don't think there will be a dramatic change in the economy – I don't see that we're off to the races.* ◆ *If you make changes in the rules, the tax lawyers will be off to the races again.*

rack

off the rack
1 from among the goods available in stores ◆ *We are requiring contestants to buy their outfits off the rack and banning custom-made costumes.*
2 at the usual price ◆ *Members can get discounts of up to 50 percent on the hotels' off-the-rack rates.*

rack up *sth*, *also* **rack** *sth* **up**
1 to obtain a large amount of something ◆ *We racked up a lot of miles on our last vacation.* ◆ *Laura is starting to rack the money up now.*
2 to score a large number of points ◆ *Even though Miller racked up 28 points, the team still lost.*

rack *your* **brains** See at BRAINS

radar

on *sb's* **radar (screen)**, *also* **on the radar (screen)**
among the things being considered by someone ◆ *The problem of trash disposal is on everyone's radar screen right now.* ◆ *This status puts the city on the radar screens of big corporations.* USAGE: often used with words like **not**, **off**, and **under** to mean that something is not considered: *The disease is sometimes not even on a doctor's radar screen.* ◆ *Some of these companies operate under everyone's radar.*

ORIGIN: from the literal meaning of **radar** (= a system that uses radio waves to follow the movement of aircraft or other objects)

rage

all the rage, *also* **the latest rage**
very fashionable or stylish ◆ *DVDs are all the rage, and several movie companies have started releasing titles in this format.* ◆ *Flared slacks and low heels are the latest rage in women's fashion.*

fly into a rage See **fly off the handle** at HANDLE

rails

go off the rails, *also* **run off the rails**
to be spoiled by bad management ◆ *Things were going off the rails here, and no one was getting any work done.* ◆ *This is a well-intentioned system that has been run off the rails.*

on someone's radar screen

It doesn't look like education is on the new governor's radar screen.

ORIGIN: from the idea of a train leaving the rails (= metal bars) it travels on

rain

(as) right as rain
feeling well ◆ *I took some aspirin, went to bed, and in the morning I was right as rain.*

raining cats and dogs See at CATS

rain on *sb's* parade See at PARADE

rainbows

chasing rainbows
trying to achieve something that is not possible or practical ◆ *He wanted to go into show business, but friends told him to quit chasing rainbows.*

rake

rake in *sth*, also rake *sth* in
to receive something valuable in large amounts ◆ *University graduate students continued to rake in awards and honors this year.* USAGE: often used about money: *The fundraiser raked in more than $23 million for the party.* ◆ *We were raking it in after the Times ran a review saying we were "the best."*

ramp

ramp up *sth*
to increase the amount or size of something ◆ *The city ramped up security at the bridge today.* ◆ *They're launching a new video game to ramp up their profits.* ◆ Opposite **scale back *sth*** at SCALE

ranch

bet the ranch
to risk everything you have because you are certain of success; = **bet the farm** ◆ *The program was in trouble, and our feeling was, why bet the ranch on it?* ◆ *She's expecting further gains, but she wouldn't bet the ranch.*

rank

pull rank
to use the power of your job or position to make someone do what you want ◆ *Some of the seniors in our school pull rank on the younger kids and force them to run errands for them.*

ranks

break ranks
to do or say something different from what a group you belong to does or says ♦ *Two owners broke ranks and said they were against locking out the players.* USAGE: often followed by **with**: *They decided to break ranks with the alliance and work independently for a solution.*

> ORIGIN: based on the military meaning of **break ranks** (= to walk away from a straight row in which you and other soldiers have been standing)

close ranks
to show support for other members of your group ♦ *Dale urged his former rivals to close ranks behind his candidacy.*

> ORIGIN: based on the military meaning of **close ranks** (= to form a straight row with other soldiers)

join the ranks of *sth*
to become part of a larger group or organization ♦ *Their country will join the ranks of the most developed nations of the world in four or five years.*

ransom

a king's ransom
a large amount of money ♦ *A visit to one of those amusement parks can cost a king's ransom.* USAGE: often used with **worth** or **cost**, as in the example

rap

beat the rap
to avoid being punished ♦ *People think that if you have enough money and high-priced lawyers, you can generally beat the rap.* ♦ Related vocabulary **get off (scot-free)** at GET

take the rap (for *sth*)
to be blamed or punished unfairly for something you have not done ♦ *Reublinger has often taken the rap for bad decisions made by his boss.*

rat

smell a rat
to believe something is wrong ♦ *When my husband started working late three or four times a week, I smelled a rat.*

not give a rat's ass
See at ASS

rate

at any rate
more exactly; = **at (the very) least** ♦ *I don't think they liked my idea – at any rate, they weren't enthusiastic.*

rattle

rattle off *sth*, also rattle *sth* off
to say something quickly ♦ *She rattled something off in French that I didn't understand.* USAGE: often used when someone gives a list of facts or other related information from memory: *Walter could rattle off the statistics of players from the 1920s and '30s.* ♦ Related vocabulary **reel off** *sth* at REEL

rattle *sb's* cage
See at CAGE

raw

a raw deal
unfair treatment ♦ *If you feel you've had a raw deal, you can always sue me.* USAGE: often used with **give** or **get**: *Workers who felt they were getting a raw deal quit.*

in the raw
as it actually is ♦ *Politics in the raw is all about power and deal-making.*

> ORIGIN: from the literal meaning of **in the raw** (= naked)

ray

a ray of sunshine
someone or something that makes you feel hopeful ♦ *The company's earnings provided a ray of sunshine for investors on Friday.* ♦ *Sara's visit was a ray of sunshine in her grandmother's day.*

rays

catch some rays slang, also catch a few rays
to lie or sit outside in the sun ♦ *This*

summer, there are plenty of festivals and outdoor concerts where you can catch some rays while enjoying the music.

reach

reach out (to *sb***)**
to make a special effort to communicate with or help someone ♦ *I was going through a hard time, and Johnny really reached out to me during that period.* ♦ *He used his dance company as a way of reaching out to African-American youth.*

within reach
almost possible or available ♦ *Everyone says agreement is within reach, but it's hard to believe.* ♦ *The price for the house was almost within reach, but a bit more than they could afford.* ♦ Related vocabulary **for the taking** at TAKING

read

read *sth* **into** *sth*
to give your own meaning to something rather than what was intended ♦ *Experts warned against reading too much into Friday's election results.* ♦ *People can read into his comments anything they want to, but no decision has been made.* USAGE: usually used with **too much** or **anything**, as in the examples

read up on *sth*
to learn about something by reading a lot ♦ *I've been reading up on Quebec's history.*

read between the lines See at LINES

read *sth* **(from) cover to cover** See at COVER

read *your* **mind** See at MIND

read the fine print See at FINE PRINT

read *sb* **the riot act** See at RIOT ACT

ready

at the ready
ready for use ♦ *Military police leapt out of the car, their weapons at the ready.*

real

for real esp. spoken
1 actually or truly ♦ *When they told me I had an unlimited budget I knew this was not for real.* USAGE: often said in reaction to what someone else says: *"I don't think I'm going to the party." "For real?"*
2 as good as it seems ♦ *Any time an unknown player does something amazing, people wonder if he is for real.*

reality

in reality
actually ♦ *The solution seemed simple, but in reality it was almost impossible to make it happen.* ♦ Related vocabulary **as a matter of fact** at MATTER, **in (point of) fact** at FACT, **in truth** at TRUTH

reap

reap what *you* **sow**
to experience the results of your own actions ♦ *If we neglect our environment, we will surely reap what we sow.* USAGE: usually used to say that something bad is likely to result from an activity

> ORIGIN: from the idea that the quality of the seeds that you **sow** (= put into the ground) grow into the kind of plants that you are able to **reap** (= cut and collect)

rear

bring up the rear
to be at the back of a group of people moving from one place to another ♦ *They walked down the hall, with Ray bringing up the rear.*

rear its (ugly) head See at HEAD

reason

for some reason (or other)
there could be many explanations why ♦ *For some reason or other, my son prefers to have a huge lizard rather than a dog or cat for a pet.*

listen to reason
to be influenced by arguments ♦ *It's too bad we had to take this problem*

to court, but that man wouldn't listen to reason. USAGE: often used in the form **not listen to reason**, as in the example

stand to reason
to seem likely to be true ◆ *It stands to reason that the more experience you have, the better you'll be at solving problems.*

with good reason, *also* **for good reason**
because of something obviously true ◆ *Roberta refused to respond to the charge, and with good reason – it was true.*

within reason
to the degree that good judgment would allow ◆ *With a good exercise program, you can eat anything you want, within reason, and not gain weight.*

rebound

on the rebound
1 becoming stronger or better again ◆ *Wall Street is on the rebound a day after stock prices plunged to new lows.* ◆ *Improved housing and rising rents are both signs of a community on the rebound.*
2 recovering from the recent end of a romantic relationship ◆ *You're a great guy, but I'm still on the rebound and I'm just not ready to start seeing anyone.*

reckon

reckon with *sb/sth*
to consider the influence or power that someone or something has ◆ *He failed to reckon with the bureaucratic skills of the military.* ◆ *You have to reckon with these angry people who just don't like change of any kind.*

a force to be reckoned with See at FORCE

record

for the record
1 officially and publicly ◆ *He is a Congressman known for saying what other politicians will not say for the record.*
2 esp. spoken ◆ so that the facts are clear ◆ *Just for the record, I was not even born when the events I'm describing happened.*

off the record
not intended to be known publicly or recorded officially ◆ *She claims the newspaper published comments about the incident that were supposed to be off the record.* ◆ Opposite **on (the) record**

on (the) record
known or recorded officially and publicly ◆ *He is on the record as saying that I was not involved in this decision.* ◆ *The number of murders this year is the lowest on record for this city since the 1920s.* USAGE: sometimes used in the phrase **go on the record** (= make something known officially and publicly): *These women are willing to go on the record with charges against their boss.* ◆ Opposite **off the record**

set the record straight
to tell the true facts that have not been accurately reported ◆ *If we are wrong and Brian would like to set the record straight, he should come talk to us.* ◆ Related vocabulary **set *sb/sth* straight** at SET

a matter of record See at MATTER

red

in the red
experiencing the situation of spending more money than you earned ◆ *Tourism is down and many hotels are operating in the red.* ◆ *The phone company found itself about $1.8 billion in the red.* ◆ Opposite **in the black** at BLACK

see red
to become very angry ◆ *Some Internet customers are seeing red as a result of the new virus that slowed Web traffic last week.*

paint the town (red) See at TOWN
roll out the red carpet (for *sb*) See at RED CARPET

red carpet
roll out the red carpet (for *sb*)
to give a special welcome to someone important ◆ *This city has rolled out the red carpet for women's fashion buyers and the media.*

> ORIGIN: based on the literal meaning of **red carpet** (= a thick red covering for a floor or other surface that is put down for important guests to walk on)

reduce
reduce *sb* to *sth*
to force someone into a worse condition than usual ◆ *He had to sell his home to pay his legal fees and was reduced to parking cars for money.* ◆ *Sheila's cries reduced him to silence.*

reel
reel in *sb/sth*, *also* reel *sb/sth* in
1 to pull someone or something toward you ◆ *We snagged the alligator near its tail and reeled it in.* ◆ *Rob took his hand, reeled him in, and gave him a big hug.*
2 to attract someone or something ◆ *Car dealers have to work harder to reel in customers when the economy is in bad shape.*

> ORIGIN: from the use of a **reel** (= an object shaped like a wheel) used to pull in the fishing line when a fish is caught

reel off *sth*, *also* reel *sth* off
1 to say a list of things quickly and easily ◆ *He reeled off the names and ages of his seven grandchildren.* ◆ Related vocabulary **rattle off *sth*** at RATTLE
2 to do something quickly and easily ◆ *In the American league, Boston has reeled off four straight victories.*

refer
refer to *sth*
to look at something for information or help ◆ *He referred to the dictionary for the correct spelling of the word.*

refer to *sb/sth*
to mention or talk about someone or something ◆ *I think you're referring to a TV interview on a news program last week.* ◆ *Do you think he was referring to me?*

refer *sb* to *sth*
to bring someone's attention to something ◆ *I refer the reader to chapter 6.*

refer *sb* to *sb/sth*
to give someone the name of someone else or of an organization ◆ *My doctor referred me to a cancer specialist.* ◆ *She was referred to the Rare Books department of the public library.* USAGE: people are usually referred to someone or something that will help them, as in the examples

refer *sth* to *sb/sth* slightly formal
to ask that a problem or idea be considered by someone or something else ◆ *The Senate voted to refer the issue to a subcommittee.* ◆ *All inquiries should be referred to the central office in Philadelphia.*

refer to *sb/sth* as *sb/sth*
to call someone or something by a particular name ◆ *Some people referred to them as freedom fighters, but to me they were terrorists.* ◆ *The area south of 9th Street is referred to as the South Slope.* ◆ *His real name is Charles, but his friends refer to him as "Chuck."*

reference
in reference to *sth* slightly formal
mentioning or talking about something ◆ *The author made the statement in reference to Silverman's latest book.* ◆ *She says the use of the word "repatriate" in reference to Quebec is historically inaccurate.*

reflect
reflect on *sth*, *also* reflect upon *sth*
to think seriously about something ◆ *Her essay invites the reader to*

reflect on the importance of art in people's lives.

reflect on *sb/sth*
to influence the reputation of a person, group, or organization ◆ *The outstanding work of our scientists reflects well on the entire university.* ◆ *If someone on our staff does a bad job, it reflects badly on all of us.* USAGE: always used with an adverb and said of both good and bad influences on a reputation

regard

in that regard slightly formal
in connection with something previously said ◆ *I think he's very, very good at working with the community, and he's done an excellent job in that regard.* ◆ *It's only natural to take a look at how your neighbors did, and in that regard, Mississippi can be thankful that it did not do as poorly as Louisiana.*

in this regard slightly formal
in connection with this ◆ *The movie has pretty low musical values, but it has plenty of company in this regard.* ◆ *I always had enough to eat, so I was much better off in this regard than many poor children in our neighborhood.*

with regard to *sth* slightly formal, also **in regard to** *sth*
considering or relating to something; = **with respect to** *sth* ◆ *Parents are concerned about protecting their kids with regard to stuff that is available on the Internet.* ◆ *It certainly should make the law clearer with regard to what is and what is not a disability.* ◆ Related vocabulary **in terms of** *sth* at TERMS

regardless

regardless of *sth*
without being influenced by something ◆ *We treat everyone equally, regardless of what their language is, regardless of their skin color or background.* USAGE: sometimes spoken as **irregardless of**, which is not considered standard English

regards

as regards *sth* slightly formal
in connection with something ◆ *As regards the governor's recommendations, we plan to act on them soon.*

rein

ORIGIN
These idioms are based on the literal meaning of **rein** (= a long, thin piece of leather used to control the movements of a horse).

give *sb/sth* **(a) free rein**, also **give (a) free reign to** *sb/sth*
to allow someone or something complete freedom ◆ *The owners gave the chef free reign to create a new menu.* ◆ *She was afraid to give free rein to her feelings.*

keep a tight rein on *sb/sth*
to control someone or something carefully ◆ *Clarke has consistently pointed to the need to keep a tight rein on government finances.* ◆ *He kept a tight rein on his daughter.*

rein in *sb/sth*, also **rein** *sb/sth* **in**
to control someone or something ◆ *We should rein in our spending, balance our budget, and stop borrowing.* ◆ *Critics say they have run the company as a personal kingdom, pocketing the profits and ignoring anyone who tried to rein them in.*

reins

take over the reins
to begin controlling an organization or a country ◆ *She offered good advice to the new Speaker as he took over the reins of leadership in the House of Representatives.*

ORIGIN: based on the idea that the person who handles the **reins** (= straps) that control a horse has control of the vehicle the horse is pulling

relate

relate to *sb*
to understand and feel sympathy for someone; = **identify with** *sb* ◆ *The kids need a teacher who can relate to them.*

relate to *sth*
to feel that you understand a situation; = **identify with** *sth* ◆ *You're looking for a job? I can relate to that!*

relation
in relation to *sth*
1 compared with something ◆ *She checked the map to see where Miami is in relation to Orlando.*
2 slightly formal and how that connects to something ◆ *This is a report about the effects of changing weather patterns in relation to farming.* ◆ Related vocabulary **in connection with** *sth* at CONNECTION

relieve
relieve *you* **of** *sth*
to steal something from you ◆ *This morning, a pickpocket relieved me of $100.*

religion
sb **gets religion**
someone's behavior suddenly changes because of a better understanding of something ◆ *After the attacks, the administration suddenly got religion about tracking down terrorists' bank accounts.* USAGE: usually said to show you think someone should have changed their behavior sooner

> ORIGIN: based on the literal meaning of **get religion** (= to suddenly become very religious)

remains
it remains to be seen
it is still unclear ◆ *It remains to be seen whether the heating system is really fixed or will have to be replaced.*

reproach
beyond reproach
not to be criticized ◆ *These were men of outstanding character who were beyond reproach.*

reserve
in reserve
available for use if needed ◆ *I know how much money I will earn, how much I can spend, and what I need to keep in reserve.*

respect
with all due respect
with the admiration that is owed ◆ *With all due respect, I think there are some facts you have not considered.* USAGE: used to disagree politely with someone

with respect to *sth* slightly formal, *also* **in respect to** *sth*
considering or relating to something; = **with regard to** *sth* ◆ *There is another question with respect to this plan that must be answered before any decision can be made.* ◆ *Do you really believe your memory is clear in respect to what happened?* ◆ Related vocabulary **in terms of** *sth* at TERMS

respects
pay *your* **respects**
to express your admiration or friendly feeling for someone ◆ *First I paid my respects to her parents and then went into to town to see some other people.* ◆ *Fans waited in the cold to pay their final respects to this fine athlete.* USAGE: sometimes used in the form **pay your final respects** (= to express your admiration for someone who has died)

rest
give it a rest
stop doing something ◆ *I was worrying about my brother all the time and needed to give it a rest.*

lay *sb* **to rest**
to bury a dead person ◆ *Hattie died peacefully at age 93 and was laid to rest in the church cemetery.*

lay *sth* **to rest,** *also* **lay to rest** *sth*
to solve or end something ◆ *The trial will lay all worry to rest that the wrong man was accused of this crime.*

rest assured
to be certain something will happen ◆ *I know this fellow well, and you can*

retreat

rest assured he will give you good advice.

the rest is history
everyone knows what happened next ◆ *The Beatles toured the US, made records, had zillions of groupies, and the rest is history.*

I rest my case See at CASE

God rest sb's soul See at GOD

rest in peace See at PEACE

rest on your laurels See at LAURELS

retreat

beat a (hasty) retreat
to quickly leave ◆ *When the cold grows overwhelming, visitors can beat a retreat to Joe Mulligan's warm bar and restaurant.*

> ORIGIN: based on the military meaning of **beat a retreat** (= to drum a signal to soldiers that they are to move back from a fight, usually one they have lost)

retrospect

in retrospect
looking back on something that happened ◆ *I think that, in retro-*

spect, we were wrong to insist that she move to an apartment.

return

in return (for *sth*)
in exchange for something ◆ *As a teenager, he worked at a nearby golf course in return for lessons.*

return the compliment See at COMPLIMENT

return the favor See at FAVOR

revel

revel in *sth*
to get great pleasure from a situation or an activity ◆ *She usually got the jobs she wanted, and she reveled in them.*

> ORIGIN: based on the literal meaning of **revel** (= to dance, drink, sing, and enjoy yourself in a noisy way)

rhyme

no rhyme or reason, *also* **without rhyme or reason**
without any reasonable explanation or purpose ◆ *Because the cave was formed by gases that ate away*

revel in something

Company executives reveled in the success of their new product.

the rock, there seems to be no rhyme or reason to its shape.

riddance

good riddance esp. spoken
I'm happy that someone or something is gone ♦ *Peter and his nasty dog have finally moved out. Good riddance!* USAGE: the full form of the phrase is **good riddance to bad rubbish**, which is sometimes used

ride

along for the ride
involved only for the enjoyment of it ♦ *My husband is speaking at the dinner and I'm just along for the ride.* USAGE: often used with **go** or **come**: *The city council was happy to go along for the ride and do nothing when times were good.*

ride on *sth*
to depend on the result of something else ♦ *Who could have predicted that the result of a presidential election would ride on a court's decision?*

ride out *sth*, also **ride** *sth* **out**
to continue to work or exist through something difficult or dangerous ♦ *He rode out the recession very well, and, in fact, his business actually grew.* ♦ *There was a big storm, but the ship managed to ride it out.*

ride roughshod over *sb/sth*, also **run roughshod over** *sb/sth*
to act without caring about how you will effect someone or something ♦ *He was a bully and rode roughshod over his workers whenever he felt they weren't working hard enough.*

ride up
to slowly move higher, out of position ♦ *The sweater would ride up in back and she'd have to yank it down – up and down and up and down all day.* ♦ *One problem with the design of seat belts is that the lap belt can ride up over the stomach and injure the passenger.* USAGE: usually said about clothing

take *sb* **for a ride**
to cheat or deceive someone ♦ *I trusted him to invest money for me, but he took me for a ride.*

ride a wave of *sth* See at WAVE

ride *sb's* **coattails** See at COATTAILS

ridiculous

from the ridiculous to the sublime See **from the sublime to the ridiculous** at SUBLIME

riding

riding high
doing very well ♦ *The president is still riding high in the polls.*

right

in *your* **own right**, also **in** *its* **own right**
because of your own ability or effort ♦ *His whole family were writers, but he became even more famous in his own right.* ♦ *This hospital is an extremely advanced critical care center in its own right.*

right away, also **right off**
immediately ♦ *She wanted to leave right away and not wait for her sister.* ♦ *You could tell right away that something was wrong.*

right on
exactly right or correct; = **(right) on the money** ♦ *His prediction on the outcome of the elections was right on.*

rights

have *sb* **dead to rights**, also **catch** *sb* **dead to rights**
found in the act of doing something wrong ♦ *The police had him dead to rights selling drugs.*

ring

give *sb* **a ring** esp. spoken
to telephone someone; = **give** *sb* **a buzz** ♦ *She's been sick for a couple of days, so why don't you give her a ring?* ♦ *I'm calling to find out what tonight's homework is, so if you could give me a ring and let me know I would really appreciate it.*

ringer

have a familiar ring (to it)
to seem as if you have heard it or experienced it before ◆ *Passing notes to friends in class may have a familiar ring to it, but these days students use text messages on their phones to send forbidden messages.* ◆ Related vocabulary **ring a bell** at BELL

ring hollow, *also* **ring false**
to seem dishonest, not true, or wrong ◆ *The Rockets sounded like a defeated team – they talked of the possibility of a comeback, but the words rang hollow.* ◆ *Her characters and situations all ring false and her movie just seems painful and pointless.* USAGE: often used in the forms **a hollow ring** or **a false ring** (= a dishonest or not sincere quality): *Her story about the hostages is certainly exciting, but it has a hollow ring.* ◆ Opposite **ring true**

ring true
to seem to be accurate or sincere ◆ *The book rang true because the author had actually experienced the ordeal of being marooned on an island.* ◆ *Cooper's reassuring words didn't ring true with everyone.* USAGE: often used with **not**, as in the example, and often used in the forms **the ring of truth** or **a ring of truth**: *Speaking as a parent of boys, I can tell you her comments have the ring of truth.* ◆ Opposite **ring hollow**

ring up *sth*
to earn or lose a particular amount of money ◆ *His division, which employs about 300 people worldwide, rang up $50 million in sales last year.*

ring up *sth*, *also* **ring** *sth* **up**
to record the prices of items being bought ◆ *Their groceries had already been rung up at the cash register.* ◆ *If a sales clerk forgets to ring something up do you call it to his or her attention?* USAGE: from pushing keys on an old-fashioned **cash register** (= a machine that records a sale and stores the money received), which made a ringing sound

ring a bell See at BELL

ring off the hook See at HOOK

throw *your* **hat in the ring** See at HAT

ringer

a dead ringer for *sb/sth*
someone or something that looks exactly like someone or something else ◆ *Our waiter was a dead ringer for Humphrey Bogart.* ◆ *My silver-blue '64 Buick was a dead ringer for the one Sinatra drove in that movie.*

rings

run rings around *sb/sth*
to show much more skill or ability than someone or something else ◆ *International gangs of art thieves have run rings around national police.* ◆ *Olympic hockey runs rings around the game played by professionals.*

riot act

read *sb* **the riot act**, *also* **read the riot act to** *sb*
to strongly warn someone to stop behaving badly ◆ *Alice read Randi the riot act, telling her, "If you don't like it here, you can just go back where you came from."* ◆ *The secretary of state said she plans to read the riot act to the country's leaders during meetings next week.* ◆ Related vocabulary **lay down the law** at LAW

> ORIGIN: based on the **Riot Act** (= an English law of 1715 that provided a way to deal with a crowd of people who were causing trouble)

rip

rip *sb* **off** slang, *also* **rip off** *sb*
1 to cheat or deceive someone ◆ *If your kids lie to you, you feel emotionally ripped off.* ◆ *She offers advice on how you can keep restaurants from ripping you off.*
2 to steal from someone ◆ *He admitted he had ripped off a drug smug-*

gler and blown up his boat. ✦ *I have a great idea for a book, but I don't want the publisher to rip me off.*

rip *sth* off slang, *also* **rip off *sth***
to steal something ✦ *Two students ripped off a fund for leukemia patients.* ✦ *I ripped off the idea from an old friend.*

let it rip See at LET

ripe

ripe for *sth*
ready for something to happen ✦ *She thinks the whole unemployment insurance system is ripe for an overhaul.* ✦ *Nobody was sure if the television audience was ripe for something different.* ✦ *Kinshasa is a city ripe for change.*

rise

give rise to *sth* slightly formal
to cause something to exist ✦ *Her experiences have given rise to the passion she expresses in her poetry.* ✦ *Stem cells produce more cells of the same kind – liver stem cells give rise to liver cells, skin stem cells give rise to skin, and so on.* ✦ Related vocabulary **give birth to *sth*** at BIRTH

rise above *sth*
to not allow something unpleasant to influence you ✦ *She rose above personal tragedy by following the principles of self-reliance, discipline, and education.* ✦ *Phillips had little hope of rising above poverty.*

rise to *sth*
to react to a difficult situation by working harder to succeed ✦ *It was a tough race, but Jean rose to the challenge and rode her horse beautifully.* ✦ *He's handled many crises before, but can he rise to the task this time?* ✦ Related vocabulary **rise to the occasion** at OCCASION

rise to the bait See at BAIT

rise to the occasion See at OCCASION

risk

run the risk (of *doing sth*)
to make possible a particular result ✦ *When doctors fail to follow government guidelines, they run the risk of being sued by their patients.* USAGE: sometimes followed by a clause beginning with **that**: *By giving students more freedom, we run the risk that sometimes they will fail.*

river

sell *sb* down the river
to do something that hurts someone who trusted you ✦ *Workers complained that their leaders sold them down the river in the latest contract negotiations.* ✦ Related vocabulary **sell out *sb*/*sth*** at SELL

road

down the road
in the future; = **down the line** ✦ *I was asked to gather statistical data that could be useful down the road.* USAGE: often a time in the future is mentioned: *This is a great invention, but a marketable product is several years down the road.*

go down that road
to do a particular thing ✦ *We're thinking of investing in real estate, but before we go down that road we need some professional advice.* USAGE: also used in the forms **go down the road** or **go down a road**: *Some of these parents were in trouble with the law, and I see their kids going down the road, too.*

hit the road
to begin traveling ✦ *I'd love to stay longer, but it's really time to hit the road.*

on the road
traveling to different places ✦ *The band spends three months a year on the road.* ✦ *Busy professionals prefer e-mail because they can work at home, at the office, or on the road.* USAGE: often used to describe traveling entertainers or sales representatives

on the road to *sth*
starting to achieve something ✦ *The doctors say she's on the road to recovery.* ✦ *Executives believe the*

company is on the road to improved sales.

the end of the road See at END

rock

between a rock and a hard place having only two very unpleasant choices; = **between the devil and the deep blue sea** ◆ *Schools for problem kids are between a rock and a hard place – they can be sued if children run away and get hurt, but have no power to keep the door locked.*

don't rock the boat See at BOAT

rock bottom

hit rock bottom, *also* **reach rock bottom** to reach the lowest possible level or be in the worst possible situation ◆ *She used illegal drugs for eight years and quit before she hit rock bottom.* ◆ *The department has reached rock bottom, with employees being fired and supervisors facing criminal charges.* USAGE: also used in the form **be at rock bottom**: *Grain prices are now at rock bottom.*

rocket scientist

it doesn't take a rocket scientist to *do sth*, *also* **you don't have to be a rocket scientist to** *do sth* it is easy to understand something ◆ *It doesn't take a rocket scientist to understand that fewer and fewer schools can afford to maintain competitive athletic programs.* USAGE: sometimes used in the form **it's not rocket science**: *A five year old could put this puzzle together – it's not rocket science.*

rocks

on the rocks
1 likely to fail because of serious problems ◆ *At the time, it seemed like capitalism was on the rocks.* ◆ *It became clear that her 15-year marriage to David was on the rocks.* USAGE: most often refers to relationships between people or organizations, as in the examples
2 with ice ◆ *I'll have a whiskey and soda on the rocks.* USAGE: used only to refer to alcoholic drinks

roll

on a roll
1 experiencing a period of success or good luck ◆ *They were on a roll, winning nine games in a row.* ◆ *With a growing economy and a dropping crime rate, the city has been on a roll.* ◆ Related vocabulary **have a good thing going** at THING
2 talking for a period of time ◆ *My mother loved to gossip, and she had a hard time stopping once she was on a roll.*

> ORIGIN: based on the idea that something which is rolling tends to continue rolling

ready to roll
1 prepared to start doing something ◆ *Once you have the software loaded, you're ready to roll.*
2 prepared to leave ◆ *Give me a call when you're ready to roll.*

roll around to happen or arrive again ◆ *When warm weather rolled around, Jim would start exercising again.* USAGE: used to describe something that happens regularly, such as a holiday or the seasons

roll back *sth*, *also* **roll** *sth* **back** to return something to a previous condition ◆ *Her staff has pushed to roll back environmental protections.* ◆ *It's unusual for any company to roll their prices back.* USAGE: often said about prices or laws

roll in to arrive or appear in large amounts or in a continuous flow ◆ *Fog rolled in along the coast.* ◆ *Bitter winter weather is rolling in over much of the eastern United States this week.* ◆ *He was certain that hard work would keep the money rolling in.*

roll out *sth*, *also* **roll** *sth* **out**
to offer a new product or service to the public ◆ *The provider plans to roll out its new Internet access service next month.* ◆ *They've experimented with the system in regional markets, and will roll it out nationally this fall.*

roll over *sth*, *also* **roll** *sth* **over**
to take profits from an investment and invest them in something similar ◆ *After calling my financial advisor, I decided to roll over those treasury bonds.* ◆ *Investors sometimes take cash out of retirement plans rather than roll the funds over.* USAGE: usually said about profits that would be taxed if they were not invested again

roll back the clock See at CLOCK

roll out the red carpet (for *sb***)** See at RED CARPET

roll over in *sb's* **grave** See **spin in** *sb's* **grave** at GRAVE

roll up *your* **sleeves** See at SLEEVES

roll with it See **roll with the punches** at PUNCHES

roll with the punches See at PUNCHES

rolled
(all) rolled into one
combined ◆ *Sports Day in Wannego was like Mardi Gras, the Summer Olympics, and the World Series rolled into one.* ◆ *She was the movie's producer, director, and writer all rolled into one.*

rolling
get *sth* **rolling**
to start an activity ◆ *The program is just getting rolling – we've only worked with a few kids so far.*

rolling in *sth*
having a lot of money or wealth ◆ *The business is rolling in cash.* ◆ *It's pretty obvious that these people aren't rolling in luxury.* USAGE: sometimes used in the form **rolling in it** (= very rich): *Mary's new husband is rolling in it.*

get the ball rolling See at BALL
rolling in the aisles See at AISLES

roof
a roof over *your* **head**
a place to live ◆ *At least we have a roof over our heads and the children have something to eat.*

go through the roof
to increase to a very high level ◆ *The price of that new stock went through the roof.* ◆ *Police say the crime rate in our area has gone through the roof.* USAGE: often used to refer to prices or costs

hit the roof, *also* **go through the roof**
to suddenly become very angry; = **hit the ceiling** ◆ *I'm afraid he'll hit the roof when he finds out our vacation is canceled.* ◆ *Officials went through the roof when a local newspaper published the report.*

raise the roof
1 to show great enthusiasm ◆ *The whole college is ready to raise the roof at next weekend's homecoming celebrations.*
2 to complain loudly ◆ *He didn't care if his boss raised the roof or even threatened to fire him, he knew he was right.*

rooftops
shout *sth* **from the rooftops**, *also* **scream** *sth* **from the rooftops**
to tell people about something that excites you ◆ *Alex was so happy, he wanted to shout the news from the rooftops.*

roost
rule the roost
to be the person who makes the decisions ◆ *Jimmy might be the boss at work, but at home it's his daughters who rule the roost.*

come home to roost See at COME

root
root for *sb/sth*
to support or encourage a person or

team ♦ *I always root for the home team.* ♦ *When you take the test tomorrow, we'll be rooting for you.* USAGE: often used when talking about a sports competition

root out *sth*, also **root** *sth* **out**
to find and remove a problem ♦ *She promises to root out corruption in state government.* ♦ *Retreating forces can blend into the landscape, making it more difficult to root them out.*

take root
to become established; = **take hold** ♦ *The organization took root all over the world and began expanding its many programs.* USAGE: often refers to an idea or set of beliefs: *Has democracy truly taken root in the region?*

> ORIGIN: based on the literal meaning of **take root** (= to start to grow roots in the ground)

roots

put down roots
to feel that you belong in a place ♦ *He hasn't put down roots anywhere because he has trouble making new friends.* USAGE: sometimes used in the form **pull up roots** (= to move away from a place in which you felt comfortable): *It's hard to pull up roots after living in the area for ten years.*

> ORIGIN: based on the literal meaning of **put down roots** (= to start to grow roots in the ground)

rope

rope in *sb/sth*, also **rope** *sb/sth* **in**
to persuade a person or group to do something ♦ *They're running ads that they hope will rope in the undecided voters.* ♦ *Once they're interested in the product, we try to rope them in and sell it to them.* USAGE: also used in the form **rope someone into doing something**: *He roped me into helping him clean up the yard.*

ropes

learn the ropes
to understand how to do a particular job or activity ♦ *It'll take some time for the new receptionist to learn the ropes.* USAGE: sometimes used in the forms **know the ropes** (= to understand how something is done) and **show someone the ropes** or **teach someone the ropes** (= to teach someone how something is done): *You'd better find someone to show you the ropes if you're going to fix the car yourself.*

on the ropes
doing badly and likely to fail ♦ *His political career is on the ropes.*

> ORIGIN: from the idea of a weakened prize fighter who leans against the ropes that surround the boxing ring

rose

(come up) smelling like a rose, also **(come out) smelling like a rose**
to end something positively or as a winner ♦ *Everyone thought he was guilty, but Smith still came up smelling like a rose.* ♦ *Hahn made a terrible play in the first half, but he was smelling like a rose by the finish.*

rote

by rote
automatically and without understanding ♦ *The children had learned number facts by rote and could calculate quickly.*

rough

in the rough
in a situation that is not comfortable or pleasant ♦ *I do not enjoy a camping vacation in the rough.* ♦ *Our new representative has had a hard time in the rough of Washington politics.*

rough *sth* **in**, also **rough in** *sth*
to begin the first work on some-

thing ◆ *First the plumber roughed in the drain pipe and water pipes.* ◆ *Make a sketch, rough it in, and then add the details.*

rough it
to live in a way that is simple and not very comfortable ◆ *They prefer roughing it on their travels, taking a tent rather than using hotels.*

rough *sth* **out**, *also* **rough out** *sth*
1 to make a first plan for an activity ◆ *Tyler started to rough out a list of schools she might want to attend.*
2 to create something in its approximate, but not finished, form ◆ *We watched as a carver began to work on the block of stone, roughing the sculpture out.*

rough *sb* **up**, *also* **rough up** *sb*
to attack someone physically but without causing serious injury ◆ *He was only thirteen the first time gang members roughed him up.* ◆ *It is reported that police officers roughed up several protesters.*

round

round and round
in a circle; = **around and around** ◆ *The children spun round and round until they were dizzy.* ◆ Related vocabulary **go around and around** at GO, **go (around) in circles** at CIRCLES

round out *sth*, *also* **round** *sth* **out**
to complete something ◆ *The visit to the ancient temple was the perfect thing to round out our vacation.* ◆ *It's a good article but I would have rounded it out with a paragraph about repairing the damage from the earthquake.*

round up *sb/sth*, *also* **round** *sb/sth* **up**
to gather people, animals, or things together into one place ◆ *Two dogs helped round up the sheep.* ◆ *Time to round everybody up! Dinner is ready!*

round up *sth*, *also* **round** *sth* **up**
to increase an amount to the next higher whole number ◆ *Round all of the numbers up to the nearest tenth.* ◆ *All measurements have been rounded up and are not exact.*

(all) year round See at YEAR

a square peg (in a round hole) See at PEG

rounds

make the rounds, *also* **do the rounds**
1 to be passed from person to person ◆ *The rumor making the rounds in Washington is that the ambassador will be leaving.*
2 to go from place to place ◆ *Tony and I made the rounds of the cheap bars in the city.* ◆ *Every new executive must do the rounds of all the departments in the company.*

make *your* **rounds**, *also* **do** *your* **rounds**
to visit or call certain people or places ◆ *Doctors make their hospital rounds every morning.*

row

in a row
in a series without interruption ◆ *They've won six games in a row.* USAGE: often used with periods of time: *I haven't had a good meal for three days in a row.*

a tough row to hoe
a difficult situation to deal with ◆ *The author said that he knew it would be a tough row to hoe when he began research for this book.*

rub

rub it in
to make someone feel even worse about something; = **rub salt into** *sb's* **wounds** ◆ *I wanted to rub it in a bit, so I said, "I'll be thinking of you working as I lie on the beach this afternoon."*

rub off (on *sb***)**
to be learned or obtained without any effort ◆ *I like to think that my love of reading will rub off on my children.* USAGE: usually used of a skill, an interest, or a quality

rub sb out, also **rub out sb**
to kill someone ♦ *She got into serious trouble when she ran an ad that said, "Looking for someone to rub out your Ex?" as a joke.* USAGE: generally used when referring to criminals who employ someone to kill an enemy

there's the rub
here is the difficulty ♦ *You can't get a job unless you have experience. And there's the rub – how do you get experience if you can't get a job?* USAGE: also appears as **here's the rub** and **that's the rub**: *The factory is ready to go, but here's the rub – there's no market for the products.*

rub elbows with sb See at ELBOWS

rub salt into sb's wounds See at SALT

rub shoulders with sb See at SHOULDERS

rub sb the wrong way See at WAY

Rubicon

cross the Rubicon slightly formal
to make a decision that cannot be changed later ♦ *When I quit editing and decided to be a writer, I had crossed the Rubicon to an uncertain future.*

ORIGIN: based on Julius Caesar's crossing of the Rubicon River in 49 B.C.E., which began a war

rug

cut a rug
to dance ♦ *Twenty disco classics on one CD. Now there's music to cut a rug to.* USAGE: also used in the form **cut a mean rug** (= to dance very well): *This flamenco dancer cuts a mean rug.*

pull the rug (out) from under sb/sth, also **pull the rug (out) from under sb's feet**
to suddenly take away important support from someone ♦ *The school pulled the rug from under the local team by making them pay to practice in the school gym.*

sweep sth under the rug
to hide something embarrassing; = **sweep sth under the carpet** ♦ *The scandal was swept under the rug because of the important people involved in it.*

rule

as a (general) rule
usually ♦ *As a rule, we go away in June, but this year, we will take a trip in the fall.*

rule out sth, also **rule sth out**
to stop considering something as a possibility ♦ *My doctor has ruled out drinking tea or coffee.* ♦ *Let's see how much the trip will cost before we rule it out.*

rule the roost See at ROOST

rules

bend the rules
to allow something to be done that is not usually allowed ♦ *We don't usually let students take books home, but I'll bend the rules this time.*

run

give *you* a run for *your* money
to be as good at something as someone who is known to be extremely good ♦ *He was a very good actor and could have given any professional a run for his money.*

have a good run, also **have a great run**
to experience success ♦ *Our industry is probably going to have a good run for the next several years.* ♦ *Gumbel had a great run as host of that morning talk show.*

have the run of *somewhere*
to be allowed to go anywhere in a place ♦ *Drug dealers have the run of the area after dark.*

in the long run
finally ♦ *Good management in the long run brought improved conditions for the workers.* ♦ Opposite **in the short run**

in the short run
for a short period of time ♦

Although gasoline prices may rise in the short run, they should begin to fall again by the end of the year. ◆ Opposite **in the long run**

make a run at *sth*
to try to achieve something ◆ *I never thought I'd win the prize, but I'm happy I got to make a run at it.*

(make a) run for it
to hurry away from something ◆ *We'd better run for it or we'll get wet.* ◆ *After a few days in the prison camp, Riney decided to make a run for it.*

on the run
1 avoiding being found ◆ *A very dangerous man was on the run last night after escaping from prison.* USAGE: usually refers to avoiding the police ◆ Related vocabulary **on the lam** at LAM
2 at a disadvantage ◆ *The mayor is on the run in this campaign and may even lose the election.* ◆ *Competition from catalog businesses has department stores on the run.*
3 while busy doing something else ◆ *He eats on the run, grabbing a sandwich in his car.*

run across *sb*
to meet someone without planning to ◆ *You don't run across many people who don't own a TV.*

run across *sth*
to find something without specifically looking for it ◆ *While looking for a present for my father, I ran across the most interesting book.*

run afoul of *sb/sth* slightly formal to act in a way not allowed by rules or the law; = **fall afoul of** *sb/sth* ◆ *Rodman ran afoul of the team's rules and was kept out of the next game.* ◆ *He ran afoul of his supervisor, who complained to the mayor about his work.*

run after *sb*
to try to get the attention or love of someone ◆ *He's about to make a fool of himself, running after a married woman.*

ORIGIN: based on the literal meaning of **run after someone or something** (= to chase someone or something)

run amok
to act in a wild or dangerous manner ◆ *There were 50 little kids running amok at the snack bar.*

run around
to go from place to place ◆ *I'm tired of running around on crutches.* ◆ *They are not just running around hoping for work, they're people with a serious business proposal.*

run around with *sb*
to spend a lot of time with someone ◆ *Mom likes to know the kids I'm running around with.*

run away (from *sb/sth***)**
1 to leave a person or place secretly and suddenly ◆ *Vinnie ran away from home when he was 16.*
2 to avoid someone or something unpleasant ◆ *You can't run away from your problems by watching videos all day.* ◆ *It is a disease and there is no cure, but you must not run away from people with AIDS.*

run *sth* **by** *sb*
to show someone something or tell them about it to get their opinion ◆ *Would you run that by me again?*

run counter to *sth*
to be the opposite of something ◆ *The article presents facts that run counter to what many of us believed had happened.*

run deep
to be very strong or well established ◆ *His worries ran deep but were hidden by his cheerful personality.*

run *you* **down**
to make you very tired ◆ *All of these crises in the family have really run her down.*

run down *sb*, also **run** *sb* **down**
to injure or kill someone with a vehicle ◆ *He's accused of running down two pedestrians while driving drunk.* ◆ *She tried to run us down!*

run down *sb/sth*, *also* **run** *sb/sth* **down**
1 to unfairly criticize someone or something ◆ *People run down the justice system all the time, but it works relatively fairly.* ◆ *Some people can only feel better about themselves if they're running you down.*
2 to search for and find someone or something ◆ *We spend a lot of money each year running down students who are out of school illegally.* ◆ *The software giant spent months running down bugs in the program and fixing them.* ◆ *The cops tried to run these guys down, but they had no luck.*

run down (*sth*)
to use the power that makes something work ◆ *We left the car lights on and ran down the battery.* ◆ *I wound up the toy dog and watched it jump until it ran down.*

run down *sth*, *also* **run *sth* down**
1 to explain something ◆ *I'll run down my research quickly.* ◆ *T. J. ran it all down for him, explaining the different costs of each option.*
2 to reduce something ◆ *We are going to start running down our savings if prices don't stop rising.* ◆ *I want to run our supplies down some more before we reorder.*

run dry
to be all used completely ◆ *We have been told the Social Security trust fund will run dry in a few more years because so many people will be retiring.*

run high
to be very strong ◆ *Frustration and anger run high when people lose hope.* USAGE: used mostly of feelings, as in the example

run into *sb*
to meet someone by chance ◆ *I ran into Mike on Seventh Avenue.*

run into *sth*
1 to experience something unexpectedly, esp. something unpleasant ◆ *The center ran into some financial trouble and had to borrow money.*
2 *also* **run to *sth*** to cost or reach a certain amount ◆ *Their salaries run into thousands per week.* ◆ *Costs on the project ran to the millions.*

run low
to be almost used up ◆ *Food stocks are running low already and we'll probably run out in April.*

run off
to leave suddenly ◆ *She punched me in the shoulder and ran off.*

run *sb* off, *also* **run off *sb***
to force someone to leave suddenly ◆ *Barlow wouldn't leave, so she ran him off by threatening to call the police.* ◆ *Dad tried to run off some people who were camping on our land, but they wouldn't leave.*

run off *sth*
to score points quickly in a competition ◆ *Iowa ran off 12 points and took the lead.*

run off *sth*, *also* **run *sth* off**
to make electronic or print copies of something ◆ *I'll just run these copies off before the meeting starts.* ◆ *He ran off 50 copies of the cassette and mailed them to agents.*

run off with *sb*
to leave your partner or home to begin a new relationship with someone ◆ *He has run off with a woman he met at the office.*

run off with *sth*
to take something that does not belong to you ◆ *The dog ran off with my shoe.*

run out (of *sth*)
to have no more of something ◆ *He just ran out of ideas.* ◆ *Time simply ran out.*

run out on *sb*
to leave or stop supporting someone who depends on you ◆ *Bob ran out on his wife and family.*

run over *sb/sth*, *also* **run *sb/sth* over**
to drive over someone or something with a vehicle ◆ *Pfeifer tried to run*

him over, but Fred luckily escaped. ♦ *I ran over a rabbit and was in tears all the way home!*

run *sb* ragged
to make someone work very hard ♦ *When Kayo first started working here, everyone ran her ragged.* USAGE: also used in the form **run yourself ragged**: *When Charlie finished law school, he didn't have to run himself ragged to find a job.*

run through *sth*
1 to practice something ♦ *We ran through our lines once, then started filming.*
2 to use all of something quickly ♦ *I still don't see how you could run through $5000 in a week.* ♦ *Alex ran through a large inheritance.*

run up *sth*
to cause something to reach a high level or large amount ♦ *Carol ran up a huge phone bill last month, calling the UK and Mexico.*

run up against *sb/sth*
to experience difficulty with someone or something ♦ *Sometimes you run up against a colleague who just doesn't want you to succeed.* ♦ *I ran up against some regulations that were incredibly stupid.*

run with it
to do something independently ♦ *You just have to give them the job and let them run with it.*

running

in the running
having a chance to win ♦ *This movie must be in the running for best documentary.* USAGE: said about a competition or election ♦ Opposite **out of the running**

out of the running
with no chance to win ♦ *This defeat puts Williams out of the running for the trophy.* ♦ Opposite **in the running**

a running battle (with *sb/sth*)
See at BATTLE

hit the ground running See at GROUND

off and running See at OFF

running on empty See at EMPTY

running on fumes See at FUMES

up and running See at UP

Russian roulette

play Russian roulette
to take foolish and dangerous risks ♦ *She accused the hospital of playing Russian roulette with the health of poor children.*

> ORIGIN: based on the literal meaning of **Russian roulette** (= a dangerous game of chance in which you hold a gun containing one bullet to your head and shoot, winning if the bullet does not come out)

rustle

rustle up *sth*, *also* rustle *sth* up
to make or get something quickly ♦ *Instead of eating out, she rustled up a romantic little dinner.* ♦ *They want $100 by tomorrow, and I can't rustle that amount up so quickly.*

S, s

sack

hit the sack
to get into bed; = **hit the hay** ◆ *When I hit the sack, I read for a few minutes, then turn out the light.*

sack out
to go to sleep ◆ *You can bring your sleeping bags and sack out on the living room floor.*

saddle

back in the saddle
doing something you stopped doing for a period of time ◆ *Friedman's career seemed to be finished a month ago, but he's back in the saddle and playing for Houston.*

in the saddle
in control ◆ *It looks like those who oppose environmental controls are going to be in the saddle.* ◆ Related vocabulary **in the driver's seat** at SEAT

> ORIGIN: based on the idea that someone who is in the **saddle** (= seat fastened on the back of a horse) controls the horse's movements

saddle sb/sth with sth
to give someone or something a difficult responsibility ◆ *Student aid often comes as loans, which can saddle students with debt for years.* ◆ *I hope I'm not going to be saddled with all the cooking on this vacation.* ◆ *The company was saddled with many lawsuits.*

safe

safe and sound
not hurt ◆ *After three days of searching for them, the hikers were found safe and sound.*

better safe than sorry See at BETTER

in safe hands See at HANDS

play it safe See at PLAY

(just) to be on the safe side See at SIDE

safety

(there is) safety in numbers
being in a group reduces risk ◆ *We stuck together because we were new in the city and felt there was safety in numbers.*

safety in numbers

Seals raise their young in large groups because they understand there is safety in numbers.

said

easier said than done
less difficult to talk about than to do ◆ *Gun control may be a good idea, but actually getting the guns out of the peoples' hands is easier said than done.*

like I said esp. spoken
as I mentioned before ◆ *She said something about not being responsible for the problem, but like I said, I wasn't paying much attention.*

sth to be said for sth
reasons why something has advantages ◆ *There's a lot to be said for living alone.* ◆ *There is something to be said for a news organization that doesn't follow the network pack.*
USAGE: can also be used in a negative way: *There is very little to be said for this argument.*

when all is said and done
when everything has been considered ◆ *When all is said and done, we can't reduce the number of nurses without lowering the quality of patient care.* ◆ Related vocabulary **at the end of the day** at END, **in the end** at END, **in the final analysis** at ANALYSIS

you said it esp. spoken
I agree with you completely; = **you can say that again** ◆ *You said it, Mac, she really is a terrific singer, and I worry that I won't be nearly as good.*

sail

sail into sth
to change to a new condition ◆ *The economy, for all its strengths, was sailing into trouble.*

sail into somewhere
to enter a place quickly and confidently ◆ *He sailed into the press conference on Friday, grinning at the journalists.*

sail through sth
1 to go quickly and smoothly through something ◆ *In the early evening light, we watched bats sail through the air, scooping up insects.* 2 to easily succeed in something ◆ *The new voting machines sailed through their first election day test last Tuesday.*

ORIGIN: based on the idea of a boat sailing smoothly on the water

set sail
to begin a trip on a ship or boat ◆ *Later he left California and set sail for Australia, searching for gold.*

ORIGIN: based on the literal meaning of **set sail** (= put up the sails of a boat to use the wind to move forward)

sail close to the wind See at WIND

sake

for old times' sake
as a way of remembering something pleasant from the past ◆ *I thought we'd take the train, just for old times' sake.*

for sth's own sake
because something is worth doing ◆ *Arnold is dedicated to writing for its own sake, and doesn't worry about whether he can sell what he writes.*

for the sake of argument
in order to consider the possibility ◆ *Assume, for the sake of argument, that what she says is true.*

for Christ's sake See at CHRIST
for God's sake See at GOD
for goodness sake See at GOODNESS
for Pete's sake See at PETE

sale

close a sale
to succeed in selling something to someone ◆ *It's an easy job – just bring out the shoe the customer chooses, and then close the sale with a thank you.*

salt

rub salt into sb's wounds
to make someone feel even worse about something; = **rub it in** ◆ *It's too bad Charlie couldn't come, but*

same

let's not tell him they let us in for free – there's no point rubbing salt into his wounds.

salt away *sth*, *also* **salt** *sth* **away**
to save something, esp. money, for use at a later time ♦ *It's not easy paying a mortgage, raising a young child, and salting away enough money for your retirement.*

the salt of the earth
the best people ♦ *Farmers were described as the best, the salt of the earth, particularly when their products were needed to feed the army.*

> ORIGIN: based on the high value salt had in the past, and used in the Bible

worth *your/its* **salt**
someone or something that deserves respect ♦ *Virtually any wine shop worth its salt carries at least a few wines from New Zealand.* ♦ *Any judge worth his salt would immediately report an attempt to influence the jury.*

same

same here esp. spoken
I agree ♦ *"I thought that movie was awful." "Same here."*

the same to you esp. spoken
I wish something as good for you ♦ *"I hope you have a great new year." "Thanks so much, and the same to you."* USAGE: used as a polite way of answering someone who has wished that something good happens to you

say

before you can say *sth*
surprisingly quickly; = **before you know it** ♦ *This bow shoots so fast, the arrow is in the target before you can say "gee whiz!"* USAGE: often the word or phrase that follows **before you can say** is related to the situation you are talking about: *In summer, food goes bad before you can say "heat wave!"*

have the final say, *also* **have the last say**
to have the authority to make decisions ♦ *Brown wanted to have the final say on the film's script, music, and costumes.* ♦ *In many families, the mother has the last say on the children's education and activities.*

I'll say esp. spoken
I agree ♦ *"We produce a wide variety of food on our farm." "Boy, I'll say – everything from melons to beans to meat!"*

> ORIGIN: based on the full form **I will say the same thing**

needless to say
obviously ♦ *Needless to say, I'm excited to be back.*

never say die
to refuse to stop trying to do something ♦ *What I liked best about hiking with this group of people was that they would never say die!*

never say never
do not ever say that you will not ever do something ♦ *At the present time, he has no intention of running for mayor, but never say never.* USAGE: used mainly in business and politics

say a lot about *sth*
to show or express something ♦ *In general, I think the way someone dresses says a lot about their attitude.*

say *sth* **to** *yourself*
to think about something ♦ *Just yesterday I said to myself that I need to get someone to fix the steps, and today this one has split.* USAGE: usually said about an effort to remember something you should do ♦ Related vocabulary **think to yourself** at THINK

say when
to stop or end something ♦ *Should it continue forever? When do you say when?*

sorry to say, *also* **sad to say**
I regret telling you this ♦ *Sorry to say, the violin was never found.*

to say nothing of *sth*
and also something else ♦ *It is difficult to escape the cold, to say nothing of the wind and rain.* USAGE: used to add emphasis to something you have just said ♦ Related vocabulary **not to mention** *sb/sth* at MENTION

to say the least
to not mention as much as you could about something ♦ *The dinner was tasteless, to say the least.*

you can say that again esp. spoken I agree with you completely; = **you said it** ♦ *"That was an absolutely delicious lunch." "You can say that again!"*

I dare say See at DARE

(just) say the word See at WORD

need I say more See at NEED

(say) enough is enough See at ENOUGH

say *your* **piece** See at PIECE

that is (to say) See at IS

scale

scale back *sth*, *also* **scale** *sth* **back**
to reduce the size or amount of something ♦ *The search for the child was scaled back sharply today, with almost a third of the volunteers heading home.* ♦ *The program was very effective, but the plan now is to scale it back.* USAGE: also used in the form **scale down**: *The original jury award of $10 million was scaled down to $250,000 by the judge.* ♦ Opposite **ramp up** *sth* at RAMP

scale up *sth*, *also* **scale** *sth* **up**
to make something larger, esp. a design or model ♦ *A number of companies manufacturing a line of popular small cars have simply scaled up those models.* ♦ *Engineers did not completely understand what would happen if they scaled their design up.*

scales

tip the scales
to cause a change, esp. in making something more likely to happen; = **tip the balance** ♦ *She says the city's reputation helped tip the balance when the company was deciding whether to move the factory.*

tip the scales at *sth*
to be measured as being a particular weight; = **weigh in at** *sth* ♦ *He's added more muscle to his frame, and now tips the scales at 268 pounds.*

scare

scare away *sb/sth*, *also* **scare** *sb/sth* **away**
to cause someone or something to go or stay away; = **scare off** *sb/sth* ♦ *Video cameras may be helpful to police, but they do not scare away robbers.* ♦ *He scared them away by yelling and firing into the air.*

scare *sb/sth* **away from** *sth/doing sth*
to cause someone or something not to do something ♦ *If people are fully informed, that will increase their confidence and not scare them away from taking the drug.*

scare off *sb*, *also* **scare away** *sb*
to cause someone not to invest money in something ♦ *A TV show as experimental and unusual as this one could scare off advertisers.* ♦ *The country's financial crisis has scared away potential foreign investors.*

scare off *sb/sth*, *also* **scare** *sb/sth* **off**
to cause someone or something to go or stay away; = **scare away** *sb/sth* ♦ *In summer, when you walked through a field of dry grass, you stamped your feet to scare off snakes.* ♦ *A deadly outbreak of "bird flu" in Hong Kong has killed six people and scared off tourists.* ♦ *Intensive border patrols probably scared smugglers off.*

scare up *sth*
to find or obtain something that is not easily available ♦ *At the very*

scared

least, I'm sure he'll have some original ideas on how to scare up some cash. ♦ We discovered it was impossible to scare up an audience for the game. ♦ Related vocabulary **scrape together** *sth* at SCRAPE

scare the hell out of *you* See at HELL

scare the pants off *sb* See at PANTS

scare *you* **to death** See at DEATH

scared

scared shitless rude slang
extremely frightened ♦ *I was scared shitless when I first moved out here, but things still worked out fine in the end.*

scared stiff
extremely frightened ♦ *Jill awoke from a dream that left her afraid – scared stiff, in fact.*

> ORIGIN: from the idea that you are **stiff** (= unable to bend or change your position) because you are too frightened to move

scared to death See at DEATH

scene

burst onto the scene
to suddenly become famous ♦ *Marsalis burst onto the scene in the early 1980s and proved that jazz could have its own superstars.*

make a scene
to be loud and rude with other people or in public ♦ *My father made a scene, then raced upstairs, slamming the door so hard that the window broke.*

make the scene
to be active in a social activity ♦ *She hopes to be behind the wheel, making the scene with her friends, after she gets her driver's license.*

on the scene
in a place where something is happening ♦ *Reporters arrived on the scene within minutes of the explosion.* ♦ *The US commander on the scene has requested 2,000 more troops.*

set the scene (for *sth***)**
1 to make something possible or likely to happen ♦ *The recent resignation of two cabinet members has set the scene for a pre-election crisis.*
2 to describe a situation so that people can understand what is happening ♦ *Let me just set the scene briefly and my colleague will add some details later.*

scenes

behind the scenes
quietly, in a way that does not attract attention ♦ *Diplomats have been working hard behind the scenes in preparation for the talks.*

scent

throw *sb* **off the scent**
to give someone false or confusing information so that they will not discover something ♦ *The police were thrown off the scent for a while by two of the witnesses, who were found later to be lying.*

> ORIGIN: based on the literal meaning of **throw a dog off the scent** (= to cause a dog to lose the smell that leads it to a person or animal)

schedule

ahead of schedule
happening or done earlier than the time that was planned ♦ *The sale will help us to repay the loan ahead of schedule.* ♦ Opposite **behind schedule**

behind schedule
happening or done later than the time that was planned ♦ *The project is behind schedule because several people are off sick.* ♦ Opposite **ahead of schedule**

on schedule
happening or done at the time that was planned or intended ♦ *The trains run pretty much on schedule, except when the weather is really bad.*

scheme
in the scheme of things
in a general view of the situation ◆ *She just got here and hasn't figured out where she belongs in the scheme of things.* USAGE: often used with the adjectives **grand**, **larger**, or **overall**, usually to suggest that something is not very important: *A two-week delay will not matter in the overall scheme of things.*

school
teach school
to instruct students in a school ◆ *Buller left journalism to teach school, and he wrote several books about his experiences.*

science
have *sth* down to a science
to be able to manage all the details of doing something very well ◆ *We have traffic management at the new stadium down to a science.* ◆ Related vocabulary **have *sth* down pat** at HAVE

score
know the score
to know all the important facts in a situation ◆ *You know the score – no payments are made until after the article is published.*

settle a score, *also* settle old scores
to punish someone because they have done something to hurt you in the past ◆ *Muhammad Ali was eager to settle a score with Joe Frazier.* ◆ *After losing the race for mayor four years ago, running again this year was partly a matter of settling old scores.* USAGE: often used in the form **have a score to settle**: *The family was mistreated, and they have a score to settle with the government.* ◆ Related vocabulary **get even (with sb)** at GET

score points See at POINTS

scrape
scrape by
1 to have only enough money to buy the basic things you need to live ◆ *Even with both of us working, we earn just enough to scrape by.*
2 to come very close to failing ◆ *She only scraped by in the last election and no one expects her to win this time.*

scrape together *sth*, *also* scrape *sth* together
to gather something that is not easily available, esp. money ◆ *He managed to scrape together $20 for the train and came back home.* ◆ *Many immigrants have difficulty scraping enough money together for the application.* USAGE: also in the form **scrape up something**: *Somehow these families managed to scrape up the tuition fee.* ◆ Related vocabulary **scare up *sth*** at SCARE

scrap heap
on the scrap heap, *also* in the scrap heap
in a place for things that are not wanted any more ◆ *Congress is threatening to throw the president's budget on the scrap heap.*

> ORIGIN: from the literal meaning of **scrap heap** (= a pile of things that are no longer wanted)

scratch
from scratch
from nothing ◆ *We decided to build a newspaper pretty much from scratch.* USAGE: often used in the form **start from scratch**: *Can we fix the current computer system, or would it be better to start from scratch?*

up to scratch
at an acceptable standard or quality ◆ *We're giving him a week to bring the team up to scratch.* USAGE: often used in the form **not up to scratch**: *I'm afraid your last essay wasn't up to scratch.* ◆ Related vocabulary **on a par with sb/sth** at PAR

scratch *your* head See at HEAD
scratch the surface See at SURFACE

screw

screw around (with *sb***)** slang
1 to annoy someone by wasting their time ◆ *You'll be sorry if you screw around with Captain Legore.*
2 to have sex with someone who is not your regular partner ◆ *I think I saw the guy that she's been screwing around with.*

screw around (with *sth***)** slang
to waste time ◆ *Stop screwing around and finish your work.* ◆ *They spent the whole morning screwing around with Jeff's motorcycle.*

screw it rude slang
I do not care what happens or what someone does ◆ *She didn't want to see the movie, but I thought, screw it, I'm going anyway.* USAGE: usually used when the speaker is annoyed

screw up *sb*, *also* **screw** *sb* **up**
to confuse or hurt someone ◆ *She really screwed him up when she left him.* ◆ *Their parents' divorce really screwed up the kids.*

screw up (*sth***)**, *also* **screw** *sth* **up**
to spoil or damage something ◆ *You couldn't screw up much worse than I did.* ◆ *Somehow the lawyer screwed up my appointment again.* ◆ *This is detailed work, and people screw it up once in a while.*

screw you rude slang
I am very annoyed by you ◆ *You don't like it? Well, screw you!* ◆ Related vocabulary **up yours** at UP

screw up (your) courage See at COURAGE

screw up *your* **face** See at FACE

screws

tighten the screws on *sb/sth*, *also* **put the screws on** *sb/sth*
to make it harder for someone to do something ◆ *Government agencies need to tighten the screws on illegal immigrants.* ◆ *We are putting the screws on that country to end its history of helping terrorists.* USAGE: sometimes used in the form **put the screws to someone or something**: *The owners could really put the screws to the players.*

sea

at sea
confused ◆ *With no data they could depend on, they were utterly at sea.*

between the devil and the deep blue sea See at DEVIL

seal

seal of approval
a statement or action that shows a good opinion of something ◆ *We can finalize the trip to China once we get Bernard's seal of approval.* ◆ *With the seal of approval of a government grant, arts organizations find it easier to raise funds.*

> ORIGIN: based on the literal meaning of **seal of approval** (= an official mark showing that something has been accepted)

seal *sb's/sth's* **fate** See at FATE
your **lips are sealed** See at LIPS
signed and sealed See at SIGNED

sea legs

get *your* **sea legs**
to get used to a new situation ◆ *After graduating from college he went to Chicago to get his sea legs by working in radio.*

> ORIGIN: based on the literal meaning of getting used to being on a moving ship

seams

bursting at the seams
containing an unusually large number of people or things ◆ *My whole family came to stay for the wedding and our house was bursting at the seams.*

> ORIGIN: from the idea that if you wear something much too small for you, it is most likely to tear at a **seam** (= place where two pieces of material are sewn together)

come apart at the seams
to be in a bad condition and about

to fail or lose control ◆ *Large segments of the world economy seem to be coming apart at the seams.* ◆ Related vocabulary **come apart** at COME

ORIGIN: from the idea that when the **seams** (= places where two pieces of material are sewn together) in clothing come apart, it can no longer be used

search
search high and low (for *sth*)
to try very hard to find something; = **look high and low (for *sth*)** ◆ *Janet searched high and low, but she couldn't find the kitten and finally had to ask the man.*

season
in season
1 available fresh locally ◆ *Strawberries are in season here in May and June.* USAGE: usually said about food
2 at the time of year when something is popular ◆ *In season, the rooms with an ocean view are more than $300 a night.*
3 at the time of year when hunting or fishing is legal ◆ *Trout are now in season, which means the rivers are full of people fishing.* ◆ Opposite **out of season**

out of season
1 not available fresh locally ◆ *Asparagus is out of season now and really expensive.*
2 at the time of year when something is not popular ◆ *We like going to beach towns out of season.*
3 at the time of year when hunting or fishing is not legal ◆ *He got fined for killing a deer out of season.* ◆ Opposite **in season**

open season (on *sb/sth*)
a situation in which someone or something is criticized or treated unfairly ◆ *City newspapers have declared open season on the mayor.* ◆ *She feels it's almost like someone has declared open season on anyone who looks like a foreigner.*

ORIGIN: based on the literal meaning of **open season** (= the time of year when hunting is legal)

seat
fly by the seat of *your* pants
to do something difficult without the necessary experience or ability ◆ *None of us had ever worked on a magazine before so we were flying by the seat of our pants.*

in the catbird seat
in a position of power or influence ◆ *Throughout the 1990s, the company was in the catbird seat, with no serious competitors in its field.*

in the driver's seat
in control of a situation ◆ *Huge consumer demand for electricity has put energy companies in the driver's seat.* ◆ Related vocabulary **in the saddle** at SADDLE

in the hot seat, *also* **on the hot seat**
in a difficult position ◆ *He suddenly found himself in the hot seat, facing angry residents who wanted him to resign.*

keep *you* on the edge of *your* seat
See at EDGE

second
second to none
better than anything or anyone else ◆ *The hotel's restaurant is second to none.*

wait a second *esp. spoken*
I have just thought of something important; = **wait a minute** ◆ *Wait a second – when was the last time he stayed here?* USAGE: usually used to interrupt someone

have second thoughts See at THOUGHTS

just a second See **just a minute** at MINUTE

on second thought See at THOUGHT

without a second thought See at THOUGHT

second fiddle

play second fiddle (to sb/sth)
to be in a less important position than someone or something else ◆ *Radio has been playing second fiddle to television for decades now.* USAGE: sometimes used without **play**

> ORIGIN: based on the literal meaning of **second fiddle** (= the lower part for a violin, a musical instrument with strings)

second wind

get a second wind, *also* **get *your/its* second wind**
to have increased energy or strength after feeling tired or weak ◆ *The automobile industry seems to have gotten a second wind.* ◆ *Fred somehow got his second wind about halfway through the race.*

see

as far as I can see
in the way that I understand ◆ *As far as I can see, he has done nothing to lower our confidence in him.*

see about *sb/sth*
to get information about someone or something ◆ *I'll see about movie times and call you back.* ◆ *I know Janet and Tom aren't interested in bicycling, but let's see about Helen.*

see fit
to decide ◆ *You can leave it here or take it with you, whichever you see fit.*

see it coming
to know that something bad is about to happen ◆ *I wasn't surprised when they divorced – you could see it coming.*

see *sb* off, *also* **see off *sb***
to go with someone to the place where they will begin a trip ◆ *My parents saw me off at the airport.* ◆ *Families gathered at the dock to see off the sailors.*

see *sb* out
to go to the door with someone who is leaving ◆ *Wait just a second, I'll see you out.* ◆ *Please don't get up. I can see myself out.*

see through *sb/sth*
to understand the hidden truth about someone or something ◆ *She saw through his excuse as an effort to put the blame on someone else.*

see *sb* through *sth*
to support someone through a difficult time ◆ *He was a real friend to see me through my long illness.*

see *sth* through
to do something until it is finished ◆ *Despite health problems, she saw the project through.*

see to *sth*
to be sure that something is done ◆ *Would you see to those inquiries before you leave today?* USAGE: often used in the form **see to it**: *Tom was a good friend, so we saw to it that he got some help when he needed it.* ◆ *See to it that you are here promptly at nine o'clock tomorrow.*

seed

go to seed
to get into a much worse condition ◆ *I almost didn't recognize John. He's really gone to seed since his wife left him.*

> ORIGIN: based on the literal meaning of plants that **go to seed** (= stop producing flowers and start producing seeds)

plant a seed
to do something that will develop more in the future ◆ *I'm not just trying to sell tickets, I hope to plant a seed that will build audiences for opera.*

seeds

sow the seeds (of *sth*), *also* **plant the seeds**
to do something that will cause a particular result in the future ◆ *Religious conflict sowed the seeds of the government's downfall.* ◆

Officials say they are planting the seeds for freedom and democracy.

seeing
seeing that, *also* **seeing as (how)** considering that ◆ *We should go to the concert, seeing that we've already paid for the tickets.*

seen
have to be seen to be believed, *also* **must be seen to be believed** so extreme that it is difficult to accept ◆ *Our spacious new offices have to be seen to be believed!*
have seen better days See at DAYS
it remains to be seen See at REMAINS

seize
seize up to suddenly stop moving or working ◆ *I hit two keys at the same time and my computer just seized up.* ◆ *Her leg seized up and she had to be carried out.*

sell
sell out to accept money to stop following your principles ◆ *So many musicians simply sell out to the demands of the industry and abandon their art.*
sell out *sb/sth*, *also* **sell** *sb/sth* **out** to stop being loyal to someone or something ◆ *He accused Congress of selling out the American people to lawyers who opposed the bill.* ◆ *I could sell you all out and go straight to the police with this information.* USAGE: often money is the advantage that is gotten: *Anyone who would sell out his own country for money deserves to go to prison for life.* ◆ Related vocabulary **sell** *sb* **down the river** at RIVER
sell out (of *sth***)** to sell all of something, so that there is none left ◆ *We sold out of the souvenir T-shirts in the first couple of hours.* ◆ *During the summer the campgrounds are sold out each night.* ◆ *Her cruises regularly book up months in advance and almost always sell out.*
sell *sb/sth* **short** to not appreciate the qualities of someone or something as much as they deserve ◆ *I think her presentation really sold Morocco short.* USAGE: sometimes used in the form **sell yourself short** (= not have reasonable confidence in your abilities): *She doesn't succeed in interviews because she always sells herself short.*
sell *sb* **a bill of goods** See at BILL
sell *sb* **down the river** See at RIVER
sell like hotcakes See at HOTCAKES
sell *your* **soul (to the devil)** See at SOUL

send
send around *sth*, *also* **send** *sth* **around** to cause something to be seen by a number of different people ◆ *The teachers sent around a letter comparing their salaries to the teachers' in neighboring towns.* ◆ *He finished the manuscript and began sending it around to publishers.*
send away for *sth* to request something by mail ◆ *She sent away for applications to six colleges.*
send back *sb/sth*, *also* **send** *sb/sth* **back** to return someone or something to the place they came from ◆ *A year after he got out of prison, he was sent back for dealing in drugs.* ◆ *Some computer ads allow users to click on a button and send an e-mail back to the advertiser.* ◆ *If that steak isn't cooked enough, you should send it back.*
send *sb/sth* **flying** to cause someone or something to move very quickly ◆ *An explosion rocked the building, sending him flying into a desk.*

send for *sb*
to request or demand that someone come to you ♦ *Knowing he was extremely ill, we sent for his family.*

send for *sth*
to request that something be sent or brought to you ♦ *She sent for catalogs and read lots of books before she started the garden.*

send in *sb*, *also* **send *sb* in**
to cause someone to go to a place ♦ *The government was sending in as many as 3,000 troops.* ♦ *His doctor sent him in for more tests at the hospital.*

send in *sth*, *also* **send *sth* in**
to mail something to a place ♦ *I sent in my entry form, but I don't expect to win anything.* ♦ *You have to send it in before July 1st.*

send off *sth*, *also* **send *sth* off**
to mail something ♦ *She sent off copies of the drawing to several friends.* ♦ *She wrote a 500-word article on Indian baskets and sent it off with photographs.*

send *sb* off
to cause someone to go away to a place ♦ *Her parents sent her off to summer camp every August.*

send on *sth*, *also* **send *sth* on**
to mail something you have to another place ♦ *He promised to send on the rest of documents tomorrow.* ♦ *As soon as you get the check, send it on.*

send *sb* on *sth*
to cause someone to do something ♦ *He'll give Rufus some money and send him on a dozen errands.* ♦ *The troubles of modern life have sent many people on a search for spiritual peace.* ♦ Related vocabulary **send *sb* on *their* way** at WAY

send out *sth*, *also* **send *sth* out**
to mail something ♦ *Frank sends out about 400 Christmas cards every year.* ♦ *I sent the checks out by overnight mail.* USAGE: usually said about sending a lot of things

send *sb* out, *also* **send out *sb***
to ask or demand that someone go somewhere ♦ *Mom sent me out to weed the garden.* ♦ *Judge Carey had the jury sent out of the courtroom.*

send *sb* packing
to tell someone to go away ♦ *There were some kids at the door asking for money, but I sent them packing.* ♦ *He got caught cheating on the test and was sent packing.* USAGE: often said about someone you are annoyed with

send a message See at MESSAGE
send a signal See at SIGNAL
send *your* love to *sb* See at LOVE
send shivers down *your* spine See at SHIVERS

sense

in a sense
considering a situation in a particular way ♦ *It is tragic, in a sense, to see a family business destroyed.*

in the strict sense, *also* **in the strictest sense**
according to the most limited and exact meaning of a word or idea ♦ *"Conservative" in the strict sense of the word is not a label that fits her.* ♦ *The novel is not tragic in the strictest sense, but it is certainly full of sadness.* USAGE: usually used to say that someone or something does not have the characteristics of this limited meaning

make sense
to be reasonable ♦ *This deal clearly makes sense in the long term.* USAGE: often used with words that describe amounts, like **some**, **much**, or **any**: *Her idea doesn't make any sense.*

make sense of *sth*
to understand something ♦ *The community is trying to make sense of the tragedy.*

talk sense
to be reasonable ♦ *Abdullah is liked by the people who work for him be-*

cause he talks sense. ◆ *I think it's time someone talked sense to us about conserving energy.*

talk some sense into *sb*
to help someone think about something in a reasonable way ◆ *My best friend talked some sense into me, and I was able to smooth things over with my mom.*

senses

come to *your* **senses**
to start to understand that you have been behaving in a stupid way ◆ *Once Jack came to his senses, he was happy to admit that he'd been wrong.*

take leave of *your* **senses** slightly formal
to become crazy ◆ *My friends wondered if I had taken leave of my senses.*

serve

serve *you* **right**
you deserve the punishment that you received ◆ *After the way she treated him, it would serve her right if he left her.* USAGE: often said with an attitude of pleasure because someone you do not like is suffering

serve up *sth*, also **serve** *sth* **up**
to offer something ◆ *The TV miniseries will be serving up five hour-long programs.* ◆ *Hitchcock served up a pitch that Perez hit over the fence for a home run.* ◆ *Filmgoers demand realism, and Lee serves it up without flash or tricks in his latest movie.*

> ORIGIN: based on the literal meaning of **serve up** (= to provide food or drink)

if memory serves See at MEMORY
serve time See at TIME

service

at *sb's* **service**
ready to help someone as soon as they ask ◆ *In this business, the customer comes first, and our employees need to remember that we are at their service.*

press *sb* **into service**
to persuade or force someone to do something ◆ *Murphy pressed his sister into service to do the research.*

press *sth* **into service**
to use something for an unusual purpose ◆ *A few buses and trucks were pressed into service, but the vast majority of refugees walked.*

put *sth* **into service**
to begin to use something ◆ *The boat was sold to a Danish firm and put into service as a ferry on the North Sea.* USAGE: usually said about something that is provided regularly

see service slightly formal
to be a member of the military ◆ *He saw service during the Seven Years War and became an aide to Frederick the Great.*

set

set about *sth/doing sth*, also **set about to** *do sth*
to begin to do or deal with something ◆ *Beall has set about the delicate task of getting the companies to work together.* ◆ *After putting up the tent, she set about making a fire.* ◆ *I bought a computer, got a book of instructions, and set about to learn how to use it.*

set *sb/sth* **against** *sb/sth*
to cause one person or group to oppose another ◆ *His health-care plan would divide older Americans and set senior against senior.* ◆ *The disagreement has turned into a public feud that has set members against each other.*

set *sb/sth* **apart (from** *sb/sth***)**
to show someone or something to be different or special ◆ *Those selected as leaders of the future have qualities that set them apart.* ◆ *He's the one in the big white hat and bow tie, which sets him apart from all the men in dark suits.*

set aside *sth*, *also* **set** *sth* **aside**
1 to save something for a particular purpose ◆ *It's wise to set aside some money for unexpected expenses that may come up in the future.* ◆ *After melting the chocolate, set it aside and beat the eggs.* ◆ Related vocabulary **put aside** *sth* 2 at PUT, **put** *sth* **toward** *sth* at PUT
2 to not allow something to influence an activity ◆ *We need to set aside our differences and work together.* ◆ *Ancient rivalries still threaten the cause of peace, but we must set them aside.* ◆ Related vocabulary **lay aside** *sth* at LAY
3 to cause a previous legal judgment to have no effect ◆ *The court set aside his conviction and ordered a new trial.*

set *sb/sth* **back**, *also* **set back** *sb/sth*
to delay or stop the progress of someone or something ◆ *Then I needed a second operation, which really set me back.* ◆ *New violence has set back the peace process.*

set *you* **back** *sth*
to cost you an amount of money ◆ *A marriage license will only set you back $30.* ◆ *The gas-powered generator would set him back at least $5 million.*

set down *sth*, *also* **set** *sth* **down**
to write or print something ◆ *He set down his memories of his trip to Italy as a child.* ◆ *When you get a chance, set your ideas down on paper.* ◆ Related vocabulary **lay down** *sth* at LAY

set forth *sth* slightly formal
to explain or state something officially ◆ *Our views were set forth by our attorney in her March 13th letter.* ◆ *The board set forth the conditions for her release.* ◆ *Selina based her argument on the rights set forth in the First Amendment of the Constitution.* USAGE: usually said about something stated in writing

set in
to begin ◆ *If the wound is not treated, infection may set in.* ◆ *In winter, darkness sets in so early!*

set off, *also* **set out**
to start going somewhere ◆ *He got a Guggenheim fellowship and set off for Mexico to write a novel.* ◆ *You need to be fit and well rested before you set off on a hiking trip.* ◆ *When the car broke down, he set out on foot for help.*

set *sb* **off**
to cause someone to become excited and upset ◆ *My sister was an unpredictable young woman, and I never knew what would set her off.*

set off *sth*, *also* **set** *sth* **off**
1 to cause an explosion ◆ *The investigation determined that he probably did not set off the blast deliberately.* ◆ *Apparently the bomb was placed in a locker and someone set it off with a cell phone.*
2 to cause sudden activity ◆ *Rumors set off a wave of selling on the stock exchange.* ◆ *If you keep your phone in a pocket and lean up against something, you may accidentally set it off.*
3 to cause something to be noticed or make it more attractive ◆ *You look terrific with those black slacks, and the bright blue blouse sets off your eyes.*

set out *sth*, *also* **set** *sth* **out**
1 slightly formal ◆ to give the details of or explain something, esp. in writing ◆ *Your contract sets out the terms and conditions of your employment.*
2 to put something in a particular place ◆ *The waiter cleared the table and set out silverware for their next course.* ◆ *Put your trash in a garbage bag and set it out by the curb.*

set out to *do sth*
to begin doing something that is part of a plan ◆ *When Mary set out to become a writer, she had no idea*

how difficult it would be to earn a living.

set *sth* right
to correct something to make it the way it should be; = **put *sth* right** ◆ *They believe that the world is unjust, and try to set it right whenever they get a chance.* USAGE: often used in the form **set things right**: *In many western movies, local people faced with gangs of bandits would hire a gunman to set things right.*

set *sb*/*sth* straight
to tell someone the true facts about a situation that they had not understood correctly ◆ *If you think we won't be affected by what's happening in Asia, our chief economist would like to set you straight.* ◆ Related vocabulary **set the record straight** at RECORD

set to work
to begin doing something ◆ *They set to work bringing order to an organization that didn't even know how many computers it had.* ◆ *She pulled out her brushes and paper and set to work making a studio out of her hotel room.*

set up *sth*, *also* set *sth* up
1 to establish or create something ◆ *The welfare system is set up to encourage people to find work as soon as they can.* ◆ *He set up his practice as an architect in New York City in the 1890s.* ◆ *His father's money was used to set him up in business.*
2 to arrange or prepare something ◆ *They set the meeting up for 9 a.m. tomorrow.* ◆ *We have a little area set up for serving food.* ◆ *They set up the tents next to the river.*

set *sb* up
to trick someone into a situation in which it appears they have done something wrong ◆ *She denied using drugs and claimed she had been set up by the police.*

set upon *sb*/*sth*
to attack someone or something ◆ *I saw an old man set upon by muggers in an alley.* ◆ *Demonstrators wearing ski masks set upon a stopped police car.*

settle

settle down
to accept responsibilities and behave in a more regular way than you have in the past ◆ *Larry met his wife in San Antonio, where they have settled down and started a family.*

settle (*sb*) down
to get someone to behave more calmly ◆ *He was so upset that one of his brothers had to settle him down.* USAGE: often used as an order: *OK, class, settle down.*

settle down to *sth*
to give something all of your attention ◆ *I settled down to read about the festival and what I could do there.* USAGE: often said about a meal: *After work, we all settle down to a home-cooked dinner.*

settle for *sth*
to agree to or accept something, although it is not exactly what you want ◆ *Patients will have to settle for fewer tests because rising costs have made them too expensive.*

settle in
to begin to feel comfortable in a new place ◆ *When you start college, it takes a few weeks to settle in.*

settle into *sth*
to become comfortable in a new place or situation ◆ *Catherine had settled into their booth and was reading her menu.* ◆ *We settle into a routine of early morning workouts followed by lectures.* ◆ *The space shuttle settled into a 184-mile-high orbit.*

settle on *sth*, *also* settle upon *sth*
to make a decision or come to an agreement about something ◆ *My parents finally settled on my punishment – I would use my summer wages to pay for the repairs.* ◆ *The*

sew

a shadow of your former self

"You're so thin that you're just a shadow of your former self."

two sides have not yet settled on a price.

settle a score See at SCORE

settle *your* stomach See at STOMACH

when the dust settles See at DUST

sew

sew up *sth*
to remove all doubt about the successful result of something ♦ *Schall hopes to sew up the nomination for governor this week.* ♦ *The company hopes to have a deal sewn up by the end of the year.*

shack

shack up (with *sb*) slang
to live with and have a sexual relationship with someone you are not married to ♦ *I was surprised to hear you're shacking up with Kathy.* ♦ Related vocabulary **set up housekeeping** at HOUSEKEEPING

shades

shades of *sb/sth*
this suggests memories of another person or thing ♦ *The president's behavior suggests he has something to hide – shades of the Watergate scandal.*

ORIGIN: based on the meaning of **shade** (= spirit of a dead person) used esp. in literature

shadow

a shadow of *your/its* former self
a smaller, weaker, or less important form of someone or something ♦ *With most of its best players traded away, the team was reduced to a shadow of its former self.*

beyond the shadow of a doubt, *also* **without a shadow of a doubt**
so that it is obviously true ♦ *Letters in her father's own handwriting would prove his guilt beyond a shadow of a doubt.*

in the shadow of *sb*
receiving little attention because someone else is better known or more skillful ♦ *Tom was a good lawyer, but he was always in the shadow of his famous father.* USAGE:

often used after **live**: *Living in the shadow of a glamorous sister, Hilda was quiet and shy.*

in the shadow of *sth*
1 near something ♦ *Her house is located in the shadow of the state capitol.*
2 influenced by something bad that has happened or could happen ♦ *The children of the survivors lived their lives in the shadow of the Holocaust.* ♦ *The organization is trying to protect civil rights in the shadow of terrorism.*

shaft

get the shaft
to be treated very unfairly ♦ *Congress acted, and the average taxpayer once again got the shaft.*

shake

shake down *sb*, also **shake** *sb* **down**
to get money from someone by using threats ♦ *His crimes ranged from murder to shaking down gamblers.* ♦ *He claimed that a government official shook his company down for $10,000 in campaign contributions.*

shake off *sth*, also **shake** *sth* **off**
to free yourself from something ♦ *Investors failed to shake off worries about the economy.* ♦ *As she was running, she felt a pain in her left leg, but she hoped to shake it off if she slowed up.* USAGE: usually said about something unpleasant

shake up *sb*, also **shake** *sb* **up**
to upset someone ♦ *The kids were pretty shaken up by the accident.* ♦ *Patrick's death shook me up pretty badly.*

shake up *sth*, also **shake** *sth* **up**
to cause big changes in a situation or organization ♦ *The company announced that it would shake up top management and cut 1,000 jobs.* ♦ *Every new boss likes to shake things up a bit when they take over.*

more *sth* **than** *you* **can shake a stick at** See at STICK
shake *sb's* **hand** See at HAND
shake hands See at HANDS
shake *your* **head** See at HEAD
shake the foundations of *sth* See at FOUNDATIONS

shakes

no great shakes
not very good ♦ *He was a very creative chef but no great shakes at managing a business.*

shame

it's a crying shame esp. spoken
it is a great misfortune ♦ *It's a crying shame when someone has worked hard and then loses everything because of someone else's dishonesty.*

put *sb* **to shame**
to cause someone to be embarrassed ♦ *I thought I was in pretty good shape for hiking, but Astrid, who is in her 70s, put me to shame.*

shame on *you* esp. spoken
you should feel embarrassed by something you have done ♦ *Protesters chanted "shame on you" at the university's president.* ♦ *Shame on me for not checking the schedule and getting there half an hour late.*

shape

bent out of shape
very angry or upset ♦ *My boss ignored my comments, but I don't feel that it's worth getting all bent out of shape over it.*

shape up
1 to develop ♦ *The state of the economy is shaping up as a major political issue.* ♦ *Everyone's waiting to see how the new football season will shape up in September.*
2 to improve your behavior or performance ♦ *He promised me he was going to shape up and stay out of trouble.*
3 to get into better physical condition ♦ *The astronauts shape up be-*

fore a mission by working with small weights and doing exercises.

whip *sb/sth* into shape
to quickly improve someone or something ♦ *The district brought in a new principal to whip the school into shape.* ♦ *His crew includes a bunch of misfits whom he whips into shape in time to win the contest.* ♦ *These three new programs will help you whip your hard disk into shape.* USAGE: usually said about improvements that happen because of hard work

in any way, shape, or form See at WAY

shapes

all shapes and sizes
a large variety ♦ *Digital marketing includes banner ads of all shapes and sizes and e-mail, among other options.* USAGE: often used in the form **come in all shapes and sizes** (= exist in a large variety of types): *Investors come in all shapes and sizes.*

share

do *your* share
to do what is expected of you to help ♦ *Taxpayers in this town are already doing their share and more, and we're asking the state to do their part.* ♦ *With everybody on the team doing their share, it's fun to be a part of it.* ♦ Related vocabulary **do *your* bit** at BIT, **do *your* part** at PART

have *your* share of *sth*
to have enough of something ♦ *My husband and I have had our share of job changes and periods of unemployment in recent years.* USAGE: sometimes, for emphasis, used in the form **have more than your share** (= have too much): *This community has more than its share of kids in trouble.*

shave

close shave See **close call** at CALL

shebang

the whole shebang esp. spoken
all of something, including everything connected with it; = **the whole nine yards** ♦ *We've got offices all over the world, and we're tying the whole shebang together with a high-speed computer network.* ♦ *Anderson has explored the black experience in America's intellectual, cultural, and political life – the whole shebang.*

shelf

off the shelf
in a form that is ready to be used ♦ *Most of the technology needed can be bought off the shelf.* USAGE: usually used to show that something is not specially made for a particular use

put *sb* on the shelf
to cause someone not to be available ♦ *A sore left knee put him on the shelf for two weeks, and he has missed six games.*

put *sth* on the shelf
to delay something ♦ *The library's plan to show three films next week has been put on the shelf.*

shell

shell out *sth*
to pay money ♦ *The insurance giant estimates that in Texas alone it will have to shell out $85 million to settle these claims.* ♦ *How much does the company expect to shell out for a solution to the problem?* USAGE: usually said about large amounts of money

shine

take a shine to *sb*
to like someone immediately ♦ *Amy took a shine to Nick, but her friends weren't so sure he was the right guy for her.*

ship

a sinking ship
an organization that is failing ♦ *She says the school is a sinking ship,*

and has no money to hire additional teachers.

jump ship
to leave a job or activity suddenly ◆ *Although most of our employees are satisfied with their jobs, half of them would probably jump ship if something becomes available elsewhere.* ◆ *The original star of the TV series jumped ship after the first season.* USAGE: often said about someone who goes to work for another company

> ORIGIN: based on the literal meaning of **jump ship** (= to leave a ship without permission while it is temporarily in a port in the middle of a trip)

ship *sb/sth* **off to** *somewhere*, *also* **ship off** *sb/sth*
to send someone or something to a place ◆ *When Pauline was twelve, her father shipped her off to relatives in Baltimore.* ◆ *The kids were arrested, convicted, and shipped off to reform school.* ◆ *Students should ship off their applications well before the deadline.*

shirt

keep *your* **shirt on**
to stay calm ◆ *The meeting may be pretty unpleasant, so promise me you'll keep your shirt on.* ◆ Related vocabulary **keep** *your* **cool** at COOL

lose *your* **shirt**
to lose all the money you put into something ◆ *I lost my shirt because I didn't know anything about publishing at the time.* USAGE: usually said about money that was invested

shit

full of shit rude slang
completely wrong, false, or worthless; = **full of crap** ◆ *You don't know what you're talking about – you're full of shit!* ◆ Related vocabulary **full of it** at FULL

holy shit rude slang
what a surprise or how very unpleasant ◆ *Holy shit! The whole basement is flooded!*

in deep shit rude slang
in a lot of trouble ◆ *If you get caught carrying that stuff, you'll be in deep shit.*

no shit rude slang
1 something is very surprising and hard to believe ◆ *He's coming here tonight? No shit!*
2 the truth ◆ *This is no shit – we're going to have the money for you tomorrow.*

not give a shit (about *sb/sth***)** rude slang
to not be interested in someone or something; = **not give a damn (about** *sb/sth***)** ◆ *I don't give a shit what they do.* ◆ *For the most part they didn't give a shit about me.* USAGE: although almost always negative, sometimes used without **not**: *Who gives a shit about what she says?* ◆ *Nobody around here gives a shit about politics.*

the shit out of *you* rude slang
as much as possible ◆ *The cops had steel bats, and they beat the shit out of us.* ◆ *The mob of yelling, angry people scared the shit out of me.*

the shit hits the fan rude slang
extremely unpleasant things happen and become known ◆ *The company's busy season was upon them once more, and the shit was hitting the fan.* ◆ Related vocabulary *sth* **hits the fan** at FAN

tough shit rude slang
I have no sympathy ◆ *I know you don't want to go, but tough shit!* ◆ Related vocabulary **tough luck** at LUCK

a crock (of shit) See at CROCK

shivers

send shivers down *your* **spine**, *also* **send shivers up** *your* **spine**
to feel very frightened or excited ◆ *Here's a tale of medical incompetence that should send shivers down your spine.* ◆ Related vocabulary

shoe

make *your* hair stand on end at HAIR

shoe

the shoe is on the other foot
the situation is now the opposite of what it was before ◆ *Now that I don't smoke, the shoe is on the other foot and I don't want people smoking around me.*

shoes

fill *sb's* shoes, *also* **step into *sb's* shoes**
to do what someone else has done as well as they did ◆ *He was a great coach, and it's not going to be easy to get someone to fill his shoes.*

in *sb's* shoes
having the same experience as someone else ◆ *If I put myself in their shoes, I think I would have done just what they did.* ◆ *You're not alone – lots of people are in your shoes, looking for work.*

shoestring

on a shoestring
by using very little money ◆ *The theater company operates on a shoestring.*

shoot

shoot down *sth*, *also* **shoot *sth* down**
1 to destroy an aircraft or weapon in the sky by shooting it ◆ *In the movie, he pulls out a portable rocket launcher and shoots down the helicopter.* ◆ *If we detect an incoming missile, we must be able to shoot it down.*
2 to refuse to accept something ◆ *The baseball owners shot down a plan to add two more teams to each league.* ◆ *At a public meeting, residents shot down two different designs for rebuilding the area.*

shoot for *sth*
to try to achieve something ◆ *Tennessee's women's basketball team is shooting for another season of straight victories.*

shoot up
1 to increase very quickly in size or amount ◆ *The boy shot up two inches over the summer.* ◆ *Temperatures shot up into the mid-90s today.* ◆ *With new technology, productivity shot up.*
2 to rise quickly and forcefully ◆ *Flames were shooting up from the burning house.*

shoot up *sth*, *also* **shoot *sth* up**
1 slang ◆ to take an illegal drug by using a needle ◆ *Some athletes are suspected of shooting up steroids to improve their strength.* USAGE: also used in the form **shoot someone up** (= give someone a drug by using a needle): *Jim was the first one to shoot me up with heroin.*

ORIGIN: based on the medical meaning of **give a shot** (= give medicine using a needle)

2 to fire guns, causing great damage to a place ◆ *Old western movies usually have a scene where some bad guys ride in and shoot up the town.*

shoot daggers at *sb* See at DAGGERS

shoot from the hip See at HIP

shoot hoops See at HOOPS

shoot *yourself* in the foot See at FOOT

shoot *your* mouth off See at MOUTH

shoot the breeze See at BREEZE

shop

close up shop, *also* **shut up shop**
to stop doing business ◆ *Poulin says high taxes and global competition have forced him to close up shop.* ◆ Opposite **set up shop**

set up shop
to establish a business or an organization ◆ *Some companies have set up shop in other countries, like China.* ◆ *UN agencies have set up shop all over the world.* ◆ Opposite **close up shop**

shop around
to compare the price and quality of similar items before buying one ♦ *You should certainly shop around before buying a new computer.*

talk shop
to talk about work when not working ♦ *Two New York Yankee pitchers will be there to sign autographs and talk shop with fans.*

shore

shore up *sth*, *also* **shore** *sth* **up**
to make something stronger by supporting it ♦ *Part of the roof collapsed, and emergency workers had to shore up walls to prevent further damage.* ♦ *Central banks try to shore the economy up by lowering interest rates.*

short

for short
in a form of less length ♦ *The continuous connection to the Internet offered by the phone companies is called the Asymmetric Digital Subscriber Line, or ADSL for short.*

in short
briefly ♦ *In short, we have to decide whether to continue losing money or change the way we do business.* ♦ Related vocabulary **in brief** at BRIEF, **in a word** at WORD

nothing short of *sth*
strongly showing this quality; = **nothing less than** *sth* ♦ *She is nothing short of amazing in her latest movie.* USAGE: used to emphasize the quality mentioned

short for *sth*
as a less long form of a word or name ♦ *They call their baby Libby, short for Elizabeth.* ♦ *The group is known as MADD, short for Mothers Against Drunk Driving.*

short of *sth*
1 not having enough of something ♦ *Men, women, and children were forced from their homes and were desperately short of food and water.* ♦ Related vocabulary **shy of** *sth* at SHY
2 not including something ♦ *There has to be some sort of punishment, short of execution.*

short on *sth* **(and long on** *sth* **else)**
having too little of one thing and a lot of another ♦ *The opposing team was short on athleticism.* ♦ *Her dresses, made of cotton, were short on style and long on wear.* ♦ Related vocabulary **long on** *sth* **(and short on** *sth* **else)** at LONG

short shrift

get short shrift
to receive very little attention ♦ *Bus riders feel they've been getting short shrift from the transit agency for years, and they are angry about the new fare increase.*

give *sb/sth* **short shrift**, *also* **give short shrift to** *sb/sth*
to give very little attention to someone or something ♦ *Many historians have given women short shrift or ignored their role in events altogether.* ♦ *The town council gave short shrift to the suggestion to establish a homeless shelter.*

shot

a shot across the bow
a warning to stop doing something ♦ *The lawsuit is a shot across the bow to businesses that are competing unfairly.*

> ORIGIN: based on the military practice of aiming **a shot across the bow** (= a small explosion in front of a ship) to force it to stop

a shot in the arm
a strong positive influence ♦ *Winning this award is a big shot in the arm for our students.*

a shot in the dark
an attempt to do something without knowing much about it ♦ *When I applied for the scholarship, it was just a shot in the dark – I had no idea*

shots

how important and competitive it was.

give *sth* a shot
to make an attempt to do something; = **take a shot at *sth*** ♦ *Jason's father always thought he would be a great baseball player, and encouraged Jason to give it a shot.*

give *sth* your best shot
to try as hard as possible to achieve something ♦ *We gave it our best shot, but we still don't know what's wrong with the computer.*

like a shot
very quickly and eagerly ♦ *If I had the chance to go to Paris, I'd be there like a shot.*

not by a long shot
not at all ♦ *"Do you think it's as good as her last movie?" "No, not by a long shot."* USAGE: sometimes used in the form **not do something by a long shot**: *We haven't eliminated the disease by a long shot.*

take a shot at *sth*, *also* have a shot at *sth*
to make an attempt to do something; = **give *sth* a shot** ♦ *I wasn't sure of the answer, but I thought I'd take a shot at it anyway.* ♦ *He's proven himself to be a talented actor and now he's having a shot at directing.* ♦ Related vocabulary **give *sth* a whirl** at WHIRL

shots

call the shots
to make the important decisions ♦ *The company was more successful when just one or two people were calling the shots.* ♦ Related vocabulary **call the tune** at TUNE, **run the show** at SHOW

shoulder

a shoulder to cry on
someone who gives you sympathy when you are upset ♦ *My father had just died and I needed a shoulder to cry on.*

put *your* shoulder to the wheel
to work hard at something ♦ *You'd be surprised what you can get done when you really put your shoulder to the wheel.*

stand shoulder to shoulder
to support one another during a difficult time ♦ *The whole town stood shoulder to shoulder while the rescue workers struggled to free the trapped miners.*

a chip on *your* shoulder See at CHIP

give *sb/sth* the cold shoulder See at COLD SHOULDER

shoulders

on *sb's* shoulders, *also* **on the shoulders of *sb***
as a personal responsibility for someone ♦ *A district attorney has an awful burden on his shoulders.* ♦ *The success or failure of the entire peace agreement will rest on the shoulders of the peace keepers.*

rub shoulders with *sb*
to meet or be with someone socially; = **rub elbows with *sb*** ♦ *The receptions offered a chance for business people to rub shoulders with business people from other countries.*

shrug *your* shoulders
to not care or feel unable to do anything ♦ *The reason most people aren't excited about the election is that both candidates leave them shrugging their shoulders.* ♦ Related vocabulary **shrug *sth* off** at SHRUG

> ORIGIN: based on the literal meaning of **shrug your shoulders** (= to move your shoulders up as you move your head down to show you do not care or are discouraged)

square *your* shoulders
to show determination and a lack of fear ♦ *When the judge asked her if she was guilty or not guilty, she squared her shoulders, looked the judge in the eye, and said, "Not guilty."*

head and shoulders above *sb/sth* See at HEAD

show

run the show
to be in charge of an organization or an activity ◆ *Although the new president of our club has not taken office yet, she's running the show already.* ◆ Related vocabulary **call the shots** at SHOTS, **call the tune** at TUNE

show *sb* around *somewhere*
to lead someone through a place ◆ *She insisted on showing us around Amsterdam.* ◆ *Guides were assigned to show new students around the campus.*

show off
to do something to attract attention to yourself ◆ *He shows off all the time, and you wonder if he's ever just a regular, real person.*

show off *sth*, also show *sth* off
to cause something to be seen and admired ◆ *The ballet music gives the Kirov's male dancers a chance to show off their astonishing leaps.* ◆ *She was wearing a deep-purple dress that showed off her slim figure.* ◆ *Oscar was so proud of the car that he couldn't wait to get to school to show it off.*

show up
1 to arrive for a gathering or event ◆ *We waited all day and he never showed up.* ◆ *Demonstrators also have regularly shown up in front of her home.*
2 to appear or be seen ◆ *The virus does not show up in blood tests.* ◆ Related vocabulary **come up** 2 at COME, **crop up** at CROP

show *sb* up
to do something that embarrasses someone or makes them seem stupid ◆ *He's always boasting about how much money he's earned – like he's trying to show you up.*

steal the show
to get all the attention and praise at an event or performance ◆ *She has a small part, but she steals the show from the lead actors.*

***sth* goes to show (you)** See at GOES

have *sth* to show for *sth* See at HAVE

show *your* face See at FACE

show *your* mettle See at METTLE

show *sb* the door See at DOOR

show *sb* the ropes See **learn the ropes** at ROPES

show (*sb*) the way See at WAY

show *sb's*/*sth's* true colors See at COLORS

show *sb* who's boss See at BOSS

shrug

shrug *sth* off, also shrug off *sth*
to act as if something is unimportant or not a problem ◆ *Although constantly troubled by a lack of money, he was able to shrug it off with a joke.* ◆ *The runner has been trying hard to shrug off a back injury that doesn't seem to go away.* ◆ Related vocabulary **shrug *your* shoulders** at SHOULDERS

shuffle

lost in the shuffle
ignored or forgotten ◆ *In conflicts between doctors and insurance companies, patients' needs may be lost in the shuffle.* USAGE: often used in the form **get lost in the shuffle**: *Maybe your name got lost in the shuffle when we typed the list.* ◆ See illustration, page 372

ORIGIN: based on the idea of losing a playing card when the cards are **shuffled** (= moved around)

shut

shut down
to stop working or operating ◆ *If the air conditioning system fails to turn on, the computers will overheat and shut down.* ◆ *The radio station shut down all broadcasting last week.*

shut off (*sth*), also shut *sth* off
to stop the operation of a machine or system ◆ *Did you shut off the light in the bedroom?* ◆ *To repair the leak they have to shut the water off in the entire building.*

lost in the shuffle

"I'm sorry, but I think your order must have gotten lost in the shuffle."

shut *sb/sth* **off**, *also* **shut off** *sb/sth*
to separate someone or something from others ◆ *A major interstate highway shuts the area off from the rest of the city.* ◆ *When her husband died she shut herself off from everyone.* ◆ *They just wanted to shut off all the people who had serious mental illnesses.*

shut *sb* **out**, *also* **shut out** *sb*
1 to prevent someone from being a part of something ◆ *She shut him out of her world and had nothing to do with him.* ◆ *A group of African-American lawyers charged that the law firm shut them out.* ◆ *Movies like his are so unusual that they're basically shut out of consideration for an Oscar.*
2 to prevent a competitor from scoring any points ◆ *The Braves shut out the Dodgers today, 7–0.*

shut out *sth*, *also* **shut** *sth* **out**
1 to prevent something from entering a place ◆ *The thick glass windows shut out most of the traffic noise.* ◆ *My eyes can't stand bright light, so I keep the curtains closed to shut the sunlight out.*
2 to not think about something ◆ *She can't shut out the memory of the accident.*

shut (*sb***) up**
to stop talking or making noise, or to make someone do this ◆ *I wish you'd shut up and listen.* ◆ *He called me a fool, and that shut me up.*

shut *sb/sth* **up**
to keep people or animals in a separate place ◆ *Every day she went up to a little room on the third floor where she shut herself up to work.* ◆ *At night we always kept the dog shut up in its cage.*

shy

shy away from *sb*
to avoid someone ◆ *She shied away from reporters during her brief visit to this country.*

shy away from *sth/doing sth*
to avoid something ◆ *I tend to shy away from big guitar solos on records.* ◆ *At first, some companies shied away from selling merchandise on the Internet, but not for long.*

shy of *sth*
having less of something than is needed or expected ◆ *The bill was four votes shy of a majority.* ◆ *He was a large man, just shy of six feet tall.* ◆ Related vocabulary **short of** *sth* 1 at SHORT

sic
sic *sb/sth* **on** *sb*
to cause someone or something to attack someone ◆ *I'm gonna sic Uncle Steve on you kids if you don't behave.* ◆ *He tried to sic the agency on her to draw attention away from himself.*

> ORIGIN: based on the literal meaning of **sic** (= to order a dog to attack)

sick
sick (and tired) of *sb/sth*
annoyed by someone or something; = **fed up (with** *sb/sth*) ◆ *They visited so often that she was sick of them by the end of the summer.* ◆ *I'm sick and tired of hearing the same old excuses!* USAGE: usually said about something that you have accepted for too long ◆ Related vocabulary **sick to death of** *sth* at DEATH
as sick as a dog See at DOG
call in sick See at CALL
make *you* **sick** See at MAKE
sick at heart See at HEART
sick to death of *sth* See at DEATH
sick to *your* **stomach** See at STOMACH

side
come down on the side of *sb/sth*
to support someone or something ◆ *The government came down on the side of oil companies that want to drill on public lands.* ◆ Related vocabulary **come down on** *sb/sth* at COME
err on the side of *sth*
to choose an action that may be too extreme ◆ *If we're not sure what's needed, let's err on the side of being too prepared.* USAGE: usually used in the form **err on the side of caution**: *I decided to err on the side of caution and spend less than my full allowance.*
get up on the wrong side of (the) bed, *also* **wake up on the wrong side of (the) bed**
to begin the day feeling unhappy and uncomfortable ◆ *I got up on the wrong side of bed yesterday, and everything that could go wrong did!* ◆ Related vocabulary **out of sorts** at SORTS
(just) this side of *sth*
almost but not quite the quality mentioned ◆ *He was just this side of being bubbly when I spoke to him.*
(just) to be on the safe side
so that you can prevent something unpleasant from happening ◆ *Just to be on the safe side, ask your doctor to test your iron levels.*
on *sb's* **good side**, *also* **on the good side of** *sb*
in a situation in which someone is pleased with you ◆ *It's a good idea to get on your manager's good side when you start a new job.* USAGE: the opposite meaning is expressed by **on someone's bad side** (= in a situation in which someone is angry or annoyed with you): *You don't want get on her bad side – she can be really mean to people she doesn't like.*
on *your* **side**
helping you or giving you an advantage ◆ *To get this project approved, you'll need to have Richard on your side.* ◆ *I thought of a way to get the older boys on my side.* ◆ Related vocabulary **time is on** *your* **side** at TIME
on the side
1 in addition to your regular job or activities ◆ *He drives a bus, but he's a tour guide on the side.*
2 served separately but intended to be eaten together ◆ *I'll have a green salad with dressing on the side.*

sidelines

on the side of the angels
supporting what is kind, right, or good ◆ *She was on the side of the angels even though it was neither profitable nor popular.*

on the wrong side of the law
in a situation in which you are doing something illegal ◆ *Being on the wrong side of the law is not unusual for many people in this part of town.*

side with *sb*
to agree with or support someone; = **take *sb*'s side** ◆ *When workers have sued companies for violating their privacy, judges have usually sided with the employer.* USAGE: the opposite meaning is expressed by **side against someone** (= to disagree with or not support someone): *As much as I hate to side against a friend, I feel she is wrong.* ◆ Related vocabulary **take sides** at SIDES

take *sb*'s side, *also* **take the side of *sb***
to agree with or support someone; = **side with *sb*** ◆ *I took Bob's side when I heard his account of the events.* ◆ Related vocabulary **take sides** at SIDES

the bright side, *also* **a bright side**
the good parts or features of a mostly unpleasant situation ◆ *There's a bright side to this – at least you can learn from your mistake.* USAGE: often used in the form **look on the bright side**: *They tried to look on the bright side when their flight was rerouted to another city.*

the other side of the coin
a different and usually opposite idea about a situation ◆ *Being a parent is such a huge responsibility, but the other side of the coin is that it is one of the most exciting and enjoyable things you can do.* ◆ Related vocabulary **two sides of the same coin** at SIDES

the wrong side of the tracks, *also* **the other side of the tracks**
the poor area of a city or town ◆ *She was brought up on the wrong side of the tracks in a small southern town.* USAGE: sometimes used in the forms **the wrong side of town** or **the wrong side of the street**: *Her family was clearly from the wrong side of town.*

> ORIGIN: based on the idea that a poor area is often divided from the rest of a town by railroad tracks

this side of *sb/sth*
other than someone or something ◆ *Nobody this side of a Roman emperor wants athletes to die for the sake of entertainment.* ◆ *Her sound is as funky as anything this side of James Brown.*

a thorn in *sb*'s/*sth*'s side See at THORN

time is on *your* side See at TIME

sidelines

on the sidelines
not actively involved in something ◆ *The majority of Western countries decided to stay on the sidelines during the crisis.*

> ORIGIN: based on the literal meaning of **sidelines** (= the lines that mark the outer edges of a playing field)

sides

take sides
to support one person, group, or opinion over another ◆ *My mother never took sides when my brother and I argued.* USAGE: usually refers to an argument or fight ◆ Related vocabulary **side with *sb*** at SIDE, **take *sb*'s side** at SIDE

talk out of both sides of *your* mouth, *also* **speak out of both sides of *your* mouth**
to say different things to different people about the same subject ◆ *How can we trust him when we know he talks out of both sides of his mouth?*

two sides of the same coin
different but closely related fea-

tures of one idea ◆ *Rewards and punishments are two sides of the same coin – both are used to control people, and neither works very well.* ◆ Related vocabulary **the other side of the coin** at SIDE

sigh

breathe a sigh of relief
to feel comfortable again after worrying about something ◆ *Coastal residents breathed a sigh of relief when the hurricane was downgraded to a tropical storm.* ◆ *Her children breathed a quiet sigh of relief when she made arrangements to get help.*

sight

a sight for sore eyes
something you are happy to see ◆ *The many taxis in the city are a sight for sore eyes when it's raining.*

at first sight
when someone or something is seen for the first time ◆ *For my brother and sister-in-law, it was love at first sight.* ◆ *At first sight I thought the test was easy, but there were some tricky questions.* ◆ Related vocabulary **at first glance** at GLANCE, **at first blush** at BLUSH

catch sight of *sb/sth*
to see someone or something only for a moment ◆ *I caught sight of someone with red hair and knew it was you.*

know *sb/sth* **by sight**
to recognize someone or something ◆ *I've never spoken to him, but I know him by sight.* USAGE: usually used to suggest that you know what someone looks like but not what type of character someone has

lose sight of *sth*
to stop considering something ◆ *Members of the peace-keeping force have lost sight of the fact that they are here to help people.* ◆ *Despite the very personal nature of her work, she never lost sight of the larger community her work would benefit.*

USAGE: usually said about an important fact or idea

not a pretty sight
1 unpleasant to look at ◆ *A state trooper guarding the crash site said, "It's not a pretty sight out there."*
2 very bad or unpleasant ◆ *The first reviews of the new on-line magazine are in, and it's not a pretty sight.*

not stand the sight of *sb/sth*
to strongly dislike someone or something ◆ *Most people can't stand the sight of blood.* ◆ *Right now, I can't stand the sight of you.* USAGE: sometimes used in the form **not bear the sight of someone or something**: *Ever since he insulted me, I can't bear the sight of him.*

on sight
as soon as someone or something is seen ◆ *The law now requires all pigeons in the area to be shot on sight.* ◆ *Even very young children can recognize certain words on sight.*

out of sight
at a very high level ◆ *Medical costs are out of sight.* ◆ *Daytime temperatures in the desert will be out of sight by mid-June.*

out of sight, out of mind
not able to be seen and so not thought about ◆ *Some people working at home start to feel they are out of sight, out of mind as far as their boss is concerned.*

sight unseen
without seeing or examining something first ◆ *He purchased the Longfellow manuscript sight unseen from a collector in Houston.*

love at first sight See at LOVE
no end in sight (to *sth***)** See at END

sights

ORIGIN
These idioms are based on the literal meaning of **sights** (= the part of a gun through which you look to help you aim at something).

in *your* **sights**
1 in a situation in which you will

sign

attack ◆ *He has already written about two of the largest insurance companies, and made no secret that he has other insurers in his sights.* **2** in a situation in which you intend to get or achieve something ◆ *He settled for the bronze medal but still had the world record in his sights.*

lower *your* sights, *also* **set *your* sights lower**
to accept something that is not as good as what you originally wanted ◆ *With so few jobs around she's had to lower her sights.* USAGE: the opposite meaning is expressed by **raise your sights** (= to try to get something better than you had originally expected)

see the sights
to visit or look at places that are famous or popular ◆ *After we checked into the hotel we went out immediately to see the sights.*

set *your* sights (on *doing sth*), *also* **have *your* sights set (on doing something)**
to decide what you want to get or achieve something ◆ *I think they set their sights too high – they'll never find someone for the job who has all those skills.* ◆ *Once she sets her sights on something, she won't stop until she gets it.* ◆ *I hear she has her sights set on becoming a journalist.*

sign

a sign of the times
something that shows what a society is like now ◆ *Young people are so rude, but I guess it's just a sign of the times.* USAGE: most often refers to negative characteristics

sign away *sth*, *also* **sign *sth* away**
to give up your claim to something by writing your name on a document; = **sign over *sth*** ◆ *He tricked her into signing away the property that she intended to leave to her friend.* ◆ *You're signing your rights away when you sign that form.* USAGE: sometimes used in the form **sign your life away** (= give up all your rights): *It felt like we had to sign our lives away to get a loan from the bank.*

sign in
to write your name on an official list when entering a place ◆ *Messengers are required to sign in at the front desk.* USAGE: sometimes used in the form **sign someone in** (= to write someone's name on an official list when they enter a place): *An elegantly dressed young woman signed us in at the door.* ◆ Opposite **sign out**

sign off
to end a television or radio broadcast ◆ *Both news programs came on the air at 4:36 p.m. and both signed off at 4:59 p.m.* ◆ *What will the network air on Tuesdays now that one of its most popular programs is signing off?*

sign off (on *sth*)
to officially agree to or support something ◆ *Mary has to sign off on any expenses over $2,500.* ◆ *A judge must sign off on a search of anyone's property.* ◆ *If all parties sign off, the settlement would end eight years of court battles.* USAGE: often used when someone agrees to something by putting their signature on an official document

sign out
to write your name on an official list when leaving a place ◆ *Make sure you sign out if you leave the office after 8 p.m.* USAGE: sometimes used in the form **sign someone out** (= to write someone's name on an official list when they leave a place): *Can you sign me out, Mitch?* ◆ Opposite **sign in**

sign over *sth*, *also* **sign *sth* over**
to give up your rights to something by writing your name on a document; = **sign away *sth*** ◆ *He signed over his death benefits in exchange for cash.* ◆ *She agreed to sign the deed over to me.*

sign (sb) up, *also* sign up sb
to join or invite someone to join a group or organization ◆ *Kathy signed up for the soccer team this year.* ◆ *The team signed him up for two years.* ◆ *Local officials worked to sign up students to the summer jobs program.* USAGE: often used when someone puts their signature on an official document

sign on the dotted line See at LINE

signal
send a signal
to do something that is likely to influence someone's attitudes or behavior; = **send a message** ◆ *The people in Pennsylvania sent a signal in this election that they wanted health-care reform.* ◆ *Making polluters pay to recycle old electronics products sends a strong signal to the companies to change the way they do business.* USAGE: said about actions whether they are intentional or not

signed
signed and sealed
1 having official approval ◆ *We won't get paid until the contract is signed and sealed.* USAGE: usually refers to an agreement or contract
2 completed or made final ◆ *He'll make a decision next week, but until then the matter isn't signed and sealed.*

> ORIGIN: based on a literal meaning of **sign and seal** (= to put your signature and an official mark on a document that shows it is legal)

sin
live in sin
to live with and have a sexual relationship with someone without being married ◆ *They know that others their age view their relationship as living in sin.* USAGE: often considered to be an old-fashioned phrase

since
since when
for how long have you believed ◆ *Since when do you have the right to tell me what to do?* ◆ *But really, since when is $250 too expensive for a nice watch?* USAGE: used in the form of a question when you do not believe a particular attitude or situation is right or true

sing
sing out (sth)
1 to shout or call loudly ◆ *He'd bring his daughters hot chocolate in their tent, singing out, "Time to get up!"*
2 slightly formal to make known ◆ *Adler tried in a scholarly way to sing out the joys of studying philosophy.*

sing the blues See at BLUES

sing sb's/sth's praises See at PRAISES

single
single out sb/sth, *also* single sb/sth out
to choose someone or something for special attention ◆ *Rosa was singled out by the teacher because her art project was so creative.* ◆ *I don't know why they singled it out, but my report was severely criticized at the meeting.*

siphon
siphon off sth, *also* siphon sth off
to take something that was intended for someone or something else ◆ *The dictator and his close friends siphoned off up to 20 percent of the annual budget.* ◆ *The donated food was mostly siphoned off and sold, while the needy got almost nothing.* USAGE: sometimes used without **off**: *A third-party candidate siphoned southern support.* ◆ *She siphoned more than $15,000 from a patient's trust fund.*

> ORIGIN: based on the literal meaning of **siphon** (= a tube used to move liquid from one container to another)

sit

not sit well (with *sb*)
to be difficult for someone to agree with or accept ◆ *The idea of declaring war does not sit well with many voters.* ◆ *Having the state's future decided in Washington, D.C., doesn't sit well with the people of Alaska.* USAGE: sometimes used in the form **not sit right with someone**: *Hiring more federal workers wouldn't sit right with conservatives.*

sit back
to stop being active ◆ *We haven't had many opportunities to sit back and talk to each other.* ◆ *We're not so good that we can afford to just tell people we're the greatest and then sit back.*

sit back and *do sth*
to take no action and allow something to happen ◆ *You can't just sit back and let them close down the library.* ◆ *Americans shouldn't just sit back and allow this technology to run their lives.*

sit (idly) by (and *do sth*)
to take no action ◆ *I felt we simply couldn't sit by and see the peace process threatened.* ◆ *We can't afford to sit idly by while dangerous people threaten our way of life.*

sit in (for *sb*)
to do someone's job or fulfill a responsibility for them ◆ *The vice president will sit in for the president at today's meeting.* ◆ *Their drummer was sick so they asked if I could sit in.*

sit in (on *sth*)
to go to a group event without being officially involved ◆ *Do you mind if I sit in on your class?*

sit through *sth*
to stay until the end of something ◆ *It's hard for little kids to sit through a whole baseball game.* USAGE: often said about something you do not enjoy: *We had to sit through another boring lecture.*

sit tight
to wait patiently and take no action ◆ *You just sit tight while I go get help.*

sit up
to stay awake past the time that you usually go to sleep ◆ *We sat up talking half the night.* ◆ *Many nights I sat up until dawn, trying to get my term papers finished on time.*

sit on *your* hands See at HANDS

sit in judgment (of *sb*) See at JUDGMENT

sit in judgment (of *sth*) See at JUDGMENT

sit up and take notice See at NOTICE

sitting

at one sitting, *also* **in one sitting**
during a short period of time ◆ *A month's supply of that drug taken at one sitting would kill you.* ◆ *I read the book in one sitting and couldn't get to sleep after I finished it.*

sitting pretty
in a good situation ◆ *She's sitting pretty as one of the music world's fastest-rising stars.* ◆ *These investments can provide cash to keep you sitting pretty once you retire.*

situation

a no-win situation
a condition in which all possible results are bad for the people involved ◆ *If she doesn't do anything, the North Side will be unhappy, and if she does do something, the South Side will be unhappy. Either way she's in a no-win situation.*

six

six of one, (and) half a dozen of the other
two things are almost the same or equal ◆ *I also compared the two stereos, and in most respects it's six of one, half a dozen of the other.*

> ORIGIN: based on the idea that **half a dozen** (= half of 12) is equal to **six**

six feet under See at FEET

size

cut *sb/sth* **down to size**
to make someone or something less important or detailed ◆ *When he started the job he thought he knew everything, but we soon cut him down to size.* ◆ *Sometimes we have to cut our grand dreams down to size.*

size up *sb/sth*, *also* **size** *sb/sth* **up**
to examine someone or something so you can make a judgment about them ◆ *After sizing up the opposition, Abe suggested a strategy.* ◆ *Warren looked the man over, trying to size him up.*

try *sth* **(on) for size**
to test something so you can form an opinion about it ◆ *I don't think everyone would be happy working here, but you should try it on for size and see if it's right for you.*

> ORIGIN: based on the literal meaning of **try on something** (= put on clothes to see if they fit and look good)

skeleton

a skeleton in the/*sb's* **closet**
a secret that would cause embarrassment if it were known ◆ *People almost always have skeletons in their closets, parts of their lives they don't want to reveal.*

sketch

sketch out *sth*, *also* **sketch in** *sth*
to describe something in a general way ◆ *Dean sketched out a rough plan of where we should go and what we should see while we were there.* ◆ *The president sent the defense secretary to the Senate today to sketch in details of the program.*

> ORIGIN: based on the literal meaning of **sketch** (= to draw quickly and with only a few details)

skids

hit the skids
to fail ◆ *His career really hit the skids after his divorce.* USAGE: often used in the form **on the skids** (= failing): *I can't believe that a whole industry is on the skids.*

skim

skim off *sth*, *also* **skim** *sth* **off**
to take something valuable ◆ *The colleges with very high standards skim off the best high school graduates.* ◆ *State and local governments skim tax money off the company's profits.*

> ORIGIN: based on the literal meaning of **skim off** (= to remove something floating on a liquid)

skin

get under *your* **skin**
to annoy you very much ◆ *He really got under my skin when he said women were bad drivers.*

(have) a thick skin
able to ignore personal criticism ◆ *People will tell you they don't like your clothes or your voice or the color of your eyes, so you need to have a thick skin to survive.* ◆ *During the two years he was the spokesperson for the police, he developed a very thick skin.*

it's no skin off *your* **nose**
it does not matter to you ◆ *I don't care if he doesn't want to come to the wedding. It's no skin off my nose.*

make *your* **skin crawl**
to be very frightening or disgusting ◆ *Just thinking about the weird way he talked made her skin crawl.*

soaked to the skin
to be extremely wet ◆ *I forgot my umbrella and got soaked to the skin when I had to go out this afternoon.*

under the skin
as part of your basic character ◆ *They look like two people who would have nothing to do with each other, but under the skin, they have some things in common that surprise even them.*

skip

skip it
do not worry about it ◆ *"Why is New York called the Empire State?" "What did you say?" "Skip it – it's not important."* ◆ Related vocabulary **never mind (*sb/sth*)** at MIND

> ORIGIN: based on the literal meaning of **skip something** (= to not have or do something)

skip out (on *sb*)
to suddenly leave someone ◆ *Our roommate skipped out on us just before the rent was due.*

skip out (on *sth*), *also* **skip out (of *sth*)**
to avoid something ◆ *He's been skipping out on hockey practice to go skateboarding.*

skip over *sb/sth*
to omit or not choose someone or something ◆ *I skipped over the boring parts of the exhibition.* ◆ *The director skipped over me when choosing a managing editor.*

sky

the sky's the limit, *also* **the sky is the limit**
there is no limit ◆ *Smaller sailboats can be reasonably priced, but for bigger boats the sky's the limit.*

out of a clear blue sky See **out of the blue** at BLUE

pie in the sky See at PIE

slack

cut *sb* some slack esp. spoken
to give someone additional freedom ◆ *I'm going to cut you some slack. Because it's the last day of classes, we don't have to talk anything serious today.* ◆ *If you and your kids don't agree about their futures, cut them some slack – explain your views, but don't try to force them to agree.*

pick up the slack, *also* **take up the slack**
to do something when someone else cannot or will not do it ◆ *With our best player injured, other players picked up the slack.* ◆ *Who will take up the slack when our grant money runs out?*

slack off
1 to work less hard than is usual or necessary ◆ *Workers tend to slack off on Mondays and Fridays.*
2 to become less severe or extreme ◆ *If this rain would slack off, we could finish the work outside.*

slap

a slap in the face
an insult ◆ *She considered it a real slap in the face when she wasn't invited to join us.*

a slap on the wrist
a gentle warning or light punishment ◆ *I got a slap on the wrist for arriving late again.* USAGE: sometimes used in the form **slap someone on the wrist**: *Instead of firing him, she only slapped him on the wrist.*

slap *sb/sth* down, *also* **slap down *sb/sth***
to refuse to accept someone's plan or idea ◆ *The judge slapped down every objection raised by the defense attorney.* ◆ *They applied for a permit and the building department slapped them down.*

a slap on the back See **a pat on the back** at PAT

slate

wipe the slate clean
to forget all past problems or mistakes and start something again ◆ *Rogers hoped he could wipe the slate clean and forget about his failed business.* USAGE: also used in the form **have a clean slate**: *She wanted to have a clean slate to start with.*

sleep

go to sleep
1 to start sleeping ◆ *There was too much noise for me to go to sleep.*
2 to lose all feeling in a hand or leg after being in one position for too

long ◆ *Sometimes my hand goes to sleep if I rest my head on it.*

lose sleep (over *sb/sth***)**
to be worried and unable to relax because of something ◆ *An asteroid could hit the earth, but it's not something you should lose sleep over.*

put *sb* **to sleep**
1 to bore someone very much ◆ *I tried reading one of her novels, but it just put me to sleep.* ◆ *All those technical discussions put everyone to sleep.*
2 to help someone sleep ◆ *The sound of the crickets puts me to sleep every night.*

put *sth* **to sleep**
to kill an animal medically; = **put** *sth* **down** ◆ *Mitzie is an old, sick cat, and I think we may have to put her to sleep.*

sleep around
to have sex with a lot of different people ◆ *Just because I'm an actor doesn't mean I sleep around.*

sleep *sth* **off**
to sleep until something stops having an effect on you ◆ *She slept off the effects of the medicine.* USAGE: often used in the form **sleep it off**: *He's got a terrible headache and probably needs to sleep it off.*

sleep on it
to wait before making an important decision ◆ *Don't give me an answer now – sleep on it and we can talk some more later in the week.*

sleep over
to stay the night in someone else's home ◆ *If you don't want to drive home this late at night, you're welcome to sleep over.* ◆ Related vocabulary **stay over** at STAY

sleep with *sb*, also **sleep together**
to have sex with someone; = **go to bed with** *sb* ◆ *He was sleeping with his secretary.* ◆ *Her husband and her sister were sleeping together, so no wonder she left him!*

not sleep a wink See at WINK
sleep like a log See at LOG

sleeve

sth up *your* **sleeve**
something secret you can use ◆ *If this plan doesn't work out I've still got a few ideas up my sleeve.* USAGE: often used in the forms **the card up your sleeve** or **the ace up your sleeve** (= a secret advantage you can use): *That recommendation from my teacher was the ace up my sleeve.*

wear *sth* **on** *your* **sleeve**
to make your feelings or beliefs known to everyone ◆ *Some people feel the need to wear their patriotism on their sleeve.* USAGE: often used in the form **wear your heart on your sleeve** (= to make your emotions known to others): *I don't like wearing my heart on my sleeve.*

sleeves

roll up *your* **sleeves**
to prepare for hard work ◆ *After the election, the mayor rolled up his sleeves and began immediately to put his promises into action.* ◆ See illustration, page 382

> ORIGIN: based on the idea that people often literally **roll up their sleeves** before doing difficult physical work

slightest

not in the slightest
not in any way; = **not in the least**
◆ *The whole stupid argument didn't interest me in the slightest.*

slings

slings and arrows
unpleasant, negative attacks ◆ *He was surprised by the slings and arrows directed at him by several economists.*

> ORIGIN: from the phrase "the slings and arrows of outrageous fortune" in Shakespeare's play "Hamlet"

slip

roll up your sleeves

There's a lot to do – I guess it's time to roll up my sleeves and get busy.

slip

give *sb* the slip
to escape from someone who is watching or following you ◆ *Reporters kept trying to follow the agents, and the agents drove in circles trying to give them the slip.*

slip away
1 to leave quickly and quietly ◆ *On the last night of conference, I decided to slip away for a few hours.* ◆ Related vocabulary **duck out (of somewhere)** at DUCK
2 to be no longer available ◆ *We're trying to keep the tradition alive, but it's starting to slip away.* ◆ *I let a great opportunity slip away.*
3 to slowly become less strong or able ◆ *She found her health rapidly slipping away.* ◆ *Every day a little more of his strength slips away.*
4 to die ◆ *The doctors worked quickly, but the old man was slipping away.*

slip into *sth*, also slip *sth* on
to put on clothing quickly and easily ◆ *Nancy slipped into her pajamas.* ◆ *Don't you think you'd better slip something on before you go to the door?*

slip off
to leave quickly and quietly ◆ *After lunch, Frank slipped off for a short nap.*

slip off *sth*, also slip out of *sth*
to remove clothing quickly and easily ◆ *Before I knew it he had slipped out of his shirt and put his arm around me.* ◆ *She slipped her gloves off and set them on the table.*

slip out
1 to leave quickly and quietly ◆ *I'll try to slip out at lunchtime and see if I can find her.*
2 to unintentionally become known ◆ *It slipped out during her interview that she had been fired from her last job.*

slip up
to make a mistake ◆ *It was unusual for him to slip up that way and forget a meeting.*

let *sb* slip through *your* fingers
See at FINGERS

let *sth* slip through *your* fingers
See at FINGERS

let *sth* **slip** See at LET

slip *your* **mind** See at MIND

slippery slope
on a slippery slope
in a situation that is likely to become more difficult or complicated ◆ *We started arguing, and then we got on the slippery slope of what's fair and what's not fair.* ◆ *So far, we have taken only the first few steps toward a society in which different people would have different rights, but we are on a slippery slope.* USAGE: sometimes used without **on**: *Where does this slippery slope end?*

slough
slough off *sth*, also **slough** *sth* **off**
to ignore something or behave as if it was unimportant ◆ *Politicians sloughed off public anger over the hospital cutbacks until several newspapers ran articles about it.* ◆ *He wrecked the car and then tried to slough it off like it was nothing.*

slug
slug it out
to compete against someone or something for first or highest position ◆ *Will the rest of the country find these teams interesting enough to watch them slug it out on TV for seven games?* ◆ *Two new mystery novels are slugging it out in the bookstores.* ◆ Related vocabulary **duke it out** at DUKE, **fight it out** 2 at FIGHT

> ORIGIN: based on the literal meaning of **slug it out** (= to fight, esp. by hitting with the hands)

sly
on the sly
secretly ◆ *She's been going out with him on the sly.*

smack
smack of *sth*
to have some of the characteristics or qualities of something ◆ *The book smacks of having been written by a committee rather than an author with a point of view.* USAGE: often said about a negative characteristic or quality, as in the example

smile
wipe the smile off *your* **face**, also **wipe that smile off** *your* **face**
to stop looking happy or pleased ◆ *You'll feel so good, you won't be able to wipe the smile off your face.*

smiles
all smiles
very happy ◆ *My boss has been all smiles lately, but I keep wondering why!*

smoke
blow smoke
to deceive others ◆ *He wanted everyone to believe he had a lot of experience, but I think he was just blowing smoke.*

go up in smoke
to be wasted ◆ *The research project was canceled, and five years of hard work went up in smoke.* ◆ Related vocabulary **go down in flames** at FLAMES

holy smoke
what a surprise ◆ *Holy smoke! Look at all of those geese!*

smoke and mirrors
something that is meant to confuse or deceive people ◆ *Is this crisis just so much smoke and mirrors, or is it true that the government will run out of money?* USAGE: usually involving a large organization rather than only one person

smoke *sb* **out**
to force someone to stop hiding ◆ *He didn't just walk into the police station and surrender, we had to smoke him out of hiding.* ◆ *To prevent such attacks, you have to smoke out the bad guys before they reach their targets.*

smoke out *sth*
to find something ◆ *The company*

smooth

is trying to smoke out a buyer for its weaker divisions.

where there's smoke, there's fire
if it looks like something is wrong, something probably is wrong ♦ *People like to think where there's smoke, there's fire, so they will always believe you were involved even if you weren't.*

smooth

smooth out *sth*, also **smooth** *sth* **out**
to make differences smaller ♦ *The two countries are working hard to smooth out their disagreements.* ♦ *A monthly average of sales smooths the highs and lows out and gives a more accurate idea of business activity.*

> ORIGIN: based on the literal meaning of **smooth out** (= to make regular).

smooth over *sth*, also **smooth** *sth* **over**
to make problems seem less serious ♦ *He's on a three-day visit to smooth over a crisis.* ♦ *They failed to agree on the main issue, and he certainly wasn't going to ignore it or try to smooth it over.*

snag

hit a snag
to experience a difficulty ♦ *Our plans for Patty's surprise party hit a snag when we discovered she would be away that weekend.*

snap

snap out of *sth*
to stop experiencing something, esp. something unpleasant ♦ *Davis snapped out of a two-year slump to win at the golf tournament.* USAGE: usually used in the form **snap out of it** and sometimes given as advice: *She's filled with grief, and just can't seem to snap out of it.* ♦ *Are you feeling guilty about not spending time with the kids? Well, snap out of it!*

snap up *sth*, also **snap** *sth* **up**
to buy or obtain something as soon as it is available ♦ *His new thriller is so popular, fans have snapped up copies as fast as bookstores get them.* ♦ *As soon as the World Series tickets went on sale, fans snapped them up.*

snappy

make it snappy esp. spoken
to do something quickly ♦ *Make it snappy, will you, because I need help right now.*

sneeze

nothing to sneeze at
something that deserves serious attention ♦ *An extra two thousand bucks a year is nothing to sneeze at.*

sniff

sniff out *sb/sth*, also **sniff** *sb/sth* **out**
to discover someone or something, usually only after a special effort ♦ *Part of their job is to sniff out talented new writers.* ♦ *The FBI knew they had a double agent in their midst, but it took years to sniff him out.* ♦ Related vocabulary **nose around** at NOSE

snowed

snowed under
having too much work to do ♦ *She wants me to take some time off but I'm snowed under with work at the moment.*

> ORIGIN: based on the literal meaning of **snowed under** (= covered by so much snow that people cannot get out or move around).

snuff

snuff out *sth*, also **snuff** *sth* **out**
to put an end to something ♦ *The bomber triggered his explosion and snuffed out the lives of 167 innocent people in that building.* ♦ *Before he could reach the top in his career, a scandal almost snuffed it out.*

soften

ORIGIN: based on the literal meaning of **snuff out** (= to stop a flame from burning)

up to snuff
at or to an acceptable level of quality ◆ *We have a part in designing and manufacturing products and then checking to make sure they're up to snuff.* ◆ *Utah's bridges are in trouble, and it would cost $88 million to bring the worst cases up to snuff.* USAGE: often used in the negative: *Earnings weren't up to snuff in the last quarter.*

so

and so forth, *also* **and so on**
and other similar things ◆ *Obviously they're not doing a good job and so forth, but I don't really like having to fire anyone.* ◆ *Insurance is getting harder to obtain, and you may not qualify for benefits and so on.* USAGE: also used in the forms **and so on and so forth** and **and so on and so on**: *Economic growth makes us all richer, provides jobs, and so on and so forth.* ◆ *The "talking computer" is supposed to help you by saying "That's good" and "That's not right" and so on and so on.*

or so
approximately ◆ *We raised $500 or so for charity.* ◆ *Twenty people or so showed up for the lecture.* ◆ *We see each other once a month or so.* USAGE: always follows a noun, often relating to a number: *It was 90 or so miles to Albany.*

so and so esp. spoken
someone whose name is not known or said ◆ *People were always saying, "I know so and so is talking behind my back."* ◆ *When you get an invitation it's usually for so and so and a guest.*

soak

soak up *sth*, *also* **soak** *sth* **up**
1 to enjoy something ◆ *I just want to lie on the beach and soak up the sun.*
◆ *What does he think of all the praise he's getting? He's soaking it up.*
2 to learn and remember something easily and quickly ◆ *Jill soaks up everything that's said in class.* ◆ *Music came naturally to him, and when he heard something, he soaked it up and could play it.*
3 to use all of something ◆ *The price of heating oil will not rise until the cold weather soaks up the huge amount waiting to be sold.* ◆ *There was a budget surplus, but the needs of the military will surely soak it up.*

socks

knock *your* socks off
to completely surprise or please you very much ◆ *The magazine is beautiful and combines color and unusual design in a way that knocks your socks off.* USAGE: also used with other verbs to say that something is done in an extreme way or to a great degree: *I worked my socks off to get my degree.*

knock *sb's/sth's* socks off, *also* **beat *sb's/sth's* socks off**
to completely defeat a competitor ◆ *Japan and Korea knocked the socks off the United States in tests of science and math.*

soft

soft on *sth*
to not oppose something strongly enough ◆ *His opponents accused him of being soft on crime because he opposed the death penalty.* USAGE: often used with **crime**, and often used in a political context, as in the example

soften

soften the blow
to make something unpleasant easier to accept ◆ *Although tuition rates are going up, more scholarships will be available to soften the blow.* ◆ *Not only were they losing their jobs, but they could not count on any financial cushion to soften the blow.*

soften sb/sth up, *also* **soften up sb/sth**
to weaken someone or something ◆ *Constant bombing was designed to soften the enemy up and weaken him.* ◆ *The ads were just a way to soften up public opinion to accept a big price increase.*

soldier
soldier on
to continue to do something in a determined way, esp. when you know you may not succeed ◆ *She was working with these gorgeous guys, and she managed to soldier on despite being a bit intimidated by them.*

some
and then some
and even more ◆ *It looked like 20,000 people and then some were crowded into the stadium.* ◆ *Investors in the business got their money back and then some.*

somehow
somehow or other
in a way you do not know ◆ *This girl at my school has somehow or other fallen in love with me.* ◆ Related vocabulary **something or other** at SOMETHING

something
something else
unusual ◆ *You think you're something else, but you're really just like all the rest of us.*

something or other
something whose exact nature you do not know or have forgotten ◆ *He's a professor of something or other and now he's living in China.* ◆ Related vocabulary **somehow or other** at SOMEHOW

(do you) know something See at KNOW

have something to prove See at HAVE

leave something to be desired See at LEAVE

make something of *yourself* See at MAKE

make something out of nothing See at MAKE

something to do with See at DO

start something See at START

somewhere
somewhere between
1 within the range of ◆ *They're priced somewhere between ten and fifteen dollars each.*
2 approximately like two different things ◆ *He made a sound somewhere between a gurgle and a cough.*

song
for a song
very cheaply ◆ *Land in the territory could be bought for a song in those days.*

soon
as soon as
when ◆ *We'll come as soon as we can.* ◆ Related vocabulary **as soon as possible** at POSSIBLE

as soon as *sth*
immediately after something ◆ *As soon as the kids fall asleep, the phone rings.*

as soon as possible See at POSSIBLE
speak too soon See at SPEAK
would just as soon See at JUST

sooner
no sooner than *sth*
not before a particular time ◆ *The new drug is expected to be ready no sooner than early next year.*

no sooner *do sth* than *do sth else*
immediately after one thing happens another thing happens ◆ *I had no sooner gotten my bags unpacked than I felt as if I had never been on vacation.* ◆ *He was no sooner graduated than he was on his way to California.* ◆ *She no sooner completed one project than she invested the profits in the next.*

sooner or later
at some time in the future ◆ *Don't*

worry, sooner or later the cat will come home.

sorrows
drown *your* sorrows
to drink a lot of alcohol because you want to stop feeling sad ◆ *Frank insisted that I accompany him to his house, where I could drown my sorrows.* USAGE: sometimes said about eating or drinking something other than alcohol: *I decided I'd drown my sorrows in a bucket of chocolate ice cream.*

sort
of a sort
having some but not all of the characteristics of something ◆ *Officials portrayed the meetings as progress of a sort, although the bargaining has not yet begun.* USAGE: used after a noun being described, as in the example
sort of
to some degree; = **kind of** ◆ *It seemed to be sort of a cross between an oyster and a mushroom.* USAGE: sometimes used to show that you are not certain about something: *I'm sort of at an age where I just want things to be a little more orderly.*
sort *sth* out, *also* sort out *sth*
to deal successfully with a problem or a situation ◆ *We know that our boys have gotten into trouble with the law, but our family is working on sorting it out.* ◆ *Detectives are still sorting out who was involved in the crime.* USAGE: often in the form **sort things out**: *We haven't had many chances to talk to each other and sort things out.*

sorts
out of sorts
in an unhappy mood ◆ *He was feeling a little tired and sore and out of sorts.* ◆ Related vocabulary **get up on the wrong side of (the) bed** at SIDE

soul
bare *your* soul
to express your secret thoughts and feelings ◆ *Although people are willing to bare their souls about subjects like rape, grief is still a difficult subject to talk about.* ◆ Related vocabulary **lay bare *sth*** at LAY
sell *your* soul (to the devil)
to accept immoral behavior in order to succeed ◆ *If the day comes when I begin to sell my soul like the other managers do, that's the day I'll quit.*

> ORIGIN: from the literal idea of exchanging your **soul** (= spirit) with the **devil** (= the origin of evil) to get something you want

sound
sound off
to express your opinion forcefully ◆ *On the Internet, people can sound off, in real time, about whatever they want.*
sound *sb* out, *also* sound out *sb*
to carefully discover what someone thinks or knows ◆ *I thought it might be good to sound him out about having you come to work for us.* ◆ *His policy was to sound out top business leaders before making any new economic proposals.* USAGE: used to describe a way of asking about someone's opinions without upsetting or angering them
safe and sound See at SAFE
sound asleep See at ASLEEP
sound the death knell for *sth* See at DEATH KNELL

soup
in the soup
experiencing a difficult situation ◆ *As soon as the airlines started to make a profit, they put themselves right back in the soup with a new round of mergers.* USAGE: often used with **right back**, as in the example
soup up *sth*, *also* soup *sth* up
to make something more powerful ◆

They had to soup up the air-conditioning to keep her computers from overheating in the summer. USAGE: usually used to describe an improvement to a car or other machine

south
go south
1 to lose value or quality ◆ *She decided to sell her stocks at the end of the year because she felt the market was going south.*
2 to stop working ◆ *Ralph was on a business trip to New York when his laptop computer went south.*

spade
call a spade a spade
to tell the unpleasant truth about something ◆ *Let's call a spade a spade – Brad is a very poor student.*

spades
in spades
in large amounts or to a very great degree ◆ *He complained that Allan had stolen some of his ideas, but Silverman didn't mention that he had done the same in spades.* ◆ *All Freya really wanted was results, and results were what I gave her – in spades.*

sparks
sparks fly
there is an angry argument ◆ *Neither actor liked the other, so when they co-starred as lovers in a new movie, sparks flew.*

speak
not to speak of *sth* slightly formal and possibly even more importantly ◆ *It's hard to imagine a country that would use those weapons on its own people, not to speak of its neighbors.* USAGE: used to introduce and emphasize another possibility

so to speak
this is one way to say it; = **in a manner of speaking** ◆ *My grandfather is 74, and he plays golf every day – it's a sport you can play even as you head into the sunset, so to speak.* ◆ *Even if New Yorkers obeyed all the rules, New York would still be, so to speak, an unruly city.* USAGE: used to suggest that some people may not think this is a good way to say something ◆ Related vocabulary **if you will** at IF, **in other words** at WORDS

speak for *sb/sth*
to express the opinions or wishes of someone ◆ *I can't speak for my boss on something that is so personal.* ◆ *Tokarczyk believed that her poetry could speak for the nation.*

speak for *yourself*
to say what you really believe or think is true ◆ *She should tell us what happened – I mean, she's an adult, she can speak for herself.* USAGE: sometimes used to say you do not agree with what someone else has said: *"Without makeup a woman cannot be pretty." "Speak for yourself. I think she's beautiful with no makeup at all."*

speak out
to say publicly what you think about something ◆ *Gail admitted that she agreed with Kris, but she didn't speak out at the meeting.* USAGE: often followed by **against**: *It's important to speak out against racism at every opportunity.*

speak too soon
to say something that is quickly proven to be not true ◆ *A few days ago I said my job is pretty stress-free, but I spoke too soon – the stress level at work has gone way up this week.*

speak up
to express your opinion ◆ *He went there to speak up for human rights, and he was arrested for doing it.* ◆ *If you need help, you have to speak up or no one will know.*

> ORIGIN: based on the literal meaning of **speak up** (= to talk more loudly)

(*sth*) to speak of
to have so little of something that it

is not worth talking about ◆ *There was no snow to speak of this winter.* ◆ *I really don't have any job benefits to speak of.* USAGE: usually following a noun in a negative statement, as in the examples, but sometimes used alone in conversation: *"Do you get a lot of headaches?" "No, not to speak of."*

actions speak louder than words See at ACTIONS

speak *your* mind See at MIND

speak of the devil See at DEVIL

speak out of turn See at TURN

sth* speaks for *itself See at SPEAKS

speak the same language See at LANGUAGE

speak volumes See at VOLUMES

speak with one voice See at VOICE

speaking

speaking as *sb*
with the experience of this type of person ◆ *What would you like to see happen, speaking as a someone who has lived in the area for a long time?*

speaking of *sth* esp. spoken
related to the subject being discussed ◆ *Casey is at a birthday party – speaking of birthdays, Abe's is Friday.* USAGE: used to introduce a slightly different subject

strictly speaking
if I want to be completely accurate in what I am saying ◆ *They're still married, strictly speaking, but they've been living apart for years.*

in a manner of speaking See at MANNER

on speaking terms See at TERMS

speaks

sth* speaks for *itself
something does not need explanation ◆ *Her behavior speaks for itself, and it doesn't matter what anyone else thinks about it.* ◆ *Is the experiment a success? I think the numbers speak for themselves.* USAGE: often used in the form **let something speak for itself**: *The record company didn't push her album, they simply put it out and let the music speak for itself.*

spectacle

make a spectacle of *yourself*
to do something that attracts people's attention and makes you look stupid ◆ *She did not scream and shout or otherwise make a spectacle of herself.* ◆ Related vocabulary **make a fool of *yourself*** at FOOL

speed

full speed ahead
with all possible energy and enthusiasm; = **full steam ahead** ◆ *The company decided to go full speed ahead on plans to make pasta in the United States.*

pick up speed
to increase in value or degree ◆ *Stocks picked up speed in the final hour of trading this afternoon.*

up to speed
having the most recent information ◆ *It took a long time for the FBI to get up to speed on computer crime.* ◆ *We'll bring you up to speed on the day's top stories after this commercial break.* ◆ Related vocabulary **stay abreast of *sth*** at STAY

spell

spell out *sth*, *also* **spell *sth* out**
to explain something in detail ◆ *Students have been given a fact sheet that spells out how AIDS is transferred.* ◆ *The company has a very strict dress code, and they spell it out for you when you start working there.*

spill

spill over
to reach or influence a larger area ◆ *The fighting may spill over the border and start a wider war.* ◆ *Layoffs in one industry often spill over into other industries.*

spill *your* guts See at GUTS

spill the beans See at BEANS

spin

spin
spin off *sth*, *also* **spin** *sth* **off**
1 to form a separate company from parts of an existing company ♦ *The company will consider spinning off its music recording and retail businesses early next year.*
2 to produce something additional ♦ *"Star Trek" seems capable of spinning movies and TV series off endlessly.*

spin out *sth*, *also* **spin** *sth* **out**
to give the details of a story or idea ♦ *LaRouche liked to spin out crazy theories all the time.* ♦ *We were dazzled by his ability to take a simple idea and spin it out into something amazing.*

spin (*your*) wheels
to use a lot of effort but not get anything done ♦ *For almost an hour now he had been spinning his wheels, accomplishing nothing.* ♦ *Seattle was spinning wheels while Texas beat New York to take a two-game lead in the division.*

spirit
(when) the spirit moves *you*
when you want to or feel ready to ♦ *When the spirit moved her, she would work through the night.* ♦ *Public opinion can take a sharp turn any time the spirit moves them.*

spite
in spite of *sth*
even while recognizing something bad ♦ *In spite of the problems they've faced, they are happy with the life they lead.* ♦ *The drug maker won't change the labeling on its product, in spite of six recent deaths tied to the drug.* USAGE: used to say that the something bad will not strongly influence you

splash
make a splash
to get a lot of public attention ♦ *His latest novel was making a splash in literary circles and is on the best-seller list.*

spleen
vent *your* spleen
to express your anger ♦ *Now you can vent your spleen about driving conditions on area freeways – you can e-mail the director of the Department of Transportation.*

> ORIGIN: from the idea in the past that the **spleen** (= an organ in the body) was the place where evil intentions began

spoil
spoil *sb* rotten
to do everything possible to satisfy someone's desires ♦ *Those children are spoiled rotten by their grandparents.* ♦ *Dad always spoiled us rotten, and Mom was the one who disciplined us.*

spoon
born with a silver spoon in *your* mouth
to have opportunities that you did not earn but that you have from the influence of your family ♦ *Bill was not born with a silver spoon in his mouth – he came from a poor family and earned his success through hard work.*

> ORIGIN: from the idea that silver spoons were given at birth to wealthy children

spot
hit the spot
to be exactly what is wanted or needed ♦ *That apple pie really hit the spot.* ♦ *This kind of testing for new products really hits the spot.*

in a tight spot, *also* **in a tough spot**
in a difficult situation ♦ *If there is a shortage of fuel, everyone who drives to work will be in a tight spot.* ♦ *Bob's in a tight spot right now because he has fallen behind in his work.* ♦ Related vocabulary **in a bind** at BIND, **put *sb/sth* in a hole** at HOLE

on the spot
1 in the place where something has just happened ◆ *Police arrested the robber on the spot.*
2 immediately ◆ *Huge numbers of people donated blood on the spot.* ◆ *We fell in love with the puppy and bought him on the spot.*

put *sb* on the spot
to cause someone difficulty or embarrassment ◆ *She asked if I would vote for her, which really put me on the spot because I had decided not to.*

rooted to the spot
not able to move ◆ *Mary was afraid and wanted to run away, but she was rooted to the spot and watched as the building collapsed.*

spotlight
put a spotlight on *sb/sth*
to direct attention to someone or something ◆ *The newspaper articles put a spotlight on the bad condition of our school buildings.* ◆ Related vocabulary **shed light on *sth*** at LIGHT

spread
spread (*yourself/itself*) too thin
1 to try to do too many different things at the same time ◆ *Max has spread himself thin and needs to focus on just a couple of his best ideas.* ◆ *The company has expanded into many different areas and has probably spread itself too thin.*
2 to not have enough people or equipment to do a job well ◆ *The police are spread thin and cannot provide enough protection.*

spread the word See at WORD
spread *your* wings See at WINGS

spruce
spruce up *sb/sth*, also spruce *sb/sth* up
to improve the appearance of someone or something ◆ *She needed to spruce up her image so she bought tons of new clothes and got a great new hairstyle.* ◆ *The city has to spruce itself up for the Olympics next year.*

spur
on the spur of the moment
without any planning ◆ *I found her old telephone number and called her on the spur of the moment.* ◆ Related vocabulary **at a moment's notice** at NOTICE, **at the drop of a hat** at DROP

spur *sb/sth* on, also spur on *sb/sth*
to encourage someone or something ◆ *I yelled at the dog to drop my hat, but that seemed to spur him on to chew it up.* ◆ *Having more women in government may spur on other women with an interest in entering politics.*

square
square off
to oppose someone directly ◆ *Two teams of students square off and earn points for answering questions correctly.* ◆ *Candidates are supposed to square off in a debate and focus on the issues.*

> ORIGIN: from the meaning in boxing of **square off** (= to take a position that shows you are ready to fight)

square with *sth*
to agree with something ◆ *Tom's explanation does not square with his earlier statement.* ◆ *Her view fails to square with historical reality.*
USAGE: usually used in the negative

a square peg (in a round hole)
See at PEG

squared
squared away
perfectly arranged or organized ◆ *Just when you think your kids are squared away and you can relax, one of them decides to do something crazy.*

square one
back to square one
returned to the beginning ◆ *The in-*

squeeze

vestigation was back to square one when Mrs. Earle proved she wasn't anywhere near the crime. ◆ Related vocabulary **go back to the drawing board** at DRAWING BOARD

squeeze

put the squeeze on *sb/sth*
to put pressure on someone or something ◆ *I hate telephone calls that put the squeeze on me to contribute to something, even to something obviously good.* ◆ *Higher numbers of commuters using buses and trains have put the squeeze on public transportation.*

squeeze *sb/sth* **out (of** *sth***)**, *also* **squeeze out** *sb/sth*
to prevent someone or something from having an opportunity ◆ *High prices for houses squeezed many people out of the market.* ◆ *Big Fellow Hamburger Stands tried illegally to squeeze out its competitors.*

squeeze *sth* **out of** *sb/sth*
to get something with great effort from someone or something ◆ *Albert was good at thinking of ways to squeeze money out of his father in England.* ◆ *Fred didn't like to tell the truth, and you had to squeeze it out of him.*

stab

make a stab at *sth*, *also* **have a stab at** *sth*
to try something new or different ◆ *We are making a stab at high-speed rail service.*

stab *sb* **in the back** See at BACK

stack

stack up (against *sth***)**
to compare with something else ◆ *We wondered how London restaurants stacked up against Atlanta's.*

stage

at this stage of the game esp. spoken
at a particular place in a process ◆ *At this stage of the game, it's really too late to switch computer software.*

set the stage for *sth*
to prepare the way for something else to happen ◆ *This new information sets the stage for a long and interesting trial.*

> ORIGIN: from the preparation of the stage in a theater for the performance of a play

take center stage
to be the center of interest ◆ *Collecting food and clothes for disaster victims has taken center stage in our town.* ◆ *A new line of electric cars took center stage at the automobile show.*

stake

at stake
in danger of being lost ◆ *About 3000 jobs are at stake if the company moves to another state.*

stake a claim (to *sth***)**
to announce that something belongs to you ◆ *Every kind of group you can think of has staked a claim to space on the Internet.* USAGE: also used in the form **stake your claim**: *He staked his claim as a liberal.*

> ORIGIN: based on the literal meaning of **stake a claim** (= to mark with posts a piece of land belonging to the government that you claim for yourself)

stake *sb* **out**, *also* **stake out** *sb*
watch someone, often secretly ◆ *A television news crew staked her out from a next-door neighbor's yard.* ◆ *For a week, police staked out the suspect.*

stake out *sth*
1 to claim something belongs to you ◆ *To avoid a long wait to eat lunch, one of you stakes out a table and the other gets the food.* ◆ *Lars staked out a cot in a third-floor bedroom and tried to make it seem like his own space.*
2 to secretly watch a place ◆ *Private detectives staked out their house,*

went through their garbage, and interviewed their neighbors.

stakes
pull up stakes
to leave the place where you have been living ♦ *They lived in Los Angeles for several years before pulling up stakes for Nova Scotia.*

raise the stakes
to increase in importance or danger ♦ *Employees who lost all their pensions have raised the stakes for the company by going to court and filing a lawsuit.* ♦ Related vocabulary **up the ante** at ANTE

stamp
stamp out *sth*, also **stamp** *sth* **out**
to stop or destroy something ♦ *How long have we been trying to stamp out drugs?* ♦ *Everyone enjoys these games, although some people want to stamp them out.*

stand
I stand corrected esp. spoken
I admit that I was wrong ♦ *I stand corrected – the company was established in 1927, not 1926, as I had mistakenly thought.*

make a stand
to make a determined effort to defend something or to stop something from happening ♦ *There comes a time in every close game when a team has to rise up and make a stand.*

not stand for it, *also* **not stand for** *sth*
to refuse to accept something ♦ *I won't have you using that kind of language, I simply won't stand for it!* ♦ *When I was a child, my mother just wouldn't stand for rude behavior.*

stand around
to stay in one place doing little or nothing ♦ *After the fire was put out, most of the fire fighters left, and the few remaining just seemed to be standing around.*

stand by
1 to let something happen or to be unable to do anything to stop something from happening ♦ *It was such a terrible fire that the firefighters had to stand by and let the fire burn itself out.*
2 to be ready to be used if necessary ♦ *During the fireworks display, the fire department trucks stood by, in case something went up in flames.*

stand by *sb/sth*
to support someone or something; = **stick by** *sb/sth* ♦ *I think people admire the fact that she stands by her husband.* ♦ *At a news conference, he stood by his criticism of the government.*

stand for *sth*
1 to represent something ♦ *She explained that DIN stands for "do it now."* ♦ *Traditionally, images of lions stand for royalty.*
2 to support particular principles or values ♦ *I'm not sure whether that group stands for more or less regulation of the power industry.* ♦ *He wanted his party to stand for human rights.*

stand out
to be easily seen or noticed ♦ *His bright red hair helps him stand out at comedy clubs.* ♦ *It simply stands out as an excellent school among many very good schools.* ♦ Related vocabulary **stick out** at STICK

stand over *sb*
to watch someone closely ♦ *Had someone been standing over her while she slept or did she just imagine it?*

stand pat slightly formal
to leave something just as it is, without any change ♦ *While he stood pat, other people found a better way to solve the problem.*

stand up
to prove to be true or correct ♦ *The way this contract is written now, it wouldn't stand up in court.* ♦ *Detectives checked his alibi and it stood up, so they let him go.*

standby

stand *sb* **up,** *also* **stand up** *sb*
to fail to meet someone you had arranged to see ♦ *Chuck and I had a date for dinner and he stood me up.* ♦ *The mayor stood up the visitors because of an emergency city council meeting.*

stand up and be counted
to publicly state your opinion ♦ *It is difficult sometimes to stand up and be counted when you know most people disagree with you.* ♦ Related vocabulary **have the courage of your/its convictions** at COURAGE

stand up for *sb/sth*
to defend or support someone or something; = **stick up for** *sb/sth* ♦ *Sometimes you have to stand up for your rights.* ♦ *I stood up for him because he had a right to his opinion.*

stand up to *sb/sth*
to oppose someone or something without fear ♦ *I know Jim would stand up to absolutely anyone, even his boss, if he believed he was right about something.*

take a stand
to publicly express an opinion ♦ *Finally, somebody is going to have to say this is the right thing to do, to take a stand.*

standby

on standby
ready to be used if needed ♦ *I always have a backup tape drive on standby, just in case.* ♦ *The UN asked various countries to keep some military forces on standby for possible peacekeeping duty.*

stands

as it stands
as something is now ♦ *We have to accept or turn down this proposal as it stands.* ♦ Related vocabulary **as things stand** at THINGS

stars

see stars
to seem to see bright flashes of light in front of your eyes ♦ *Corky hit his head hard enough to see stars.*

thank *your* **lucky stars**
to be grateful for having good luck ♦ *I thanked my lucky stars that no one took my bag when I stupidly left it on a park bench.*

written in the stars
intended to be ♦ *Do you really believe our fates are written in the stars and will happen no matter what we do?*

start

off to a flying start
beginning very well ♦ *This year he's off to a flying start, playing very well and winning his first five games.*

start over
to begin something again ♦ *If I make even one mistake on this, I've got to start over.* USAGE: for more emphasis, often in the form **start all over**: *We had to start all over several times until we got it right.*

start something
to begin an argument or fight ♦ *He's always starting something – he doesn't know when to keep quiet.*

starters

for starters
as a beginning; = **for openers** ♦ *If they want to be involved, for starters, they might join Saturday's antiwar protest downtown.* USAGE: often used in the form **that's just for starters**: *You've got to put down a deposit of $500, and that's just for starters!* ♦ Related vocabulary **to begin with** at BEGIN

state

a sad state of affairs esp. spoken, *also* **a sorry state of affairs**
a bad situation that you find upsetting ♦ *It's a sad state of affairs when schools don't provide a basic education for their students.* USAGE: sometimes used in the form **a sad state**: *Things have reached a sad state when you have to pay a bribe to get something done.*

lie in state
to place a person's body where it

can be seen by the public ♦ *The President's body lay in state in the Capitol for three days and thousands walked by his coffin to pay their respects.*

the state of play *esp. spoken*
the present situation ♦ *With the state of play on the battlefield the way it is, the rebels will not give up but will keep attacking.*

stave

stave off *sth, also* **stave** *sth* **off**
to keep something away or keep something from happening ♦ *The Federal Reserve lowered interest rates to boost the economy and stave off a recession.* ♦ *Death is natural and inevitable – we can't stave it off forever.* ♦ Related vocabulary **fend off** *sth* at FEND, **ward off** *sb/sth* at WARD

stay

stay abreast of *sth*
to have the most recent information about something; = **keep abreast of** *sth* ♦ *Regional conferences provide the opportunity for everyone to stay abreast of the latest developments in our field of research.* ♦ Related vocabulary **up to speed** at SPEED

stay over
to spend one or more nights in a place away from home ♦ *She decided to stay over in Boston for the long weekend.* ♦ *Ask your mom if you can stay over with us tonight.* ♦ Related vocabulary **sleep over** at SLEEP

stay put
to stay where you are ♦ *Just stay put until I get the car.*

stay the course See at COURSE

stead

in *sb's/sth's* **stead** *slightly formal*
in the place of someone or something else ♦ *We gave Mr. Neil a power of attorney to deal with the landlord in our stead while we were out of the country.*

stand *sb* **in good stead** *slightly formal, also* **hold** *sb* **in good stead**
to be useful or helpful in the future ♦ *His recommendation will stand you in good stead when you apply for a job.*

steam

blow off steam, *also* **let off steam**
to do or say something that helps you get rid of strong feelings or energy ♦ *I've told her she can call me and talk any time she wants to blow off some steam.* ♦ *After a long car trip, the kids need to run around a bit and let off steam.*

> ORIGIN: based on the **steam engine** (= a machine that uses steam), which would explode if steam were not allowed to escape into the air

full steam ahead
with all possible energy and enthusiasm; = **full speed ahead** ♦ *The real estate market has heated up, and building is going full steam ahead.* USAGE: sometimes used in the form **it's full steam ahead**: *It's full steam ahead for Internet service providers today.*

> ORIGIN: based on the literal use of full steam in ships, which makes them go at their top speed

pick up steam
to improve at a quicker rate ♦ *In the third month the campaign really started to pick up steam.*

run out of steam
to lose the energy or interest to continue; = **run out of gas** ♦ *She'd been talking for two hours and was just starting to run out of steam.*

steam up *sth, also* **steam** *sth* **up**
to become covered with a thin layer of small water drops ♦ *Going into the warm room steamed my glasses up.* ♦ *They were sitting in the back seat of the car and the windows were all steamed up.*

steamed

under *your* own steam
without help from anyone else ◆ *Don't bother organizing a ride for us – we can get there under our own steam.*

a head of steam See at HEAD

steamed

(all) steamed up
angry or upset ◆ *She got all steamed up because he arrived over an hour late.*

steer

steer clear (of *sb/sth*)
to avoid someone or something ◆ *I'd steer clear of Joe if I were you – he's in a terrible mood.* ◆ *They invited me to comment on the proposals, but I think I would rather steer clear.* USAGE: usually the person or thing you avoid is dangerous or likely to cause trouble

stem

(from) stem to stern
completely ◆ *We overhauled the car from stem to stern.* ◆ Related vocabulary **from top to bottom** at TOP

ORIGIN: based on the literal meaning of **from the stem to the stern** (= from the front end to the back end of a ship)

stem from *sth* slightly formal
to result from something ◆ *His fear of snakes stems from an incident in his childhood.*

step

a step in the right direction
an action that is expected to bring good results ◆ *Both sides agreed that continuing the talks was a step in the right direction.*

in step with *sb/sth*
1 in agreement with someone or something ◆ *She is very much in step with the times.*
2 at the same speed or level as someone or something else ◆ *He found it hard to keep in step with the changes.* ◆ *Gasoline prices rose in step with oil prices.*

ORIGIN: based on the literal meaning of moving your legs at the same time as someone you are walking with

one step ahead
slightly better prepared or more successful than someone else ◆ *The filmmaker manages to keep one step ahead of his critics by constantly trying new ideas.* USAGE: often used with the verbs **be**, **keep**, or **stay**: *In this business, you have to be one step ahead of the competition.*

out of step (with *sth*)
1 not having the same ideas or beliefs as a group you are part of ◆ *The governor's remarks show she is seriously out of step with voters.*
2 not aware of something ◆ *Many parents are surprisingly out of step with the reality of drugs in their children's lives.* USAGE: often used as a criticism: *My dad's clothing store, once successful, is now dismissed as old and out of step.*

step back, *also* **take a step back**
to pause in an activity, esp. to consider what to do next ◆ *We need to step back and look at all our options.*

step by step, *also* **one step at a time**
gradually or slowly ◆ *These changes need to be made step by step.* USAGE: also used in the form **a step at a time**: *He wanted to rush through the job, but I encouraged him to take it a step at a time.*

step down
to stop doing a job or stop having a position ◆ *She stepped down as captain of the team.*

step in
to become involved ◆ *An outside buyer stepped in to save the company.* ◆ Related vocabulary **step up to the plate** at PLATE

step on it
to hurry in order to get something done quickly; = **step on the gas** ◆

We'd better step on it or we'll still be here when they get back.

step out
to leave a place, esp. for a short time ♦ *Mr. Taylor just stepped out of the office to get the mail.*

step up *sth*, *also* **step** *sth* **up**
to make something larger, faster, or more effective ♦ *Following the explosion the airport authorities stepped up security.* ♦ *We had to step our defense up and move the ball better.* USAGE: also used in the form **step it up**: *The coach said that if we don't step it up in the second half we're in trouble.*

watch *your* **step**
to be careful in a situation that could be dangerous ♦ *You have to watch your step when you're dealing with him, as he has an awful temper.* ♦ Related vocabulary **watch** *your* **back** at BACK

step into the breach See at BREACH

step on the gas See at GAS

step on (*sb's***) toes** See at TOES

step up to the plate See at PLATE

steroids

on steroids
in a much more powerful or extreme form ♦ *The brownies and pecan rolls are sweets on steroids, with calorie and fat totals as high as a full meal.* ♦ *She looks like a movie star on steroids, a beautiful woman with big hair and a man-eating personality.*

> ORIGIN: based on the literal meaning of **steroids** (= chemical substances taken to improve the strength or energy of competitors in sports)

stick

more *sth* **than** *you* **can shake a stick at**
a very large number of something ♦ *I don't know why she wants more shoes – she's already got more pairs than you can shake a stick at.*

stick around
to stay somewhere and wait ♦ *You go ahead – I'll stick around until Candice shows up.*

stick by *sb/sth*
to support someone or something; = **stand by** *sb/sth* ♦ *He stuck by his earlier statements and never changed his story.* ♦ *She stuck by him through all the years of his illness.*

stick it out
to continue to do something to its end ♦ *I didn't really like the movie, but I stuck it out.* USAGE: often used in the phrase **stick it out to the bitter end**

stick it to *sb*
to punish someone who did something wrong earlier ♦ *If you fail to pay enough estimated tax, the IRS will really stick it to you.* ♦ Related vocabulary **get back at** *sb* at GET, **get even** at GET

stick out
to be very easily noticed because of being different ♦ *Dye your hair orange and you'll really stick out in a small town like this.* ♦ Related vocabulary **stand out** at STAND

stick to *sth*
to follow or continue with something without changing it ♦ *Would you stick to the point, please?* ♦ *It's going to be hard to stick to the schedule with this much work.*

stick together
to support each other ♦ *If we all stick together, we can succeed.*

stick up *sb/sth*
to steal from a person or place, using a weapon as a threat ♦ *Some guy tried to stick up a coffee shop and got caught.* ♦ Related vocabulary **hold up** *sb/sth* 1 at HOLD

stick up for *sb/sth*
to support or defend someone or something; = **stand up for** *sb/sth* ♦ *Her friends stuck up for her when other people said she was guilty.*

stick with *sb/sth*
to continue to be closely involved

with someone or something ◆ *Stick with me, and we'll do lots of interesting things.* ◆ *Once Stephen takes up a hobby, he sticks with it.*

stick *sb* with *sb/sth*
to force someone to do something or to have responsibility for someone ◆ *She claims that big power companies cut costs and stick their customers with high prices.* ◆ *They go out dancing and stick me with the baby.*

a carrot and stick (approach) See at CARROT

get the short end (of the stick) See at END

make *sth* stick See at MAKE

stick in *your* craw See at CRAW

stick in *your* mind See at MIND

stick *your* neck out See at NECK

stick out like a sore thumb See at THUMB

stick to *your* guns See at GUNS

still

(but) still and all
despite that ◆ *Her performance wasn't that original but still and all, the audience was really impressed.*

sting

take the sting out of *sth*
to slightly improve something that is unpleasant ◆ *It was a difficult loss, but the support of the fans really took the sting out of it.*

stink

kick up a stink
to cause an argument about something that seems wrong ◆ *The consumer group kicked up a stink about the defective tires on SUVs.*

raise a stink, *also* **make a stink**
to complain angrily about something ◆ *Parents really should raise a stink about violence on children's TV shows.*

stink up *sth*, *also* **stink *sth* up**
1 to make a place smell unpleasant ◆ *Take the garbage out before it stinks up the entire house.*

2 to do something very badly ◆ *Every time I begin a new job, I worry that I'm gonna stink it up, you know?*
USAGE: sometimes used to suggest that an experience causes you to react as you would to a bad smell: *The Dolphins stunk up Rich Stadium by losing 40-0.*

stir

cause a stir, *also* **create a stir**
to cause unusual interest or excitement ◆ *Rufus was arguing with his older daughter about her boyfriend, and it caused a stir in the family.*
USAGE: often used with **quite** for emphasis: *Her latest novel has created quite a stir.*

stir up *sb/sth*, *also* **stir up a hornet's nest**
to cause a situation that upsets many people ◆ *One official claimed that foreign activists were stirring up trouble.* ◆ *The threat of censorship stirred up a hornet's nest of criticism on the Internet.*

stitches

in stitches
laughing so much that it is difficult to control yourself ◆ *The movie will keep you in stitches from beginning to end.*

stock

stock up (on *sth*)
to buy a large amount of something so that you will have enough for future use ◆ *When there's a storm coming we always stock up on food and candles.*

take stock (of *sth*)
to examine a situation carefully ◆ *After two days of record snowfalls, millions of Americans began digging out and taking stock of storm damage.*

stomach

a strong stomach
the ability not to be upset by unpleasant things ◆ *You have to have a strong stomach to invest in the stock market these days.*

stoop

not have the stomach (for *sth***),** *also* **have no stomach (for** *sth***)**
to not feel strong or brave enough to do something unpleasant ♦ *The soldiers did not have the stomach for another fight.* USAGE: sometimes used in the form **not have the stomach to do something**: *I don't think I've got the stomach to argue with her again about money.* ♦ Related vocabulary *your* **heart isn't in it** at HEART, **not have the heart (to do** *sth***)** at HEART

on an empty stomach
when you have not eaten anything ♦ *He left early this morning and drove three hours on an empty stomach.*

settle *your* **stomach**
to make your stomach feel less upset ♦ *She found that a cup of tea usually settled her stomach.*

sick to *your* **stomach**
feeling like you are going to vomit ♦ *When you saw the way his ankle was broken, you got sick to your stomach.*

stone

leave no stone unturned
to do everything possible in order to achieve or find something ♦ *Both sides have vowed to leave no stone unturned in the search for peace.*

set in stone
firmly established and very difficult to change; = **set in concrete** ♦ *The schedule isn't set in stone, but we'd like to stick to it pretty closely.* USAGE: sometimes with other verbs, such as **write, carve,** or **etch**: *Our business plan isn't carved in stone – we can still make adjustments if we need to.*

a heart of stone See at HEART

get blood from a stone See at BLOOD

kill two birds with one stone See at BIRDS

stoop

stoop to *sth*
to do something that makes your moral standards lower ♦ *They have stooped to using threats of violence in order to get their way.* USAGE:

leave no stone unturned

"Keep looking – we'll leave no stone unturned until we find that necklace."

often used in the forms **stoop to someone's level** or **stoop to the level of dong something**: *The president shouldn't stoop to the level of exchanging insults.*

> ORIGIN: from the literal meaning of **stoop** (= to bend forward and down to make yourself smaller)

stop

put a stop to *sth*
to stop something; = **put an end to sth** ◆ *I wish I could put a stop to those annoying phone calls.*

stop at nothing (to do *sth***)**
to be willing to do anything to get what you want ◆ *She sets herself a goal and then stops at nothing to achieve it.* USAGE: often used in the form **will stop at nothing**: *Those people will stop at nothing, including murder, to harm you.*

stop by (*somewhere***)**, also **stop in (at** *somewhere***)**
to visit a place briefly ◆ *Stop by on your way home and I'll give you that book.* ◆ *Can you stop in at the courthouse for a minute today?*

stop over
to stay at a place briefly on the way to somewhere else ◆ *Marj decided to stop over in Pittsburgh to see an old friend.*

stop short
to stop suddenly ◆ *She ran toward him but stopped short when she saw the gun.* ◆ Related vocabulary **stop (dead) in** *your* **tracks** at TRACKS

stop short of *doing sth*
1 to decide not to do something ◆ *I stopped short of telling him what I really felt about him.*
2 to almost do something, or partly do something without completing it ◆ *The punishments are quite severe but they stop short of losing your job.* USAGE: sometimes used in the forms **stop well short of** or **stop just short of**: *The government is stopping just short of threatening to go to war.*

stop (dead) in *your* **tracks** See at TRACKS

stop on a dime See at DIME

stops

pull out all the stops
to make every effort to achieve something ◆ *Both sides promise to pull out all the stops, running more TV and newspaper ads and making more phone calls to supporters.*

store

in store (for *sb/sth***)**
planned or likely to happen ◆ *We have a big surprise in store for you.* ◆ *She's got a difficult few months in store, with her husband's illness.*

mind the store
to be responsible for the operation of a business or organization ◆ *The governor was on vacation then, and he was clearly not minding the store.*

storm

take *sb/sth* **by storm**
to be suddenly and extremely successful ◆ *The Beatles took the US by storm in the early 1960s.*

up a storm
with a lot of energy ◆ *Her dog barks up a storm every time the phone rings.* ◆ *They were sitting in a corner, talking up a storm.* USAGE: used after action verbs, as in the examples

weather the storm, also **ride out the storm**
to continue to exist and not be harmed during a difficult period ◆ *Johnson apparently has weathered the storm over his careless remarks.*

story

it's the same old story, also **it's an old story**
this bad situation has happened many times before ◆ *It's the same old story – the women do all the work and the men just sit around talking.* ◆ Related vocabulary **the same old same old** at OLD, **the same old thing** at THING

that's another story
that is an explanation I will make at some other time ♦ *Strangely enough, we bumped into each other again in Amsterdam, but that's another story.* USAGE: usually used when you have just said as much about something as you feel is necessary

the story of *sb*'s life
something that repeatedly happens to someone ♦ *She's involved with another guy who says he's going to divorce his wife soon – that's the story of her life.*

to make a long story short esp. spoken
as a way to avoid a long explanation, I am going to give only the basic facts ♦ *To make a long story short, I was young and ambitious and I thought I could beat the guy.*

straight

the straight and narrow (path)
behavior that is correct and moral ♦ *You have to keep to the straight and narrow if you want to stay on her good side.*

give it to *sb* straight See at GIVE
go straight See at GO
keep a straight face See at FACE
set *sb/sth* straight See at SET
set the record straight See at RECORD
(straight) from the horse's mouth See at MOUTH
think straight See at THINK

straighten

straighten *sb* out, *also* **straighten out *sb***
to cause someone's behavior or character to improve ♦ *I thought marriage would straighten him out but it hasn't.* ♦ *He plays the part of an uncle trying to straighten out a troubled teenager.*

straighten *sth* out, *also* **straighten out *sth***
1 to end uncertainty or confusion about something ♦ *I'm sorry if our letter was confusing, but I'll straighten that out now.* ♦ *Sometimes I'll feel there's something I need to straighten out because no one's sure what to expect.*
2 to arrange or organize something that is in disorder ♦ *It took her a while to straighten out her father's accounts.* ♦ *When her husband died, there were problems with his will, and it took her a year to straighten them all out.*

straighten up
to start behaving in a more acceptable or correct way ♦ *If you don't straighten up, I'm going to suspend you from this school.*

straighten up *sth*, *also* **straighten *sth* up**
to make things neat ♦ *Be sure to straighten up your room before you leave.* ♦ *It was only four-thirty, and she still had time to straighten things up before the guests arrived.*

straight face

keep a straight face
to avoid showing any emotion, esp. amusement ♦ *I thought it would be funny to tell him he failed the course, but it was hard to keep a straight face when I was talking to him.*

straits

in dire straits
in extreme danger or difficulty ♦ *Officials in Washington say the peace process is in dire straits.* USAGE: sometimes used in the forms **dire economic straits** or **dire financial straits**: *He's been out of work for eight months, and his family is in dire financial straits.*

strangely

strangely enough
in a way that is unusual or surprising ♦ *His mother, strangely enough, seemed to be happy that he got arrested.*

stranger

stranger

no stranger to *sth*
familiar with something or with some place ◆ *She's certainly no stranger to hard work.* ◆ *The nation's disease-fighting agency is no stranger to epidemics.* ◆ *He's no stranger to British pubs.*

straw

straw in the wind
something that shows you what might happen in the future ◆ *There were straws in the wind that suggested a strike was likely.* USAGE: usually used in the plural, as in the example

straws

grasping at straws, *also* **clutching at straws**
1 trying to find some way to succeed when nothing you choose is likely to work ◆ *Jerry, grasping at straws, searched the backup tapes from last week, looking for the missing files.*
2 trying to find reasons to feel hopeful about a bad situation ◆ *She thinks he might still be interested because he calls her now and then but I think she's clutching at straws.*

strength

go from strength to strength
to become increasingly successful ◆ *The firm has gone from strength to strength since she took over as manager.*

on the strength of *sth*
because of something that has influenced or persuaded you ◆ *On the strength of last month's sales figures, we decided to expand our business.* ◆ *He was offered a teaching position on the strength of his experience in sales and marketing.*

a pillar of strength See at PILLAR

stretch

at a stretch
continuously; = **on end** ◆ *Sometimes I work for ten hours at a stretch.* ◆ *I can't concentrate for more than 15 minutes at a stretch.*

not by any stretch (of the imagination), *also* **by no stretch (of the imagination)**
even if you try, it is still difficult to accept ◆ *She was never a great player, not by any stretch of the imagination.* ◆ *He's nice-looking but by no stretch of the imagination could you describe him as handsome.* ◆ *Our survey was purely random and by no stretch scientific.* USAGE: sometimes used in the form **by any stretch (of the imagination)** (= even possibly): *It's the only plan that could, by any stretch, be relied upon to work.*

stretch *your* **legs** See at LEGS

stride

hit *your* **stride**
to start to do something confidently and well ◆ *She began writing novels in the 1930s but really only hit her stride after the war.*

take *sth* **in (*your*) stride**
to calmly deal with something unpleasant and not let it have a bad effect on you ◆ *There's plenty of work to do, but she seems to take it all in her stride.* ◆ *Cooper has learned to take such criticism in stride.*

strike

strike down *sth*, *also* **strike** *sth* **down**
to decide that a law, rule, or order is not legal ◆ *The court struck down the law, saying that it was unconstitutional.*

strike home
to be understood completely and have a strong effect; = **hit home** ◆ *Her tearful expression made it clear that his nasty remarks had struck home.* ◆ Related vocabulary **come home (to** *sb***)** at COME

strike it rich
to become suddenly and unexpectedly rich or successful ◆ *Many im-*

migrants dream of striking it rich in America.

ORIGIN: based on literal meaning of **strike it rich** (= to find gold in the ground)

strike out
1 to begin moving or acting with energy or determination ♦ *At dawn they struck out on foot toward the town.*
2 to fail ♦ *In the past our ads have been successful, but we struck out this time.*

ORIGIN: from an expression used in baseball, referring to a play in which the hitter fails to hit the ball

strike out on *your* own
to begin a new and independent activity ♦ *Instead of joining the family business, I decided to strike out on my own.*

strike up *sth*
to begin something ♦ *She struck up a relationship with an artist soon after she arrived in Paris.* ♦ *We walk into the room and a brass band strikes up a rendition of "Parker's Mood."* ♦ *I was hoping he'd strike up a conversation.*

strike a blow against *sb/sth* See at BLOW
strike a chord See at CHORD
strike *sb's* fancy See at FANCY
strike gold See at GOLD
strike the right note See at NOTE
strike while the iron is hot See at IRON

string

string out *sth*, *also* string *sth* out
1 to make something continue ♦ *Zeb hoped he could string out his vacation as long as possible.* ♦ *The legal process could string this dispute out for years.*
2 to be spread in a long, thin line ♦ *Most of Canada's population is strung out along its border with the United States.* ♦ *The early fast pace soon strung the field of runners out over more than a mile.*

strings

no strings attached
no special demands or limits that you have to accept ♦ *The donation has no strings attached, so the charity can use the money for whatever purpose it chooses.* USAGE: sometimes used in the form **with strings attached** (= with special demands or limits): *Many special offers come with strings attached, so be aware of this before you buy.*

pull strings
to use your influence over important people in order to get something or to help someone ♦ *I may be able to pull a few strings for you if you need the document urgently.*

pull the strings, *also* **pull *sb's* strings**
to control the actions of a person or group, often secretly ♦ *I'd like to know who's pulling the strings in that organization, because it's not the elected committee.* ♦ *He wanted to make his own decision, with no one pulling his strings.*

ORIGIN: based on a comparison with the movements of a marionette (= a small model of a person or animal moved by strings by attached to its body)

stripes

earn *your* stripes
to do something to show that you deserve a particular rank or position ♦ *She earned her stripes as a local reporter before becoming a foreign correspondent.*

ORIGIN: based on the idea that soldiers wear **stripes** (= strips of material sewn onto a uniform that show rank)

stroke

a stroke of luck, *also* **a stroke of fortune**
something good that happens to you

strokes

when you do not expect it ◆ *To walk in and get a job like that was an incredible stroke of luck.*

in one stroke, *also* **at one stroke**
immediately ◆ *In one stroke, farmers will go from $100,000 in revenues to nothing.* USAGE: sometimes used in the forms **at a (single) stroke** or **in a stroke**: *Rejecting the treaty would undo years of effort in a stroke.*

strokes

different strokes (for different folks)
different things are done or liked by different people ◆ *The man walks backward for exercise. Different strokes for different folks!*

in broad strokes, *also* **with broad strokes**
in a general way, without giving details ◆ *Mostly, he talked in broad strokes about how his faith supports him every day.*

> ORIGIN: based on the idea of painting with **broad strokes** (= wide marks made with a wide brush)

stub

stub out *sth*, *also* **stub** *sth* **out**
to stop something from burning or smoking by pressing it against something ◆ *She used the edge of the ashtray to stub out her cigarette.* ◆ *He dropped the cigar on the street without stubbing it out.*

stuck

stuck with *sb/sth*
forced to have or deal with someone or something you do not want or like ◆ *Taxpayers may be stuck with a $330,000 bill for the Olympic festival.* ◆ *If you're late for dinner, you'll be stuck with the leftovers.*

stuff

do *your* **stuff**
to do something that you are expected to do ◆ *She came on stage, did her stuff, and was out of the theater within an hour.* USAGE: usually said about something that you do well

know *your* **stuff**
to know a lot about a subject or be an expert at doing something ◆ *When it comes to restoring grand pianos, he really knows his stuff.*

strut *your* **stuff**
to show other people what you can do well ◆ *I thought you'd be up there on the dance floor, strutting your stuff!* ◆ *It was a chance for the city to strut its stuff with a series of public concerts and festivals.* ◆ *Investment managers were eager to strut their stuff before their corporate board in Chicago last Thursday.*

> ORIGIN: from the literal meaning of **strut** (= to walk proudly in a way that attracts attention)

stumble

stumble across *sb/sth*, *also* **stumble on** *sb/sth*
to meet someone or find something unexpectedly ◆ *Lee has stumbled across a plot to sell high-tech US weapons to international terrorists.* ◆ *Border Patrol agents stumbled on the drugs when they were on a routine patrol.*

stump

on the stump
traveling to different places to speak to people in order to get their political support ◆ *On the stump in North Dakota, the senator took time out to talk to our reporter.*

> ORIGIN: based on a politician standing on a **stump** (= cut end of a tree) in order to be seen

style

cramp *sb's* **style**
to prevent someone from doing something freely, esp. something they enjoy ◆ *Bringing her mother along on the trip would definitely cramp her style.*

subject
subject *sb/sth* **to** *sth*
to cause someone or something to experience something ◆ *How do you feel about subjecting people to random drug testing?* ◆ *My daughter's only three, but I've already subjected her to all sorts of music, from bebop to hip-hop.* USAGE: often said about experiencing something unpleasant: *The company's accounts were subjected to close investigation.*

sublime
from the sublime to the ridiculous
from something that is very good to something that is very bad or silly ◆ *The performances at the festival ranged from the sublime to the ridiculous.* USAGE: also used in the form **from the ridiculous to the sublime**

subscribe
subscribe to *sth*
to agree with or support an opinion, belief, or theory ◆ *I subscribe to the notion of lying down when the urge to exercise strikes me.*

such
as such
1 being exactly what is mentioned or suggested ◆ *There's no dining room as such, but we've made a dining area just outside the kitchen.*
2 considered alone or by itself ◆ *The size of their family as such is not a factor in our decision to give them financial aid.*

suck
suck *sb* **into** *sth*, also **suck** *sb* **in**
to cause someone to become involved in something or do something ◆ *I got sucked into their argument because I was a friend of the family.* ◆ *I didn't return the salesman's phone calls because I didn't want to be sucked in.* USAGE: usually used as **get sucked into something** or **be sucked into something**, as in the examples, and often said of someone who becomes involved without fully understanding the situation

suck up (to *sb***)**
to praise someone in order to win their approval or good opinion ◆ *She's always sucking up to the boss, telling him how wonderful he is.*

sudden
all of a sudden
happening or done quickly and without any warning; = **all at once** ◆ *All of a sudden we heard a loud explosion that shook the building.*

suit
follow suit
to do the same as someone else has just done ◆ *If other stores lower their prices, we'll have to follow suit.*

> ORIGIN: based on the literal meaning of **follow suit** (= to play a card of the same type as someone else just played in a card game)

suit *yourself*
to be satisfactory for you ◆ *He was always able to arrange things to suit himself.* USAGE: often showing you are annoyed: *Suit yourself – as you usually do.*

sum
sum up (*sth***)**, also **sum** *sth* **up**
to give a brief but complete statement ◆ *The last paragraph should sum up the main points of your argument.* ◆ *He's a small man with a big ego – that about sums him up.* ◆ *To sum up, Eleanor has promised to revise the designs, and Bernard will finalize the text.*

in sum See **in summary** at SUMMARY

summary
in summary slightly formal, also **in sum**
briefly ◆ *In summary, this book is a good introduction to bird watching.*

sun

sun
everything under the sun
everything that exists or that you can imagine ◆ *We talked about everything under the sun.* USAGE: often **every something under the sun**: *She seems to have an opinion on every subject under the sun.*

supply
in short supply
not readily available ◆ *Money is in short supply until I get paid.*

sure
sure enough
as expected ◆ *He said he left the book on the desk, and sure enough, there it was.*

for sure
without any doubt; = **for certain** ◆ *We're coming to visit you for sure this summer.* USAGE: often used in the form **that's for sure**: *They don't want any of us there this weekend, that's for sure.* ◆ Related vocabulary **you bet** at BET, **you bet your (sweet) ass** at ASS

sure as hell See at HELL

surface
scratch the surface
to deal with only a small part of a subject or a problem ◆ *All the payments we've made so far have hardly scratched the surface of the total we borrowed.*

surprise
take (sb) by surprise
to do something not expected ◆ *His resignation took us all completely by surprise.*

suspicion
above suspicion
not believed to have done anything wrong ◆ *The fact that you were once famous doesn't mean you're above suspicion.*

swallow
hard to swallow
1 difficult to accept ◆ *The terms of the agreement were hard to swallow, but I needed the work.* ◆ *My father's anger was very hard to swallow.*
2 not easy to believe ◆ *We found her excuse hard to swallow.* ◆ Related vocabulary **take *sth* with a grain of salt** at GRAIN

swallow up *sb/sth*, *also* **swallow *sb/sth* up**
to take in or absorb someone or something ◆ *The suburbs are swallowing up all the farmland and open space in the region.* ◆ *She walked down the street, and the crowd just swallowed her up.*

a bitter pill (to swallow) See at PILL

swallow *your* pride See at PRIDE

swath
cut a (wide) swath, *also* **cut a (wide) swathe**
1 to attract a lot of interest or attention ◆ *The two beautiful sisters cut a wide swath through our little town, and every male wanted to take them out.* ◆ *The new game is unusually inventive and has cut a wide swath in the video game market.*
2 to cause a lot of destruction, death, or harm in a particular place ◆ *Violent thunderstorms cut a swath of destruction through the area, blowing down trees and damaging houses.*

> ORIGIN: based on the literal meaning of **swath** (= a line or strip of grass that has been cut)

sway
hold sway
1 to control ◆ *Each group that held sway over a particular strip of the Mississippi River controlled who used it.*
2 to have great influence ◆ *Ten years after she correctly predicted the crash, she still holds sway among stock brokers.*

swear

swear by *sth*
to strongly believe in something ♦ *Though there's no scientific evidence for this method of finding water, some farmers swear by it.* ♦ *Some teachers swear by stickers as a teaching tool and use them to teach kids everything.*

swear *sb* **in**, *also* **swear in** *sb*
to get a formal promise from someone to be honest ♦ *A ceremony to swear in the new governor took place Wednesday.* ♦ *The witness took the stand after the court clerk swore her in.*

swear off *sth*
to decide to stop doing or using something ♦ *He says he has sworn off candy.* ♦ *She won $10,000 on the slots and was so shocked, she swore off gambling completely.*

swear up and down
to say as strongly as possible ♦ *He swore up and down that he didn't know the guy at all.*

> ORIGIN: based on the meaning of **swear on the Bible** or sometimes **swear on a stack of Bibles** (= to promise that a statement is true)

sweat

no sweat esp. spoken
there is no problem or difficulty ♦ *We'll be back by six, no sweat, but if there's a problem, we'll call you.*

sweat out *sth*, *also* **sweat it out**
to anxiously wait for something ♦ *I sent in my application and now I have to sweat out the two months until I get an answer.* ♦ *We really had to sweat it out because it wasn't clear until the end that we would actually win.*

work up a sweat
to put a lot of effort into something ♦ *The volunteers are working up a sweat to make sure everything is ready on time.*

in a cold sweat See at COLD SWEAT
sweat blood See at BLOOD

sweep

sweep away *sth*, *also* **sweep** *sth* **away**
1 to get rid of something ♦ *You will have to sweep away all your anger in order to improve your relations with your family.* ♦ *There was almost no wind to sweep the smog away.*
2 to destroy something ♦ *The decision to close the lab meant that twenty years' work was swept away in a moment.* ♦ *Francis spent his last few years at home, until heart failure swept him away.*

sweep *sb* **off** *their* **feet** See at FEET
sweep *sth* **under the carpet** See at CARPET
sweep *sth* **under the rug** See at RUG

swept

swept away
made extremely emotional or enthusiastic; = **carried away** ♦ *You couldn't help being swept away by the beauty of the place.*

swept up (in *sth***)**
suddenly very involved in something ♦ *Billings went there for a vacation and got so swept up in the place that he never left.*

swim

swim in *sth*
to have too much of something ♦ *The company is swimming in cash and trying to figure out what to do with it.* ♦ *Every meal was swimming in grease.*

swing

in full swing
moving quickly forward ♦ *In Moscow, a building boom is in full swing.*

swing at *sb/sth*, *also* **take a swing at** *sb/sth*
to try to hit someone or something ♦ *They were arguing, and then I saw him swing at Howie.* ♦ *He took a swing at the window so he could*

switch

asleep at the switch

Let's hope he's not asleep at the switch when we need him.

get into the house, and then he remembered the key hidden under the doormat.

swing by (*somewhere*)

to visit a place briefly ◆ *I told Paul we'd swing by his office about five today.* ◆ *George said he planned to swing by later.*

the swing of things

the usual way that something is done ◆ *I was just getting into the swing of things when they moved me to another department.* ◆ *Jim immediately began collecting samples, and I was soon in the swing of things.* USAGE: usually used in the forms **in the swing of things** or **into the swing of things**, as in the examples

switch

asleep at the switch

not paying attention; = **asleep at the wheel** ◆ *Health experts were asleep at the switch when the disease began to spread rapidly again.*

ORIGIN: based on the idea of someone going to sleep while they are responsible for operating the **switch** (= device) that allows a train to move from one track to another

switch gears See at GEARS

swoop

in one fell swoop

all at the same time ◆ *I prefer to see someone in charge so we can deal with everything in one fell swoop.*

ORIGIN: based on the literal meaning of **fell swoop** (= a quick, sudden downward movement by an attacking bird)

swords

cross swords (with *sb*) slightly formal

to argue with someone ◆ *The candidates crossed swords on several issues, including taxes, guns and immigration.*

system

beat the system
to get what you want by not following the usual rules ◆ *If you have money and know the right people, you have a much better chance of beating the system.* ◆ *Ellen always has some scheme that she thinks will help her beat the system.*

buck the system
to fight against the usual way of doing something ◆ *Tom spent much of his working life bucking the system, which explains why he didn't get many promotions.*

get *sth* out of *your* system
to do enough of something so that you do not want to do it any more ◆ *After last night, I think I can say that I got my desire to party out of my system.*

systems

(it's) all systems go
everything is ready for something to begin ◆ *Once the new software is installed, it's all systems go.*

T, t

T

to a T
perfectly ♦ *That hat suits you to a T.* ♦ *The qualities she described fit my daughter to a T.* USAGE: usually used with **fit** or **suit**, as in the examples

tab

pick up the tab (for *sth*)
to pay money for something ♦ *We shouldn't have to pick up the tab for the new road if only one family will be using it.* USAGE: sometimes used in the form **pick up the bill (for something)**: *Taxpayers will have to pick up the bill for political campaigns.*

table

bring *sth* to the table
to provide something that will be a benefit ♦ *Our partners brought useful skills to the table.* ♦ *You have to bring definite suggestions to the table.*

come to the table
to meet to discuss how to solve a problem or end a disagreement ♦ *Carlson urged them to come to the table to resolve the issue.* USAGE: also used in the form **come back to the table** (= to continue discussions that had stopped): *The strikers decided to come back to the table.*

on the table
being discussed or considered ♦ *I'd like to put another idea on the table to see what you think.*

set the table
to put dishes, knives, forks, and spoons on a table before a meal ♦ *You make the salad and I'll set the table.*

under the table
secretly and often illegally ♦ *A lot of these people work 80 hours a week, and they are paid under the table.*

tables

turn the tables (on *sb/sth*)
to change a situation so that someone's position is the opposite of what it was ♦ *She turned the tables by playing a better game and recently has won most of her matches.* ♦ *Hendricks turned the tables on the media when he borrowed a camera from a TV crew and started filming.* ♦ *Dan was always the one in trouble, but now the tables are turned and he's doing very well.*

wait (on) tables
to serve meals to people in a restaurant ♦ *She earned the money for college by waiting tables.*

tabs

keep tabs on *sb/sth*
to watch a person or a situation carefully ♦ *Websites use software that keeps tabs on who visits the site.* ♦ *Once you buy a stock, you need to keep tabs on it.*

tack

(as) sharp as a tack
very intelligent ♦ *He may be old in years, but he's still as sharp as a tack and knows what he's talking about.*

tack on *sth*, also tack *sth* on
to add something that is extra or does not belong ♦ *When we got the bill there was an extra 18% tacked on as a service charge.* ♦ *You should ask that question at the meeting and not tack it on to an e-mail.*

tag

tag along (with *sb/sth*)
to follow or go with a person or group when you were not invited ♦ *Do you mind if I tag along? I'd like to see the show at the museum too.* ♦ *We don't want any kids to tag along with us today.*

tail

tail off
to gradually lessen; = **taper off** ♦ *Sales of new cars always tail off when people are worried about losing their jobs.*

turn tail
1 to suddenly leave ♦ *The only thing I could do was to turn tail and run from my attacker.*
2 to suddenly change from supporting something to opposing it ♦ *The senator turned tail on his party.*

***your* tail between *your* legs**
feeling ashamed and embarrassed ♦ *After playing so badly for the entire game, the team walked off with their tails between their legs.*

> ORIGIN: based on the behavior of dogs, who will put their tails between their legs when someone speaks angrily to them

tailor-made

tailor-made for *sb/sth*
particularly suited to someone or something ♦ *Business schools are offering courses tailor-made for a firm's executives.* ♦ *The contest was tailor-made for Alexander, who was not well known and had little funding.*

tailspin

go into a tailspin
to quickly become worse ♦ *The country's nickel industry went into a tailspin, with production falling for five years in a row.* ♦ *His career went into a tailspin when he joined the New York Mets.* USAGE: sometimes used to describe someone's mental condition: *I imagine the news sent Barry into a tailspin.*

> ORIGIN: based on the literal meaning of **tailspin** (= a sudden fall by an aircraft in which the back points up and the aircraft turns around and around)

take

hard to take
difficult to believe ♦ *The reports that this extremely successful company is near bankruptcy are very hard to take.* ♦ *The humiliation of her son's crime was very hard to take.*

not take anything for granted
to question everything, including what is usually accepted as true ♦ *He did not take his luck for granted and worked constantly to be an even better dancer.* USAGE: also used in the form **take nothing for granted**: *The president took nothing for granted and worked hard to gain the support of Congress.* ♦ Opposite **take *sth* for granted** 2

not take kindly to *sth*
to be angered by something ♦ *Gomez, who had a great deal of experience, did not take kindly to advice.*

take after *sb*
to be like or to look like someone in your family ♦ *Most of my children take after my husband, both in appearance and character.*

take *sb* apart
to try to understand a person by examining their personality and character ♦ *That psychiatrist wanted to take me apart to see what makes me tick.*

> ORIGIN: based on the literal meaning of **take something apart** (= separate the parts of something)

take *sth* apart, *also* **take apart *sth***
to examine something carefully in order to completely understand it ♦ *I decided to take apart this popular word "subculture" and see what it really means.*

> ORIGIN: based on the literal meaning of **take something apart** (= separate the parts of something)

take *sb* aside
to bring someone away from other people ♦ *If Pops makes a mistake, Walker will take him aside during a break and quietly encourage him.*

take *sth* as it comes
to deal with something as it happens ◆ *At my age you can take every day as it comes and not try to guess about what will happen tomorrow.*

take away from *sth*
1 to make something less important ◆ *I don't want to take away from his achievement, but I think he should have thanked his colleagues for their help.* ◆ *Wearing that kind of outfit takes away from your dignity and self-respect.*
2 to reduce something ◆ *You know the company will cut jobs because it will not allow anything to take away from profits.*

> ORIGIN: based on the literal meaning of **take away** (= to remove or subtract one thing from another)

take *sth* away from *sb/sth*
to reduce the praise earned by a person or group ◆ *She did a lot to help people, and no one should ever try to take that away from her.* ◆ *We made some mistakes, but I don't want to take anything away from Iowa State – they played a great game.*

take *sb* back, *also* take back *sb*
to start a relationship again ◆ *Why on earth would you take him back when he's been such a rat?* ◆ *Mary took back her husband after he stopped drinking.*

take back *sth*, *also* take *sth* back
1 to say that something you said was wrong ◆ *I take it back – this is a darn good car.* ◆ *She wanted to take back her words – it wasn't easy to learn Chinese.*
2 to get control over something you controlled earlier ◆ *Democrats hope to take back the House of Representatives in the next election.* ◆ *Once we give them up to the government, we will never be able to take those rights back.*

take *you* back (to *sth*)
to cause you to remember ◆ *That song takes me back to my miserable adolescence.*

take charge (of *sth*)
to do something to control a situation or organization ◆ *Germany, Switzerland, and France still have the best teams, and they will take charge of these games.* ◆ *When the union needed someone to clean up its finances, I took charge of the whole mess.*

take down *sb*, *also* take *sb* down
1 to spoil or destroy someone's life ◆ *Some journalists just want to find a celebrity's weak points and take him or her down.* ◆ *She claims there was a government plot to take down outspoken community leaders.*
2 to defeat a competitor ◆ *Today in tennis, Martinez easily took down Kournikova to win the championship.*

take down *sb/sth*, *also* take *sb/sth* down
to remove a person or group from a position of power ◆ *Stockholders are hoping to take down the company's management team.* ◆ *Bush decided it was up to American forces to take Saddam down.*

take down *sth*, *also* take *sth* down
to destroy an aircraft as it is flying ◆ *The helicopter was taken down by enemy guns.*

take effect
to start working ◆ *The medicine takes effect in less than a half hour.* ◆ *New voter registration laws took effect last year.*

take *sb* for granted
to fail to appreciate someone ◆ *When your own children are growing up, you tend to take them for granted, and then, suddenly, they are grown up.* ◆ *Politicians seem to take voters for granted, except when they face a serious challenge.* USAGE: usually said about someone who is not appreciated because you think they will always be available

take *sth* for granted
1 to fail to appreciate the value of

something ♦ *So many of us take clean water for granted.*
2 to accept something as true without questioning or testing it ♦ *We take it for granted that our children will be better off than we are.* ♦ Opposite **not take anything for granted**

take forever
to happen very slowly ♦ *I have an old microwave, the kind that takes forever to boil a cup of water.* ♦ *In rush-hour traffic, it takes forever to get home.*

take hold
to become established; = **take root** ♦ *Democracy cannot take hold there until peace has been achieved.* ♦ *It will be several years before new plants take hold in the area hit by the volcano's eruption.*

take in *sb*, *also* **take** *sb* **in**
1 to deceive someone ♦ *Do you think the teacher was taken in by your excuse?* ♦ *That sales pitch totally took us in.*
2 to provide a place for someone to live or stay ♦ *His aunt took him in when his mother died.* ♦ *I couldn't believe Tim wanted us to take in some guy who'd been living on the street.*

take in *sth*, *also* **take** *sth* **in**
1 to see something ♦ *We took in the new Scorcese movie last night.* ♦ *We drove around the island, seeing the sights and taking it all in.*
2 to understand the meaning or importance of something ♦ *I had to read the letter twice before I could take in all that it said.* ♦ *His father described the plan, but Nick's imagination couldn't take it in.*
3 to make clothes smaller ♦ *These pants fit much better since I had them taken in.*
4 to receive money from sales ♦ *The show took in $100,000 over this weekend alone.*

take it easy
1 to rest and relax ♦ *She said I looked really tired, and told me to take it easy.*
2 to be calm and not get too excited or angry ♦ *I know you're upset, but you just take it easy, I'll make you some tea, and you can tell me all about it.* USAGE: often used as an instruction: *Now just take it easy and stop waving that knife around.*
3 esp. spoken goodbye; = **take care (of yourself)** ♦ *"Well, it was nice talking to you. Take it easy." "You too. Bye-bye."* USAGE: used to end a conversation

take it or leave it
1 to lack interest in whether you have something or not ♦ *Some people who smoke can take it or leave it, so they don't mind not being able to smoke in a restaurant.* ♦ *My sister's absolutely crazy about chocolate but I can take it or leave it.*
2 to accept or refuse without any discussion ♦ *The dealer has a set price for the car, and customers can take it or leave it.*

take kindly to *sth*, *also* **take well to** *sth*
to willingly accept a particular behavior or activity ♦ *Americans don't take kindly to being told what to say.* ♦ *I don't think the state would take kindly to the mental-health system being taken over by a judge.* ♦ *In general, Renee doesn't take well to change.*

take off
1 to leave the ground and fly ♦ *The plane could not take off because of a problem with its fuel tanks.*
2 to leave suddenly ♦ *When he saw me coming, he took off in the other direction.*
3 to suddenly succeed ♦ *The style really took off among teens.*

take (*sth***) off**
to not work at your job for a period of time ♦ *I've decided to take next semester off and travel and write.* ♦ *Jim needs to take off for a little while.*

take off after *sb*
to chase someone ♦ *Several people took off after the thief and caught him before the police got there.*

take on *sb*, *also* take *sb* on
1 to fight or compete against someone ♦ *Later today, the World Cup champions take on Chile.* ♦ *When you take a fighter like that on, you could end up in big trouble.*
2 to employ someone ♦ *The law firm took on a new partner.* ♦ *She wasn't sure if she should take a new programmer on right now.*

take on *sth*
to begin to have something ♦ *A chameleon can take on the color of the leaf it is on, making it hard to see.* ♦ *Her voice took on a troubled tone.*

take on *sth*, *also* take *sth* on
1 to fight against something ♦ *You have to be well prepared to take on a large corporation.* ♦ *We understand how this disease works, and we're ready to take it on.*
2 to accept something ♦ *My sister took on the responsibility of caring for our elderly mother.* ♦ *I knew it was going to be a difficult job I wouldn't want to take it on.*

take *sb* out *somewhere*
to bring someone somewhere for food or entertainment ♦ *When the dictionary was finished, our boss took us out for dinner.* ♦ *Alex is taking her out to a concert.*

take *sb/sth* out, *also* take out *sb/sth*
to kill a person or group ♦ *With automatic fire, you can take out a whole enemy squad.*

take out *sth*, *also* take *sth* out
1 to obtain an agreement to borrow money or financially protect your property ♦ *If you buy a house, you must take out fire insurance to protect you from loss.* ♦ *He took a loan out to buy the car.*
2 to attack and destroy something ♦ *The army took out the bridges and roads surrounding the city.*

> ORIGIN: based on the literal meaning of **take out** (= remove something)

take *sth* out on *sb*
to express negative feelings by behaving badly toward someone who is not responsible ♦ *I know you're angry at your boss, but don't take it out on the kids.*

take over (*sth*), *also* take *sth* over
to get control of something ♦ *Believe me, your mother will take over your life if you let her!* ♦ *The new director made changes the minute she took over.* ♦ *We are ready to hand over power as soon as there is someone ready to take it over.*

take some doing
to need a lot of effort ♦ *It took some doing, but I finally got the manager to agree to hire you.*

take to *sb*
to like someone soon after meeting them ♦ *We took to our new neighbors very quickly.*

take to *sth*
to like to do something ♦ *The children have really taken to tennis.*

take to *doing sth*
to start doing something regularly ♦ *She's taken to walking along the beach after work.* ♦ *After he retired, he took to working in the local schools as a volunteer.*

take to *somewhere*
to go to or escape to a place ♦ *Caryn took to her room and wouldn't come out all weekend.* ♦ *The refugees took to the hills for safety.*

take up *somewhere/sth*
to fill a space or a period of time ♦ *This desk takes up most of my office.* ♦ *Just getting there would take up too much of his time.* ♦ *Most of the weekend was taken up with shopping and cleaning.*

take up *sth*, *also* take *sth* up
1 to begin to do something ♦ *She*

worked for a TV company, then took up writing and produced a series of best-sellers. ♦ *I didn't know you smoked – when did you take it up?* **2** to consider or deal with something ♦ *A group has taken up the cause of preserving open spaces in our town.* ♦ *The coach said he couldn't practice with the team, and that he needed to take the matter up with Principal Hall.* **3** to shorten a piece of clothing ♦ *The skirt dragged on the floor, so I took it up.* ♦ *I need to have these pants taken up.*

take *sb* **up on** *sth*
to accept (an offer or invitation) from someone ♦ *I think I'll take him up on his offer of a free ticket.*

take up where *sb/sth* **left off**
to continue something that was started by someone or something ♦ *Five years after their first album, the band takes up where they left with the release of their new disc.* ♦ *If the legislature won't approve the deal, the court will try to take up where the legislature leaves off and impose a settlement.*

take up with *sb*
to begin a romantic relationship with someone ♦ *Her sister has taken up with a former high school sweetheart.* ♦ *Immigrants who have left families behind in their home countries sometimes take up with new partners here.*

take it upon *yourself/itself* **to do** *sth*, also **take** *sth* **upon** *yourself/itself*
to accept a responsibility without being asked to ♦ *He took it upon himself to personally thank each person who came to the memorial service.* ♦ *The Transit Authority has taken it upon itself to be the spokesman for its riders.* ♦ *Is there a reason why some countries should take upon themselves the role of international policeman?*

taken
taken aback
confused or surprised by something unexpected ♦ *Company executives have been taken aback by the criticism.* ♦ *I asked him directly if he was looking for someone with my skills, and I think he was kind of taken aback.*

> ORIGIN: based on the literal meaning of **aback** (= backward), which is not used in modern English

taken with *sb/sth*
attracted to someone or something ♦ *Carpenter was so taken with the sculpture that he persuaded the town to sell it to him.* ♦ *I was really taken with her, and admired her talent and personality.*

takes
what it takes
everything that is needed ♦ *They run health fairs at high schools where teenagers learn about what it takes to take care of a baby.* USAGE: often used with **that's**: *You've got to spend a lot of money, because that's what it takes to make a championship team.* ♦ Related vocabulary **have (got) what it takes** at HAVE

have (got) what it takes See at HAVE

it takes two to tango See at TWO

sth **takes the cake** See at CAKE

taking
for the taking, also free for the taking
easily available ♦ *If you're interested in the job, it's there for the taking.* USAGE: often used in the form **someone's for the taking**: *Just when it looked like the gold medal was hers for the taking, she fell and twisted her ankle.* ♦ Related vocabulary **within reach** at REACH

like taking candy from a baby See at CANDY

talk

talk back (to *sb***)**
to answer rudely ◆ *They were arrested on minor charges after talking back to a police officer.* ◆ *In my family, kids just never talked back.*

> ORIGIN: based on the literal meaning of **talk back** (= to answer someone)

talk dirty
to talk about sex ◆ *He called one of those phone services where you pay to have women talk dirty to you.*

talk down *sth*, also **talk** *sth* **down**
to say that something is not very good or important ◆ *Bonds is doing everything possible to talk down his achievements.* ◆ *I love this town, and I don't like to talk things down, but there are some real problems here that need to be dealt with.*

talk down to *sb*
to speak to someone as if they were too young or stupid to understand something ◆ *I think of old people just as I think of myself, so I don't talk down to them.*

talk *sb* **into** *sth*
to persuade someone to do something ◆ *It was pretty hard to talk the kids into going to the dance, but they did go and had a great time.* ◆ *She talked the boss into buying new computers by saying we could work faster with them.* ◆ Opposite **talk** *sb* **out of** *sth*

talk out *sth*, also **talk** *sth* **out**
to discuss a problem in detail ◆ *We're trying to encourage these kids to talk out their differences.* ◆ *I can't stand endless arguments, so if you have a problem with me, let's talk it out.* ◆ Related vocabulary **talked out** at TALKED

talk *sb* **out of** *sth*
to persuade someone not to do something ◆ *She had to talk him out of quitting his job.* ◆ *I wish I'd known she was taking the drug, I would have tried to talk her out of it.* ◆ Opposite **talk** *sb* **into** *sth*

talk *sth* **over**, also **talk over** *sth*
to discuss something ◆ *We should get together and talk this over.* ◆ *They met yesterday to talk over ways of funding the school.* USAGE: usually said about a disagreement or problem

talk the talk
to say something in a way that appears to be true or real ◆ *For a woman whose criminal-law practice is only 11 months old, she sure can talk the talk.* USAGE: sometimes used in the full form **talk the talk and walk the walk** (= to say something that appears to be real or true and show it is real or true through your actions): *Most of these guys say they have religious beliefs, but only a few of them can talk the talk and walk the walk.* ◆ Related vocabulary **walk the walk** at WALK

talk tough
to speak in a way that makes others fear you ◆ *Our government is talking tough to both our enemies and our allies.* ◆ *I can talk tough and scare someone, but I can't really act tough.*

talk through *sth*, also **talk it through**
to explain or consider something in detail, esp. a problem ◆ *He had tried to get her to talk through her fears so she would see that they weren't so serious.* ◆ *I think you will have to talk it through with Sandy to see if she agrees with our plans.* ◆ Related vocabulary **walk (***sb***) through** *sth* at WALK

talk *you* **through** *sth*
to explain something in detail to someone; = **walk (***sb***) through** *sth* ◆ *Phil was looking for someone to talk him through the new computer system.*

talk up *sth*, also **talk** *sth* **up**
to support something enthusiasti-

cally ♦ *His job is to talk up new bands and get them gigs.* ♦ *She talked the idea up with as many friends and colleagues as she could.*

talk out of both sides of *your* mouth See at SIDES

talk sense See at SENSE

talk some sense into *sb* See at SENSE

talk shop See at SHOP

talk turkey See at TURKEY

talk *your* way *somewhere* See at WAY

talked
talked out
unable to say anything more ♦ *After two hours of nonstop discussion, everybody was talked out.* ♦ Related vocabulary **talk out *sth*** at TALK

talking
now you're talking esp. spoken
you have finally had a good idea ♦ *"Would you like pizza for dinner?" "Now you're talking!"*

tandem
in tandem (with *sb*/*sth*)
together ♦ *The airlines cut prices in tandem.* ♦ *This director has worked in tandem with the same composer on several films.*

tangent
(off) on a tangent
suddenly dealing with a completely different matter ♦ *We were talking about gas prices and you went off on a tangent about your vacation plans.*

tangle
tangle with *sb*/*sth*
to disagree or fight with someone or something ♦ *She's not afraid to tangle with her father.* ♦ *The two computer giants had tangled with each other in court several times.*

ORIGIN: based on the literal meaning of **tangle** (= to get things mixed together so that it is difficult to separate them)

tangled
tangled up with *sb*
involved with someone ♦ *The boy had gotten tangled up with a bad bunch of kids and was in serious trouble.* USAGE: usually said about someone who causes you trouble

tangled up with *sth*, *also* **tangled up in *sth***
involved in something that is difficult to get out of ♦ *It is a huge mistake to get tangled up with drugs.* ♦ *The Development Commission got tangled up in a controversy and lawsuit over a gravel plant located along the railroad tracks.*

tank
tank up on *sth*
to drink a great deal of something ♦ *Be sure to tank up on water before you work outdoors on a hot day!* ♦ *We tanked up on gin and tonics and then had a long nap.*

tank up (*sth*), *also* **tank *sth* up**
to fill the fuel container of a vehicle with gas or other fuel ♦ *There won't be any gas stations for miles and miles, so we'd better tank up now.* ♦ *It's always a good idea to tank up a rented car before you return it.*

tantrum
throw a (temper) tantrum
to become very angry and unreasonable ♦ *When you are a grown-up, you don't throw a tantrum if something offends you, you discuss it.* USAGE: usually the anger is expressed by shouting and crying

tap
on tap
available or expected ♦ *Temperatures will be in the 90s over much of the Mississippi River valley, with*

taper

on tap

There are several terrific movies on tap this weekend.

plenty of humidity on tap. ♦ Three more playoff games are on tap today.

> ORIGIN: based on the literal meaning of beer **on tap** (= served from a large container rather than a can or bottle)

taper

taper off
to gradually lessen; = **tail off** ♦ *The price of gasoline should taper off in the fall.* ♦ *The rain will taper off by morning and the afternoon should be sunny.*

target

(right) on target
correct or accurate ♦ *Many of Mr. Bryant's criticisms were on target but others were not fair.* ♦ *Estimates of costs for the new high school were right on target.*

task

take *sb* to task, also **take to task *sb***
to criticize someone ♦ *We have gotten many letters that take us to task for including swear words in the dic-*tionary. ♦ *The article takes to task those movie stars who look like they just rolled out of bed.*

taste

leave a bad taste in *your* mouth
to cause an unpleasant memory ♦ *Violent movies always leave a bad taste in my mouth.*

tatters

in tatters
damaged beyond repair ♦ *They argued and fought for years, and their relationship is now in tatters.*

> ORIGIN: based on the literal meaning of clothing **in tatters** (= torn in small pieces)

team

team up (with *sb*/*sth*)
to join with another person or group to achieve something ♦ *The two companies teamed up to provide a new electronic news service.* ♦ *Feer first teamed up with Laff in high school to do cartoons for the school newspaper.*

tear

tear apart *sb/sth*, *also* **tear** *sb/sth* **apart**
1 to severely criticize someone or something ◆ *The critics tore apart his first novel, but he never gave up and finally achieved great success.* ◆ *His teachers tore him apart for cheating on the test.*
2 *also* **tear** *sb/sth* **up** to hurt someone or something badly ◆ *The college was torn apart by antiwar protests.* ◆ *The families of the victims were torn apart with grief and anger and sorrow.* ◆ *Success has a way of tearing up relationships.*

> ORIGIN: based on the literal meaning of **tear apart** (= pull into pieces)

tear at *sth*
to cause you to feel emotional ◆ *There are scenes in this movie that tear at my heart because they are just like scenes from my life.*

tear *yourself* **away (from** *sb/sth***)**
to force yourself to leave a person or activity ◆ *I'm glad you managed to tear yourself away from the TV and come eat dinner with us!* ◆ *These video games offer plenty of action – you will hardly be able to tear yourself away.*

tear down *sb/sth*, *also* **tear** *sb/sth* **down**
to damage or reduce the importance of someone or something ◆ *In the end, she glamorizes the very concept she is trying to tear down.* ◆ *Many blame the media for tearing heroes down by publicizing their mistakes.*

> ORIGIN: based on the literal meaning of **tear down** (= to cause a structure to fall)

tear into *sb*
to attack someone fiercely ◆ *He tore into the witness, calling him a liar.* ◆ *I saw a small boy tear into a much larger fellow who had taken his bike.*

tear off *sth*, *also* **tear** *sth* **off**
to quickly remove something ◆ *She tore off her apron and ran outside to see what had happened.*

tear *your* **hair (out)** See at HAIR
tear *your* **heart out** See at HEART
tear *sb* **limb from limb** See at LIMB
wear and tear See at WEAR

tears

burst into tears
to suddenly cry ◆ *She burst into tears when she read the rejection letter.* ◆ *Every time I thought about it I'd burst into tears.*

in tears
crying ◆ *Some employees were in tears as they said they were resigning.* USAGE: often used in the form **break down in tears** (= to begin crying): *He broke down in tears when he learned that his father had died.*

moved to tears
feeling very emotional, like you are going to cry ◆ *She was moved to tears several times by the kindness of complete strangers who were searching for survivors of the explosions.*

tease

tease out *sth*, *also* **tease** *sth* **out**
to carefully separate particular facts from a great deal of information ◆ *What has always been interesting for me is how you can tease out the reasons for an event as you review its history.* ◆ *After a while, you learn how to tease out the errors hidden in texts.* ◆ Related vocabulary **puzzle over** *sth* at PUZZLE

teeth

armed to the teeth
having many and powerful weapons ◆ *Some of these gangs are armed to the teeth.*

cut *your* **teeth in** *sth*, *also* **cut** *your* **teeth on** *sth*
to get your first experience doing a particular kind of work or using a particular skill ◆ *He cut his teeth in politics as a campaign manager for*

a small-town mayor. ♦ *They had just graduated from law school and were anxious to cut their teeth on a case.*

gnash *your* teeth
to show you are angry or annoyed about something bad that you cannot do anything to stop ♦ *His advisers are gnashing their teeth in frustration because he refuses to attack his opponent on foreign policy issues.* USAGE: also used in the form **gnashing of teeth**: *The first test-tube baby was born in 1978, to considerable gnashing of teeth.*

grit *your* teeth
to deal with something in a determined way ♦ *When a test came along, I just gritted my teeth and studied harder because I knew I had to improve my grades.*

in the teeth of *sth*
while experiencing something difficult ♦ *The road was built in the teeth of fierce opposition from environmentalists.*

lie through *your* teeth
to say things that are not true in a way that seems sincere ♦ *Slater wasn't a doctor, he had never been to medical school, he just lied through his teeth and we believed him.*

like pulling teeth
extremely difficult ♦ *Getting our kids dressed and off to school in winter is like pulling teeth.*

put teeth into *sth*
to make a law or rule effective ♦ *The threat of fines and jail put real teeth into the laws regulating how and where children can work.*

set *your* teeth on edge
to annoy you or make you feel nervous or uncomfortable ♦ *Jason used his knife to scratch our initials into the wall, which was nice to do but made a noise that set my teeth on edge.* ♦ Related vocabulary **on edge** at EDGE

sink *your* teeth into *sth*
to start to do something with a lot of energy and enthusiasm ♦ *She'd* only had small parts in films and was hoping for a bigger, more interesting part, something she could sink her teeth into. ♦ *It's a really exciting project – I can't wait to sink my teeth into it.*

tell

I tell you esp. spoken, *also* **I'll tell you**
this is what I think ♦ *Well, I tell you, if you worked on the pier, you'd see how much junk there is floating on the water.* ♦ *It's important to have health insurance, but I'll tell you, I don't mind having dental insurance, too.* USAGE: used to emphasize what you are about to say

tell (*sb/sth*) apart, *also* **tell which is which**
to be able to see the difference between one person or thing and another ♦ *One guy's a Democrat and the other's a Republican, but it wasn't always easy to tell them apart.* ♦ *The twins are no longer as hard to tell apart as when they were little babies.* ♦ *She held out two flowers, but I couldn't tell which was which.*

tell it like it is
to describe a situation honestly without avoiding any unpleasant details ♦ *I am honest about things, and I'm going to tell it like it is as long as I am in charge of this project.*

tell me about it esp. spoken
I have had the same experience ♦ *"I love my sister, but she can be a real bother sometimes." "Oh, tell me about it."* USAGE: said in reaction to someone else's statement, as in the example

tell off *sb*, *also* **tell *sb* off**
to tell someone that their behavior is not acceptable ♦ *I was told off by my best friend, and it was a long time before I could forgive her.* ♦ *He's always been obnoxious and it's about time someone told him off.*

tell on *sb*
to give information about bad be-

havior to someone in authority ◆ *None of his friends told on Louie, not even when he slipped live grasshoppers into a mailbox.*

tell *sb* where to get off
to let someone know in a direct way that they are wrong or behaving badly ◆ *Steve's one of the few people in the office who will tell her where to get off.*

tell you what esp. spoken
this is what I think ◆ *I'll tell you what, it's a wonder Elise didn't have a heart attack when she got that bill.* ◆ *I tell you what, if you buy now I'll give you an additional 20% off the sales price.*

you never can tell
there is no way to know or be certain of something ◆ *It sounds like a nice place to live, but you never can tell – we may end up hating it.* ◆ Related vocabulary **there's no telling** at TELLING

kiss and tell See at KISS

(only) time will tell See at TIME

tell time See at TIME

telling

there's no telling, *also* **there is no telling**
it is impossible to guess ◆ *There's no telling how much damage has been done to young people by these "designer drugs."* ◆ *Even when we don't let them loose, there's no telling what kind of trouble the puppies will get into.* ◆ Related vocabulary **you never can tell** at TELL

temper

lose *your* temper
to become very angry ◆ *If she contradicted him now, he would lose his temper and his blood pressure would shoot up.*

throw a (temper) tantrum See at TANTRUM

tenterhooks

on tenterhooks
anxiously waiting for news about someone or something ◆ *She was on tenterhooks until her son called and said he was not hurt.*

> ORIGIN: based on the literal meaning of **tenterhook** (= a hook that holds cloth that is stretched to dry), suggesting that someone's emotions are tightly stretched like a piece of cloth held by tenterhooks

term

in the long term, *also* **for the long term**
involving a long period of time ◆ *Better teacher training will make a big difference to the school in the long term.* ◆ *For the long term, we hope our plans will create a large number of jobs.* ◆ Related vocabulary **take the long view** at VIEW

in the short term, *also* **for the short term**
in the near future ◆ *In the short term, the tax would bring money into the treasury, but after that, it would cost the government more each year.*

over the long term
for a long period of time; = **for the long haul** ◆ *Experts say it's the best place over the long term to put your savings.*

over the short term
for a brief period of time only ◆ *Profits will rise over the short term, but over the long term, no one really can predict.*

terms

come to terms with *sth*
to begin to accept and deal with something difficult or unpleasant ◆ *She's never really come to terms with her son's death.* ◆ *It's very hard coming to terms with the fact that you'll never have children.* ◆ Related vocabulary **come to grips with *sth*** at GRIPS

in no uncertain terms
very clearly ◆ *She was told in no un-*

certain terms that the magazine had no interest in her short stories.

in terms of *sth*
in relation to something ◆ *Cheryl was speaking in terms of improving students' grades by teaching them how to study.* ◆ *Getting laid off from his job affected him more emotionally than in terms of the loss of income.* ◆ Related vocabulary **with regard to** *sth* at REGARD, **with respect to** *sth* at RESPECT

on good terms (with *sb***)**
friendly with someone or with each other ◆ *Although she is on good terms with her parents now, Angie said she doesn't want to live with them, even for a short time.* ◆ *Even after their divorce, they remained on good terms.* USAGE: also **on bad terms (with someone)**, with the opposite meaning: *She and her brother have been on bad terms for many years.*

on speaking terms
friendly enough to talk ◆ *We have heard from various people that the coach is barely on speaking terms with his best pitcher.* USAGE: often used in the form **not on speaking terms**: *The two nations have not been on speaking terms for a couple of decades.*

territory

come with the territory, *also* **go with the territory**
included as a regular part of a job or activity ◆ *Steven knew when he became a doctor that telephone calls at any hour came with the territory and to be prepared for them.*

test

pass the smell test
to be morally acceptable ◆ *Robinson's removal as an independent investigator doesn't pass the smell test, and many believe it was done for political reasons.* USAGE: often used in negative sentences, as in the example

put *sb/sth* **to the test**
to find out how good someone or something is ◆ *Those icy roads certainly put my driving to the test.* ◆ *An explosion in the subway put police and firefighters to the test.*

stand the test of time, *also* **withstand the test of time**
to continue to work well over a long period of time ◆ *Look for software that has stood the test of time, not something new and unproven.* ◆ *So we want it to be a good house, one that's going to stand the test of time.*

test the waters See at WATERS

thanks

no thanks to *sb/sth*
despite someone or something ◆ *Well, we've finished the painting, no thanks to Sandra, who suddenly decided she had to go away for the weekend!*

thanks to *sb/sth*
because of someone or something ◆ *Thanks to Sandy, I found this great apartment.* ◆ *Thanks to his fitness, Roberto recovered from the injury fairly quickly.*

that

that's it esp. spoken, *also* esp. spoken **that's about it**
everything necessary or related to a subject has been mentioned ◆ *I read the comics in the Sunday paper – that's it.* ◆ *Well, I've told you all the news about us. That's about it.*

that's that esp. spoken
nothing more can be said about this ◆ *You are not allowed to stay up to see that movie and that's that.* USAGE: used to show you are very determined

them

with the best of them
in a way that is equal to any other person's effort ◆ *If we need a seat on the subway, I can fight for seats with the best of them.*

then

(but) then again
after thinking more about something ◆ *She'd look better if she lost maybe ten or fifteen pounds, but then again who wouldn't?* ◆ *It would be fun to see them – then again, I don't really have the time.* ◆ Related vocabulary **on second thought** at THOUGHT

then and there
immediately ◆ *The minute I saw her, I decided I had to tell her then and there that I wanted to marry her.* ◆ Related vocabulary **(right) here and now** at HERE

and then some See at SOME

(every) now and then See at NOW

theory

in theory
possibly ◆ *They could, in theory, have been paid twice if someone hadn't caught the error.* ◆ Opposite **in practice** at PRACTICE ◆ Related vocabulary **in principle** at PRINCIPLE

there

from there to here
from that point or situation to this very different one ◆ *The special shopping service was very popular and really got us from there to here.*

thick

in the thick of it, *also* **in the thick of** *sth*
completely involved in an activity or a situation ◆ *At first George didn't want to have anything to do with planning our wedding, but he's in the thick of it now.* ◆ *Although he denies it, the company's treasurer was in the thick of the illegal activities.*

through thick and thin
including both good times and bad times ◆ *Dogs are real friends because they are loyal to you through thick and thin and don't expect more than food and approval in return.* USAGE: sometimes used in the form **stick together through thick and thin** (= to support one another in good or bad times): *The brothers promised they would stick together through thick and thin.*

thing

amount to the same thing, *also* **come to the same thing**
to be nearly the same thing, after you consider it ◆ *She wanted him to suffer and she wanted to punish him, which amounts to the same thing.*

a thing of the past
something that does not exist or happen any more ◆ *Your friendly local telephone operator may be a thing of the past, but you still can dial "0" and talk to a real person if you need to.* ◆ *Unfortunately, torture is not a thing of the past.*

do *your* own thing
to follow your interests, esp. without worrying about what other people think ◆ *I know artists who won't let anyone or anything interfere with doing their own thing, even if it means not having any money.* ◆ Related vocabulary ***your* own person** at PERSON

except for one thing
not including something in particular ◆ *The car is beautiful and perfect, except for one thing – the price.*

for one thing
one reason is ◆ *For one thing, sun screens block more of the sun's damaging rays, so they are much more effective.* ◆ *I like smaller companies – they're more personal for one thing.*

have a good thing going
to do or have something that is successful ◆ *This director has a good thing going with one film nominated for an Oscar and two others earning him a lot of money.* USAGE: also used in the forms **the better thing going** or **the best thing going**: *If you have to commute to the city, the train is the best thing going.* ◆ Related vocabulary **on a roll** 1 at ROLL

have a thing about *sth*
to have a strong opinion about something ◆ *I've always had a thing about fresh raspberries, so now I grow them in my garden.* ◆ *She won't come to the beach with me because she has a thing about getting sand between her toes.* USAGE: usually refers to something that is an unusual characteristic

(it's) one thing after another
bad things keep happening ◆ *Ever since my car was stolen last year, it's been one thing after another.*

not know the first thing about *sth* esp. spoken
to know nothing about something; = **not know beans about *sth*** ◆ *I don't know why you're asking Alice, she doesn't know the first thing about sports.*

one thing leads to another
an event or activity results in another that you have usually not planned ◆ *I agreed to help him paint his house and one thing led to another until I ended up helping him fix up his kitchen.*

(the) first thing (in the morning)
before doing anything else ◆ *The first thing tomorrow, you'll have to cancel our reservations.* ◆ *White had a habit of playing his trumpet first thing in the morning, which really irritated his neighbors.*

the funny thing is esp. spoken
what I am about to say is really strange ◆ *But the funny thing is, I still love my job, because I still feel I am doing something important.* ◆ *And the funny thing is, the guy spending the least money on TV ads is the one who's ahead in the opinion polls.*

there is no such thing
the situation you are talking about does not exist ◆ *There is no such thing as a completely truthful politician, he maintained.*

the same old thing
something that is extremely familiar ◆ *I'm just doing the same old thing, and soon I'm going to die of boredom!* ◆ *Every summer it's the same old thing – shouts of kids enjoying the pool in the hot weather.* ◆ Related vocabulary **it's the same old story** at STORY, **the same old same old** at OLD

the thing is esp. spoken
this is what must be considered ◆ *The thing is, my car is being repaired, so how can I get groceries for the weekend?* USAGE: sometimes used in the form **another thing is**: *Another thing is, I had told her about your operation just the day before.*

too much of a good thing
too much of something that in smaller amounts is good ◆ *We had hoped for a snowstorm, but now we have too much of a good thing and can't go out at all.* ◆ *Some people believe that the Internet offers too much of a good thing, specifically, free speech.*

the greatest thing since sliced bread See at BREAD

things

(all) other things being equal
if in all other ways two situations are the same or similar ◆ *All other things being equal, a professor can get higher ratings from students by giving higher grades.* USAGE: also used in the form **all things being equal**: *All things being equal, children are better off having both a mother and father in the home.*

all things considered
after carefully thinking about all the facts or opinions ◆ *Actually, Fitch thinks his family is doing fine right now, all things considered.*

all things to all people
everything that every person wants ◆ *The baseball museum is all things to all people, which means that both old and young can enjoy this visual history of the game.* USAGE: often as

a negative: *A political party cannot be all things to all people.*

as things stand
as the situation is ◆ *As things stand now, I can't imagine we'll be ready to leave until Friday at the earliest.* ◆ Related vocabulary **as it stands** at STANDS

first things first
the most important thing should be thought about or done before any other ◆ *You may need to get a better Internet service, but first things first – see if the one you have can do what you want.*

just one of those things esp. spoken
something that happens unexpectedly ◆ *I couldn't keep the dog from running toward the car. It was just one of those things.*

of all things
surprisingly ◆ *The biggest change in the band came when Dee Dee left in 1989 to become, of all things, a rapper.* ◆ Related vocabulary **of all people** at PEOPLE, **of all places** at PLACES

see things
1 to notice something, esp. something that someone else would not notice ◆ *And when I'm playing hockey, my eyes watch the puck, and I see things I hardly realize I'm seeing.*
2 to imagine something is present or happening when it is not ◆ *Everyone is afraid of something, and most people see things at one time or another.*

in the scheme of things See at SCHEME

the swing of things See at SWING

the way things are (going) See at WAY

think

have another think (coming)
to need to consider something again ◆ *If you expected praise just for doing your job, you had another think coming.* ◆ *I really do know what I'm talking about, and if you don't agree, you had better have another think.*

not think twice about *sth*
to do something quickly without considering it very much ◆ *With such a good offer from a buyer, I didn't think twice about selling the farm.*

think again
you are wrong ◆ *If you believe that the term "marketing" should not be applied to an idea, think again.*

think back
to remember something ◆ *When I think back on it, I realize I should have noticed that you were unhappy.* ◆ *Melissa and Jay both fell silent, thinking back to the dreadful time when Jack had almost died.*

think better of it, *also* **think better of** *sth*
to decide that something is not a good idea ◆ *He considered quitting college but thought better of it.*

think big
to form plans that are extremely difficult to achieve ◆ *She could never have imagined owning her own business, but her husband encouraged Janice to think big.*

think for *yourself*
to decide for yourself your opinion about something ◆ *You are old enough and have had enough experience to think for yourself and don't let anyone else do it for you!*

think long and hard
to carefully consider something ◆ *Allen liked to think long and hard about each question, and his answers were always carefully expressed.*

think nothing of *sth/doing sth*
to do something unusual or dangerous without worrying about it ◆ *Howell thinks nothing of taking off to London or Paris to look for rare and wonderful antiques.* ◆ *Randy thought nothing of hanging from a*

steel beam 400 feet above ground during his career as an iron worker.

think out loud esp. spoken
to say your thoughts aloud ◆ *I'm thinking out loud now, but it looks as if I can meet you Tuesday.*

think *sth* **over**, also **think over** *sth*
to consider something carefully; = **think** *sth* **through** ◆ *She really ought to think it over before she quits school.* ◆ *Dunham was looking at me, thinking over what he had heard and deciding what it meant.* USAGE: often used in the form **think it over**: *She made an offer to buy our house, and I promised to think it over.*

think positive
to be hopeful that good things will happen ◆ *I try to think positive, so if something goes wrong, I try to fix it or, if I can't, I just forget it.*

think straight
to use your mind effectively ◆ *The actor said she was so surprised to be nominated for an award that she still can't think straight.* USAGE: usually used in a negative way, as in the example

think *sth* **through**, also **think through** *sth*
to consider something carefully, esp. before making an important decision; = **think** *sth* **over** ◆ *We can't afford a mistake, so think things through and make sure you have everything ready.* ◆ *You should think through all these questions before you send your proposal to a publisher.* USAGE: also used in the form **think out something**: *He's trying to think out all the options available before deciding on one.*

think to *yourself*
to make a judgment about something without talking about it with anyone else ◆ *I thought to myself, who knows, maybe he is right.* ◆ Related vocabulary **say (*sth*) to yourself** at SAY

think twice (about *sth*)
to consider something more carefully ◆ *You may want to think twice before buying one of California's new earthquake insurance policies.* USAGE: often used as a warning, and sometimes used in the form **think twice before doing something**: *He said he is sorry and will think twice before giving such advice again.*

think up *sth*, also **think** *sth* **up**
to invent something ◆ *She used to think up funny things just to make him laugh.* ◆ *Sitting in the school yard, I thought up a scheme to get the older boys on my side.* ◆ *They had to do something fast, and they were smart to actually think that up.* ◆ Related vocabulary **dream up** *sth* at DREAM

think well of *sb/sth*, also **think highly of** *sb/sth*
to have a very good opinion of someone or something ◆ *Although Scott has a high regard for the Navy, I understand the Navy doesn't think well of his film about the submarine service.* ◆ *We think very highly of our new chorus director.* ◆ Related vocabulary **think the world of** *sb* at WORLD

hear *yourself* **think** See at HEAR
think on *your* **feet** See at FEET
think outside the box See at BOX
think the world of *sb* See at WORLD

this

this and that
one thing and another ◆ *You see a lot of activity in the park, people riding bikes, playing ball, doing this and that.*

this is
this person is ◆ *Harry, this is my cousin, Joan.* ◆ *This is my friend, Robert.* USAGE: usually used in introducing someone by their name or by their relationship to you

at this stage of the game See at STAGE
you don't need this See at NEED
in this day and age See at DAY
in this regard See at REGARD
(just) this side of *sth* See at SIDE
not long for this world See at WORLD

thorn
a thorn in *sb's/sth's* side, *also* **a thorn in the side of *sb/sth***
someone or something that continually causes problems ♦ *Most teachers usually have one student in their class who is a thorn in their side.* ♦ *The town finds the casino a thorn in its side, even though it brings huge numbers of tourists to the town.* ♦ *Health inspectors are a thorn in the side of most restaurant owners.*

thought
lost in thought
not aware of what is happening around you because you are thinking about something else ♦ *I didn't answer right away because I was lost in thought.*
on second thought
after having thought about something again ♦ *On second thought we decided that it would be too expensive to fly, so we took a bus instead.* ♦ Related vocabulary **(but) then again** at THEN, **have second thoughts** at THOUGHTS
perish the thought
do not even think about it ♦ *I don't think either parent would ever, perish the thought, tell that kid "no."*
who would have thought esp. spoken
I am very surprised at what has happened ♦ *Who would have thought that this disaster would affect so many members of our community?*
without a second thought
without stopping to consider whether something is wise or right ♦ *She doesn't worry about money –* *she'll spend a hundred bucks on a dress without a second thought.*
food for thought See at FOOD

thoughts
have second thoughts
to consider changing a decision you have already made ♦ *Sean Elliott appears to be having second thoughts about retirement.* ♦ *Some of the biggest companies are having second thoughts about jumping into the Internet access business.* ♦ Related vocabulary **on second thought** at THOUGHT

thrash
thrash out *sth*, *also* **thrash *sth* out**
to reach an agreement after a long or difficult discussion ♦ *The meeting lasted all night, but by morning, the two sides had thrashed out their differences and agreed on a new contract.* ♦ *They're close to making a deal, and we just hope they can thrash it out without going to trial.*

thread
hang by a thread
to be in danger of having something unlucky or bad happen ♦ *Roberta was told that her job hung by a thread, and she needed to be more serious about it.* ♦ *For several days after the accident, his life hung by a thread.*
lose the thread (of *sth*)
to not be able to understand what someone is saying because you are not giving it all your attention ♦ *Jeb wasn't listening at all and lost the thread of what his father was saying.*

threshold
on the threshold of *sth*
near the beginning of something ♦ *Tyler is on the threshold of becoming a very successful singer.*

> ORIGIN: based on the literal meaning of **threshold** (= the part of the floor at the entrance to a room or building)

throat

clear *your* throat
to give a small cough ♦ *She cleared her throat before she began to speak.* ♦ *I wanted to say something, so I cleared my throat to get everyone's attention.*

grab *you* by the throat
to completely hold your attention or emotions ♦ *Jealousy grabbed him by the throat and destroyed his marriage.* USAGE: also used in the forms **take you by the throat** or **hold you by the throat**: *This is an adventure that takes you by the throat and doesn't let you go until the end of the film.*

throats

at each other's throats
in angry disagreement ♦ *The neighbors are at each other's throats over who should repair the fence.*

through

through and through
completely ♦ *He's a military man through and through.*

throw

throw away *sth*, *also* throw *sth* away
to fail to use an opportunity ♦ *Milton threw away his chance of promotion by being late almost every day.* ♦ *It's a chance to audition for the Metropolitan Opera – don't throw it away.* ♦ Related vocabulary **blow it** at BLOW

ORIGIN: based on the literal meaning of **throw away something** (= to get rid of something)

throw in *sth*, *also* throw *sth* in
to include something extra ♦ *If you subscribe now, the phone company throws in 90 days of free Internet access.* ♦ *She would throw some French fries in to keep the customers happy.*

throw *yourself* into *sth*
to do something with a lot of energy and enthusiasm ♦ *I threw myself into the Spanish classes and after three months I could carry on a simple conversation.*

throw off *sth*, *also* throw *sth* off
to quickly remove something ♦ *The boys threw off their clothes and jumped into the lake.* ♦ *Dad threw the cover off and there was a beautiful new bike – just for me!* ♦ Opposite **throw on *sth***

throw on *sth*, *also* throw *sth* on
to quickly put on something ♦ *He leapt out of bed and threw his clothes on.* ♦ *She threw on a raincoat and*

at each other's throats

Those two have been at each other's throats all afternoon.

ran outdoors to get the cat. ♦ Opposite **throw off** *sth*

throw open *sth* **to** *sb/sth*
to make something available to someone or something ♦ *Ticket sales will be thrown open to the public next week.* ♦ *The artist threw open his studio to me and taught me to be a serious painter.*

throw *sb* **out**, *also* **throw out** *sb*
to force someone to leave ♦ *At least four kids have been thrown out of school for cheating on exams.* ♦ *The worst part of Edsel's job is having to throw out the drunks when the bar closes.*

throw out *sth*, *also* **throw** *sth* **out**
1 to offer something ♦ *Sally threw out some good ideas for discussion at the next meeting.* ♦ *Let me just throw this concept out to you and see if you like it.*
2 to decide a legal case will not be heard ♦ *The judge threw the lawsuit out because it was silly.*

throw *sb* **together**, *also* **throw together** *sb*
to bring people together in a manner that is not planned ♦ *The refugees were thrown together in large camps.* ♦ *We'd throw together people from different parts of our lives and have a great big party.*

throw *sth* **together**, *also* **throw together** *sth*
to create something quickly without preparation ♦ *We came home late and I just threw something together for us to eat.* ♦ *It was one of those low-cost movies that studios often throw together.*

throw up (*sth***)**, *also* **throw** *sth* **up**
to vomit ♦ *The bus ride was making him feel sick, and he was afraid he was going to throw up.* ♦ *I fed the baby some fruit, but she threw it up.*

throw up *sth*
to build something quickly ♦ *The houses were thrown up in a matter of months and were not well built.*

thumb

stick out like a sore thumb, *also* **stand out like a sore thumb**
to be easily noticed as different ♦ *Ted wore old jeans to the party, and he stuck out like a sore thumb among all the well-dressed guests.*

thumb through *sth*
to quickly look at a pile of papers or the pages of a magazine or book ♦ *Quinn thumbed through his messages until he found the slip with Ritter's phone number on it.* ♦ *Bella had to wait for Jill so she passed the time thumbing through magazines.*

under *sb's/sth's* **thumb**, *also* **under the thumb of** *sb/sth*
completely controlled by someone or something ♦ *That girl is totally under her mother's thumb.*

thumb *your* **nose at** *sb/sth* See at NOSE

thumbs

all thumbs
awkward in handling things ♦ *Can you thread this needle for me? I'm all thumbs.*

(give a) thumbs down to *sb/sth*
to show disapproval of or opposition to someone or something ♦ *My husband gave a big thumbs down to my idea of getting a new car.* USAGE: often used in the form **give the thumbs down (to something)**: *Voters gave the thumbs down to building a new firehouse.* ♦ Opposite **(give a) thumbs up to** *sb/sth*

(give a) thumbs up to *sb/sth*
to show approval of or support for someone or something ♦ *Voters gave a thumbs up to building swimming pool for the town.* USAGE: often used in the form **give the thumbs up to (something)**: *We have been given the thumbs up and will begin work next week.* ♦ Opposite **(give a) thumbs down to** *sb/sth*

twiddle *your* **thumbs**
to do nothing ♦ *Dan spent a whole day twiddling his thumbs, waiting for a package to be delivered.*

tick

tick off *sth*, *also* **tick** *sth* **off**
to name a list of things ◆ *She ticked off six reasons for saying no.* ◆ *She had lots of objections, and she ticked them off one after another.*

tick *sb* **off** esp. spoken, *also* **tick off** *sb*
to make someone angry ◆ *It just ticks me off to think that anyone who wants to can read my e-mail.* ◆ *It was only a suggestion, not a criticism, and she didn't think it would tick off everyone at the meeting.*

what makes *sb* **tick** See at MAKE

ticket

just the ticket
exactly what is needed ◆ *If you love a splash of color, this striped T-shirt is just the ticket.* ◆ Related vocabulary **just what the doctor ordered** at DOCTOR

tide

stem the tide
to stop something from increasing ◆ *This law may stem the tide of pollution of our beautiful river from the factories built along its banks.*

tide *sb* **over**, *also* **tide over** *sb*
to supply someone with something they need for a short period ◆ *We were lucky and got a small loan to tide us over until our customers began to pay us.* ◆ *They're seeking food aid to tide over the starving population until the next harvest.*

turn the tide
to completely change the direction of something ◆ *The new medicine turned the tide for my father, and he was out of the hospital in a few days.* ◆ *Better rifles for the army helped turn the tide of the war.* USAGE: usually said about a condition, opinion, or process

tie

tie *sb* **down**, *also* **tie down** *sb*
to limit someone's freedom ◆ *We were tied down by an impossible schedule and had to put off all vacations.* ◆ *He always thought marriage would tie him down and said it was too bad he was so stupid for so long.*

> ORIGIN: based on the literal meaning of **tie down** (= to hold in place with rope)

tie *sb/sth* **in with** *sb/sth*
to connect or influence one person or thing with another ◆ *The company can tie this new acquisition in with its other businesses.* ◆ *Do we have any information to tie Bernard in with Kelly?* ◆ *Scientists say that this crazy weather is tied in with warmer temperatures in the Pacific Ocean.*

tie *sth* **to** *sth*
to connect one thing to another ◆ *Any increase in pay is tied to doing a better job.*

tie *you* **to** *sth*
to connect you to something ◆ *Police found bloody clothes in Duggan's closet, and that's how they tied him to the killings.* ◆ *Melanie wished she weren't tied to home and could travel a little.*

tie up *sb*, *also* **tie** *sb* **up**
to limit someone's ability to act ◆ *I was tied up in meetings all morning.* ◆ *We were late because traffic tied us up for two hours!*

tie up *sth*, *also* **tie** *sth* **up**
to limit the use of something ◆ *All our savings are tied up in buying a house right now.* ◆ *My daughter can tie the phone up for hours.*

tie the knot See at KNOT

tie *sb* **(up) in knots** See at KNOTS

tightrope

walk a tightrope
to act carefully to avoid creating enemies or a dangerous situation ◆ *The show has always walked a tightrope between old-fashioned humor and modern comedy.* ◆ *The organization's director must walk a tightrope between various religious groups.*

ORIGIN: from the literal expression **walk a tightrope** (= to walk on a tightly stretched wire that is high off the ground)

tilt

(at) full tilt
as fast or hard as possible ♦ *In order to produce more new cars, factories are running at full tilt.* ♦ *Bill left the house late, as he usually does, and had to run full tilt to catch his train.*

time

ahead of time
before something happens ♦ *We'd better buy our tickets ahead of time if we want to avoid waiting in a long line.*

ahead of *your* time, *also* **before *your* time**
having very modern ideas ♦ *The inventor was years ahead of his time in realizing the importance of being able to record sound.* ♦ *Taylor's ideas have been before his time on many occasions.*

(all) in good time
within a reasonable period of time ♦ *Max didn't worry about getting an answer today or tomorrow, because he knew it would come in good time.* USAGE: often said to someone who is not being patient: *They said the package will come all in good time and there's no way to hurry it up.*

all the time esp. spoken
1 esp. spoken ♦ very often ♦ *We shop in that store all the time.* ♦ *This coat is really warm, and I wear it all the time.*
2 continually ♦ *The kids watch TV all the time.* ♦ *She just didn't want to stay home with children all the time.*

all the time in the world
an unlimited amount of time ♦ *She made me feel as if she had all the time in the world for me, even though she's very busy.*

at a time
during any one period ♦ *He prac-ticed every day for four or five hours at a time.* ♦ *The shelter cares for up to 60 children at a time.* USAGE: often used in the phrase **one thing at a time**: *Things will go better if you work on one thing at a time.*

at no time
never ♦ *At no time did I ever say or suggest or even hint that she should lie about what I was doing.*

at one time
in the past ♦ *At one time this ranch had dozens of cowhands, but now it has fewer than ten.*

at one time or another
on different occasions ♦ *Studies show nearly half of all Americans have had trouble sleeping at one time or another.* ♦ Related vocabulary **at times** at TIMES

before *your* time
during a period when you were not active or alive ♦ *I don't know how old the bridge is, but I know it was built well before my time.*

bide *your* time
to wait patiently to do something ♦ *She decided to bide her time until her children were all in school before she went to graduate school.*

big time slang
a lot ♦ *He owes her big time for all the favors she's done for him.* ♦ *I got screwed big time when I signed that agreement.*

buy time
to obtain a longer period before something happens ♦ *We were quickly running out of money but managed to buy time by getting a small loan.*

do you have the time esp. spoken
can you tell me what time it is ♦ *Do you have the time? I forgot my watch.*

every time *you* turn around
surprisingly often ♦ *Every time you turn around, another building is going up and another city garden has disappeared.*

find the time (to *do sth*), *also* **find time to *do sth***
to have a suitable period available to do something that you want to do ♦ *He finds time to paint in the mornings before he comes to work.* ♦ *I wonder how she finds the time to work and write.* USAGE: often used to mean there is not enough time to do what you want to do: *Finding the time to exercise is never easy.*

for the time being
at this time; = **for the moment** ♦ *This is probably about as good a deal as we're going to get, at least for the time being.* ♦ Related vocabulary **for the present** at PRESENT

from time to time
sometimes ♦ *He has been bothered from time to time by pain in his back.*

give *sb* a hard time
to make things difficult for someone ♦ *Josh's pals were giving him a hard time about his girlfriend.* ♦ *We were trying to help Tim, not just giving him a hard time about his bad grades this year.*

have a hard time *doing sth*
to have difficulty doing something ♦ *With all the traffic noise, Mr. Packard had a hard time hearing the reporters' questions.*

have (the) time
to have a period long enough to do something ♦ *I don't have time to keep calling him several times a day.* ♦ *I'll take care of that as soon as I have the time.*

have the time of *your* life
to enjoy yourself very much ♦ *I gave my mother a trip to London, and she had the time of her life.*

in due time slightly formal
after a certain period; = **in due course** ♦ *We turned south and in due time found ourselves walking along the shore of the lake.*

in no time
very quickly ♦ *I pulled my blanket around me and in no time was fast asleep.*

in time (for *sth*), *also* **in time to *do sth***
before it is too late ♦ *I'm glad you made it in time.* ♦ *He planned to arrive in time to have dinner with his sister.* ♦ *I hope she gets here in time to see the show's opening number.* USAGE: often used in the form **just in time** (= almost too late): *He was just in time for his flight.*

(it's) about time esp. spoken
this should have happened long ago ♦ *It's about time that women's sports were treated the same as men's.* ♦ *I think it's about time that our country invested in education.* USAGE: often used to show someone is annoyed by a situation, as in the examples ♦ Related vocabulary **at (long) last** at LAST, **it is high time** at HIGH TIME

keep time
1 to stay even with a musical beat ♦ *Many in the crowd swayed and kept time to the music by tapping their feet.*
2 to record how long something has taken ♦ *When I go running I like to keep time on my watch.*

kill time
to do something while waiting ♦ *We were early for our appointment, so we killed time at a bookstore.*

lose time
to take longer ♦ *We lost a lot of time because we went north instead of south and had to turn around and go back.*

make time for *sth*
to allow time for something in particular ♦ *On the flight back to Washington, the president made time for reporters' questions.* ♦ *I try to make time to run at least four times a week.*

make up for lost time
to do as much as possible that you were not able to do before ♦ *Ms Wesley published her first novel when she was 70 and quickly made up for lost time by writing nine more.*

mark time
to not do anything important while you wait ◆ Mrs. Jamison marked time while waiting to take up her new job. ◆ Related vocabulary **tread water** at WATER

> ORIGIN: based on the military phrase **mark time** (= to march in the same place, moving your legs up and down without going forward)

not give *sb* the time of day
to feel unfriendly toward someone ◆ After the way Phyllis talked about me, I wouldn't give her the time of day.

on borrowed time
not likely to be active or working much longer ◆ Sales were down by a whole lot, putting the company on borrowed time. ◆ I think our hot water heater is on borrowed time. USAGE: often used in the form **living on borrowed time** (= not likely to live very long): He knew he was living on borrowed time after two heart attacks.

once upon a time
long ago ◆ I had worked for some big companies once upon a time, but later I was self-employed. USAGE: often used to begin a children's story: Once upon a time, in a far-off kingdom, there lived a beautiful princess.

(only) time will tell
it is necessary to wait to find out something ◆ Farmers are experimenting with a new type of corn, and only time will tell whether it's better than the old one.

on *your* own time
when you are not working for your employer ◆ I'm impressed with the number of working people who take courses on their own time.

on time
when expected or scheduled ◆ If I don't leave right away, I won't get to work on time. ◆ Here's Jane, right on time. Now we can go to the movie. ◆ The train is almost never on time on the weekend.

pass the time
to do something to keep busy while waiting ◆ While she was home with a broken leg, she passed the time reading, listening to music, and writing letters.

pass the time of day (with *sb*)
to talk in a friendly way with someone ◆ She often stopped to pass the time of day with her neighbors.

play for time
to try to obtain more time ◆ We had to play for time in the meeting because we were waiting for important papers to be delivered.

pressed for time
feeling that you have to hurry and are late ◆ I was pressed for time to finish my business and catch my plane.

serve time, *also* **do time**
to spend a period of time in prison ◆ He was serving time for a series of burglaries in the neighborhood.

take the time (*to do sth*)
to spend enough time to do something ◆ If you take the time to read the directions carefully, you won't have any trouble installing the software. USAGE: used to emphasize that someone should be careful or exact in doing something, and often used to show you are annoyed because someone was not careful: People should at least take the time to understand why we do things this way before they start criticizing us.

take *your* time
to not hurry ◆ Carlin took her time before she answered him. ◆ Take your time – this is a big decision, and you don't want to rush into it.

take time out
to stop an activity temporarily ◆ Some women take time out from their careers when their children are very young.

times 434

tell time
to be able to read the time from a watch or clock ◆ *Kate was so proud of herself when she learned to tell time.*

the time is ripe
the conditions are very good ◆ *I think the time is ripe to look for a larger house.*

time after time
on repeated occasions ◆ *Time after time she was involved with men who did not appreciate her.* ◆ Related vocabulary **again and again** at AGAIN, **over and over (again)** at OVER

time and (time) again
very often ◆ *Time and again I have had to remind my son to study before going out with his friends.*

time flies esp. spoken
a certain period has passed surprisingly quickly ◆ *I can't believe your daughter is old enough to be in college already! How time flies!*

> ORIGIN: based on the saying **time flies when you are having fun**

time is on *your* side
you will do better by waiting ◆ *Your parents think time is on their side, that you'll give up and stop asking if they wait long enough.* ◆ *Because waiting is likely to bring a higher price, we believe that time is on our side.* ◆ Related vocabulary **on *your* side** at SIDE

***sb's/sth's* time is up**
an activity is finished ◆ *From the day he joined the army to the day his time was up, he was a fine soldier.*

time on *your* hands
a period when you have nothing you must do ◆ *These kids have too much time on their hands, and they get into trouble.* ◆ *For the traveler with time on his hands, try a boat ride on the river that surrounds the city.*

time's up esp. spoken, *also* **time is up**
no more minutes are available ◆ *My time's up, and I have to leave now.* ◆ *Time is up on today's quiz – hand in your papers.*

waste no time in *doing sth*, *also* **lose no time (in) *doing sth***
to immediately begin an activity ◆ *Caroline wasted no time in tackling her new job.* ◆ *Will came right from the airport to the office and lost no time getting back to work.*

a matter of time See at MATTER

a race against time See at RACE

in the fullness of time See at FULLNESS

in the right place at the right time See at PLACE

in the wrong place (at the wrong time) See at PLACE

it is high time See at HIGH TIME

(just) in the nick of time See at NICK

stand the test of time See at TEST

walk and chew gum (at the same time) See at GUM

times

at times
during some periods ◆ *The couple had lived apart at times during their married life.* ◆ *At times, in front of the class, I get very nervous.* ◆ Related vocabulary **at one time or another** at TIME

behind the times
old-fashioned ◆ *When it comes to women's rights, my grandfather is way behind the times.*

change with the times, *also* **keep up with the times**
to accept and use new ways ◆ *Hospitals are changing with the times and are much friendlier, more informal places.* ◆ *If you do not keep up with the times, you will lose customers.*

fall on hard times
to be in a very difficult period ◆ *When he fell on hard times, he worked for a while in a local store.*
USAGE: usually used to describe a

period in which someone has lost a job and has too little money
nine times out of ten
almost always ◆ *When a company has to lay off workers, nine times out of ten women employees are the first to be fired.*
times have changed
conditions now are very different from those of the past ◆ *Years ago nobody in my neighborhood locked their doors, but times have changed and everyone has a burglar alarm.*
a sign of the times See at SIGN
for old times' sake See at SAKE

tip

just the tip of the iceberg
a small part of something much larger ◆ *This technology is the tip of the iceberg, the very beginning of modern telecommunications.* ◆ *The list of thefts goes on and on, and the examples you have read about are just the tip of the iceberg.*

> ORIGIN: based on the literal meaning of **the tip of the iceberg** (= the small part of a large mass of ice floating in the sea that can be seen above water)

on the tip of *your* **tongue**
about to be said ◆ *Her name is right on the tip of my tongue – Helen something or other, what is her last name!*
tip off *sb*, also **tip** *sb* **off**
to give information to someone ◆ *Rawson tipped off the Bennetts about this great place to have lunch in Old San Juan.* USAGE: often said about information given to the police or other authorities: *Someone called the police to tip them off that the painting was in a locker at the bus station.*
tip *your* **hand** See at HAND
tip the balance See at BALANCE
tip the scales See at SCALES

tire

tire of *sb/sth* slightly formal
to become bored or upset with someone or something ◆ *I am so tired of him that one day I shall simply ignore him.* ◆ *She was tired of people telling her what to do.*
tire *you* **out**
to feel that you do not have any energy ◆ *Painting the living room in one day really tired Dad out.*

to

to and fro
in one direction and then in the opposite direction ◆ *The children were running to and fro, knocking over all the chairs.*

toast

the toast of *somewhere*
the person who is most admired somewhere ◆ *His charm and wit made him the toast of Paris.* USAGE: sometimes used in the form **the toast of the town**: *After rave reviews of her play, she is the toast of the town.*

today

here today, gone tomorrow
appearing or existing only for a short time ◆ *He had a string of girlfriends, but they were always here today, gone tomorrow.*

toes

on *your* **toes**
aware and energetic ◆ *Acting classes and occasional work in clubs keep the actor on her toes.* ◆ *Bob always looked for difficult assignments because he believed that challenging work helped him stay on his toes professionally.* ◆ See illustration, page 436
step on (*sb's***) toes**
to upset someone, esp. by getting involved in something that is their responsibility ◆ *It's hard to make changes in the department without stepping on a lot of toes.* ◆ *He's willing to step on toes to get things done.*

together

together with *sth*
and also something; = **along with**

toilet — 436

on your toes

Catherine's new job really keeps her on her toes.

sth ♦ *The cost of food together with drinks and prizes made it an expensive party.*

toilet
down the toilet
wasted or lost; = **down the drain** ♦ *Appearing on that talk show is usually a sign that your career is already down the toilet.* USAGE: often used with **go**: *He never showed up to drive us, and our plans for the evening went down the toilet.*

in the toilet, *also* **into the toilet**
in a bad condition ♦ *The economy is rapidly going in the toilet and the country is in a mess.*

token
by the same token
because of this same situation or condition ♦ *University athletes are happy to be in the news, but by the same token, they must not be distracted from their studies.* ♦ *When he liked a woman, he loved her, and, by the same token, when he disliked a woman, he hated her.*

in token of *sth* slightly formal
as a sign or proof of something ♦ *She shaved her head in token of her grief.*

told
all told
as a total ♦ *All told, there were 550 people there.*

toll
take its toll, *also* **take a toll**
to cause harm or suffering ♦ *Divorce takes its toll on the children involved.*

Tom
every Tom, Dick, and Harry
anyone ♦ *Draw the curtains or we'll have every Tom, Dick, and Harry peeking in the window.* USAGE: usually said about any person you do not know or think is unimportant, and sometimes used in the form **any Tom, Dick, or Harry**: *I want a qualified plumber to do the job, not just any Tom, Dick, or Harry.*

tomorrow
like there's no tomorrow, *also* **as if there is no tomorrow**
quickly and eagerly, without thinking ♦ *She's spending money like there's no tomorrow and I don't know how to stop her.*

here today, gone tomorrow See at TODAY

ton

(hit *you*) like a ton of bricks
to shock you so much that you do not know how to react ✦ *The death of her father hit her like a ton of bricks.*

weigh a ton
to be very heavy ✦ *This suitcase weighs a ton!* USAGE: usually said about something you have to lift or carry

tone

set the tone (for *sth*)
to establish a particular mood or character for something ✦ *The governor's speech was intended to set the tone for the party's national convention next week.* USAGE: sometimes used with an adjective before **tone**: *The announcement of last month's sales figures set an optimistic tone for the meeting.*

tone down *sth*, *also* tone *sth* down
to make something less forceful or offensive ✦ *The foul language in the original play has been toned down for television.* ✦ *Your presentation has to be convincing, so don't tone it down.*

tongue

bite *your* tongue
to stop yourself from speaking ✦ *his lack of reply seemed to indicate that he was angry and was biting his tongue.*

hold *your* tongue
to say nothing or to stop speaking ✦ *He wanted to tell her the secret but wisely decided to hold his tongue.*

loosen *your* tongue
to cause you to talk without thinking carefully about what you are saying ✦ *The vodka really loosened her tongue and I found out exactly what happened that night.*

(with) tongue in cheek
in a way that is not serious, although it appears to be ✦ *Karl explained, tongue in cheek, that he was busy with housecleaning.*

tools

tools of the trade, *also* **the tools of *sb's* trade**
the things that are needed in order to do a job ✦ *Eileen's dress-making shop had buttons and thread and needles and scissors, all the tools of the trade.*

tooth

fight (*sb/sth*) tooth and nail
to use a lot of effort to oppose someone or achieve something ✦ *We fought tooth and nail to keep our share of the business.* ✦ *They vowed to fight the new legislation tooth and nail.*

long in the tooth, *also* **long of tooth**
to be very old ✦ *Don't you think she's a bit long in the tooth to be a romantic heroine?*

> ORIGIN: based on the idea that teeth grow longer in some animals as they get older

top

at the top of *your* lungs, *also* **at the top of *your* voice**
as loudly as you can ✦ *She sang the national anthem at the top of her lungs.*

blow *your* top
to become very angry ✦ *Arley invited us to visit her in Italy, and when my wife said it was impossible for her to go, I blew my top* ✦ *Almost all bosses blow their tops once in a while.* ✦ Related vocabulary **go ballistic** at BALLISTIC

from top to bottom
in every part ✦ *We searched the house from top to bottom but we couldn't find the letter.* ✦ Related vocabulary **(from) stem to stern** at STEM

off the top of *your* head esp. spoken
based on what you remember ✦ *I couldn't tell you what the final score was off the top of my head.* ✦ *Off the*

top of my head I could probably only name about three women artists.

on top of *sth*
aware of or in control of a situation ♦ *The stock market has been unpredictable, and you really have to stay on top of your investments.* ♦ *If Sheila's not staying on top of the applications, I think we should hire an assistant.*

on top of that
in addition to the bad thing already mentioned ♦ *We missed the bus, and on top of that it started raining.*

over the top
too extreme ♦ *To blame one person for the collapse of the business seems way over the top.* ♦ *I listened to her speech, and some of her language was just over the top.*

put *sb/sth* **over the top**, *also* **push** *sb/sth* **over the top**
to cause someone to have enough of something to achieve a goal ♦ *The award put his popularity over the top in a dramatic way.* ♦ *We're trying to make a deal that pushes our team over the top.* USAGE: sometimes used in the form **get someone over the top**: *We managed to get the two sides talking, but that wasn't enough to get us over the top.*

(sitting) on top of the world
in a happy position of advantage ♦ *With these figures and their other recent successes, the company is sitting on top of the world.*

the top of the heap
the highest rank within a group ♦ *How does Stephen plan to keep the company at the top of the heap?* USAGE: often used in the form **at the top of the heap**, as in the example ♦ Opposite **the bottom of the heap** at BOTTOM

the top of the hour
the time when an hour begins on the clock ♦ *We'll update the weather again at the top of the hour.* ♦ Related vocabulary **the bottom of the hour** at BOTTOM

the top of the ladder
the highest level or position ♦ *After thirty years with the company, he's near the top of the ladder.* ♦ Opposite **the bottom of the ladder** at BOTTOM

(the) top of the line
the very best of something ♦ *The four acts for the opening of the jazz festival were all top of the line.*

top off *sth*, *also* **top** *sth* **off**
1 to add enough liquid to make a container full ♦ *Rhodes refilled his glass and topped off Carey's.* ♦ *We have enough gas to get there, but we ought to top it off so we won't have to stop again tomorrow.*
2 to make something complete and satisfying ♦ *An incredible cherry pie topped off the meal.*

to top it all (off), *also* **to top it off**
1 and the worst thing is ♦ *The washing machine flooded, my car broke down, then to top it all off I locked myself out of the house.*
2 and the best thing is ♦ *Students get to meet the world's top scientists and researchers, and to top it off, the conference is free.* ♦ Related vocabulary **cap** *sth* **off** at CAP
USAGE: used before you tell the best or worst of one or more related things, as in the examples

(from) top to toe See **(from) head to toe** at HEAD

torch

pass the torch (to *sb***)**
to give responsibility to someone ♦ *The president of the company announced his retirement, saying it was time to pass the torch to someone younger.*

toss

toss and turn
to be unable to sleep because of worrying ♦ *Bernard was tossing and turning all night.*

toss around *sth*, *also* **toss** *sth* **around**
1 to consider or think about some-

thing ♦ *Some of us have been tossing around suggestions for improving the show.* ♦ *The morning newspapers print the news, and then commentators toss it around on the evening TV news shows.*
2 to use words without thinking carefully about them ♦ *The financial press tossed around words like "crash" and "disaster."* ♦ *Students toss bad words around freely.*

toss off *sth*, also **toss** *sth* **off**
to do or say something quickly, easily, and sometimes without thought ♦ *He simply tossed off a comment about what women want and it got him into a lot of trouble.* ♦ *He had a great memory for jokes, and could just toss them off one after the other.*

toss out *sb/sth*, also **toss** *sb/sth* **out**
to get rid of someone or something ♦ *She tossed out my old chair.* ♦ *Mrs. Curtis tossed him out of class for laughing.*

toss out *sth*, also **toss** *sth* **out**
1 to refuse to accept or consider something ♦ *The judge tossed out the case two weeks ago.* ♦ *We received thousands of proposals for the memorial, but tossed most of them out because they were dull or inappropriate.*
2 to suggest something as a possibility ♦ *We tossed out half a dozen titles and then discussed what we thought about each one.* ♦ *Now that you've had a chance to look at the memo, I'll toss an idea out to start the discussion.*

total

in total
the whole number or amount of something ♦ *Last week only 45 people in total came to see the exhibit.*

totem pole

low on the totem pole
least important ♦ *He's the low man on the totem pole here.* ♦ *AIDS deaths are low on the totem pole compared with cancer and heart disease.*

> ORIGIN: based on the literal meaning of **totem pole** (= a wooden pole with images of people and animals cut or painted on it)

touch

in touch (with *sb***)**
in communication with someone ♦ *I'm sorry we haven't been in touch over the past few years.* ♦ *We stay in close touch with the New York office.* ♦ *How can I get in touch with your sister?* USAGE: usually used with the verbs **be**, **keep**, **stay**, and **get**, as in the examples ♦ Opposite **out of touch (with** *sb***)**

in touch (with *sth***)**
having recent knowledge about something ♦ *I try to keep in touch with the latest developments in the music scene.* ♦ *A president must stay in touch to know what citizens want or need.* ♦ Opposite **out of touch (with** *sth***)** 1

lose touch (with *sb***)**
to no longer communicate with someone ♦ *I lost touch with Katie after she moved to Canada.*

lose touch (with *sth***)**
to no longer have recent knowledge about something ♦ *He has never lost touch with Mexican culture and traditions.*

lose *your* **touch**
to no longer be able to do something as well as you could before ♦ *In her latest book, O'Reilly seems to have lost her touch for creating interesting characters.*

out of touch (with *sb***)**
no longer in communication with someone ♦ *I've been out of touch with Willner for a long time and don't even know where he lives now.* USAGE: usually used with the verb **be**, as in the example ♦ Opposite **in touch (with** *sb***)**

out of touch (with *sth***)**
1 not informed about something ♦ *The report shows that the committee is out of touch with recent develop-*

ments in space technology. ♦ Opposite **in touch (with** *sth***)**
2 not reflecting what is true or actual ♦ *These statistics are wildly out of touch with reality and cannot be used.* ♦ *Everything the patient says shows how much he is out of touch.*
3 lacking a connection ♦ *The writing in this story is out of touch, like an accident report or a doctor's notes.*

touch down
to reach the ground ♦ *Our plane touched down about 40 minutes after it was supposed to.* ♦ *In Florida, tornadoes touched down in at least three counties yesterday.*

touch off *sth*, *also* **touch** *sth* **off**
to cause something violent or destructive to start ♦ *Plans for a new homeless shelter touched off a storm of protest.* ♦ *Windblown wires touched off the blaze.* ♦ *There was a dramatic fall in stock prices, and no one is sure what touched it off.*

> ORIGIN: based on the literal meaning of **touch off** (= to cause an old-fashioned gun to fire)

touch on *sth*
1 to speak briefly about something ♦ *During the interview, we only touched on how much I would be paid.*
2 to be connected to ♦ *Although his book is about an event of many years ago, it touches on similar events of today.*

touch up *sth*, *also* **touch** *sth* **up**
to improve something by making small changes ♦ *We didn't redo the kitchen, just really touched it up by painting the cabinets.* ♦ *Chris went to the ladies' room to touch up her makeup.*

not touch *sth* **with a ten-foot pole** See at POLE

touch a (raw) nerve See at NERVE
touch base (with *sb***)** See at BASE

tough

tough it out
to be strong while experiencing difficulties ♦ *Should we tough it out, or should we close the store and go out of business now?*

tour

on tour
going to several places to perform ♦ *The band is currently on tour in Australia.* ♦ *Our local women's basketball team is on tour right now, playing exhibition games in a number of cities.*

tow

in tow
following or going along under someone's control ♦ *She usually goes shopping with her three children in tow.*

> ORIGIN: based on the literal meaning of a vehicle or ship **in tow** (= being pulled with a rope or chain)

towel

throw in the towel
to admit defeat or failure ♦ *The union was forced to throw in the towel and settle their bitter dispute with the company.*

> ORIGIN: based on the literal meaning of **throwing a towel into the ring** in boxing (= signaling that a fighter can no longer continue by throwing a towel into the area where the fight takes place)

town

all over town
in or to many parts of a city or town ♦ *People all over town thought I was crazy to buy that old hotel.* ♦ *Now you won't have to drive all over town to find that dress.* ♦ Related vocabulary **all over** at ALL

go to town (on *sth***)**
to do something eagerly and as completely as possible ♦ *Angie and Phil have really gone to town on their wedding.* USAGE: often used to describe an activity that involves spending a large amount of money

on the town
going to bars or other places of en-

tertainment in a town or city for pleasure ◆ *I went out on the town and didn't get home till 3:00 in the morning.* ◆ *I invited my house guests for a big night on the town.*

paint the town (red)
to go out and celebrate without control ◆ *Jack finished his exams today so he's gone out to paint the town red.* USAGE: usually said about celebrations that include a lot of drinking

the only game in town See at GAME

toy

toy with *sb*
to encourage someone to believe you care about them when you do not ◆ *Don't fool yourself by thinking he wants a serious relationship – he's famous for toying with women.* ◆ Related vocabulary **lead *sb* on** at LEAD

toy with *sth*
1 to think about something but not seriously ◆ *We're toying with the idea of going to Peru next year.*
2 to handle something or move it around without any clear purpose ◆ *As he was speaking, he toyed nervously with a button on his jacket.*

track

keep track (of *sb/sth*)
to continue to be informed or know about someone or something ◆ *I've never been very good at keeping track of how I spend my money.* ◆ *You've moved so many times, how can I possibly keep track?* ◆ *He's had so many different jobs that it's difficult to keep track.* ◆ Opposite **lose track (of *sb/sth*)**

lose track (of *sb/sth*)
to no longer be informed or know about something or someone ◆ *I've lost track of most of my college friends.* ◆ Opposite **keep track (of *sb/sth*)**

off the beaten track
not known or popular with many people; = **off the beaten path** ◆ *Her tastes in reading tend to be off the beaten track.*

on the right track
doing something correctly or well ◆ *I think he is going to help us work together and get us back on the right track for the final weeks of the baseball season.* ◆ *Tax cuts for the rich will not put the economy on the right track.*

on the wrong track
not correct about something ◆ *If you suspect my son was involved, you are on the wrong track.*

on track
developing or making progress as expected ◆ *His recovery from the accident is right on track and he should be back at work in about three weeks.* ◆ *He's on track to become the world heavyweight boxing champion.* USAGE: often used in the form **back on track**: *We're behind schedule on this job, so we need to get back on track right after the holidays.*

track down *sb/sth*, also **track *sb/sth* down**
to find someone or something after searching for them ◆ *I'm trying to track down one of my old classmates from college.* ◆ *My library assistant tracked down several references for me* ◆ *My mother wanted to find the family who had taken care of my father during the war, and somehow she was able to track them down.*

on the fast track See at FAST TRACK
have the inside track See at INSIDE TRACK

tracks

cover *your* tracks
to hide or destroy anything that shows where you have been or what you have been doing ◆ *Roberts covered his tracks by throwing the knife in the river and burying his wife's body miles from his home.*

stop (dead) in *your* tracks
to suddenly stop moving or doing

trade

something ♦ *When I heard the loud scream, I stopped dead in my tracks.* USAGE: often used in the forms **stop someone (dead) in their tracks** or **stop something (dead) in its tracks**: *The memo was supposed to stop the protest in its tracks.* ♦ Related vocabulary **stop short** at STOP

the wrong side of the tracks See at SIDE

trade

ply *your* trade slightly formal
to do your usual work ♦ *Fishermen in small boats ply their trade up and down the coast.*

trade down
to exchange something expensive for something that costs less ♦ *The family traded down to a smaller house, cutting their mortgage payments in half.*

trade in *sth*, also **trade *sth* in**
to return something as part of a payment for something similar ♦ *I traded in my wonderful little sports car for a much more practical van.* ♦ *The store wouldn't give me a refund on the camera, but they offered to let me trade it in.* USAGE: usually said about a device, a piece of equipment, or a vehicle

trade on *sth*, also **trade upon *sth***
to use something for your own advantage ♦ *The mayoral candidate ran the kind of campaign that trades on most people's fear of crime.* ♦ *George traded upon his family's powerful connections.*

trade up
to replace something with something better or more valuable ♦ *When Phil needed a new car, he decided to trade up and bought a luxury car.*

tools of the trade See at TOOLS
trade places See at PLACES
tricks of the trade See at TRICKS

tradition

break with tradition
to do something different from what is usually done ♦ *They were among the first to break with tradition and use clay to make contemporary sculpture.*

trail

blaze a trail
to do something different ♦ *The hospital has blazed a trail in children's care by giving them many things to do and allowing visitors at any hour.*

trail off, *also* **trail away**
to become quieter ♦ *His voice trailed off weakly and we could not hear the rest of what he said.* ♦ *The wail of the sirens finally trailed away almost completely.*

trap

fall into the trap of *doing sth*
to become involved in something ♦ *Don't fall into the trap of deciding to buy a more expensive house than you can afford because someone says it is a good investment.*

travel

travel light
to bring very few things with you when you go on a trip ♦ *My new car has lots of cargo space, which is great for people like me who don't travel light.*

tread

tread carefully, *also* **tread warily**
to avoid saying or doing anything that could cause difficulties ♦ *Some companies continue to tread carefully when doing business on the Internet.* USAGE: sometimes used in the form **tread cautiously**: *You should tread cautiously when discussing financial matters with him.*

tread water See at WATER

tree

up a tree
in a difficult situation ♦ *If the insurance company won't pay for the damage, I'll be up a tree.*

travel light

When I fly to Europe on business, I always try to travel light.

trial
on trial
being judged in a court of law ◆ *He was on trial for burglary.*

stand trial
to appear in a court of law to be judged guilty or not guilty of doing something ◆ *He is scheduled to stand trial for murder this summer.*

trick
do the trick
to achieve the desired result; = **do the job** ◆ *At first my brother didn't want to help out, but a phone call from my wife did the trick and he showed up the next morning.*

every trick in the book
every way possible ◆ *He tried every trick in the book to get her to sign the contract.* USAGE: usually said about an attempt to deceive someone

the oldest trick in the book
a way of deceiving someone that is not new ◆ *It was the oldest trick in the book – one man distracted me while another stole my wallet.*

tricks
tricks of the trade
methods that help you to do a job better or faster ◆ *As a journalist, you learn the tricks of the trade pretty quickly or you don't get your stories.*

up to *your/its* old tricks
doing something you or it has done before ◆ *House Republicans are up to their old tricks again, promising to cut taxes for everyone and then giving most of the tax cuts to the very wealthy.* USAGE: usually said about an attempt to deceive someone

trip
trip *sb* up, *also* **trip up *sb***
to cause someone to make a mistake ◆ *The lawyer used what he knew about her personality to trip her up in court.* ◆ *I did fine on most of the test, but I tripped up on the last problem.*

> ORIGIN: based on the literal meaning of **trip someone up** (= to cause someone to fall)

trot
hot to trot rude slang
1 sexually exciting or sexually excited ◆ *He met a woman who he said was hot to trot.*

2 eager to begin something ◆ *When asked about the band's recording plans, Weir said he was hot to trot, but everyone else wanted to wait.*

trot out *sb/sth*, *also* **trot** *sb/sth* **out**
to bring someone or something to the attention of others, so they can see or admire it ◆ *The military trotted out all their experts to testify for the new weapons system.* ◆ *She trotted her espresso machine out this morning and made us all coffee.*

trouble

ask for trouble, *also* **look for trouble**
to behave in a way that will cause you problems ◆ *Drinking before driving is asking for trouble.* ◆ *Phil wondered why Deegan was always looking for trouble.* ◆ Related vocabulary **ask for** *sth* at ASK

go to the trouble (of *doing sth***)**, *also* **take the trouble (to** *do sth***)**
to make an effort to do something ◆ *If anyone had gone to the trouble of looking up his record, the police would not have released him.*

the trouble with *sb/sth*
one annoying characteristic of someone or something ◆ *The trouble with this place is they don't care about the people who work here.*

truck

have no truck with *sb/sth* slightly formal
to refuse to become involved with someone or something ◆ *Our committee will have no truck with racist attitudes.* USAGE: usually said about someone or something you do not approve of

true

true enough
correct or accurate, but not completely explaining something ◆ *It's true enough that he had doubts about the project, but we have to look further to understand why he resigned so quickly.*

a dream come true See at DREAM
come true See at COME
ring true See at RING
show *sb's/sth's* **true colors** See at COLORS
too good to be true See at GOOD
true to form See at FORM
true to *your* **word** See at WORD

truth

in truth slightly formal
actually ◆ *We kept climbing but, in truth, we knew we could not reach the top of the mountain before sunset.* ◆ Related vocabulary **as a matter of fact** at MATTER, **in (point of) fact** at FACT, **in reality** at REALITY

try

try on *sth*, *also* **try** *sth* **on**
to put on clothes to see how they look or fit ◆ *Try on those shoes.* ◆ *It's silly to buy something that expensive without trying it on.*

try out (for *sth***)**
to compete for something ◆ *Jim tried out for the school play.* USAGE: usually said about competing to play on a team or perform in a show

try *sth* **out on** *sb*
to get someone's opinion about something ◆ *I've got some new jokes I'd like to try out on you.*

try *your* **hand at** *sth* See at HAND
try *your* **luck** See at LUCK
try *sth* **(on) for size** See at SIZE
try the patience of *sb* See at PATIENCE

tubes

go down the tubes esp. spoken, *also* **go down the tube**
to fail or become much worse ◆ *His business is going down the tubes and he's about to lose his house.* ◆ *Prices are going up and the service is terrible – everything's going down the tubes.*

tuck

tuck in *sb*, *also* **tuck** *sb* **in**
to cover a child comfortably in bed

♦ I tucked in Josh and Amy after reading them a story. ♦ Who's going to tuck me in while you're gone?

tucked
tucked away
hidden or difficult to find ♦ Van's house is tucked away at the end of the road.

tune
call the tune
to have the most power and authority in a situation ♦ In this part of the mortgage market, the banks call the tune. ♦ Related vocabulary **call the shots** at SHOTS, **run the show** at SHOW

carry a tune
to be able to sing accurately ♦ For such a complicated song they should at least find someone who can carry a tune.

change *your* tune
to change your opinion completely ♦ They'll change their tune when they see that their advice is making people angry with them.

dance to *sb's* tune, *also* **dance to the tune of *sb***
to always obey someone who has power over you ♦ Powerful local residents seem to have the city council dancing to their tune. ♦ In the future, people will ask why we danced to the tunes of this president.

in tune (with *sb/sth*)
having a good understanding of someone or something ♦ Carl was thoroughly in tune with new developments in art. ♦ He's more in tune with his players today because he's seeking out their opinions.

to the tune of *sth*
in the approximate amount mentioned ♦ We're in debt to the tune of $50,000. USAGE: usually used with amounts of money, as in the example.

tune in (to *sth*), *also* **tune into *sth***
to turn on and watch or listen to television or radio ♦ Millions of viewers tuned in, hoping to learn more about the princess's death. ♦ We usually tune into the morning news when we wake up.

tuned in (to *sb/sth*), *also* **tuned into *sb/sth***
very aware of someone or something so that you understand them well ♦ She's tuned in to all the latest fashions. ♦ Our staff are trained to be tuned into the needs of children.

tune out (*sb/sth*)
to stop paying attention to someone or something ♦ Beverly always tunes out in the middle of her music lesson. ♦ He's been tuning me out ever since I tried to talk to him about his drinking.

tune up (for *sth*)
to prepare for something ♦ The coach feels confident that the team is tuned up for tonight's game.

tune up *sth*, *also* **tune *sth* up**
to adjust an engine or vehicle so that it works as well as possible ♦ I haven't tuned up my car in two years. ♦ The motorcycle isn't running right, but she can't afford to tune it up.

turkey
talk turkey
to discuss a problem seriously with the intention of solving it ♦ The session was businesslike, and according to one official, "They talked turkey."

go cold turkey See at COLD TURKEY

turn
at every turn
every place or every time that something is possible ♦ Since the divorce she has avoided the press at every turn.

in turn
1 one after the other ♦ She spoke to each of the guests in turn.
2 slightly formal ♦ as an equal or related effect ♦ Yiddish has borrowed words from German, and German has in turn borrowed from Russian.

turn

♦ *The agency wants to put pressure on local business people, so they, in turn, will put pressure on state officials.*

speak out of turn, *also* **talk out of turn**
to say something that you should not have said ♦ *I'm sorry if I spoke out of turn, but somebody had to tell him the facts.* USAGE: sometimes used to describe something you did not have the authority to say: *The company president said there had not been any delays, and that the project manager had spoken out of turn.*

turn against *sb*
to change from supporting to opposing someone ♦ *A lot of his supporters turned against him.*

turn *sb/sth* **against** *sb/sth*
to cause someone or something to oppose someone or something else ♦ *He took all of our proposals and turned them against us.* ♦ *Advisors have been trying to turn the president against increased military spending.*

turn *sth* **around**, *also* **turn around** *sth*
to cause a situation or organization to change in a positive direction ♦ *They were losing badly but they turned things around in the second half of the game.* ♦ *We've hired a new director who we hope will turn around the failing company.*

turn *sb/sth* **away**, *also* **turn away** *sb/sth*
to refuse to see or talk to someone, or to consider something ♦ *If anyone comes to the door, just turn them away.* ♦ *She has turned away every opportunity to improve her English in the last ten years.*

turn down *sb/sth*, *also* **turn** *sb/sth* **down**
to refuse to accept or agree to something, or to someone's idea ♦ *The bank turned down their request for a loan.* ♦ *Go ahead and ask her out,* *if you're prepared for her to turn you down.*

turn in
to go to your bed in order to sleep ♦ *I'm getting sleepy – I think I'll turn in.*

turn in *sth*, *also* **turn** *sth* **in**
to give or return something to someone in authority ♦ *We have another week to turn in the report.* ♦ *He found a stack of twenty-dollar bills and he doesn't want to turn it in.*

turn in *sb*, *also* **turn** *sb* **in**
to take or report someone to the police or other authority ♦ *I would feel very nervous about turning in my neighbors to the police.* ♦ *He learned that the police were looking for him and turned himself in.*

turn *sb/sth* **loose**, *also* **turn loose** *sb/sth*
to give up control of someone or something, so they can do what they want ♦ *He turned the horse loose in the field.* ♦ *The trouble began when the newspaper turned loose a dozen reporters to investigate the incident.*

turn *sb* **off**, *also* **turn off** *sb*
to cause someone to lose interest or sympathy ♦ *Her offensive remarks really turned me off.* ♦ *Her opening statement completely turned off the jury.*

turn *sb* **on**
to cause someone to feel excited and very interested ♦ *What turns the kids on these days?*

turn on *sb*
to attack or criticize someone suddenly ♦ *He suddenly turned on me and accused me of not supporting him when he needed it.* ♦ *The country's leaders worry that the people could quickly turn on them.*

turn on *sth*
to depend on something in an important way ♦ *The success of the talks turns on whether both sides are willing to compromise.*

turn out
to happen or become known to hap-

pen in a particular way ◆ *She assured him that everything would turn out all right.* ◆ *It turns out that Ray had borrowed the money from one of his students.*

turn out (for *sth*)
to come, appear, or be present for something ◆ *A lot of students turned out for the demonstration.* ◆ *The last time she performed here the whole town turned out.*

turn out *sth*, also **turn *sth* out**
to produce or make something ◆ *Which university turns out the most successful scientists?* ◆ *The factory is turning the dolls out as fast as it can.*

turn *sb* out (of *somewhere*)
to force someone to leave a place ◆ *They turned him out of the shelter when they discovered he was using drugs.* ◆ *She was forced to leave home, turned out at the age of 16.*

turn *sb*/*sth* over, also **turn over *sb*/*sth***
to put someone or something under the control of someone ◆ *As soon as Roger came home his Dad turned him over to the police.* ◆ *Eventually she turned over the company to her son.*

turn to *sb*/*sth*
to go to someone or use something in order to get help ◆ *Some young people turn to Jesus, others turn to drugs.* ◆ *In times of stress, we turn to these principles for guidance.*

turn up
to appear or come to your attention ◆ *She said she'd let me know if anything new turned up.* ◆ *Look who just turned up – my old friend Buzz Galbraith!*

turn up *sth*, also **turn *sth* up**
to find something, usually after looking ◆ *A three-hour search turned up no sign of a bomb.* ◆ *Our first look at the records did not turn anything up.*

turns

take turns (*doing sth*)
to do something one person after another ◆ *The mothers in our group take turns driving the children to school.* ◆ *When they play on the swings, we try to make sure the kids take turns.*

twain

never the twain shall meet
these two things or people will never exist together or agree with each other ◆ *Psychologists believe in therapy, chemists believe in drugs, and never the twain shall meet.*

twinkling

in the twinkling of an eye
very quickly ◆ *This machine will do all the calculations in the twinkling of an eye.*

two

it takes two to tango
both people involved in a bad situation are responsible for it ◆ *"She blames Tracy for stealing her husband." "Well, it takes two to tango."*

ORIGIN: based on the literal meaning of **tango** (= a South American dance for two people)

put two and two together
to understand something by using the information you have ◆ *I didn't tell her George had left, but she noticed his car was gone and put two and two together.*

two can play at that game
if one person does something wrong, someone else can do the same thing ◆ *So she's been spreading rumors about me, has she? Well, two can play at that game.*

U, u

umbrage
take umbrage at *sth* slightly formal
to feel insulted by something someone has said or done ♦ *The mayor took umbrage at the suggestion that the new park was not well designed.*

unison
in unison
together at the same time ♦ *The audience rose to its feet in unison, applauding and cheering.* ♦ *All the babies in the nursery were wailing in unison.*

unthinkable
do the unthinkable
to do something unexpected ♦ *Some stores are doing the unthinkable – they're lowering their price.*

up
not up to *sth*, also **not up for** *sth*
not able or eager to do something ♦ *After a long day at the office, I'm not really up to a late movie.*

on the up and up
honest or legal ♦ *There is no way to be sure that a salesman is on the up and up.*

(right) up there with *sb/sth*
as good or as bad as someone or something else ♦ *He's up there with the most important sculptors of our age.* ♦ *I thought that wine was right up there with vinegar and turpentine as a taste treat.*

up against *sb/sth*
in opposition to someone or something ♦ *In the music competition, Tyler was up against some of the best singers in the country.* ♦ *Next week, our field hockey team will go up against the best team in this area.*

up and around, also **up and about**
out of bed and beginning to move around ♦ *A day after the surgery Mom was up and around, but she'll have to use crutches for a while.* USAGE: usually said about someone who has been ill or injured

up and coming
beginning to achieve success or popularity ♦ *It's an up and coming business center that has attracted many new offices and stores.* ♦ *Many fans think Jimmy is an up and coming country singer.*

up and running
actively working ♦ *My computer was finally up and running again, and I could attack the huge batch of work I had to finish.* ♦ *It took several years to get his law practice up and running.*

up to *sb* **(to do** *sth***)**
someone's responsibility to do something ♦ *It's up to the judge to decide whether her prison sentence should be reduced.* ♦ *It's not up to us to make that decision.*

up to *sth*
doing or planning something secretly ♦ *We knew the boys were up to something because we hadn't seen them all morning.* ♦ *What are you up to in there? Open the door!*

up yours rude slang
I do not care what you say or think ♦ *"If it's at all possible, I'll do it, you know I will." "Oh, Rob, up yours. Just do it, if you're going to, or else stop talking about it."* ♦ Related vocabulary **screw you** at SCREW

upper hand
have the upper hand
to have power and control over someone or a situation ♦ *By half time, the Italian soccer team seemed to have the upper hand.* USAGE: also used with **get** and **gain**: *There is always worry over who will get the upper hand in the oil markets.* ♦ *Fire fighters from more than six states finally gained the upper hand on the forest fire.*

ups

ups and downs
the mixture of good and bad things that happen ◆ *Ups and downs are to be expected in life, but that doesn't make the down parts any easier.* ◆ Related vocabulary **the ebb and flow of** *sth* at EBB

upside

turn *sth* **upside down**
to change something completely; = **turn** *sth* **inside out** ◆ *His experience in the war turned his world upside down.* ◆ *The crash of the dotcom companies turned lives upside down.* ◆ Related vocabulary **turn** *sth* **on its head** at HEAD

uptake

slow on the uptake
not able to understand something quickly ◆ *I tried to explain how the new software works to my manager, but he's a little slow on the uptake.* USAGE: also used in the form **quick on the uptake** (= able to understand something quickly): *He was quick on the uptake and able to realize right away what was wrong.*

use

have no use for *sb/sth*
to have a very low opinion of someone or something ◆ *To my mother, my friends were simply a bunch of bums, and she had no use for them.* ◆ *He has no use for gossip, which he thinks is a waste of time.*
ORIGIN: based on the literal meaning of **have no use for something** (= to not be able to use something)

it's no use, *also* **there's no use**
there is no reason to ◆ *It's no use asking me about it because I don't know anything.* ◆ *There's no use resisting someone so much stronger than you are.*

use up *sth*, *also* **use** *sth* **up**
to use all of something so that none of it is left ◆ *New ink cartridges often cost $25 to $35 each and can be used up quickly if you print a lot of photos.* ◆ *Many seniors quickly use up their money on prescription drugs.* ◆ *She gets three weeks of vacation but she uses it up before the year was half over.*

used

used to *do sth*
to have done something in the past ◆ *A young lady who used to work in my office had seven brothers!* ◆ *We used to visit our parents at Christmas every year.*

used to *sth/doing sth*
familiar with something ◆ *He's used to beginning without me because I'm almost always late.* ◆ *His clothes and manners show he's used to being a celebrity.* ◆ *It's not easy getting used to cold weather if you've been brought up in a hot climate.*

usher

usher in *sth*, *also* **usher** *sth* **in**
to signal the beginning of something ◆ *We will usher in the new year with champagne and dancing.* ◆ *Another powerful storm system ushered in wind and rain, causing great damage here.*

usher *sb* **in**
to show that someone is welcome ◆ *He opened the door wide and with a welcoming arm, ushered them in.* USAGE: also used in the form **usher someone into something** (= to welcome someone to the start of something): *Graduation ceremonies are designed to usher the new graduates into adult life.*

usual

as usual
in the ordinary or expected way ◆ *As usual, she was wearing jeans.* ◆ *He was wrong about the time, as usual, and so we missed the first part of the concert.*

V, v

vacuum
in a vacuum
without any connection to other people or events ◆ *These kids are growing up in a vacuum, without any guidance from their parents or anyone else.*

vain
in vain
1 without success ◆ *Melissa shifted about, trying in vain to find a comfortable position.* ◆ *Government agents tried in vain to kidnap him.*
2 without any useful result ◆ *Clegg said Friday's military operation went well, and that these soldiers did not die in vain.* ◆ *The president himself must make the argument, or all our work will be in vain.*

variance
at variance with sb/sth
different from or not agreeing with someone or something ◆ *What she told the police was totally at variance with the truth.* ◆ *My opinions seem to be completely at variance with my friends' opinions.*

veil
draw a veil over sth slightly formal
1 to hide something ◆ *Dense fog drew a veil over the landscape.*
2 to avoid talking about something ◆ *I think we should draw a veil over this conversation and pretend it never happened.* ◆ Related vocabulary **keep (sth) under wraps** at WRAPS
lift the veil
to make something known that was secret before ◆ *The company lifted the veil on its planned online magazine.*

vengeance
with a vengeance
with great force or energy ◆ *Susan works out with a vengeance when she goes to the gym.*

verge
on the verge of doing sth
almost doing or experiencing some-

in a vacuum

Janice has been working in a vacuum.

thing ♦ *He was on the verge of making a comment but stopped, realizing it would be a mistake.*

very
very well
1 probably ♦ *Stress could very well have triggered her heart attack.* ♦ *The robber might very well have been in the house when the police arrived.*
2 clearly ♦ *The little boy knew very well that the neighbors didn't like his father.*

vicinity
in the vicinity of *sth*
approximately a certain amount ♦ *The price for a house here is in the vicinity of $150,000.* USAGE: used with money, percentages, and numbers

ORIGIN: based on the literal meaning of **in the vicinity of** (= near)

view
in view of *sth*
considering something ♦ *In view of the late hour, we'll have to put off that discussion until our next meeting.* ♦ Related vocabulary **in (the) light of** *sth* at LIGHT
on view
in a place to be seen by anyone ♦ *Plans for the new park are on view at the library this week.*
take a dim view (of *sth***)**
to disapprove of something ♦ *Most bosses take a dim view of long lunches.*
take the long view, *also* **take the longer view**
to think about the effects that something will have in the future ♦ *If you take the long view, computer training for your staff is an investment in increased productivity.* ♦ Related vocabulary **in the long term** at TERM
a bird's eye view See at EYE

virtue
by virtue of *sth* slightly formal
because of ♦ *Many people believe that he will avoid jail by virtue of his money and connections.*

visit
pay (*sb/sth***) a visit** slightly formal, *also* **pay a visit (to** *sb/sth***)**
to go to see someone or something ♦ *Yesterday a police detective paid us a visit and asked a lot of questions.* ♦ *The three elderly women decided to pay a visit to a spa and had a great time.* ♦ Related vocabulary **pay a call on** *sb/sth* at CALL

voice
a (lone) voice in the wilderness, *also* **a voice (crying) in the wilderness**
someone who expresses an idea or opinion that is not popular ♦ *For many years, she was a lone voice in the wilderness who wrote about the need for better urban planning.*
speak with one voice
to express the same opinion ♦ *It is a very rare event when my family speaks with one voice about anything.* USAGE: must refer to two or more people, as in the example

void
fill the void, *also* **fill a void**
to replace or provide something necessary ♦ *It is impossible to fill the void left by my sister's death.*

volumes
speak volumes
to express something very clearly and completely ♦ *The happy expressions on both their faces spoke volumes about their marriage.* ♦ *He didn't say anything about what happened at the meeting, but his furious expression spoke volumes.* USAGE: usually said about expressing something without words

vouch
vouch for *sth*
to support the truth of something ♦ *An accountant must vouch for the accuracy of any financial report.* ♦ *I've known him for years and can vouch for his honesty.*

W, w

wade

wade into *sth*, *also* **wade in**
to become involved in something in a forceful and determined way ◆ *She wades into a complicated project with great enthusiasm.* ◆ *If there's a problem, my mother is the one to wade in and try to solve it.*

wade through *sth*
1 to read detailed or complicated information ◆ *We don't have enough staff to wade through the data.* ◆ *If you can wade through the ads, there's useful information here about the history of the Internet.*
2 to move through a large group ◆ *We waded through a crowd of thousands.* ◆ *The players have to wade through a sea of fans after games.*

> ORIGIN: based on the literal meaning of **wade** (= to walk in water that is not deep)

wagon

off the wagon
drinking alcohol again, after having stopped ◆ *If she falls off the wagon again, she'll just have to pick herself up and try to stop drinking.* USAGE: usually said about someone who has an alcohol problem ◆ Opposite **on the wagon**

on the wagon
not drinking any alcohol, after a period of drinking regularly ◆ *He's been on the wagon for ten years now.* USAGE: usually said about someone who has an alcohol problem ◆ Opposite **off the wagon**

wagons

circle the wagons
to stop communicating with people not in your group to avoid their ideas or beliefs ◆ *Americans are feeling it is an especially good time to spend time with family, to circle the wagons.*

> ORIGIN: based on the custom of bringing **wagons** (= vehicles pulled by horses) into a circle when they are being attacked

wait

lie in wait
1 to stay hidden, ready to attack ◆ *Police said the suspect was lying in wait in a dark hallway.* ◆ *This person was found behind a wall, as if he were lying in wait for someone.*
2 to delay doing something until the best time for it ◆ *The smart thing to do is lie in wait for the right time to ask for a raise.* ◆ Related vocabulary **lie low** at LIE

wait and see
to be patient until a later time ◆ *Nothing can be done about it now, so you'll just have to wait and see.*

wait on *sb*
to serve someone ◆ *She waited on customers all day at the department store.* ◆ *He sits there in front of the TV and expects me to wait on him!* ◆ Related vocabulary **wait on** *sb* **hand and foot** at HAND

wait *sb* **out**, *also* **wait out** *sb*
to allow time to go past until someone does something ◆ *I have time and he doesn't, so I'll wait him out until he agrees to sell the business to me.* ◆ *She hoped to wait out her opponent, but that has not worked.*

wait out *sth*, *also* **wait** *sth* **out**
to allow time to go past until something happens or ends ◆ *Should we leave now or wait out the storm?*

hurry up and wait See at HURRY
wait a minute See at MINUTE
wait a second See at SECOND
(wait) in the wings See at WINGS
wait on *sb* **hand and foot** See at HAND
wait (on) tables See at TABLES

wake

in the wake of *sth*
following or as a result of something ♦ *The airport lowered parking rates in the wake of many complaints from drivers who felt the rates were far too high.*

wake up to *sth*
to become aware of something important ♦ *I wish Dad would wake up to the fact that the car is about to fall apart.*

wake up and smell the coffee See at COFFEE

walk

take a walk
to leave; = **take a hike** ♦ *The manager threatened to take a walk, so the owner of the team offered him a better contract.*

walk all over *sb/sth*
1 to treat someone or something without respect ♦ *You shouldn't let him walk all over you like that.* ♦ *This new law would walk all over our civil rights.*
2 to defeat a person or team badly ♦ *The Nighthawks walked all over the Tigers last night with a 5–0 victory.*

walk away with *sth*, also **walk off with** *sth*
to win or get something easily ♦ *The German soccer team is favored to walk away with the championship.* ♦ *She got a minor injury and walked off with a million-dollar insurance settlement.*

walk off with *sth*
to take something without asking ♦ *Who walked off with my drink?*

walk out
1 to leave an event before it is finished ♦ *It was such a bad movie that I felt like walking out in the first fifteen minutes.*
2 to refuse to work because of a disagreement with your employer ♦ *Airline pilots are threatening to walk out next week.*

walk out on *sb/sth*
to suddenly end your relationship with someone or something ♦ *She walked out on her husband and two children after 12 years of marriage.* ♦ *Why would anyone walk out on a seven-year contract that includes a share of the profits?*

walk the walk
to show that something is true through your actions ♦ *He says the team will be just as good without Groncki as they were with him, but we'll have to see if the team can walk the walk.* USAGE: sometimes used in the full form **talk the talk and walk the walk** (= to say something that appears to be real or true and show it is real or true through your actions): *Most of these guys say they have religious beliefs, but only a few of them can talk the talk and walk the walk.* ♦ Related vocabulary **talk the talk** at TALK

walk (*sb***) through** *sth*
to explain or study something completely ♦ *The lawyer prepared himself for the trial by walking through his opening statement.* ♦ *Could you please walk us through the schedule for tomorrow?* ♦ Related vocabulary **talk it through** at TALK

walk and chew gum (at the same time) See at GUM

walk a thin line (between *sth***)** See at LINE

walk a tightrope See at TIGHTROPE

walk on air See at AIR

walk on eggshells See at EGGSHELLS

walk the plank See at PLANK

wall

drive *you* **up the wall**
to make you very unhappy and full of anxiety or anger ♦ *Working in front of a computer screen all day drives me up the wall.* ♦ Related vocabulary **drive** *you* **to distraction** at DISTRACTION

go to the wall
to be defeated or destroyed ◆ *They believe in a completely free market, and would let the weakest groups or individuals go to the wall.*

go to the wall (for *sb/sth*)
to do as much as is possible ◆ *Friends and colleagues were ready to go to the wall for Hal, but he didn't want anyone's help.*

nail *sb* to the wall
to punish or hurt someone severely ◆ *I was so angry, I just wanted to nail the crooks to the wall.*

off the wall
strange or very different ◆ *Even though many people thought he was off the wall, they also thought he had very interesting ideas.*

a fly on the wall See at FLY

the writing on the wall See at WRITING

with *your/its* back against the wall See at BACK

wand

wave a magic wand
to solve a difficult problem with no effort ◆ *Unfortunately, you can't just wave a magic wand and get rid of poverty.*

> ORIGIN: from the practice of waving a **wand** (= a special stick) when someone is doing a magic trick

want

(do you) want to bet slang, *also* (you) wanna bet
I think you are wrong ◆ *"She wouldn't go out with you if you paid her." "Want to bet?"* USAGE: often used with **how much**: *"No bank would be stupid enough to lend him any money." "How much do you want to bet?"*

want for *sth* slightly formal
to lack something that you need ◆ *We didn't have much, but we never wanted for food.*

ward

ward off *sb/sth*, *also* ward *sb/sth* off
to try to keep away someone or something that would hurt you ◆ *He raised his arm at the elbow to ward off the blow.* ◆ *They have a "No Trespassing" sign out front to ward off anyone who happens by.* ◆ *She often gets headaches, so she carries a bit of fresh ginger wherever she goes to ward them off.* ◆ Related vocabulary **fend off** *sb* 2 at FEND, **stave off** *sth* at STAVE

warm

warm *sb* up, *also* warm up *sb*
to cause someone to become more relaxed and friendly ◆ *It is a good idea to warm up an audience with a few amusing stories before talking about serious things.* ◆ *Do you think meditation might help warm him up before he gets out there to speak?*

warm up (*sth*), *also* warm *sth* up
to briefly exercise as preparation for something ◆ *She warms her voice up before a concert by singing scales and making funny noises.* ◆ *He always warmed up for about 15 minutes before his morning run.*

> ORIGIN: based on the literal meaning of **warm something up** (= to cause the temperature of something to increase)

warm up to (*sb/sth*)
to begin to like or enjoy someone or something ◆ *It took a couple of days for us to warm up to each other, but now we're very good friends.* ◆ *Some people have warmed up to the idea of extending the school year, but many still oppose it.* USAGE: sometimes used in the form **warm someone up to something** (= to prepare someone so they will like something): *I think you should warm them up to the idea, and not just surprise your parents when they get here.*

on the warpath

You've never seen my mother when she's on the warpath – look out!

warpath
on the warpath
angry and ready to argue or fight ◆ *Hollywood studios are on the warpath, trying to bring an end to the illegal copying of movies.* ◆ *The little girl went on the warpath in defense of her brother.*

warts
warts and all
including all faults or other unpleasant facts ◆ *Because no one is perfect, you have to accept people warts and all.*

> ORIGIN: from the fact that **warts** (= small, hard lumps that grow on the skin) are thought of as being ugly

wash
wash down *sth*, also **wash** *sth* **down**
to drink a liquid to help you swallow something ◆ *It was a great meal washed down with several glasses of wine.* ◆ *He got two aspirin and washed them down with a glass of water.*

wash out (of *sth***)**
to leave a program or activity because you failed to meet its standards ◆ *I didn't make it through flight school – I washed out.* ◆ *After washing out of the military academy, he joined his father's business.*

wash out (*sth***)**, also **wash** *sth* **out**
to cause an activity or event not to happen because of rain ◆ *Even the golf tournament was washed out this week.* ◆ *Storms washed the picnic out.*

wash up
to clean your hands ◆ *She told the children to wash up for dinner.*

wash up (*sth***)**, also **wash** *sth* **up**
1 to be moved and left in another place by the flow of water ◆ *Following the sinking of the ferry, a number of bodies washed up on shore.* ◆ *Scattered around the bridge is a lot of debris that washed up.*
2 to clean the dishes after a meal ◆ *Who's turn is it to wash up?* ◆ *I started washing up the supper dishes.*

wash *your* **hands of** *sb/sth* See at HANDS

waste

go to waste
to not be used ◆ *It's wrong to let good food go to waste.* ◆ *The companies have spent millions of dollars on new equipment that lets nothing go to waste.*

lay waste (to *sth*)
to destroy something ◆ *Last night, rabbits laid waste to the lettuce I was going to pick today.* ◆ *The army laid waste to the countryside as it moved south.*

waste away
1 to gradually become thin and weak ◆ *He stopped eating and wasted away until he looked like a shadow.*
2 to be damaged or rubbed away by weather ◆ *Good soil can waste away quickly if it's not cared for properly.*

waste *sth* on *sb*
to not be noticed or appreciated ◆ *I wouldn't waste this material on high school students – they don't have the background to understand it.* USAGE: often used when speaking of something of special quality: *The difference between a really fine French wine and one that's not as good is wasted on me.*

waste *your* breath See at BREATH
waste no time in *doing sth* See at TIME

watch

keep (a) close watch on *sb/sth*, also keep (a) close watch over *sb/sth*
to guard or follow carefully someone or something ◆ *With an international team keeping close watch on polling stations, voters chose from an array of 12 candidates.* ◆ *Republicans are warning the president to keep a close watch on spending.* USAGE: sometimes used in the form **keep a watch on**: *He wants to keep a watch on who comes and goes from the office.* ◆ Related vocabulary **keep an eye out (for *sb/sth*)** at EYE

watch out esp. spoken
be aware ◆ *They say a storm is coming, so watch out and don't take any chances.* USAGE: sometimes used as an order: *Andy saw the car coming toward them, and yelled, "Watch out!"* ◆ Related vocabulary **look out** at LOOK

watch out for *sb/sth*
1 to feel responsibility for someone or something; = **look out for *sb/sth*** ◆ *Carol's father made me promise I'd watch out for her and make sure she had whatever she needed.*
2 to be careful in order to avoid a problem ◆ *You've got to watch out for viruses when downloading files to your computer.* ◆ *Watch out for that dog – he's not very friendly.*
3 to be aware of someone or something ◆ *I used to tell everyone, "Watch out for this girl. She's going to be a great tennis player one day."*

watch over *sb/sth*
to protect and feel responsible for the care of someone or something ◆ *She had to watch over her four young children.* ◆ *He watched over his vegetable garden, trying to think up ways to keep the deer away from it.*

watch *your* back See at BACK
watch *sb* like a hawk See at HAWK
watch *your* step See at STEP

water

blow *you* out of the water
1 to completely surprise you ◆ *Her singing blew me out of the water – I haven't heard anyone sing like that since Sarah Vaughn.*
2 to defeat or completely confuse you ◆ *We were blown out of the water by that team – they didn't make one mistake the whole game!* ◆ *Those directions blew us out of the water. We couldn't follow them at all.*

blow *sth* out of the water
to destroy something ◆ *The virus*

blew my computer's hard drive completely out of the water. ◆ My lawyer blew their case right out of the water with his witnesses.

dead in the water
without any chance for success; = **dead on arrival** ◆ I guess our plans for summer vacation are dead in the water.

in hot water
in a difficult situation in which you are likely to be punished ◆ Those e-mails complaining about your boss can land you in hot water.

not hold water
to not seem to be true or reasonable ◆ That argument isn't likely to hold water with my father! ◆ A lot of the stuff I believed in when I was 17 just doesn't hold water today. ◆ Related vocabulary **hold up** 2 at HOLD

throw cold water on *sth*, *also* **pour cold water on** *sth*
to criticize or stop something that some people are enthusiastic about ◆ The proposal seemed reasonable enough, but authorities quickly threw cold water on it.

tread water
to be active but without making progress or falling farther behind ◆ Sales are about the same as last year, and the company is pretty much treading water. ◆ Related vocabulary **mark time** at TIME

> ORIGIN: based on the literal meaning of **tread water** (= to stay in one place in water by moving your legs quickly)

water down *sth*, *also* **water** *sth* **down**
to make something weaker ◆ Some people say the new regulations water down several laws that protect people who rent apartments in the city. ◆ Once the bill is introduced, he's worried that lawmakers will water it down.

> ORIGIN: based on the literal meaning of **water down something** (= to add water to a liquid to weaken things mixed in it)

water under the bridge
something that has happened and cannot be changed ◆ I should probably have asked for more money when I was offered the job, but hey, that's water under the bridge now.

a fish out of water See at FISH
come hell or high water See at HELL
make *your* **mouth water** See at MOUTH
throw out the baby with the bath water See at BABY

waterfront
cover the waterfront
to deal with all parts of a subject or area of interest, not omitting anything ◆ The FBI cannot expect a handful of agents to cover the waterfront in investigating terrorism.

waters
muddy the waters
to make a situation more confusing ◆ He's just trying to muddy the waters so we won't notice all the bad things he's done. USAGE: sometimes used with a modifier: The controversy has muddied the social waters of communities throughout this region. ◆ Related vocabulary **muck** *sth* **up** at MUCK

test the waters
to try something new ◆ We are testing the waters to see if online ads increase sales. ◆ Related vocabulary **float an idea** at IDEA

> ORIGIN: based on the literal meaning of **test the waters** (= to put your toe into water to see how cold it is)

wave
catch the wave
to understand and behave according to the most modern fashions in

wavelength 458

social behavior ◆ *The company's move was aimed at catching the wave of consumers rushing to the Web.* ◆ *Is the topic hip enough for TV to want to catch the wave?*

> ORIGIN: based on the literal meaning of **catch a wave** (= to start riding a board across the rolling surface of the sea)

ride a wave of *sth*, *also* **ride the wave of** *sth*
to be helped by being connected to something attractive or interesting ◆ *The president rode a wave of good feeling among voters that made it impossible for him to lose the election.*

> ORIGIN: based on the literal meaning of **ride a wave** (= to stand on a board moving across the rolling surface of the sea)

wavelength
on the same wavelength
in agreement ◆ *Writing the screenplay was easy because Bill and I were on the same wavelength.* ◆ Related vocabulary **on the same page** at PAGE

waves
make waves
to shock or upset people with something new or different ◆ *Her clothes have made waves on the fashion scene around the world.* USAGE: often used in the form **not make waves**: *We decided not to make waves with our parents and agreed to have a real wedding.* ◆ Related vocabulary **don't rock the boat** at BOAT, **keep your nose clean** at NOSE

wax
wax and wane
to become stronger and then weaker ◆ *Religious influence on politics has waxed and waned since the founding of this country.*

way
along the way
while something is happening ◆ *Enjoy the concert, but please call me along the way to let me know how you are.* ◆ *I'm new at this parenting thing and I'm bound to make a few mistakes along the way.*

any way you slice it, *also* **any way you cut it**
in whatever manner you consider this; = **no matter how you slice it** ◆ *Any way you slice it, there are going to be some very unhappy people when the prizes are announced.*

a way of life
accepted as a regular part of something ◆ *Unfortunately, arguments and anger have been a way of life at the art center for several years.*

> ORIGIN: based on the literal meaning of **a way of life** (= how a person lives)

bluff *your* **way**
to deceive others to get what you want ◆ *Some teens used false IDs to bluff their way into casinos.* USAGE: usually followed by a phrase starting with **through**, **out of**, or **into**, as in the example

buy *your* **way** *somewhere*
to pay money so you can join or leave an organization ◆ *In the past, men could legally buy their way out of serving in the army.* ◆ *Some said he bought his way into the law firm.*

by the way esp. spoken
in addition but of less importance ◆ *By the way, I heard that Phyllis may be moving to Dallas.* ◆ *What did you have for dinner, by the way?*

claw *your* **way** *somewhere*
to use all your energy and determination to achieve something ◆ *Little by little, the county is clawing its way out of the damage caused by the flood.* ◆ *She clawed her way to the top of the company.*

clear the way (for *sb/sth***)**
to make it possible or easier for someone or something to follow ◆ *Approval of the financing helped clear the way for the new construc-*

tion. ◆ *Our grandmothers who demanded the vote cleared the way for today's women to become politicians, professionals, and judges.*

come a long way
to make a lot of progress and improvement ◆ *The five-member rock group has come a long way since recording its first album.* ◆ *Computer graphics have come a long way in the last few years.*

either way
whatever happens ◆ *Give me a call either way and let me know if you want to come with us.* USAGE: the same meaning can be also expressed by **at (the very) least**, **come hell or high water**, **come what may**, **in any case**, and **in any event**

every which way
in many different directions ◆ *The forest fire spread, and frightened animals were running every which way.*

feel *your* way
to do something slowly and carefully ◆ *I've only been at the job two months, so I'm still feeling my way.*

ORIGIN: from the literal meaning of **feel your way** (= to move forward in a dark area by touching things with your hands)

get in the way (of *sth*)
to prevent something from happening ◆ *Anger often gets in the way of understanding a situation.* ◆ *We had almost reached an agreement, but some unimportant details got in the way.*

get *sth* out of the way
to finish something first so that you can do something else ◆ *I got my required courses out of the way, and now I can study the things I'm really excited about.*

get *your* own way
to succeed in being allowed to do what you want ◆ *He's enormously likable and charming and usually gets his own way.*

give way
to break or fall down suddenly ◆ *Those wooden steps are old, and I'm afraid one of them will give way, so we need to replace them this weekend.*

give way to *sth*
to be replaced by something ◆ *My excitement gave way to fear when I drove a car for the first time.*

go all the way
to have sex ◆ *In the old days, couples spent a lot of time kissing but didn't go all the way.*

go a long way toward *sth*, also go a long way to *sth*
to be very helpful in achieving something ◆ *The fire insurance went a long way toward repairing all the damage.* ◆ *The extra money will go a long way to buying a house.*

go back a long way
to know someone for a long time ◆ *Justin and I go back a long way – we were at college together.*

go out of *your* way to *do sth*
to try very hard to help other people or make them comfortable ◆ *Our hosts went out of their way to make us feel welcome.* ◆ *Many teachers really go out of their way to help their students.*

have a way with *sb/sth*
to be especially good in dealing with someone or something ◆ *My son has a way with little kids.* ◆ *She had a way with words that was fantastic.*

in a bad way
having difficulties ◆ *We were in a bad way until Sergio joined the team, and then we began to win our games.*

in any way, shape, or form
in any possible manner or under any conditions ◆ *Neither Bill nor Ann is prepared for this in any way, shape, or form.* USAGE: often used in the form **not in any way, shape, or form**: *The new principal said that*

she would not in any way, shape, or form tell teachers how to teach their subjects.

in a way
considered in this manner ♦ *I suppose, in a way, I was more of a sister to you than Joan was.* ♦ *I think that's sad in a way.*

in the way
using or filling space ♦ *I pushed our dinner dishes into a corner where they wouldn't be in the way.*

in *sb's* way, *also* **in the way of *sb***
in a position that prevents someone from moving or making progress ♦ *Several people stood right in my way, so I couldn't move.* ♦ *Why would anyone put any barriers in the way of parents who want to adopt these children?*

in the way of *sth*
1 like something ♦ *I realize this makes no sense to you – it is in the way of a private joke between my wife and me.* ♦ *Do you have anything in the way of house plants that don't need much light?*
2 relating to something ♦ *They did little in the way of training.*

in the worst way
very much ♦ *After a day in the hot sun, he needed a shower in the worst way.*

know *your* way around (somewhere)
to be familiar with a place ♦ *He'd be a good guide for tourists because he really knows his way around the city.*

know *your* way around *sth*
to have knowledge about how something works ♦ *You don't have to know your way around a slide rule to enjoy these exhibits.*

laugh all the way to the bank
to be pleased about the profit earned from doing something ♦ *Team owners complain about the latest TV deal, but in fact they are laughing all the way to the bank.* ♦ *After we sold the house, my wife cried and I laughed all the way to the bank.*

lead the way
1 to be the best ♦ *That research group leads the way in developing new software.*
2 to be the most popular ♦ *For women, a natural look in hairstyles led the way this spring.*

lead the way (*somewhere*)
to go first to show how to get somewhere ♦ *Joseph led the way to the nearest corner, away from the crowd of people.*

learn (*sth*) the hard way
to obtain knowledge or understanding through experience ♦ *We'd never done anything like this, so we learned how to build a house the hard way.* ♦ *Since he won't take advice from anyone, I guess he is going to have to learn the hard way.*
USAGE: often used in the form **find (something) out the hard way**: *He found out the hard way that he needed help.*

look the other way
to ignore something wrong or unpleasant ♦ *When someone is having a serious problem, friends sometimes try to look the other way.*

make *its* way *somewhere*
to reach a place or condition ♦ *The product should be making its way into retail stores in a few months.* ♦ *Mary's poems finally made their way into print.*

make *your* way (*somewhere*)
to move in a particular direction ♦ *In the midst of war in Europe, he somehow made his way back to the United States and joined the army.*

make way for *sth*
to create space for something else ♦ *Some fine old buildings have been torn down to make way for an ugly new parking garage.*

not know which way to turn
to not know what to do ♦ *The uncertainty has left many companies not knowing which way to turn.*

way

no way esp. spoken
not possibly; = **my foot** ◆ *Now he's asking me to lend him my car. No way!* USAGE: often used in the form **there's no way**: *There's no way I could have paid for it.*

one way or another
using any method available ◆ *One way or another, I'm going to finish this job by next week.* USAGE: usually used when you know something will happen or get done, but you do not know exactly how

one way or the other
1 which of two possibilities will happen or be chosen ◆ *They've had a week to think about it, and now they must decide one way or the other.* ◆ *It doesn't really matter to me one way or the other.*
2 whatever method is used ◆ *One way or the other, this project must be finished by March first.* ◆ Related vocabulary **in any case** at CASE, **in any event** at EVENT

on the way, *also* **on** *your/its* **way** *somewhere*
happening or arriving soon ◆ *They have three kids, and another on the way.* ◆ *This software is well on its way to driving me crazy.* ◆ *We're on our way from the airport, so save some supper for us!*

on *your* **way**
leaving or away ◆ *Give me a kiss and I'll be on my way.* ◆ *They stayed with us for a week and then went on their way.*

open the way for *sth*, *also* **open the way to** *sth*
to create an opportunity for something to happen ◆ *New regulations will open the way for more people to live and work here.* ◆ *These talks have opened the way to ending war in the region.*

out of the way
1 not near any cities or large towns ◆ *We decided to vacation in a quiet place in Maine that is really out of the way.*
2 completed ◆ *I'm glad my final exams are out of the way.*

out of *sb's* **way**
not in the direction in which someone is going ◆ *Robert insisted on taking me home, even though it was about 10 miles out of his way.*

pave the way for *sb/sth*
to make it possible or easier for someone or something to follow ◆ *The procedure helped pave the way for successful open heart surgery using the heart-lung machine.* ◆ Related vocabulary **lay** *sb/sth* **open (to** *sth***)** at LAY

pay its way
to earn as much money as something costs to produce ◆ *In one city at least, public transportation has paid its way for years.*

pay *your* **way**
to pay for all your expenses ◆ *The army paid my way through medical school.*

pick *your* **way**
to walk very carefully and slowly ◆ *He helped me pick my way over the stream.*

point the way (to *sth***)**
to be among the first to show how something can be done ◆ *This research points the way to more effective treatment.*

prepare the way (for *sb/sth***)**
to create an opportunity for something to happen ◆ *His comments prepared the way for the two organizations to work together.* ◆ *Her election prepared the way for me and others like me.*

rub *sb* **the wrong way**
to annoy someone ◆ *He was known as a moody and selfish player who rubbed teammates the wrong way.*

ORIGIN: based on the idea that if you **rub the wrong way** on a cat's fur, you annoy it

send *sb* **on** *their* **way**
to cause someone to leave ◆ *Dad gave me $15 and sent me on my way.*

♦ *All the tests showed that her heart was functioning normally, so the doctors sent her on her way.* ♦ Related vocabulary **send *sb* on *sth*** at SEND

show (*sb*) the way
to teach someone how to act in particular situations ♦ *As an older, more experienced girl, Cheri wanted to show Lauren the way to success as a teenager.*

smooth the way for *sb/sth*, also **smooth *sb's/sth's* way**
to make conditions easier for something to happen ♦ *Parents can do a lot to smooth the way for their children when they start school.* ♦ *To smooth our way, many people offered to drive us to and from the hospital.*

take *sth* the wrong way
to fail to understand a statement or situation correctly ♦ *A lot of people take his confidence the wrong way, mistaking it for arrogance.* ♦ *She feels like every word she says is taken the wrong way.*

talk *your* way *somewhere*
to use persuasion to do or avoid something ♦ *Phillips talked his way into a military site that does not permit visitors.* ♦ *She tried to talk her way out of a speeding ticket but the police officer gave it to her anyway.*

the way things are (going), also **the way things stand**
as the situation is now ♦ *The way things are going, soon most people will be working at home.* ♦ *The way things stand, I don't think we'll be able to leave for vacation until Monday.*

which way the wind is blowing
how something will probably develop ♦ *It wasn't hard to tell which way the wind was blowing when the judge spoke to the jury.* ♦ *Peter quickly saw which way the wind was blowing and tried to comfort the worried parents.*

***sb* will go a long way**
to be very successful ♦ *She is an excellent actor, and I know she'll go a long way.*

in the family way See at FAMILY

(way) out in left field See at LEFT FIELD

ways

change *your* ways, also **mend *your* ways**
to improve your behavior ♦ *If he wants to continue living here, he's going to have to change his ways.*

cut both ways
to have both advantages and disadvantages; = **work both ways** ♦ *The Internet cuts both ways – it not only opens borders, it draws boundaries between the people who have it and those who do not.*

go *your* separate ways
to end your relationship ♦ *We were good friends in college, but after graduation we went our separate ways.* ♦ *The two firms went their separate ways about 18 months ago.*

have it both ways
to satisfy two opposing groups or opinions ♦ *Americans want to have it both ways, saying they strongly believe in certain principles while reserving the right not to apply them in difficult situations.* USAGE: often used in the form **not have it both ways**: *I don't see how critics can say that it won't be effective and that it will be too tough – you can't have it both ways.* ♦ Related vocabulary **square the circle** at CIRCLE

no two ways about it
there is no doubt about something ♦ *She just fell madly in love with him, no two ways about it.*

quite a ways esp. spoken
a long distance ♦ *We're quite a ways from the Mexican border here.*

ways and means
methods of achieving something ♦ *She spent years exploring ways and*

means of improving children's nutrition.

work both ways
1 to have a similar or equal effect on each side ◆ *Asking for sacrifices has to work both ways – workers and management both have to accept cuts.*
2 to have both advantages and disadvantages; = **cut both ways** ◆ *Installing the new computer system works both ways – we'll have better control of our business, but we'll lose some of our best workers.*

parting of the ways See at PARTING

see the error of *your/its* **ways** See at ERROR

wayside

fall by the wayside
1 to no longer be active ◆ *Plans for at least one other power plant have fallen by the wayside.* ◆ *Most of the company's smaller rivals have fallen by the wayside.*
2 to stop trying ◆ *Students who fall by the wayside often do not see any reason why they should finish their courses.* ◆ *"I've seen a lot of bands split up and fall by the wayside," the singer said.*

wear

wear and tear
damage from work or use ◆ *The house showed lots of wear and tear from the large family who lived in it.* ◆ *Your body suffers a lot of wear and tear from playing football.*

wear *sb* **out**
to make someone very tired ◆ *Those kids wore their grandmother out.* ◆ *The journey wore him out, and he went straight to bed as soon as he got to the hotel.*

wear out *sth*, also **wear** *sth* **out**
to use something so much that it can no longer be used ◆ *Randy's been cooking in a kitchen that's so old, almost everything in it has simply worn out.* ◆ *He wore out a pair of running shoes every three months.*

USAGE: sometimes used without **something**: *On rough roads, tires wear out fast.*

wear thin
to become less effective ◆ *It was a constant struggle to get him to do his homework, and finally my patience wore thin.* ◆ *The sort of character Hugh plays has been done so many times, it's beginning to wear thin.*

none the worse (for *sth***)** See at WORSE

the worse for wear See at WORSE

wear *your* **heart on** *your* **sleeve** See at HEART

wear *sth* **on** *your* **sleeve** See at SLEEVE

wear out *your/its* **welcome** See at WELCOME

wear the pants See at PANTS

weasel

weasel out (of *sth***)**
to escape responsibility for something ◆ *He used all kinds of excuses to weasel out of paying his bills.*

weather

under the weather
not healthy ◆ *It's hard to keep working when you're under the weather* ◆ See illustration, page 464

weather the storm
to be all right despite experiencing serious problems or great difficulties ◆ *Bob lost his job, but somehow his family weathered the storm.*

wedded

wedded to *sth*
strongly or closely attached to something ◆ *Many teachers are wedded to the ideas and methods they learned in college and find it hard to try anything new.* ◆ *People in this country are really wedded to their cars.*

wedge

drive a wedge between *sb/sth*
to cause a division between people or groups ◆ *Frank had to travel a lot*

under the weather

Ellen was feeling under the weather today.

and this finally drove a wedge between him and his wife. ♦ *The issue of global warming has driven a wedge between our government and the rest of the world.*

weed

weed out *sb/sth*, *also* **weed** *sb/sth* **out**
to remove someone or something not wanted ♦ *The school needs to weed out wasteful spending.* ♦ *You need to be able to weed people out if they can't do a good job.*

week

week after week
repeatedly for many weeks ♦ *The play was a smash hit, and I tried week after week to get tickets, but I still haven't seen it.* ♦ Related vocabulary **day after day** at DAY, **month after month** at MONTH, **year after year** at YEAR

week by week
every week ♦ *Week by week, the child gained strength.* ♦ Related vocabulary **day by day** at DAY, **month by month** at MONTH, **year by year** at YEAR

weigh

weigh *sb* **down**, *also* **weigh down** *sb*
1 to be very heavy for someone to carry ♦ *She checked her bags because she knew they would weigh her down.* ♦ *The number of keys he carried would have weighed down a band of sturdy men.*
2 to make someone feel tired and weak ♦ *He was weighed down by worries about money.* ♦ *Old, sad memories weighed her down.*

weigh down *sth*, *also* **weigh** *sth* **down**
to slow the operation or growth of an organization ♦ *The company was weighed down with debt.* ♦ *Health-care costs weigh the economy down.*

weigh in
to offer an opinion in a discussion or argument ♦ *Mr. Pierce weighed in with a warning that many companies would not be able to meet the deadline.* ♦ *One angry woman weighed in to remind us that a lot of what we'd read was not true.*

weigh in at *sth*
to be measured as being a particular weight; = **tip the scales at** *sth* ◆ *Both fighters weighed in at 162 pounds.* ◆ *The baby weighed in at 6 pounds, 9 ounces.*

weigh on *sb*
to cause someone anxiety or worry ◆ *Her daughter's illness definitely weighed on her mind.*

weigh on *sth*
to push something down ◆ *High energy prices weigh on a company's profits by increasing production costs.* USAGE: usually used in connection with financial markets or prices

weigh a ton See at TON

weigh *your* **words** See at WORDS

weight

carry weight
to be important and have influence ◆ *Her opinion carries a lot of weight with the boss.* ◆ *A partnership without a written agreement carries no legal weight.* USAGE: usually used with **some**, **little**, and other modifiers, as in the examples

pull *your* **weight**
to do your fair share of work ◆ *In a busy restaurant, everyone has to pull their weight.*

throw *your* **weight around**
to use your position or influence to unfairly get what you want ◆ *Most of the time the department manager just throws his weight around to remind you he can always fire you.*

throw *your* **weight behind** *sb/sth*
to use your influence to support someone or something ◆ *A number of top performers have thrown their weight behind a live concert to fight hunger around the world.*

worth *your/its* **weight in gold**
extremely useful or valuable ◆ *User-friendly software is worth its weight in gold.* ◆ *Experienced singers are worth their weight in gold because they bring strength to the choir.*

ORIGIN: based on the idea that gold is the most valuable metal

welcome

wear out *your/its* **welcome**
to stay somewhere too long, making people tired of seeing you ◆ *By the time Buzz left, he had worn out his welcome with almost everyone.* ◆ *The TV comedy hasn't worn out its welcome, probably because its characters are so good.*

you're welcome
I was happy to do it; = **no problem** ◆ *"Thanks for returning the video." "You're welcome!"* USAGE: usually used as an answer to someone saying **thank you**

well

all very well
acceptable ◆ *It's all very well to give money to help people, but there needs to be some way of helping them to help themselves.* USAGE: said about something that is good but not enough by itself

well and truly
completely ◆ *Most Australians would say that Australia has been well and truly independent since the beginning of the 20th century.*

were

as it were esp. spoken
1 in some way ◆ *In my district, we almost vote where we live, as it were – it's right across the street from my house.*
2 to some degree ◆ *That's an interesting combination, as it were, of the two ideas.*

weren't

if it weren't for *sb/sth*
the situation would have been different without someone or something ◆ *If it weren't for him, I would probably be living on the streets.* ◆ *I'd keep a garden if it weren't for having too much to do.* USAGE: also

used in the form **if it hadn't been for someone or something**: *If it hadn't been for Judy, Betsy was sure she would have left the city.*

wet

all wet *esp. spoken*
completely wrong ◆ *Anyone who talks about reducing taxes now is all wet.*

get *your* feet wet See at FEET

wet behind the ears See at EARS

whack

out of whack
1 not working well or not in good condition; = **out of kilter** ◆ *Lifting boxes in and out of the truck threw his back out of whack.*
2 not matching; = **out of kilter** ◆ *What we were told just now is basically out of whack with the facts.*

whale

a whale of a *sth* *esp. spoken*
1 an unusually good something ◆ *Perry's done a whale of a job for us.* ◆ *We had a whale of a time, and we were sorry when we had to leave.*
2 an unusually large something ◆ *There's a whale of a difference between being a partner in a law firm and just being another lawyer.*

what

so what *esp. spoken*
it does not seem important ◆ *She's got a big career and yeah, she has a voice, so what?* ◆ *Maybe he's a little obnoxious sometimes, but so what?*

what about *sb/sth* *esp. spoken*
can you explain or give your opinion about someone or something ◆ *That's fine for you, but what about the rest of us?* ◆ *What about the idea that as a nation we watch TV rather than read?*

what for
why ◆ *We were peacefully protesting and the cops arrested us, so I asked, "What for?"*

what if
imagine what would happen in the event that ◆ *What if our plane is delayed and we can't make the connection?* ◆ *A scary dream was bad enough, but what if it came true?*

what's more
the next fact is at least as important or even more important ◆ *Military action will hurt ordinary people, and what's more, it won't solve the problem.*

what's what *esp. spoken*
the information about a person or situation ◆ *You finally met her boyfriend, so now you know what's what.* ◆ *He's been in this business for a long time and really understands what's what.* ◆ *It will be hard for investors to tell what's what in the current stock-market crisis.*

what's up *esp. spoken*
what is happening ◆ *I'll be over there sometime today just to see what's up.*
USAGE: sometimes used as a greeting: *"Hey, Edsel, what's up?" "Nothing much. How are you?"* ◆ sometimes spelled **wassup** to show how it sounds

wheat

separate the wheat from the chaff
to choose what is of high quality over what is of lower quality ◆ *As we learn more about computer programs for the classroom, we are able to separate the wheat from the chaff and get the right software for our kids.*

wheel

asleep at the wheel
not paying attention; = **asleep at the switch** ◆ *Why was our government asleep at the wheel when the crisis began?*

> ORIGIN: based on the literal meaning of **asleep at the wheel** (= sleeping while driving a vehicle)

behind the wheel, *also* **at the wheel**
driving a vehicle ◆ *Mia was behind*

the wheel, and Kim was studying the map.

reinvent the wheel
to discover how to do something that has already been discovered ◆ *We've had a lot of experience with disasters, and don't have to reinvent the wheel every time something happens.*

put *your* shoulder to the wheel See at SHOULDER

wheel and deal See at WHEELING

wheeling

wheeling and dealing
looking for and using a good opportunity ◆ *He was always wheeling and dealing to get financial support.* USAGE: usually said about business or financial opportunities, and also used in the form **wheel and deal**: *If you want to be successful in this business, you have to wheel and deal.*

wheels

spin *your* wheels
to waste time doing something that is not effective ◆ *For almost an hour he had been spinning his wheels on the telephone when he could have fixed the problem himself in less than hour.*

the wheels are turning
something is happening ◆ *By the late 1940s the wheels were turning that would make space flight possible by the end of the 1950s.*

whether

whether or not
if something does or does not happen ◆ *Whether or not she wins the championship, she'll still be one of the best swimmers we've ever had in the school.* USAGE: often used in the form **whether something or not**: *Whether you like it or not, I'm taking the car tonight.*

while

(every) once in a while
sometimes; = **every so often** ◆ *Every once in a while I've been tempted to take an art class.* ◆ Related vocabulary **(every) now and then** at NOW

quite a while esp. spoken
a long time ◆ *I hadn't seen Rebecca in quite a while, but she hadn't changed much.*

while away *sth*
to spend time in a relaxed way ◆ *Commuters while away the time they are stuck in traffic by listening to their favorite radio station.*

worth *your* while
of benefit to you ◆ *It would be worth your while to see if you can still get tickets to the show.* ◆ *You could make this trip more worth your while if you arranged to see more than one client.*

strike while the iron is hot See at IRON

while *you* are at it See at AT

whip

crack the whip
to use your authority to cause people to do more or do what you want ◆ *He is one editor who knows how to crack the whip, so his authors generally hand in their assignments on time.*

whip up *sth*, also **whip *sth* up**
1 to quickly prepare something to eat ◆ *They got up at 3:30, Pete whipped up breakfast, and they left for the airport by 4:00.* USAGE: also used in the form **whip someone up something**: *Let's ask Marion to whip us up a little snack.*
2 to cause something to increase in strength or violence ◆ *Huge waves, whipped up by the unusually strong winds, pounded the beaches.* ◆ *The press whipped up public opinion to the point where we were in danger of rioting in the streets.* ◆ *The crowd was pushing forward, and some people tried to whip things up even further.*

whip *sb/sth* into shape See at SHAPE

whirl

whirl
give *sth* a whirl
to try something ◆ *Tan had given up technical writing to give fiction a whirl.* USAGE: often used in the form **give it a whirl**: *We've always wanted to take a cruise in the Caribbean, so we decided to give it a whirl.* ◆ Related vocabulary **take a shot at *sth*** at SHOT

whisker
within a whisker of *sth*
close to something ◆ *Yesterday, the price of oil came within a whisker of its all-time high.* ◆ *An asteroid came within a whisker of crashing into the earth.*

whistle
blow the whistle (on *sb/sth*)
to show to the public dangerous conditions or illegal activities ◆ *I knew my company was polluting the water, but I was afraid I would lose my job if I blew the whistle on it.* USAGE: usually something bad is shown in the hope of correcting it

whistling
whistling in the dark
to be confident about something although you have no good reason to be confident ◆ *He wasn't very sure of his chances at the time – he was really just whistling in the dark, hoping to get some support.*

whittle
whittle *sth* down, *also* **whittle *sth* away**
to gradually reduce or destroy something ◆ *By halftime our team's lead had been whittled down to only two points.* ◆ *College is so expensive, after two years, my college fund has been whittled away to almost nothing.* USAGE: also used in the form **whittle away at something**: *Over the past year, we've whittled away at our debts.*

> ORIGIN: based on the literal meaning of **whittle** (= to shape a piece of wood by cutting strips or small pieces from it with a knife)

whole
as a whole
considering all parts together ◆ *Unemployment here is much higher than for the country as a whole.*

on the whole
in important ways ◆ *On the whole, I think my dinner party was a success.*

a (whole) new ballgame See at BALLGAME

go whole hog See at HOG

(made up) out of whole cloth See at CLOTH

the whole ball of wax See at BALL

the whole bit See at BIT

the whole kit and caboodle See at KIT

the whole nine yards See at YARDS

the whole picture See at PICTURE

the whole shebang See at SHEBANG

whoop
whoop it up
to celebrate or enjoy yourself in a noisy and enthusiastic way ◆ *The proposal's supporters whooped it up like cheerleaders when the governor said he supported it.* ◆ *I won't be whooping it up this week – I have too much to do.*

why
why not esp. spoken
there is no reason not to ◆ *"Do you want Italian food tonight?" "Sure, why not!"* ◆ *If you're so unhappy there, why not leave right now?*

whys
the whys and wherefores (of *sth*)
the reasons for something ◆ *The movie doesn't spend much time worrying about the whys and wherefores of its stars' behavior.*

wild
wild about *sb/sth*
to like someone or something a lot ◆ *He's totally wild about her!* ◆ *I'm not wild about apples.*

wildfire

like wildfire
everywhere very quickly ♦ *The new dance has caught on like wildfire in all the popular clubs.* ♦ *Scandal spreads like wildfire around this office.*

> ORIGIN: based on the literal meaning of **wildfire** (= a fire that burns out of control)

will

against *your* will
without your permission or agreement ♦ *Police searched my mother's bags against her will.*

at will
at any time or in any way you want ♦ *Most actors are able to cry at will.* ♦ *Gangs of rebels attack at will because the army is too weak to control them.*

willies

give *you* the willies
to make you feel frightened or nervous; = **give *you* the creeps** ♦ *Driving at night on country roads gives me the willies.* USAGE: also used in the form **get the willies** (= to become frightened or nervous): *I get the willies whenever I think of having to take exams.*

win

win out
to succeed after great effort ♦ *In the end, greed won out over doing the right thing.*

win *sb/sth* over, *also* **win over *sb/sth***
to succeed in changing opinion ♦ *The senator made a stirring speech but failed to win over enough votes to pass his bill.* ♦ *The argument she used to win them over was not about who was right and who was wrong.*

wind

get wind of *sth*
to learn about something secret ♦ *As soon as we got wind of the concert, I ordered tickets.*

in the wind
likely to happen soon ♦ *Did he know that a promotion and pay raise were in the wind?*

(leave *sb* to) twist in the wind
1 to keep someone waiting for a decision or answer; = **leave *sb* hanging** ♦ *Carolyn was left twisting in the wind for about a week, and so were several other people who interviewed for the job.*
2 to be forced to exist without support or help ♦ *Some workers were fired and left to twist in the wind after many years on the job.* ♦ *People know she's ambitious and are afraid she might leave the company twisting in the wind if a better job came along.*

sail close to the wind
to take risks ♦ *We thought she was sailing a bit close to the wind in her business deals, but she claimed everything was legal.* USAGE: often refers to doing something that may not be legal or acceptable

> ORIGIN: based on the literal meaning of **sail close to the wind** (= to sail a boat as near as possible to the direction the wind is coming from)

take the wind out of *your* sails
to make you feel less confident or determined ♦ *I was really mad at him, but he greeted me with flowers, which immediately took the wind out of my sails.*

> ORIGIN: based on the literal meaning of **take the wind out of someone's sails** (= to slow down a competing boat by catching the wind in your own sails and preventing it from filling the other boat's sails)

wind down (*sth*)
to end or cause something to end gradually ♦ *The storm finally began to wind down after four hours of heavy rain.* ♦ *We wound down our affairs in Europe and left for home.*

wind up
to reach a place or condition; = **end up** ◆ *If he continues to spend money this way, he's going to wind up in bankruptcy.* ◆ *How did you ever wind up in this little town in the middle of nowhere?*

wind up (*sth*), *also* **wind *sth* up**
to end or finish something ◆ *The meeting just wound up, so let's go to lunch now.* ◆ *We should be able to wind the discussion up by 10 o'clock.*

get a second wind See at SECOND WIND

straw in the wind See at STRAW

throw caution to the wind See at CAUTION

which way the wind is blowing See at WAY

window

out the window
gone, wasted, or no longer in existence ◆ *It is as if everyone's good judgment has flown out the window.* ◆ *If we quit now, we might as well just toss three months' work out the window.*

winds

to the four winds
in all directions ◆ *It would be a disaster if we allowed all that know-how to be scattered to the four winds.* ◆ Related vocabulary **the four corners of the earth** at CORNERS

wine

wine and dine *sb*
to entertain someone expensively ◆ *The company wined and dined us, hoping to convince us we should accept the job.*

wing

on the wing
in motion ◆ *He started to run, but a rifle shot caught him on the wing.*
USAGE: based on the literal meaning of **on the wing** (= flying): *The sight of so many enormous birds on the wing filled me with awe.*

under *your* wing
helped and protected by you ◆ *One of the children in the class will usually take a new girl or boy under their wing for the first few weeks.*
USAGE: also used in the forms **under someone's wing** or **under the wing of someone**: *Everyone who lost their home in the fire was taken under the wing of a local church.*

ORIGIN: based on the idea of a bird that protects its babies by spreading its wings over them

wing it
to invent a way to deal with a situation you are not prepared for ◆ *I didn't have time to write a speech, so I just had to wing it in front of a large audience.* ◆ *Some actors can wing it, others go completely silent when something happens on stage that isn't supposed to happen.* ◆ Related vocabulary **on the fly** at FLY

wings

clip *your* wings
to limit your freedom ◆ *She was afraid that motherhood would clip her wings.*

ORIGIN: based on the literal meaning of **clip a bird's wings** (= to cut the feathers that make it possible for a bird to fly)

spread *your* wings
to do new and different things ◆ *Since I retired, I've been able to spread my wings and am busier than I was when I worked.*

(wait) in the wings
to be ready to do something when the opportunity comes ◆ *Other companies were waiting in the wings to sell similar drugs at much lower prices.* ◆ *The novel has sold well in the hardcover edition, and a paperback edition waits in the wings.*

ORIGIN: based on the idea of an actor who **waits in the wings** (= areas to each side of a stage) before appearing on stage

wink

not sleep a wink
to not sleep at all ◆ *I was so excited about our trip that I didn't sleep a wink last night.* USAGE: sometimes used in the forms **not get a wink of sleep** or **not have a wink of sleep**: *Poor Henry didn't get a wink of sleep on the plane.*

wipe

wipe out
to have a very serious accident ◆ *Jim wiped out on the ice and broke his leg.* ◆ *He was driving crazily and wiped out on a curve.* USAGE: usually someone **wipes out** because they are going too fast

wipe out (sb/sth), also **wipe sb/sth out**
1 to destroy someone or something ◆ *We were ordered to wipe out a small enemy force hiding in the village.* ◆ *The floods wiped whole villages out.*
2 to cause someone to lose or spend all their money ◆ *My neighbor was totally wiped out by the last recession.* ◆ *A night out with Paul and Michelle just about wiped us out.*

wire

down to the wire
until the last possible moment ◆ *The election was so close, it went down to the wire and was decided by a court.* ◆ *We had very little time to get the place decorated for the party, which meant that everyone worked right down to the wire.*

ORIGIN: based on the racing meaning of **wire** (= a thread that marks where a race ends)

wisdom

in your/its (infinite) wisdom
using your or its knowledge or intelligence ◆ *The city government, in its wisdom, decided to close the library and now kids can't use it for research or just plain reading.* ◆ *When I said we needed a bigger house, my wife replied, in her infinite wisdom, that we did not have enough money.* USAGE: usually used humorously to show that something was not based on great knowledge or intelligence, as in the examples

wise

be wise to sb/sth, also **get wise to sb/sth**
to know about and not be fooled by someone or something ◆ *He called in sick almost every Monday, and the boss quickly got wise to him.* USAGE: often used in the forms **wise up (to something/someone)** or **wise someone up (to something/someone)**: *I finally wised up to their scheme.* ◆ *It's time they wised him up to what's really going on.*

wiser

be none the wiser, also **not be (any) the wiser**
1 to fail to understand something ◆ *Isabel must have explained her idea three times to me, but I'm afraid I'm none the wiser.* ◆ *If you take the label off the jar and say you made it yourself, your guests won't be any the wiser.*
2 to not be aware of something ◆ *The health department gave the restaurant a health warning, but customers were none the wiser.* USAGE: often said about efforts to be sure that no one is aware: *I figured I could just get rid of the stuff, and you'd be none the wiser.*

wish

I would not wish sth on sb
I would not want someone to experience something unpleasant ◆ *Getting stranded in the snowstorm was so awful, I wouldn't wish it on anyone.* ◆ *I wouldn't wish having to go through a lawsuit on my worst enemy!*

witness

bear witness to sth
to show by your existence that

wits

something is true ◆ *The survivors of this disaster bear witness to a terrible event we would like to forget.*

wits

frighten *sb* out of *their* wits, *also* **scare *sb* out of *their* wits**
to cause extreme fear in someone ◆ *Don't sneak up behind me like that – you frightened me out of my wits!*

gather *your* wits
to make an effort to be calm and think ◆ *I was really scared, but I knew I had to gather my wits and try to figure out what to do.*

have *your* wits about *you*, *also* **keep *your* wits about *you***
to be able to think clearly ◆ *The engines failed, but the pilot had his wits about him and managed to get them started again.* ◆ *She managed to keep her wits about her and was able to escape unharmed.*

live by *your* wits, *also* **live on *your* wits**
to exist by taking advantage of any opportunity you have ◆ *Kids thrown on the streets with no family to support them have to live by their wits.*

woe

woe betide *sb*, *also* **woe be unto *sb***
bad things will happen to someone ◆ *Woe betide anyone who plays Ann's CDs without asking her first.* ◆ *And woe be unto anyone who messes with my desk!*

wolf

cry wolf
to ask for help when you do not need it ◆ *Growers who cry wolf today about the lack of water will probably be selling their vegetables in a few months.* ◆ *He said the mayor's grim predictions about what would happen if the bill isn't passed amounted to crying wolf.*

> ORIGIN: from the children's story "The Boy Who Cried Wolf," in which a boy who was watching some sheep called for help when there was no wolf (= wild animal) attacking them and then got no help when a wolf did attack the sheep because no one believed him

a wolf in sheep's clothing
someone or something that seems to be good but is actually bad ◆ *The financial advisor we hired turned out to be a wolf in sheep's clothing who stole from the people he promised to help.*

wolves

throw *sb* to the wolves
to put someone in a situation where there is nothing to protect them ◆ *Are illegal foreign workers going to be thrown to the wolves, or will we try to regulate their employers?*

woman

the woman on the street, *also* **the woman in the street**
an ordinary woman ◆ *Her research looks at what the woman on the street thinks about the police.* ◆ Related vocabulary **the man on the street** at MAN

***your* own woman** See ***your* own person** at PERSON

wonder

it's a wonder
it is surprising ◆ *After having so many problems with the house, it's a wonder they ever got to live in it.* ◆ Opposite **(it's) no wonder**

(it's) no wonder
it is not surprising ◆ *It's no wonder ticket prices are so high when you see what the players are being paid.* ◆ *No wonder I couldn't find my keys! They were in the car all along.* ◆ Opposite **it's a wonder**

wonders

work wonders, *also* **do wonders**
to cause improvements or have a very good effect ◆ *He's only been*

here for a couple of months and already he's worked wonders. ♦ Drinking lots of water does wonders for the skin.

wood

knock (on) wood esp. spoken I hope my good luck will continue ♦ We haven't had any problems with the car so far, knock on wood. ♦ I'm expecting, knock wood, to be offered the job next week. USAGE: used when you think difficulties are likely

not see the wood for the trees See **not see the forest for the trees** at FOREST

woods

not out of the woods
1 slightly better but not yet well ♦ The operation went fine, but she's not out of the woods yet – the next 24 hours will tell us whether or not she'll recover. USAGE: said about someone's health
2 improving but not yet good ♦ Our sales went up last month, but the company is not out of the woods yet. USAGE: said about financial problems and sometimes used in the form **out of the woods** (= in good condition): If we continue to watch our expenses, we should be out of the woods in a month.

woodwork

come out of the woodwork, also **crawl out of the woodwork** to appear suddenly and unexpectedly ♦ If you try to lose weight, people will come out of the woodwork to offer advice. USAGE: usually said about someone who was not invited or wanted

> ORIGIN: based on the idea of insects that suddenly come out from under boards in a house where they have been hidden

wool

pull the wool over *sb's* eyes to deceive someone ♦ These people who claim to have paranormal or supernatural powers are just pulling the wool over people's eyes.

word

break *your* word to fail to keep a promise ♦ He has broken his word so many times that

come out of the woodwork

When Mitch won the lottery, long-lost friends and family came out of the woodwork, hoping for some of the money.

words

no one can believe him any more. ◆ Opposite **keep *your* word** ◆ Related vocabulary **go back on *sth*** at GO

breathe a word
to tell a secret ◆ *If you breathe a word of this to anyone, the whole deal will fall apart.* USAGE: often used in the form **not breathe a word**: *We were warned not to breathe a word about the party.*

from the word go
since the very beginning; = **from the get-go** ◆ *I knew from the word go that she would be hard to work with.*

get a word in edgewise
to find an opportunity to say something ◆ *Harold talked so much that nobody else could get a word in edgewise.*

hang on (*sb's*) every word
to listen very carefully to what someone says ◆ *He hung on every word I said.* ◆ *Larry only likes girls who hang on his every word.*

have a word (with *sb*)
to speak with someone privately to tell them something ◆ *I don't think she's interested but I'll have a word with her.*

in a word
briefly described ◆ *The final report was, in a word, ridiculous.* ◆ Related vocabulary **in brief** at BRIEF, **in short** at SHORT

(just) say the word
to tell someone that you want something ◆ *If you want me to pick up some fish for dinner, just say the word.* ◆ *You only have to say the word and I'll come and help you paint the kitchen.*

keep *your* word
to do what you promise to do ◆ *He is someone who keeps his word – you can rely on that.* ◆ Opposite **break *your* word**

leave word (with *sb*)
to give someone a message ◆ *If I can't get back in time I'll leave word with Susan.*

put in a good word (for *sb*)
to say positive things about someone ◆ *I'm applying for a job in your department, so please put in a good word for me.* USAGE: often you **put in a good word** with someone who has a position of authority

spread the word
to tell others about something ◆ *The meeting will be held on Thursday, so if you see anyone who should be there, spread the word.*

take *sb's* word for it, *also* **take *sb* at *their* word**
to believe someone ◆ *If she says she's sick, you have to take her word for it.* ◆ *I took him at his word when he said he could translate Russian.*

the last word in *sth*
the best or most modern example of something ◆ *In the '70s, the magazine was widely viewed among young people as the last word in humor.*

true to *your* word
as you promised ◆ *True to his word, he paid back the money I had loaned him.*

word for word
exactly as spoken or written ◆ *She copied it word for word from the encyclopedia.*

***sb's* word is law**
what someone says must be obeyed ◆ *There's no use questioning anything around here, because my boss's word is law.*

a man of his word See at MAN

mum's the word See at MUM

words

eat *your* words
to admit that what you said is wrong ◆ *I may eat my words, but I don't think Holly is going to be able to do this.*

have words (with *sb*)
to speak to someone angrily ◆ *The coach had words with several of his players when the game was over.*

in other words
said in a different, clearer way ◆ *Does she have the right work experience and skills – in other words, can she do the job?* ◆ Related vocabulary **if you will** at IF, **in a manner of speaking** at MANNER, **so to speak** at SO

in so many words
directly or very clearly ◆ *He told me, in so many words, to mind my own business.* USAGE: often used in the form **not in so many words**: *She didn't say it in so many words, but it was clear that she thought I was wrong.*

lost for words
unable to think of something to say; = **at a loss for words** ◆ *Chris was lost for words at Kathy's incredible rudeness.* USAGE: usually said because something has surprised you

mark my words slightly formal
give your attention to what I am saying because it is true and important ◆ *That girl's going to cause trouble, you mark my words.*

not mince words
to say what you mean as clearly and simply as possible ◆ *Tom didn't mince any words – he told us right at the beginning of the meeting that he was quitting his job.* USAGE: sometimes used in the form **mince words** (= to say something that is not clear): *The report minces words, trying not to offend anyone.*

put words in sb's mouth, also **put words into the mouth of sb**
to say what you think someone else should say ◆ *I never suggested that she should move – don't try to put words in my mouth.* USAGE: sometimes used in the form **put words into someone's mouth**

take the words (right) out of sb's mouth
to say exactly what someone else is about to say ◆ *I was just going to mention that, but you took the words right out of my mouth.*

too sth for words
having this characteristic to an extreme degree ◆ *Their argument was too ridiculous for words.* ◆ *A lot of people think they're too weird for words.*

ORIGIN: based on the idea that an extreme characteristic cannot be expressed in words

weigh your words
to think carefully about what you will say ◆ *I had weighed my words because I didn't want any confusion over what I intended to do.*

actions speak louder than words
See at ACTIONS

a man of few words See at MAN

at a loss for words See at LOSS

work

all in a day's work
unusual for other people to have to do but not unusual for you ◆ *A fancy dinner with a Hollywood celebrity is all in a day's work for this reporter.*

all work and no play (makes Jack a dull boy)
it is not good to work all the time ◆ *You need to get out and have fun – you know, all work and no play.*

do the dirty work
to do the unpleasant or difficult things ◆ *Well, usually I do the dirty work and someone else gets the credit for getting it done.* USAGE: often used in the form **do someone's dirty work** (= to do the unpleasant or difficult things that are someone else's responsibility): *Naturally, he has assistants who do his dirty work.*

have your work cut out for you
to have to do something you know will be difficult ◆ *If that report is going to be finished by tomorrow, she has her work cut out for her.*

make short work of sb/sth
to deal with someone or something

quickly ◆ *We made short work of the food that was put in front of us.* ◆ *The boxer made short work of his challenger.*

work out
1 to develop in a satisfactory way ◆ *It was too bad that my plan didn't work out.* ◆ *Is your new job working out well?*
2 to get physical exercise ◆ *I work out at the gym twice a week.*

work out *sth*, *also* **work** *sth* **out**
to find a solution to something ◆ *The committee met today and worked out a statement that everyone liked.* ◆ *You can use a calculator to work out the problem, or you can work it out on paper.*

work (*yourself***) up**
to make yourself excited or upset ◆ *You've worked yourself up over just meeting a girl for a drink?* ◆ *I can't work up any enthusiasm for this plan.*

work up *sth*, *also* **work** *sth* **up**
to develop something ◆ *It took me a month to work up an outline of my book.* ◆ *She made a sketch, and hoped to work it up into a full-size painting when she got home.*

set to work See at SET
work both ways See at WAYS
work hand in glove with *sb/sth* See at HAND
work like a charm See at CHARM
work *your/its* **magic** See at MAGIC
work the problem See at PROBLEM
work up a sweat See at SWEAT
work wonders See at WONDERS

works

gum up the works
to prevent a machine or system from operating correctly ◆ *The project was going really well until that software upgrade gummed up the works.* ◆ Related vocabulary **gum up** *sth* at GUM

in the works
being developed or scheduled to happen in the future ◆ *Plans are in the works to improve reporting of HIV and AIDS cases.* ◆ *There are rumors that big salary increases are in the works.* ◆ Related vocabulary **in the pipeline** at PIPELINE

world

dead to the world
sleeping to the greatest degree possible ◆ *Guy was curled up on the sofa, dead to the world.*

do *sb* **a world of good**
to make someone feel much better ◆ *A vacation in the mountains will do you a world of good.*

for all the world like *sth*
very much like something ◆ *He stood with his legs apart and his head thrown back, looking for all the world like a victorious warrior.* ◆ *She looks for all the world an old-fashioned school teacher.*

have the world at *your* **feet**
to be extremely successful and so able to get what you want ◆ *This young Broadway actress already has the world at her feet.* USAGE: also used in the form **the world is at your feet**: *If you get this book published the world will be at your feet.*

in the world
in any conditions; = **on earth** ◆ *What in the world did he think he was doing?* ◆ *Why in the world would she say that?* ◆ *How in the world did you guess that it was me calling you?* ◆ *Who in the world does he think he is, speaking to me like that!* ◆ *Where in the world will they get the energy they need?* USAGE: used to express great surprise that something could happen or exist

make a world of difference
to have an important effect; = **make all the difference (in the world)** ◆ *Some food, some milk, and some warmth made a world of difference to the small stray cat.* ◆ *The rains made a world of difference to worried farmers.*

not long for this world
about to stop working or existing ♦ *I'm afraid that my laptop is not long for this world.*

out of this world
1 extremely good ♦ *Their chocolate cake is just out of this world!*
2 extremely expensive ♦ *The price of gasoline is out of this world right now.*

set the world on fire
to be very exciting or successful ♦ *The new video game format set the world on fire with huge sales at Christmas.*

the world is *your* oyster
you have the ability and the freedom to do exactly what you want ♦ *The world is your oyster when you're young and healthy and free to go anywhere.*

think the world of *sb*
to have a very high opinion of someone ♦ *Steve Tay is an excellent doctor and his patients all think the world of him.* ♦ Related vocabulary **think well of *sb/sth*** at THINK

what's the world coming to
I am shocked and disappointed ♦ *What's the world coming to when you can't leave your house for five minutes without someone trying to break in and rob you?*

all the time in the world See at TIME

for anything (in the world) See at ANYTHING

make all the difference (in the world) See at DIFFERENCE

not the end of the world See at END

(sitting) on top of the world See at TOP

worlds

worlds apart
completely different ♦ *The most expensive entertainment system and what most of us have are worlds apart and can't be compared.* ♦ *The two women were single mothers but in every other respect were worlds apart.*

the best of both worlds See at BEST

the worst of both worlds See at WORST

worry

not to worry
there is no problem ♦ *He lost his wallet, but not to worry – he's already called the credit-card companies.*

worse

none the worse (for *sth*)
not damaged or hurt despite something ♦ *It was cold and windy during the parade but we were none the worse for the weather.* USAGE: often used in the form **none the worse for wear** (= in good condition despite hard use or a difficult experience): *He seems to be none the worse for wear after his car wreck.*

the worse for wear
1 damaged from use ♦ *The old picnic table is looking the worse for wear, but it should last another year.*
2 tired from hard work ♦ *After our dog had her puppies, she definitely looked the worse for wear.*

a fate worse than death See at FATE

for better or (for) worse See at BETTER

go from bad to worse See at GO

worst

at worst, *also* **at the worst**
in the least satisfactory conditions ♦ *There's no harm in sending them your resume – you might get an interview, and at worst, they'll ignore it.* ♦ Opposite **at best** at BEST

fear the worst
to feel sure that what was least wanted has happened or will happen ♦ *When the doctor called, she feared the worst.*

if worst comes to worst
if the least wanted situation develops ♦ *If worst comes to worst, we*

can ask Dad to send us some more money.

the worst of both worlds
the least satisfactory parts of two different things ♦ *By making his parents and his teachers angry with him, Jim seemed to have the worst of both worlds.* ♦ Opposite **the best of both worlds** at BEST

***your* own worst enemy** See at ENEMY

in the worst way See at WAY

worth
for what it's worth
whether or not this is of value ♦ *For what it's worth, I think you can't trust that man.* ♦ *And my son says, for what it's worth, that he won't do that again.*

(it's well) worth it
1 it is useful or important ♦ *Writing the book is a lot of work, and there are times when Hart wonders if the effort is worth it.* ♦ *If you want to have a good time traveling, it's well worth it to spend time reading guidebooks before you go.*
2 it is rewarding despite the difficulties involved ♦ *It was a long climb up the hill, but the view from the top was worth it.* ♦ *Even though he knows that love can hurt, he still believes it's well worth it.*

get *your* money's worth See at MONEY

not worth the paper *sth* is printed on See at PAPER

worth a damn See at DAMN

worth *your/its* salt See at SALT

worth *your/its* weight in gold See at WEIGHT

worth *your* while See at WHILE

wounds
lick *your* wounds
to avoid or ignore other people after an unpleasant experience ♦ *Mary's film career was a failure, and she went home to lick her wounds in private.*

> ORIGIN: based on the idea of an injured animal that **licks its wounds** (= cleans an injury with its tongue)

wrap
it's a wrap
this is successfully completed ♦ *After three months of planning and two years of building, it's a wrap and we've moved into our new home.* ♦ *It was a wrap for the latest unmanned mission to Mars.*

> ORIGIN: based on the literal meaning of **it's a wrap** (= the filming of this movie or part of a movie is completed)

wrap up *sth*, also wrap *sth* up
to complete or stop doing something ♦ *The president will wrap up his visit to China on Thursday.* ♦ *It's late and I have to get home, so let's wrap it up and finish tomorrow.*

> ORIGIN: based on the literal meaning of **wrap something up** (= to put paper around something to cover it)

wraps
keep (*sth*) under wraps
to hide something ♦ *The studio is keeping details of the new movie under wraps until its release in May.* ♦ *The painting was bought by someone who wants to keep his name under wraps.* ♦ Related vocabulary **draw a veil over *sth*** at VEIL

take the wraps off *sth*
to make something known that had been secret ♦ *Today the company took the wraps off their new electric car.*

> ORIGIN: based on the literal meaning of **wraps** (= coats or other clothes worn to keep warm)

wrestle
wrestle with *sth*
to work hard to do something difficult ♦ *The new governor will be*

wrestling with the state's disastrous financial condition. ♦ *These are the big issues that society will have to wrestle with.* ♦ *More than 200 firefighters wrestled with the blaze for more than two hours.*

ORIGIN: based on the literal meaning of **wrestle** (= to fight someone by trying to hold them to the ground)

wring

wring *sth* **out of** *sb*
to persuade someone to give you what you want ♦ *She is a very original comedian and can wring laughs out of any audience.* ♦ *The trick in fundraising is to wring money out of people who don't want to give it away.*

ORIGIN: based on the literal meaning of **wring something out** (= to twist cloth that is wet to get the water out of it)

wring *your* **hands** See at HANDS

wringer

through the wringer
experiencing something very difficult or unpleasant ♦ *Our tech people have been putting the new servers through the wringer.* ♦ *Mr. Gold went through the wringer to get immigration papers for his parents.* USAGE: usually used with **put** or **go**, as in the examples

ORIGIN: based on the literal meaning of **wringer** (= a device that presses water from clothing that has been washed)

writ

writ large slightly formal
expressed in a bigger or more obvious way ♦ *She believed that cultures are just personalities writ large.* ♦ *The genius of the story is that it's about ordinary life writ large.* USAGE: usually used after a noun, as in the examples

write

nothing to write home about
not something that is especially good or exciting ♦ *The food was all right but nothing to write home about.* USAGE: often used as a humorous way to describe something that is obviously bad: *War is nothing to write home about.*

write in (*sth***)**
to send a letter or electronic message to an organization or business ♦ *A lot of customers write in their complaints and get nothing from the company in response.* ♦ *Write in today and let us know what you think.*

write *sb/sth* **off**, *also* **write off** *sb/sth*
to decide that someone or something is not important ♦ *Most critics wrote him off as a minor artist until he received that huge grant.* ♦ *Everyone had pretty much written off the team after they lost their tournament last week.* ♦ *Americans no longer dream of their children becoming president – in fact, many write it off as not worth the effort.*

write off *sth*, *also* **write** *sth* **off**
1 to accept that a debt will not be paid ♦ *Last year the bank wrote off $17 million in bad loans.* ♦ *I'll probably never see the money I loaned my brother, so I guess I'll write it off.*
2 to charge something as a business expense ♦ *You can write off your cell phone and all the costs of service for it.* ♦ *I'm giving the furniture to a local church and writing it off as a donation.*
3 to decide that something will not be successful ♦ *For a long time, both political parties have written off the Greens.* ♦ *Since they behave oddly, people tend to write them off as weirdos, but many members of the group are important business people.*

write up *sth*, *also* **write** *sth* **up**
to tell about something by writing it

writing

♦ *We had such a wonderful trip, I wanted to write it up in my diary before I forgot a lot of details.* USAGE: often said about creating a finished document: *We have to write up the lab report for this chemistry experiment.*

writing

in writing
in the form of a document ♦ *Any agreement can be canceled, even one in writing.* ♦ *If you want to examine these papers, you must ask in writing for permission to do it.* ♦ *She saw so little of her father that, when she wanted something, she would put her request in writing.*

the writing on the wall, *also* **the handwriting on the wall**
the likelihood that something bad will happen ♦ *Area residents can see the writing on the wall and realize that if they don't cooperate with the police, these crimes will continue.* ♦ *As leaders, they should have seen the handwriting on the wall and come up with an alternative course of action.* USAGE: often used with **see**, as in the examples

> ORIGIN: based on a story in the Bible about Daniel, who reads **the handwriting on the wall** that predicts the end of the kingdom of Babylon

wrong

in the wrong slightly formal
responsible for something bad ♦ *He was the first leader to state publicly that his country was in the wrong in the war.* ♦ *Although she is portrayed as a victim, many of her friends think she may have been in the wrong.*

Y, y

yards
the whole nine yards *esp. spoken* all of something, including everything connected with it; = **the whole shebang** ◆ *When you join the gym, they show you all the equipment, tell you how to use it, the whole nine yards.* ◆ *They rushed him to the emergency room with lights flashing, sirens wailing, a police escort, the whole nine yards.* USAGE: often used in the phrase **go the whole nine yards**: *So we moved to the suburbs and went the whole nine yards – we had two cars, a pool in the back yard, even cookouts in the backyard.*

year
year after year
repeatedly for many years ◆ *She got tired of performing the same music year after year.* ◆ *Aaron just did his job, year after year after year.* ◆ Related vocabulary **day after day** at DAY, **week after week** at WEEK, **month after month** at MONTH

year by year
every year ◆ *Year by year there has been an increase in violence shown in the movies and on TV.* ◆ Related vocabulary **day by day** at DAY, **month by month** at MONTH, **week by week** at WEEK

year in, year out
every year for a long time ◆ *Year in, year out, he has been one of the best players in baseball.*

(all) year round
during the whole year ◆ *The farm is open to the public year round on weekends.* ◆ *In the Southwest, it's a lot easier to get outside all year round.*

years
in years
for a very long time ◆ *The February issue of the magazine is easily its best in years.* ◆ *The two friends hadn't seen each other in years.*

getting on in years
becoming old ◆ *She's getting on in years, but she's healthy.*

yet
as yet
1 until now ◆ *Ziemacki has not given this plan a name as yet.*
2 still ◆ *We hope to raise funds for the project, but the exact plans are as yet unclear.*

yours
all yours
available for you to use ◆ *"Can I use the bike?" "It's all yours."*

yours truly
me ◆ *Even though he never graduated from high school, his business ability rivaled anyone's, yours truly included.* ◆ *Some folks, such as yours truly, can't resist a clever pun or play on words.* USAGE: usually used as a humorous way of referring to yourself

yourself
by *yourself*
alone ◆ *You're old enough to go by yourself on the train.* ◆ *They were left by themselves for three days.*

to *yourself*
for use by you only ◆ *Now that Neil and Sam are away, you've got time to yourself, for a change.* ◆ *When my parents were away, I had the whole house to myself.*

knock *sb/yourself* out See at KNOCK

Z, z

zero

zero in (on *sth*)
to direct your attention to one particular thing ◆ *My son's teacher was able to zero in and deal with his problems.* ◆ *She needs to really zero in on what's important instead of going off on a lot of tangents.*

zone

zone out
to not notice or stop being interested in what is happening around you ◆ *When I'm dancing I zone out and feel like I'm the only one in the room.* ◆ *I just flew in from Europe this morning, so don't get upset if I just zone out in the middle of the meeting.*

zoom

zoom in (on *sth*)
to view something more closely ◆ *The software lets you zoom in so you can check the details of any part of the picture.*

> ORIGIN: based on the literal meaning of **zoom in** (= to move quickly toward something)

Subject Index

This subject index groups idioms according to the categories listed below. By using this index, you should be able to find an idiom that expresses a particular meaning. The index does not include all the idioms in this book; only the idioms that fit one of these categories are shown here. The **boldface** word in each idiom shows the headword it is entered under in the dictionary.

beginning	483	knowing	491
behavior	484	looking	492
dealing with	485	moving	492
death	486	near	492
differences	486	physical condition	492
difficult	486	problems	493
easy	487	saying	493
emotional condition	487	similarities	495
failing	488	speed	495
fighting	489	success	495
finishing	489	thinking	496
going away	490	time	497
having	490	truthfulness	498
hearing	490	writing	498
including everything	491		

beginning

at the **point** of *sth*
back to **square** one
break into *sth*
break out
break the ice
bring it on
bring on *sth*
burst into *sth*
burst out *doing sth*
dive into *sth*
early on
fish or cut **bait**
for **openers**
for **starters**
from **day** one
from **scratch**
from the **get-go**
from the **ground** up
from the **word** go
get a **jump** on *sb/sth*
get **cracking**
get down to **business**
(get) in on the **ground floor**

get on with *sth*
get *sth* off the **ground**
get *sth* **rolling**
get the **ball** rolling
get *your* **feet** wet
give **birth** to *sth*
give *sb/sth* the **green** light
go ahead (with *sth*)
go at it
go back to the **drawing board**
have (the) first **crack** at *sth*
here **goes**
here **goes** nothing
hit the **ground** running
hit the road
jump in with both **feet**
kick in
kick off *sth*
launch into *sth*
lead off (*sth*)
light a **fire** under *sb*
off and running
off to a **flying** start

Subject Index

off to the **races**
on the **brink** of *sth*
out of the (starting) **blocks**
out of the (starting) **gate**
put *sth* into **service**
ready to roll
(right) off the **bat**
set about *sth/doing sth*
set in
set off
set out to *do sth*
set **sail**
set *sth* in **motion**
set up shop
settle down to *sth*
since when
spring to **life**
start over
start **something**
strike out on *your* own
strike up *sth*
take effect
take **root**
take up *sth*
the **wheels** are turning
to **begin** with
touch off *sth*
turn over a new **leaf**
usher in *sth*
without further **ado**

behavior

a **chip** on *your* shoulder
a **glutton** for punishment
a **heart** of gold
a **heart** of stone
a pain in the **ass**
act out
act up
as if *you* own the **place**
ask for *sth*
ask for trouble
be *yourself*
bear up
bear with *sb/sth*
bend over backwards
bitch and moan
blow off steam
bore *sb* to **death**
boss *sb* around
breathe down *your* **neck**
brush off *sb/sth*
call *sb* names

clean up *your* **act**
curry **favor** (with *sb*)
cut off *your* **nose** to spite *your* face
do *your* **damnedest**
dote on *sb/sth*
drive *sb* to **drink**
drive *you* crazy
eat *you* alive
fall all over *yourself* (to *do sth*)
flex *your/its* muscles
fool with *sb*
frown on *sth*
fuck with *sb*
full of *yourself*
get off *your* **high horse**
get on *your* **high horse**
get *your* **act** together
give *sb* a piece of *your* **mind**
give *sb/sth* the **cold shoulder**
go **all** out
go (around) in **circles**
go easy on *sb*
go overboard
go to *your* **head**
goof off
grin and **bear** it
ham it up
hat in hand
have a **heart**
have **ants** in *your* **pants**
have **blinders** on
have the **courage** of *your/its* convictions
high and mighty
hold *your* **head** high
horse around
in the **doghouse**
in *your* **face**
jerk *sb* around
jump all over *sb*
keep a **low** profile
keep *your* **distance** (from *sb/sth*)
keep *your* **head**
keep *your* **nose** clean
keep *your* **nose** out of *sth*
keep *your* **nose** to the grindstone
kick *sb* around
kiss (*sb's*) **ass**
lash out (at *sb/sth*)
laugh at *sb*
laugh at *sth*
let *your* **hair** down
lick *your* **chops**
look down *your* **nose** at *sb/sth*

Subject Index

lose *your* **head**
make a scene
make a **spectacle** of *yourself*
make an **ass** of *yourself*
make **light** of *sth*
make *your* **peace** with *sb*
mean well
mess with *sb*
mind your own **business**
muck around (with *sth*)
muck *sth* up
muddle through (*sth*)
not **bat** an eye
not **done**
not give *sb* the **time** of day
not lift a **finger**
of *sb's/sth's* own **accord**
on *sb's* **case**
on the **attack**
on the **ball**
on the **go**
on *your* best **behavior**
on *your* **guard**
on *your* **toes**
overstep *your/its* **bounds**
pick on *sb*
play hard to get
play **hardball**
play it **cool**
play it safe
play the **fool**
poke *your* **nose** into *sth*
push (*sb*) around
put on a brave **face**
put *your* **best** foot forward
ride roughshod over *sb/sth*
risk *your* **neck**
sb can't be **bothered** to *do sth*
sb gets **religion**
scream bloody **murder**
show *sb* up
show *sb* who's **boss**
show *sb's/sth's* true **colors**
shrug *sth* off
straighten up
stab *sb* in the **back**
stick *your* **neck** out
take **advantage** (of *sb*)
take **advantage** (of *sth*)
take no **prisoners**
take **pity** on *sb*
take *sb* for a **ride**
take *sb* for **granted**
the **straight** and narrow (path)

throw a (temper) **tantrum**
thumb *your* **nose** at *sb/sth*
treat *sb* like **dirt**
turn the other **cheek**
turn *your* **back** on *sb/sth*
twist *sb's* **arm**
up to no **good**
walk all over *sb/sth*
walk on **eggshells**
wear *your* **heart** on *your* sleeve

dealing with
at the **helm** (of *sth*)
attend to *sth*
bite the bullet
block out *sth*
call the shots
call the **tune**
carry the **ball**
come to **grips** with *sth*
drag *your/its* feet
drag *your/its* heels
follow up (on *sth*)
have a **way** with *sb/sth*
have *sb/sth* on *your* **hands**
have the final **say**
in the driver's **seat**
keep *sth* at **arm**'s length
let *sb/sth* slide
live in the past
look after *sb/sth*
lose *your/its* **grip**
make it *your* **business** to *do sth*
make short work of *sb/sth*
mind the store
on *sb's* **shoulders**
on the back **burner**
on the front **burner**
on **top** of *sth*
out of *your* **hands**
pass the **buck**
pick up the **slack**
provide for *sth*
put aside *sth*
put *your* (own) **house** in order
run the **show**
shy away from *sth/doing sth*
step up to the **plate**
take **care** of *sb/sth*
take **charge** (of *sth*)
take *sth* as it comes
take *sth* into *your* own **hands**
take the **bull** by the horns

Subject Index

take the **initiative**
the **buck** stops with *sb*
treat *sb* with kid **glove**s
wade into *sth*
wade through *sth*

death
(as) **dead** as a doornail
blow *sb* away
breathe *your* last
bump off *sb*
die off
die out
do *sb* in
end it all
give up the **ghost**
have **blood** on *your* hands
have one **foot** in the grave
in **memory** of *sb*
keel over
kick the **bucket**
lay down *your* life
lay *sb* to **rest**
lie in state
life and limb
pass away
pick *sb/sth* off
put *sb* to **death**
put *sb/sth* out of *their/its* **misery**
put *sth* to **sleep**
put *your* **life** on the line
rest in **peace**
rub *sb* out
sb's **number** is up
six **feet** under
take *sb/sth* out
take *your* **life** in *your* hands

differences
a **change** of pace
a different **ball** of wax
a **fish** out of water
a (whole) new **ballgame**
as **opposed** to *sth*
at **cross** purposes
at **variance** with *sb/sth*
blaze a **trail**
break with tradition
compare **apples** and oranges
different **strokes** (for different folks)
easier said than **done**

for a **change**
less than *sth*
(like) a **breath** of fresh air
march to a different **drummer**
never the twain shall **meet**
(off) on a **tangent**
other than
quite a **change**
set *sb/sth* apart (from *sb/sth*)
something else
stick out
stick out like a sore **thumb**
that's another **story**
the other **side** of the coin
two **sides** of the same coin
worlds **apart**

difficult
a bitter **pill** (to swallow)
a **heck** of a *sth*
a **hell** of a *sth*
a living **hell**
a **needle** in a haystack
a tough **row** to hoe
at all **costs**
at any **cost**
at any **price**
close **call**
do the dirty **work**
down on *your* **luck**
fall on **hard** times
get off easy
go from **bad** to worse
hard put to *do sth*
hard to swallow
hard to take
have a hard **time** *doing sth*
have *your* **work** cut out for *you*
hell on wheels
hit a **snag**
in dire **straits**
in the **face** of *sth*
like pulling **teeth**
move **mountains**
out of *your* **league**
paint *sb/yourself* into a **corner**
sweat **blood**
through the **wringer**
too hot to **handle**
tough **sledding**
with *your/its* **back** against the wall

Subject Index

easy
a **piece** of cake
(as) **easy** as pie
(as) plain as **day**
black and white
breeze through *sth*
do sth with *your* **eyes** closed
easy **does** it
hands down
it doesn't take a **rocket scientist** to *do sth*
lighten *your* load
like taking **candy** from a baby
the path of **least** resistance
(there's) **nothing** to it

emotional condition
a **lump** in *your* throat
ache for *sb/sth*
all **smiles**
(all) **steamed** up
(as) cool as a **cucumber**
(as) happy as a **clam**
(as) nutty as a **fruitcake**
(as) tough as **nails**
at **ease**
at **home**
at loose **ends**
at **peace** with *sth/yourself*
at *your* wit's **end**
bent out of shape
beside *yourself*
blow *your* top
boggle the **mind**
bottle up *sth*
bound and determined
break down
break *your* heart
breathe a **sigh** of relief
breathe easy
bug out
burn out (*sb*)
burn *sb* up
carried away
charged up
cheer up (*sb*)
chill out
choke (*you*) up
climbing the walls
cool down
crazy about *sb/sth*
deep down
down in the **dumps**
down on *sb/sth*
drive *you* up the **wall**
eat it up
fall in **love** (with *sb*)
fed up (with *sb/sth*)
feel for *sb*
flip out
fly off the handle
foam at the **mouth**
freak (*sb*) out
frighten *sb* out of *their* **wits**
get a **charge** out of *sth*
get a **grip** (on *yourself*)
get a **kick** out of *sth*
get off on *sth*
get on *your* **nerves**
get under *your* **skin**
get up on the wrong **side** of (the) bed
get up *sth*
get (*you*) going
get *your* **goat**
give a **damn** (about *sb/sth*)
give *you* the **creeps**
give *you* the **willies**
glory in *sth*
go **ape**
go **ballistic**
go **bananas**
go off the deep **end**
go postal
go to **pieces**
got it bad
green with **envy**
hang *your* head
hate *sb's* **guts**
have a **cow**
have a **fit**
have **butterflies** in *your* stomach
have **egg** on *your* face
have *sth* **hang**ing over *your* head
head over heels (in love)
hit the roof
hopped up
hot and bothered
hot under the **collar**
ill at **ease**
in a **cold** sweat
in a **fog**
in a **quandary**
in **earnest**
in good **conscience**
in **tears**
in the **doldrums**

Subject Index

it's no skin off *your* **nose**
jacked up on *sth*
keep *you* on the **edge** of *your* seat
keep *your* **cool**
keep *your* shirt on
keyed up
kick *yourself*
knock *sb* off *their* **feet**
knock *your* **socks** off
laugh off *sth*
look forward to *sth*
lose *your* **cool**
lose *your* **heart** (to *sb*/*sth*)
lose *your* **nerve**
lose *your* **temper**
love at first sight
love *sb* to **death**
mad about *sb*/*sth*
(make) *your* **blood** run cold
make *your* **day**
make *your* **hair** stand on end
make *your* **skin** crawl
mean **business**
moved to tears
no hard **feelings**
not give a **damn** (about *sb*/*sth*)
not have the **stomach** (for *sth*)
not know if *you* are **coming** or going
not **know** what **hit** *you*
not **know** whether to laugh or cry
not **take** kindly to *sth*
off **balance**
on **cloud** nine
on **edge**
on **pins** and needles
on **tenterhooks**
on the **warpath**
over the **edge**
over the **moon**
peace of mind
perk up (*sb*)
pick *you* up
piss *you* off
put *sb* out
put the **fear** of God into *sb*
quicken the **pulse**
raise *your* **hackles**
rub *sb* the wrong **way**
ruffle (*sb's*) **feathers**
scare the **pants** off *you*
scare *you* to **death**
scared shitless
scared stiff

scared to **death**
see **red**
send shivers down *your* spine
sick (and tired) of *sb*/*sth*
sick at **heart**
sick to **death** of *sth*
(sitting) on **top** of the world
spin in *sb's* **grave**
spoiling for a **fight**
sweep *sb* off *their* **feet**
swept away
take **heart**
take leave of *your* **senses**
take **pride** (in *sb*/*sth*)
take *sth* in (*your*) **stride**
take **umbrage** at *sth*
take *your* **breath** away
tear *your* **hair** (out)
tear *your* **heart** out
through rose-colored **glasses**
tick *sb* off
tickled to **death**
tie *sb* (up) in **knots**
tire of *sb*/*sth*
try the **patience** of *sb*
tug at *your* **heartstrings**
up in **arms**
vent *your* **spleen**
walk on **air**
weigh on *sb*
with open **arms**
work (*yourself*) up
wring *your* **hands**
your **eyes** pop out of *your* head
your **heart** bleeds (for *sb*)
your **heart** goes out to *sb*
your **heart** sinks
your **heart** skips a beat
your **nose** is out of joint

failing

beat a dead horse
bite the dust
blow up in *your* **face**
break *your* **word**
burn out (*sth*)
conk out
crash and **burn**
dead in the water
dead on **arrival**
done for
down the toilet
drop the **ball**

Subject Index

fall **apart**
fall by the wayside
fall flat (on *your* face)
fight a losing **battle**
get off on the wrong **foot**
go **belly** up
go down in **flames**
go down the **tubes**
go into a **tailspin**
go under
hit the **skids**
in **vain**
let *sth* slip through *your* **fingers**
lose **face**
lose **ground**
miss the **boat**
out of the running
run *sth* into the **ground**
sth will never **fly**
strike out
take a **beating**
the **party** is over
throw in the towel
to no **avail**
wash out (of *sth*)

fighting

a running **battle** (with *sb/sth*)
above the **fray**
at each other's **throats**
at **loggerheads**
beat *sb's* **brains** out
come to **blows**
cross **swords** (with *sb*)
do **battle** (with *sth*)
fall out with *sb*
fight it out
go after *sb/sth*
have it out (with *sb*)
keep the **peace**
kick (*sb's*) **ass**
kick (*sb's*) **butt**
lay a **finger** on *sb*
lay into *sb*
let *sb* have it
lock **horns** (with *sb*)
mend (*your*) **fences**
mix it up
pick a **fight** (with *sb*)
raise *your* **hand** against *sb*
set upon *sb/sth*
sparks **fly**
take **issue** with *sb*

take the **gloves** off
tangle with *sb/sth*

finishing

(a) **nail** in the coffin of *sth*
break off (*sth*)
break up with *sb*
break with *sb/sth*
call it a day
cap *sth* off
carry through *sth*
choke off *sth*
clear the **decks**
close a **sale**
close the **door** on *sth*
close up **shop**
die hard
dispose of *sth*
drop out (of *sth*)
end of story
finish *sb/sth* off
fizzle out
follow through (on *sth*)
fresh from *sth*
fresh out of *sth*
get *sth* out of the **way**
get *sth* over with
give out
go by the **board**
go the **distance**
hang it up
hang up
hear the last of *sb/sth*
in the **can**
it's a **wrap**
knock off (*sth*)
lay *sth* to **rest**
leave off (*doing sth*)
let out
mop up (*sth*)
no **end** in sight (to *sth*)
once and for all
over (and done) with
pack it in
polish off *sth*
put an **end** to *sth*
put *sth* to **bed**
round out *sth*
run dry
run its course
run out of steam
sb's/sth's **time** is up
sew up *sth*

Subject Index

sign off
so **much** for *sth*
sound the **death knell** for *sth*
squared away
step down
stop on a **dime**
talked out
that's **that**
the **beginning** of the end
the **curtain** falls (on *sth*)
the **end** of the line
time's up
wash *your* **hands** of *sb/sth*
wind down (*sth*)
wind up (*sth*)
wrap up *sth*

going away

beat it
break away (from *sb/sth*)
break loose
buzz off
clear out
cut *sb/sth* loose
drop dead
duck out (of *somewhere*)
get away from it all
get lost
get out of my **face**
get the **hell** out of *somewhere*
go to the **devil**
hang around
jump **ship**
kiss off *sb/sth*
leave the **nest**
on *your* **way**
pack *your* **bags**
piss off
pull out
pull up **stakes**
push off
run away (from *sb/sth*)
run off
run out on *sb*
send *sb* **packing**
show *sb* the **door**
slip away
slip off
slip out
step out
take a **hike**
take a **walk**
take off
take *your* **leave**
tear *yourself* away (from *sb/sth*)
turn on *your* **heel**
turn **tail**
walk out

having

blessed with *sth*
crawling with *sth*
endowed with *sth*
fall into *sb's* **hands**
get **ahold** of *sth*
get *your* **fill** (of *sth*)
get *your* **hands** on *sth*
go without (*sth*)
have it in *you*
have *sth* to show for *sth*
have *sth* to spare
hold all the **cards**
hold onto *sth*
imbue *sb/sth* with *sth*
in the **hands** of *sb*
on *your* **person**
run out (of *sth*)
short of *sth*
shy of *sth*
sth to **call** *your* own
(*sth*) to **speak** of
take on *sth*
under *your* **belt**

hearing

a **fly** on the wall
all **ears**
drown out *sth*
get an **earful**
hang on (*sb's*) every word
have an **ear** for *sth*
hear *sb* out
hear *sth* through the **grapevine**
in one **ear** and out the other
keep an **ear** out for *sb/sth*
lend an **ear** to *sb/sth*
make out *sth*
music to *sb's* **ears**
never hear the **end** of it
out loud
prick *your* **ears** up
trail off

Subject Index

including everything
across the **board**
all but *sth*
all in **all**
all of the **above**
all **things** considered
all told
as a **whole**
chapter and verse
cover all the **bases**
cover the waterfront
every **inch** of *somewhere*
every last
every **trick** in the book
everything but the **kitchen** sink
everything under the **sun**
from **A** to Z
(from) **stem** to stern
from top to **bottom**
have *your* **cake** and eat it too
hook, line, and sinker
in **depth**
in **detail**
lock, stock, and barrel
pay off *sth*
pay up
run the **gamut**
that's it
the whole **ball** of wax
the whole **bit**
the whole **kit** and caboodle
the whole nine **yards**
the whole **shebang**
warts and all

knowing
a **feel** for *sth*
a **mystery** to *you*
as **far** as I can see
be **wise** to *sb/sth*
bring *sth* forward
bring *sth* home (to *sb*)
by **heart**
cut through *sth*
dawn on *you*
do *your* **homework**
draw a **blank**
feel *sth* in *your* **bones**
find *yourself*
for **certain**
forewarned is forearmed
get a **fix** on *sth*
get a **grip** (on *sth*)
get a **handle** on *sth*
get a **line** on *sb/sth*
get it
get the **drift**
get the **message**
get the **picture**
get *your* **arms** around *sth*
go **blank**
go figure
have a **head** for *sth*
have all the **answers**
have (got) *sb's* **number**
have *sth* **down** pat
hit *you* (right) between the **eyes**
I **dare** say
in the **back** of *your* mind
in the **know**
it **goes** without saying
it is understood that
know best
know better (than to *do sth*)
know different
know *sth* backwards and forwards
know *sth* **inside** out
know *sth* like the **back** of *your* hand
know the **score**
know what *you* are doing
know what *you* are talking about
know *your* stuff
learn a/*your* **lesson**
lost on *you*
make **heads** or tails (out) of *sth*
not have a **clue**
not have the **faintest** idea
not have the foggiest **notion**
not know **beans** about *sth*
not know the first **thing** about *sth*
not see the **forest** for the trees
off the **record**
on (the) **record**
onto *sb*
onto *sth*
open *your* **eyes** (to *sth*)
out of *your* **depth**
pin down *sth*
put *your* **finger** on *sth*
read **between** the lines
read the **fine** print
read the small **print**
read up on *sth*
see the **light**
see through *sb/sth*
slow on the **uptake**
stay abreast of *sth*

Subject Index

the **genie** is out of the bottle
up to **speed**
wake up to *sth*
what *sb* is **driving** at
what's what
with *your* **eyes** (wide) open
you never can **tell**
your **feet** on the ground
your **finger** on the pulse (of *sth*)

looking
a **bird**'s eye view
at a **glance**
catch sight of *sb/sth*
feast *your* **eyes** on *sb/sth*
from the **corner** of *your* eye
get a **load** of *sth*
get an **eyeful**
give *sb/sth* the **once-over**
have *your* **eye** on *sb*
keep an **eye** on *sb/sth*
keep an **eye** out (for *sb/sth*)
keep one **eye** on *sb/sth*
keep *your* **eyes** peeled (for *sth*)
lay **eyes** on *sb/sth*
look right through *sb*
look *sb* over
look *sth* over
look the part
make out *sb*
nose around
on **view**
pore over *sth*
see **things**
shoot **daggers** at *sb*
sight unseen
tell (*sb/sth*) apart
watch *sb* like a **hawk**
wipe the **smile** off *your* face

moving
bog down *sb/sth*
cart *sb* off
cart *sb/sth* away
change hands
door to **door**
follow *your* nose
get *your* **ass** *somewhere*
go around and around
go astray
hoof it
make a **beeline** for *sb/sth*

make as if to *do sth*
make for *sth*
make **way** for *sth*
make *your* **way** (*somewhere*)
on the **stump**
on the **wing**
pick *sb* up
play musical **chairs**
press on
push on
reel in *sb/sth*
rooted to the **spot**
run around
sail into *sth*
sail through *sth*
stand around

near
around the **corner**
at *sb*'s **elbow**
at *your* **fingertips**
cheek by jowl
(hard) on the **heels** of *sth*
hot on *your* **heels**
in hot **pursuit** (of *sb/sth*)
in the **ballpark**
in the **bosom** of *sb/sth*
in the **shadow** of *sth*
neck and **neck**
on **hand**
on the **scene**
on the **threshold** of *sth*
on the **verge** of *sth*
on *your* **doorstep**
within a **whisker** of *sth*
within striking **distance** (of *sth*)

physical condition
a clean **bill** of health
alive and well
(as) right as **rain**
(as) strong as an **ox**
at **death**'s door
bounce back (from *sth*)
catch *your* **breath**
done in
feel (more) like *yourself*
fuck up *sb*
get over *sth*
huff and puff
hung over
in one **piece**

Subject Index

in the **pink** (of *sth*)
in *your* right **mind**
knock *sb* out
knock *sb* up
knock *sb/yourself* out
lay *sb* up
lose *your* **mind**
on an empty **stomach**
on the **mend**
on *your/its* **feet**
out of **breath**
out of it
out of sorts
pass out
put *your* **feet** up
run a **fever**
run *sb* **ragged**
run *yourself* into the **ground**
sack out
safe and sound
settle *your* stomach
sick to *your* **stomach**
soaked to the **skin**
take it easy
tire *you* out
under the **knife**
under the **weather**
up and around
wear *sb* out

problems

a **bone** of contention
a **bone** to pick with *sb*
a **cloud** on the horizon
a **fly** in the ointment
a **load** off *your* mind
a **monkey** on *your* back
a **thorn** in *sb's/sth's* side
a tough **nut** (to crack)
add fuel to the **fire**
add **insult** to injury
behind the **eight ball**
between a rock and a hard place
between the devil and the deep **blue** sea
cross that **bridge** when *you* come to it
cut the **Gordian knot**
drive a wedge between *sb/sth*
face the music
go haywire
go wrong
hell to pay
in a **bind**

in a **pickle**
in a tight **spot**
in deep **shit**
in **hot** water
in the **hot** seat
in the **soup**
iron out *sth*
lose **sleep** (over *sb/sth*)
make something out of nothing
no **sweat**
on the **rocks**
open (a) **Pandora's box**
open (up) a **can** of worms
out of the frying pan (into the **fire**)
over a **barrel**
parting of the ways
patch up *sth*
play **havoc** with *sth*
put *sb* on the **spot**
put *sb/sth* in a **hole**
rear its (ugly) **head**
sad **state** of affairs
save the **day**
set off **alarm bells**
set *sb/sth* against *sb/sth*
shoot *yourself* in the **foot**
shoot *yourself* in the foot
slings and arrows
smooth over *sth*
sort *sth* out
sth hits the **fan**
talk out *sth*
the **eye** of the storm
the **trouble** with *sb/sth*
up the **creek** (without a paddle)
when the **chips** are down
wreak **havoc**

saying

at a **loss** for words
bare *your* **soul**
beat around the bush
bend *sb's* **ear**
bite *your* tongue
blah, blah, blah
break the **news**
breathe a **word**
bring *sb* up to date
butter *sb* up
cast **aspersions** on *sb/sth*
cat got *your* tongue
chime in
clam up

Subject Index

clear the **air**
clue *sb* in
cut in
cut to the **chase**
dish the **dirt** (on *sb/sth*)
draw *sb/sth* out
dress *sb* down
eat **crow**
fill *sb* in
flesh out *sth*
float an **idea**
get a **word** in edgewise
get at *sth*
get *sth* off *your* **chest**
give it to *sb* straight
give **notice** (to *sb*)
give *sb* **hell**
give *sb/sth* away
go into *sth*
go on (and on) about *sth*
go **public** (with *sth*)
harp on *sth*
have a **word** (with *sb*)
have **words** (with *sb*)
have *your* **day** in court
heap *sth* on *sb/sth*
hold forth
hold *your* **tongue**
if you will
in a **manner** of speaking
in **chorus**
in **other** words
keep quiet (about *sth*)
keep *sth* from *you*
keep *sth* to *yourself*
keep *your* **mouth** shut
keep *your* own **counsel**
kiss and tell
launch into *sb*
lay down *sth*
lay down the **law**
leave it at that
let **fly** (with) *sth*
let it be known
let *sb* in on *sth*
let *sth* slip
let the cat out of the **bag**
like I **said**
loosen *your* tongue
make a **case** for *sth*
make no **bones** about *sth*
make **noises** about *sth*
mention (*sb/sth*) in passing

mouth off
mum's the word
name **names**
need I say more
needless to say
not mince **words**
off the **cuff**
on everyone's **lips**
on the **tip** of *your* tongue
open up
open *your* **mouth**
pardon me
pop the **question**
preach to the **choir**
preach to the **converted**
put in a **good** word (for *sb*)
put **words** in *sb's* mouth
put *your* two **cents** in
rattle off *sth*
reel off *sth*
refer to *sb/sth*
run *your* **mouth**
save *your* **breath**
say *your* **piece**
shoot the **breeze**
shoot *your* **mouth** off
shut (*sb*) up
sing out (*sth*)
sketch out *sth*
so to speak
sorry to **say**
sound off
speak for *sb/sth*
speak for *yourself*
speak out
speak up
speak *your* **mind**
spell out *sth*
spill the **beans**
spill *your* **guts**
spin out *sth*
spread the word
take a **stand**
take the **words** (right) out of *sb's* mouth
talk back (to *sb*)
talk *sth* over
talk tough
that **is** (to say)
think out loud
tick off *sth*
to make a long **story** short
under *your* **breath**

Subject Index

weigh in
your lips are sealed

similarities
a chip off the old **block**
a dead **ringer** for *sb/sth*
(all) of a **piece**
(all) other **things** being equal
along the lines of *sth*
along those **lines**
amount to *sth*
amount to the same thing
and **so** forth
and the **like**
as if
been there, done that
border on *sth*
bring *sth* into **line**
by the same **token**
cut from the same **cloth**
fall into **line**
follow in *sb's/sth's* footsteps
follow suit
have *sth* in **common** (with *sb/sth*)
in good **company**
in **kind**
in **line** with *sth*
in *sb's* **shoes**
in the same **ballpark**
in the same **boat**
in the same **league** (as *sb/sth*)
in **tune** (with *sb/sth*)
it's the same **old** story
keep **pace** (with *sb/sth*)
(like) two **peas** in a pod
meet *your* **match**
of a **sort**
of one **mind**
on a **par** with *sb/sth*
on the same **page**
on the same **wavelength**
return the **favor**
(right) **up** there with *sb/sth*
same **difference**
sb after *your* own **heart**
sb's **answer** to *sb/sth*
shades of *sb/sth*
six of one, (and) half a dozen of the other
speak the same **language**

sth **goes** for *sb/sth else*
take after *sb*
the **likes** of *sb/sth*
two of a **kind**

speed
a **mile** a minute
all of a sudden
at a **moment**'s notice
at a snail's **pace**
(at) full **tilt**
at the **drop** of a hat
before you can **say** *sth*
behind in *sth*
fast and furious
flat out
floor it
get a **move** on
hop to it
hurry up and *do sth*
in a **flash**
in a New York **minute**
in short **order**
in the **blink** of an eye
in the **twinkling** of an eye
keep up (with *sb/sth*)
leave *sb/sth* in the **dust**
let it rip
like a **bat** out of hell
like a **shot**
like mad
like nobody's **business**
like there's no tomorrow
like wildfire
make it **snappy**
on the **double**
on the **fly**
pick up
pick up **steam**
(put) the **pedal** to the metal
quick on the **draw**
set *sb/sth* back
step by **step**
step on it
step on the **gas**
take forever
think on *your* **feet**

success
a **feather** in *your* cap
a **flash** in the pan
against the **odds**

Subject Index

ahead of the **game**
ahead of the **pack**
beat the system
big in *sth*
bring off *sth*
by **hook** or by crook
carry off *sth*
carry the day
come a **cropper**
flying high
gain **ground**
get ahead
get off on the right **foot**
get somewhere
get to first **base**
give *sth your* **best** shot
go from **strength** to **strength**
go great **guns**
go **places**
grasping at **straws**
have a good **run**
have the **last** laugh
hit a home run
hit pay dirt
hit the jackpot
hold promise
home **free**
if **all** else fails
in the **fast** lane
in the **running**
in *your* **sights**
it's **do** or die
keep up with the **Joneses**
land on *your* **feet**
lead the pack
leave *your/its* **mark** (on *sb/sth*)
make a **go** of *sth*
make a **name** for *yourself*
make a **splash**
make **good**
make good *sb's sth*
make it
make it **big**
make or break *sth*
make out
make something of *yourself*
make *your* **mark**
never say **die**
not **hack** it
not have a **prayer**
on a **roll**
on the **fast track**
over the **hump**
pan out

pay off
pull off *sth*
push *sb's* **buttons**
put *your* **shoulder** to the wheel
rest on *your* laurels
rise to *sth*
sb will go a long **way**
set *your* **sights** (on *doing sth*)
stand the **test** of time
(still) go**ing** strong
strike **gold**
take *sb/sth* by **storm**
the **toast** of *somewhere*
up and **coming**
win out
win the **day**
with flying **colors**
work out
work *your/its* **magic**
your name in **lights**

thinking

a **flight** of fancy
as far as *you* are **concerned**
bring to **mind** *sb/sth*
come to **mind**
connect the **dots**
figure out *sth*
food for thought
for my **money**
get it into *your* **head**
get *sb's* **hopes** up
get *your* **mind** around *sth*
give *sb* **pause**
have another think (**coming**)
have in **mind** *sb/sth*
have *your* **wits** about *you*
hear *yourself* think
I **tell** you
keep *sth* in **mind**
look upon *sb/sth* as *sth*
make a mental **note**
make **sense** of *sth*
make up *your* **mind**
mull over *sth*
occur to *you*
on **second** thought
out of sight, out of **mind**
put *sb/sth* out of *your* **mind**
put **two** and **two** together
puzzle out *sth*
puzzle over *sth*
rack *your* **brains**

Subject Index

reflect on *sth*
see the **glass** (as) half empty
see the **glass** (as) half full
size up *sb/sth*
spring to **mind**
sth comes into *your* **head**
take *your* **mind** off *sb/sth*
think for *yourself*
think **long** and hard
think *sth* over
think *sth* through
think **straight**
to my **mind**
toss around *sth*
toy with *sth*
try *sth* (on) for **size**
weigh *your* words
without a **second** thought
your **mind** goes blank

time
a **matter** of time
a **race** against time
ahead of **time**
(all) in **good** time
all the time
all the **time** in the world
(all) year **round**
along the **line**
around the clock
as of
as **soon** as
as soon as **possible**
at **length**
at (long) **last**
at **once**
at one **time**
at **present**
at the **crack** of dawn
at the **latest**
at the **moment**
at the **outside**
before **long**
before *you* **know** it
bright and early
buy time
by and **by**
come down the **pike**
count down (to *sth*)
day after **day**
day and night
day by **day**
day in, **day** out

dead of winter
down the **line**
down the **road**
draw *sth* out
drop-dead **date**
for the long **haul**
for the **moment**
for the **present**
for the **time** being
from the **cradle** to the grave
fuck around
get around to *doing sth*
getting on toward
in **advance** (of *sth*)
in due **course**
in **due** time
in **just** a minute
in **just** a moment
in **living** memory
in no **time**
in **perpetuity**
in the **dead** of night
in the **fullness** of time
in the **interim**
in the long **run**
in the long **term**
in the **meantime**
in the **meanwhile**
in the short **run**
in the short **term**
in this **day** and age
in **time** (for *sth*)
in **years**
it is **high** time
just a **minute**
just a **moment**
(just) in the **nick** of time
just now
look ahead
look back
lose **time**
make a *sth* of it
month after **month**
month by **month**
night after **night**
night and day
no sooner *do sth* than *do sth else*
of **late**
of **old**
on and **on**
on **end**
on the **dot**
on the **horizon**
on the **hour**

Subject Index

on the spur of the **moment**
once in a **blue** moon
once upon a time
one **day**
only just
over the long **term**
over the short **term**
quite a **while**
sb will be **along**
so **far**
so **long**
sooner or later
take **leave**
the **bottom** of the hour
the **calm** before the storm
(the) first **thing** (in the morning)
the **glory** days (of *sth*)
the **height** of *sth*
the **here** and now
the **last** minute
the other **day**
the **top** of the hour
time flies
to **date**
until the **cows** come home
(until *you* are) **blue** in the face
week after **week**
week by **week**
when the **dust** settles
year after **year**
year by **year**
year in, **year** out

truthfulness

a **crock** (of shit)
a **man** of his word
an **article** of faith
as a **matter** of fact
back up (*sth*)
bear out *sth*
believe it or not
believe me
beyond **question**
blow **smoke**
call a spade a spade
call into **question** *sth*
(do you) **know** something
face **facts**
fall for *sth*
get **real**
get to the **bottom** of *sth*
give the **lie** to *sth*
honest to **God**

honest to **goodness**
in (point of) **fact**
in **truth**
it is *your* **understanding**
lay it on the **line**
level with *sb*
lie through *your* **teeth**
like **hell**
(made up) out of whole **cloth**
make up *sth*
no **kidding**
not hold **water**
on the **level**
pass *yourself* off as *sb*
play **games**
pull *sb's* **leg**
put (all) *your* **cards** on the table
ring hollow
ring true
sell *sb* a **bill** of goods
set *sb/sth* straight
set the **record** straight
so help me (**God**)
square with *sth*
sth **goes** to show (you)
swear up and down
take *sth* as **gospel**
take *sth* with a **grain** of salt
take the **fifth** (amendment)
talk out of both **sides** of *your* mouth
tell it like it is
the **long** and the short of it
true enough
vouch for *sth*

writing

a **matter** of record
draw up *sth*
drop *sb* a **line**
fill in *sth*
fire off *sth*
in **black** and white
in **writing**
mark up *sth*
put **pen** to paper
put *sth* down
set down *sth*
set forth *sth*
sign in
sign out
take down *sb/sth*
write in (*sth*)
write up *sth*